CRIMINAL CONDUCT AND SUBSTANCE ABUSE TREATMENT FOR ADOLESCENTS

The Provider's Guide

Pathways to Self-Discovery and Change

Harvey B. Milkman and Kenneth W. Wanberg

This document was prepared under contract number OE IHM NC030000031 with the Colorado Department of Human Services, Alcohol & Drug Abuse Division. Funding for this project was $37,000.00 through the Colorado Department of Public Safety, Division of Criminal Justice, Office of Juvenile Justice.

For information:

Sage Publications, Inc.
2455 Teller Road
Thousand Oaks, California 91320
E-mail: order@sagepub.com

Sage Publications Ltd.
1 Oliver's Yard
55 City Road
London EC1Y 1SP
United Kingdom

Sage Publications India Pvt. Ltd.
B-42 Panchsheel Enclave
Post Box 4109
New Delhi 110017
India

Printed in the United States of America
Library of Congress Cataloging-in-Publication Data
Milkman, Harvey B.
Pathways to self-discovery and change:
Criminal conduct and substance abuse treatment for adolescents: The provider's guide
Harvey B. Milkman, Kenneth W. Wanberg
p. cm.
Includes Bibliographical References and Index.
ISBN # 1-4129-0615-6 (pbk.)
1. Problem youth—Substance use. 2. Problem youth—Behavior modification. 3. Cognitive therapy for teenagers. 4. Substance abuse—treatment. 5. Social work with juvenile delinquents. I. Wanberg, Kenneth W. II. Title.
HV4999.Y68M57 2005
364.36—dc22   2004019819

Correspondence should be sent to:
The Center for Interdisciplinary Studies
899 Logan Street, Suite 207
Denver, Colorado 80203
(303) 830-8500/Fax (303) 830-8420
e-mail: cisdenver@msn.com

04 05 06 07 10 9 8 7 6 5 4 3 2 1

Harvey B. Milkman, Ph.D. is Professor of Psychology at Metropolitan State College of Denver and Director of the Center for Interdisciplinary Studies, Denver, Colorado. Kenneth W. Wanberg, Th.D., Ph.D. is a private practice psychologist and Director of the Center for Addictions Research and Evaluation (CARE), Arvada, Colorado.

Project Editor: Karen Storck
Layout and Graphic Design: Barbara Barr
Chapter 4: Substance Abuse and the Adolescent Brain
Stanley Sunderwirth, PhD
Professor of Chemistry
Indiana University-Purdue at Columbus
e-mail: ssunder@iupui.edu
Neurobiological illustrations for Chapter 4:
Kenneth Axen, PhD
Adjunct Professor, *Department of Health and Nutrition Sciences, Brooklyn College, NYC*
Consultation, research and writing assistance: Barbara Gagliardi and Karen Storck
Research and technical assistance: Brent Carey, Michelle Tolar, and Robert Nicholls
Project Manager, Colorado Alcohol and Drug Abuse Division: Katie Wells
Project Manager, Office of Juvenile Justice, Colorado Division of Criminal Justice: Pat Carvero

TABLE OF CONTENTS

Introduction: Promoting Adolescent Resiliency 1

SECTION I   THEORETICAL AND RESEARCH PERSPECTIVES 17

Chapter 1   Risk and Resiliency During Adolescence 19

The Experience of Adolescence 21

Scope of Adolescent Problem Behavior 21

Problem Behavior Theory 23

The Offset of Risk and Resiliency in Adolescent Adjustment 25

Summary of Risk Factors for Delinquency and Substance Abuse in Adolescents 27

Empirical Studies of Resiliency: Buffers Against Adolescent Problem Behavior 33

A Strengths-Based approach to Juvenile Justice and Treatment Services 36

Chapter Review 37

Chapter 2   Mental Health and Adolescent Problem Behavior 39

The Scope of Adolescent Mental Health Issues 41

Disruptive Behavior Disorders and Diagnostic Criteria 42

Personality Disorders 49

Post Traumatic Stress Disorder 50

The MMPI-A: Use for Diagnosis and Treatment Planning 54

Psychotherapeutic Medications for Children and Adolescents 54

Chapter Review 56

Chapter 3   Substance Abuse and Adolescent Problem Behavior 59

The Scope of Adolescent Substance Abuse 61

Imminent Drug Threats 61

Factors Associated with the Onset of Adolescent Substance Abuse 69

Adolescent Drinking and Driving 71

Relationship of Age to Adolescent AOD Abuse and AOD Use Disruption 74

Adolescent Drug Use and Criminal Conduct 77

AOD Abuse Across American Subcultures 80

Chapter Review 82

Chapter 4   Substance Abuse and the Adolescent Brain 85

The Human Brain: A Fast Idiot 87

The Adolescent Brain 92

Alcohol 95

Methamphetamine: Need a Sudafed? 98

Cocaine: "Gift of the Gods" 99

Marijuana: Reefer Madness Revisited 101

Opiates: Everyone Makes Them 103

Ecstacy: Let's Party 104

Inhalants: How Stupid Can You Get? 105

Hallucinogenic Drugs: Chemical Vision 106

Tobacco: The Ultimate Drug 108

Chapter Review 110

Chapter 5   **Delinquency Crime and Violence** 113

Characteristics of Juvenile Delinquency 115

Adolescence and Deviant Subculture 118

Correlates of Juvenile Delinquency and Crime 121

Theories of Adolescent Crime 123

Developmental Aspects of Adolescent Crime 126

Transient versus Stable Patterns of Delinquency and Crime 127

Trends in Juvenile Violence 133

Implications for Treatment and Policy 139

Chapter Review 141

Chapter 6   **Gender and Adolescent Problem Behavior** 143

Adolescent Girls and Delinquency 145

The Nature of Female Offense 145

Gender Comparisons Across Risk and Drug Involvement 147

Risk Factors and Correlates of Juvenile Offending Among Females 150

Gender Norms and Sexual Violation 151

Sexual Assault During Childhood 152

Experiences with Violent Trauma in Childhood:
A Major Route for Girls into Criminal Conduct 154

Female Gang Participation 157

Trauma within the Juvenile Justice System 159

Implications for Treatment and Policy: A Gender-Focused Treatment Platform 161

Chapter Review 162

Chapter 7   **Youth Culture and Diversity** 165

Defining Culture and the Importance of Cultural Awareness 167

Adolescent Subcultures 169

Cultural Competence 172

Chapter Review 173

Chapter 8   **Perspectives On The Assessment** 175

Overview 177

Objectives of Screening and Assessment 177

The Structure and Content of Assessment: Data Sources and Report Subjectivity 178

Valuing Client Self-Disclosure When Discerning Veridicality or the "True Picture" 179

Convergent Validation and the Process Model of Assessment 180

Self-Report as a Valid Estimate of the "True Condition" 181

Guidelines for Using Psychometric Assessment Instruments 181

Determining Inclusion into a Substance Abuse Category 182

The Process and Structure of Assessment 187

Special Focus Areas for Juvenile Justice System Clients 196

Chapter Review 199

SECTION II THE TREATMENT PLATFORM FOR ADOLESCENT SERVICE DELIVERY 201

Chapter 9 Foundations of Cognitive-Behavioral Therapy 203

Historical Roots of Cognitive-Behavioral Therapy...205

Contemporary CBT: Integrating Cognitive and Behavioral Principles and Approaches 206

Underlying Principles of Cognitive-Behavioral Therapy 207

Therapeutic Focal Points in CBT..211

What Works in Psychotherapy: Empirical Support for the Use of CBT.................214

Chapter Review..215

Chapter 10 Core Strategies for Delinquency, Crime and Substance Abuse Treatment 217

Integrating Education and Therapy in the CBT Model 219

Seven Core Strategies in the Education and Treatment Process 220

Chapter Review..234

Chapter 11 Cognitive-Behavioral Perspectives on Adolescent Treatment 235

Treatment Efficacy with Juvenile Justice Clients: Past and Present 237

Evidence for a Cognitive-Behavioral Approach to Adolescent Treatment 238

Key Features of Cognitive-Behavioral Treatment for Adolescents 241

Summary of Cognitive-Behavioral Principles Targeted at
Delinquency, Crime and Substance Abuse 242

Chapter Review..244

Chapter 12 Treatment Systems and Modalities 247

Individual Approaches to Treatment 249

Family Systems Theory and Family Therapies 252

Residential Treatment 257

Chapter Review..258

Chapter 13 Exemplary Treatment Programs 261

Exemplary Youth Treatment Programs 263

Nationally Recognized Programs..269

Chapter Review..270

SECTION III PROGRAM IMPLEMENTATION 271

Chapter 14 Operational Guidelines and Procedures for Program Delivery 273

Chapter Overview..275

Characteristics of the Effective Juvenile Justice Treatment Counselor 275

The Process and Structure of Program Delivery 279

Ethical and Legal Considerations in Screening and Assessment 284

Client Participation Guidelines and Ground Rules 287

Program Structure and Delivery Guidelines 287

Intake and Admission Methods and Procedures 288

Principles of Effective Group Management and Leadership 289

Operational Model for Assessment 290

Chapter Review..296

Chapter 15 The Treatment Curriculum 297

Initiation of Treatment: Challenge to Change 299

Cognitive-Behavioral Skill Development: Commitment to Change 300

    Cementing Gains: Ownership of Change: 300

    Getting Started 301

    Curriculum Description 304

    Chapter Review...316

References 319

Index 359

Appendix A 371

    Referral Evaluation Summary (RES)...372

    Intake Personal Data Form 373

    Consent for Release of Confidential Information 374

    Client Rights Statement 375

    Consent for Program Involvement 376

    Health Insurance Portability and Accountability Act (HIPAA) 377

    Parent Consent Form 378

    Full Disclosure Statement Sample...379

    Notice of Federal Requirements Regarding Confidentiality.......................................380

Appendix B 381

    Substance Use Survey (SUS)...382

    Scoring Directions for the Substance Use Survey (SUS)...386

    Adolescent Self-Assessment Questionnaire (ASAQ) 387

    Scoring Instructions for Adolescent Self-Assessment Questionnaire..........................391

    Social Response Questionnaire (SRQ) 392

    Scoring Guide and Scale Interpretation for Self-Assessment Questionnaire 394

LIST OF TABLES

0.1   Elements of Effective Treatment 5

0.2   Target Populations 10

0.3   Minimum Symptom Admission Criteria..10

0.4   Principles of Intervention (National Institute of Justice) 10

1.1   Risk and Resiliency Factors for Adolescent Problem Behaviors 26

1.2   Summary of Risk Factors for the Development of Problem Behavior 32

1.3   Positive Building Blocks of Human Development 35

2.1   Oppositional Defiant Disorder: DSM-IV-TR Diagnostic Criteria 43

2.2   Conduct Disorder: DSM-IV-TR Diagnostic Criteria..44

2.3   Attention Deficit hyperactivity Disorder: DSM-IV-TR Diagnostic Criteria 48

2.4   Medications and Behavioral Treatment for ADHD 50

2.5   Key Characteristics of Post Traumatic Stress Disorder 52

2.6   Psychiatric Medications Commonly Used for Children and Adolescents 55

3.1   Monitoring the Future Study 2003 Prevalence of Various Drugs for 12th Graders 62

3.2   Commonly Abused Drugs 63

3.3   Cross-Sectional Study of AOD Involvement and Disruption Across Age Groups 75

3.4   Incidence of Juvenile Arrests in the U.S—1997 78

3.5   Differences in Psychosocial Risk and Protection for Substance Abuse Across Gender and Ethnicity 81

4.1   Effect of Various Drugs on Dopamine Levels in the Nucleus Accumbens 93

4.2   Effect of Various Activities on Dopamine Levels in the Nucleus Accumbens 93

4.3   Site of Action of Drugs in the Reward Cascade and Percentage Increase in Dopamine in the Nucleus Accumbens 94

5.1   Projected Percentage of Each Racial Population Who Will be Under Age 18 in 2010 117

5.2   Ethnicity of Juveniles in Public Schools vs. Probation Referrals to AOD Treatment 118

5.3   Comparison of Mean Self-Concept Score Across Offense Category..123

5.4   Mean Total Self-Concept Scores Among Violent Youth 123

5.5   Summary of Social Influences on Development of Adolescent Crime and Violence 126

5.6   Predictor Variables for Recidivism in Juvenile Delinquency in Adolescents Aged 13 to 17 Years 133

5.7   Ranking of Child Murder of Juveniles by Age 135

5.8   Interaction of Age and Type of Risk Factor for Best Predictors of Juvenile Violence 136

5.9   Characteristics of Adolescent Homicide (Higher than Average % of Perpetrators Below Age 18) 137

5.10 Summary of Trends in Juvenile Violence 140

6.1   Variation in Self-Reported Criminal Behaviors by Sex..146

6.2   Rates of Birth/1000 Females Ages 15-17..151

6.3   Percentage of Perpetrators by Age in the Sexual Assault of Juveniles 154

6.4   Types of Abuse Suffered by Adolescent Female Offenders 155

6.5   School Failures and Types of Abuse..157

7.1   Videotapes and Teaching Tools 173

8.1   Diagnostic and Statistical Manual-IV Criteria for Substance Abuse..184

8.2   Diagnostic and Statistical Manual-IV Criteria for Substance Dependence 184

8.3   Simple Screening Self-Report Instruments for Adolescent Assessment with
an Alcohol and Other Drug (AOD) Focus or Component 192

8.4   Differential Screening Self-Report Instruments for Adolescent Assessment with
an Alcohol and Other Drug (AOD) Focus or Component 192

8.5   Differential Screening and In-Depth Structured Interview-Based Instruments for
Adolescent Assessment with an Alcohol and Other Drug (AOD) Focus or Component 194

8.6   Differential In-Depth Assessment Instruments for Adolescent Assessment with
an Alcohol and Other Drug (AOD) Focus or Component 194

8.7   Instruments for Assessing Treatment Progress and Change, During Treatment,
at Discharge or at Post-Discharge 195

8.8   Instruments That Assess Juvenile Delinquency and Criminal Conduct 197

8.9   Instruments That Assess Adolescent Mental and Behavioral Adjustment Problems...............198

12.1   Getting Principles for Problem Solving 251

15.1   Skills for Self-Management, Responsible Living and Change...302

15.2   Outline of Orientation of Topics 303

LIST OF FIGURES

1.1   Diagnostic Prevalence Rates for the 10 Most Common Disorders for ADM and
Non-ADM Service Sectors 24

3.1   Drug Involvement Scales (Probation) Compared Across Three Ethnic Groups 76

3.2   AOD Disruption for Three Groups Across Age Groupings 76

3.3   Drug Involvement Scale Compared Across Three Ethnic Groups (Probation Group) 82

4.1   The Neuron 87

4.2   Cross Section of the Human Brain..88

4.3   The Synaptic Junction and Chemical Transmission 89

4.4   Hypothalmus-Pituitary-Adrenal (HPA) Axis 89

4.5   The Reward Cascade 91

4.6   Action of Various Drugs on the Brain to increase Dopamine...92

4.7   Structures and Functions of the Human Brain...96

4.8   Neurotoxic Effects of Methamphetamine...99

4.9   Human Brain Areas Corresponding to the Mouse Brain Areas Damaged by Methamphetamines 99

4.10 Cocaine in the Brain 100

4.11 Severity of Cognitive Deficits Varies by Level of Marijuana Use 103

4.12 Brain Damage in a Toluene Abuser 106

4.13 Molecular Structures 107

4.14 Nicotine 109

4.15 Causes of Death Attributable to Cigarette Smoking...110

5.1   Prevalence of Delinquency Among Gang and Nongang Youth Ages 13 to 18, SSDP Sample 120

5.2   Percentage of Youth Ages 13 to 18 Who Joined a Gang, SSDP Sample 121

5.3   Crime by Age 129

5.4   Comparison of Deviancy Patterns 134

6.1   Gender Comparisons (Treatment) Across Risk Scales 148

6.2   Gender Comparisons (Probation) Across Risk Scales 148

6.3   Gender Comparisons (Treatment) Across Drug Involvement Scales 149

6.4   Gender Comparisons (Probation) Across Drug Involvement Scales 149

8.1   The Convergent Validation Model 181

8.2   Components of the Juvenile Justice Substance Abuse Assessment Process 188

8.3   Conceptual Framework for Comprehensive and In-Depth Assessment of Juvenile Justice Clients 191

10.1   The Cyclical Process of Growth and Change in Treatment 221

10.2   Model of Cognitive Structures and Processes..227

10.3   Cognitive-Behavioral Process of Learning and Change:
       How Thoughts and Behaviors Are Strengthened 228

10.4   Marlatt's Cognitive-Behavioral Model of the Relapse Process 230

10.5   Cognitive-Behavioral Model for Relapse and Recidivism...231

10.6   Steps and Pathways for Relapse and Recidivism Prevention 233

12.1   Conceptual Model of the MST Treatment Process 258

14.1   Profile of the Juvenile Justice Provider and Counselor 276

14.2   Conceptual Framework for the Pathways to Self-Discovery and Change 285

14.3   Substance Use Survey (SUS)—Intake Testing 292

14.4   Colorado Youth Offender—Level of Service Inventory (CYO-LSI)—Intake Testing 292

14.5   Adolescent Self-Assessment Profile—II (ASAP II) Admission Testing.......................293

14.6   Adolescent Self-Assessment Questionnaire (ASAQ)—Intake Testing 294

14.7   Social Response Questionnaire (SRQ)—Intake Testing..294

14.8   Adolescent Self-Assessment Questionnaire (ASAQ)—Intake Testing 294

14.9   Colorado Youth Offender—Level of Service Inventory (CYO-LSI)—Six Months Retest.......................295

14.10 Social Response Questionnaire (SRQ)—Six Months Retest 295

14.11 Treatment Response Questionnaire (TRQ) Monthly Rating by Primary Counselor 295

14.12 Client Manager Assessment Questionnaire (CMAQ) Six Months Post-Discharge 296

14.13 Follow-Up Assessment Questionnaire (FAQ)—Six Months Post-Discharge Self-Report 296

Promoting Adolescent Resiliency

Introduction: Promoting Adolescent Resiliency

Chapter Outline

Definitions and Terminology

Program Rationale

Provider's Guide and Participant's Workbook

Fundamental Principles for Criminal Conduct and Substance Abuse Treatment

Elements of Youth-Focused Treatment

General Principles for Understanding Teenage Problem Behaviors

1Correlations Among the Various Problem Behaviors

Cultural and Gender

- Race, ethnicity and teenage problem behaviors
- Gender considerations

Target Groups & Admission Criteria

Principles of Intervention

How this Provider's Guide is Organized

Chapter Descriptions

Chapter Objectives

- To introduce *Pathways to Self-Discovery and Change (PSD-C): The Provider's Guide and Participant's Workbook*;
- To review principles of effective treatment for substance abuse, criminal conduct and emotional distress;
- To summarize evidence-based treatment programs for teenagers;
- To define essential components of an effective treatment program for youthful offenders;
- To overview the current treatment platform presented in this manual;
- To define target groups and principles of effective intervention for PSD-C; and
- To summarize the content of this Provider's Guide.

DEFINITIONS AND TERMINOLOGY

While it is possible to conceptualize a general beginning and end to the period conventionally referred to as "adolescence," there are no definite boundaries. Some consider the entire second decade of life (i.e., 10 to 20 years of age) as the adolescent stage, while a more general and conservative range is 12 to 18 (Spear, 2000). The construct of adolescence is widely used in research and academic forums to denote the 12 to 17 year age group, often subdivided into youth who are 12 to 14 years of age and 15 to 17 years of age.

What is adolescence? Early approaches and theories depicted this period of life as a time of turmoil and stress, a time of turbulent transition (Hall, 1916), where sexual desires are strengthened and the severance of parental dependency leads to interpersonal turmoil (Freud, 1958). Other prominent theorists focused on the inevitability of turmoil during this developmental period (Erickson, 1950; Sullivan, 1947). Even though these biological and psychoanalytic based theories have forged a current and popular image of adolescence being a time of stress and turmoil, they have little empirical support in research (see Schulenberg, Maggs, Steinman & Zucker, 2001).

A more common perspective, and one that is more congruent with the current research and theory, is that adolescence is not characterized by turmoil and stress. Rather, it is a period of human development where biological, social and psychological changes and challenges occur, that these changes are multidimensional and multidirectional and that they are a function of the dynamic interaction of the individual with his or her contextual world (Schulenberg et al., 2001). This developmental-contextual view provides a basis for understanding resiliency, stability, change and problem behavior in adolescence.

In the judicial domain, penal codes differ between states as to when an individual moves from juvenile to adult jurisdiction. About three-fourths of the states (including Colorado) have set 18 as a maximum age for defining juveniles, with two states setting cutoffs at 19. Seven states use age 17 and four states (including New York) use 16 as the upper limit for the legal definition of a juvenile (Dryfuss, 1990). Youth themselves (ages 13 to 19) show more affinity for the term "teenager" than for either "juveniles" or "adolescents." Hence, the terms "teenager" and "adolescent" are used interchangeably throughout this guide. We use the term "youthful offender" to denote youth who are under court jurisdiction serving their sentences as juveniles.

Delinquency, Crime and Substance Abuse Treatment for Adolescents: Pathways to Self-Discovery and Change: PSD-C) is designed for youth ages 14 to 18, who have co-morbid involvement with substance abuse and criminal conduct. In some instances, when either a younger adolescent (e.g., 12 to13 years of age) or an older teen (e.g., 19 yrs.), is grouped with an intermediate-age adolescent treatment cohort, the PSD-C program would be appropriate for an expanded age range.

PROGRAM RATIONALE

Participation of juveniles (ages 14 to 18) in antisocial behavior has reached such high proportions that it appears to be normative at this time (Loeber & Farrington, 1998). Mental disorder is frequently co-existent with substance abuse and crime. Relapse and recidivism rates remain high—higher and sooner than for their adult counterparts (Glicken & Sechest, 2003)—suggesting that currently operating treatment programs have yet to reach their full potential. It is widely accepted that cognitive-behavioral therapy (CBT) has promise for improving the odds for adolescents and older teens who manifest multiple problem behaviors (e.g., Kashani, Jones, Bumby, & Thomas, 2001).

Criminal Conduct and Substance Abuse Treatment: Strategies for Self-Improvement and Change (SSC) (Wanberg and Milkman, 1998) is recognized as the standard of care for adult substance abusing offenders by the *Colorado Alcohol and Drug Abuse Division, Department of Corrections* and *Office of Probation Services*. The program (SSC) provides a manualized protocol for delivering group-focused cognitive-behavioral treatment in prisons, community corrections and outpatient settings throughout the United States. However, when utilized with youthful offenders, treatment providers generally report that although the cognitive restructuring and social skills material as developed in the SSC curriculum is vital, the presentation format does not adequately address the needs of the teenage population, e.g., attention span, vernacular, interactive learning style, and examples relevant to youth culture.

Some programs have opted to adapt less comprehensive CBT curricula for reasons of expediency, cost considerations, and the perception of increased responsivity to teenage treatment needs, e.g., *Thinking For a Change* (Bush, Glick & Taymens, 1997). However, treatment outcomes appear to be compromised by the lack of developmentally appropriate models for teenage programming. Reasons cited for poor treatment outcomes include: 1) intervention may have begun too late; 2) the program being utilized was originally intended for use with adults; and 3) long-term negative consequences rarely influence a teen's behavior (Dennis, Dawud-Noursi, Muck & McDermeit, 2003).

The field of adolescent treatment is further complicated by the emergence of a variety of CBT models, designed to meet special needs of teenage clients and their families, e.g., *Behavioral Therapy for Adolescents* (Azrin et al., 1996); *Functional Family Therapy* (Sexton, & Alexander, 2002); *Multisystemic Therapy* (Henggeler et al., 1996; 1998), etc. These are deployed in various treatment settings without reconciliation of similarities or differences in conceptual models, theoretical constructs or styles of presentation. Consequently, youth who participate in treatment services at different entry points or levels of care in the mental health/substance abuse/criminal justice system may experience an array of treatment curricula, some originally designed for adult populations (e.g., *Thinking for a Change*, Bush et al., 1997; SAMHSA) only loosely connected by a common CBT framework. When going from one level or type of service to another, e.g., outpatient substance abuse treatment to probation, probation to incarceration, or incarceration to parole, the treatment models may appear quite different; most likely resulting in confusion and further alienation within the population of treated youth.

There is need for a developmentally appropriate CBT model designed to meet the special needs of teenagers who are affected with substance abuse, mental disorder and/or criminal conduct. Cognitive-behavioral skills can be effectively taught to young people providing that the material is presented in an interactive format, drawing on themes that have both immediate and long-term importance to adolescents and young adults. *Delinquency, Crime and Substance Abuse Treatment for Adolescents: Pathways for Self-Discovery and Change (PSD-C)*—Provider's Guide and Participant's Workbook, is designed to bridge many of the gaps between the diverse array of CBT approaches. Rather than attempting to replace these curricula with a "one size fits all" approach, PSD-C provides the basis for implementing a *cognitive restructuring and social skills laboratory for practicing, rehearsing and integrating* the various CBT models as they exist in the ecosystem of therapeutic operations.

PROVIDER'S GUIDE AND PARTICIPANT'S WORKBOOK

The purpose of *Pathways for Self-Discovery and Change (PSD-C)* is to create an outcome-based program for delivering effective cognitive restructuring and social skills training to adolescent substance abusing offenders (14 to 18 years of age). While the program is developed as a stand-alone model (i.e., the primary blueprint for group treatment in residential or outpatient settings), it can also serve as an additional service component that can be nested within an existing treatment model that relies on one or more different CBT curricula.

THE PROVIDER'S GUIDE attempts to pinpoint those at greatest risk by taking up the challenge of identifying psychological, biological, socio-cultural, economic and political factors that contribute to the onset of teenage problem behavior. Causal models for an array of problem behaviors are presented, followed by a review of primary treatment protocols widely used in contemporary *practice*. Guidelines are developed for implementation of a standardized treatment curriculum specifically designed for youthful offenders who manifest multiple problem behaviors, including emotional distress, delinquency and crime. PAR utilizes a cognitive-behavioral orientation as the platform from which to initiate change. In addition to presenting the theoretical and research basis for implementing a comprehensive, youth-focused CBT

So I think I want to stop drinking. In fact, I know I want to stop drinking. Besides, pretty soon, they're going to put me on probation, then I'll have to take tests every couple of days. I don't get the warm and numb feelings anymore, and it's just not fun.

curriculum, the *Providers Guide* presents operational guidelines for implementation of the PSD-C program, e.g., confidentiality, rights of privacy, intake, session delivery, treatment progress, outcome and follow-up procedures. This *Guide* works in tandem with the *Participant's Workbook—Pathways to Self-Discovery and Change (PSD-C)*.

THE PARTICIPANT'S WORKBOOK (PSD-C) provides a written and richly illustrated format through which clients can better understand and reflect on each of 32 (approximately 90 to 120 minutes in length) youth-focused CBT treatment sessions. *PSD-C* supplies clients with a visual and written record of all treatment objectives, content information, modeling and role plays, discussion points, interactive exercises, reflective assignments and a place to record their ideas, insights, short- and long-term goals, and progress during the entire treatment episode. *The Workbook* is geared to a broad range of reading and conceptual abilities. Using comic strip illustrations and gripping stories (presented through the narrative voice of teenagers who experience a variety of problems with substance abuse, criminal conduct and

mental health issues), clients are engaged in active discussion about the situations, thoughts, emotions, and behaviors that have become embroidered in their patterns of substance abuse and criminal conduct.

FUNDAMENTAL PRINCIPLES FOR CRIMINAL CONDUCT AND SUBSTANCE ABUSE TREATMENT

Table 0.1 presents a summary of effective treatment strategies for individuals with a history of substance abuse, criminal conduct and mental health issues, which have been integrated into the *PSD-C* program. These elements are comprehensively reviewed in *Chapter 8—Perspectives on Youth Assessment* and *Chapter 9—The Cognitive-Behavioral Model for Self-Discovery and Change*.

Table 0.1   Elements of Effective Treatment

- **Multi-dimensional assessment**—identifies the multiple conditions of a teenager's problems and strengths, including cognitive, emotional, behavioral, socio-cultural, and biological factors;

- **Differential assessment**—designed to develop individually focused treatment plans;

- **Rapport building in the therapeutic alliance**—utilizes the principles of therapeutic support and motivation to develop trust in the therapeutic alliance;

- **Motivational enhancement**—through mutual respect, feedback, advice, emphasis on personal responsibility, multiple treatment options, empathy and support for self-management;

- **Integration of correctional and therapeutic approaches**—addresses both the needs of society as well as the needs of the individual adolescent;

- **Cognitive-behavioral therapy**—focuses on cognitive restructuring and social skills training as the keys to initiating change;

- **Relapse and recidivism prevention**—develops individualized plans for maintaining recovery when released back to the community;

- **Strength-based orientation**—capitalizes on the strengths already present within the client, as well as enriching other personal qualities that may aid in lasting improvement and change;

- **Stages of change**—clients and therapy groups generally proceed through identifiable stages of change during recovery, which must be acknowledged and addressed as integral to the treatment process.

ELEMENTS OF YOUTH-FOCUSED TREATMENT

Drawing on evidence-based treatment models for youthful offenders, *PSD-C* provides a research-based protocol for the delivery of adolescent focused treatment to youth (ages 14 to 18) who manifest multiple and severe problem behaviors. The cognitive behavioral treatment platform presented in this manual utilizes a holistic approach to identify, reduce, buffer, and redress risk factors for the development of adolescent problem behavior. In the following section, we present general principles for understanding adolescent problem behaviors and guidelines for development of a specific focus on relevent treatment for delinquency and substance abuse in teenage clients.

GENERAL PRINCIPLES FOR UNDERSTANDING ADOLESCENT PROBLEM BEHAVIOR

Most problem behaviors of youth are exaggerated by the media. Steinberg (1999) suggests several general principles to help distinguish severe problems of adjustment in adolescence from more transitory difficulties of growth that most people experience at some point in their lives. These principles help develop a perspective from which to view adolescent problem behavior.

- Be aware of the distinction between intermittent experimentation vs. enduring patterns of problem behavior. Experimentation is normal and generally does not produce long-term difficulty (Dacey & Kenny, 1997). Even sporadic engagement in crime generally does not produce lifelong criminal behavior (Steinberg, 1999).

- Investigate whether a particular adolescent's behavior began in adolescence or farther back in earlier periods of development. Generally, the earlier the onset, the more problematic the troublesome behavior will be (Moffit, 1993)). This is true not only for criminal behavior, but for other adjustment problems as well; for example, chronically depressed adolescents frequently are found with childhood anxiety problems (Steinberg, 1999).

- Keep in mind that most of the difficulties experienced in adolescence will be resolved by early adulthood. Those individuals whose problem behavior continues into adulthood are most likely to have experienced problematic environments during childhood and adolescence (Steinberg, 1999).

- Understand that problem behavior does not result from adolescence itself (such as "raging hormones," an innate need to rebel against authority, or an inevitable "identity crisis"). Theories that parallel the onset of puberty with inevitable difficulty have not received empirical support. The effect of hormones on adolescent psychological development is relatively minimal (Steinberg, 1999). When an adolescent engages in seriously dangerous or delinquent behavior, or experiences serious mental health problems, the most likely reason is that something is seriously wrong in her or his social environment.

- Some researchers suggest that it may be important to distinguish adolescents who display only one type of problem behavior (such as depression alone, or substance use alone) from adolescents who indicate co-morbidity (i.e., more than one concurrent disorder, e.g., substance abuse with violence, or depression with delinquency). Research shows that juveniles with co-morbid disorders have generally experienced much more disruption and environmental damage during their formative years (Ge, Best, Conger & Simons, 1996). From this, researchers have concluded there may be differences in the etiology of concurrent disorders that may require particular types of intervention (e.g., Capaldi, 1991).

- A distinction that may be important in determining the severity of an adolescent's problem behavior is between those adolescents who engage in problem behavior defined from the standpoint of parents but not peers (such as loitering, drinking, smoking and sexual activity), and those adolescents who engage in problem behavior that is understood to be problematic by both parents and peers (e.g., violence and serious crime) (Basen-Engquist, Edmundson & Parcel, 1996; Steinberg, 1999).

Social Learning Perspective: Promoting alternative recreational activities, improving self-efficacy, building social competence, and providing broadening cultural experiences are the most effective strategies for stress management, delinquency and drug abuse prevention. There is a shift to a social competence model, which includes a developmental, ecological and skills-based approach to working with teenage problem behaviors, with corresponding emphasis on the identification of individual risk and resiliency factors and on the effective matching of programs to accommodate these needs.

Person-oriented perspective: This program applies a person-oriented approach (Bergman, 2000; Asendorpf, 2000) to treatment with teenagers engaged in problem behavior and crime. It assumes that the individual is the organizing principle that can explain pathways to crime, and why some persons are more prone to antisocial development than others (Magnusson, 2000). Therefore, person-oriented therapy investigates the extent to which self-descriptions (Pulkkinen, Maennikkoe, & Nurmi, 2000) predict antisocial behavior, and provides information to treatment providers for identifying the necessary targets for redress in an individual adolescent who enters the criminal or juvenile justice systems. The use of narratives or personal life stories in this context has been found to be useful for discovering and understanding the meaning of an individual's experience (Lieblich & Josselson, 1997). These stories can provide insight into an individual's: personality construction; ethnic identity; gender identity; gender and race dynamics in the adolescent subculture (Camarena, Sarigiani, & Petersen, 1997); dynamics of resilience (e.g., among survivors of abuse) (James, Huser, Liem, & O'Toole, 1997); processes of reform (Maruna, 1997).

Interpretation of an adolescent's troubles is based on the adolescent's own words concerning his or her life condition. This provides effective means to personalize the therapeutic process and helps the adolescent develop a sense of meaning and purpose (Lieblich & Josselson, 1997).

The person-based focus of this treatment platform will also incorporate the diversity involved in an essential understanding by treatment providers of: cultural awareness; dynamics of adolescence, race, ethnicity and gender, including ageism, racism and sexism in the lives of adolescents; effects of immigration and biculturalism on the development of problem behavior; dissimilarities between problem behavior in inner city vs. suburban and rural contexts; expanded meanings of the word "culture" (to include a wide variety of adolescent sub-cultures, such as "stoners," "Goths," "punks," etc.).

Strengths-based perspective: While internal predispositions and the life experiences of some adolescents may render them vulnerable for delinquent activity, criminal conduct and substance abuse, these adolescents frequently possess a powerful reserve of self-reliance and strength that have enabled them to survive the harsh life on the streets. The treatment platform presented here helps adolescents harness this reserve into a strengths-based orientation from which to grow toward a better life.

- *Cognitive-behavioral treatment platform*: How can cognitive-behavioral principles be used in treatment with adolescents and young adults? Cognitive-behavioral treatment has been a powerful strategy for productive change within a wide range of anti-social and criminal activities, as well as mental and physical health applications. This manual will demonstrate how these strategies may be tailored to create an adolescent-focused treatment curriculum that is relevant and compatible with the needs of this population.

- *Important developmental tasks and transitions of adolescence:* Effective adolescence is predicated upon the acquisition of skills to manage stage-related issues in socio-emotional, economic, cognitive, mental health and biological domains.

- *Self-development:* Youth are helped to re-encounter important milestones of development that may have been compromised or missed altogether, in order to redress resulting distortions to self-concept (such as low self-esteem, negative identity construction, identification with the subculture of violence etc.). Internal and external forces that mitigate against positive changes in self-concept will also be explored.

- *Developing healthy relationships with others*: This component of the program will help youthful offenders to:

  - Identify elements of unhealthy and high-risk relationships, including unreasonable or counter-productive demands and expectations of others;

  - Discover ways in which the social scripts for behavior that are defined within the "code of the streets" may set an individual up for crime and delinquency, as well as recidivism and relapse;

  - Learn skills and abilities necessary to develop healthy and productive relationships, which enable troubled youth to encounter more positive experiences with others. As experiences within more conventional settings become more positive, it is expected that the motivation to avoid antisocial activities will be developed and sustained.

- *Successful transition to healthy, crime-free living:* Treatment programming that prepares adolescents and young adults for successful transition upon exit from correctional and/or juvenile justice services is crucial in effecting reasonable expectation of successful (crime and substance-free) living within the community. Through participation in a number of hands-on activities, youthful offenders will gain practice in effecting these changes.

- *Utilizing community resources:* This component aims at helping youthful offenders to utilize the community resources (such as school counselors, recreational centers, teen rap sessions, etc.) that may facilitate effective coping with the difficulties that they are likely to encounter in the world outside of the subculture of violence.

- *Preparation for healthy living in the community*: The provision of transitional services for youth leaving the juvenile justice system (in order to prepare them for healthy living upon exit) is a crucial aspect of any treatment program with this population.

CORRELATIONS AMONG THE VARIOUS PROBLEM BEHAVIORS

Problem behaviors tend to cluster into several different categories. One cluster, which involves *school failure and absenteeism, defiant behavior, early sexual activity, violence and delinquency* (Luster & Small, 1995; Morris et al., 1995) has been labeled as *"under controlled"* (Robins et al., 1996), because each of these problems appears to stem from a *failure of impulse control.*

Another perspective that attempts to explain the clustering of these phenomena is presented in Jessor and Jessor's *Problem Behavior Theory* (Jessor & Jessor, 1997), which postulates that *unconventionality* in adolescents and their environments underlies all of these behaviors. Characteristics such as *acceptance of deviance; low levels of connection to conventional institutions, such as family, church and school; political views that defy everyday social norms; and participation in deviant behavior* comprise unconventionality in the individual (Steinberg, 1999). Alcoholic, abusive or transitory families, communities with high levels of stress, gang activity, violence and/or drug availability, and deviant peers (all of which support engagement in problem behavior) constitute unconventional environments. Other factors known to cluster with unconventional cognition and behavior are: *sensation seeking, risk tak-*

ing, drug use, and drunk driving (Brack, Brack & Orr, 1994). The underlying source of unconventionality has been hotly debated. Three general theoretical perspectives explain its occurrence:

- **Problem behavior within the individual:** A basic predisposition toward engaging in deviant behavior (whether biologically or environmentally derived) exists within the at-risk youth. An older view is that unconventionality may stem from an inherited disposition toward deviance. Other versions of a biological interpretation (sometimes referred to as "bottom-up" explanations) look to differences in individual arousal and sensation-seeking tendencies. More recent theories emphasize problematic childhood environments such as family and community violence, deviant (substance abusing or criminal) parents and peers, etc. This model explains problem behavior as a misdirected but adaptive response to a bad situation.

- **Spiraling of consequences:** Kandel, et al. (1991) suggests that there is no need to postulate an underlying predisposition toward deviant behavior (whether biologically or environmentally derived). This model stresses the eventuality that some sorts of problem behavior tend to elicit others (such as cocaine and alcohol use underlying an increased likelihood of an adolescent becoming pregnant, or engagement in delinquent activity landing an adolescent in a juvenile facility which exposes them to criminal peers). Thus, early and milder problem behaviors, after initial experimentation may spiral into more severe and frequent problem behaviors in a sort of domino effect (Steinberg, 1999).

- **Social control theory:** It is the lack of ties to conventional individuals and environments (peers, family and school) that underlies problem behavior (Steinberg, 1999). Weak social bonding disconnects some youth from more normative environments and experiences. Bereft of these social bonds to conventional activities, social control theory postulates that the development of unconventional attitudes and behaviors is likely. This theory is capable of predicting elevated rates of problem behavior found among adolescents in high-risk environments (such as those characterized by poverty, abuse, etc.) that are characterized by disengagement from conventional institutions (Steinberg, 1999).

Throughout this guide, each of these theories is used eclectically to develop intervention strategies. It is likely that a combination of some of the above factors may be operating in the etiology of problem behavior (Steinberg, 1999). This analysis, therefore, assumes that adolescent problem behavior is caused by multiple factors and that those factors interact in complex ways within any particular individual.

CULTURE AND GENDER

Race, Ethnicity and Adolescent Problem Behaviors

Most studies of adolescent risk have focused on the psychosocial and cognitive domains. Analyses of the effects of cultural variables (e.g., ethnic identity, ethnic values) have been comparatively rare (Scheier, Botvin, Diaz, & Ifill-Williams, 1997). Although most minority adolescents do not have adjustment difficulties (Steinberg, 1999), culture may be related to a wide range of risk factors for problem behavior including: self-esteem (Bautista de Domanico, Crawford, & De Wolfe, 1994); academic achievement (Arroyo & Zigler, 1995); personal and social development (Scheier et al. 1998); psychological well-being (Bernal, Saenz, & Knight, 1991); and other mental health factors. The link between cultural variables and other risk factors for problem behavior, however, is not straight-forward, especially when it comes to ethnic identity (Scheier et al.). For example, in comparison to Anglo-American youth, certain behaviors among African American and Native American juveniles, such as early sexual activity and disengagement from school, may not be as suggestive of underlying adjustment disorder and other more severe forms of problem behavior (Neumark-Sztainer, et al., 1996). Cultural factors are undoubtedly interwoven throughout the entire fabric of adolescent development. In addition to presenting a discrete chapter on *Youth Culture and Diversity,* our approach is to discuss the importance of gender, race and ethnicity across all categories of juvenile problems (e.g., crime, substance abuse and mental disorder), as well as the relevance of culture to risk, resiliency, treatment and rehabilitation.

Gender Considerations

Female juvenile offenders constitute the largest growing segment of the juvenile population (Acoca, 1998). In the past decade, the increase of arrests of girls has been at a higher rate for almost every type of crime than for boys (Snyder, 1997). This includes arrests for violent crime, where research has long revealed far lower rates among females than males. Snyder (1997) reports that 723,000 girls younger than age 18 were arrested in 1996 alone. Thirty-one percent of juvenile offenders are female. The phenomenon of delinquent girlhood as well as differences in developmental pathways to male and female offending is explored in depth in *Chapter 6—Gender and Adolescent Problem Behavior.*

Much of what is presented in this *Provider's Guide* will have direct relevance for both females and males. However, it has become recognized that in order to improve services and reduce female recidivism, a special-needs focus for girls and women must be incorporated into the treatment policy and curriculum (Covington, 2000; White, 2001; *Center for Substance Abuse Treatment* [CSAT] - Kassebaum, 1999). This is especially important as rates of female arrest and imprisonment are on the rise, among both adolescents and adults (Covington, 2000; Kassebaum, 1999; Pollock, 1998). This project, therefore, makes the following key assertions:

- Gender-adapted relevance in treatment is required. One focus of this guide, therefore, will be to identify those specific areas where female clients may require different types of intervention, in order to achieve relevance to the contexts of their lives. As there is no direct correspondence between adolescent males' and females' experiences, "special services to a male treatment model is not sufficient" (Kassebaum, 1999, p. 17).

- Girls' needs and experiences are often fundamentally different from those of boys', not simple add-ons requiring a minor substitution of details.

- Because adolescence imposes some general demands upon an individual, (e.g., exploration of sexuality), some experiences of male and female adolescents may overlap. In addition, some particular issues may have relevance to both sexes, to the extent that both males and females may have encountered similar experiences (such as witnessing domestic violence between their parents), or developed similar problems (such as substance abuse). For example, some young males have been sexually abused as children and although there is extensive literature suggesting a male's response to this abuse may be quite different from a female's, there are some areas of overlap. In general, however, these experiences tend to elicit gender-specific responses, which must be responded to individually as they appear.

Table 0.2 Target Populations

- 14 to 18 years of age
- Committed youth
- Youth on probation
- Social Services placements
- Community Corrections
- Court-ordered outpatient treatment services
- Youth who have been or are at-risk of suspension or expulsion from school

Table 0.3 Minimum Symptom Admission Criteria

One or more of the following patterns of problem behaviors:

- Moderate to severe involvement in the criminal justice system with evidence of substance abuse;

- History of substance abuse and meets *DSM-IV* criteria for conduct disorder including: A repetitive and persistent pattern of behavior in which the basic rights of others or major age-appropriate societal norms or rules are violated as manifested by the presence of three or more of the following criteria in the past 12 months, with at least one criterion present in the past 6 months: 1) aggression to people and animals; 2) destruction of property; 3) deceitfulness or theft; 4) serious violations of the rules.

- Youth who have an identified pattern of drug use and delinquency, who are at risk of developing treatment level problems due to significant disruptions in family functioning, school adjustment, mental health adjustment, deviant behaviors, or involvement with deviant subculture.

Table 0.4 Principles of Intervention (National Institute of Justice)

- Striking a balance between accountability to the victim and/or the community with rehabilitation of the offender;

- Recognition of the importance of the juvenile justice system in the treatment process;

- An early intervention, when reversal of problem behaviors is still possible;

- A collaboration among all agencies, i.e., a single point of entry for the youth, yet with communication and involvement by both drug rehabilitation agencies and the judicial agencies;

- Relating all interventions to the youth's world: school, peers, and the family;

- Staff who are trained in unique needs of adolescents, minorities, as well as the justice system;

- Offering educational and job opportunities;

- The utilization of less restrictive programs that specifically address the occurrence and reinforcement of problem behaviors, e.g., family, school and peer groups.

TARGET GROUPS & ADMISSION CRITERIA

The intended target populations and criteria for participation in the *PSD-C* program are delineated in *Tables 0.2 and 0.3*.

PRINCIPLES OF INTERVENTION

Table 0.4 shows the *National Institute of Justice* principles of intervention that guide the development for systems-wide improvement of treatment services for at-risk youth.

HOW THIS PROVIDER'S GUIDE IS ORGANIZED

Introduction—Juvenile Problem Behavior and Juvenile Offending

The *Introduction* presents the purpose and major goals of *Pathways to Self-Discovery and Change (PSD-C)*. Strategies for intervention with the youthful offender are presented in the context of a holistic approach, including key features of the cognitive-behavioral treatment (CBT) platform as adapted for use with adolescents. An integrative approach to the treatment of adolescent problem behaviors is defined, with emphasis on a social learning perspective, relevance to race, gender and culture, a person-centered focus, a strengths-based orientation, training to aid in successful transition and preparation for healthy living in the broader community.

This *Provider's Guide* is divided into three sections:

SECTION I: THEORETICAL AND RESEARCH PERSPECTIVES

This section describes the theoretical foundations and research evidence for development and implementation of adolescent-focused treatment programming. Included are discussions of: risk and resiliency factors that mediate problem behaviors; mental heath factors associated with deviant activity; bio/psycho/social underpinnings of substance abuse and crime; the action of AOD on the developing adolescent brain; factors that predict adolescent limited and life-course persistent patterns of criminal involvement; gender differences and treatment implications for juvenile

justice clients; treatment enhancement through cultural mindfulness; and perspectives on assessing risk and resiliency for screening, in-depth treatment planning and outcome assessment.

Chapter 1—Risk and Resiliency During Adolescence

Chapter 1 examines adolescent patterns of behavior as resultant from an amalgam of individual, family, peer and community risk and resiliency factors. Adolescent problem behaviors are considered in the context of dramatic change in a person's life. Parental influence and identification with a deviant subculture are discussed as correlates of adolescent problem behavior. These factors are placed in the framework of *Problem Behavior Theory* (Jessor, 1987b), which describes the mechanisms through which some adolescents crystallize a deviant identity. Research evidence is presented for an array of risk factors along with evidence for protective factors in the individual, family and community infrastructure. Various subtypes of adolescent problem behaviors are analyzed according to specific risk factors. The chapter concludes with a discussion of the need for a strengths-based treatment model addressing delinquency, substance abuse and co-occurring mental disorder.

Chapter 2—Mental Health and Adolescent Problem Behavior

Chapter 2 begins with a statement that most adolescents navigate teenage years without major emotional or behavioral disturbance. There is, however, a large population of adolescents who manifest symptoms of mental disorder and become involved in delinquency, crime, and substance abuse. Diagnostic criteria and causal factors are examined for subtypes of mental disorder with the highest probability of intersecting with delinquency, crime, and substance abuse. Correlates and moderating factors are examined in profiles of ADHD, oppositional defiant disorder; conduct disorder, some personality disorders, and post-traumatic stress disorder. Information is provided on diagnosis and psychosocial treatments as well as a summary of the arsenal of psychotherapeutic medications used in contemporary clinical practice.

Chapter 3—Substance Abuse and Adolescent Problem Behavior

Chapter 3 investigates the phenomenon of adolescent substance use and abuse. Information is presented on prevalence and severity, followed by discussing the importance of current drug trends and the potential impact of imminent drug threats. Key factors in the etiology of adolescent-onset substance abuse are examined. These include social competence, life skills, deviant peer affiliations and positive expectancies for substance use. Adolescent problem drinking is examined, including variables associated with teenage drinking and driving. The drug-crime relationship during adolescence is explored, as is the relationship between substance abuse and violence. The possible contribution from prescription drugs to teenage violence is also addressed. Ethnic identity is explored as a potential risk or protective factor for substance abuse during adolescence.

Chapter 4—Substance Abuse and the Adolescent Brain

There are some very complex changes in brain wiring that take place during adolescence, the most profound of which seem to occur in the frontal lobes. As a consequence of such changes, alcohol and other drugs affect adolescents and adults differently. *Chapter 4* begins with an explanation of the neurochemical basis for brain functioning, followed by discussion of factors involved in adolescent brain development. Mechanisms of action are delineated for each major category of AOD abuse including: alcohol, methamphetamine, cocaine, marijuana, opiates, Ecstasy, inhalants, hallucinogens and tobacco. Each section concludes with a description of the possible long- and short-term effects of each type of substance abuse.

Chapter 5—Delinquency, Crime and Violence

Chapter 5 investigates general patterns of juvenile offending, as well as the major correlates of juvenile crime. Two major pathways of development are identified— *"life-course-persistent"* and *"adolescence-limited."* The etiology of each of these patterns of antisocial behavior is explained, and implications for treatment and policy are explored. A developmental perspective on youth violence is presented, including studies about the trajectory of violent crime over the course of childhood and adolescence. A profile of serious criminality by juvenile offenders is then presented, including neurological, psychiatric and socio-cultural components. The phenomenon of juvenile homicide is explored, as well as recidivism among adolescent violent offenders. Finally, the situation of juveniles in the criminal justice system is investigated, concluding with a discussion of implications for treatment and policy.

Chapter 6—Gender and Adolescent Problem Behavior

Chapter 6 addresses issues of gender as they pertain to juvenile problem behavior. The chapter begins with a discussion of the major psychosocial factors associated with the development of problem behavior in adolescent girls. This sets the stage for analysis of: girls and status offenses; sexual abuse factors as they contribute to female substance abuse and crime; and the interrelationships between gender, gangs and juvenile offending. The need for gender-specific programming is elaborated. Gender norms are explored in terms of how they influence patterns of juvenile substance abuse, crime and violence. Gender norms are also discussed in relationship to teen dating and the widespread phenomenon of date rape. Characteristics of sexually abusive adolescents are examined followed by a discussion of implications for treatment and social policy.

Chapter 7—Youth, Culture and Diversity

Chapter 7 views adolescent subgroups in terms of common beliefs, values, behaviors and communication patterns. Effective treatment builds upon the developmental process of forming attitudes and behavioral patterns that foster a sense of belonging and purpose during adolescence. Beginning with an analysis of the adolescent quest self-identity and social role definition, this chapter proceeds to explore cultural similarities and differences within four adolescent subgroups: violence-based; music-based; anti-authority; thrill-seeking. Due to the relative salience of peer influence compared to adult influence, a treatment focus on *commonalities of experience and purpose* among group members can promote an "in-group" identity. Through a strength-based perspective, group members become aligned with positive attitudes about treatment and the common goal of achieving positive treatment outcomes. The chapter delineates a continuum of cultural competence among counseling personnel with guidelines presented for how treatment providers can improve their counseling proficiencies by becoming mindful of their own cultural proclivities as well as the cultural orientations of each member of the treatment group. The three elements germane to cultural proficiency are *understanding, respect and support.*

Chapter 8—Perspectives on Assessment of the Juvenile Offender

Chapter 8 provides a theoretical framework and model for the assessment of juvenile justice system (JJS) youth with substance abuse issues. The goals and objectives of screening and assessment, the key data sources for assessment, and issues of report subjectivity are discussed. The *convergent validation* model is presented, which addresses the dilemma of establishing a valid information base about the client and the problem of self-report validity. Guidelines related to the use of assessment instruments and basic approaches to determining whether to include an adolescent in the category of having a substance abuse problem are described. Difficulties in the use of the *DSM-IV* for diagnosing substance misuse in adolescents and issues around error risks in assessment decisions are also examined. Various levels of evaluation, including preliminary screening, differential assessment, process and outcome measures are outlined. *Chapter 8* includes an annotated reference list of instruments that can be used at various levels of assessment. Specific areas of risk-resiliency assessment are outlined and discussed.

SECTION II: THE TREATMENT PLATFORM FOR ADOLESCENT SERVICE DELIVERY

This section explains the basic principles of cognitive-behavioral treatment including the primary focal points of *cognitive restructuring* and *social skills training*. The integration of therapeutic and didactic approaches as well as the synthesis of correctional and therapeutic strategies results in improved relapse and recidivism prevention outcomes. Visual schemas, used throughout the program, are introduced to clarify how thinking and behavior are related to learning and change. A visual blueprint of the sequential model for *relapse and recidivism prevention* is also provided. This section goes on to explain how generic CBT principles are adapted for juvenile justice clients, and how these basic approaches are operationalized for individual, family and residential treatment applications. The formats for *exemplary treatment programs* are discussed across a range of service delivery settings.

Chapter 9— Foundations of Cognitive-Behavioral Treatment

Chapter 9 explains the historical roots and major constructs that define contemporary cognitive-behavioral treatment (CBT). Behavioral and cognitive approaches have merged to form the *primary psychotherapeutic model* for criminal conduct, substance abuse and mental disorder. A comprehensive description of the basic principles of cognitive-behavioral therapy is followed by an introductory discussion of the major focal points of CBT: *cognitive restructuring and social skills training.*

Chapter 10—Core Strategies for Delinquency, Crime and Substance Abuse Treatment

Chapter 10 defines the meanings and distinctions between education, counseling and psychotherapy, then shows how PSD-C utilizes a psycho-educational model, combining therapeutic and didactic approaches. Core elements of the education and treatment platform are discussed, followed by a comprehensive analysis of the underlying principles of the cognitive-behavioral model for growth and change. Methods to achieve *cognitive restructuring* are examined, followed by discussion of how behavioral outcomes create and sustain old or new pathways to emotion and behavior. A visual schema is presented as a *conceptual tool* for understanding the CBT process of growth and change. The cognitive-behavioral blueprint for relapse and recidivism prevention is explained, pinpointing the primary targets of change in the PSD-C curriculum. *Chapter 10* concludes with a discussion of the necessary convergence of therapeutic and correctional (sanctioning) approaches for optimal treatment outcomes.

Chapter 11—Cognitive-Behavioral Perspectives on Adolescent Treatment

Chapter 11 begins with the assertion that there is dire need for treatment programs *geared specifically for adolescents*. At present, there is strong support for the use of cognitive-behavioral techniques; however, cultural and developmental considerations call for adaptations to fit adolescent experience. *Chapter 11* explores how the basic principles of CBT operate in teenage culture. Attraction to a deviant subculture, and initiation into substance abuse, promiscuous sexuality, gangs and criminal conduct can be seen as attempts (albeit maladaptive ones) to survive, given the *cognitive assessment* of living in a harsh and punishing environment. As alienation and social problem behaviors become repetitive, the adolescent may increasingly fail to perceive positive behavioral alternatives. Negative self-identities may be supported by fleeting feelings of "well-being" (as a result of successful criminal behavior). Some teens come to believe that they "have been driven into" (rather than chosen) crime and other problem behaviors, and that these patterns are necessary for survival. Support, concern and accurate information, rather than blame and confrontation, can move an adolescent into increased personal responsibility and self-efficacy. Counselors and treatment providers fulfill the functions of evaluation, education, consultation, coaching and support. They may also serve as role models, who demonstrate positive coping skills for dealing with adversity and challenge throughout the life trajectory. *Chapter 11* concludes with discussion of the need to ensure a post-treatment environment that *supports and re-kindles* positive treatment outcomes.

Chapter 12—Treatment Systems and Modalities

Chapter 12 discusses operational models for an array of adolescent intervention services, each utilizing CBT as the primary intervention tool. *Individual treatment* usually includes some facet of *motivational enhancement* (a set of principles that promote client engagement, including willingness to discuss relevant treatment issues and developing a plan for continued therapeutic progress). *Problem Solving Skills Training* (PSST) provides the framework for teaching a step-by-step approach to negotiate difficult interpersonal situations. Pro-social solutions are fostered through modeling, role-playing, coaching, practice and direct reinforcement. The basic premise of the *family systems approach* (included in most contemporary family therapy models) is that *improvement in the dynamics of the family* will result in increased resiliency for all involved. In the domain of *residential treatment*, the therapeutic community (TC) is a highly structured long-term treatment approach (6 to 18 months) where the community itself acts as *therapist and teacher*. Modifications to the original adult model include specific services for youth such *as education and family support* services. There is increased emphasis on recreation, less confrontation, more supervision and evaluation, more assessment for psychological disorders, greater family involvement, more psychotropic medications, and an integration of academics and techniques for cognitive restructuring.

Chapter 13—Exemplary Treatment Programs

Chapter 13 summarizes five exemplary adolescent treatment programs that are currently under empirical study by the *National Institute on Alcohol Abuse and Alcoholism* (NIAAA) and the *Center for Substance Abuse Treatment* (CSAT). The evaluation and manualization of these programs have been funded by the *Adolescent Treatment Model* (ATM) whose goals include: (a) identifying exemplary treatment models

for adolescents; (b) collaborating with providers to formalize and disseminate manuals; (c) evaluating the effectiveness as well as the cost-effectiveness of the models; and (d) to ensure that study findings are disseminated. Two additional programs are summarized: *Thinking for a Change* (T4C) and *Motivational Enhancement Therapy/Cognitive Behavioral Therapy* (MET/CBT 5). These programs cover a wide range of therapeutic approaches. The overview of these exemplary models will assist counselors in understanding the intricacies and nuances involved in providing adolescent-focused treatment for substance abuse and behavioral problems.

SECTION III: PROGRAM IMPLEMENTATION

This section presents procedural guidelines for how to deliver the 32-session PSD-C curriculum in the framework of a three-phase model for: (a) client involvement and problem recognition; (b) skill-building; and (c) internalization of understandings, skills and attitudes to sustain treatment gains outside the structures provided by therapeutic and/or judicial supervision. Admission procedures include: establishing consent for program involvement; implementing client rights notifications; and presenting full disclosure statements of provider qualifications and relevant professional certifications. A standardized client assessment protocol is outlined including recommendation of specific evaluation instruments and strategies. Different program schedules are provided including recommendations for presentation in an open group format. Specific principles of group leadership are outlined. Finally, this section provides concrete suggestions for how to set the tone for optimal client engagement, as well as a brief description of the content of each treatment session.

Chapter 14—Operational Guidelines for Program Delivery

Chapter 14 addresses implementation and operational procedures for delivery of the complete PSD-C curriculum. Characteristics of the effective counselor are outlined with discussion of the need to establish a balance between the correctional and therapeutic roles of the provider. *Chapter 14* discusses adaptation of the *stages of change* model to fit the context of adolescent development, i.e., the distinction between changing established patterns of thinking and acting vs. expediting transition from "adolescent-limited" experimentation with deviant identity. Ethical and legal issues in working with adolescent substance-abusing offenders are presented. Methods of admitting clients, establishing program involvement consent, implementing confidentiality and client rights notifications, and dispensing provider full disclosure statements are also outlined. Variations in program presentation are described. Basic principles of effective group management and leadership, within the framework of a manual-guided curriculum, are summarized. An operational approach to the assessment of clients is described, including specific instruments that are recommended at the various levels of assessment, i.e., screening, differential assessment, process and outcome data collection. A case study is presented that clearly demonstrates this assessment process. Provider facilitation and utilization of the *Self-Portrait* (client self-assessment) and *Plan for Change* (individual treatment plan) are discussed.

Chapter 15—The Treatment Curriculum

Chapter 15 begins with guidelines for how to establish an atmosphere of safety, trust and rapport in adolescent treatment settings. The theoretical framework and content of the treatment curriculum is presented as clients move through *Phase I: Challenge to Change, Phase II: Commitment to Change, and Phase III: Ownership of Change.* An outline of the cognitive-behavioral skills developed throughout the program is provided. *Chapter 15* describes techniques to enhance the treatment process, including a summary of orientation topics, which can be used by treatment providers as a checklist for how to engender client participation, present program guidelines and explain the theoretical basis for the *Pathways to Self-Discovery and Change* approach to treatment. The final section presents the rationale for each chapter in the *Participant's Workbook* with a content description for each treatment session.

SECTION I: THEORETICAL AND RESEARCH PERSPECTIVES

What's done to children, they will do to society.

—*Karl A. Menninger*

Risk and Resiliency During Adolescence

1

Chapter One:
Risk and Resiliency During Adolescence

Chapter Outline

Introduction

The Experience of Adolescence

Scope of Adolescent Problem Behavior
- Alcohol or other drugs
- Antecedents and correlates of adolescent drug abuse
- Gateway experiences
- Parent and peer influences
- Delinquency and crime
- Mental disorder

Problem Behavior Theory

The Offset of Risk and Resiliency in Adolescent Adjustment
- Risk and resiliency defined
- Identification of high-risk youth
- Mitigating risk by focusing on resiliency
- Risk and resiliency assessment

Summary of Risk Factors for Delinquency and Substance Abuse in Adolescrents
- Individual
- Family
- Psychosocial
- Core risk factors germane to research and assessment
- Different models for understanding risk factors

Empirical Studies of Resiliency
- Individual protective factors
- Family protective factors
- Psychosocial protective factors
- Positive building blocks of human development
- The relationship between risk and resliliency-protective factors

A Strengths Based Approach to Juvenile Justice and Treatment Services

Chapter Review

Chapter Objectives

- To provide an overview of adolescent problem behavior—its characteristics and prevalence;

- To present correlates of adolescent problem behavior such as parental influence and identification with the deviant subculture;

- To describe the interactions of personality, behavior, and perceived environment in relationship to risk and resiliency during adolescence;

- To describe the increased probability of adolescent problem behaviors in relationship to multiple risk exposures;

- To show the research evidence for an array of risk factors;

- To present evidence for protective factors in the individual, family and community infrastructure;

- To present a summary of risk and resiliency factors for subtypes of adolescent problem behavior; and

- To demonstrate theneed for an adolescent, strength-based treatment model thataddresses delinquency, substance abuse and co-occurring mental disorders.

INTRODUCTION

Most of our sentimentalists, friends of humanity and protectors of animals have been evolved from little sadists and animal tormentors.

- Sigmund Freud
Thoughts for the Times on War and Death
(1915, p. 212)

This chapter begins by setting adolescence in the context of rapid and dramatic change in a person's life. The scope of adolescent problem behaviors (drugs, crime and mental disorder) is delineated, addressing childhood antecedents and gateway experiences. The frequent appearance of attention deficit/hyperactivity and other disruptive behavior disorders in juvenile justice and public health treatment sectors is discussed as well as the common co-occurrence of *mental disorder and substance abuse.* Jessor's (1998) *Problem Behavior Theory* (PBT) is used to explain pschosocial factors that contribute to adolescent substance abuse and crime. PBT posits three interactive spheres that are causally related to multiple patterns of juvenile problem behavior: *the behavior system, the perceived environment,* and the *personality system.* The countervailing forces, or *risk* (e.g., individual, family, community) and *resiliency* (e.g., prosocial bonding, and solidity of community infrastructure), are reviewed, followed by a discussion of client risk and resiliency factors that are appropriate targets for therapeutic intervention. The chapter concludes with discussion of the elements of a strengths-based approach to juvenile justice and treatment services.

THE EXPERIENCE OF ADOLESCENCE

What are the factors—individual, family, school and the community—that lead some youth to major problems in living? Anna Freud (1958) described all adolescents as *"normal psychotics."* In fact, large-scale investigations of adolescent mental health (e.g., PowersHauser & Kilner, 1989; Roberts, Attkisson & Rosenblatt, 1998) do not confirm the severity of this indictment. The majority of meta-analytic and epidemiological studies report that the prevalence estimate of psychiatric disorders in the general child/adolescent population ranges from 5% to 8% for severe emotional distress (Costello, 1999; Friedman et al., 1996) and approximately 20% for any diagnosis manifesting some degree of psychological impairment (Costello et al., 1996; Shaffer, Hauser, &

Kilner, 1996). "Epidemiological studies reveal that only about 10% to 20% of adolescents exhibit some type of severe emotional disturbance—approximately the same percentage as in the adult population" (Powers et al. 1989, p. 201).

Offer (1987) warns that a generalized view of adolescence as naturally rife with mental disorder incorrectly leads us to *normalize* grave emotional and behavioral disturbance, blinding practitioners by failing to identify and help those adolescents in true crisis. Nonetheless, in consideration of the high rates of drug involvement, criminal conduct, and suicide, adolescence is sometimes tumultuous, aptly characterized by Hall (1916) as a period of *"Sturm und Drang"* (Gr. *Storm and Stress*). Psychological models provide insight into the formidable challenges posed by the unique confluence of psychological, biological and social forces signatory of adolescence. Erikson (1963) views the major developmental task of adolescence as the successful formation of *ego-identity,* or a prosocial stance toward the world, versus *ego-diffusion,* or *identity crisis* in which the individual has no clear concept of his or her role in life.As Erickson (1963) notes "The prime danger of this age, therefore is identity confusion, which can express itself in excessively prolonged moratoria; . . . in repeated impulsive attempts to end the moratorium with sudden choices. . . (p. 13).

Although emotions are often topsy-turvy during teenage years, thinking becomes more complex (Piaget, 1952). Young adults, in their natural transition from "concrete" to "abstract," develop the capacity for hypothetical reasoning, deduction and conclusions. They can ponder the future of the world and the history of the universe. Still, their concepts may be astonishingly simplistic. Adolescents are vulnerable to becoming true believers in black-or-white scientific, political, or religious ideologies, with a penchant for magical thought, particularly regarding their own omnipotence. Adolescence represents a window of vulnerability, whereby vast numbers of youth perform dangerous personal and social experiments.

SCOPE OF ADOLESCENT PROBLEM BEHAVIOR

Alcohol or other drugs

According to the *National Household Survey on Drug Abuse* (U.S. Department of Health and Human Services, 2001b), 7.1% of the population aged 12 and older reported using *illicit drugs during the prior month,* up from 6.3% in 1999. Marijuana use was most common, representing 76% of all current users. Marijuana usage increased from 4.8% in 1999 to 5.4% in 2001. Among 12-17 year olds, 10.8% were described as current illicit drug users. According to the *Monitoring the Future Study* (Johnston , O'Malley, & Bachman, 2002), the *lifetime use of any known illicit drug for 12th graders is 53%, with marijuana, LSD and cocaine showing lifetime use rates for 12th graders of 47.8%, 8.4% and 7.8% respectively. These rates were double those shown of 8th graders.* Lifetime usage of alcohol *increases* from 47% of the population of 8th graders to 78.4% of 12th graders. The steep increase in use rates from the 8th to 12th grade justifies *targeted prevention/intervention/treatment* efforts during adolescence, which may yield maximum benefits to youth and society. The use of *any illicit drugs* during the previous 30 days was 10.4% for 8th graders and 25.4% for 12th graders. When including *inhalants*, the figures rise to 12.6% for 8th graders and 25.9% for 12th graders. *Past month marijuana usage was 8. 3% and 21.5% for 8th and 12th graders, respectively.* 1.2% of 8th graders and 6% of 12th graders report *using marijuana daily* (Johnston et al., 2002).

Alcohol remains an *even larger problem* among teenagers than illicit drugs. 7% of 8th graders and 30.3% of 12th graders report *having been drunk* during the previous 30 days. *Alcohol usage during the previous month was 19.6% for 8th graders and 48.6% for 12th graders. 12.4% of 8th graders and 28.6% of 12th graders report having had five or more drinks in a row during the previous two weeks* (Johnston et al., 2002).

Antecedents and correlates of adolescent drug abuse

Ray & Ksir (2002) assert that individuals who are at *risk for drug abuse are also at risk for other deviant behaviors;* fighting, stealing, vandalism, and early sexual activity are correlated with drug use and heavier alcohol use. Therefore, the pattern of deviance-prone activity might have both a variety of causes and a variety of behavioral expressions, one of which is drug use. Other indicators of deviant behavior generally appear before drug use. Children often achieve poor grades or get into trouble for fighting or stealing before they first experiment with alcohol, cigarettes or other substances. In most cases, the conduct problems and grade problems are not caused by drug use.

Gateway experiences

Ray and Ksir (2002) found that only 1% of students began their substance use with marijuana or another illicit drug. It is as though they first had to go through the gateway of using alcohol and in many cases, cigarettes. Cigarette smokers were about twice as likely as the nonsmokers to move on to smoking marijuana. In the senior class of 1994, those who were daily smokers of a pack or more of cigarettes were about 15 times more likely than non-smokers to have used cocaine and about four times as likely to have smoked marijuana. From the *National Household Survey on Drug Abuse (U.S. Department of Health and Human Services),* (2001b), among youth aged 12 to 17, just over one-third had ever tried cigarettes, but those who had tried cigarettes were more than 10 times as likely to have also tried marijuana. Early alcohol use and cigarette smoking are common indicators of the general deviance-prone pattern of behavior that also includes an increased likelihood of smoking marijuana or trying cocaine. In the senior class of 1994, a student with a D average was about 14 times as likely as a student with an A average to be a pack-a-day smoker.

Parent and peer influences

It is generally true that adolescents are more influenced by their parents when it comes to *long-term* goals and plans, but their peers have more influence over *their immediate lifestyle* and day-to-day activities. As adolescence progresses, peer influences become stronger. The best predictors of drug use are *peer variables.* Having peers with *antisocial attitudes* is the *strongest predictor* of drug use (Ray and Ksir, 2002).

Delinquency and crime

According to the *Office of Juvenile Justice and Delinquency Prevention (U.S. Department of Justice), (1997),* there are about *30 million* youth in the U. S. between the ages of 10 and 17. The estimated number of juvenile arrests in 1995 was 2. 7 million. About 1 in 7 juvenile arrests were for a crime involving *violence or the threat of violence.* Ten percent of high school students carried a weapon on school property in the past month. In the same year, 1 in 12 high school students *were threatened or injured with a weapon at school.*

As shown in the *Surgeon General's (U.S. Department of Health and Human Services),* (2001c) report on juvenile crime and violence, in 1998, over *30%* of 12th graders were reported to have *hit an instructor,* gotten into a *serious fight* in school or at work, *taken part* in a fight, hurt somebody badly enough to need *bandages or a doctor*, or used a *knife or gun* or some other weapon to get something from a person. *Fifteen percent* were reported to have committed an *assault with injury*, and 5% committed *robbery with a weapon*. In 1998, *one out of every six youth* (10 to 17 years of age) who was arrested, was arrested for violent crimes (*U.S. Department of Health and Human Services, 2001c*).

Mental disorder

The *Diagnostic Interview Schedule for Children* was administered between October 1997 and January 1999 to 1,618 randomly selected youths aged 6 to 18 years who were participants in at least one of the following five public sectors of care: *alcohol and drug services (AD); child welfare (CW); juvenile justice (JJ); mental health (MH); and public school services for youth with serious emotional disturbances (SED)*. Fifty-four percent of the participants met criteria for at least one disorder. Attention-deficit/hyperactivity disorder (ADHD) and other disruptive behavior disorders, (conduct disorder and oppositional defiant disorder), *at 50 %*, were extremely high for youth in public sectors of care. Rates were generally higher in sectors that are designated to serve mental health needs, but the prevalence of mental health disorders was also high in sectors not specifically designed to meet this need (e.g., CW & JJ). While there were no significant differences in the rates of "any study disorder" associated with age group or gender, there were significant differences for specific diagnoses. The rates of ADHD decline by age while the rates of CD are higher among adolescents than in younger children. The rate of PTSD is higher among older teenagers and the rates of major depression also increase with age. Rates of ADHD and CD were significantly higher among males and the rates of PTSD, separation anxiety, and major depression were significantly higher among females.

Figure 1.1, Diagnostic Prevalence Rates for the 10 Most Common Disorders for ADM and Non-ADM Service Sectors, shows the prevalence rates for each of the most common diagnostic categories for youth who were identified as being "active" in at least one of the alcohol/drug/or mental health settings (ADM) compared to youth who were "active" in child welfare or juvenile justice settings (non-ADM).

PROBLEM BEHAVIOR THEORY

A long history of multivariate research (e.g., Horn & Wanberg, 1969; Botvin, 1983; Newcomb, Maddahian, & Bentler, 1986) points to multiple causes, patterns and outcomes of substance abuse, delinquency and mental disorder within the teenage population. Using the *Adolescent Self-Assessment Profile*, Wanberg (1992, 2000) identified *six independent risk factors* for continued adjustment problems into adulthood: family disruption; mental health problems; deviant and antisocial behavior; negative peer influence; poor school adjustment; and history of alcohol or other drug abuse. *Problem Behavior Theory* (Jessor, 1987a) provides a psychosocial framework for exploring the interaction of risk and resiliency factors, which operate as countervailing forces in the development of prosocial or antisocial patterns of behavior.

Problem behavior, defined by Jessor (1987a, 1994, 1998) as behavior that departs from the social and legal norms of the larger society, is theoretically caused by three systems of psychosocial influence:

THE BEHAVIOR SYSTEM includes a *problem behavior* structure that gives examples of problem behavior, and also a *conventional behavior* structure that exemplifies conventional behavior.

THE PERSONALITY SYSTEM includes the *motivational-instigation* structure, determined by value placed on achievement and independence; the *personal belief structure*, related to a person's concept of self relative to society; and *personal control structure*, which gives a person reasons to not participate in problem behavior.

THE PERCEIVED ENVIRONMENT system includes two structures: *distal*, inclusive of a person's relationship to their support network; and *proximal*, which deals with a person's environment in relationship to available models of behavior.

Since problem behaviors are related, isolating drug abuse or juvenile delinquency as independent problem behaviors, without considering the behavior system along with associated personality and perceived environment structures, would be counterproductive to any attempts at treatment or rehabilitation. When the *personality system* and the *perceived environment system* clash, behavioral problems become evident. Relative to adolescent substance abuse and crime, factors that significantly increase the probability of continued involvement in a deviant lifestyle include:

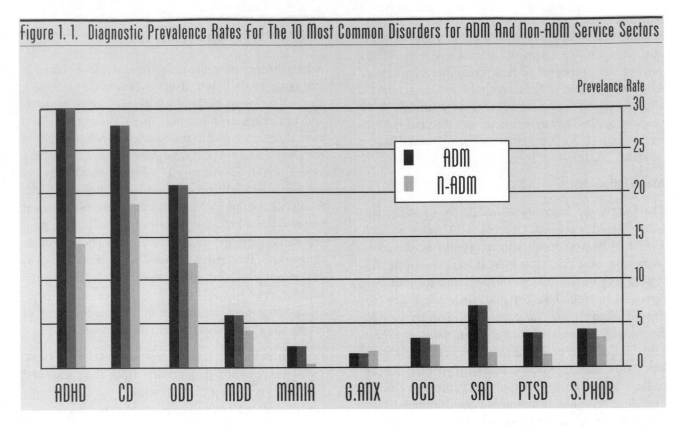

Figure 1.1. Diagnostic Prevalence Rates For The 10 Most Common Disorders for ADM And Non-ADM Service Sectors

- **Behavior structure:** featuring *normalized images of drug use and criminal conduct;*

- **Personality structure:** characterized by *low value placed on achievement and success along with a poorly developed personal control structure;*

- **Perceived environment:** steeped in *role models and opportunities* (including work environment and living situation) that *manifest substance abuse and criminal conduct*

By treating all *spheres of influence* (not just substance abuse and criminal conduct), a broad array of antisocial patterns is expected to diminish.

Although *risk factors* play a strong role in the determination of adolescent problem behaviors, their influence is *moderated by protective* factors, which are also important determinants of adolescent adjustment. According to Jessor (1998) risk factors that contribute to the formation of deviance are: low self-esteem, low success expectations, a sense of alienation and desperation (*personality system*); orientation towards antisocial friends and parents, and peer models with problem behavior (*perceived environment*); disconnection with conventional institutions and the lack of success in school (*behavior system*).

Protective/Resiliency factors are: relationships with adults, supportive family relationships, the perception

of a normative control from the outside, conventional friends' models of behavior, good school results, being involved in prosocial groups and in positive social activities, positive attitude towards school and intolerance to deviance, religious faith, and voluntary activity. Jessor shows that protective factors *interact with risk factors* in such a way that *when protection is high,* there is *no impact of risk* on problem behavior, whereas when there is no protection, there is a *linear relationship between risk and problem behavior.* These results stress attention toward **promotion of protective factors** rather than more conventional approaches that focus almost exclusively on reduction of risk.

THE OFFSET OF RISK AND RESILIENCY IN ADOLESCENT ADJUSTMENT

Understanding the various factors that place youth at risk for developing problem behavior is an essential first step toward effective intervention. In particular, recognition of the early signs of disruptive problem behaviors (e.g., attention deficit hyperactivity; oppositional defiant or, conduct disorder) is of vital importance, as timely intervention may stem long-term progression from aggressive and noncompliant behavior into more severe behavioral and social problems during late adolescence and into adulthood (Holmes, Slaughter, & Kashani, 2000).

Risk and resiliency defined

Research with large and distinct populations (both within and outside of the US) reveals a relatively consistent set of risk factors for adolescent problem behavior (Scheier, Botvin, Diaz & Ifill-Williams, 1997). Jessor, Turbin and Costa (1998) identify some of the mechanisms that may be involved in the development of risk for or protection from problem behavior.

RISK is defined as any characteristic that:

- Evokes or encourages problem behavior;

- Elicits behavior that is incompatible with staying in school; and

- Produces circumstances that compromise school engagement.

PROTECTION is defined in direct opposition, referring to any factor that:

- Promotes development of individual constraints on problem behavior;

- Supplies social controls against the development of problem behavior;

- Focuses the adolescent on alternative activities;

- Elicits activities that are incompatible with problem behavior; and

- Promotes and reinforces orientation toward conventional institutions and codes of behavior (Jessor et al., 1998, p. 195).

Identification of high risk youth

Kashani, Jones, Bumby and Thomas (2001) reviewed relevant psychosocial risk factors for the development of youth violence, and concluded that theoretical approaches reliant on single dimensions of prediction are insufficient to encompass or explain this phenomenon. They suggest use of a multi-dimensional psychosocial framework, with factors ranging from the individual and family levels to the school, peer, community, and cultural levels. Utting (1996) encompasses this range within four general areas of risk: *individual, familial, educational, and socio-economic/community*. In accordance with these formulations, *Table 1.1* presents a four-tiered summary of risk and protection for adolescent problem behavior.

Multiple Exposures to Risk: Fox and Levin (2001) summarize the many factors that may separate some adolescents from more prosocial alternatives and styles of responding.

- Behavioral interference and frustration

- Relative deprivation and economic need associated with poverty

- Minimal levels of social bonding to conventional individuals, attitudes and institutions

- Repeated head trauma

- Various types of personality disorder (e.g., a lack of moral restraint and empathy)

- Poor skills for everyday social functioning

- Growing up in a subculture of violence

In a meta-analysis of 66 longitudinal studies of non-incarcerated adolescents Hawkins, Herrenkohl, et al., 2000 reported that the more individual risk factors to which an individual is exposed, the greater the probability of becoming involved in violent conduct. Regarding criminal involvement, by comparing aggressive vs. non-aggressive adolescent offenders, Venezia (2001) found that while no one factor carried enough variance to provide for good prediction in itself, a combination of the total number of risk factors to which an adolescent is exposed is more strongly correlated with criminal involvement. From this, a "total risk variable" was proposed, which simply adds the presence of individual risk factors into a sum.

Mitigating risk by focusing on resiliency

Griffin, Scheier, Botvin and Diaz (2000) emphasize the importance of targeting both **risk and resiliency** in attempting to deter adolescent problem behavior. Psychosocial factors that *confer social competence, self-esteem, and adaptive cognition*, as well as factors that provide for *job or other organizational attachment* (Sampson & Laub, 1993), may serve to buffer adolescents from the negative effects of risk. Such *protective factors* have been associated with lower levels of problem behavior, as well as with positive treatment outcomes (Jessor, Van Den Bos, Vanderryn, Costa & Turbin, 1997). These empirical findings have been interpreted as the *mitigating effects of protective factors* to promote *resiliency*. This moderation of *risk by protection* is found to hold across gender, race and ethnicity (Jessor et al., 1995).

A study that probed the relationship between *cognitive protective factors* and outcomes with regard to problem behavior (Jessor et al., 1998) found a correlation between adaptive (constructive) cognition and lower levels of problem behavior involvement. In a longitudinal study involving high school students in an urban

Table 1.1   Risk and Resiliency Factors for Adolescent Problem Behaviors

INDIVIDUAL

- Biological, e.g., age, sex, learning disability, hyperactivity, attention deficits

- Psychological, e.g., self-concept, relevant personality factors, mood and emotional adjustment

- Cognitive, e.g., locus of control, alcohol expectancies

- Behavioral, e.g., early onset of aggressiveness, noncompliance, substance use

- Life experience, e.g., early contact with the juvenile justice system

PSYCHOSOCIAL

- Familial, e.g., quality of attachment and social bonds, parental control

- Educational e.g., academic failure, school discipline referrals and truancy

- Peer, e.g., delinquent vs. conventional peer associations

COMMUNITY

- Socio-economic status and poverty;

- Neighborhood, e.g., neighborhood stress ,community violence, etc.

- Gang activity

DEMOGRAPHIC

- Various aspects of teen culture (e.g., the subculture of violence) that may provide access to delinquent peers and role models

- Ethnic norms and values that can provide protective buffering against these influences

school district (Jessor et al., 1998), both risk and protective factors were analyzed for interactions with student outcome. Negative outcomes correlated with socioeconomic disadvantage and with low self-esteem, low expectations for success, a sense of hopelessness, and association with delinquent peers while positive effects were found for protective factors. Other studies have investigated the influence of protective factors among first-time adolescent offenders (aged 13 to 17 years). The strategic inclusion of (*family involvement*) protective factors along with risk factors during the treatment process allowed for better rates of program completion, lower recidivism and later reductions of serious crime (Pobanz, 2001). These findings further support the interpretation that *identifiable protective factors* may play a significant role in producing

resilience against problem behavior in adolescence.

Treatment implications: In order to deliver comprehensive and effective services, intervention that helps an adolescent develop both psychosocial and cognitive protective factors should be used alongside treatment that attempts to reduce risk directly (Jessor et al., 1998). These efforts should be geared toward both the individual and contextual levels, providing the adolescent with an environment that not only helps to develop patterns of protective cognition and behavior, but also fosters and sustains their use. In this regard, commitment of social resources along such avenues as *attempting to increase school engagement and connectedness, providing opportunities for prosocial activities (such as community volunteer opportunities) as well as instruction geared toward enhancing cognitive and psychosocial development* may be well worth their return in reduced adolescent involvement in problem behavior (Jessor et al., 1998). This public health strategy may be especially effective in social contexts of high socioeconomic disadvantage, as moderation of risk is more vivid among economically disadvantaged adolescents (Jessor et al., 1998). Therefore, targeting both risk and protection may be even more important when working with teens that lack other types of protection, e.g., those living in poverty or without social ties and family bonds—precisely those adolescents who are at highest risk. A first step in designing an effective treatment regimen for substance abusing and/or delinquent adolescents is comprehensive evaluation of the factors that increase vulnerability, balanced with assessment of individual, family and community assets that can reduce the effects of deprivation and negative influences.

Risk and resiliency assessment

Apparent differences in *developmental trajectories* of criminal behavior suggest the existence of two distinct groups of adolescent offenders:

- "Teen culture" — those who seem to be experimenting with delinquency as a mechanism of separation from home and family (i.e., "experimenters," Probanz, 2001) also known as "*adolescence-limited*" trajectory of development (Moffitt, 1993).

- "Criminal career" — those whose delinquent behavior develops into a lifetime of criminal offense, i. e., "chronic offenders" (Probanz, 2001), also known as the "*life-course-persistent*" pathway of development (Moffitt, 1993; Patterson & Yoerger, 1993).

This distinction in the pathways of adolescent development necessitates that **risk assessment** be done on at least two levels. An adolescent who has become visible to social services must be screened for:

- The probability of worsening of problem behaviors (such as alcohol use escalating into alcoholism, drunk driving or drug abuse; or drug use escalating into drug sales); and

- The likelihood of escalation of problem behavior into criminal behavior and serious violence.

Jessor et al. (1998) hypothesize that risk and protection are likely to exert *reciprocal influence* upon each other in progressions toward adolescent lifestyles and behavior. For this reason, protective factors are an important component of risk assessment as well as in treatment.

Risk assessment procedures may be enhanced by adding analysis of protective factors to those of risk, in order to comprise a composite profile that affords enhanced prediction of whether an adolescent is merely experimenting or embarking on a lifetime career of criminal conduct (Probanz, 2001). The section below summarizes evidence for specific *individual, family, and psychosocial risk factors*, combinations of which exponentially increase the probability of delinquency and/or substance abuse within the adolescent population.

SUMMARY OF RISK FACTORS FOR DELINQUENCY AND SUBSTANCE ABUSE IN ADOLESCENTS

INDIVIDUAL RISK FACTORS

Biological

Sensation Seeking (SS): Jessor et al. (1998) contends that *SS* behavior can interfere with healthy adolescent development, and Spence (1998) finds sensation seeking to be one of the most important risk factors for engagement in problem behavior. For many teenagers, the surrounding social environment serves to inhibit recklessness. For some, however, the social environment promotes risk taking and thrill seeking. A thrill-oriented environment, when combined with personal characteristics such as egocentrism, may exacerbate the tendency to engage in rash and radical behaviors. This orientation toward risk may propel the adolescent into delinquent activity for the thrill of it. An orientation toward sensation seeking in tandem with the behavior of reckless peers, predicts irresponsible and dangerous adolescent behavior (Arnett, 1992). Epstein, Griffin and Botvin (2001) found *risk taking* to be an important predictor of alcohol use among inner-city minority adolescents. Arnett (1990) found a correlation between the inclination to drive while under the influence of alcohol and the impetus toward sensation seeking. Drunk driving was strongly correlated with subscales designed to measure *thrill and adventure seeking, disinhibition and boredom susceptibility*.

Depression: Some forms of depression that are attributed to biological underpinnings (endogenous) are related to substance abuse and criminal conduct (Scheier et al., 1997).

Head trauma: In some instances, head trauma (or exposure to environmental pollutants) has been implicated in abrupt and atypical explosions of rage (Fox & Levin, 2001).

Psychological

Self-concept: Several researchers site low self-esteem (unfavorable self-view) as a major risk factor for problem behavior (Scheier et al., 1997; Jessor et al., 1998). In a study spanning from 7th through 10th grades, correlations between alcohol, personal competence and self-esteem were investigated, with particular focus on change in these dimensions over time. Increasing levels of alcohol use were associated with decreases in perceived personal self-competence over time (Scheier & Botvin, 2000).

Self-concept and juvenile delinquency: Findings regarding the enhanced self-image of some adolescents who are involved in juvenile crime (Anderson, 1999; Bynum & Weiner, 2002) suggest that issues regarding self-concept and delinquency are complex, as opposed to previous suggestions such as:

- *Containment theory*—positive self-image will buffer an adolescent against peer associations that lead to delinquency and crime (Reckless, 1967);

- *Negative self-image* is at the root of delinquency, with delinquency serving as some sort of compensatory mechanism for self-perceived deficits (Kaplan,1980); and

- Delinquents "*cannot or have not gained the sense of a central self*" which affirms their personal uniqueness or value (Levy, 1997, p. 684).

The discovery of *enhanced self-image* in delinquent teens (Anderson, 1999; Bynum & Weiner, 2002) suggests that violence and criminal conduct may serve as a psychological mechanism for coping with poverty, harsh environments at home, or the threat of family or neighborhood violence (Prothrow-Stith, 1995; Feigelman, Howard, Xiaoming, & Cross, 2000). In Anderson's (1994, 1999) research with a sample of inner-city African American youth, he notes that violence was used as a *defensive posture* to gain respect and avoid victimization, i. e., the "code of the streets." Fagan & Wilkinson (1998) observe that frequent experiences with violence may impel youth to assimilate more deeply such a "street code" for self-protection. Bynum & Weiner (2002) found statistical correlations between high scores on the *Tennessee Self-concept Scale* and violent delinquency.

Cognitive deficits: Cognitive ability was found to predict criminal involvement (Levitt & Lochner, 2001).

The correlation between cognitive deficits and antisocial behavior holds across social class, race, and academic level (Lynam, Moffitt, & Stouthamer-Loeber, 1993). *Self-defeating thought patterns* often contribute to elevated risk for problem behavior (Jessor et al., 1998). Among these are:

- Low expectations of success;

- General sense of hopelessness; and

- Positive expectancies for cigarette, alcohol and drug use.

Low levels of personal competence skill: Poor communication skills, such as low levels of assertiveness and refusal skills are among the most prominent of risk factors for early onset drug and alcohol abuse, as well as other problem behaviors (Scheier et al., 1997).

Social orientation: Various directions of interpersonal focus may place adolescents at increased risk for problem behavior (Jessor, et al., 1998). Among these are:

- Greater orientation to friends than to parents;

- Greater orientation to friends as models for problem behavior; and

- Disengagement from school.

Behavioral problems: Early contact with the juvenile justice system is one of the strongest predictors of life-course persistent criminality and other adolescent adjustment difficulties (Loeber & Farrington, 1998). Six percent of males experience their first arrest before adolescence. This may be the best predictor of long-term criminal conduct (Moffitt, Caspi, Harrington & Milne, 2002).

Health behavior: A study of 7th to 12th graders found that insufficient personal health behavior (self-care) was itself correlated with engagement in problem behavior (Jessor, Donovan & Costa, 1996). Early sexual activity and/or promiscuity have also been associated with problem behavior (Jessor et al., 1998).

FAMILY RISK FACTORS

Maternal age at birth: Being born to a teenaged mother (who is likely to have a poor education), an individual (at age 18) is found to have lower levels of educational achievement, higher risk for substance abuse, juvenile crime and mental health problems. These risks were from 1.5 to 8.9 times higher than for those birthed by a mother over 30 years of age. These correlations may be related to the types of child-rearing environments and practices characteristic of younger maternal age. Generally, younger mothers provided environments that were less nurturing, less supportive and more volatile than those of older mothers (Fergusson & Woodward, 1999). Similarly, maternal age is associated with higher risk for child abuse (Connelly & Straus, 1992), which itself is implicated in the development of adolescent problem behavior.

Insecure attachment in infancy: Childhood attachment problems are correlated with childhood onset of disruptive behavioral problems, as well as the development of later delinquent and aggressive activities and reduced development of empathy and connectedness to others (Fonagy, Targct, Steele & Steele, 1997a). Qualities of attachment and social bonds have been found significant in predicting behaviors and attitudes of offending vs. non-offending adolescents (Utting, 1996). Disorganized attachment patterns tend to be associated with aggressive behavioral development (Lyons-Ruth, 1996).

Parental characteristics and behaviors of family members: A mother with a psychiatric diagnosis places an individual at four times the risk of engaging in serious criminal behavior (Preski & Shelton, 2001). *Parental substance abuse, criminal conduct and incarceration* arc associatcd with early emergence of adolescent substance abuse (Sommers & Baskin, 1991). In a 19-year study of 9- to 18-year-olds and their parents, parental involvement in criminal activity tends to transfer across generations (Wu, Ping, Kandel & Denise, 1995). *Parental use of cigarettes* has been shown to transmit across generations (Wu et al.).

Degree of parental supervision: Low levels of parental monitoring are associated with the emergence of adolescent substance abuse (Sommers & Baskin, 1991). Higher levels of parental monitoring were associated with lower levels of delinquency (Griffin, 2000). Higher levels of parental monitoring were associated with less drinking in males; spending time at home alone predicted more cigarette smoking in females only (Griffin et al., 2000).

Experiences with trauma and abuse, and domestic violence in the home: Family distress tends to predict adolescent difficulty in anger management (Thornberry et al., 1999) as well as adolescents use of violence toward their parents as an "adaptation to family strain" (Brezina, 1999). Trauma experienced within the family of origin is implicated in the development of adolescent problem behavior in several ways. A major class of problem behavior—the so-called "status offenses"—are strongly linked to the adolescent experiencing abuse of one form or another within the context of home and family. Covington (1998) defines status offenses as acts that would not be offenses if committed by adults, such as promiscuity, truancy, or running away. There are few alternatives in society for a child who is running away from physical abuse, sexual assault or other forms of psychological trauma that may occur in the contexts of home and family. A huge percentage of "runaways" are fleeing from such abuse. Most runaways are teenage girls (58%), who are between 16 and 17 years old (68%) (Covington, 1998). Of these girls, 29% did not find a safe place to stay. Yet the act of "runaway" alone is grounds for the charge of status offense.

Another reason youth may be found on the streets is a phenomenon known as *"thrown aways,"* i. e., "a child who was told to leave home, or whose caretaker refused to let come home . . . or whose caretaker made no effort to recover the child when the child ran away, or who was abandoned" (Snyder & Sickmund, 1999, p. 38). Though clearly engaging in self-defensive action by trying to survive on the streets, and frequently an act of health in trying to escape from a destructive situation, it is the child or adolescent who gets in trouble and is often returned to the abusive home without redress. Family abuse or neglect is also associated with early emergence of adolescent substance abuse (Sommers & Baskin, 1991).

Corporal Punishment and Child Abuse: In *Beating The Devil Out of Them*, Straus (2001) discusses the normative use of corporal punishment (such as spanking and slapping) and its effect on families and children. He documents common norms and social myths regarding spanking that portray it as a "minor," even "virtuous," form of aggression, and addresses the consensual validation for its use that stems from common parental beliefs (such as "everybody does it," "spare the rod, spoil the child," etc.), as well as supporting structures for the use of corporal punishment stemming from religious institutions, such as Protestant Fundamentalism (Grasmick, Bursik, Jr., & Kimpel, 1991; Ellison & Sherkat, 1993; Greven, 1991). Others have investigated the role of parental experiences with corporal punishment in their own childhood histories in the development of attitudes toward corporal punishment of their own children (Stattin, Janson, Klackenberg-Larsson, & Magnusson, 1995).

Although Straus (2001) documents that today, parents are generally using less corporal punishment, hitting of children and adolescents is still widespread (Straus & Donnelly, 1993; Stattin et al., 1995) and is hidden by a "conspiracy of silence" (Straus, 1991, 2001). Straus asserts that the price of such disciplinary "virtue" includes *adolescent depression and suicide, generalized alienation, as well as the fusion of sex and violence*. Drawing from decades of research considering the effects of child maltreatment, Straus (2001) concludes that this type of discipline in families contributes to the development of *aggressiveness, delinquency and criminal conduct* (conclusions also supported by the *American Psychiatric Association*, 1991; Berkowitz, 1993; Baumrind, 1991).

Supportive evidence for Straus's conclusions is strong. Several studies explore the connection between coercive punishment and adolescent aggressiveness; these effects have been observed to emerge as aggression toward peers as early as kindergarten (Strassberg, Dodge, Pettit, & Bates, 1994). Punitive discipline was associated with the development of delinquent and criminal behavior in a 28-year longitudinal study by Laub & Sampson (1995). Further evidence of the relationship between family violence and the development of problem behavior has been documented by Kashani & Allan (1998). Other investigations focus on the *relationship between spanking and lifetime psychiatric disorder* (MacMillan et al., 1999), as well as the relationship between childhood *spanking and depression, hopelessness, and reduced purpose in life* among adolescents (DuRant, Getts, Cadenhead, & Emans, 1995). Cohen and Brook (1995) found evidence that correlations between corporal punishment and adolescent problems may be influenced by both the gender and the age of the child who is being disciplined (whether in childhood, early, or late adolescence).

Although the appropriateness of corporal punishment in child discipline is still being debated (Larzelere, 1994), Straus presents convincing evidence regarding the negative effects of corporal punishment, i.e., delinquency and criminal conduct, by comparing these outcomes to those for teenagers who grow up without aggressive coercion. Further evidence comes from the social outcomes observed in Sweden after the 1979 ban placed on the use of corporal punishment in that country (Haeuser, 1990). Longitudinal studies have determined that since the ban was put in place, adolescent involvement in criminal conduct, drug and alcohol use, sexual assault and suicide have diminished among teens aged 13 to 17 years (Durrant, 1999, 2000).

PSYCHOSOCIAL RISK FACTORS

School difficulties: Being suspended, expelled or held back in school are all associated with increased probability of being detained in a juvenile facility (Rodney & Mupier, 2000). School discipline referrals have also been found useful in identifying teens who are at risk for delinquency (Sprague et al., 2001). In a study designed to explore the relationship between school behaviors (measured by number of school discipline referrals and teacher nominations) and later referrals to juvenile authorities for illegal activities, Sprague and colleagues were able to identify youth who may indicate a propensity toward antisocial/violent behavior.

Peer associations and teen culture: Several aspects of teen culture provide a *powerful socializing* influence. Using explanations of differential association, Erickson, Crosnoe and Dornbursch (2000) found that peer relationships were key to explaining a significant portion of adolescent problem behavior. Exposure to deviant peers was strongly correlated with the development of problem behavior, while ties to conventional peers instead may provide buffering against this development. The behavior of deviant peers was correlated with both adolescent substance use and delinquency, especially among males.

Socioeconomic disadvantage: Poverty has multiple effects, both direct and indirect, which may add to overall risk for problem behavior. The isolation of the urban setting from outside cultural influences may restrict an individual's access to alternative modes of behavior, as well as to alternative means of coping. Poor schools and few employment opportunities result in economic and social deprivations that may serve to justify or even "necessitate" (in the eyes of a juvenile) participation in gangs and crime (Glicken & Sechrist, 2003). *Poverty in family of origin* predicts early emergence of adolescent substance abuse (Sommers & Baskin, 1991) and was found to have major influence on criminal involvement among adolescents (age 13 to 17 years) (Levitt & Lochner, 2001). Socioeconomic disadvantage was found to correlate with *lower levels of school engagement, higher levels of problem behavior and lower probability of successful adaptation to adolescence* (Jessor, et al., 1998). Other mechanisms for the effects of poverty may be:

- Overly stressed parents experiencing extreme financial strain (possibly working multiple jobs) may be unable to provide adequate nurturance or monitoring of adolescent behavior;

- Poverty may upset the fabric that holds communities together, leading to fragmented institutions and services, denying adolescents outlets where their behavior will be supervised and guided;

- Unemployment of males is often associated with the use of compensatory aggression to display competence, status and power, all of which may act as models for (especially male) adolescent behavior;

- Neighborhood violence often associated with impoverished environments often breeds further violence as vendetta and revenge becomes increasingly cited as motivation for spiraling conflict (Steinberg, 1999).

Neighborhood: Exposure to community violence places an individual at four times the risk of engaging in serious criminal behavior (Preski & Shelton, 2001).

Ethnicity, race and culture: An exploration of the relationships between acculturative stress and adolescent problem behavior among Latino youth (Cabrera, 2001) found that juveniles who reported greater stress from acculturation engaged in higher levels of substance use, maladjusted behavior and criminal conduct.

Gang membership: Analysis of an ethnically diverse sample of adolescents that used self-report data found the following correlates of youth gang involvement:

- Neighborhood crime and danger;

- Parent-adolescent conflict; and

- Parental behavioral control (Walker-Barnes, 2000)

Table 1.2 summarizes risk factors that may be associated with various problem behaviors.

CORE RISK FACTORS GERMANE TO RESEARCH AND ASSESSMENT

Each of the following factors is defined by different constructs referred to as sub-risk factors:

- Family disruption and problems;

- Poor school adjustment - behavior and performance;

- Mood and psychological adjustment problems;

- Involvement in negative peer associations and relationships;

- Substance use and abuse involvement;

- Delinquent and deviant behavior including criminal conduct; and

- Health and physical problems.

DIFFERENT MODELS FOR UNDERSTANDING RISK FACTORS

The most common approach to understanding the relationship between problem behavior and risk factors is *causative*, e.g., that A causes B causes C, etc. With this model, and we would look for one risk factor causing another, e.g., that substance use involvement can lead to school failure. However causative connections are often more complicated.

It is more helpful to visualize the relationship of risk factors to each other and to problem behavior in a multidimensional and multivariate perspective. Different ways to conceptualize risk factors and their interactions include:

Alternative sequences: Whereas one risk factor can lead to another, the opposite can also occur. While substance use involvement can lead to school failure, school failure can lead to substance use involvement (or greater involvement).

Risk factors may be reciprocal: When substance use involvement leads to school failure, school failure can exacerbate substance abuse.

Co-occurring relationships: Two risk factors may "move together" to determine another risk factor outcome (Winters, 2001). Both substance use involvement and school failure may set the stage for involvement in criminal conduct.

Equifinality: Several types of risk factors can lead to the same outcome (Cicchetti & Rogosch, 1996; Gjerde, 1995).

Multifinality: Certain risk factors can actually work as protective factors (Cicchetti & Rogosch, 1996; Gjerde, 1995). For example, a youth whose father has a severe alcohol problem may serve to protect that youth from developing such a problem, or even to cause the youth to abstain from alcohol.

Finally, it is important to understand that risk factors and problem behaviors are often interchangeable. Substance abuse is a risk factor, but it is also a problem behavior. Thus, problem behaviors can lead to other problem behaviors.

Table 1.2   Summary of Risk Factors for the Development of Problem Behavior

MENTAL HEALTH PROBLEMS (INCLUDING SUICIDE):

Young maternal age

Parental use of corporal punishment

RUNAWAY:

Parental use of corporal punishment

Sexual trauma

Other forms of family trauma

Being "thrown away" by parents

SUBSTANCE ABUSE:

Low levels of parental monitoring

Parental use of corporal punishment

Sexual trauma

Witnessing violence between parents

Parental substance abuse, criminal conduct or incarceration

Young maternal age

Acculturative stress

Sensation seeking (risk factor for DUI)

Exposure to deviant peers (especially among males)

CONDUCT PROBLEMS OR CONDUCT DISORDER, INSECURE ATTACHMENT IN INFANCY:

Hyperactivity and/or attention deficit disorders

Reduced development of empathy

Lack of social bonding

Young maternal age

Cognitive deficits

Cruelty to animals

DELINQUENCY:

Young maternal age

Insecure attachment in infancy

Lack of social bonding

Low levels of parental monitoring

Parental use of corporal punishment

Exposure to deviant peers

Few or poor quality social ties

School difficulties

Sensation seeking

GANG INVOLVEMENT:

Neighborhood crime and violence

Feelings of vulnerability to violent victimization

Poverty

Parent adolescent conflict

Low levels of parental monitoring

School dropout

Criminal conduct

CRIMINAL CONDUCT:

*Early contact with the juvenile justice

Insecure attachment in infancy

Mother with a psychiatric diagnosis

Parental use of corporal punishment

Parental involvement in criminal activity

Low social bonding

Cognitive deficits

Exposure to community violence

Poverty

Acculturative stress

ADOLESCENT AGGRESSIVENESS (MILD):

Disorganized attachment patterns

Parental use of corporal punishment

Family stress/conflict

Multiple exposures to risk

VIOLENCE (SEVERE):

*Early contact with the juvenile justice system (between ages 6 and 11)

Lack of social ties or involvement with antisocial peers

Physical trauma during childhood, child abuse

Substance abuse

School failure

Community violence

Racial prejudice

*Multiple exposures to risk (especially frequent experiences with violence)

Head trauma—sometimes implicated in abrupt and atypical eruption of homicidal rage

SEXUAL ASSAULT:

Parental use of corporal punishment

Sexual trauma in childhood

Denotes best predictor for this type of problem behavior

EMPIRICAL STUDIES OF RESILIENCY: BUFFERS AGAINST ADOLESCENT PROBLEM BEHAVIOR

Resiliency factors fall into the same general categories as those used to assess risk, namely, protection within the *individual* (including biological and cognitive), family, and *psychosocial* (including educational, school, community and socioeconomic domains).

INDIVIDUAL PROTECTIVE FACTORS

Health-positive cognition and behavior

Engagement in *healthy behaviors* such as eating a nutritious diet, getting adequate sleep, engaging in physical exercise and personal hygiene, and the use of seatbelts is *negatively correlated* with engagement in problem behavior (Jessor et al., 1998). Protective factors in the cognitive domain center on placing positive value on health and perceiving the negative consequences of health-negative behaviors. Another important protective factor is having *parents who model health-positive behavior* (Jessor et al., 1998). Belief in self-determination of health status has been found to mitigate the relationship between neighborhood stress and adolescent alcohol use and abuse (Scheier, Botvin & Miller, 1999). This is generally accompanied by a positive orientation to health (Jessor et al., 1998), and increased likelihood of engaging in healthy behaviors.

Personal competence skills

Many studies have found an *inverse relation* between a variety of *healthy self-management skills* (such as assertiveness and refusal skills, boundary setting, self-efficacy, etc.) and *severity of problem behavior* (e.g., Griffin, Scheier, Botvin & Diaz, 2001). These associations were observed in a variety of instances, including lower rates of early onset substance use and delinquency. Because *personal competence skills provide protection against* risk by enhancing well-being, Griffin et al. (2001) suggest that intervention should involve *competence-enhancing components* in order to promote overall resilience.

Social orientation

Several elements of social activity may serve to buffer adolescents from engagement in problem behavior (Jessor et al., 1998). Among these are *positive relations* with adults, involvement in *prosocial activities* (such as those involving family and community), persistence in and *commitment to school and volunteer employment*.

Cognitive focus

Various directions of cognitive focus may buffer adolescents from engagement in problem behavior (Jessor et al., 1998). Among these are greater *orientation to family* than to friends and greater orientation to *friends who model conventional behavior*. An intolerance of deviance is likely to orient adolescents toward positive peer associations and the perception of severe consequences for violation of conventional norms, generally inhibits their expression (Jessor et al. 1998).

Empathy and internal locus of control

The ability to make decisions based upon an internalized system of *moral and ethical principles*, including the capacity to feel the suffering of others, is an important element of protection. *Internal locus of control* (the ability to rely on internal mental structures, e.g., values, ethical principles, perceptual cues) has been found to mitigate the relationship between neighborhood stress and adolescent alcohol use and abuse (Scheiee al., 1999).

Empathy deficits and participation in delinquent behaviors are generally correlated (Cohen & Strayer, 1996; Marcus & Gray, 1998). Empathy levels of adolescents involved in antisocial and/or criminal behaviors (identified using the *Interpersonal Reactivity Index—IRI*) *tend to be below the norm* for adolescent counterparts who are not engaging in such behaviors (Broom, 2000; Ellis, 1982). This appears to be true at all ages through the age of 18. What's more, empathy level appears to predict the type of offense committed. Broom shows the effectiveness of empathy training with juveniles engaged in problem behavior. This strategy has received some empirical support from programs such as *Phases of Re-socialization*—a program in Texas that uses a combination of instruction and empathy enhancement, which has been found to increase levels of empathy.

FAMILY PROTECTIVE FACTORS

Security of attachment in infancy

Secure attachment in infancy may protect an individual from development of problem behavior in adolescence. Positive outcomes may occur through several distinct mechanisms. *First*, security of attachment appears to be *negatively associated* with *exposure to high-risk* environments. *Second*, secure attachment appears to foster the development of *mental capacities* such as empathy and a sense of connectedness to others, which may reduce the motivation to engage in antisocial or criminal activity.

Third, by supplying the individual with *positive relational abilities*, secure attachment may provide necessary skills for obtaining need satisfaction that may render antisocial or criminal acts unnecessary for goal attainment (Fonagy, Target, Steele, & Steele, 1997b).

Positive family interaction and the quality of social ties

Utting (1996) draws attention to the *quality of social ties* in the lives of children and adolescents, and utilizes attachment theories to elucidate the developmental processes that foster an individual's capability to form *healthy human bonds*. Extent of mother-child interaction has been shown to reduce the probability of an adolescent serving time in juvenile detention (Rodney & Mupier, 2000).

Scheier et al. (1999) consistently found *family communication* to be an important factor in mitigating the effects of neighborhood stress (such as gang presence and perceived neighborhood toughness) among urban minority youth. Frequently, juveniles engaged in problem behavior have not developed this capacity for relationships, and are found to be lacking in the healthy social ties that might afford them some protection. Sharing family dinners was strongly associated with lower levels of aggressiveness (in males and females) as well as lower levels of delinquency in youth from single parent families (Griffin, Botvin et al., 2000).

PSYCHOSOCIAL PROTECTIVE FACTORS

Attachments to conventional individuals

Strong and *healthy social ties* have been found to provide a major source of protection against the development of problem behavior, particularly violence and aggression (Fox & Levin, 2001). Interpersonal commitments and attachments to *conventional individuals* may provide the non-offending adolescent with a link to mainstream beliefs and values. Attachment to *teachers, coaches, club leaders*, etc., may provide the adolescent with opportunities to participate in supportive social activities, which may contribute to the development of empathy (Fox & Levin, 2001). Teenagers may avoid criminal and violent behavior in order to maintain important social connections (Gottfredson & Hirschi, 1990).

Social ties to *conventional peers* may reduce adolescent substance use and delinquency by reducing the extent of exposure to maladaptive cognitions and deviant peer norms. It also prevents exposure to the destructive behavioral patterns that develop in the deviant subculture. Social ties to conventional peers are inversely related to adolescent substance use (Erickson, Crosnow, & Dornbusch, 2000). Whatever the exact mechanism, a lack of social bonding is generally associated with higher rates of violent crime and pathology (Fox & Levin, 2001). This correlation may provide some explanation as to why there are high rates of violence, suicide and murder in cities—areas that tend to attract people with few social ties (Gottfredson & Hirschi, 1990). Sampson and Laub (1993) also found that the ability to bond with others, a job or some other social institution, protects adolescents against development into a criminal lifestyle.

Community Infrastructure

Based on studies by the *Search Institute* of 460 urban, suburban and rural communities, including data collected from a sample of 254,634 school-aged children in the U. S. (most surveyed between 1992 and 1995), Benson (1998) developed a community focused model for strengthening resiliency. "A community that truly meets the needs of its youngest generation complements its strong economic infrastructure with a vibrant developmental infrastructure—that is, with community commitments and strategies that accentuate the positive building blocks of human development."

Forming this foundation is the result of collaborative effort between all the community's residents and institutions. Healthy communities focus on the development of a normative culture in which adults, organizations, and community institutions take pride in their commitments to nurturing caring and competent youth, who will in turn become responsible neighbors, citizens, parents and workers. Resilient, healthy children and adolescents experience positive building blocks of human development as shown in *Table 1.3*.

THE RELATIONSHIP BETWEEN RISK AND RESILIENCY-PROTECTIVE FACTORS

In this discussion, we treat resiliency and protective factors as the same and refer to both as *resiliency factors*. However, we recognize that resiliency factors are often reserved for identifying *strengths within individuals* and *protective factors* are often seen as more *environmentally based*.

One common perspective is to view risk and resiliency factors at opposite ends of the continuum (Winters, 2001). From a measurement standpoint, a high score on a scale that measures family problems would indi-

Table 1.3 Positive Building Blocks of Human Development

- *Daily support* and care provided by one or more involved, loving parents or other caregivers;

- *Sustained relationships* with several non-parent adults in the community;

- A *neighborhood* where everyone knows, protects, listens to, and gets involved with the young;

- *Opportunities to participate* in developmentally responsive and enticing clubs, teams and organizations led by principled, responsible, and trained adults;

- *Access* to child-friendly public places;

- *Daily affirmation* and encouragement;

- *Intergenerational relationships* in which children and teenagers bond with adults of many ages and in which teenagers bond with younger children;

- A *stake in community life* made concrete through useful roles and opportunities for involvement;

- *Boundaries, values, and high expectations* consistently articulated, modeled and reinforced across multiple socializing systems;

- *Peer groups* motivated to achieve and contribute;

- *Caring schools*, congregations, youth-serving organizations and other institutions; and

- *Opportunities* for frequent acts of service to others.

Source: Benson, P., (1998). *All Kids Are Our Kids: What Communities Must Do to Raise Caring and Responsible Children*. Jossey Bass, Inc.

cate a risk factor for a particular youth. However, a low score would indicate the absence of family problems, or even family strengths, and would indicate, for this youth, a resiliency factor. According to Winters (2001), those frameworks fit nicely into statistical models that assume linear relationships among variables. However, this conceptualization can fail to take into account the interaction among risk and resiliency-protective factors.

Another perspective is to look at resiliency factors as *operationally independent* of risk factors. Thus, the measurement of positive family involvement would be a separate factor from measuring family disruption. The problem with this model is that the two measured factors within the same domain, i. e., *family*, are usually highly correlated. When this happens, we end up with the two factors measuring the same construct, family disruption at one end and family strengths at the other end. Two highly correlated variables also pose significant problems with respect to simple linear and multivariate statistical analyses.

Another perspective is to view risk and resiliency factors as *interactive*. In this model, a resiliency-protective factor may attenuate a risk factor. This model would hold that a resiliency-protective factor would be relevant only in the presence of a risk factor upon which it has an influence (Garmezy, Masten & Tellegan, 1984; Rutter, 1990; Hawkins et al., 1992).

Still another view is to look at the relationship between risk and resiliency factors *on a continuum* and then to use one or more constructs to measure the individual's strengths (Wanberg, 2003). Again, this continuum sees risk at the high end of the scale and resiliency at the low end of the scale, or visa versa. A general, higher-order strength factor may be used; or several primary or specific strength factors can be used which tap into specific domains such as *positive self-view, identifying strong and positive relationships in friends, family, the community, etc.* The strength scales are directed at measuring only positive, self-perceived strengths, and are measures of strengths that we would like to see treatment develop or enhance. This model is of particular value at the individual assessment level.

Finally, we can view risk and resiliency factors as organized into several types (Winters, 2001). Some are *robust* in that they predict both current and future problem behavior or they might be classified as *emergent* in that they predict future outcomes but not current conditions or levels of problem behaviors. As well, some risk-resiliency factors might be seen as con-current in that they predict current levels of problem behavior but not changes in problem behaviors.

A STRENGTHS-BASED APPROACH TO JUVENILE JUSTICE AND TREATMENT SERVICES

Uncovering the multiple factors that place a teenager at risk for a broad spectrum of personal and social problems calls for development of adolescent-focused treatment aimed at improving the ratio of protective elements relative to the negative factors that can segue into drugs or criminal activity. Our traditional meth-ods of responding to delinquency and juvenile drug abuse have focused primarily on *problems* and how to reduce them, i. e., the predominant model of change has been "deficit reduction." This approach has never been particularly effective. A more productive (and engaging) means of working with the delinquent or substance-abusing teenagers is to recognize that multi-problem adolescents and their families have considerable resources that can positively change their lives. A *strength-based* perspective not only addresses the teenager's vulnerabilities and weaknesses but also recognizes youth as potential contributors to the com-munity (Wanberg, Milkman & Robinson, 1996; Milkman, 2001).

Teen and family advocates are encouraged to use the techniques of *motivational interviewing* to elicit infor-mation about what things parents and teenagers have done well, both in family and individual contexts. In developing a *comprehensive plan* for each youth, assessment is geared not only to the weaknesses or vulnerabilities that require remediation but also an evaluation of *his or her talents* that need to be nur-tured. Youth and families are *consulted* regarding every treatment decision, considering them as experts on their own case. When adolescents and their fami-lies are *praised and acknowledged* for their accomplishments and abilities, the treatment alliance becomes strengthened; they become less resistant and increasingly motivated to actively participate in the treatment program. There is *focus on a young person's future*, rather than his or her past, nurturing hope and the possibility for change. By helping youth and their families to clarify their goals and, whenever possible, utilizing the principles of *restorative justice* (rectifying the effects of past actions), youth internalize the message that not only can they look to the future with optimism but they can be responsible, make reparations for past misdeeds and make positive con-tributions to the community. Restorative justice not only fosters teen offenders' accountability to the com-munity but also leads to a sense of increased competence while developing personal responsibility for their behavior and its consequences.

By describing the scope of adolescent problem behav-iors and illustrating some of the ways in which the lives of adolescent offenders have been impacted by their more general experiences as children and teens (such as negative peer influence, poor parental role models, low academic achievement, traumatic vio-lence), it becomes clear that these experiences require specific focus in the development of effective pro-gramming for large numbers of teenagers who manifest multiple problem behaviors. While these experiences may be associated with vulnerability for antisocial behavior, criminal conduct and substance abuse, they may also provide the adolescent with a *reservoir of survival skills* that can be modified using *cognitive-behavioral interventions* into a *strengths-based orientation* for building a better life. Helping adolescents understand and recognize their own strengths and abilities can contribute toward improv-ing self-esteem, self-awareness and recognition of personal rights and responsibilities that can propel them out of high-risk situations (such as deviant peer associations and the subculture of violence) and into those that facilitate reaching their goals.

Adolescent problem behaviors such as drug abuse, mental disorder and criminal conduct are associated with multiple childhood antecedents, including low motivation toward success and achievement, minimal attachment to positive role models or institutions, and normalized images of crime and violence. A major tenet of *Pathways to Self-Discovery and Change*, how-ever, is that across the entire continuum of substance abuse and criminal conduct, from minimal rule break-ing to violent crime, positive change is, first and foremost, tied to recognizing that we are *personally responsible* for our actions. We can become healthy and productive community members by *learning to control our thoughts, feelings, and behavior*.

CHAPTER REVIEW

Adolescent patterns of behavior result from an amalga-mation of individual, family, peer and community factors of risk and resiliency. Owing to the unique confluence of biological, psychological and social forces, adolescence is often a stressful period of life. Although epidemiological studies reveal that only about 10% to 20% of teenagers exhibit some type of severe mental disorder, high prevalence rates for substance abuse and delinquent activities have powerful effects on individuals, families, communities and the society at large. Six percent of 12th graders report daily use of marijuana and nearly 30% of 12th graders report having had five or more drinks in a row during the previous two weeks (Johnston, 2002).

Teenagers who abuse drugs show a pattern of being involved in other deviations from social norms, e.g., fighting, stealing, vandalism, low school achievement, and early sexual activity. For the vast majority of adolescents who abuse drugs, alcohol and tobacco have been implicated as *gateway substances*. For example, those who report having tried cigarettes are about ten times more likely to have also tried marijuana (Ray and Ksir, 2002). Relative to long-term goals, teenagers are more influenced by their parents; however, peers have significantly greater influence regarding immediate lifestyle and day-to-day activities. Having peers with antisocial attitudes is the best predictor of drug abuse.

In the domain of juvenile delinquency and criminal activity, the estimated number of juvenile arrests (under 18 years of age) during the past few years was upward of 2. 3 million (*U.S. Department of Health and Human Services,* 2001c) with less than 5% for violent crimes. Although the rate of arrest for adolescent involvement in violence appears to have declined during the past decade, the *Surgeon General Report on Juvenile Crime and Violence* (2001) shows that among 12th graders, 15% were reported to have committed an assault with injury and 5% committed robbery with a weapon.

In the sphere of *mental disorder*, 50% of youth who participate in one of five sectors of public care (alcohol and drug services, child welfare, juvenile justice, mental health, and public school services for severe emotional disturbance) meet criteria for attention deficit /hyperactivity) or other disruptive behavior disorders (conduct disorder and oppositional defiant disorder). The rate of PTSD is higher among older teenagers while the rate of ADHD tends to decline with age.

Jessor (1998) describes teenage problem behavior as derived from three interactive systems of psychosocial influence: *the behavior system, the personality system and the perceived environment*. Since problem behaviors are related, isolating drug abuse or juvenile delinquency as independent targets for intervention, without considering the *behavior system* along with associated *personality* and *perceived environment*, would be coun-

terproductive to any attempts at treatment or rehabilitation.

An array of *protective* elements (e.g., positive relationships with adults, conventional friends, good school attitudes and results, involvement in prosocial activities, religious faith, intolerance to deviance) is shown to mitigate factors that put an adolescent at risk (e.g., low self-esteem, personality disorder, low success expectations, alienation, negative peers, disconnection with conventional institutions, growing up in a subculture of violence, relative economic deprivation, and lack of school success). Empirical study of risk and protective factors provides the platform for developing appropriate targets for treatment and other social services interventions. Research findings support the moderating function of protective factors to offset risk.

Studies of resiliency show the importance of *strengthening protective factors* for improved treatment outcomes. Significant and positive effects have been documented for: improving health-positive cognition and behavior; increasing self-management skills (e.g., assertiveness, refusal, boundary setting, self-efficacy); developing empathy and an internalized system of moral and ethical principles; improving family communication; and the development of a normative culture in which adults, organizations and community institutions take pride in their commitments to nurturing competent and responsible youth. Based on data collected by the Search Institute from a sample of more than one quarter million U. S. school children, this chapter delineates individual, family and community elements that are viewed as *positive building blocks* of human development. The final segment presents the case for the shift to a strength-based focus in adolescent treatment, utilizing the principles of motivational interviewing and restorative justice.

Mental Health and Adolescent Problem Behavior

2

Chapter Two:
Mental Health and Adolescent Problem Behavior

Chapter Outline

The Scope of Adolescent Mental Health Issues

- Internalizing disorders
- Externalizing disorders
- Substance disorders
- Co-occurring disorders

Disruptive Behavior Disorders and Diagnostic Criteria

- Oppositional defiant disorder
- Conduct disorder
- Distinctions between ODD and CD
- Conduct disorder, criminal behavior and antisocial personality disorder
- Treatment considerations for CD
- Attention deficit hyperactivity disorder (ADHD)
- ADHD and criminal conduct
- Treatment of ADHD

Personality Disorders

Post-Traumatic Stress Disorder

- Key characteristics of PTSD
- PTSD and associated patterns of problem behavior
- PTSD treatment implications
- Evaluation of PTSD treatment efficacy

The MMPI–A: Use for Diagnosis and Treatment Planning

Psychotherapeutic Medications for Children and Adolescents

Chapter Review

Chapter Objectives

- To describe the diagnostic criteria and causal factors associated with various subtypes of disruptive behavior disorders;

- To examine relationships between mental disorder, criminal activity and substance abuse during adolescence;

- To describe correlates and moderating factors involved in the profiles of ADHD, oppositional defiant disorder, conduct disorder, personality disorder and post-traumatic stress disorder;

- To discuss the effectiveness of CBT in treatment of PTSD;

- To describe psychotherapeutic medications used with children and adolescents in terms of mechanisms of action, side effects and FDA approval; and

- To evaluate the use of the MMPI-A in diagnosis, treatment planning and risk assessment.

THE SCOPE OF ADOLESCENT MENTAL HEALTH ISSUES

Most individuals go through adolescence without duress. Some, however, encounter major difficulties on psychological, psychosocial and behavioral levels. Problems such as depression, antisocial behavior and conduct disorder, substance abuse, crime and delinquency characterize this minority. These individuals may be unable to form or maintain close relationships, have negative attitudes toward themselves, their parents or society, and be without the necessary skills and abilities to navigate through school and other productive activities. While this is not the norm for adolescents, statistics concerning these types of difficulties are of serious concern to communities and the broader society.

An appreciation of the range of mental health issues that may beset juvenile offenders is important in the provision of effective treatment services. In a study of nearly 5,000 adolescents involved in the mental health and/or juvenile justice systems, 20% of those receiving *mental health services* had been *arrested recently*, and 30% of adolescents in the *juvenile justice system* were receiving *mental health services* (Rosenblatt, Rosenblatt & Biggs, 2000). On average, users of the mental health system had more arrests than non-users (Rosenblatt et al.).

Psychosocial problems and mental health difficulties in adolescence are generally divided into three broad categories of emotional-behavioral disorder: *internalizing, externalizing, and substance abuse* (Steinberg, 1999).

Internalizing disorders

These disorders, such as depression, anxiety, and phobia, involve distress in the *emotional and cognitive domains*. Self-destructive behaviors often emerge among adolescents suffering from internalizing disorders in the forms of self-hatred and suicide (Laufer, 1995), as well as self-mutilation and tattooing (Friedman, Glasser, Laufer, Laufer et al., 1996). There also appears to be comorbidity (co-occurrence) among a variety of internalizing disorders. For example, depression frequently correlates with anxiety, phobic and panic disorders, obsessive and eating disorders, suicidal tendencies and physical distress that has psychological origins (psychosomatic disorders) (Steinberg, 1999). The co-occurrence of these internalizing distress symptoms may be indicative of a syndrome labeled "over controlled" (or sometimes referred to as "stuffing" in everyday parlance), while clustering of externalizing behaviors has been labeled "under controlled" — otherwise referred to as "acting out" (Robins et al., 1996).

This co-occurrence of internalizing behaviors is reflective of a more general negative affect (Steinberg, 1999). Some individuals seem to become distressed more easily than others, and the negative affectivity that underlies this predicts greater probabilities of depression, anxiety, and other internalizing disorders (Bardone, Moffitt, Caspi, Dickson, & Silva, 1996).

Externalizing disorders

These "acting out" behaviors such as truancy, aggression and delinquency are directed *outside of the self* as a wide range of behavioral disorders, characterized by an antisocial orientation to others and society. Adolescent delinquency and crime, aggression and other forms of disorderly conduct fall under the category of externalizing behaviors and are believed to derive from a general propensity toward antisocial behavior. The association of juvenile delinquency and crime with this more generalized tendency toward antisocial behavior (such as lying, indifference toward the feelings of others, etc.) has led to a definition of antisocial behavior in this context as acts that "inflict physical or mental harm or property loss or other damage on others" (Tolan & Loeber, 1993).

Substance disorders

These disorders involve the (non-experimental) abuse of a wide range of substances, from prescription drugs (such as stimulants or sedatives), to street drugs (such as marijuana and cocaine), to legal substances (such as nicotine and alcohol). Substance disorders are characterized separately because they are just as likely to accompany behavioral (externalizing) problems, as are depression (and other internalizing problems) (Steinberg, 1999). Although substance abuse often appears alongside these other difficulties, i.e., comorbidity (Henry et al., 1993), it may also appear alone, without other behavioral or affective problems, another reason for viewing substance abuse as a separate realm of disorder (Steinberg, 1999).

Co-occurring disorders

It is important to recognize that comorbidity can encompass the presence of both externalizing and internalizing disorders within the same individual. For example, many adolescents who engage in delinquent behavior are also depressed (Hinden, Compas, Howell

& Achenbach, 1997). Some researchers have examined processes involved in other pathological forms of behavior, which appear to have their origins during adolescence, such as *suicide and self-mutilation*. These authors argue that the capacity for aggression directed toward the self rests upon and emerges alongside the rapid developmental changes in mental function during adolescence (Friedman et al., 1996). Identifying the specific variables that render some juveniles able to negotiate adolescence without difficulty, while others develop self-destructive or antisocial-aggressive lifestyles is of key importance. Among those adolescents with negative outcomes, understanding what different factors may be involved in the development of self-destructive behaviors, versus aggressive and antisocial tendencies, is of key importance for instituting effective and safe intervention techniques. Further study is needed to answer these and related questions.

DISRUPTIVE BEHAVIOR DISORDERS AND DIAGNOSTIC CRITERIA

All of the subtypes of *disruptive behavior disorders (attention deficit disorder, oppositional defiant disorder and conduct disorder)* are more common among boys. Children who are diagnosed with these disorders experience difficulty in controlling their behavior and often develop adjustment problems that persist into adulthood.

Oppositional defiant disorder

Children with oppositional defiant disorder (ODD) display a pattern of negativity, defiance and opposition that leads to problems with teachers, parents, siblings and peers. They vehemently resist restrictions or (limits) on behavior despite the "reasonableness" of the request. For example, they may refuse to wear a coat when it is snowing and when required to do so or they may have prolonged and exaggerated temper tantrums. These children have a constant tendency to "test the limits" by either ignoring or questioning what they are asked to do and by contradicting and provoking others. *Aggression-related happiness* may become manifest in pleasure derived from disturbing, annoying, teasing, or irritating others. From an early age, these children seem to *derive pleasure*, i.e., they appear happy and joyous when *engaged in taunting or fighting* with adults or their peers (Arsenio, Cooperman, & Lover, 2000). They typically lack tolerance and patience. Frustration may result in temper tantrums, prolonged arguments and explosive verbal outbursts. When confronted with the harmfulness of their actions, children with ODD often shift the blame to others whom they perceive as abusive, unreasonable, unfair or mean. The prevalence of ODD is estimated to be about 2% during the course of childhood (Seligman, Walker, & Rosenhan, 2001).

Table 2.1 presents the diagnostic criteria for ODD. These criteria describe behaviors that are quite common during the course of adolescence. This presents a challenge for accurate diagnosis, i.e., where is the line between expected teenage defiance and mental disorder? The answer is usually determined by frequency, degree of severity and duration of the disruptive behavior pattern.

Conduct disorder

Issues regarding mental health and mental illness in children and adolescents are fraught with controversy. Some question whether terms such as "psychopathology," "criminal conduct" and "psychopathy" can be aptly applied to youth, given their early (incomplete) stage of emotional and cognitive development and the harmful effects of labeling. Yet, mental health issues must be addressed, as the vast majority of adults diagnosed with antisocial personality disorder displayed major conduct disruptions in childhood (Robins 1978). Currently, the assessment of serious antisocial tendencies during childhood cluster in a syndrome known as *conduct disorder* (CD). The *Psychopathy Screening Device* has been used to assess the extent of cruelty and vindictiveness in young people aged 2 to12 years elevated profiles of which may indicate severe conduct disorder (Frick, Barry, & Bodin, 2000).

Most children, at one time or another, transgress societal norms for good behavior. In a study of 1,425 British boys, 13-16 years of age, 98% admitted to keeping something that did not belong to them, although in only 40% of the instances were the goods worth more than $2.00 (Belson, 1975). For the most part, these are isolated instances and apparently a "normal" aspect of growing up. However, conduct-disordered youth *persistently violate the rights of others*, are habitually aggressive and cruel and may repetitiously lie and cheat. CD often has its origins in ODD beginning in early and middle childhood (Dumas & Nilsen, 2003) A primary difference between ODD and CD is the scope and consequences of the disruptive behaviors. During adolescence, physical and sexual maturation create increased opportunities for disruptive and antisocial behavior. CD is characterized by

Table 2.1 Oppositional Defiant Disorder: *DSM-IV-TR* Diagnostic Criteria

A. A pattern of negativistic, hostile and defiant behavior lasting at least 6 months, during which four (or more) of the following are present:

(1) often loses temper

(2) often argues with adults

(3) often actively defies or refuses to comply with adults' requests or rules

(4) often deliberately annoys people

(5) often blames others for his or her mistakes or misbehavior

(6) is often touchy or easily annoyed by others

(7) is often angry and resentful

(8) is often spiteful or vindictive

Note: Consider a criterion met only if the behavior occurs more frequently than is typically observed in individuals of comparable age and developmental level.

B. The disturbance in behavior causes clinically significant impairment on social, academic or occupational functioning.

C. The behaviors do not occur exclusively during the course of a Psychotic or Mood Disorder.

D. Criteria are not met for *Conduct Disorder*, and, if the individual is age 18 years or older, criteria are not met for *Antisocial Personality Disorder*.

Source: American Psychiatric Association, Diagnostic and Statistical Manual of Mental Disorders, Fourth Edition, Text Revision (Washington, D.C.: American Psychiatric Association, 2000a), Copyright 2000 American Psychiatric Association. Reprinted with permission.

---

fights, threats and intimidation which are frequent at home and at school, combined with *callousness and cruelty* to people and animals, along with *theft, vandalism and willful destruction of property*. Children with CD are not only *perpetrators* but also frequent *victims of violence* such as aggravated assault, rape and murder (Dumas & Nilsen, 2003). The diagnosis is 3 times higher in boys with a range of 6 to 16 % of the general population compared to a range of 2 to 9% of girls qualifying for the diagnosis. Girls are less likely to manifest physical aggression, while they are more likely to lie and be truant.

The patterns of conduct disorder change with age. In early or middle childhood there is likely to be a high rate of lying, fighting and aggression toward animals. During adolescence, the severity of problems and the rate of conduct disorder increases dramatically, with youth becoming involved in such violent acts as muggings, armed robberies or rapes. Children with conduct disorder are at increased risk for a diagnosis

of *antisocial personality disorder* (the presence of a conduct disorder is one of the diagnostic criteria for antisocial personality disorder) when they reach adulthood (Langbehn et al., 1998). *Table 2.2* shows the DSM-IV criteria for the diagnosis of conduct disorder (APA, *DSM-IV*, 1994).

Psychosocial correlates of conduct disorder: Children and adolescents are referred to mental health systems for a wide range of conduct difficulties. Though these various behaviors are generally subsumed under the rubric of conduct disorder, children in this group are quite diverse in the underlying causes, correlates and developmental trajectories of their problem behaviors (Frick, Barry, & Bodin, 2000). Risk factors and correlates of conduct disorder span a wide range (Hinshaw, Lahey, & Hart, 1993)—from individual, genetic and neurochemical factors (Lahey, McBurnett, Loeber & Hart, 1995) into the psychosocial and environmental domains (Kazdin, 1996; Holmes, Slaughter, & Kashani, 2001). Psychosocial and environmental cor-

Table 2.2 Conduct Disorder: *DSM-IV-TR* Diagnostic Criteria

A. A repetitive and persistent pattern of behavior in which the *basic rights of others or major age-appropriate societal norms or rules are violated*, and manifested by the presence of three (or more) of the following criteria in the past 12 months, with at least one criterion present in the past 6 months.

Aggression to people and animals

(1) often bullies, threatens, or intimidates others;

(2) often initiates physical fights;

(3) has used a weapon that can cause serious physical harm to others (e.g., a bat, brick, broken bottle, knife, gun);

(4) has been physically cruel to people;

(5) has been physically cruel to animals;

(6) has stolen while confronting a victim (e.g., mugging, purse snatching, extortion, armed robbery);

(7) has forced someone into sexual activity. Destruction of property;

(8) has deliberately engaged in fire setting with the intention of causing serious damage;

(9) has deliberately destroyed others' property (other than by fire setting).

Deceitfulness or theft

(10) has broken into someone else's house or car;

(11) often lies to obtain goods or favors or to avoid obligations (i.e., "cons" others);

(12) has stolen items of non-trivial value without confronting a victim (e.g., shoplifting, but without breaking and entering; forgery).

Serious violations of rules

(13) often stays out at night despite parental prohibitions, beginning before age 13 years;

(14) has run away from home overnight at least twice while living in parental or parental surrogate home (or once without returning for a lengthy period);

(15) is often truant from school, beginning before age 13 years.

B. The disturbance in behavior causes clinically significant impairment in social, academic, or occupational functioning.

C. If the individual is age 18 years of older, criteria are not met for Antisocial Personality Disorder.

Source: *American Psychiatric Association, Diagnostic and Statistical Manual of Mental Disorders*, Fourth Edition, Text Revision (Washington, D.C.: American Psychiatric Association, 2000a), Copyright 2000 American Psychiatric Association. Reprinted with permission.

relates of conduct disorder are many. Children with conduct disorder frequently experience:

- School failure (Mandel, 1997; Maguin & Loeber, 1996);

- Peer rejection (Olson, 1992);

- Families characterized by parental psychopathology (Halperin et al., 1997);

- Parental aggression (Widom, 1997); and

- Child abuse and neglect (Widom, 1997).

Other problem behaviors that are frequently found in these juveniles include:

- ADHD;

- Depressive and anxiety disorders (Biederman, Newcorn, & Sprich, 1991);

- Oppositional defiant behavioral style (Loeber, Burke, Lahey, Winters, & Zera, 2000); and

- Aggression (a frequent correlate of antisocial behavior especially in childhood) (Coie & Dodge, 1997).

Biological correlates of conduct disorder: Extensive research has identified biological factors that may contribute to the development of conduct disorder and its related symptoms. For example, neurochemicals such as serotonin (Halperin et al., 1997; Brown, Ebert & Goyer, et al., 1982) have been implicated in the development of ADHD, juvenile aggression and suicide. Low levels of the cerebrospinal fluid 5-hydroxyindoleacetic acid have been found to discriminate between impulsive-affective vs. non-impulsive cognitively mediated aggression (Linnoila et al., 1983), and cerebrospinal monoamine metabolites have been implicated in the development of ADHD (Castellanos, Elia, Kruesi, et al., 1995). Genetic factors may also be involved. For example, the dopamine transporter gene may contribute to the development of ADD (ADHD without the presence of hyperactivity) (Cook, Stein, & Krasowski, 1995). Differences in temperament may also link to child and adolescent behavioral disruptions (Caspi, Henry, McGee, Moffitt, & Silva, 1995). Clearly, effective treatment requires assessment of biological as well as psychosocial conditions.

Recognizing these early indications of conduct difficulties (such as childhood aggression and other maladaptive responses) may provide a window for intervention that can halt the progression into full-blown conduct (CD) and antisocial personality

disorders (APD) (Holmes, Slaughter, & Kashani, 2001). Most studies suggest that the earlier the intervention, the better the prognosis (Fox & Levin, 2001).

Distinctions between ODD and CD

The distinction between ODD and conduct disorder is based on the presence of violations of legal statutes and social mores. Children with ODD *do not typically engage in repeated physical assault, destruction of property or deceit.* The two disorders, however, tend to occur in sequence, with a high frequency of children who are diagnosed with ODD gradually developing conduct disorder during adolescence. Both disorders reflect deficits in the ability to solve interpersonal problems (Matthys, Cuperus, & van Engeland, 1999) and both are associated with increased risk for antisocial behavior during adulthood. In terms of causes, research findings point to similar factors in both CD and ODD, i.e., both tend to come from unstable homes, with parental discipline characterized by inconsistency, harsh punishment and less involvement in the child's activities (Frick, Christian, & Wooton, 1999). Youth who are diagnosed with ODD or conduct disorder show reductions in indicators of serotonin activity (van Goozen, Matthys, Cohen-Kettenis, Westenberg, & van Engeland, 1999). Given the many similarities, treatment for both disorders has generally relied on behavioral principles as well as cognitive theories concerning the misinterpretation of events (Barkley, Edwards, and Robin, 1999; Christopherson & Finney, 1999).

Conduct disorder, criminal behavior and antisocial personality disorder

Empirical research regarding "psychopathy" in youth ages 3 to 17 (using the *Hare Psychopathy Checklist-Revised,* Hare, Hart, & Harper 1991) reveals correlations between conduct disorder, other psychological disorders, and adolescent participation in crime (Forth & Mailloux, 2000). The symptoms of conduct disorder as defined in the *DSM-IV* are found to correlate with engagement in criminal behavior during adolescence (Kjelsberg, 2002). The correlation between as little as three of 14 symptoms of conduct disorder (*DSM-IV*) and possession of a criminal record reached .9 in males, slightly lower in females. Theft was the strongest indicator of both general crime and violence in males, while runaway was most strongly related to general crime and violent criminality in females. Forcing another into sexual activity strongly indicated the probability of sex offending later in life. Forty-eight percent of the entire sample

(11 to 18 year olds) that displayed symptoms of conduct disorder had a criminal record of some kind (Kjelsberg, 2002).

The term "fledgling psychopath" (Lynam, 1996) aptly describes a subset of early onset conduct-disordered adolescents who manifest insensitivity, harshness, and lack of remorse combined with callous and unemotional personality characteristics such as a disconcerting lack of empathy and respect for others. They may justify cruelty to animals by saying they were "just having fun" or they "enjoyed hurting them." This, yet to be classified, subset are the target of increasing attention on the part of researchers and clinicians because the quality of parenting does not appear to modify their callousness and lack of remorse. This is not true for a majority of children with CD (Wootton, Frick, Shelton, & Silverthorn, 1997). Further, their psychological profile seems to correspond to adults who have been diagnosed with *Antisocial Personality Disorder* (APD) (Blair, Colledge, Murray, & Mitchell, 2001; Frick & Ellis, 1999). APD cannot be diagnosed before the age of 18 because it is viewed as a chronic and pervasive personality style not present in childhood or adolescence.

There are a number of biologically relevant factors that have been found closely associated with the development of APD. These results have generally been interpreted in terms of interactional processes between biological and environmental factors (Magnusson, 1996; Mason & Frick, 1994). For example, some researchers have found that style of parental discipline (the use of coercion and punishment) combine with features of a child's personality that may have biological roots (such as impulsiveness and anxiety) to predict antisocial behavior and delinquency in adolescence (Tremblay, 1995). Other theorists suggest a strictly social development model (Catalano & Hawkins, 1996), which interprets antisocial disorder as largely the result of powerful social influences.

A study designed to explore the biological correlates of antisocial personality disorder compared three groups of males (non-offenders, adolescence-limited offenders and offenders whose antisocial behavior persisted through age 30) for difference in baseline levels of autonomic activity (Magnusson, 1996). Operationalizing physiological reactivity in terms of levels of adrenaline excreted from the adrenal medulla of the kidney, there was found to be:

- A strong association between persistent antisocial behavior and low levels of autonomic reactivity (low adrenaline excretion); and

- No such relationship within the adolescence-limited offender group (Magnusson, 1996).

Neuropsychological deficits appear to correlate with antisocial behavior in early-onset offenders, but not among those whose criminal conduct comes and goes during adolescence (Piquero, 2001). These observations support the distinction between "life-course persistent" antisocial behavior and antisocial behavior that likely emanates from the powerful social pressures of adolescence ("adolescence-limited") (Moffitt, Casi, Harrington, & Milne, 2002; Patterson, 1995). Low levels of autonomic activity and other physical characteristics may have an underlying genetic derivation (Mason & Frick, 1994), which interacts with environmental experience in the development of antisocial behavior (Magnusson, 1996). Antisocial personality traits may exacerbate the drug-violence relationship (Kaplan & Damphousse, 1995).

Treatment considerations for adolescents with conduct disorder

Twenty three percent of children who manifest symptoms of *conduct disorder* or the less severe *oppositional defiant disorder* are referred for treatment (Anderson, Williams, McGee, & Silva, 1987). This is unfortunate in light of the fact that research is increasingly demonstrating improved outcomes for treated youth (Brestan & Eyberg, 1998). Successful interventions, generally derived from social learning theory, include the following goals:

- Helping the client identify situations that trigger aggressive or antisocial behavior;

- Teaching the child how to take the perspective of others and care about this perspective;

- Reducing the aggressive child's tendency to attribute hostility to others; and

- Training the child in adaptive ways of solving conflicts with others.

Each of these goals is achieved through modeling, observational learning, and positive reinforcement for the attainment of the desired behavior, and punishment or negative consequences for the continuation of negative patterns. Positive outcomes appear to be related to early involvement in treatment (soon after the child begins to exhibit antisocial behavior) combined with successful engagement of the family in the overall treatment design. Interventions that use multiple strategies are most effective (Frick, 1998). Theoretical and research perspectives along with efficacious models for treating conduct-disordered youth are covered in *Chapter 9 Cognitive-Behavioral Model for PSD-C; Chapter 10 Cognitive-Behaviorial Perspectives on Adolescent Treatment; Chapter 11 Treatment Systems and Modalities; Chapter 12 Exemplary Treatment Programs.*

Attention deficit hyperactivity disorder

To meet *DSM-IV* criteria for *attention deficit hyperactivity disorder* (ADHD), symptoms must begin before the age of 7, persist for a minimum of six months and be evident in multiple settings. Large-scale epidemiological studies conducted in multiple countries during the past thirty years show prevalence ranges for ADHD from 4.2% to 6.3% with more recent estimates (based on *DSM-IV* criteria) slightly higher. Szatmari et al. (1989) report that between the ages of 6 and 12, ADHD affects approximately 6% to 9% of boys and 2% to 3% of girls, whereas in adolescence, the disorder affects 3% of boys and 1% of girls. Biederman et al. (2002) found that girls with the disorder were: (a) Twice as likely as boys to have the predominantly inattentive subtype of ADHD; (b) less likely than boys to have oppositional defiant disorder, conduct disorder and major depressive disorder; (c) less likely than boys to have learning or school problems; and (d) at greater risk than boys for drug use and abuse problems.

As shown in *Table 2.3, DSM-IV* lists symptoms of the disorder in two distinct groups: *inattention* and *hyperactivity-impulsivity.*

Attention deficit hyperactivity disorder and criminal conduct

Clinical syndrome hyperactivity has been operationalized as a combination of poor concentration skills and motor restlessness (Magnusson, 1996). Hyperactivity, low impulse control, attention deficits and behavioral difficulties, when combined, may serve as an early indicator of developing conduct disorder (Loeber, Green, Keenan, & Lahey, 1994). Some researchers suggest that hyperactivity, especially in concert with attention deficits and other childhood problems, may act as a catalyst for the development of antisocial behavior and substance abuse. Loeber et al. (1994) found that ADHD was correlated with an early onset of conduct disorder and delinquency. The combination of *attention deficit hyperactive disorder and conduct disorder* is considered a *major risk factor* for later engagement in criminal conduct. Hyperactivity and conduct problems from age 8 to10 are correlated with

persistent offending in adolescence. (Mannuzza, Klein, Bessler, Malloy, & LaPadula, 1993) The development of later conduct problems and delinquency was worsened when early defiance was accompanied by the use of aggression. A combination of oppositional defiant disorder and physical aggression was shown to predict later conduct disorder, and one study found that attention-deficit hyperactivity disorder (ADHD) alone was sufficient to predict antisocial personality disorder in adulthood. (Mannuzza et al., 1993; Loeber et al., 1994).

Farrington, Loeber, & Van Kammen (1990) concluded that hyperactivity alone predicted an early onset of criminal conviction (between ages 10 and 13) better than did conduct problems alone. However, it is not yet certain whether hyperactivity as a single factor is associated with later conduct disorder and delinquency, or whether its function is purely catalytic in the presence of other factors as noted above. Current scientific thought views hyperactivity as a catalyst, which in the presence of attention deficits, low levels of impulse control, disobedience, and/or aggressiveness, may facilitate the development of serious conduct disorder (Mannuzza et al., 1993; Loeber et al., 1994). It is likely that hyperactivity initiates the onset of behaviors that manifest as defiance, opposition to rules, and other conduct difficulties. Punitive responses to these behaviors may initiate identification with deviance and delinquency.

A longitudinal study of later conviction for a criminal offense was carried out with adolescents who had been referred to psychiatric services for behavioral or emotional problems as children (Elander, Simonoff, Pickles, Holmshaw, & Rutter, 2000). The various symptoms associated with hyperactivity were associated with subsequent convictions (age 17 to 21 years), with compound offending (five or more separate convictions), and with the incidence of incarceration following these convictions. Additional diagnosis of conduct disorder during childhood added little to the above predictions regarding later criminality (Elander, et al., 2000).

Treatment of ADHD

In addition to the enormous burdens on parents, teachers, school and neighborhood associates, perhaps the most problematic aspect of ADHD during childhood and adolescence is the enormous interference with academic performance and peer relationships, thus setting the stage for "failure identity," rejection or social isolation. Sadness and feelings

Table 2.3 Attention Deficit Hyperactivity Disorder: *DSM-IV-TR* Diagnostic Criteria

A. Either (1) or (2):

(1) six (or more) of the following symptoms on inattention have persisted for at least 6 months to a degree that is maladaptive and inconsistent with developmental level:

Inattention

   (a) fails to give close attention to details or makes careless mistakes in schoolwork, work or other activities

   (b) often has difficulty sustaining attention in tasks or play activities

   (c) often does not seem to listen when spoken to directly

   (d) often does not follow through on instructions and fails to finish schoolwork, chores or duties in the workplace (not due to oppositional behavior or failure to understand instructions)

   (e often has difficulty organizing tasks and activities

   (f) often avoids, dislikes, or is reluctant to engage in tasks that require sustained mental effort (such as schoolwork or homework)

   (g) often loses things necessary for tasks or activities (e.g., toys , school assignments, pencils, books, or tools)

   (h) often easily distracted by extraneous stimuli

   (i) is often forgetful in daily activities

(2) six or more of the following symptoms of **hyperactivity-impulsivity** have persisted for a least 6 months to a degree that is maladaptive and inconstant with developmental level:

Hyperactivity

   (a) often fidgets with hands or feet or squirms in seat

   (b) often leaves seat in classroom or in other situations in which remaining seated is expected

   (c) often runs about or climbs excessively in situations in which it is inappropriate (in adolescents or adults, may be limited to subjective feelings of restlessness)

   (d) often has difficulty playing or engaging in leisure activities

   (e) is often "on the go" or often acts as if "driven by a motor"

   (f) often talks excessively

   (g) often blurts out answers before questions have been completed

   (h) often has difficulty awaiting turn

   (i) often interrupts or intrudes on others

B. Some hyperactive-impulsive or inattentive symptoms that caused impairment were present before age 7 years.

C. Some impairment from the symptoms is present in two or more settings (e.g., at school [or work] and at home).

D. There must be clear evidence of clinically significant impairment in social, academic, or occupational functioning.

E. The symptoms do not occur exclusively during the course of a Pervasive Developmental Disorder, Schizophrenia, or other Psychotic Disorder and are not better accounted for by another mental disorder (e.g., Mood Disorder, Anxiety Disorder, Dissociative Disorder, or a Personality Disorder.

Source: American Psychiatric Association, Diagnostic and Statistical Manual of Mental Disorders, Fourth Edition, Text Revision (Washington, D.C.: American Psychiatric Association, 2000a), Copyright 2000 American Psychiatric Association. Reprinted with permission.

of low self-worth are often profound, indicating the need for clinical intervention. The two most prominent approaches to treatment are medication and behavior therapy.

Drug and/or Behavioral Therapy: Paradoxically, many children who suffer from ADHD respond to tranquilizing medications by becoming more active. Conversely, they typically improve their capacity for attention and task focus when treated with stimulants. The most commonly prescribed stimulant is an amphetamine called methylphenidate whose trade name is Ritalin. Methylphenidate is a dopamine antagonist, i.e., it increases the levels of activity in brain systems that rely on dopamine as their neurotransmitter. Another stimulant used to treat ADHD is premoline whose trade name is *Cylert*. Like Ritalin, Cylert has been found to increase interpersonal responsiveness and goal-directed efforts along with bringing about decreases in activity level and disruptive behavior. Contrary to earlier thought, these effects are not unique to ADHD children; normal youth also increase their focus and goal-directed activity when under the influence of these drugs (Seligman & Rosenhan, 2001). Although some studies question the long-term benefits of Ritalin (e.g., Henker & Whalen, 1989), others show both short- and long-term benefits (Campbell and Cueva, 1995; Greenhill, 1998. An additional factor in understanding the most efficacious use of *Ritalin* is the finding that some youth respond to relatively small doses for optimal treatment effects, while others require considerably larger amounts.

Behavioral treatments are the main alternative to medication for ADHD. Typically, operant conditioning provides incremental rewards for reducing the frequency of such behaviors as distracting others or being inattentive. These programs have been found to be effective in treating overactivity and attention deficits, particularly in the short run (Barkley, 1998). A critical question is whether behavioral therapies are as effective as medication, or are they more useful when used in combination? Studies that compare the two approaches show that medication is more effective in treating the symptoms of ADHD; however, a *combination of drug and behavioral therapy* is most effective in reducing conduct problems that often accompany ADHD (DuPaul & Barkley, 1993; Hinshaw, Klein, and Abikoff, 1998). *Table 2.4* shows the relative benefits and liabilities of the two approaches to treatment, used separately and in combination.

PERSONALITY DISORDERS

Personality disorders during adolescence tend to correlate with an *increased incidence* of violent behavior during adolescence and early adulthood (Johnson et al., 2000). Longitudinal analysis reveals that the more *DSM-IV* personality disorder symptoms a juvenile displays in early adolescence, the more likely they are to be involved in such criminal conduct as physical assault and fighting, robbery, arson, and general threatening behavior. Youth who met diagnostic criteria for *narcissistic, passive-aggressive,* and *paranoid personality disorders* showed an association with increased risk for violent and criminal conduct, even after factors such as parental psychopathology, socioeconomic stress, sex and co-morbid psychiatric distress were controlled (Johnson et al., 2000).

By interviewing a study group of inner-city youth and their mothers every few years (the youth were studied from about 5 years of age in the 1970s, when the study began, to their early 20s), the research group was able to show links between specific personality disorders in adolescence and violent behavior during early adulthood. The two disturbances that were particularly associated with risk for violent acts and criminal behavior during early adulthood were *narcissistic* and *passive-aggressive* personality disorders. Given that *antisocial personality disorder* is not an appropriate diagnosis until after the age of 18, and its childhood precursor *conduct disorder* is clearly linked to markedly increased violent behavior during early adulthood, the study focus was on other personality disorders which have not been previously investigated.

Johnson et al. (2000) describe youth with *narcissistic personality disorder* as lacking in empathy and easily irritated when other people do not respond to their self-centered demands for special attention. They become verbally and physically abusive and often become associated with crimes involving arson and vandalism, threats to inflict harm with a weapon, initiation of fights, assault and overall escalation of violent actions. A second type of personality disorder, *passive-aggressive*, was also linked to crime and violence. Although statistically infrequent (1 to 2% of the adolescent or early adult population), people who are diagnosed as *passive-aggressive* are also likely to be *actively aggressive*. Contrary to popular belief, passive-aggressive youth are not merely "quiet saboteurs" who procrastinate, come late, simply won't appear when they are supposed to, or launch a litany of com-

Table 2.4 Medications and Behavioral Treatment for ADHD

	Stimulants	Antidepressants	Behavior Therapy	Combined Treatment
Improvement	about 80% at least moderately improved	about 50% moderately improved	about 40% moderately improved	slightly better than stimulants alone
Relapse	high	high	low to moderate	moderate
Side effects	mild to moderate	mild to moderate	low to moderate	moderate
Cost	inexpensive	inexpensive	expensive	expensive
Time scale	weeks/months	months	weeks/months	months
Overall	good	useful	marginal	good

SOURCE: Campbell and Cueva, 1995, p.10; Greenhill, 1998; Hinshaw, Klein and Abikoff, 1998; Revised with MTA cooperative group, 1999. Reprinted with permission from Seligman, Walker & Rosenhan, Abnormal Psychology, 4th Edition, Norton 2001, p. 365.

plaints against their supervisors or teachers (Johnson et al., 2000). Similar to *narcissistic personality disorder, passive-aggressive* youth showed a high risk for committing *vandalism and arson, threatening to injure people with a weapon, initiating fights, and for overall increased levels of violence during early adulthood.* Johnson et al. also found *paranoid personality disorder* to be associated with teenage crime and violence. These individuals tend to be extremely suspicious and mistrustful, sharing little personal information about themselves. They typically have difficulty with people they work with or with whom they become romantically involved and are at substantially *greater risk for initiating physical fights.*

POST-TRAUMATIC STRESS DISORDER (PTSD)

A diagnosis of PTSD is predicated upon the individual having experienced a threat to one's own life or physical integrity to which he or she responded with intense fear, horror or helplessness (*American Psychiatric Association,* 2000). A number of traumatic events are viewed as precipitants of PTSD including:

- Natural and man-made disasters such as floods;

- Violent crimes such as kidnapping, rape or murder of a parent,

- Sniper fire and school shootings;

- Motor vehicle accidents such as car and plane crashes;

- Severe burns;

- Exposure to community violence;

- War;

- Peer suicide; and

- Sexual and physical abuse.

There are three factors that have been shown to increase the likelihood that children will develop PTSD: (a) severity of the traumatic event; (b) parental reaction to the event; and (c) physical proximity to the traumatic event. Children with greater family support and less parental distress will show less severe symptoms of PTSD. The type of trauma experienced will also affect the likelihood of developing PTSD, i.e., *interpersonal traumas such as rape and assault are more likely to result in PTSD than other types of traumas.*

Very young children, who may present with relatively few PTSD symptoms, report more generalized fears such as stranger anxiety, avoidance of situations and preoccupation with words or symbols (that may or may not be directly related to the event). Elementary school-aged children experience *"time skew"* (improperly sequencing trauma events when recalling the memory and *"omen formation"* (believing that there were warning signs that predicted the trauma).

Adolescent responses to trauma, however, appear more similar to adult PTSD with a few notable exceptions. While children are likely to exhibit *"post-traumatic play,"* which is a literal representation of the harmful event through compulsive repetition of some aspect of the trauma (e.g., increase in shooting games after exposure to a school shooting), adolescents are likely to manifest "post traumatic reenactment" in which the individual behaviorally recreates some aspect of the trauma (e.g., carrying a weapon after exposure to violence. Further, adolescents are more likely than adults to exhibit aggressive and impulsive patterns of behavior (Hamblen, 1998).

As shown in *Table 2.5*, key characteristics of the disorder include *intrusive symptoms, avoidance symptoms and hyperarousal.*

PTSD and associated patterns of problem behavior

Post-traumatic stress disorder is found with high frequency among juveniles involved in problem behavior, and is most often associated with crime-related causation, such as violent and/or sexual assault during childhood (Saigh, Yasik, Anastasia, Sack & Koplewicz, 1999). In a study of risk factors associated with adolescent substance abuse and dependence, teenagers who had been physically or sexually assaulted, who had witnessed violence or who had parents with AOD problems, were at increased risk for substance abuse and dependence. The presence of PTSD increased risk for marijuana dependence or hard drug use and dependence (Kilpatrick et al., 2000). In a longitudinal study of the relationship between childhood trauma and substance abuse, children who were maltreated were at one-third greater risk for using drugs as teenagers (Kelley, Thornberry, & Smith, 1997). In another study, adolescents who reported that they had been sexually abused also reported that they began using drugs at a younger age and tended to be heavier users of drugs and alcohol as early as the eighth grade (Bensley et al., 1999). Further, the probability of being arrested for an AOD-related offense is about 39% higher for abused children than for comparison subjects (Ireland & Widom, 1994). In addition to substance abuse and the associated symptoms of PTSD, there are a number of psychiatric disorders that are commonly found in children who have experienced trauma. In addition to the commonly co-occurring disorder of depression, PTSD often appears concurrently with other anxiety disorders such as separation anxiety, panic disorder, and generalized anxiety disorder. Externalizing disorders such as oppositional defiant disorder, conduct disorder and ADHD are also quite common (Hamblen, 1998). In summary, the problems most likely to be associated with childhood trauma are PTSD and other forms of anxiety, grief and depression, aggressive and defiant behavior, physical symptoms, lowered self-esteem, substance abuse and social and academic difficulties.

In relationship to violence, *The Project on Human Development in Chicago Neighborhoods* studied self-reported exposure to violence among urban youth:

- 88% witnessed someone physically striking another person during their lifetime;

- 3% reported they had been sexually assaulted during the last year;

- 23 to 30% saw a shooting or someone being killed or shot at;

- 66% heard live gunfire;

- 8% had been shot in the past year;

- 15% were attacked with a weapon;

- 31% were hit; and

- 14% were sexually assaulted during his or her lifetime.

PTSD treatment implications

The implications of these statistics are far-reaching. Educational campaigns and exclusive reliance on criminal justice sanctions, without carefully targeted mental health services, are unlikely to positively affect this cognitive, behavioral and emotionally damaged population.

It is believed that *cognitive-behavioral treatment* (CBT) is the most effective means for helping children to decrease the consequences of childhood trauma. CBT generally includes the child directly discussing the traumatic event (exposure), anxiety management techniques (e.g., relaxation training and assertiveness training), and assistance in correcting or modifying inaccurate or distorted thoughts that emanate from the traumatic experience (e.g., "I am always unsafe,

Table 2.5 Key Characteristics of Post-Traumatic Stress Disorder

Intrusive Symptoms:

Intrusive symptoms consist of "recurrent and intrusive distressing recollections of the event, including images, thoughts or perceptions" and, in young children, repetitive play that reenacts some aspect of the trauma (APA, 2000). These repetitive images have the power to continuously re-traumatize youth even when they are safe, e.g., a 15-year-old rape victim may relive the scene of her victimization every time she closes her eyes; a 4-year old child may compulsively "beat her dolls to death" as she relives emotions connected to witnessing the repetitive and brutal beating of her mother. Intrusive symptoms may also include nightmares or flashbacks in which the youth may relive the event, often in a state of panic.

Avoidance symptoms:

A primary symptom of PTSD is the *deliberate avoidance* of thoughts, people, places and events that are reminiscent of the trauma. Adolescents, more so than younger children, may also exhibit partial or total loss of memory about the traumatic event. Additionally, there is typically a *loss of interest in people* and activities that were previously sources of comfort and pleasure. Adolescents who are afflicted with PTSD are characteristically *emotionally flat*, showing limited affect and unable to experience the same range of ups and downs as their peers. Specifically, victims of repeated sexual abuse may give the impression that they are suffering from "emotional anesthesia" in that they can't seem to come into contact with their emotional selves. There is often an accompanying sense of "foreshortened" or *limited future* in the sense of not being able to make plans beyond the moment in connection with an unpredictable and shattering worldview. The general personality constellation of adolescents who suffer from PTSD is characterized by low self-esteem, guilt feelings, and pessimism, which are attributed to a world viewed as unpredictable, dangerous, difficult to control with limited or no respite from untrustworthy adults.

Hyperarousal:

PTSD is also associated with symptoms of hyperarousal, which may include difficulties falling or staying asleep, heightened irritability, limited capacity to maintain attention and concentration, hypervigilance to danger or threats and being started easily, i.e., an exaggerated reaction to sudden noises or unexpected events.

Source: Dumas & Nilsen, *Abnormal Child and Adolescent Psychology*, Allyn and Bacon, 2003, pp. 286-288.

wherever I am"). Although Hamblen acknowledges that there is some controversy regarding the wisdom of re-exposing children to the events that frighten them, exposure-based treatments are indicated when memories or reminders of the trauma are constant sources of distress.

Children are taught relaxation skills and learn to relax while recalling their experiences. Through gradual exposure, in the context of successful relaxation training, traumatized children can learn that they do not have to respond with fear to their memories. CBT also involves challenging and correcting distorted views, such as "the world is totally unsafe," or "nobody can be trusted." CBT with children and adolescents is often accompanied by parental involvement in psycho-education regarding the symptoms and effects of PTSD. The better parents are able to cope with the trauma, the more they can give support to their children with corresponding improvements in treatment outcomes. It is therefore suggested that parents seek treatment for themselves to improve their capacity to assist their children. Special interventions may be required for children who manifest extreme and persistent PTSD-related symptoms, e.g., inappropriate sexual behavior or extreme behavioral problems .

Evaluation of PTSD treatment efficacy

McNally, Bryant, and Ehlers (2003) conducted a comprehensive review of interventions designed to mitigate acute distress and prevent long-term psychopathology associated with *Acute Stress Disorder* (ASD) and *Posttraumatic Stress Disorder* (PTSD). In consideration of the fact that the *vast majority of trauma survivors* recover from initial posttrauma reactions without professional help, the authors stress the need for controlled evaluation of commonly used interventions.

Psychological debriefing is the most widely used method for early intervention but has shown disappointing results. "Although the majority of debriefed survivors describe the experience as helpful, there is no convincing evidence that debriefing reduces the incidence of PTSD and some controlled studies suggest that it may impede natural recovery from trauma" (McNally et al., 2003, p. 45). The most recent recommendations suggest that crisis intervention workers *carefully assess trauma survivors' needs*, offering support as necessary, *without forcing disclosure* of personal feelings and thoughts about the event. Providing information about the event and its consequences is also considered important.

Cognitive-behavioral treatments for PTSD differ from debriefing in that they are delivered weeks or months after the traumatic event, in contrast to crisis intervention methods delivered within a few hours or days after a traumatic event. They are not designed to prevent disorder, but rather to help individuals whose symptoms remain problematic several weeks posttrauma.

Several controlled studies on the efficacy of CBT for trauma survivors show promising results. Severity of early posttrauma symptoms from about one to two weeks after the trauma seems to be the best indicator of need for treatment (Halligan, Michael, Clark, & Ehlers, 2003). Recent studies, including some that used randomized control trials, suggest that CBT may be effective in accelerating recovery and reducing the risk of long-term PTSD (see reviews by Ehlers & Clark, 2003; Litz, Gray, Bryant, & Adler 2002).

Foa, Hearst-Ikeda, and Perry (1995) evaluated a cognitive-behavioral protocol for treating the trauma of rape within several weeks after occurrence. The intervention was comprised of four weekly two-hour sessions that proceeded in the following sequence: education about trauma symptoms; detailed reliving of the traumatic event in memory; real-life exposure to avoided situations associated with the assault; cognitive restructuring designed to modify maladaptive beliefs; and training in relaxation and breathing skills. A description of the treatment procedure follows.

First session: Therapist educated the patient about typical acute responses to trauma and assembled a list of objectively safe situations that the patient had been avoiding since the event.

Second session: The therapist provided information and rationale for exposure therapy explaining that many symptoms may persist because the patient had not adequately processed the trauma. After teaching techniques for deep muscle relaxation and controlled breathing skills, patients were asked to close their eyes and describe the assault in the present tense as if it were recurring (imaginal exposure). As the trauma was retold, the therapist noted any cognitive distortions on the part of the patient regarding the dangerousness of the world or about the victim's perceptions of personal incompetence. Both the relaxation procedure and imaginal reliving were audiotaped and patients were asked to listen to the tapes as homework practice. They were encouraged to confront avoided situations and activities (exposure in vivo) and participated in a therapist-initiated discussion of the irrational beliefs presented by the patient during the imaginal reliving.

Third session: This began with 45 minutes of imaginal exposure followed by further cognitive therapy targeted at distorted thoughts involving patients' beliefs about the unpredictability, danger and uncontrollability of the world and extremely negative beliefs about the self. After helping patients to identify these problematic beliefs, homework involved addressing negative thinking in daily life.

Fourth session: This session included imaginal exposure, cognitive restructuring and a review of skills mastered by the patients in the program.

At 2 months postintervention, when compared to patients who did not receive CBT, fewer of those who received the CBT intervention met the criteria for PTSD (10% vs. 70%). Relative to untreated patients, the CBT group reported significantly fewer re-experiencing and arousal symptoms. However, at a5.5-month assessment, there were no significant differences in measures of PTSD between treated and untreated patients. The study suggests that although CBT may accelerate recovery, natural healing also occurs albeit at a slower rate.

In another study, Paunovic and Gillow (2002) randomly assigned crime victims with PTSD to up to 16 sessions of CBT or assigned them to a wait-list. Treatment, which started 4 to 12 weeks post-trauma consisted of: imaginal and in vivo exposure techniques. Upon completion, the CBT group was significantly improved in comparison to those who were wait-listed on measures of PTSD symptoms, anxiety, depression, quality of life, and social adjustment. Among those completing the CBT trial, only 5% of the group still had PTSD while 65% of the wait-list group were still affected.

McNally et al. (2003) concluded their extensive study of early interventions for PTSD by stating that: "Several controlled trials suggest that certain cognitive-behavioral methods may reduce the incidence of people exposed to traumatic events. These methods are more effective than either supportive counseling or no intervention" (McNally et al., 2003, p. 45).

THE MMPI-A: USE FOR DIAGNOSIS AND TREATMENT PLANNING

The MMPI-A is used as a tool in assessing characteristics of personality and psychopathology of adolescents in treatment (Butcher et al., 1992; Archer, Maruish, Imof, & Piotrowski, 1991). It has been shown to effectively differentiate juvenile offenders on the basis of offense severity (Glaser, Calhoun, & Petrocelli, 2002; Pena et al. 1996; Losada-Paisley, 1998) as well as providing accurate categorization of offense category. Studies of male adolescent offenders found that features of personality and elements of psychopathology differ across offense category (Glaser et al., 2002).

Several subscales of the MMPI-A have been found to differentiate between male adolescents who engage in criminal conduct and those who do not (Pena et al., 1996). There is a significant association between adolescent conduct problems and the *Psychopathic Deviance* subscale (MMPI-A Scale 4) (Toyer & Weed, 1998). Other analyses using the MMPI-A found prominence of *Scale 1* (*hypochondriasis*) and *Scale 8* (*schizophrenia*) in predicting psychopathic deviance among young males involved in juvenile offending (Hume, Kennedy, Patrick, & Partyka, 1996). The subscales of this instrument also have a high degree of predictive validity (79%) for differentiating male adolescents by type of offense. For example, exaggerated apprehension over health and illness (*hypochondriasis Scale 1*) and the maintenance of social distance (social

avoidance) appears to predict engagement in property crimes (Pena et al., 1996). *Psychopathic deviance* (*Scale 4*) and schizophrenia (*Scale 8*) also contributed to the identification of juvenile sex offenders, while *Scale 3* (*hysteria*) and *Scale 7* (*psychasthenia*) contributed most to identifying nonsexual offenders (Losada-Paisley, 1998).

Pena et al. (1996) conclude that the personality characteristics of male juvenile offenders (as measured by the MMPI-A) may be useful in differentiating between individuals in terms of probability of offense type: 75% of adolescent offenders were correctly linked to crimes against persons; 85% to crimes against property; and 78% to substance-related crimes. Pena et al. suggest use of an integrated assessment approach that synthesizes behavioral, biological, and psychological information. Prediction is enhanced through the addition of social factors, such as family dynamics, experiences with physical/sexual trauma, and other information about the specific adolescent's problem behavior (Pena et al. 1996). These observations suggest that treatment might be enhanced through attention to personality issues that vary according to offense type (Pena et al.).

PSYCHOTHERAPEUTIC MEDICATIONS FOR CHILDREN AND ADOLESCENTS

Epidemiological studies report that 10 to 20% of American children suffer from some form of mental disorder with 5 to 8% experiencing extreme emotional distress (Powers, 1989; Roberts, Attkisson & Rosenblatt, 1998; Costello, 1999; Friedman et al., 1996; Costello et al., 1996; Shaffer et al., 1996). Children between the ages of 5 and 19 have at least a 7.5% chance of being diagnosed with ADHD (approximately 5 million youth), with others receiving diagnosis and medication for obsessive-compulsive disorder, social anxiety disorder, post-traumatic stress disorder (PTSD), pathological impulsiveness, sleeplessness and depression. *Table 2.6* summarizes mechanisms of action, side effects and treatment indications for psychiatric medications commonly used for children and adolescents.

Table 2.6 Psychiatric Medications Commonly Used for Children and Adolescents

Name	How it Works	Side Effects	Tested/Approved
Adderall	A once-a-day amphetamine, inhibits areas of the brain responsible for organizing thoughts	Rapid heartbeat, high blood pressure, in rare cases over stimulation, sometimes addictive	Approved to treat ADHD in children 3 and older
Concerta	Keeps high levels of norepinephrine and dopamine, which reduce hyperactivity and inattention	Headache, stomach pain, sleeplessness, in rare cases, over stimulation	Approved to treat ADHD in children 6 and older
Strattera	First non-stimulant for ADHD; enhances norepinephrine levels in the brain	Decreased appetite, fatigue, nausea, stomach pain	Approved to treat ADHD in children 6 and older
Ritalin	Active agent methylphenidate; stimulates the brain to filter and prioritize incoming information	Headache, lack of appetite irritability, nervousness, insomnia	Approved to treat ADHD in children 6 and older
Methypatch	Patch form of methylphenidate, delivers continuous low doses through the skin	Similar to those for oral methylphenidate	Developed to treat ADHD but "unapprovable" by FDA
Prozac	Approved in 1987, first antidepressant aimed at regulating serotonin	Insomnia, anxiety, nervousness, weight loss, mania	Approved to treat depression and OCD in children 7 and up
Zoloft	Enhances levels of serotonin to maintain feelings of satisfaction and stability	Upset stomach, dry mouth agitation, decreased appetite	Not approved for children, based on adult data prescribed for depression, anxiety, OCD and others
Paxil	Elevates levels of serotonin (similar to Prozac and Zoloft)	Nausea, drowsiness, insomnia	Same as Zoloft
Effexor	Targets serotonin and norepinephrine to regulate mood	Nausea, constipation nervousness, loss of appetite, drowsiness	Not approved for children, prescribed for depression based on adult data
Depakote	Antiseizure medication, effective for grandiose, hyperagitated state of mania	Liver and white blood cell abnormalities, headache nausea, drowsiness	Not approved for children, prescribed for bipolar mania and seizures
Zyprexa	Mood stabilizer designed to balance brain levels of serotonin and dopamine	Weight gain, drowsiness, dry mouth, seizures	Not approved for children, prescribed for bipolar mania and schizophrenia
Lithium	Stabilizes episodes of elated, intensely joyous mood associated with mania	Nausea, loss of appetite,	Not approved for children, prescribed for childhood bipolar mania

Source: Kluger, J., Medicating Young Minds, *Time Magazine,* November 3, 2003, pp. 48-58

CHAPTER REVIEW

This chapter begins with a reminder that most adolescents manage the teen years without difficulty. It then goes on to describe a subset of adolescents who manifest symptoms of psychological distress or dysfunction, and who make up a sizeable percentage of adolescents who become involved in criminal activity and other problem behavior. Depression, conduct disorders, antisocial personality disorder, post-traumatic stress disorder and substance abuse disorders are among these patterns of adolescent disturbance. Internalizing disorders (e.g., depression), externalizing disorders (e.g., conduct disorder) and substance abuse can (and often do) occur in the same individual, concurrently.

Disruptive behavior disorders including attention deficit disorder, oppositional defiant disorder and conduct disorder are more common among males during childhood and adolescence, sharing common difficulties in controlling behavior coupled with adjustment problems that often persist into adulthood. Children with oppositional defiant disorder (ODD) display a pattern of negativity, defiance and opposition that leads to problems with teachers, parents, siblings and peers. The distinction between ODD and conduct disorder (CD) is based on the presence of violations of legal statutes and social mores. Children with ODD do not typically engage in repeated physical assault, destruction of property or deceit. During adolescence, the severity of problems and the rate of conduct-disorder increases dramatically, with youth becoming involved in such violent acts as muggings, armed robberies or rapes. The term "fledgling psychopath" aptly describes a subset of early onset conduct disordered adolescents who manifest insensitivity, harshness, and lack of remorse combined with callous and unemotional personality characteristics such as a disconcerting lack of empathy and respect for others. Disruptive behavior disorders may have an underlying genetic derivation that interacts with environmental experience in the development of antisocial behavior. The presence of certain types of personality disorders may exacerbate the drug-violence relationship.

A relatively small percentage (23%) of children who manifest symptoms of conduct disorder or the less severe oppositional defiant disorder are referred for treatment. This is unfortunate in light of the fact that research shows improved outcomes for treated youth. Successful interventions, generally derived from social learning theory, include the following goals:

- Helping the client identify situations that trigger aggressive or antisocial behavior;

- Teaching the child how to take the perspective of others and care about this perspective;

- Reducing the aggressive child's tendency to attribute hostility to others; and

- Training the child in adaptive ways of solving conflicts with others.

Each of these goals is achieved through modeling, observational learning, positive reinforcement for the attainment of the desired behavior, and punishment or negative consequences for the continuation of negative patterns.

Clinical syndrome hyperactivity is diagnosed on the basis of poor concentration skills and motor restlessness. Hyperactivity, low impulse control, attention deficits and behavioral difficulties, when combined, may serve as an early indicator of developing conduct disorder. It is likely that hyperactivity initiates the onset of behaviors, which manifest as defiance, opposition to rules, and other conduct difficulties. Punitive responses (by parents, caretakers and teachers) to these behaviors may initiate identification with deviance and delinquency. A critical question is whether behavioral therapies are as effective as medication, or are they more useful when used in combination? Studies that compare the two approaches show that medication is more effective in treating the symptoms of ADHD; however, a combination of drug and behavioral therapy is most effective in reducing conduct problems that often accompany ADHD.

Other personality disorders tend to correlate with an increased incidence of violent behavior during adolescence and early adulthood. Youth who meet diagnostic criteria for narcissistic, passive-aggressive, and paranoid personality disorders show an independent association with increased risk for violent and criminal conduct, even after factors such as parental psychopathology, socioeconomic stress, sex and co-morbid psychiatric distress were controlled.

A diagnosis of PTSD is predicated upon the individual having experienced a threat to one's own life or physical integrity to which he or she responded with intense fear, horror or helplessness. Children who were maltreated are at greater risk for using drugs as teenagers, and those who reported sexual abuse said they began heavy drug use at a younger age. Further, the probability of being arrested for an AOD-related offense is higher for abused children. The problems most likely to be associated with childhood trauma are PTSD and other forms of anxiety, grief and depression, aggressive and defiant behavior, physical symptoms, lowered self-esteem and social and academic difficulties These findings strongly suggest that educational campaigns and exclusive reliance on criminal justice sanctions, without carefully targeted mental health services, are unlikely to positively affect this cognitive, behavioral and emotionally damaged population. CBT shows promise as the treatment of choice for PTSD.

Personality characteristics of male juvenile offenders (as measured by the MMPI-A) may be useful in differentiating between individuals in terms of probability of offense type and severity of crime. Research points toward use of an integrated approach, which synthesizes behavioral, biological, and psychological information. Prediction is enhanced through the addition of social factors, such as family dynamics, experiences with physical/sexual trauma, and other information about the specific adolescent's problem behavior. Treatment outcomes may be enhanced through attention to personality issues that vary according to offense type.

When indicated, an array of psychotherapeutic medications have become strong allies, as neuroscience and psychology have become increasingly effective in the targeting of specific patterns of cognition, affect and behavioral disturbance in adolescents who struggle with mental disorder.

Substance Abuse and Adolescent Problem Behavior

3

Chapter Three: Substance Abuse and Adolescent Problem Behavior

Chapter Outline

The Scope of Adolescent Substance Abuse

- Recent trends
- Teenage drinking prevalence
- Commonly abused drugs

Imminent Drug Threats

- Club drugs
- Ritalin and other prescription drug abuse
- Methamphetamine

Factors Associated with the Onset of Adolescent Substance Abuse

- Psychosocial causal factors
- Mediating factors in adolescent AOD Abuse

Adolescent Drinking and Driving

- Alcohol-related accidents and fatalities
- Prevalence of drinking and driving among youth
- Characteristics of young DWI offenders
- Causes of drinking and driving

Relationship of Age to Adolescent AOD Abuse and Disruption

Adolescent Drug Use and Criminal Conduct

- The drug-crime connection
- Substance abuse and violence in adolescence

AOD Abuse Across American Subcultures

- Ethnic identity as both risk and protection for substance use
- Relationship of AOD abuse and disruption to ethnicity

Chapter Review

Chapter Objectives

- To describe the scope of adolescent substance abuse in terms of prevalence rates for commonly abused drugs, recent trends, and imminent drug threats;

- To examine risk and resiliency factors associated with the onset of or protection from adolescent substance abuse;

- To examine adolescent drunk driving, including psychosocial and cognitive factors that underlie an adolescent's decision to drink and drive;

- To discuss the importance of imminent drug threats including the abuse of: club drugs, Ritalin and other prescription drugs and methamphetamine;

- To explore subcultural patterns of substance use and to investigate the role of ethnicity in AOD exposure, disruption, risk and protection;

- To analyze the connections between adolescent substance abuse and crime, including violence; and

- To suggest implications for treatment of adolescent substance abuse.

THE SCOPE OF ADOLESCENT SUBSTANCE ABUSE

Recent trends

Results from the 2003 *Monitoring the Future* (MTF) survey of nearly 50,000 students in 392 secondary schools across the country marked the seventh year in a row that illicit drug use among 8th, 10th, and 12th graders remained stable or decreased. Substance abuse, however continues to play a major role in adolescent life experience.

Ecstasy use rose rapidly from 1998 through 2001, but in 2001, an increasing proportion of students began to see Ecstasy as a dangerous drug. That perception strengthened, and by 2003, the proportion of 10th and 12th grade students who reported using Ecstasy in the prior 12 months fell by more than half since 2001. Decline in use may be attributed to extensive media coverage and concerted efforts at preventive education by the *National Institute on Drug Abuse*, and anti-Ecstasy ad campaigns by the *White House Office on National Drug Control Policy, and the Partnership for a Drug-Free America* (Johnson et al., 2004).

In 2003, marijuana use showed its second year of decline in the upper grades and its seventh year of decline among 8th graders. In 2003, 13%, 28% and 35% of the 8th, 10th, and 12th graders, reported that they had smoked marijuana in the prior 12 months. Use of marijuana during the past month was reported by 21.2% of 12th graders.

Although drug use has appreciatively declined during the past seven years, this year's *halting of declines among eighth graders* is a matter of concern (Johnson et al., 2004). The fact that this group is no longer showing reductions in use could signify that drops in the upper grade levels will soon come to a halt as well. Eighth-grade annual prevalence rates for *inhalant use* increased from 7.7% in 2002 to 8.7% in 2003, with concurrent *declines in perceptions of danger* associated with such use. As well, eighth graders show unchanged use of hallucinogens (other than LSD), amphetamines, methamphetamine, tranquilizers, and alcohol use in the past 30 days. These trends appear problematic.

Johnson et al. (2003) suggest that *"generational forgetting"* may account for these recent shifts. Even though one generation or cohort of young people may comprehend the hazards associated with particular drugs, the next cohort may not have lived through the same set of events that resulted in perceptions of dan-

ger. Current trends among 8th graders may portend that *generational forgetting* is about to occur again, as it did in the early 90s.

Teenage drinking prevalence

Despite a minimum legal drinking age of 21, the prevalence of alcohol consumption among youth is high. According to the annual *Monitoring the Future Survey*, almost 50% of 12th graders reported drinking alcohol during the 30 days prior to being surveyed (Johnston et al., 2004). In addition, *binge drinking—* defined as having *four or more drinks in one sitting* for females and *five* of more drinks in one sitting for males—is widespread. This phenomenon often begins about age 13, tends to increase during adolescence, peaks between the ages or 18 and 22, and then gradually decreases (NIAAA, 1997). *Binge drinking*, at least once in the two weeks before the survey, was reported by more than *30 percent of 12th graders* (Johnston, 2000).

Table 3.1 shows the 2003 lifetime and 30-day prevalence of various drugs for 12th graders (Johnston et al., 2004).

Commonly abused drugs

Table 3.2 categorizes commonly abused drugs including their street names, DEA classification, route of administration, intoxication effects and potential health consequences.

IMMINENT DRUG THREATS

Some of the most valuable data relative to emergent drug threats is derived from trend analysis in the identification of certain subpopulations that show greater vulnerability than the wider population to particular drug use patterns. Trend analysis may elucidate imminent drug threats, which may be obscured by attending to data pertaining to the population at large Tobacco, for example, is probably the most prominent gateway drug with repeated findings that initial use of cigarettes is highly correlated with the use of other drugs (Wilson, 2003). At present, about 16% of youth 12 to 17 years of age smoke cigarettes and about 19% report using alcohol during the past month (Johnston et al., 2004). This is important in that research points to a strong relationship between cigarette smoking and the future use of marijuana. Among youth who use drugs, 60% use marijuana and twice as many 8th graders have tried marijuana as compared to a decade ago. More youth enter treatment for

Table 3.1 Monitoring the Future Study 2003 Prevalence of Various Drugs for 12th Graders

Category of Drug(s)	Percent Lifetime	Percent 30-day Use
Any illicit drug	51.1	24.1
Cigarettes	57.3	24.4
Smokeless tobacco	17.0	6.7
Alcohol*	76.6	47.5
Marijuana**	46.1	21.2
Inhalants	11.2	—
Ecstasy (MDMA)	8.3	1.3
Hallucinogens	10.6	2.1
Cocaine	7.7	2.1
Crack cocaine	3.6	0.9
Heroin	1.5	.04
Steroids	3.5	1.3
Tranquilizers	11.4	2.8
Amphetamines	14.4	—
Methamphetamine	6.2	—

* Daily use of alcohol was 3.2%

** Daily use of marijuana was 6.0%

Source: Johnston, L.D., O'Malley, P.M., Bachman, J.G., & Schulberg, J.E., (2004). Monitoring the Future national results on adolescent drug use: Overview of key findings, 2003. (NIH Publication No. [yet to be assigned.]Bethesda MD; National Institute on Drug Abuse. Website: www.monitoringthefuture.org

marijuana than for all drugs combined—with 60% of those who enter drug treatment with a primary marijuana drug problem (Wilson, 2003). Thus careful attention to trends in cigarette smoking among youth is of vital importance to educators, prevention and treatment specialists as a barometer of future drug threats and health-related issues.

Club drugs

The use of club drugs such as MDMA (Ecstasy), GBH (grievous bodily harm), Rohypnol (roofies, r-2, forget me drug), Ketamine (jet, special k, honey oil), PMA (death, mitsubishi double stack, Nexus (venus, bromo, toonies), and PCP (angel dust, rocket fuel) is often perceived as less harmful and addictive than more mainstream drugs such as cocaine and heroin. However, the quality of these drugs varies greatly as distribution networks associated with club drugs are unstable and characterized by the sale of "look alikes" or analogues, e.g., Rohypnol (supplies of pharmaceu-

tical Rohypnol have been successfully limited by the government's effort to restrict its availability). *The Drug Abuse Warning Network* (DAWN) reports drastic increases in emergency room treatment for overdoses of GHB (Wilson, 2003).

Ritalin and prescription drug abuse

Another emergent and alarming trend is the abuse of prescription drugs. *Opiate-related* pharmaceuticals such as codeine, and Oxycontin; *benzodiazepines*, such as Xanex and Valium; and *stimulants* like Ritalin (vitamin R) are frequently abused. Lifetime amphetamine use among high school seniors is reported by the *2003 Monitoring the Future Study* (Johnston et al., 2004) to be 14.4%. Ritalin and Aderall (methylphenidate)—milder stimulants than amphetamine, with potency between amphetamine and caffeine (Ray and Ksir, 2002)—are now considered the drugs of choice for treating ADHD. An informal survey conducted by *Men's Health* (Jaffe, 2002)

Table 3.2 Commonly Abused Drugs

Substance: Category & Name	Examples of Commercial & Street Names	DEA Schedule*/ How Administered **	Intoxication Effects/ Potential Health Consequences
Cannabinoids			
Hashish	Boom, chronic, gangster, hash, hash oil, hemp	I/swallowed, smoked	*Euphoria, slowed thinking and reaction time, confusion, impaired balance and coordination/cough, frequent respiratory infections; impaired memory and learning; increased heart rate, anxiety; panic attack/ tolerance, addiction.*
Marijuana	Blunt, dope, ganja, grass, herb, joints, Mary Jane, pot, reefer, sinsemilla, skunk, weed	I/swallowed, smoked	
Depressants			
Barbiturates	Amytal, Membutal, Seconal, Phenobarbital; barbs, reds, red birds, phennies, tooies, yellows, yellow jackets	II, III, V/injected, swallowed	*Reduced anxiety; feeling of well-being; lowered inhibitions; slowed pulse and breathing; lowered blood pressure; poor concentration/ fatigue; confusion; impaired coordination, memory, judgment; addiction; respiratory depression and arrest, death.*
Benzodiazepines (other than flunitrazepam)	Ativan, Halcion, Librium, Valium, Xanax; candy, downers, sleeping pills, tranks.	IV/swallowed, injected	*Also for barbiturates—sedation, drowsiness/depression, unusual excitement, fever, irritability, poor judgment, slurred speech, dizziness, life-threatening withdrawal.*
Flunitrazepam III	Rohypnol; forget-me pill, Mexican Valium, R2, Roche, roofies, roofinol, rope, rophies	IV/swallowed, snorted	*For benzodiazepines—sedation, drowsiness/dizziness*

Table 3.2 continued

Substance: Category & Name	Examples of Commercial & Street Names	DEA Schedule*/ How Administered **	Intoxication Effects/ Potential Health Consequences
Depressants (continued)			
Flunitrazepam III (continued)			For Flunitrazepam—visual and gastrointestinal disturbances, urinary retention, memory loss for the time under the drug's effects.
GHBIII	Gamma-hydroxybutyrate; G, Georgia home boy, grievous bodily harm, liquid Ecstasy		For GHB—drowsiness, nausea/vomiting, headache, loss of consciousness, loss of reflexes, seizures, coma, death.

For methaqualone—euphoria/depression, poor reflexes, slurred speech, coma. |
| **Dissociative Anesthetics** | | | |
| Ketamine | Ketalar SV; cat Valiums, K, special K, vitamin K | III/injected, snorted, smoked | Increased heart rate and blood pressure, impaired motor function/memory loss/ numbness/nausea/vomiting.

Also, for ketamine—at high doses, delirium, depression, respiratory depression and arrest. |
FCP and Analogs	Phencyclidine; angel dust, boat, hog, love boat, peace pill	I, II/injected, swallowed, smoked	For PCP and analogs—possible decrease in blood pressure and heart rate, panic, aggression, violence/loss of appetite, depression, altered states of perception and feeling; nausea; persisting perception disorder (flash-backs).
Hallucinogens			
LSD	Lysergic acid diethylamide; acid, blotter, boomers, cubes, microdot, yellow sunshines	I/swallowed, absorbed through mouth tissues	For LSD and mescaline—increased body temperature, heart rate, blood pressure; loss of appetite, sleeplessness, numbness, weakness, tremors. For LSD—persistent mental disorders.

Table 3.2 continued

Substance: Category & Name	Examples of Commercial & Street Names	DEA Schedule*/ How Administered **	Intoxication Effects/ Potential Health Consequences
Hallucinogens *(continued)*			
Mescaline	Buttons, cactus, mesc, peyote	I/swallowed, smoked	
Psilocybin	Magic mushroom, purple passion, shrooms	I/swallowed	Nervousness, paranoia
Opioids & Morphine Derivatives			
Codeine	*Empirin with Codeine, Fiorinal with Codeine, Robitussin A-C Tylenol with Codeine;* Captain Cody, Cody, schoolboy; (with giuthimide) doors & fours, loads, pancakes and syrup	II, III, IV/injected, swallowed	*Pain relief, euphoria, drowsiness*/nausea, constipation, confusion, sedation, respiratory depression and arrest, tolerance, addiction, unconsciousness, coma, death. Also for codeine—less analgesia, sedation, and respiratory depression than morphine.
Fentanyl and Fentanyl analogs	*Actiq, Duragesic, Sublimaze;* apache, China girl, China white, dance fever, friend, goodfella, jackpot, murder 8, TNT, Tango and Cash	I, II/injected, smoked snorted	
Heroin	*Diacetylmorphine;* brown sugar, dope, H, horse, junk, skag, skunk, smack, white horse	I/injected, smoked, snorted	*Staggering gait*
Morphine	*Roxanol, Duramorph;* M, Miss Emma, monkey, white stuff	II, III/injected, swallowed, smoked	
Opium	*Laudanum, paregoric;* big O, black stuff, block, gum, hop.	II, III, V/swallowed, smoked	
Oxycodone HCL	*Oxycontin;* Oxy, O.C., killer	II/swallowed, snorted, injected	
Hydrocodone bitartrate, acetaminophen	*Vicodin;* vike, Watson-387	II/swallowed	

Table 3.2 continued

Substance: Category & Name	Examples of Commercial & Street Names	DEA Schedule*/ How Administered **	Intoxication Effects/ Potential Health Consequences
Amphetamine	*Biphetamine, Dexedrine;* bennies, black beauties, crosses, hearts, LA turnaround, speed, truck drivers, uppers	II/injected, swallowed, smoked, snorted	*Increased heart rate, blood pressure, metabolism; feelings of exhilaration, energy, increased mental alertness/rapid or irregular heart beat; reduced appetite, weight loss, heart failure, nervousness, insomnia. Also, for amphetamine—rapid breathing/tremor; loss of coordination; irritability, anxiousness, restlessness, delirium, panic, paranoia, impulsive behavior, aggressiveness, tolerance, addiction, psychosis*
Cocaine	*Cocaine hydrochloride;* blow, bump, C, candy, Charlie, coke, crack, flake, rock, snow, toot.	II/injected, smoked, snorted	Increased temperature/chest pain, respiratory failure, nausea, abdominal pain, strokes, seizures, headaches, malnutrition, panic attacks.
MDMA (methylenedioxy-methamphetamine)	Adam, clarity, Ecstasy, Eve, lover's speed, peach, STP, X, XTC	I/swallowed	*Mild hallucinogenic effects, increased tactile sensitivity, empathic feelings/* impaired memory and learning, hyperthermia, cardiac toxicity, renal failure, liver toxicity
Methamphetamine	*Desoxyn;* chalk, crank, crystal, fire, glass, go, fast, ice, meth, speed	II/injected, swallowed, smoked, snorted	Aggression, violence, psychotic behavior/memory loss, cardiac and neurological damage; impaired memory and learning, tolerance, addiction.
Methylphenidate (safe and effective treatment of ADHD)	*Ritalin;* JIF, MPH, R-ball, Skippy, the smart drug, vitamin R	II/injected, swallowed, snorted	
Nicotine	Cigarettes, cigars, smokeless tobacco, snuff, spit tobacco, bidis, chew	Not scheduled/smoked, snorted, taken in snuff and spit tobacco	Adverse pregnancy outcomes, chronic lung disease, cardiovascular disease, stroke, cancer, tolerance, addiction.

Table 3.2 continued

Substance: Category & Name	Examples of Commercial & Street Names	DEA Schedule*/ How Administered **	Intoxication Effects/ Potential Health Consequences
Other Compounds			
Anabolic steroids	*Anadrol, Oxandrin, Durabolin, Depo-Testosterone, Equipoise; roids, juice*	III/injected, swallowed, applied to skin	*No intoxication effects*/ hypertension, blood clotting and cholesterol changes, liver cysts and cancer; kidney cancer, hostility and aggression, acne; in adolescents, premature stoppage of growth; in males, prostate cancer; reduced sperm production, shrunken testicles, breast enlargement; in females, menstrual irregularities, development of beard and other masculine characteristics.
Inhalants	Solvents *(paint thinners, gasoline, glues)*, gases *(butane, propane, aerosol, propellants, nitrous oxide)*, nitrates *(isoamyl, isobutyl, cyclohexyl)*; laughing gas, poppers, snappers, whippets	Not scheduled/inhaled through nose or mouth	*Stimulation, loss of inhibition; headache; nausea or vomiting; slurred speech, loss of motor coordination;* wheezing, unconsciousness, cramps, weight loss, muscle weakness, depression, memory impairment, damage to cardiovascular and nervous systems, sudden death.

*Schedule I and II drugs have a high potential for abuse. They require greater storage security and have a quota on manufacturing, among other restrictions. Schedule I drugs are available for research only and have no approved medical use; Schedule II drugs are available only by prescription (unrefillable) and require a form for ordering. Schedule III and IV drugs are available by prescription, may have five refills in 6 months, and may be ordered orally. Most Schedule V drugs are available over the counter.

**Taking drugs by injection can increase the risk of infection through needle contamination with staphylococci, HIV, hepatitis, and other organisms.

***Associated with sexual assaults.

Source: National Institute on Drug Abuse (2004). Web site, http://www.nida.nih.gov/DrugsofAbuse.html

showed student self-report estimates of Ritalin or Aderall ingestion at top-rated colleges as high as 50%. College students indicate that snorting, which leads to more rapid absorption than when ingested orally (as intended for medical use), is a popular route of administration. Rapid absorption makes the drug act more like cocaine.

Methamphetamine

According to the *2003 Monitoring the Future Study* (Johnston et al., 2004) among high school seniors, lifetime use of methamphetamine was 6.2%. Methamphetamine (meth) is a powerfully addictive stimulant that affects the central nervous system (CNS) by interfering with normal neurotransmission, creating a large release of dopamine in the brain. It was developed early in the 1900s from amphetamine and was used in nasal decongestants and bronchial inhalers. The chemical structure is similar to amphetamine but has more pronounced effects on the CNS. Accepted uses for meth include treatment of narcolepsy, attention deficit disorder and obesity. Meth is known as speed, chalk, ice, crystal, crank, and glass. It is a white, odorless, bitter-tasting crystalline powder that dissolves easily in water or alcohol. Like cocaine, it produces changes similar to the fight-or-flight response: it boosts heart rate, respiration, blood pressure and body temperatures. Both cocaine and meth boost brain levels of dopamine, creating euphoria and increased energy, but they do it in different ways. Cocaine prevents the re-uptake of dopamine; meth causes the excess release of dopamine.

Meth is made in clandestine laboratories with inexpensive over-the-counter ingredients. The illicit manufacture of methamphetamine can be accomplished in a number of ways, but most commonly is based on ephedrine/pseudoephedrine reduction. Large-scale production is dependent on ready access to bulk quantities of ephedrine and pseudo-ephedrine. Products used to manufacture methamphetamine are widely available commercially in the U.S. and include over the counter medications including ephedrine, red phosphorous, hydrochloric acid, drain cleaner, battery acid, lye, lantern fuel, and antifreeze. The chemicals are extremely volatile and amateur chemists who create makeshift laboratories are creating an atmosphere for deadly explosions or fires.

Users are attracted to what they call "neutral meth effects" which include wakefulness, physical activity, weight loss and a sense of well-being. Different ways of taking meth produce different alterations in mood.

After smoking or injecting meth, there is an experience of a rush or "flash" that lasts a few minutes. Snorting or ingesting produces a euphoria—a high, but not the intense rush. Snorting produces effects within 3-5 minutes, oral ingestion within 15-20 minutes (NIDA, 1998). Since the pleasurable effects disappear before the concentration of the drug in the blood falls, users maintain a high by binging. In the 1980s, "ice," a smokable form of meth came into use. Smoked in a glass pipe, it produces effects that can continue for over 12 hours.

Effects on the brain: The brains of former chronic meth abusers show a significant decrease in dopamine transporters, with a 24% loss in the normal number of dopamine transporters. This directly relates to slowness in motor skills and poorer performance in verbal and memory tasks. Neuron loss is substantial; there is a definite loss of disruption in performance and a statistically significant correlation between changes in dopamine transporters and functional disturbances. From a medical perspective, meth use has taken treatment practitioners beyond strategies to improve client motivation, thinking patterns and decision-making, to considerations of possible brain damage. (Chang, 2002)

Treatment for methamphetamine addiction: According to NIDA, the most effective treatments for meth addiction are cognitive behavioral interventions, which help modify thinking, expectancies, and behaviors and increase coping skills to various life stressors. They also recommend support groups as an adjunct to leading to drug-free recovery. CSAT recommends the Matrix, Model (Rawson et al., 1995), first developed in the 80s as a cocaine treatment plan, it consists of a 4-6 month program that follows normal CBT therapy protocol including techniques to manage cravings and avoiding risky activities that could trigger relapse. The intensive outpatient program was developed with an understanding of the diversity of problems that contribute to addictive disorders; thus the needs of the individual are considered in the design of each treatment plan. The intensity, duration and contents can vary for different patients although certain key elements are significantly related to treatment success and include:

- *Therapist support*—*Matrix* outcome reports have consistently found that empathic and directive support of a professional therapist is critical in developing successful recovery.

- *Group/Individual Participation*—Data from *Matrix* follow-up research showed that participation in group activities was highly related to long-term success. Individualized treatment is also available for people who are at the earliest stages of readiness for treatment.

- *12-Step or Other Spiritual Group Involvement*—Outcome reports have demonstrated that those patients who are involved in 12-Step and/or other support group activities have far better outcomes than patients who are not.

- *Relapse Prevention and Education*—Substance abusers benefit from learning about how they became addicted, how they have been affected by their addiction, what they need to do to prevent a relapse and what to do if they return to drug and/or alcohol use.

- *Family Involvement*—Research clearly indicates superior treatment outcome for patients whose families are involved in the treatment process.

- *Structure*—Chemical dependency treatment requires an explicit framework giving patients a clear understanding of the treatment requirements.

FACTORS ASSOCIATED WITH THE ONSET OF ADOLESCENT SUBTANCE ABUSE

Psychosocial causal factors

The causes of adolescent onset substance abuse have been studied extensively. Jessor (1987; 1998) reviewed the links between problem-behavior, psychosocial development, and adolescent problem drinking. Through longitudinal study Costa, Jessor & Turbin (1999) showed that *higher levels of risk*, as well as *lower levels of protection*, predicted a large portion of the variance in several aspects of drinking behavior. Most notably, *timing* in the development of an adolescent's problem drinking, as well as overall probability of the development of problem drinking during the adolescent's life course were significantly related.

The role of *social influence* in the etiology of adolescent substance abuse has been identified as *central*. Much research has focused on contributions from behavior and attitudes of siblings, parents, and peers (Griffin, Botvin, Epstein, Doyle & Diaz, 2000; Dusenbury, Epstein, Botvin, & Diaz, 1994; Duncan, Duncan, Biglan, & Ary, 1998; Conger & Rueter, 1996). Baumrind (1991) investigated the influence of *parenting style* on adolescent outcome, including

personal competence and *substance use*. Epstein, Botvin, Diaz & Schinke (1995) found that *"social popularity"* correlates with both alcohol use and heavy intoxication among inner city youth. Additionally, *difficulties in forming peer relationships* during childhood is associated with *psychosocial problems* (Woodward & Fergusson, 1999) and *deviant peer affiliation* (Fergusson, Woodward & Horwood, 1999) - factors that *increase vulnerability to substance abuse and criminal conduct* during adolescence (Woodward, Fergusson & Horwood, 2002).

Other researchers have investigated the role of *gang participation* in facilitating drug use and delinquency as well as other forms of criminal behavior and violence. (Thornberry, Krohn, Lizotte, & Chard-Wierschem, 1993; Zhang, Welte, & Wieczorek, 1999; (Thornberry, 1998; Scott, 1999). In a study of inner city youth, *perceived neighborhood risk* (including an adolescent's assessment of local gang activity, fighting, and neighborhood toughness) contributed to an adolescent's risk for abusing substances (nicotine, alcohol and cannabis), especially when combined with high levels of truancy. *Communication* within families, an *internal health locus of control* and *social concern*, however, appeared to provide some *protection* against these and other harmful life experiences (Scheier, Miller, Ifill-Williams, & Botvin, 2001; Scheier, Botvin & Miller, 1999).

Some of the risk factors associated with *heavy drinking* in older adolescents are *conduct problems during childhood, early experimentation with alcohol and nicotine* (Griffin et al. 2000), and *positive alcohol expectancies* (Griffin et al. 2000; Smith & Goldman, 1995). *Poor behavioral control* during childhood has been linked to *later drug problems* (White, 1992). *Age of first use of any substance*, including nicotine, and *age of delinquency onset*, has also been implicated in an adolescent's increased risk for substance abuse (Labouvie, Bates, & Pandina, 1997; Zhang, Wieczorek, & Welte, 1997).

Mediating factors in adolescent AOD abuse

This section discusses psychosocial factors that have either positive or negative influences on adolescent AOD abuse patterns. Following each factor is a brief description of studies that have probed the mechanisms underlying this involvement. These relationships have been interpreted primarily through cognitive-behavioral perspectives.

Social Competence: Associated with *reduced drinking* in adolescence (Scheier & Botvin, 1998; Scheier,

Botvin, Diaz, & Griffin, 1999). Psychological well-being was predicted by social competence skills, as well as predicting low levels of substance involvement (Griffin, Scheier, Botvin, & Diaz, 2001). Griffin et al. propose that social competence may provide a protective function against substance involvement by enhancing wellness and promoting resilience to the effects of other risk factors. Specific competency skills include: social confidence, perceived self-efficacy and the possession of cognitive and behavioral alternatives (Jessor, 1996). In particular, *assertiveness and communication skills* are central (Griffin, Epstein, Botvin, & Spoth, 2001).

Life Skills Training: Research conducted during the past two decades (Botvin & Griffin, 2001, 2002) reports *Life Skills Training* (LST) to be effective in prevention of adolescent drug abuse, as well as enhancement of social and personal competence skills. Youth who actively participate in LST are reported to have *lower rates of early onset* of substance use, and tend to experience *enhanced well-being*. Critics argue that the *Life Skills Training* approach "convinces the already convinced," i.e., LST is of benefit mainly to the subset of adolescents who are highly motivated to decrease substance abuse before even entering the program (Gorman, 1998).

Deficits in cognitive-behavioral self-management: Important components of LST are *cognitive-behavioral self-management techniques* and *social skills*, which play a predominant role in protecting adolescents from developing substance abuse problems (Scheier & Botvin, 1998; Scheier, Botvin, Diaz & Griffin, 1999; Griffin, Scheier, Botvin & Diaz, 2001).

Assertiveness, including refusal assertiveness (or a disinclination to use them): Underdeveloped refusal assertiveness predicts greater drinking involvement (Epstein, Griffin, & Botvin, 2001). Drug refusal efficacy is associated with low levels of alcohol use (Scheier, Botvin, Diaz & Griffin, 1999). Similarly, research with minority youth living in public housing developments found that good communication skills (such as refusal skills) significantly lowered an adolescent's overall risk against substance involvement (Williams, Epstein, Botvin, Schinke, & Diaz, 1998).

Low self-esteem: Adolescent alcohol use is *negatively correlated with high self-esteem* (Scheier, Botvin, Griffin & Diaz, 2000). Social competence, as well as *progressive growth* in social competence, positively influences the development of self-esteem. Low levels of personal competence tend to accelerate the advancement through developmental transitions toward alcohol abuse, while inadequate social skills are correlated with a more rapid deterioration in self-esteem (Scheier, et al. 2000). Low self-esteem may constitute an early condition that increases vulnerability to alcohol abuse in adolescence (Scheier, et al. 2000).

External locus of control: Jessor (1996) found that *internal locus of control* is negatively associated with substance abuse problems in adolescence.

Positive AOD expectancies: Studies that explore the relationship between *alcohol-related expectancies* and adolescent problem drinking find strong empirical foundation for the use of these cognitions in identifying adolescents who may be at risk (Griffin, Botvin, Epstein, Doyle & Diaz, 2000; Smith, & Goldman, 1995). Alcohol expectancies may serve an *initiating function* in adolescent alcohol use.

Positive outcome expectancies of substance use have emerged as a *major mediating factor* in research on social competence. Adolescents with low levels of social competence may turn to cigarette, alcohol and drug use because of *perceived social benefits* from such use, such as "having more friends, looking grown up and 'cool', and having more fun" (Griffin, Epstein, Botvin, & Spoth, 2001). These expectancies of *social reinforcement* are associated with *perception of peer norms* for alcohol use (Scheier & Botvin, 1997). Smith and Goldman (1995) found that *shifts in alcohol expectancies* following experimental intervention were associated with reduced rates of drinking among 7th to 9th graders

Griffin et al. (2001) posit that developing *interpersonal skills* that enhance social competence may inoculate youth against entry into substance use and abuse by providing *constructive alternatives for gaining peer acceptance*. Conversely, *social benefit expectancies* for AOD use may counteract the positive effects of social confidence, assertiveness and communication skills in risk assessment (Griffin et al., 2001). Positive alcohol expectancies have also been found to *counteract* the effects of various positive peer influences (e.g., perceived peer norms, perceived friends' alcohol use and attitudes about alcohol) on an adolescent's alcohol use levels, as well as knowledge regarding the medical consequences of alcohol use (Scheier & Botvin, 1997).

Family influences: A *mediating role* for alcohol expectancies on drinking behavior has been identified through *family influences*, involving activities of family members that may *justify, promote, or otherwise disinhibit* the use of alcohol, or association with friends who provide *social pressure and social modeling* for drinking behavior (Costa, Jessor, & Turbin, 1999; Smith & Goldman, 1995; Conger & Rueter, 1996).

Deviant peer affiliation: Deviant peer associations have been found to be a central factor underlying the relationship between *substance use and crime* (Fergusson, Swain-Campbell, & Horwood, 2002; Dishion, Capaldi, Spracklen, & Li, 1995).

Perceived life chances: (Jessor, 1996) found an association between *adolescent health behaviors* in general, and the larger social context, which influences their *perception of life possibilities.* Restricted perception of life's possibilities has been associated with *low self-efficacy,* an *external locus of control* and a *perceived lack of cognitive and/or behavioral alternatives,* resulting in higher levels of adolescent substance abuse.

Sense of purpose in life: Feelings of *loneliness, hopelessness and suicidal ideation* are associated with *sensation seeking,* as well as with other dangerous or health-compromising behaviors such as substance abuse (Scheier & Botvin, 1996). They are also associated with low perceived self-competence, and associated feelings of sadness or frustration. Due to the affective nature of these predictors, Scheier and Botvin (1996) advise including an *affect-based* element to cognitive-behavioral interventions.

Childhood experiences with physical and/or sexual trauma and violence: Exposure to trauma, such as physical and sexual abuse, and parental use of violence in the home are associated with the early emergence of adolescent substance abuse, problem drinking and alcoholism, probably because of its self-medicating effects (Sommers & Baskin, 1991; Stevens, 2002).

Health skills and knowledge regarding the medical consequences of substance use: Self-report studies indicate that drinking behavior is negatively correlated with the perception of risk associated with heavy drinking and drunk driving (Agostinelli, 1994). The positive correlation between knowledge of alcohol-related medical consequences and lower levels of alcohol use point towards an *educational component* as part of a cognitive-behavioral approach to treatment (Scheier & Botvin, 1997; Johnston et al., 2002).

There is a vicious cycle in these risk factors. That is, the use of substances increases various elements of risk. For example, those with low social competence are more vulnerable to become involved in drugs and the abuse of drugs. But drug abuse also *decreases* social competence. It is important to note that all of these major risk factors for juvenile substance abuse contain psychosocial and/or cognitive elements; hence, cognitive-behavioral approaches that *succeed in developing an arsenal of cognitive-behavioral and social skills* are strongly indicated for reducing AOD abuse among adolescents (Williams, Epstein, Botvin, Schinke, & Diaz, 1998; Epstein, Griffin, & Botvin, 2001).

ADOLESCENT DRINKING AND DRIVING

Alcohol-related accidents and fatalities

The estimated crash risk for *male drivers ages 16 to 20* is at least *three times higher* than the risk for male drivers age 25 and older at all BAC levels (Zador, 1991). *More than 33% of all fatalities for 15- to 20-year olds* result from motor vehicle crashes, and of these, *more than 35% are alcohol related.* In fact, *alcohol-related automobile accidents are the number one cause of death for people 15 to 24* (Snow & Cunningham, 1985; Foley, 1986; Burnet, 1988). In 1998, *14 percent of underage drivers involved in fatal crashes tested positively for alcohol in their system.*

Young impaired drivers are involved in fatal crashes at approximately *twice the rate* of drivers aged 21 and over. In 1996, for every 100,000 licensed drivers, *sixty-six 15- to 20-year-old drivers* were involved in fatal crashes compared with 28 adult drivers (NHTSA, 1998). Of 15 -to19- year-olds involved in an accident, *60% were drinking before the accident and 43% of those had BACs over the legal limit for their state* (Williams, 1989).

For all drivers, each .02% increase in BAC nearly doubles the risk of being involved in a fatal crash. For drivers ages 16–20, the risk of a fatal crash increases even more with each .02% rise in BAC (Mayhew et al., 1986; Zador, 1991; NIAAA, 1996). Paradoxically, young impaired drivers are less likely to be detained and arrested than their adult counterparts (NHTSA, 1999). This may be due to the possibility that adolescent drinkers experience less sedation and motor skills disruption (albeit greater cognitive impairment) than their adult counterparts, at equal BAC levels (White, 2003).

Prevalence of drinking and driving among youth

As previously discussed, not only is drinking prevalent among youth, many of those who drink also drive after drinking. According to the *National Highway Traffic Safety Administration* (2003) 9% of young drivers (ages 16 to 18) reported driving within two hours after drinking during the past year; and 2% *reported* riding with a driver who they thought might have consumed too much alcohol to drive safely. Among the 19% of high school seniors who were defined as *frequent binge drinkers*, drinking and being in driving situations during the 30 days before being surveyed was reported by more than 60% of the males and by almost 50% of the females. By comparison, only 20% of the males and 13% of the females who were non-binge drinkers reported having been involved in situations in which drinking and driving occurred (Johnson, 2004).

Characteristics of young DWI offenders

Farrow (1985) found that young drunk drivers are most often male, doing (or did) poorly in school, hold many jobs and drive late at night. A recurrent finding in impaired driving research has been that young drivers more frequently crash at *lower blood-alcohol concentrations* (BACs) than do older drivers, which may be attributable to driver immaturity, less experience with decision-making skills and inexperience with drinking, driving or both (Preusser et al., 1992).

Causes of drinking and driving

Adolescence is a time of great change in a person's life. One example of that change is the adolescent's shift in associations and allegiances from families to peers—along with a corresponding movement toward the norms and values of his or her peer culture. Alcohol consumption and driving are *common social norms;* positively accepted and cherished by our society and they are both introduced during adolescence. According to Klepp and Perry (1990), youth feel that drunk driving is not a problem, but just something that occurs in their communities. The repercussions of getting caught do not outweigh their reasons for drinking or for driving drunk. Often adolescents drink heavily in one episode because they are more likely to drink all that they have. This happens because they do not often have a place to store the alcohol since it is illegal for them to have it in the first place. Most underage drinkers drink at parties, in cars and in parking lots where they can easily hide the alcohol (Little & Clontz, 1994).

Cognitive errors: Adolescent males typically drive drunk more frequently than females. More males are arrested for DWIs, but the numbers of females driving drunk, being arrested for DWI and being involved in alcohol-related crashes is increasing (NHTSA, 2003). Little and Clontz (1994) find that young DWI offenders abuse alcohol to cope with problems, or to satisfy needs for risk-taking and impulsively. Farrow (1994) suggests that young people may drive while intoxicated because of the following errors in their thinking and perception.

- Failure to realize how intoxicated they are and don't know that they will be impaired while driving;

- Lack of information about alcohol and consequently fail to understand how much and what kinds of alcoholic beverages will have certain types of effects;

- Lack of empathy for the potential suffering of others caused by crash fatalities every year;

- Because they have driven after drinking before (without being caught), they think they can do it again;

- Do not acknowledge that they are impaired and reject the possibility that anything bad (arrest, an accident, etc.) could happen to them;

- Believe that drinking and driving will allow them to feel free from rules or societal norms; and

- Believe that drinking and driving will make them look good in front of their peers/friends.

Life History and Environmental Factors: Hawkins et al. (1985) identified multiple factors that put a person at risk for being a drunk driver:

- *Family* - history of problem behavior; problems with discipline from parents, parents approving of use, or use of drugs and alcohol by the parents;

- *School* - little commitment or success in school;

- *Peers* - friends who use drugs and alcohol;

- *Attitudes, beliefs, personality traits*, e.g., rebellion and alienation from society.

Early drinking onset: According to a study by the *National Highway Traffic Safety Administration* (2000), *the earlier the age of drinking onset*, the greater the likelihood of being involved in a motor vehicle crash because of drinking. Several factors may contribute to this relationship.

- Those who engage in a variety of deviant or illegal behaviors at an early age are probably more likely to engage in several such behaviors later in life.

- People who start drinking at an early age frequently drink more heavily than those who start consuming alcohol later in life, even if they are not alcohol dependent This would increase the probability that they might drive after heavy drinking (Hingson et al., in press).

- Those who begin drinking at an early age may be less likely to believe that driving after drinking increases the risk of accidents or injury. They may believe that driving while under the influence is dangerous only for people who are visibly intoxicated (Lewis, 1988).

- Some high-risk drivers may derive pleasure or an increased sense of self-importance by taking chances behind the wheel (people who drink and drive are more likely to speed and less likely to wear seat belts).

- *Heavy* consumption of alcohol may result in greater impairment of judgment for those who start drinking at an earlier age, i.e., after drinking they may be less likely to appreciate their increased crash risk than when sober (NHTSA, 2000).

Personality associated with increased risk for drinking and driving: Donovan (1983) found certain aspects of personality related to automobile accidents: *anxiety, frustration, depression, low self-esteem, and feeling out of control.* McMillan et al. (1990) found that some people who are risk takers get cues from alcohol that they should take bigger risks than they normally would. Some individuals who thought they had alcohol in their system (who were given non-alcoholic drinks without their knowing it), drove more impaired and took more risks on the road than those with alcohol in their systems (they were using simulators, not real cars, to study driving skills). Zuckerman (2000) examined the question of whether multiple forms of risk-taking activities— smoking, drinking, drugs, sexual behavior, gambling and reckless driving—are related to a generalized risk-taking tendency. Furthermore, are their specific personality types associated with a predilection for taking risks? Smoking, drinking, sex and drugs were found to work in tandem with each other. *Reckless driving, however,* was related to only one other area of risk: *drinking!* People who scored high (both men and women) on the various types of risk-taking also scored high on three personality traits - *impulsive sensation seeking, aggression-hostility, and sociability.*

Problem Behavior Theory (PBT) applied to drinking and driving: Problem behavior, defined as behavior that departs from the social and legal norms of the larger society, is theoretically caused by three systems of psychosocial influence:

BEHAVIOR

PERSONALITY

PERCEIVED ENVIRONMENT

As discussed in *Chapter 1—Risk and Resiliency During Adolescence*, when the *personality system* and the *perceived environment system* clash, *behavioral problems* become evident (Jessor, 1987).

The adolescent DWI offender is an individual with a predominate behavior structure featuring *normalized images of drinking and driving*; low value placed on achievement and success; a poorly developed personal control structure; and a perceived environment steeped in role models and opportunities (including work environment and living situation) that support drunk driving. Since problem behaviors are related, *isolating drunk driving* as a single problem behavior, without considering the *behavior system* along with associated *personality* and *perceived environment structures*, would be counterproductive to treatment efficacy. By focusing on *cognitive restructuring and coping skill* development in all areas of problem behavior (not just drinking behavior), non-alcohol-related accidents and problems are expected to decrease as well.

Cognitive deficits in adolescent DWI offenders: According to Jessor (1996), young people who drink and drive have *specific cognitive deficits* that enable DWI behavior, e.g., inadequate life management skills; poor social competence; positive expectancies regarding substance abuse; inadequate self-management techniques; low self-esteem; poor assertiveness and refusal skills; low appreciation for the seriousness of DWI; restricted sense of perceived life chances; and lack of purpose in life. Other key factors involved in the etiology of adolescent driving while intoxicated are discussed below.

Attribution of responsibility: Perception of the seriousness of DWI as a dangerous and criminal behavior is positively correlated with attributions of responsibility for the perpetrator-driver. This suggests that *education regarding crime seriousness* may enhance adolescent perception of responsibility for DWI behavior (Gebotys, 1987), thereby reducing rates of participation.

Threat to perceived self-competence: In a study named *"Wadda ya mean I can't drive: Threat to competence as a factor in drunk driving intervention,"* perceived level of *threat to competence* was evaluated as a component in intervention effectiveness (Shore, 1998). The study found that high levels of perceived threat to competence were associated with low effectiveness of intervention. The study suggest that prevention strategies should be designed to improve peer attempts at intervention with friends, as well as detecting some of the underlying factors (such as low self-esteem, the use of bravado to mask self-doubt, etc.) that may contribute to increased resistance to intervention (Shore, 1998).

Risky cognitions: Risky cognitions have been found to play a predominant role in the decision to drink and drive (Arnett, 1990). Adolescents who drive while drinking are more likely to expect a positive outcome for this behavior, such as *social status* (Jessor, 1996), *fun or thrills,* and are less likely to realize how intoxicated they are. They tend to think that drinking and driving will allow them to *break free of social rules and norms,* and that drinking and driving will make them *more desirable* in the eyes of their friends. Most importantly, adolescents who drive while drinking are *less likely to grasp* its potentially dangerous or lethal outcomes such as an auto accident, injury or death, or DWI arrest (Arnett, 1990; Agostinelli, 1994).

Motivational biases in cognition: Research reveals that self-serving motivational biases in cognition affect an adolescent's judgments of risk regarding drinking and driving (Agostini, 1994). For example, teenagers might justify their driving while intoxicated by rationalizing that someone has to help get their friends to and from parties and that they are most qualified to do so.

Sensation seeking: The tendency to drive while intoxicated is correlated with scores on both the *Sensation Seeking Scale* (SSS) and the *Thrill and Adventure Seeking—Disinhibition and Boredom Susceptibility* subscales (Arnett, 1990). What's more, risk taking is *negatively correlated with refusal assertiveness* (Epstein, Griffin, & Botvin, 2001).

Tendency to use DWI as a "rite of passage": Adolescents who drive while drinking are more likely to use their streets and communities as venues for *"rites of passage"* activities, such as speeding, drag-

racing, "road rage," etc. These tendencies tie in with predilections for distorted cognition and sensation seeking noted above, and are likely exacerbated by low self-esteem, or the failure to find a sense of purpose through other means or activities.

RELATIONSHIP OF AGE TO AOD USE AND AOD USE DISRUPTION

Within the general population of adolescents, there is evidence that the *number of drugs* used and *drug use prevalence tends* to increase across age. Some researchers have pointed to these findings as support for the "gateway" theory of AOD involvement. Does this finding that there is a gradually escalating increase in AOD use and disruption hold up within groups that have been identified as having drug use problems?

To address this question, a study was completed on three large adolescent samples (*Probation, Committed Offenders and AOD Outpatients*) screened for AOD problems. The project was designed to determine differences within these groups across age cohorts as to the number of drugs used and extent of disruptive symptoms resulting from drug use (Wanberg, 2004). This cross-sectional analysis of age cohorts (13 to 18) within three population samples is summarized in *Table 3.3.*

The *Probation* group represents youth who were referred by probation workers to a TASC (*Treatment Alternatives to Street Crime*) agency because of being screened as having AOD use problems. This group would be expected to have less psychosocial problems and lower levels of AOD involvement and disruption. The Committed Offenders represents a group who had been screened, among all *committed offenders,* as having AOD problems. The AOD *Treatment* group represent youth referred to statewide adolescent AOD treatment agencies.

When comparing these three groups on two scales of the *Adolescent Self-Assessment Profile* (ASAP: Wanberg, 1998) measuring the *Number of Drugs* used and the degree of AOD Disruption, the *Probation Group* scores lower across these scales. Across most AOD use and disruption scales, the *Committed Offenders* and the *AOD Treatment groups* generally do not differ.

The three samples were studied using these two scales with respect to within-group changes across age cohorts. The first scale measures the *Number of Drugs*

Table 3.3	Cross-Sectional Study of AOD Involvement and Disruption Across Age Groups							
GROUP SCREENED FOR AOD	**AGE 13**	**14**	**15**	**16**	**17**	**18**	**n**	
Probation	102	249	494	657	694	298	2494	
Committed Offenders	41	102	225	285	295	65	1013	
AOD Treatment	179	406	618	713	687	350	2953	

an individual reports using at least once. For example, if a youth reports having used alcohol, marijuana and cocaine at least once, his score would have been three.

The second scale measures the degree of *AOD Disruption* from drug use. The scale is comprised of 20 AOD use symptoms, each variable scored as to the number of times they have experienced the symptom in a lifetime, for example, the number of times having a blackout when using drugs.

Figure 3.1 provides the results of the mean *number of drugs used at least once* across age cohorts within each of the three samples. *Probation* clients, on the average, scored lower than the other two groups on all age cohorts except for age 14, where the AOD *Treatment* group scores higher than the other two groups and *Age Cohort 18* where there is no differences across groups.

Figure 3.1 shows that there is a statistically significant incremental increase across the age cohorts within the *Probation group*, but not within the *Committed Offender* or *AOD Treatment* group. That is, for the latter two groups, 13-year-olds report having used as many of the 17 drugs at least once as 14-, 15-, 16-, 17- or 18-year-olds. Thus, 13- and 14-year-olds in these two groups have *equal exposure to the use of drugs* as are 17- and 18- year-olds. The extent of drug involvement in the *AOD Treatment and Committed* juvenile offender groups is the same across all age groups. This is not the case for *Probation* youth, where 17-year-olds report the use of a higher number of drugs than 13-year-olds.

Figure 3.2 indicates that the findings are similar when comparing within group changes across age cohorts for a scale measuring the *degree of disruption* from AOD use. Within *Probation*, as we progress from age cohort 13 to 18, older youth report a higher degree of symptom involvement. However, for the *AOD Treatment* group, younger clients do not statistically differ from older clients with respect to degree and

number of symptom involvement. For *Committed Offenders*, although the changes in mean scores on the *Disruption* scale does not statistically differ across age groups, it is clear that 16- and 17-year-old *Committed Offenders* report higher disruption scores than 14-year-olds. Yet, among *Committed Offenders*, 13-year-olds have higher *AOD Disruption scores* than 14-year-olds and the same scores as 18-year-olds.

These findings show that for groups where we would expect to find AOD involvement and disruption to be high (i.e., AOD *Treatment and Committed Offender*), we find no statistically significant increase of reported *number of drugs used at least once* or reported symptoms of disruption across the age cohorts. For groups identified as having more severe AOD problems, as is the case for the AOD Treatment group, younger youth have as *extensive drug exposure* and AOD *use disruption* as older youth.

For a group where we would not expect as severe of involvement in AOD use and disruption, as is the case with *Probation* youth, younger youth in this sample do not have the extent of AOD disruption as do older youth. Yet, these data indicate that the older *Probation* youth catch up with the AOD *Treatment and Committed* youth. In fact, with respect to AOD drug use disruption, we see that older *Probation* youth have even higher scores than both *Committed Offenders* and *AOD Treatment* youth. What might be operating here is that 18 year olds in the *Committed Offender* and *AOD Treatment* group most likely had the benefits of treatment (or correctional/treatment monitoring), versus the *Probation* group, and thus are reporting lower AOD disruption scores than *Probation*. This may be interpreted as providing some evidence that treatment is working.

Finally, the "gateway" theory may not be as applicable for those youth who become involved in AOD use at the *problematic* level. The *number of drug involvement*, and the *degree of disruption* from drug use is

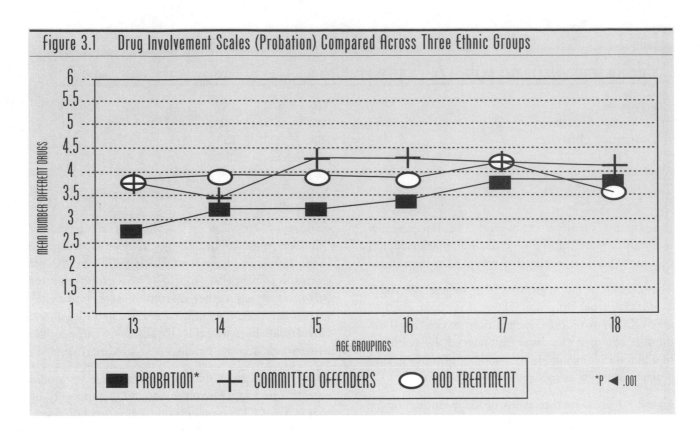

Figure 3.1   Drug Involvement Scales (Probation) Compared Across Three Ethnic Groups

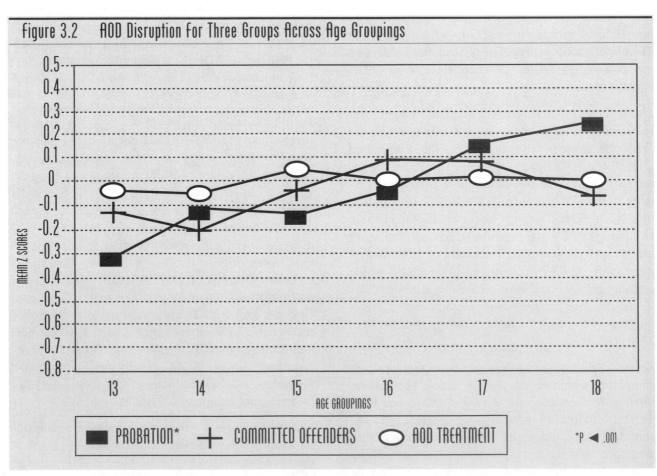

Figure 3.2   AOD Disruption For Three Groups Across Age Groupings

just as high for younger than for older youth. Older youth in samples identified as *AOD problematic* do not indicate the number of drugs that they have tried to be any higher than younger youth in these samples. Younger youth have already "passed through the gate," so to speak, in these samples.

ADOLESCENT DRUG USE AND CRIMINAL CONDUCT

Psychosocial influences are heavily implicated in adolescent drug use, and in the drug-crime connection, most notably through the mechanisms of *deviant peer attitudes and role modeling* (Stacy & Newcomb, 1995; Fergusson, Swain-Campbell & Horwood, 2002). Some research suggests that in adolescent subculture drug use and crime may serve as "deviant adaptations" which provide elements of status, psychological escape, safety and resources under hostile conditions (Kaplan, 1995; Inciardi, Horowitz & Potteiger, 1993). A review of literature on the connection between drug usage and other problem behaviors identifies four basic explanatory mechanisms (Zucchi, 1996):

- **Problem Behavior Theory**

  Depicts adolescent drug use as an expression of a more generalized orientation toward *unconventional behavior and delinquency* (Jessor & Jessor, 1977; Jessor, 1996, 2002);

- **Social Learning Theory**

  Explains adolescent drug abuse and delinquency in terms of the *modeling influences* to which an adolescent is exposed, including direct behaviors and attitudes toward drug use, as well as the phenomenological effects of drug use itself (Akers, Krohn, Lanza-Kaduce, & Radosevich, 1979; Ray & Ksir, 2002);

- **Stage Theory**

  Drug abuse and crime are viewed as the result of a terminal progression—from the use of cigarettes to beer to marijuana, cocaine and other drugs (Kandel, 1975; Kandel & Yamaguchi, 1993; Ray & Ksir, 2002);

- **Multiple Pathway Theory**

  Considers the total number of risk factors that adolescents may encounter on their way toward eventual drug abuse and criminal conduct (Farrell, Danish, & Howard, 1992; Wanberg, 1991; 1998; Wanberg & Milkman, 1998, 2004).

There is support in the literature for each of these models, although Zucchi (1996) reports that the *multiple pathway theory* (which subsumes many aspects of the other theories) is probably most useful for understanding adolescent drug use and criminal conduct. Similarly, other researchers have used both *social control* and *differential association* theories in combination to explain transitions in substance abuse and delinquency (Erickson, Crosnoe & Dornbusch, 2000).

The drug–crime connection

Table 3.4 shows the 1997 national incidence of substance-related juvenile arrests, as well as arrests for other problem behaviors often associated with intoxicants.

Several lines of research suggest a general connection between adolescent substance use and engagement in criminal conduct (White, Tice, Loeber, & Stouthamer-Loeber, 2002). Wanberg (1992, 1998) found a robust correlation of .63 between scales measuring substance abuse and criminal behavior in juvenile offenders. Shope and Bingham (2002), Swisher (1988) and Jessor (1987) argue that specific categories of criminal activity, e.g., drunk driving, drug abuse violations, disorderly conduct are part of a *larger syndrome of negative behaviors*. Corwyn and Benda (2002) investigated the relationship between AOD behavior and crime. Their results support Jessor's (1996) construct of a *general delinquency syndrome*; however, they found moderating influences of both gender and race that may reduce levels of overlap among these behaviors. Potential relationships between adolescent alcohol and cannabis use, cannabis sales and engagement in criminal conduct have also been examined. Both cross-sectional and longitudinal correlations among these variables were found (Dembo et al., 2002). The link between drug abuse and delinquency is further supported by self-report data, e.g., juvenile drug users are more likely than non-users to report breaking the law (Snyder & Sickmund, 1999).

Researchers have implicated crack cocaine as particularly involved in the drug-crime relationship as the dynamics of the crack drug market have drawn many adolescents into drug sales and arms possession (Blumstein, 1995; Dembo, Hughes, Jackson & Mieczkowski, 1993). There are several explanations for this phenomenon:

- Crack became a particularly desirable drug within many adolescent subcultures, which required that it be relatively inexpensively sold in small "single-hit" doses;

Table 3.4 Incidence of Juvenile Arrests in the U.S. - 1997

Statistics report only the most serious crime for which an adolescent was arrested.

Substance-Related Offense	Total # Juvenile arrests (1997)
Drug Abuse Violations	220,700
Drunkenness	24,100
Violation of Liquor Laws	158,500
Driving Under the Influence	19,600

Other Problem Behaviors (often associated with the use of intoxicants)	
Disorderly Conduct	215,100
Aggravated Assault	75, 900
Other Assaults	241,800
Motor Vehicle Theft	66,600
Vandalism	136,500
Curfew/Loitering law violations	182,700
Runaway	196,100

Source: National Center for Juvenile Justice - Juvenile Offenders and Victims: 1999 National Report

- Such small doses required an unusually high number of street merchants for efficient distribution;

- Adolescents were recruited as street sellers because they were able to "blend into" these adolescent communities without detection and they were willing to work for lower remuneration;

- It was believed that adolescents would receive weaker penalties if they got caught;

- Many adolescents were ready and willing to bear these risks due to the expected rewards of quick cash and free "highs";

- Adolescent recruits were frequently provided with firearms in the course of carrying out these new-found activities (Blumstein, 1995; Fox & Levin, 2001; Sheley & Wright, 1995; Dembo, Hughes, Jackson & Mieczkowski, 1993).

The provision of firearms to some youngsters quickly spread to others, even among those uninitiated to the drug trade (Hemenway, Prothrow-Stith, Bergstein, Adler & Kennedy, 1996). Some adolescents felt they needed guns for self-protection, others used guns for offense, and others used firearms possession as a route toward status among their peers (Fox & Levin, 2001).

Recent studies have examined the relationships between *deviant peer association, adolescent sub-*

stance use and criminal conduct (Fergusson, Swain-Campbell & Horwood, 2002). Several behaviors were correlated with deviant peer association, among them: nicotine dependence, alcohol and cannabis abuse, and both property and violent crime. The influence of deviant peer association appeared to be *strongest among younger adolescents*, for all outcomes except nicotine dependence. This study suggests that deviant peer affiliations may place adolescents at risk for adjustment difficulties that may underlie the development of substance abuse, criminal violence and other delinquent behaviors, especially at early ages. Wanberg (1991, 1998) found high correlations between scales measuring *negative peer association* and *criminal conduct* (.49) and *negative peer association and substance abuse* (.45).

Self-report data also indicates an elevated tendency to engage in criminal behavior while under the influence of drugs or alcohol (McCord, 1995; White, Tice, Loeber, & Stouthamer-Loeber, 2002). Through longitudinal research, McCord (1995) probed the relationship between problem drinking and criminal conduct over the life course, starting at ten years of age and continuing through middle age. The study reveals the presence of a longitudinal trajectory encompassing such phenomena as *childhood onset of disruptive behavior, juvenile delinquency, and alcoholism and/or criminality in adolescence and adulthood.* The empirical identification of this trajectory led McCord (1995) to conclude that problem drinking likely increases the tendency to engage in criminal behavior.

Substance abuse and violence in adolescence

In analyzing data on youth who were incarcerated in state prisons for murder, researchers have found that a full 45% were under the influence of drugs during the time they committed their crime (Inciardi, 1984; Inciardi & Saum, 1996). Other researchers have investigated the interrelationships of alcohol, street drugs, and violence (White, 1997), and drugs have been implicated in the etiology of certain instances of violent behavior (White, 1998; White, Loeber, Stouthamer-Loeber, & Farrington. 1999). Studies of self-report data similarly indicate an especially elevated tendency to engage in criminal aggression while under the influence of alcohol or drugs (excepting cannabis) (White, Tice, Loeber, & Stouthamer-Loeber, 2002). The illegal activities that are associated with adolescents who are under the influence of drugs tend to be characterized by:

- Aggressive assaults against other persons (rather than theft or other property crime);

- Aggressive offenses that involve more than one perpetrator;

- Adolescent perpetrators who associate with more deviant peers;

- Impulsivity; and

- Heavier levels of alcohol and drug involvement overall (White, et al. 2002).

Adolescents who perpetrate aggression while under the influence of drugs and/or alcohol also report being arrested at a higher frequency than adolescents involved in these behaviors without substance involvement. These researchers (White et al., 2002) conclude that the mechanisms underlying substance use and criminal conduct among adolescents are multifaceted and complex.

Other researchers have explored the influence of *crack cocaine* on tendencies to aggress (Glicken & Sechrist, 2003). They maintain that chronic cocaine use may actually cause violence through a mechanism known as *cocaine psychosis*. They note that the hallucinations and paranoia associated with this condition may underlie a generalized hostile attribution bias, which causes them to misattribute the ambiguous gestures and comments of others as direct threats to them-

selves or their competence. Delusions that others (including family, peers, police and other community representatives) are plotting against them may generate a violence response, as (perceived) self-defense against these "assaults" (Glicken & Sechrist, 2003).

Some inconsistent results regarding the drug-violence relationship have been reported in the literature. Do drugs cause violence or are there other factors that underlie both drug use and violent behavior? These questions have been investigated by researchers who suggest that such inconsistencies may be due to moderating influences in this relationship by third factors, such as negative self attitudes and antisocial tendencies in the drug user (Kaplan & Damphousse, 1995).

Glicken and Sechrist (2003) offer three major mechanisms at the root of the drug-violence connection:

- *Pharmacological*—the physiological effects of drug use, both proximal and cumulative, may predispose an individual toward violent response (Mocan & Corman, 1998);

- *Economic*—much crime is motivated by the desire for drugs or money to obtain drugs;

- *Systemic*—crime is part and parcel of the subculture that supports marketing and trafficking in drugs.

Prescription drugs, crime and violence: Psychotropic drugs, which are frequently used among youth to treat depression and attention deficit disorders, have also been examined as possible triggers of violent behavior (Fox & Levin, 2001). There is evidence for this in numerous anecdotes. For example, Sam Manzie, a 15-year-old boy, was taking Paxil when he sexually assaulted and strangled another child. T.J. Solomon, a 15-year-old boy, was taking Ritalin when he commenced a school shooting, wounding six of his classmates. Kip Kinkel, a 14-year-old boy, was being treated with both Ritalin and Prozac when he murdered his parents, then took his homicidal rampage to school. Eric Harris, an 18 year old, was taking Luvox when he and his friend Dylan Klebold executed the shootings at Columbine High School in Littleton, Colorado, killing 12 students and a teacher (Fox & Levin, 2001). Each of these adolescent males was being treated with a psychiatric medication just before engaging in their seemingly senseless acts of violence.

(T)he case against psychiatric medications would be stronger if it weren't for the fact that killers who were being treated at the time they committed murder typically had all of the usual

warning signs associated with such crimes. In almost every case, there was a good reason why a psychiatrist had prescribed a psychotropic drug: the killer had been profoundly depressed, disappointed, and discouraged about the future. (Fox & Levin, 2001, p.17)

Would these acts have occurred without the intervention of these medications? It is difficult to tell. Clearly, the potential of an increasing reliance on pharmacological interventions must be analyzed further before any definitive conclusions about their effects can be drawn.

AOD ABUSE ACROSS AMERICAN SUBCULTURES

Rates in the use of alcohol and other intoxicating substances diverge between ethnic groups, and various aspects of culture appear to be involved. European Americans, when compared with African and Hispanic Americans, scored significantly higher on alcohol involvement and lower on levels of cocaine involvement. African Americans, on the other hand, scored significantly higher on cocaine involvement and lower on levels of alcohol involvement than the other two groups (Wanberg & Milkman, 1998). Some factors that have been identified at the root of these differences may be *acculturative stress* (Cabrera, 2001); the power of particular *social influences* within a cultural context (Epstein, Botvin, Diaz & Schinke, 1995; Dusenbury, Epstein, Botvin & Diaz, 1994); *health-related knowledge* concerning the effects of alcohol (Epstein, et al. 1995); and *ethnic identity* (Scheier, Botvin Diaz & Ifill-Williams, 1997).

Acculturative stress may be a primary factor in the development of substance abuse among Latino youth (Cabrera, 2001). Research designed to investigate this hypothesis revealed several significant findings:

- Higher levels of acculturative stress were associated with higher levels of alcohol use;

- Females experienced more acculturative stress than did males; and

- Youth with greater exposure to the English language experienced less acculturative stress than did youth with less experience (Cabrera, 2001).

Peer and other social influences were shown to exert significant influence on the substance-abusing behavior among New York City Latino youth, including Puerto Rican, Dominican, Colombian and Ecuadorian

6th and 7th graders (Dusenbury et al., 1994). Similar results have been found among economically disadvantaged inner-city minority youth, especially Black and Hispanic 7th graders (Epstein et al., 1995). Analysis of self-report data revealed that social influences (peers as well as parents) were primary in the prediction of alcohol use; in fact, the drinking behavior of the person an adolescent "admired most" served as the best predictor of that adolescent's drinking status. Such results led these researchers to propose that education on such *social influence pressures*, and the provision of *non-drinking role models*, may be important components in curbing adolescent substance abuse among minority populations (Epstein et al., 1995).

Health-related knowledge concerning the effects of alcohol were also associated with anti-drinking attitudes among inner-city minority populations, and these attitudes significantly reduced levels of drinking in these populations (Epstein et al., 1995). In addition, African Americans scored higher in social skills than Hispanic Americans, while Hispanic Americans displayed higher levels of personal competence (Scheier et al., 1997).

Although rates of substance abuse and substance of choice appear to vary between cultures, a general pattern of similarity is found in the *severity of alcohol abuse* problems for African American and Hispanic American adolescents within treatment populations. Wanberg (1992) found no appreciable differences in scores across these two ethnic groups on the DISRUPT Scale (measures symptoms and negative consequences of substance use) but did find that European Americans scored higher than these two groups on DISRUPT (which measures the nine criteria for substance use dependency in the *DSM III-R*).

Ethnic identity as both risk and protection for substance use in adolescence

Studies examining the relationship between ethnic identity and substance abuse in adolescence have generated mixed results. There may be *increased pressure* to engage in substance-abusing behaviors among some ethnic communities (Felix-Ortiz & Newcomb, 1995), and some cultural factors such as *acculturative stress* (Cabrera, 2001) may be associated with increased levels of substance abuse. However, other studies have found that cultural factors such as *ethnic identity* may be correlated with lower levels of substance use (Scheier, Botvin, Diaz, & Ifill-Williams, 1997), perhaps through the mechanism of engaging pride and a sense of purpose through understanding the values and responsibilities associated with one's culture.

Chapter 1—Risk and Resiliency During Adolescence presented the hypothesis that cultural factors such as ethnic identity may provide a buffer against some types of risk for maladaptive behavior. Scheier et al. (1997) found that adolescent resistance to substance use may be improved in some instances when combined with a *strong sense of ethnic identity*. Concerning alcohol use, ethnic identity moderates the adverse effects of pro-alcohol expectancies, low levels of alcohol knowledge, and poor social skills. Similarly, with regard to marijuana, ethnic identity may mitigate the adverse effects of peer influences, inadequate personal competence and poor social skills. In some instances, ethnic identity alone effectively predicted levels of cannabis and alcohol use. Scheier et al. (1997) concluded that cultural factors, such as ethnic identity, may perform a key role in the trajectories of early-stage substance use, abuse and resistance.

Table 3.5 analyzes some differences in psychosocial risk factors for substance abuse across gender and ethnicity (Griffin, Scheier, Botvin & Diaz, 2000; Scheier et al., 1997).

Relationship of AOD use and disruption to ethnicity

A robust finding in the research literature is that European Americans show a higher degree of involve-

Table 3.5 Differences in Psychosocial Risk and Protection for Substance Abuse Across Gender and Ethnicity

Alcohol

- African American youth were found to have fewer risk factors and more protective factors against alcohol use, as well as the lowest levels of alcohol use overall;

- Anglo American youth were found with the most risk factors for alcohol use, as well as the highest levels of alcohol use overall;

- Hispanic American females reported greater social pressures for alcohol use than other groups;

- Hispanic youth were found to have the fewest protective factors against alcohol use and their levels of alcohol use appeared to be between African-American and Anglo-American youth overall.

Cannabis

- Both African American males and females reported more social pressure in their environment to use marijuana than did Hispanic-American youth;

- Both Hispanic American males and females reported more social pressure in their environment to use alcohol than did African American youth, and African American females reported more pressure than did African American males.

Gender Effects

- African American and Hispanic American males reported more positive cognitive-affective responses to the use of marijuana; while females of both races reported more positive cognitive-affective responses to the use of alcohol.

Age Effects

- The above differences in psychosocial risk appear to increase with age. From 7th to 8th grade, Hispanic youth were found with increased social pressures toward alcohol use, greater competence risk, and more distress. African American adolescents in the 8th grade had more social pressures to use marijuana than in the 7th grade and greater social skills risk. Gender differences also increased across these two grade levels.

Source: Griffin, Scheier, Botvin & Diaz, 2000; Scheier et al., 1997

ment in AOD use. Using the *Probation* sample of the Wanberg (2004) study of age cohorts and the *Adolescent Self-Assessment Profile* (ASAP) scales, the three ethnic groups of Anglo American, African American and Hispanic American, were compared across the *Degree of Involvement* on six drug-use category scales and a scale measuring degree of AOD use disruption. Each of the drug-use category scales is measured by six involvement variables. The AOD *Disruption Scale* is measured by 20 AOD use symptoms.

Figure 3.3 provides results from this study. European American *Probation* youth score *significantly higher* across the degree of involvement in alcohol, amphetamines and hallucinogens than African American and Hispanic American youth. The three groups do not differ with respect to the degree of involvement in marijuana. African American youth score significantly lower on the cocaine and inhalant involvement scales. As to overall AOD disruption, measured by the 20 disruptive symptoms from AOD use, European Americans score higher than the other two ethnic groups and African American youth score lower than the other two groups.

Very similar results were found when European Americans were compared with other ethnic groups across the same scales within the *Committed Offender* and *AOD Treatment groups*. What is most significant is that the two groups do not differ on degree of marijuana involvement.

CHAPTER REVIEW

Substance Abuse and Adolescent Problem Behavior begins with presentation of the major findings from the *2003 Monitoring the Future Study*. Drug use has significantly declined during the past seven years; however, a halt of reductions in the major drug categories along with an increase in prevalence rates for inhalant use among 8th graders are causes for concern. These findings may be explained by "generational forgetting." Even though one generation may comprehend the hazards associated with particular drugs, the next group may not have lived through the same set of events to appreciate the dangers of drug involvement. Perhaps the most imminent drug threat exists in the realm of widespread tobacco consumption. About 16% of youth report that they smoked cigarettes and 19% report use of alcohol during the past month. There is a strong relationship between cigarette smoking and the future use of mar-

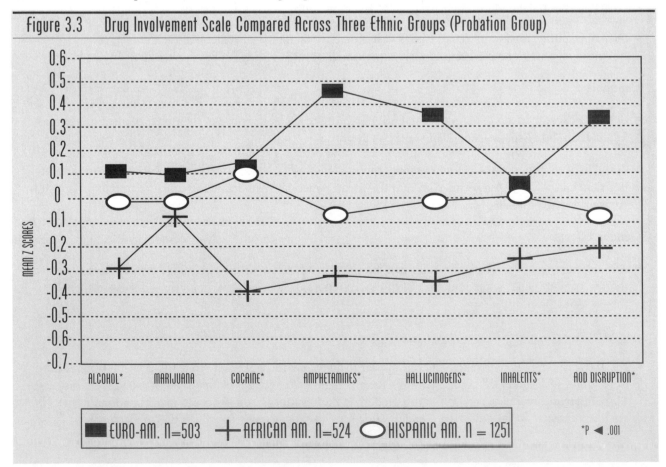

Figure 3.3   Drug Involvement Scale Compared Across Three Ethnic Groups (Probation Group)

ALCOHOL*   MARIJUANA   COCAINE*   AMPHETAMINES*   HALLUCINOGENS*   INHALENTS*   AOD DISRUPTION*

■ EURO-AM. N=503   ┼ AFRICAN AM. N=524   ⬭ HISPANIC AM. N = 1251   *P ◄ .001

ijuana. More youth currently enter treatment for problems with marijuana than all other drugs combined. Other emergent threats reside in the widespread use of club drugs such as MDMA (Ecstasy), GHB, Rohypnol, Ketamine, PMA and PCP, which advocates believe to be less harmful and addictive than more mainstream drugs such as heroin or methamphetamine. Another emergent and alarming trend is in the abuse of prescription drugs. Opiate-related pharmaceuticals such as codeine and Oxycontin, stimulants such as Ritalin and Aderall, and benzodiazepines such as Xanex and Valium are commonly abused. Methamphetamine, for which lifetime use among high school seniors in 2003 was 6.2%, is a powerfully addicting drug, potentially resulting in impaired brain functioning including neuronal loss as well as reduction in the normal number of dopamine transporters.

Among the many factors associated with adolescent substance abuse, the role of *social influence* has been identified as central. An array of psychosocial factors has been identified as mediating teenage resiliency or vulnerability relative to substance abuse (i.e., social competence, life-skills training, self-management skills, assertiveness, self-esteem, locus of control, AOD expectancies, family influences, deviant peer affiliation, perceived life chances, childhood abuse, health knowledge and self-care skills). Each factor contains *cognitive elements* that can be *practiced and learned*, resulting in increased resiliency and decreased risk.

Of particular concern is the widespread practice of adolescent drinking and driving. The estimated crash risk for male drivers ages 16 to 20 is at least *three times higher* than the risk for male drivers age 25 and older, at all BAC levels. More than 33% of all fatalities for 15 to 20 year olds result from motor vehicle crashes and of these, more than 35% are alcohol related. Alcohol-related automobile accidents are the number one cause of death for young people ages 15-24. Causes of drinking and driving are attributed to a widely held belief among adolescents that drinking and driving is not a problem, but just something that occurs in their communities. Because teenagers often do not have a place to store alcohol, and when drinking alcohol, they are usually outside the perimeter of adult supervision, they often drink all they have. From a cognitive perspective, young drinking drivers are subject to the following errors in thinking: failure to realize how intoxicated they are; lack of information about how alcohol affects brain, mind and body; lack of empathy for potential suffering by others; thinking they can "get away with it" because they have in the past; failure to acknowledge they are impaired; belief that drinking and driving frees them from social norms and will make them look good in front of their peers.

Teenagers who use drugs and alcohol at *problematic* levels are apt to have *significant involvement* (number of drugs used) and *disruption* (symptoms resulting from use) as early as 13 years of age. In fact, among *committed* and *AOD treatment* youth, there is little difference in number of drugs used and symptoms of disruption among 13- to 18-year-old youth. The literature reveals four basic explanatory mechanisms for teenage drug abuse: (a) *problem behavior theory* (deviant peer attitudes and role modeling); (b) *social learning theory* (modeling influences); (c) stage theory (progression for cigarettes and alcohol to marijuana and other drugs; and (d) *multiple pathway theory* (considers multiple risk factors).

Relative to drugs and crime, several lines of research suggest a general relationship between adolescent substance abuse and criminal conduct. Studies routinely show an elevated tendency to engage in criminal behavior while under the influence of alcohol or drugs (with the exception of cannabis). Three primary mechanisms are hypothesized to be at the root of the drug-violence connection: (a) *pharmacological* (physiological effects may predispose uses to violent actions); (b) *economic* (crime is often motivated by the desire for drugs or money to obtain them; (c) *systemic* (crime is part of a subculture that supports drug trafficking and marketing).

Although most research supports Jessor's (1996) construct of a general *delinquency syndrome*, there appears to be moderating influences from both gender and race.

European Americans, when compared to African and Hispanic Americans scored significantly higher on alcohol involvement and lower on levels of cocaine involvement. African Americans, however, scored higher on levels of cocaine involvement and lower on levels of alcohol involvement than the other two groups. However, in a sample of youth who were assigned to *probation*, African Americans scored significantly lower on cocaine and inhalant involvement scales.

Divergence in rates of alcohol and other intoxicating substances between ethnic groups appear to be related to particular cultural influences. Some factors that have been identified are *acculturative stress, peer and other social influences, and health-related knowledge.* While such factors as acculturative stress, in association with ethnic and minority affiliation, may present a risk for increased substance abuse, under some circumstances, *ethnic identity forms a buffer* against maladaptive behavior. Concerning alcohol use, ethnic identity has been shown to moderate the adverse effects of pro-alcohol expectancies, low levels of alcohol knowledge, and poor social skills. Similarly with regard to marijuana, ethnic identity may mitigate the adverse effects of peer influence, inadequate sense of personal competence and poor social skills.

Substance Abuse And The Adolescent Brain

4

by Stanley Sunderwirth, PhD
Indiana University–Purdue University, Columbus

Chapter Four:
Substance Abuse And The Adolescent Brain

Chapter Outline

The Human Brain: A Fast Idiot
- The joy of dopamine

The Adolescent Brain
- Brain development during adolescence
- Implications for drug abuse and other risky behavior

Alcohol
- Brain chemistry 301: alcohol and neurotransmission
- Alcohol and the adolescent brain
- Learning and memory: alcohol and adolescence
- The dangers of binge drinking
- Summary of alcohol effects

Methamphetamine: Need a Sudafed?

Cocaine: Gift of the Gods
- Crack—faster/stronger
- Cocaine high
- Health effects of cocaine
- Crack babies revisited
- Cocaine and neuronal growth
- Summary of cocaine effects

Marijuana: Reefer Madness Revisited
- Effects on the brain
- Withdrawal effects from marijuana usage
- Effects on cognition
- Marijuana and the endocrine system
- Marijuana and the immune system
- Long-term effects on health
- Summary of marijuana effects

Opiates: Everyone Makes Them
- Opiates and the brain
- Heroin: the ultimate pipe dream
- Summary of heroin effects

Ecstasy: Let's Party
- Health effects
- Summary of Ecstasy effects

Inhalants: How Stupid Can You Get?
- Nitrites: non-prescription Viagra
- Inhalants and the brain
- Summary of inhalant effects

Hallucinogenic Drugs: Chemical Vision
- Hoffmann's nightmare
- Effects of LSD
- Other mind-altering drugs
- PCP: "zombie"—an accurate description
- Ketamine: let me fix you a drink
- Dextromethorphan: cough syrup anyone?
- Summary of effects of hallucinogenic drugs

Tobacco: The Ultimate Drug
- Effects on the brain
- Other health effects of smoking
- Summary of tobacco effects

Chapter Review

Chapter Objectives

- To understand how the human brain works; and
- To understand how alcohol and other drugs affect the body, with emphasis on the adolescent brain.

THE HUMAN BRAIN: A FAST IDIOT

Your brain creates your world. It is the hardware of your soul. It is the very essence of you as a human being. It is the brain, which distinguishes us as humans, not skin color, body structure or facial characteristics.

—Daniel Amens
Change Your Brain, Change Your Life

Before discussing the powerful effects of drugs on the mind and body, we take some time to explain the basic design of the brain, which has been described as more complex than the entire known universe. According to Avram Goldstein (1982), "The language of the brain is chemistry." Indeed, the brain is a giant pharmaceutical factory constantly manufacturing chemicals that result in moods such as fear, anger, shame, despair, joy, depression, mania and any other mood to which the human species is subjected. However, in this chapter we are interested in how drugs manufactured *outside the brain* (possibly in your neighbor's SUV), affect mood and behavior. To comprehend how these external chemicals affect the internal chemistry of the brain, we need to understand how the brain itself works. So prepare yourself for *Neurochemistry 101.*

Although the metaphor is not perfect, it is helpful to consider the brain as an electrochemical computer as well as a chemical factory (Milkman & Sunderwirth, 1993). Its 100 billion or so nerve cells, which constitute the brain's hardware, are able to store more information than all the libraries in the world combined. Each of these nerve cells (neurons) is in turn composed of three basic elements (*Figure 4.1*). The nucleus of the cell (cell body) constitutes a *miniature brain* within a larger brain. It is the cell body that "decides" to transmit a message (an electrical impulse) from one nerve cell to the next, i.e., "fire." Or the cell body may decide to ignore it, i.e., not to "fire." This is the only decision the cell body needs to make, but it needs to make that decision very quickly. For example, you don't want to wait five minutes to remove the hand you unknowingly placed on a hot stove, while the cell body takes its time deciding to transmit the message to the next neuron and ultimately on to the brain. Like a computer, the cell body is "a fast idiot." It has to make one of only two possible decisions, i.e., to "fire" or not to "fire." Connected to the cell body is a long fiber, the axon, through which the message must travel on its way to the next neuron. The message is transferred from one of the many branches at the end of the axon of the sending neuron to one of a number of branches on the receiving cell. These branches are called dendrites; each neuron may have up to *10,000 dendrites.* If we consider the possibilities of interaction between the 100 billion neurons found in the human brain with 10,000 dendrites per neuron, we have the possibility of quadrillions of connections—different ways to send messages to different "receivers," with different results. Clearly, as we have said, the brain is the most complex entity in this universe.

Incredibly, this process of communication between neuron and neuron is carried out without any direct physical contact between the two cells—as if this were all taking place in a city of trillions of people, all talking to each other on cellular telephones! Neurons are separated by a gap known as the synapse or synaptic junction. The message is carried from one neuron to the next by molecules known as neurotransmitters, which in our computer analogy may be considered as

Figure 4.1 The Neuron

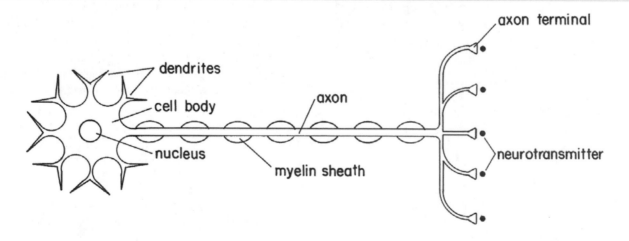

the software of the brain. Chemical changes that occur in these neuronal spaces determine how we respond to each "message." This process of communication between neurons, known as neurotransmission, is largely responsible for the brain functions that determine what we are as individuals, including our personalities, intellect, and character. It is precisely because the neurons are separated by a synapse—in other words, they are not "hardwired"—that the brain ends up with nearly limitless options for neurotransmission, which results in the limitless complexity of the human species.

We are our neurotransmission. What we are as human beings is reflected in the way our neurons communicate and form new pathways as well as utilize old ones. Francis Crick (1995) summarizes the relationship between self and neurotransmission as follows:

The astonishing hypothesis is that you, your joys, and your sorrows, your memories and ambitions, your sense of personal identity and free will, are in fact no more than the behavior of a vast assembly of nerve cells and their associated molecules. As Lewis Carroll's Alice might have phrased it, "You're nothing but a pack of neurons."

—Francis H. C. Crick
"The Astonishing Hypothesis"

In order for us to understand the effect of drugs on the brain, we need to know how the brain works, and especially the role of neurotransmitters. Let us consider a very important neurotransmitter, norepinephrine (NE), which is found in a part of the brain known as the locus coeruleus (*Figure 4.2*). One of NE's primary functions is to produce arousal and excitability, including the "fight or flight" phenomenon associated with the release of adrenaline. The ability of NE to stimulate the "fight or flight" response is an evolutionary survival mechanism. The rise in NE levels in times of danger and/or stress results in an increase in adrenaline, which raises blood pressure and increases heart rate. This forces more oxygen-carrying blood into the muscles, which in turn enables our pre-historic ancestors to fight if the attacker is a small bear or "run like hell" if it is a saber-tooth tiger. To understand how NE, as well as other neurotransmitters, is involved in communication between neurons, let us continue in *Neurochemistry 101.*

Figure 4.2   Cross Section of The Human Brain
(showing major components of the limbic system)

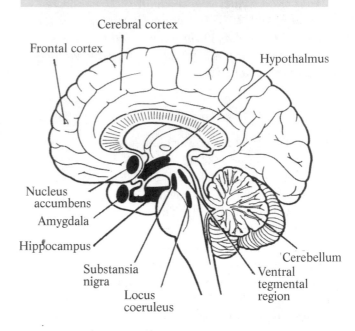

As we have said, the language of the brain is chemistry and therefore the flow of information (impulse) from one neuron to the next must be chemical. This action is illustrated in *Figure 4.3*, indicating what occurs at a single synaptic junction between two neurons during the saber-tooth tiger episode. Chemical messages flow from the axon on the top (presynaptic) neuron across the synapse to the dendrite of the postsynaptic neuron on the bottom and then on to the cell body of the postsynaptic neuron. As the impulse reaches the presynaptic terminal, specific channels open in the membrane of this neuron, which allows doubly charged calcium atoms (ions) to enter the cell. This in turn stimulates the release of the neurotransmitter—in this case, NE (illustrated by curve-shaped molecules)—into the synapse. NE moves across the synapse, carrying the message to the postsynaptic neuron. Embedded in the outer membrane of this neuron are hundreds of complex chemicals (proteins) that act as receptors for NE. These receptors have specific shapes that exactly complement the shape of NE. This enables the molecules of NE to attach themselves to these receptors in much the same way that a key fits into a lock. In fact, the key must not only fit the lock perfectly but must also open the door, just as many Cadillac keys will fit the ignition of Buicks but will not start the engines. The same is true of neurotransmitters and receptors.

Norepinephrine not only fits the locks but also opens the doors (ion channels) of the postsynaptic cell.

Figure 4.3 The Synaptic Junction and Chemical Transmission

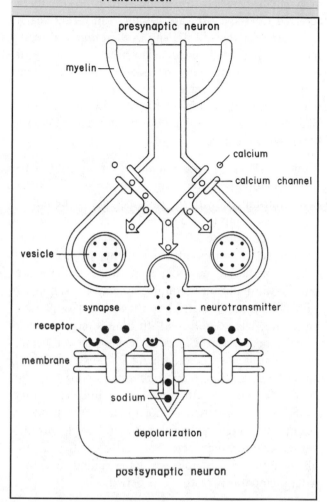

presynaptic neuron

myelin

calcium

calcium channel

vesicle

synapse — neurotransmitter

receptor

membrane

sodium

depolarization

postsynaptic neuron

In the case of neurotransmission, the more molecules of NE released into the synapse, the sooner these receptor sites are occupied—and the more rapidly the neurons will fire. In the case of NE, the more aroused you will be and able to run from the saber-tooth tiger or your abusive boss [joke]. Just exactly how does this increase in NE neurotransmission bring this about?

The increased level of NE signals an organ in the brain known as the hypothalamus (H) to send messages to another organ in the brain, the pituitary gland (P), which in turn causes the adrenal glands (A) sitting on top of the kidneys to produce adrenaline. The activation of this system, known as the HPA axis (*Figure 4.4*), accelerates the heart rate, bringing oxygen and other nutrients to the various parts of the body, increasing strength, and decreasing reflex time. Following the escape from the tiger, or your boss, you are unable to sleep for many hours, because the chemicals (NE) produced by this episode cascade back and forth across the synapse, keeping the rate of neurotransmission high, your eyes wide awake, and your brain pulsating.

What makes neurotransmission so remarkable is the speed with which this seemingly very cumbersome and complex process occurs. It is like running a

Figure 4.4 Hypothalmus-Pituitary-Adrenal (HPA) Axis

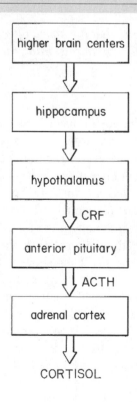

higher brain centers

hippocampus

hypothalamus

CRF

anterior pituitary

ACTH

adrenal cortex

CORTISOL

Opening these cell doors allows certain ions (potassium, sodium, and chloride) to go in and out of this cell. If enough channels (doors) are opened and enough ions go in and out, the electrical nature of the cell's outer membrane is altered (depolarized). This enables the message to be sent to the cell body of the postsynaptic cell, where it is processed with input from thousands of other cells, all undergoing the same process.

Before the membrane of the postsynaptic cell can "fire" (become depolarized and send its impulse to the cell body), a critical number of the many receptor sites must be occupied by NE. The more molecules of this neurotransmitter (NE) that we can shove into the synapse, the quicker this critical number of sites will be occupied. Imagine trying to fill the holes of an egg carton by dropping ping-pong balls from ten feet. Many of the balls will not land in the holes of the egg carton. If we want to fill the carton quickly, we need to drop more ping-pong balls in a given period of time.

marathon race in which there are a thousand streams to cross. At each stream, the runner must gather rocks (neurotransmitters) from the first shore (presynaptic terminal) to build stepping-stones to the next shore (postsynaptic terminal). The encounter with the tiger (boss) increases the number of "neuronal" rocks that are available on the shore where the runner arrives (presynaptic neuron); the more rocks available, the more rapidly will the runner be able to build a path to cross over the stream.

Of course, most activities in which we engage do not alter our consciousness to the level of arousal brought on by the attack of the tiger or serious confrontation with our boss. The tiger scenario should, however, give you some idea of how the mind and body can be energized, how mood can dramatically shift, and how the moment can be seized—all through the power of brain chemistry. It should be noted that this elevation of neurotransmission (i.e., mood) is brought about without resorting to stimulant drugs such as cocaine or methamphetamine. In today's society, we are often tempted to alter our mood by the use of drugs, which, as we shall see, can increase neurotransmission in certain parts of the brain that result in pleasurable experiences. Let us now turn our attention to the effect of drugs on the brain (*Neurochemistry 102*). It turns out that most of the mood alterations brought about by drugs are due to the role of a neurotransmitter known as dopamine (DA).

The joy of dopamine

The most pleasure that life has to offer is an adequate flow of dopamine into the nucleus accumbens.

S. G. Sunderwirth

Understanding the joyful feelings evoked by brain chemistry begins with a search for a site in the brain responsible for this pleasure. The presence of a "pleasure center" in the brain was demonstrated by Olds and Milner (1954) at *McGill University*. They found that a rat with an electrode implanted into a certain region of the brain would continually press a lever in order to receive electrical stimulation. Routtenberg (1978) of *Northwestern University* later showed that, given a choice between a lever that delivered food for survival and one delivering brain stimulation, rats would forgo food in favor of the "reward" of brain stimulation. In other words, they chose Ecstasy over survival. Rats, it seems, may become as addicted to an artificial (and ultimately fatal) paradise as humans.

In these experiments, the preference for "prolonged Ecstasy" occurred only if the electrode was placed in a very small part of the brain, which Routtenberg referred to as the "Reward Center." In recent years, the search for the specific site in the brain that regulates mood has led scientists to a complex array of neuronal clusters known as the limbic system (*Figure 4.2*). This region of the brain is believed to control emotions and is often referred to as the "reptilian brain," since we share this primordial brain with other living creatures.

Blum (1991) has proposed a model for reward (pleasure) involving the interaction of several neurotransmitters with the various parts of the limbic system that compose the reward center. Blum proposes that the release of dopamine into the nucleus accumbens, an important reward site, plays a major role in mediating our moods. (Although there are other reward sites in the limbic system, for simplicity we will limit our discussion to the action of dopamine on the *nucleus accumbens*.) In Blum's model, which he calls the "Reward Cascade," feelings of well-being, as well as the absence of craving and anxiety, depend on an *adequate supply of dopamine* flowing into the nucleus accumbens. In humans, an imbalance that would lead to a deficit of dopamine would produce anxiety and a craving for substances (alcohol, cocaine, heroin, amphetamine, etc.) or activities, (e.g., gambling, crime, promiscuous sex, hang gliding, etc.) that would temporarily restore this deficit.

A modified version of the *Reward Cascade* (*Figure 4.5*) by Milkman and Sunderwirth (1998) helps us to understand this complex interaction of neurotransmitters. Let's start with serotonin, that ubiquitous neurotransmitter about which thousands of articles have been written. The introduction of Prozac and other selective serotonin reuptake inhibitors (SSRIs) has made serotonin (5-HT) a household word. In the hypothalamus, serotonin neurons stimulate the release of methionine enkephalin (or simply enkephalin), which in turn inhibits the release of GABA (gamma-aminobutyric acid) in the limbic system. (It seems that we have one more chemical to consider.) What is GABA? The brain must have synapses that retard neurotransmission as well as increase it; otherwise we would be in even more of a constant state of emotional turmoil than we are. GABA is the neurotransmitter utilized by these inhibitory synapses; it's our own internal "Valium," regulating our mood through inhibition of the release of neurotransmitters such as dopamine and norepinephrine.

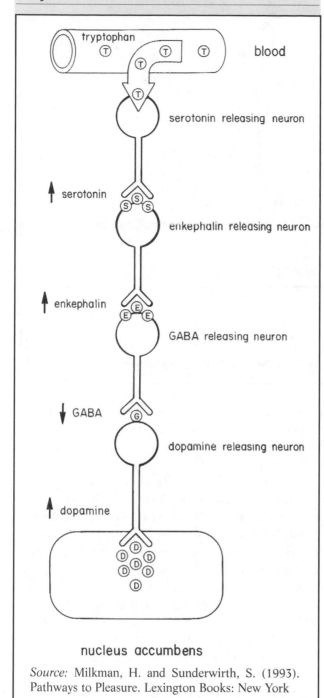

figure 4.5 The Reward Cascade

tryptophan

blood

serotonin releasing neuron

↑ serotonin

enkephalin releasing neuron

↑ enkephalin

GABA releasing neuron

↓ GABA

dopamine releasing neuron

↑ dopamine

nucleus accumbens

Source: Milkman, H. and Sunderwirth, S. (1993). Pathways to Pleasure. Lexington Books: New York

Now that we have struggled through these technical terms, let's see what they really mean in terms of our emotional state. As we follow the *Reward Cascade*, the most important concept to keep in mind is that an adequate supply of dopamine in the *nucleus accumbens* is necessary for feelings of well-being. Studies have shown that increased levels of dopamine in the nucleus accumbens can lead to increased pleasure and reward as well as decreased anxiety. Most drugs of abuse as well as certain activities increase the supply

of DA in the *nucleus accumbens. Tables 4.1 and 4.2* summarize these effects.

Figure 4.6 is an illustration of where various drugs act on the brain to increase DA in the *nucleus accumbens*. It is now generally accepted that DA is the master chemical of pleasure and that the "high" from drugs is caused by this increase in DA.

How does the *Reward Cascade* work to produce this flow of DA into the nucleus accumbens? As we have said, the process is initiated by the neurotransmitter serotonin (5-hydroxytryptamine or 5-HT), which is produced in the brain from the amino acid, trypto-phan, and is enhanced by antidepressants such as Prozac. Once we have a supply of serotonin, what does this do for us? How does it help us not only to sleep but in general to reduce feelings of anxiety and craving? In the *hypothalamus*, serotonin-releasing neurons impinge on enkephalin neurons, enhancing the release of enkephalin (*Figure 4.5*). In *Figure 4.5*, the up and down arrows indicate an increase or decrease, respectively, of the appropriate neurotrans-mitter molecules. The primary function of enkephalin neurons in the brain is to inhibit the release of neuro-transmitters from any neuron with which they interact; the more enkephalin released from these neu-rons, the more inhibition they exert on neurons on which they impinge (*Figure 4.5*). Now, how does GABA fit into this neurochemical puzzle? Conveniently, GABA-releasing neurons, as well as other neurons, have receptor sites for enkephalin mol-ecules. As the number of these GABA receptor sites occupied with enkephalin molecules increases, the release of GABA decreases. But GABA keeps the release of dopamine in check through another inhibitory synapse. Therefore, as GABA decreases due to either enkephalin increase or opiate ingestion, we can expect the release of dopamine to increase. In other words, the enkephalin has inhibited the inhibitor (GABA). This process works with the logic of a dou-ble negative and results in a positive increase in dopamine at the *nucleus accumbens*, which brings about a decrease in feelings of restlessness and anxiety as well as a general increase in feelings of well-being. Serotonin is the battery that starts the engine (*Reward Cascade*) that brings about enhanced dopaminergic neurotransmission.

Although serotonin starts the *Reward Cascade* engine, the real power behind the pleasure pathway is enkephalin, that internal opiate produced by our brains in response to both internal and external stim-uli. It is this euphoric effect that has resulted in

Figure 4.6 Action of Various Drugs on the Brain to Increase Dopamine

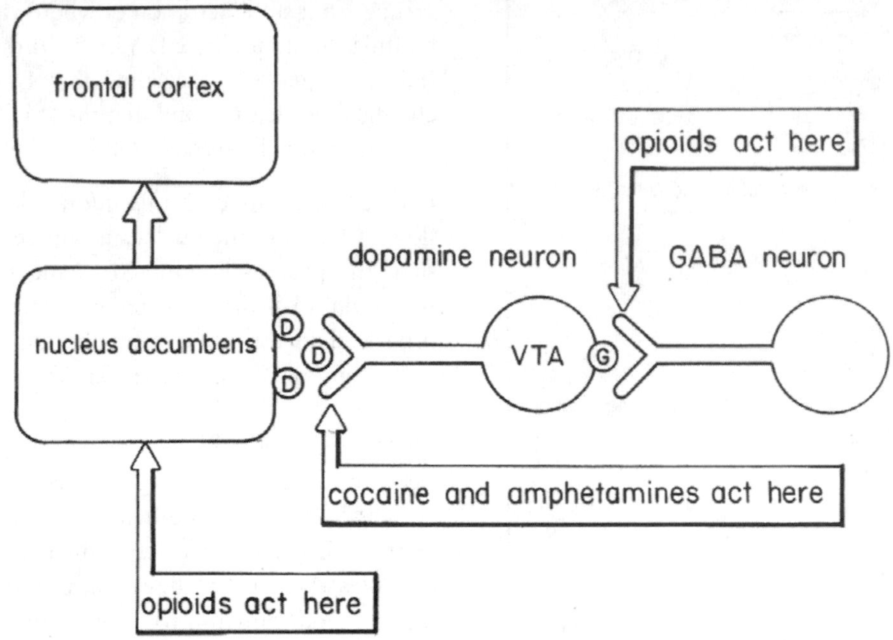

Source: Goldstein, A. (1994). Addiction From Biology to Drug Policy. New York: W.H. Freeman and Company

enkephalins and their cousins, the endorphins, being referred to as "The Keys to Paradise." Enkephalins and endorphins, although structurally different, are often grouped together under the generic name endogenous or internal opiates.

Much to our credit—and eternal regret—humankind has been able to find drugs (morphine) and even manufacture drugs (heroin) that have chemical structures similar to our own enkephalins (endorphins) and, as we shall see later, can produce the feelings of euphoria even more intense than our internal opiates.

The fundamental concept is that drugs or behavior, which elicits pleasure and/or reward, are accompanied by an increase of dopamine in the *nucleus accumbens*. *Table 4.1* shows the wide variety of drugs which cause an increase in dopamine in the *nucleus accumbens*, which are ultimately interpreted by the user as rewarding.

We have referred several times to the concept that activities and/or certain behaviors can mimic the neurochemistry of drugs of abuse. Activities as varied as crime and eating have been shown to increase the level of dopamine in the *nucleus accumbens*. *Table 4.2* shows the various activities that also bring about this increase. Obviously, hugging your child will not give you the same sensation as a line of cocaine. Although

both are accompanied by an increase in dopamine in the *nucleus accumbens*, other pathways in the brain are also involved. To be sure, nothing in brain chemistry is simple. But in this chapter, let's stick to the effect of drugs of abuse on the brain and the dopaminergic reward system. *Table 4.3* adapted from the work of DiChiara (1988), Tanda et al. (1997) and Joseph (1996) indicate the sites of action and the percent increase in dopamine compared to controls (absence of drugs). It is clear that *amphetamine has the greatest influence* (900+%), followed by cocaine, heroin and marijuana. Methamphetamine (not shown in *Table 4.3*) has even a greater effect than amphetamine. Although alcohol is not as powerful as a stimulant for DA release, the amount in which it is consumed in this country makes it the second most serious drug problem in the U.S. after nicotine.

THE ADOLESCENT BRAIN

Brain development during adolescence

The human brain will have more neurons at birth than any time in life. The baby overproduces neuronal connections (synapses) as the brain responds to new environmental stimuli. Then, at about the age of three, the brain begins to eliminate those connections that

Table 4.1 Effect of Various Drugs on Dopamine Levels in the Nucleus Accumbens

DRUGS AND DOPAMINE

Drug	Effect on Dopamine (DA) Levels in the Nucleus Accumbens
Cocaine	Increase
Heroin	Increase
Marijuana	Increase
Amphetamine	Increase
Nicotine	Increase
Alcohol	Increase

Source: Review in Time, 5/5/97

Table 4.2 Effect of Various Activities on Dopamine Levels in the Nucleus Accumbens

ACTIVITIES AND DOPAMINE

Activity	Effect on Dopamine (DA) Levels in the Nucleus Accumbens
Sex	Increase
Crime	Increase
Risk-Taking	Increase
Gambling	Increase
Hugs	Increase
Eating	Increase

Source: Review in Time, 5/5/97

are not being used, in a typical case of "use it or lose it." It was previously thought that no major changes in either organization or function occurred after adolescence. Although the overall size of the brain changes very little after childhood, there are important changes in neuronal connections occurring between childhood and adulthood. These changes are especially noticeable in the frontal lobes of the neocortex. There are other dramatic changes occurring in the brains of adolescents. For example, Geidd (1999) found that the *corpus callosum*, which relays information between the two hemispheres of the brain, also undergoes growth during adolescence. The *cerebellum* (*Figure 4.2*), which is involved in motor coordination, also undergoes changes during adolescence. It has also been shown using rat studies (Teicher et. al., 1995) that dopamine receptors increase in the striatum and the *nucleus accumbens* in an age that corresponds to

adolescence in humans. Also, GABA receptors increase in the *cerebellum*, the *medial septal nucleus* and other subcortical structures.

A second spurt of synaptic formation occurs just *before puberty*, followed by loss of up to 1% of gray matter (neurons) per year during adolescence. This process enables the brain to consolidate learning by pruning unused synapses and strengthen and protect used synapses by wrapping the neurons in myelin (white matter). The myelin sheaths protect the neurons of the gray matter and enhance neurotransmission.

The growth and pruning of synapses is only a part of brain development. Changes in the architecture of the brain have an equal or greater impact on adolescent behavior. It has been shown by functional magnetic resonance imaging (fMRI) that the *pre-frontal cortex*

Table 4.3 Site of Action of Drugs in the Reward Cascade and Percentage Increase in Dopamine in the Nucleus Accumbens

DRUGS AND DOPAMINE

<u>Control:</u> (Absence of Drugs)

Serotonin ↑ → Enkephalin*↑ → GABA ↓→ DA ↑

<u>Amphetamine:</u> Enhances release and blocks reabsorption of DA

Serotonin ↑ → Enkephalin*↑ → GABA ↓→ DA ↑↑ (900+%)[2]

<u>Cocaine:</u> Prevents reuptake of DA

Serotonin ↑ → Enkephalin*↑ → GABA ↓→ DA[1] ↑↑ (200+%)[2]

<u>Nicotine:</u> Stimulation of exicitatory ACH receptors on DA cell bodies

Serotonin ↑ → Enkephalin*↑ → GABA ↓→ DA[1] ↑↑ (100%)[2]

<u>Nicotine:</u> Stimulation of exicitatory ACH receptors on DA cell bodies

Serotonin ↑ → Enkephalin*↑ → GABA ↓→ DA ↑↑ (100%)[2]

<u>Heroin:</u> Increases DA through opioid receptors

Serotonin ↑ → Heroin (Enkephalin*) [1]↑↑→ GABA ↓↓→ DA ↑↑ (160%)[2]

<u>Marijuana:</u>

Serotonin ↑ → THC (Enkephalin*)[1]↑↑→ GABA ↓↓→ DA ↑↑ (130%)[2]

<u>Prozac:</u> Inhibits reuptake of serotonin

Serotonin[1] ↑↑ Enkephalin* ↓↓→ GABA ↓↓→DA ↑↑

<u>Morphine:</u> Inhibits the inhibitor (GABA), therefore increasing DA

Serotonin ↑ → Mor (Enkephalin*) [1]↓↓→ GABA ↓↓→ DA ↑↑ (60+%)[2]

<u>Alcohol:</u> Increases serotonin

Serotonin ↑ → THIQ (Enkephalin*) [1]↑↑→ GABA ↓↓→ DA ↑↑ (100%)[2]

* an opioid   [1] site of action   [2] % increase over control

Source: Di Chara, G. et. al. Proceedings of the National Academy of Science, USA, 85, 5274-5278 (1988); Joseph, M.H. et. al. Human Psychopharmacology. Vol. II S55-S63 (1996); and Tanda, G. et. al. Science. Vol. 276, 2048-2050 (1997).

begins growing just before puberty (Geidd et al., 1999). The pre-frontal cortex controls higher functions such as rational thinking, planning, organization, working memory, behavioral inhibition, and also assists in modulating emotions. The continuing maturation of the prefrontal cortex enables older adolescents to exert more control over emotional impulses and make more rational decisions as they mature. This is good news for parents. Since the development of the frontal lobes, which are involved in rational decision-making, continue into the twenties, the troubled teenager will very likely mature into a responsible adult. As the cortex begins to control the amygdala, the impulsive and emotionally dictated behaviors give way to cortically dominated rationality.

Implications for drug abuse and other risky behavior

It has been suggested that the younger teenager's ability to make sound judgments is compromised by the *immaturity of the frontal cortex*. This concept is supported by the use of functional magnetic resonance imaging (fMRI) which records activity in the working brain. When processing emotional decisions, adults have a greater activity in their frontal lobes than adolescents processing the same decisions. Adults also have lower activity in their amygdala (the part of the brain involved in emotions) than teenagers when confronted with the same emotional decision. The data imply that the immaturity of the *frontal lobes* of the adolescent prevents him/her from reliably making rational decisions. Instead, the decisions are processed in the amygdala, the emotional part of the brain Geidd et al., 1999).

As an example, when pressured by peers to engage in a harmful activity, such as drug use, an adult has the ability to weigh the desire to conform against the perceived harmful effects, and hopefully arrive at a rational decision. On the other hand, because of *immature frontal lobes,* the adolescent may not have the same capacity to respond in as rational a manner. In this case, the more developed amygdala is likely to be the region of the brain that processes the decision, and the emotional desire to conform overcomes the weak response from the frontal cortex. In other words, "the amygdala has hijacked the cortex" and the adolescent takes poorly calculated risks as in delinquent actions, drug abuse or lapses in self-care and concern for the welfare of others.

ALCOHOL

Possibly the most distressing aspect of alcohol abuse is its effect on the brain. The bad news is that brain damage leading to cognitive impairment can result from even mild to moderate drinking (Evert, 1995). Such impairment interferes with those mental activities that involve acquiring, storing, retrieving, and being able to use information. The good news is that some cognitive impairment due to alcohol is reversible (Volkow, 1995). The really bad news is that *not all* alcohol-related brain damage is reversible. The most devastating and irreversible effect of heavy alcohol consumption on the brain is a disorder known as *Wernicke-Korsakoff Syndrome*, which is a disorder that prevents the affected person from remembering new information for more than a few seconds (Oscar-Berman, 1990). It has also been demonstrated by Pfefferbaum (1992) that most alcoholics' brains are smaller and this shrinkage is most notable in the *outer layer of the frontal lobe (Figure 4.7)*, which may explain the cognitive decline in long-term alcoholics.

Another piece of bad news is that although alcohol abuse declined slightly in the 2-year period between 2000 and 2002, binge drinking on college campuses continues to kill 1,400 college students between the ages of 18-24 every year in the U.S. (NIAAA, 2003). In addition, 600,000 students in this age group are injured, 600,000 are assaulted, 70,000 are sexually assaulted, 400,000 practice unsafe sex, and more than 100,000 report that they are not sure if they consented to sex, all while under the influence of alcohol. The following alcohol-related problems and the numbers of college students affected in this age group are included in the NIAAA (2003) report:

- Negative health—150,000 students

- Drunk driving—2.1 million

- Police involvement/public drunkenness and/or DUI—110,000

- Suicide attempts while under the influence of alcohol or drugs

- Property damage sustained by institutions

- Vandalism while under the influence

- Alcohol abuse/dependence

While students in this age category are approaching the end of what we generally consider adolescence,

Figure 4.7 Structures and functions of the Human Brain

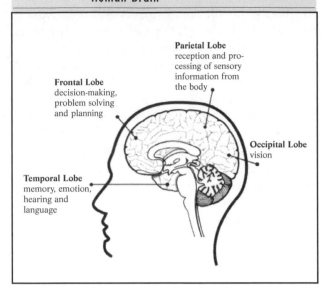

several parts of their brains are still undergoing transitions to adulthood and alcohol exerts a greater negative influence on their brains than that of older adults.

Brain chemistry 301: alcohol and neurotransmission

Now that we have discussed the negative effects of alcohol, let's see if we can handle an advanced course (*Brain Chemistry 301*) on how alcohol affects neurotransmission. However, as usual, before we can do this, we need to look at some more elements of brain chemistry. The brain controls our moods and emotions by a process called *synaptic homeostasis* (Sunderwirth, 1991). To survive, the brain needs a mechanism to calm us down when we become overly excited after the saber-tooth tiger escapade. On the other hand, we cannot sit around in a state of relaxed bliss if we intend to feed our Neolithic family. Two of the neurotransmitters involved in restoring and maintaining synaptic homeostasis are gamma-aminobutyric acid (GABA) and glutamate. We have seen how GABA inhibits dopamine-producing neurons. It turns out that GABA is the major inhibitor of neurotransmission in the brain. On the other hand, glutamate and its chemical cousin, N-methyl-D-aspartic acid (NMDA) are the major excitatory neurotransmitters.

Our hope is to maintain a balance of these two neurotransmitters in order not to "doze off" in times of danger or "fly off the handle" while watching TV. To understand how our two opposing neurotransmitters work, let's go back to *Figure 4.3*. When glutamate

attaches itself to a post-synaptic receptor site, it allows positive ions to enter the receiving neuron. If enough positive ions (Na+) flow into the receiving neuron, the membrane of this post-synaptic neuron becomes depolarized and the neuron will "fire." That is, it will send the impulse on to the next neuron. Therefore, glutamate is called an excitatory neurotransmitter. On the other hand, when GABA attaches to a post-synaptic receptor, it opens channels which allow negative ions (Cl-) to flow in. If enough of these receptor sites are occupied and enough negative ions enter the post-synaptic neuron, it will not fire. For this reason, GABA, is called an inhibitory neurotransmitter.

Braun (1996), in his very readable book, *Buzz*, does an excellent job of describing the effect of alcohol on glutamate and GABA receptors as well as the "rush" associated with alcohol. When alcohol enters the brain, it attaches itself to glutamate receptors in many parts of the brain and distorts the structure of the receptor. This alteration of the receptor is just enough to prevent glutamate from activating the neuron. Remember the Cadillac key in the Buick ignition? It will fit but not allow the engine to "fire." This inhibition occurs in many parts of the brain involving speech, coordination, heart rate, and most serious, the ability to learn. The ability to learn and retain information is the function of the brain's *hippocampus* (See *Figure 4.2*). Any damage to this structure affects the ability of the brain to convert new information into long-term memories. Damage to the *hippocampus* would then have a negative effect on memory formation and may explain the phenomena of alcoholic blackouts experienced by acute alcohol poisoning. White (2002) has summarized research conducted over the past few decades which leads to the conclusion that disruption of normal neuronal activity in the hippocampus is partially responsible for alcohol-induced impairment of memory. Interestingly, alcohol primarily interferes with the establishment of new memories more than remembering previous information.

Other brain structures involved in memory are the *frontal lobes* (*Figure 4.7*), which are also involved in cognitive processes besides memory. Damage to the frontal lobes may be responsible for the cognitive impairment in chronic alcoholics. Neuronal connections between the *frontal lobes* and the *hippocampus* (Shastri, 2002) indicate that memory and cognition involve both of these brain structures. Therefore it is not surprising that chronic alcohol use has been associated with frontal lobe damage (Kubota et. al., 2001) due to shrinkage.

Another neurotransmitter involved in hippocampal function is the previously mentioned cousin of glutamate called N-methyl-D-aspartic acid (NMDA). NMDA is involved in a hippocampal learning process called *long-term potentiation* (LTP) (Martin, and Morris, 2002). If a memory such as an order or a verse from a favorite poem is repeated, the neuronal connections responsible for the memory become strengthened and the ability to recognize the order or repeat the verse becomes easier. This process illustrates why repetition can be a valuable learning tool. It is known that alcohol retards LTP by interfering with the activation of the NMDA receptors in the hippocampus (Smartwelder et. al., 1995).

Alcohol and the adolescent brain

As discussed earlier, the adolescent brain is not fully developed, but is undergoing developmental changes that extend into young adulthood (Geidd et. al., 1999). Therefore, it would not be unreasonable to expect that drugs such as alcohol, which have a direct effect on the brain, would have a greater affect on the developing adolescent brain than on the mature adult brain. An analogy might be to consider the varying effects of damaging chemicals on a piece of clay during the process of forming a finished vase. When the clay is removed from the potter's wheel, it is still moist and may be molded into any number of shapes. Care must be taken not to add too much water, since some of the smaller molecules of the clay will dissolve. Firing of the vessel not only removes water but causes chemical reactions which result in the formation of new chemical bonds that solidify and strengthen the entire vessel. Because of the formation of these bonds during firing, water and even strong chemicals have very little effect on the finished vase.

Now suppose that a harsh chemical such as a strong acid is placed in the vessel right after it has been formed on the potter's wheel (birth to adolescence) and before it has been matured (achieved adulthood) by firing in the furnace. Very likely the acid would dissolve many of the molecular components which have not been stabilized by bond formation through firing. But once the vessel has been fired (matured in the human brain), many of the chemicals which had such a devastating effect on the raw clay would have little if any effect on the finished vase.

In a similar manner, evidence indicates that alcohol and other drugs have a *greater effect* on the undeveloped adolescent brain than on the mature adult brain (Markweise et. al., 1998). Ongoing changes in the immature brain would make the adolescent brain more vulnerable than that of adults to alcohol (and other drugs) damage (Spear, 2000a).

Learning and memory: alcohol and adolescence

The *hippocampus* is the primary region of the brain involved in learning and memory. Alcohol has been shown to affect memory by disrupting the functioning of the hippocampus (White & Best, 2000). Therefore, alcohol-induced memory impairments may be the result of neurotoxic effects on the hippocampus. There is evidence that adolescents who abuse alcohol have a *decrease in the size* of their hippocampus (DeBellis et. al., 2000).

As mentioned earlier, a model for changes in *hippocampal* structure during learning is called *long-term potentiation* (LTP). Alcohol is known to have a greater effect on LTP of adolescents than on adults (Swartzwelder et. al., 1995; Pyapali et. al., 1999). In fact, alcohol has been implicated in loss of brain cells in many of the areas of the brain besides the hippocampus. These other neuronal losses are in the cerebral cortex, hypothalamus, cerebellum, amygdala and the locus cerulus (Harper, 1998). A key neurotransmitter involved in LTP is believed to be the glutamate cousin, NMDA. Alcohol exerts a disrupting influence on the NMDA receptor, therefore interfering with the activation of the cell and a corresponding reduction in LTP. It has been shown (Swartzwelder et. al., 1995) that alcohol has a *greater effect* on the NMDA receptor in the hippocampus of adolescents than on adults. Thus, it is not a quantum leap to believe that alcohol has a greater effect on learning and memory on the adolescent brain than on the adult brain. In experiments using rats, Markweise et al. (1998) showed that alcohol impaired the ability of adolescent rats to navigate a water maze more than adults. It is not unreasonable to assume that effects found in animal studies would be similar to those expected in humans. After all, at a basic level, the neurobiology of memory formation between humans and animals should not be that different.

While it seems clear that adolescents are more vulnerable than adults to alcohol-induced learning and memory impairments, it seems that adolescent rats are less sensitive to the sedative effects of alcohol than adult rats (Little et. al., 1996; Swartzwelder et. al., 1998; Silveri and Spear, 1998). As we have seen, the neurotransmitter responsible for calming us down after the Bengal tiger episode is gamma-aminobutyric acid (GABA), which is our internal tranquilizer. In adults, alcohol enhances the sedative effects of GABA more than in adolescents. This decrease in the effect of alcohol on GABA receptors of adolescents compared to adults would allow adolescents to drink more than adults before passing out. Alcohol also appears to have *less effect on the motor coordination* of adolescents than on adults (White et al., 2002b). This would allow adolescents to drink more than adults before they exhibit typical signs of intoxication. However, the ability to drink larger amounts without becoming intoxicated enables the teenager to continue drinking alcohol. On the other hand, this increased ability to consume alcohol would have more of an increased neurotoxic effect on the brains of teenagers than on adults. Therefore, alcohol is doubly damaging to teenagers: more alcohol ingested into a brain that is already more sensitive to alcohol.

The dangers of binge drinking

As documented in the previous chapter, too many young people are caught up in binge drinking.

Because the adolescent brain is undergoing rapid changes, it is especially vulnerable to *alcohol neurotoxicity* with accompanying long-term consequences. Binge drinking has become a serious health problem among late teens on college campuses as well as at high school parties. Repeated binge drinking, sometimes called "chronic intermittent exposure" (CIE) results in withdrawal seizures that are believed to be responsible for many of the negative effects of alcohol ingestion on the central nervous system (CNS). Using laboratory animals, Becker and Hale (1993) showed that *repeated withdrawals* from alcohol caused a *higher rate of seizures* than continuous exposure to alcohol. In humans, those with a history of detoxifications showed a greater tendency to have seizures while undergoing withdrawal (Brown et. al., 1988). Binge drinking, which is characterized by repeated withdrawals, has been shown in rats to be associated with impaired learning (Bond, 1979). This CIE-induced cognitive impairment in adolescent rats has been shown to extend into adulthood (White et al., 2000). Once again, it is reasonable to expect that similar impairments would be present in adults who had previous CIE episodes. In humans, those with a *history* of *binge drinking* showed greater impaired memory function while intoxicated compared to others.

Summary of alcohol effects

Alcohol exerts its damaging effects on both the brain and the body. It exerts its effect on the brain by damaging and destroying neurons in the *hippocampus and*

frontal cortex. These areas of the brain are responsible for learning, memory and cognition. Alcohol also has serious health effects on the rest of the body including heart, liver disease and increased incidence of strokes.

METHAMPHETAMINE: NEED A SUDAFED?

One of the most serious drug problems, besides alcohol, in the U.S. today is methamphetamine (ice, meth, speed, crystal), which is easily manufactured in homes, barns, pick-ups, and SUVs using a common cold remedy (*Sudafed*), easily available chemicals such as anhydrous ammonia and lithium batteries. Unlike cocaine, which is imported from Colombia, Bolivia and Peru by way of countries such as Haiti, "meth" is produced primarily in the United States.

As a close relative of amphetamine, we would expect meth to have many negative effects on the body, especially the brain and the cardiovascular system. Besides addiction, serious effects from meth usage include rapid and irregular heart beat, and increased blood pressure resulting in irreversible damage to small blood vessels in the brain, which in turn may result in strokes. Other damaging effects include increased wakefulness, insomnia, convulsions, tremors, confusion, anxiety, aggressiveness and paranoia. Possibly the most serious health problem from chronic methamphetamine abuse is damage to the neurons of the brain. Previous studies have shown that meth causes damage to neurons in several parts of the brain, including the *frontal cortex*, which is responsible for cognitive functioning and decision-making capacity. It was also known to damage cells in the striatum. Damage to these cells could lead to movement disorders resembling *Huntington's chorea* and *tardive dyskinesia*. Cadet (1997) has shown that methamphetamine not only damages neurons but actually destroys them through a process called "apoptosis" (*Figure 4.8*).

In experiments using rodents (mice), Cadet showed that neuronal death was also prominent in the *frontal cortex* and *hippocampus*, which is utilized in the formation of long-term memory. There is also extensive damage in the *striatum* (*Figure 4.9*). Cell death in the frontal cortex, which is involved in cognition and reasoning, is especially troublesome during adolescence since this area is undergoing rapid changes at this time of life. Immature development makes this part of the brain especially vulnerable to apoptosis.

Figure 4.8 Neurotoxic Effects of Methamphetamine

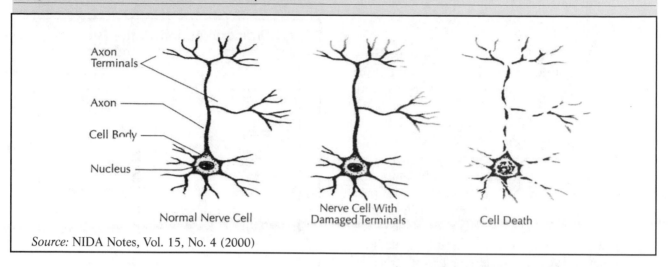

Normal Nerve Cell   Nerve Cell With Damaged Terminals   Cell Death

Source: NIDA Notes, Vol. 15, No. 4 (2000)

Another serious consequence of meth usage is damage to the nerve endings of dopamine-producing cells and that this damage persists for *at least three years* after drug intake has ceased. This damage to dopamine-producing cells is similar to that caused by Parkinson's disease and may be responsible for the addicting aspects of methamphetamine usage. These earlier studies of the effects of methamphetamine on the brain have been confirmed by Chang (2002) using a technique called *Perfusion Nuclear Magnetic Imaging* (pNMI), which measures blood flow into important brain regions.

If meth is so harmful, then why is it so popular among not only teens but adults as well? The answer is the same as with most drugs of abuse. It rapidly increases the flow of dopamine into the nucleus accumbens (*Figure 4.6*), resulting in euphoria that lasts from 8-24 hours, unlike cocaine in which the high lasts 20-30 minutes (NIDA, 1998).

COCAINE: "GIFT OF THE GODS"

In the early 16th century when Francisco Pizarro encountered the Quechua (usually referred to as the Inca) people of present-day Peru, he found that the royalty used the extract of a local shrub known today as *Erythroxyion coca* or simply the coca plant. This was the first contact of Europeans with this drug, which was soon to become one of the most widely abused drugs in the world. In Peru, the extract of the coca plant was considered to be "the gift of the gods" and was used in religious ceremonies as well as for medicinal purposes. The use of cocaine was initially

Figure 4.9 Human Brain Areas Corresponding to the Mouse Brain Areas Damaged by Methamphetamines

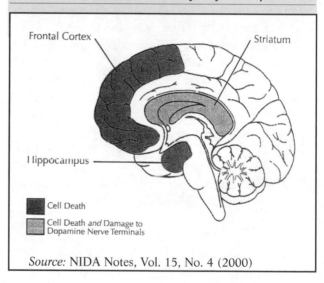

Source: NIDA Notes, Vol. 15, No. 4 (2000)

banned by the Spanish conquerors, but they soon learned that the enslaved natives could not work the gold mines in the rarified air of Peru without the stimulation of coca leaves that were distributed several times a day to the workers. The returning conquistadors called the drug "the elixir of life." They introduced the coca leaf to Europe where it soon became a fashionable social beverage.

Sherlock Holmes used cocaine and doctors even prescribed it as an antidote to morphine addiction. Cocaine was readily available in the late nineteenth century and early twentieth century either over the counter or in beverages such as Coca-Cola, which was introduced in 1886. It was claimed to be a brain tonic and a cure for nervous affliction. A typical serving of

Coca-Cola contained about 60 mg of cocaine. Today *Coca-Cola* contains only the name "coca" not the drug.

Crack: faster, stronger

Cocaine is found in the coca plant as the free-base form where it constitutes less than one percent of the leaf. After being extracted, the paste is treated with hydrochloric acid. This forms cocaine hydrochloride, an organic salt. This is the form in which it arrives in the United States as a white powder. Cocaine can be extracted from the leaves in hot water to make coca tea, a popular beverage in Peru. Cocaine becomes dangerous when extracted and concentrated to form pure cocaine hydrochloride. This form is usually snorted since it is not sufficiently volatile to smoke. The hydrochloride salt may be converted to "crack" by a general chemical reaction (acid plus base) learned by every beginning student of chemistry. Treatment of the acid salt with any household base such as ammonia or sodium bicarbonate releases the hydrochloric acid to form the volatile "free base," known as crack, which, once extracted with ether and dried, can now be smoked to give a much faster high than can be obtained snorting. Sounds easy, right? Actually, it is very easy for anyone in a chemistry laboratory equipped with an exhaust hood. The problem arises when inexperienced "chemists" evaporate the ether extract to get the pure cocaine. Ether is very volatile and flammable and many serious accidents have resulted from igniting the ether during extraction. Richard Pryor suffered severe burns while attempting to evaporate the ether extract with a flame.

Cocaine high

How does cocaine react in the brain to give such an immediate and intense high? Let's return to *Brain Chemistry 101* for an answer. Briefly stated, cocaine obtains its high by increasing the availability of, guess what, *dopamine.* No surprise there. When dopamine is released from the presynaptic neurons (*Figure 4.6*) of the dopamine-producing nerve cells in an area of the brain known as the ventral *tegmental area* (VTA), it causes a flow of dopamine into the reward center, the *nucleus accumbens* where it produces the expected high. After activating the cells of the nucleus accumbens, dopamine is transported back into the presynaptic VTA cells by transporter receptors. Cocaine blocks these transporter receptors (*Figure 4.10*), which prevents dopamine from being reabsorbed. Since it stays in the synapse, it is able to be used over and over again and to continually activate the neurons of the *nucleus accumbens*, giving the user the intense high characteristic of cocaine use.

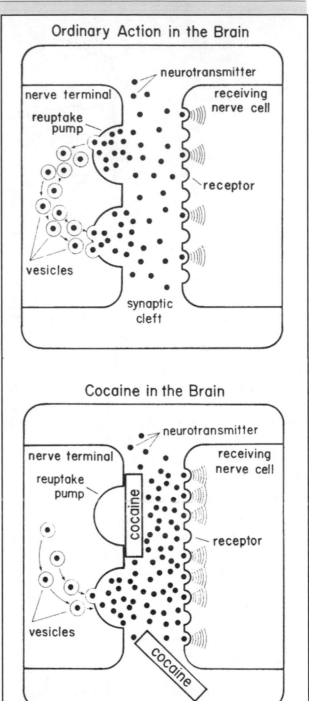

Figure 4.10 Cocaine in the Brain

Ordinary Action in the Brain

Cocaine in the Brain

Health effects of cocaine

Obviously, cocaine, like most drugs of abuse, even caffeine, exerts its major effect on the brain. Because of the intense high associated with the drug, addiction can occur during a single binge episode. Once addicted, the user finds himself or herself in a continuing spiral of increased usage to obtain the previously obtained high and especially to avoid the effects of withdrawal. These effects include severe depression, with the resulting intense craving to resume using. Prolonged usage can produce paranoia, especially among crack users, who may become aggressively paranoid.

Crack babies revisited

In the 1980s, scary reports about the effects of cocaine on the brains of the developing fetus were widespread. Women whose fetuses were allegedly damaged by cocaine usage during pregnancy were subject to criminal prosecution. Then in the 1990s, the pendulum swung in the opposite direction in terms of the brain damage suffered by the fetuses of women who used cocaine. It is now clear that cocaine may not be the "sledge hammer" for the developing brain, but clearly does have serious negative effects on the brain later on in the life of the exposed child. These include *behavioral problems* such as aggression, inability to stay focused, and impulsivity. In addition, crack, exposed children were more anxious and depressed (Chasnoff, 1997). Mayes (1995) reported that "crack" babies at 3 to 6 months of age showed more signs of *irritability* than those in the control group whose mothers were exposed to alcohol, nicotine and drugs other than cocaine. At 12 to 18 months, the "crack" babies were having more *trouble focusing* their attention than the control group.

Cocaine and neuronal growth

As we have seen, cocaine acts by increasing the supply of dopamine in the synaptic junction of neurons. This enables more dopamine receptors to be activated, which in turn brings about the "high" characteristic of cocaine. In research on animals, the number of dopamine receptors, designated as D1, were normal in rabbits exposed to cocaine, but the exposed receptors do not transmit their signal as efficiently as those in normal brains. According to Levitt (1997), this may result in the abnormal growth of the dendrites, which causes them to weave around each other to accommodate this abnormal growth. This is believed to have a significant effect on their circuitry. This abnormal growth of the dendrites was found in the anterior cingulated cortex, which is the area of the brain involved in learning and attention. This abnormal growth and interweaving of neurons would be especially significant for adolescents. As we have seen, the cortex of adolescents is undergoing rapid changes. Any alteration in the normal growth patterns could have significant effects on cognition.

Summary of cocaine effects

Cocaine exerts its effects on the brain by increasing the amount of dopamine flowing into the *nucleus accumbens*, a major reward center. Negative effects on the fetus have not met with universal agreement over the past 20 years. However, there is general agreement that maturing "crack" babies exhibit *attention deficits, irritability and aggression*. Cocaine interferes with the normal growth of dendrites, especially in the area of the brain involved in learning and attention. This is especially troubling for adolescents whose brains are in the process of rapid development.

MARIJUANA: REEFER MADNESS REVISITED

Effects on the brain

According to the *Drug Abuse Warning Network (DAWN, 2003)*, the most frequent drug-related visits to hospital emergency rooms for youths 12 to 19 are for marijuana abuse. In 2001, there were over 26,000 visits by youths in this age group to emergency rooms for marijuana or marijuana in combination with other drugs.

A National Conference on the *Effects of Marijuana on the Brain, Endocrine System, and Immune System* (1995) summarizes the effects of chronic marijuana abuse. Since marijuana in sufficient doses is hallucinogenic, we would expect that the main ingredient (*tetrahydrocannabinol* or THC) responsible for this effect would have receptors in the brain. Such receptors have been found in the *hippocampus*, the *cortex* and the *cerebellum*. These are the areas of the brain involved in *memory, cognition and coordination*. Our brains are programmed to react to THC by conveniently providing receptors for a naturally occurring cousin of THC, *anadamide*, named after the Sanskrit word for "bliss."

Withdrawal effects from marijuana usage

One of the hallmarks of addiction is the presence of negative physiological and psychological effects upon removal of the drug. The sometimes proclaimed view that marijuana is non-addicting is contradicted by observed withdrawal effects. Kouri et. al. (1999) found that long-term marijuana users became more aggressive during withdrawal than did former users. Haney et. al. (1999) found that chronic users experience other withdrawal symptoms such as anxiety, stomach pain, and irritability. More recently Budlex et. al. (2001) showed that during abstinence and while living at home, marijuana smokers experienced *sleep difficulties, decreased appetite, and increased anger, aggression and irritability*. These studies on withdrawal effects clearly indicate that contrary to earlier opinions, marijuana is an addictive drug.

Effects on cognition

One area in which there is little if any difference of opinion is that of the effect of marijuana on the brain with the accompanying deficits in cognition. This observed impairment is not surprising since research in animal studies have shown that marijuana causes structural damage to the *hippocampus*, a brain region involved in memory and learning. Compared to light abusers of marijuana, Bolla et al. (2002) found that heavy abusers suffered deficits in verbal and visual memory, executive functioning, visual perception, psychomotor speed, and manual dexterity (*Figure 4.11*). These impairments existed for at least 28 days and possibly longer. An interesting observation by Bolla and co-workers was that *cognitive impairment* from smoking marijuana was greater among those students with lower IQ scores than those with higher scores. Bolla believes that those with higher IQs have more "cognitive reserves" and the impairment from marijuana will not be as obvious as with lower cognitive reserves, i.e., lower IQs. Earlier research by Pope (2001) indicated that cognitive impairment from heavy marijuana use seemed to *disappear after one month*.

According to Pope (1996), it is very clear that heavy marijuana use decreases the ability to learn and remember while under the influence of the drug. The problem is not so much getting the abuser to remember a previously learned item; the basic problem is "getting them to learn in the first place." Therefore, students who smoke marijuana might be expected to get lower grades in school than those who abstain. This has been found to be true.

Marijuana and the endocrine system

Murphy (1995) speaking at the *National Conference on Marijuana Use* indicated that several studies have shown that the *reproductive system* of marijuana users may be affected by alteration of the secretion of hormones from the pituitary gland. This gland secretes a number of hormones that control reproductive function in humans. These include follicle stimulating hormone (FSH), luteinizing hormone (LH), and prolactin, all of which play a role in the secretion of both the female hormone, estrogen and the male hormone, testosterone. Clearly, tinkering with *Mother Nature* at this basic level is a prescription for disaster.

Marijuana and the immune system

The human immune system is a complicated system that enables the body to resist the invasion of bacteria, viruses, and other microbes. This system also offers protection against tumors by inhibiting cancer growth. Cabral, speaking at the *National Conference* (1995) presented evidence that the ingredient in marijuana that is responsible for the negative effects observed in the immune system is our familiar hallucinogenic compound THC. Not exactly a surprise. The *scavenger* cells of the immune system, which are responsible for ridding the body of pathogens, are subject to *damage by exposure to THC*. Marijuana has also been shown to have a negative effect on *T- and B-lymphocytes*, which are important in fighting bacterial and viral infections.

Because marijuana use is often associated with sexual promiscuity, impairment of the immune system creates an additional risk factor that may be associated with the spread of herpes, Type B hepatitis and AIDS.

Long-term effects on health

Although there may be some conflicting evidence on long-term brain damage from smoking marijuana, there is no difference of opinion on the damage to the lungs. These effects from long-term abuse are similar and in many cases worse than in the case of cigarette smoking. Marijuana smokers experience *frequent respiratory illnesses*, daily coughing with phlegm production, obstructed breathing pathways, and frequent lung infections. Other effects on the lungs of marijuana smoking include acute pneumonia, inflammation of airways, chronic bronchitis, acute chest illnesses and possibly emphysema. The carcinogenic molecules and tars in marijuana smoke make smokers especially vulnerable to lung cancer, as well as head and neck cancers.

Summary of marijuana effects

There is overwhelming evidence that chronic marijuana usage has serious negative effects on memory, learning and cognition. There is some dispute regarding how long these effects last. However, with animal studies showing destruction of cells in the hippocampus, there can be little doubt that long-term marijuana smoking impacts the ability to remember and especially to learn new information. One of the most deleterious effects of marijuana smoking is permanent damage to the lungs including respiratory illness, obstructed breathing, lung cancer, frequent pneumonia, bronchitis and possible emphysema.

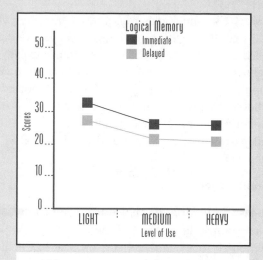

Heavy marijuana users scored below light users on all measures of verbal memory, although they had no problems recognizing previously learned material.

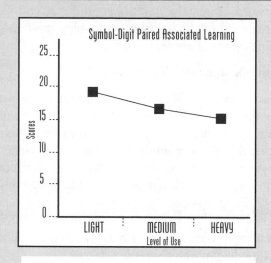

Heavy marijuana use effects affected visual learning and memory.

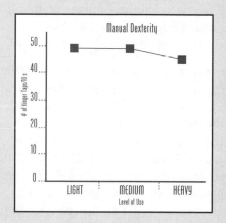

Heavy marijuana use was associated with lower performance on manual dexterity measures.

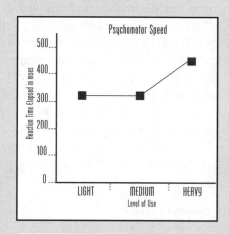

Heavy marijuana users showed slower reaction times on a test of simple reaction time

Source: Volume 18. Number 5 NIDA NOTES (2002)

OPIATES: EVERYONE MAKES THEM

Opiates include heroin and morphine, as well as our internal opiates, enkephalin and endorphins. In fact, the term endorphin is a contradiction of the words, "endogenous morphine." Recently, prescription opiates such as *Vicodin* and *Oxycontin* have hit the illegal street trade and are replacing the old standby, heroin, as the opiate of choice among adolescents.

Opiates and the brain

To understand the effect of opiates on the brain, let's return to the *Reward Cascade* (Figure 4.5) discussed in *Neurochemistry 101,* and the role of GABA. As we have seen, opiates including our own opiates (endorphin and enkephalin) act on the brain by binding to opiate receptors and inhibiting the release of neurotransmitters from those neurons on which they have receptor sites. If these neurons happen to also impinge on GABA neurons, the release of GABA is inhibited. GABA inhibits the release of our pleasure-inducing neurotransmitter, dopamine (DA). So, if we *inhibit the inhibitor*, we get an increase in the flow of DA into the reward center, the *nucleus accumbens*, and feel intense pleasure. Let's begin by looking at a long-standing opiate of abuse, heroin.

Heroin: the ultimate pipe dream

Heroin is a synthetic derivative of morphine, known as diacetylmorphine. The *Adolph Von Bayer Company* made it by the same process they used to make Bayer Aspirin. This is not to imply that there is any relationship between the two in terms of physiological action. Heroin was first marketed as a non-addicting form of morphine and was even found in some cough syrups. It soon became apparent that not only was heroin (diacetylmorphine) addicting but, was actually more addicting than morphine itself.

Heroin is administered by smoking, snorting, injection or sniffing. For those who use injection as the method of delivery, many inject up to 4 times a day. Intravenous injection provides euphoria within 7 to 8 seconds, whereas smoking requires 10 to 15 minutes for the euphoria to peak. Injection continues to be the primary method of heroin administration among addicts, although recently there has been a trend *towards snorting/sniffing* as a preferred method of administration. This tendency to move away from injection has prompted drug traffickers to produce high-purity heroin that is being marketed to middle-class Americans as a "non-addicting" way to use the drug.

Summary of heroin effects

Heroin crosses the blood-brain barrier soon after injection and binds to opiate receptors (*Figure 4.6*) where it soon produces the expected "rush" as well as suppression of pain. It can also *depress respiration,* which can be fatal, especially if combined with alcohol. Clouded mental functioning is a short-term consequence of heroin usage, as is occasional nausea and vomiting. The most obvious and detrimental long-term effect is addiction, characterized by compulsive drug seeking and use. Physical dependence requires the abuser to continue taking the drug to avoid withdrawal symptoms, which include restlessness, bone pain, explosive diarrhea, vomiting, cold flashes and goose bumps. These withdrawal symptoms peak within 24 to 48 hours and subside after about a week. Some serious effects of intravenous heroin injections are infectious diseases such as HIV/AIDS and hepatitis. Collapsed veins, abscesses and bacterial infections are common among those who inject heroin.

ECSTASY: LET'S PARTY

Ecstasy (B-bombs, disco biscuit, essence, go, wheels, "X," Scooby snacks, sweeties, hug drug, love drug) is called a "party drug" since it is often present at all-night dance parties or "raves" which are growing in popularity among teenagers. It is reported and believed by many adolescents that Ecstasy produces euphoria and boosts energy allowing users to dance and party all night. Users also claim that it is a sex enhancer.

Health effects

Ecstasy is the drug of choice for many late teens and other young adults. Most of these users are not aware of the risk for negative effects on health. Chemically, Ecstasy is 3,4-methylenedioxymethamphetamine (MDMA). The significant part of the name is "methamphetamine," which should be a red flag. As a derivative of "meth," it would be expected to exhibit many of the deleterious effects of that drug, which were discussed earlier. This it does well, with a few added zingers of its own.

Since any drug that causes the type of mood swing attributed to Ecstasy obviously has a great effect on the brain, let's examine these effects first. It is believed that the major contributor to the euphoria experienced by MDMA users is our familiar neurotransmitter serotonin. The euphoria brought about by Ecstasy is due, at least in part, by the *rapid release of serotonin* from nerve endings. This over-stimulation of these nerves causes what appears to be *irreversible damage to the nerve endings* (McCann et al., 1998). Even if the serotonin neurons do re-grow, they don't grow back normally and in the right location in the brain. Some studies in monkeys have shown that after only 4 days of exposure to Ecstasy, brain damage was apparent 6 to 7 years later (NIDA, 2000), pointing to the strong possibility of permanent brain damage in humans.

It has also been shown that unborn rats exposed to *MDMA* during what corresponds to the *third trimester of human pregnancy* suffered memory and learning deficiencies throughout their adult lives (Broening et. al., 2001). Rodgers (2003) has shown that "people who regularly take Ecstasy report experiencing long-term memory difficulties and are 23% more likely to report problems with remembering things than non-users." Even after at least 2 weeks of abstinence, users have significant memory problems.

Ricaurte (2000), in a widely cited work, reported that monkeys who were exposed to Ecstasy suffered severe damage the part of the brain that produces serotonin, and that Ecstasy kills dopamine-producing cells after only one night's dose. Damage to these cells would put users at risk for Parkinson's disease, which is characterized by non-functioning or poorly functioning dopamine neurons. However, Ricaurte's work has been widely criticized as it was later discovered that the primates used in his study were injected with methamphetamine and not Ecstasy (*Chronicle of Higher Education*, 2004).

An added health risk for Ecstasy users is the fact that the drug is often *consumed with other drugs,* especially marijuana and/or alcohol, an especially deadly combination for permanent brain damage. Liechti et al. (2001) also reported that women seem to be *more susceptible* than men to the subjective effects of Ecstasy such as perceptual changes, thought disturbances and fear of loss of body control.

Many of the emergency admissions to hospitals are not for Ecstasy-induced memory deficits but for dehydration, due to disruptions in body temperature and cardiovascular regulation (NIDA, 2001). The extremely high room temperatures often found at "raves" as well as the stimulating effects of the drug greatly increases the severity of dehydration. These conditions are very conducive to hypertension, hyperthermia, as well as heart or kidney failure. In addition, "ravers" compensate for this expected dehydration by drinking excessive amounts of water, which in some cases results in swelling of the brain.

Summary of the effects of Ecstasy

Escalating use of Ecstasy among college and high school students would indicate that the drug is rapidly becoming the drug of choice within this age group. According to one study, MDMA causes what appears to be irreversible and long-term damage to dopaminergic neurons and damage to serotonergic nerve endings. Therefore, it would not be surprising if users suffer long-term memory and other cognitive deficits. However, some of this research has been criticized. So what are we to believe? The conflicting data does show damage to serotonin-releasing neurons. However, the extent of this damage is controversial. Other effects on health that seem to be substantiated are dehydration, hypertension, brain-swelling, hyperthermia, heart and kidney failure. Considering the potential damage to the brain and the rest of the body, use of Ecstasy appears to present considerable risk.

INHALANTS: HOW STUPID CAN YOU GET?

Inhalants, which are volatile substances that produce *breathable vapors*, include paint sprays, paint thinners and removers, spray paints, deodorant, vegetable oil, gasoline, glues and other aerosols. In addition, certain medical anesthetics found in commercial and household uses are abused. These include chloroform, ether, and nitrous oxide (laughing gas) and aliphatic nitrites.

Nitrites: non-prescription Viagra

Nitrites, which include cyclohexyl, amyl and butyl nitrite, are often used to enhance sexual performance. Nitrites act much like Viagra by dilating blood vessels and relaxing muscles. Cyclohexyl nitrite is found in room deodorizers, while amyl nitrite is sometimes prescribed by doctors for heart pain. Both amyl and butyl nitrites are packaged in small bottles (butyl nitrite) and are referred to as "poppers."

Inhalants and the brain

One of the most dangerous as well as widely used inhalants is the organic aromatic compound, *toluene.* It is used commercially to make TNT (trinitrotoluene), an explosive used in military bombs. Although quite different than TNT, toluene does a number on the brain not unlike that of TNT on a city. But first, let's see if we can explain why anyone would use inhalants such as toluene. Toluene and most other inhalants (except nitrites) activate the brain's dopamine reward system. That should not come as any surprise at this point. The rapid high produced by inhalants *resembles* that of *alcohol intoxication*. This high is followed by drowsiness, lightheadedness, apathy, impaired functioning, and judgment, disinhibition and belligerence. The other short-term effects of inhalant abuse are too numerous to mention here, but include dizziness, slurred speech, increased lethargy, muscle weakness and stupor. Heart failure and death can occur within minutes after a prolonged "sniffing." While long-term effects include weight loss, irritability, decreased coordination, depression, and withdrawal, the real bomb, figuratively speaking, is the damage to the brain.

Toluene's effects on the brain are shown in *Figure 4.12.* The brain actually shrinks in size with chronic toluene abuse. The neurons are destroyed in a manner similar to that of buildings in a city being destroyed by TNT. Since toluene affects nearly all areas of the brain, it is like a "dumb bomb," indiscriminately destroying everything it hits. This is really bad news, since the two areas we need to preserve are the *hippocampus,*

Figure 4.12 Brain Damage in a Toluene Abuser

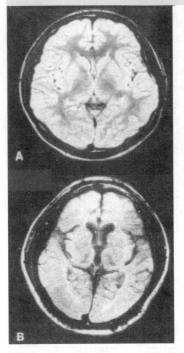

Brain images show marked shrinkage of brain tissue in a toluene abuser (B) compared to a nonabusing individual (A). Note the smaller size and the larger (empty) dark space within the toluene abuser's brain

Source: NIDA Research Report - Inhalant Abuse: NIH Publication No. 00-3818, Printed 1994, Revised, 2004 Photos: Courtesy of Neil Rosenberg,

for memory, and the *frontal cortex*, for cognition. These are the areas of the adolescent brain that are not mature. In a manner similar to the effect of chemicals on the pottery vessel before firing, inhalants damage the "uncured" brain more than the adult brain.

Summary of inhalant effects

Inhalants exert their effect on the brain by activating the dopamine reward system. In many ways, the high produced by inhalants resembles that produced by alcohol, but is much more damaging to the neurons in the brain. This damage is due to the damage to the protective myelin sheath which surrounds nerve fibers in the brain and other parts of the nervous system. Many health care workers believe that adolescent inhalant users are the most brain-damaged of the adolescent drug users, and much of this damage is irreversible.

HALLUCINOGENIC DRUGS – CHEMICAL VISION

When Hernan Cortez entered Mexico in the early 16th century, he found the inhabitants involved in religious ceremonies that included use of psychedelic plants such as magic mushrooms and the buttons of the peyote cactus. The Aztecs were especially known for

using magic mushrooms (*Psilocybe mexicana*) in their religious ceremonies. The Nahuatl (language of the Aztecs) name for the mushrooms was *teonanactl* which means "flesh of the gods." In 1958, Albert Hofmann, a Swiss chemist who had discovered LSD, isolated the active ingredients of the mushroom, psilocybin (*Figure 4.12*).

The inhabitants of Mexico as well as the southwest United States also used peyote cactus buttons in their religious ceremonies. The active ingredient of the cactus buttons was identified in 1986 by A. Heffter, a German scientist. The compound, mescaline, was named after the Mescaleno Apaches who were known to use the buttons in their religious ceremonies. The chemical structure of mescaline was determined in 1918 by E. Spaeth, another German, and is similar to the chemical structure of our brain's own neurotransmitter, serotonin (*Figure 4.13*). It is also interesting to note that the active ingredients of "magic mushrooms" are also structurally related to serotonin as is that infamous hallucinogen, LSD.

Hoffman's nightmare

Albert Hofmann, the Swiss chemist who isolated the active ingredient in magic mushrooms, also synthesized LSD (lysergic acid diethylamide) from compounds that he isolated from ergot, a fungus that grows on rye grass. Five years after Hofmann created the drug, he accidentally ingested a small amount of the compound and experienced the first recorded "trip" with LSD (Hofmann, 1980).

My surroundings . . . transformed themselves in more terrifying ways. Everything in the room spun around, and the familiar objects and pieces of furniture assumed grotesque, threatening forms. They were in continuous motion, animated, as if driven by an inner restlessness . . .. Even worse than these demonic transformations of the outer world were the alterations that I perceived in myself, in my inner being. Every exertion of my will, every attempt to put an end to the disintegration of the outer world and the dissolution of my ego, seemed to be wasted effort. A demon had invaded me, had taken possession of my body, mind, and soul.

Albert Hofmann

Figure 4.13 Molecular Structures

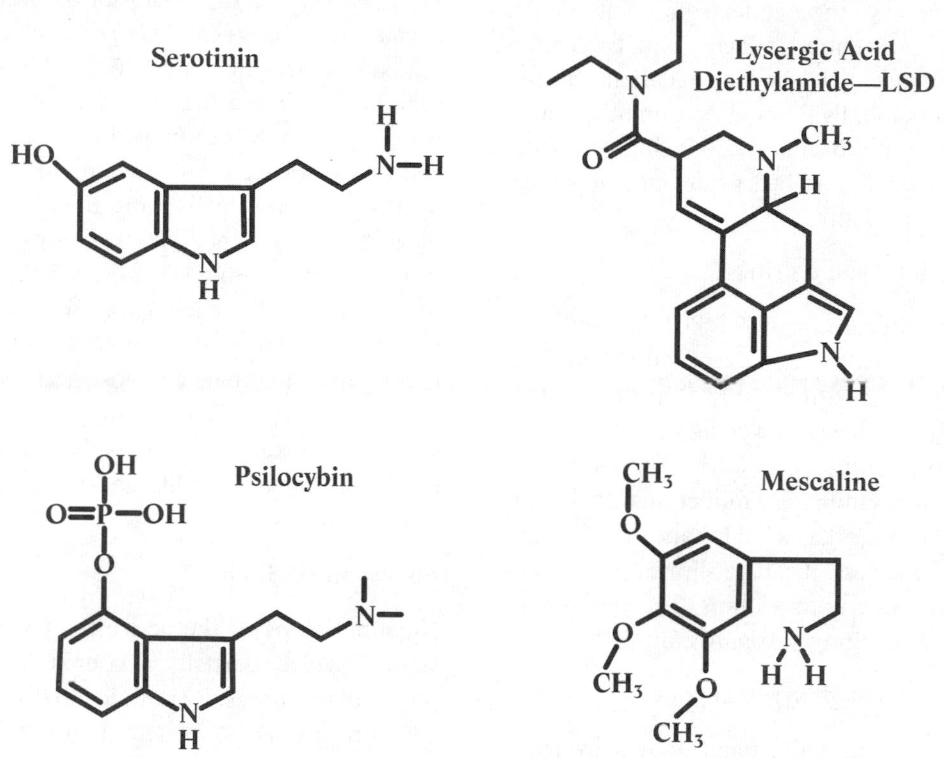

Serotinin

Lysergic Acid Diethylamide—LSD

Psilocybin

Mescaline

Hallucinogenic drugs are much like the neurotransmitter serotonin in their molecular structure as well as where and how they act in the brain.

Effects of LSD

Because of the structural similarity between LSD and serotonin, it is not surprising that scientists believe that LSD, as well as the other plant-derived hallucinogens, acts on serotonin receptors (Sanders-Bush, 1994) in two brain regions. One is the *cerebral cortex*, which as we have indicated is involved in cognition, perception and mood. The other is the *locus ceruleus*, an area of the brain that receives external stimuli. This would partially explain why LSD users experience short-term effects such as rapidly changing moods and are also over-stimulated by colors, sounds and smells that are intensified by the drug. Long-term effects include tolerance, including tolerance to psilocybin and mescaline but not to marijuana and amphetamine, which do not target serotonin receptors. A quick glance at the chemical structures shown in *Figure 4.13* will explain why this is to be expected.

Other long-term effects are persistent psychosis and occasional "flashbacks." The psychosis is characterized by distortion of reality as well as the ability to

think rationally. Some users experience long-lasting psychotic states including dramatic mood shifts, visual disturbances and hallucinations.

Other mind-altering drugs

Two other mind-altering drugs, PCP (phenylcyclidine) and ketamine were originally developed in the 1950s and 1960s to be used in surgery as general anesthetics. They are often referred to as hallucinogenic drugs because they cause feelings of detachment from reality and distortions of space, sounds, sight and body image. Because of these effects, which are not true hallucinations, PCP and ketamine are known as "dissociative" rather than hallucinogenic drugs.

PCP: "Zombie" an accurate description

Known by such street names as *zombie, dummy dust, angel dust, boat, peace, PCP* acts on the brain by altering the receptor sites for the neurotransmitter glutamate (*Figure 4.13*). These receptors are associated with the way we perceive pain, as well as in emotion and cognition, which affects our ability to learn and to remember. It is not surprising that the rush from PCP is caused by the increase in the release of the neurotransmitter, dopamine, into the *nucleus accumbens*. Generally, these effects are felt within minutes and last several hours or even days. Even after one year of abstinence, the user may experience memory loss and depression. PCP has effects on other parts of the body besides the brain. These include elevated body temperature, increased heart rate and dangerous increases in blood pressure.

Ketamine: Let me fix you a drink

A less violent chemical cousin of PCP is ketamine known as "K," "Special K," and even "cat valium." It was developed in 1963 to replace PCP in surgery and is used in human anesthesia as well as veterinary medicine (cat valium). Although its effects are similar to PCP, the effects of ketamine are milder and of shorter duration. It has been used as a "date rape drug." Since it is tasteless and odorless, it can be slipped into drinks to bring about amnesia in its victims. The victim may not remember the resulting sexual assault.

Dextromethorphan: cough syrup anyone?

The amount of dextromethorphan found in most cough syrups is not harmful. However, abuse can occur using the "extra strength" variety. If the dosage exceeds four ounces of dextromethorphan, dissociative effects similar to PCP and ketamine may result. However, the chance of this amount of the drug being ingested with the normal cough suppressant is very unlikely.

Summary of effects of hallucinogenic drugs

Plant-derived hallucinogenic drugs have been used by ancient societies for many hundreds of years. Many of these societies such as the Aztecs of Mexico as well as our Native American tribes used mushrooms and peyote cactus buttons in their religious societies to create visions, which they believed enabled them to communicate with their gods. LSD was synthesized by a Swiss chemist who accidentally ingested some of it and experienced the first "acid trip." LSD affects the *cerebral cortex* and the *locus ceruleus*, resulting in short-term effects such as rapid mood changes and over-stimulation of sights, sounds and smells. Other mind-altering drugs are PCP (phenylcyclidine) and ketamine. Even the cough syrup ingredient, dextromethorphan, can be abused to produce dissociative effects.

TOBACCO: THE ULTIMATE DRUG

We have saved a discussion of tobacco until the last because it is the *crème de la crème* of addictive drugs. Smoking causes from 450,000 to 500,000 deaths per year in the United States and over 3 million worldwide. By 2025, it is estimated that if the present trend continues, tobacco will account for over 10 million deaths per year. This is more than all other legal and illegal drugs combined. Smoking tops the list of deaths from preventable diseases closely followed by diet and inactivity with the accompanying diseases associated with obesity. The *Center for Disease Control* has estimated that the medical cost ($3.45) and loss of productivity ($3.73) is $7.18 per pack of cigarettes smoked. Smoking also causes the average male smoker to lose 13 years of life and the average woman to lose 14.5 years.

Effects on the brain

Nicotine is one of the active ingredients of cigarette smoke, which partially accounts for the addicting power of cigarettes. By now, if you don't know that the addicting power of tobacco is due to an increase of dopamine (DA) in the *nucleus accumbens* (NAc), you should re-enroll in *Neurochemistry 101*. Nicotine directly stimulates the flow of DA into the NAc (see *Figure 4.14*). Nicotine also stimulates the release of the excitatory neurotransmitter, glutamate (glu), which triggers additional release of DA. But as we have seen, GABA (produced by the ventral tegmental area (VTA)) moderates DA release. The VTA initially enhances GABA release to moderate the increase of DA produced by nicotine. However, within a few minutes nicotine kicks in to inhibit the release of GABA (Mansvelder et. al., 2000; 2002). As we have seen, inhibiting the DA-releasing inhibitor results in high DA levels in the NAc. The combination of these effects, i.e., (a) direct stimulation of DA release and (b) inhibiting the inhibitory effects of GABA on DA, result in an increase in DA in the NAc and an amplification of the rewarding properties of nicotine (Mansvelder, 2002).

It gets even worse. There appears to be an unknown substance in cigarette smoke which blocks the action of monoamine oxidase (MAO) which is responsible for breaking down (destroying) DA in order to maintain a balance of this neurotransmitter. So now it seems that smoking is a *triple-sided sword*: one to directly enhance DA, one to inhibit the DA inhibitor and the third to block the DA destroyer (MAO). It

figure 4.14   Nicotine

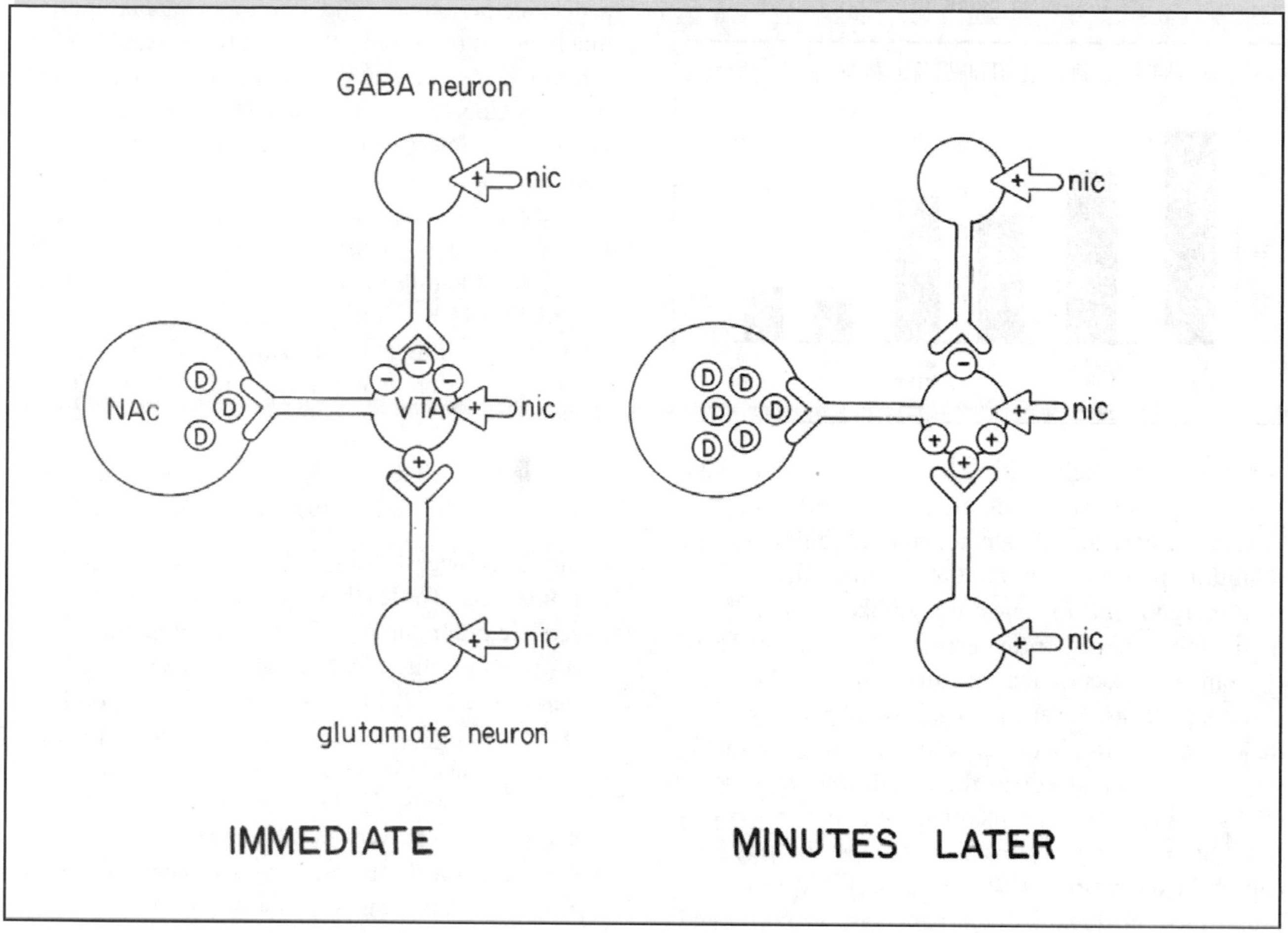

GABA neuron

NAc

VTA

nic

glutamate neuron

IMMEDIATE

MINUTES LATER

would not be possible for the best pharmaceutical company in the world to design a better combination of drugs (nicotine and the unknown MAO inhibitor) to produce addiction.

Even this is not the end of the nicotine story with its multitude of effects on the brain. Many smokers, even though they know that smoking is really stupid, will claim that smoking makes them temporarily smarter and more alert. Actually, this is probably true. It is known that the chemical structure of nicotine is similar to that of the neurotransmitter acetylcholine, which is involved in many brain functions including memory and mental alertness. Because of the similarity in chemical structure, nicotine is able to attach itself to and activate acetylcholine (cholinergic) receptor sites. On the other hand, Ott (2004) and his colleagues have shown that smoking *retards mental functioning in the elderly* five times faster than in elderly non-smokers. They also observed a close response in that those who smoked more declined faster than those who smoked less. This is especially significant as we observe an increase in the average age of the pop-

ulation in the U.S. and around the world. But as is the case with all addicting drugs, continued activation of either the DA-enhancing neurons or the cholinergic receptors changes the sensitivity of these neurons to nicotine, which results in tolerance, dependence and addiction.

Other health effects of smoking

The truly devastating effects of smoking are not the multifaceted action of nicotine in the brain. *Figure 4.15* from the *Center for Disease Control* shows serious effects of smoking in the health of smokers in the U.S. in the early 1990s. Obviously, lung cancer is the greatest hitter, followed by heart disease. In terms of health effects and deaths, cigarette smoking is the most serious drug problem in the U.S. today.

Summary of tobacco effects

Tobacco is the most widely used of the drugs of abuse and is responsible for more deaths and financial expenditures due to health problems and lost productivity than all other legal and illegal drugs combined.

Figure 4.15 Causes of Death Attributable to Cigarette Smoking

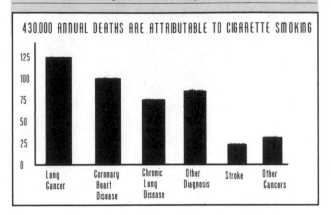

430,000 ANNUAL DEATHS ARE ATTRIBUTABLE TO CIGARETTE SMOKING

Nicotine is an excellent drug to activate the dopamine reward system by direct stimulation of dopamine release, release of glutamate and inhibition of the inhibitory neurotransmitter, GABA. In addition, there is a component of cigarette smoke that inhibits monoamine oxidase from destroying dopamine. These combined effects make nicotine one of the most addicting drugs, legal or illegal, in our society. The major health effects of tobacco are due to smoking (and chewing) and not to the nicotine. In fact, some evidence indicates that nicotine may increase cognition. Smoking is responsible for most of the lung cancer in the world as well as cancer of the larynx, esophagus, bladder, kidney, pancreas, stomach and uterine cavity. It is also the major cause of chronic bronchitis and emphysema.

CHAPTER REVIEW

To understand the effects of drugs on the adolescent brain, it is necessary to have a basic knowledge of how the human brain works as well as the concept of adolescence. The human brain has been compared to a computer using only on and off signals between the billions of neurons that make trillions of connections. The software of the brain can be represented by various kinds of molecules known as neurotransmitters. The neurotransmitters carry the message from one neuron to the other with lightning speed. The neurotransmitter believed to be responsible for the "rush" of most drugs is *dopamine*. Dopamine is produced in one area of the brain (the *ventral tegmental* area) and sent to a major reward center (the *nucleus accumbens*) where it produces feelings of pleasure and well-being. In addition to drugs, many activities (eating, hugging, sex, even crime) produce a flow of dopamine into the *nucleus accumbens*.

Adolescence is both a cultural concept as well as a biological condition. The cultural view of adolescence as a distinct period in child development has received much more attention in the last 50-60 years than was the case before, say 1930-1940. Children simply went from childhood to adulthood. Of course, we now know that adolescence is a time of rapidly changing hormones in the body and even more rapid changes in several parts of the brain. The ability of the teenager to make rational decisions is compromised by the inability of the *immature frontal cortex to control* the amygdala, which is the part of the brain involved in emotions. For this reason, many decisions by adolescents are made on an emotional rather than a rational basis.

The usage as well as the effect of drugs on the human brain and on the body is organized as follows:

- *Alcohol*: Biggest drug killer of college students: 1,400/year. Those that survive often suffer irreversible brain damage. In the general population, it is estimated that alcohol kills 100,000 people per year in the U.S. This is in addition to 16,000 killed and 1 million injured as a result of traffic accidents in which alcohol was a factor. The annual cost of alcohol abuse in the U.S. alone is estimated to be $185 billion. Alcohol ranks second after tobacco in the deaths attributable to drugs. Alcohol effects are especially damaging to adolescents, whose brains are undergoing rapid changes.

- *Cocaine*: Introduced to Europe through the conquest of Peru by Francisco Pizarro, who observed the natives of that country chewing the leaves of the coca plant. The most deadly form is "crack" which is "free base" and can be smoked. Cocaine causes its effect by *blocking the reuptake of dopamine* into the pre-synaptic neuron (*Figure 4.10*), therefore prolonging the "high." Once again, cocaine is especially hazardous to adolescents since it interferes with the normal growth of dendrites in their rapidly developing brains.

- *Marijuana:* The active ingredient of marijuana is *tetrahydrocannibal* (THC), which attaches to *anandamide* (Sanskrit for "bliss") receptors in the brain to bring about its effects. Long-term use of marijuana affects the brain by producing deficits in cognition. The other deleterious effects of smoking marijuana are on the endocrine system, the immune system, and especially on the lungs.

- *Opiates:* Include morphine, heroin, Vicodin, Oxycontin and our own internal endorphins and enkephalins. Opiates exert their influence on the brain by inhibiting GABA neurotransmission. This in turn causes a cascade of dopamine to flow into the *nucleus accumbens*, bringing about the euphoria characteristic of opiates. It was estimated in 1998 that 87% of the 130,000 users in the past month were under the age of 26. In that same year it was estimated that 14% of all hospital emergency room admissions were for heroin abuse. In 1999, it was estimated that 2.3% of 8th graders, 2.3% of 10th graders and 2.0% of 12th graders had used heroin at some time in their lives.

- *Ecstasy*: The party drug is believed to deliver its euphoria by enhancing serotonin release from serotonergic nerve endings in the brain. This over-stimulation causes irreversible damage to these neurons. There is some controversy regarding the actual amount of nerve damage since some of the earlier research has come under considerable criticism. One of the major causes of Ecstasy-related emergency room admissions is dehydration, due to the combined high temperature found at "raves" and the stimulation of the drug.

- *Inhalants*: Including paint sprays, nitrites, aerosols, glue, etc., are especially damaging to the protective lining (myelin sheath) of the nerve fibers in the brain, including those in the hippocampus and the frontal cortex.

- *Hallucinogens*: Include the synthetic compound LSD as well as plant-derived compounds such as psilocybin (magic mushrooms) and mescaline (peyote cactus buttons). The Swiss chemist, Albert Hofmann, who synthesized LSD (lysergic acid diethylamide) accidentally ingested some of the compound and experienced the first recorded "acid high." LSD acts on the neurons in the *cerebral cortex* and the *locus ceruleus* to bring about alterations of the perception of external stimuli. Other mind-altering drugs are: phenylcyclidine (PCP), ketamine (known as a date rape drug) and even the common ingredient in cough syrup, dextromethorphan, has been abused. These three mind-altering drugs are, strictly speaking, not hallucinogens but are classified as dissociative drugs since their major effect is to produce feelings of detachment from reality.

- *Tobacco*: The major killer-drug in the U.S. today, causing 450,000 to 500,000 deaths per year in the U.S. alone and over 3 million worldwide. The active ingredient of tobacco is nicotine, which acts in several ways to enhance dopamine levels in the *nucleus*

accumbens. It directly stimulates dopamine release, enhances glutamate release and inhibits GABA release. There is another ingredient in cigarette smoke that inhibits the dopamine-destroying enzyme, monoamine oxidase. All of these effects increase the level of dopamine in the *nucleus accumbens*. Because of the action on *cholinergic* receptors, nicotine brings about a temporary improvement in cognition. However, more recent research has shown that nicotine retards mental functioning in the elderly. The most serious effect of smoking is not the nicotine, but is the result of the hazardous chemicals in the smoke. Smoking is the leading cause of lung and other cancers in the U.S. and is a major contributor to heart disease. In terms of health effects, tobacco is the most serious drug problem in the U.S. today.

Delinquency, Crime and Violence

5

Chapter five:
Delinquency, Crime and Violence

Chapter Outline

Characteristics of Juvenile Delinquency

- Motivations for juvenile crime
- Juvenile crime and recidivism
- Juvenile delinquency and criminal careers
- Public perception of juvenile crime
- Criminal processing
- Minority overrepresentation in statistics on crime
- Relationship of deviancy with risk factors

Adolescence and Deviant Subculture

- Mechanisms of deviant peer association
- Gang membership and deviant activity

Correlates of Juvenile Delinquency and Crime

- School discipline referrals and delinquency
- Deviant peers, substance abuse and juvenile delinquency
- Juvenile problem behavior and gender development
- Delinquency and self-concept

Theories of Adolescent Crime

- General strain theory
- Relative deprivation
- Social control theory
- Differential association theory
- Social learning theory

Developmental Aspects of Adolescent Crime

- Biological influences: neurotransmitters and hormones
- A bio/psycho/social synthesis

Transient Versus Stable Patterns of Delinquency and Crime

- Relationships between age and crime
- Bio/psycho/social factors in "life-course persistent" patterns of juvenile delinquency
- Bio/psycho/social factors in "adolescent limited" patterns of juvenile delinquency
- Alternative proposals for categorizing adolescent offenders
- Recidivism: the continuity of criminal behavior over time

Trends in Juvenile Violence

- Prevalence and types of juvenile violence
- Juvenile victims of crime
- Risks and predictors for adolescent violence
- Teens and firearms
- Characteristics of teen homicide
- Adolescents and mass murder: School shootings and other catastrophic episodes
- Personal and social responsibility for violent adolescent behavior

Implications for Treatment and Policy

Chapter Review

Chapter Objectives

- To describe the major features that characterize juvenile delinquency and crime, including motivations, recidivism, public perception of juvenile crime, criminal processing and minority over-representation;
- To examine psychosocial correlates of delinquency and crime;
- To explore theories that have been proposed to explain the phenomena of teen crime;
- To examine developmental aspects of adolescent crime;
- To differentiate transient vs. stable patterns of delinquency and crime;
- To examine violent juvenile offending; and
- To discuss the treatment implications of the multiple factors involved in adolescent crime and violence.

CHARACTERISTICS OF JUVENILE DELINQUENCY

It is "rarely creative, frequently self destructive, mostly mundane"

- Emler & Reicher, 1995 p. 2

Glicken and Sechrist (2003) define juvenile delinquency as a set of "minor violations against accepted societal norms, values and practices." Adolescent arrests tend to center around *property crimes and other less serious offenses*; less than .5% of all adolescents in the U.S. is arrested for violent offenses (Howell, 1995). Nevertheless, law violations are more frequently found among adolescents than among any other age group in society. While part of these statistics may be explained by adolescent participation in *status offenses* (such as runaway and truancy, which would not be considered crimes if performed by an older age group), there is still an elevated rate of participation for juveniles in both violent and property crimes beyond rates in the general population (Steinberg, 1999). A full *50% of all violent crimes* committed in the U.S. are attributed to individuals under age 24 (Federal Bureau of Investigation, 1993), most of which are gun related (Steinberg, 1999). The incidence of property crimes, such as vandalism, theft and arson, as well as violent crimes, such as physical and sexual assault and homicide, tends to increase at about age 13 (especially among males), then declines in young adulthood.

Data derived from other sources tend to provide different indications of the extent of juvenile delinquency. It is estimated that a full 2/3 of juvenile crimes are never reported to the police but are otherwise dealt with through reprimands and other such informal responses (Steinberg, 1999). Official arrest records provide only a partial view of the situation. Self-report data (with confidentiality assured) provide a very different picture (although probably flawed by other sources of inaccuracy, such as "wannabe" reporting). Such studies, however, depict juvenile involvement in crime as a somewhat normative type of behavior, with 60 to 80% of juveniles reporting some type of delinquent behavior in their past; some estimates go to 90% (Dacey & Kenny, 1997), and 50% of male juveniles admitting to some type of violent assault (Steinberg, 1999). Despite such high rates of experimentation with delinquent activity, most adolescents who do experiment with crime do so just once (or a very few times). Thus, only a small proportion of adolescents—estimated at about 10% (Steinberg,

1999); 5 to 8%—"life-course persistent" offenders (Moffitt, et al., 2002; Moffitt, 1993) are responsible for most of the criminal behavior in this age group (Steinberg, 1999; Dacey & Kenny, 1997). It is this group that receives major focus in this chapter.

The offense categories that make up the bulk of juvenile offending are:

- Less serious offenses, such as status offenses or offenses that primarily produce harm to the self, such as prostitution;

- Non-aggressive offenses, e.g., property crime aimed toward self-preservation on the streets, shoplifting and other forms of minor theft aimed at enhancing material possessions;

- Juvenile delinquency which may include the aforementioned two levels, but also includes crimes directly aimed at damage toward property or other persons, such as vandalism and physical assault; and

- Gang membership, which adds elements related to group crimes as well as drug trafficking, and serious violent crime, such as violent assault, rape and murder.

Motivations for juvenile crime

Lopez and Emmer (2000) examined the *motivations, emotions and cognitions* that drive adolescent male offenders to commit their crimes. Several delinquent crime contexts emerged. Examining adolescent offenders' perspectives on their own behavior, Lopez and Emmer (2000) identified distinct trends in adolescent definition, interpretation and justification for their delinquent conduct. Interviews conducted with adolescent males (aged 14 to 20 years) involved in criminal conduct revealed the following six crime contexts:

- Emotion-driven violent assault;

- Belief-driven violent assault;

- Emotion driven/property theft;

- Reward driven/property theft;

- Reward driven/drug dealing; and

- Mixed-motive mixed-crime contexts

Juvenile crime and recidivism

Juvenile offenders are of particular concern because their tendency to reoffend generally arises *sooner after release* than for adults (Glicken & Sechest, 2003). Youthful offenders also present with *greater likelihood of multiple problems,* including: emotional, interpersonal, medical, psychiatric and substance abuse problems (Huizinga & Jakob-Chien, 1998; Altschuler & Armstrong, 1991). These types of problems are found disproportionately among incarcerated juvenile offenders.

Juvenile delinquency and criminal careers

The classification of behaviors known as "juvenile delinquency" usually terminates by age 18 for most adolescents (Farrington, 1996). Juvenile offending that continues into the mid-20s, however, may rest on a general antisocial tendency with biological predispositions, generally initiated and maintained through high-payoff immediate rewards and a social learning process that leads to impaired decision making and criminogenic cognitive styles (Farrington, 1996). The *adolescence-limited* versus *life-course-persistent* patterns of antisocial behavior apply to delinquency and criminal conduct as well as more general problem behaviors (Kjelsberg, 1999).

Once an adolescent's career in crime is initiated, individual rates of conviction are found to be relatively constant over time (Barnett, Blumstein, & Farrington, 1996). This continuity of delinquent behavior over time may be a function of *certain catalysts,* which serve to energize these behaviors that otherwise might dwindle with time (Loeber, 1996). Hyperactivity, delinquent peer affiliations and enmeshment in the deviant subculture, chronically hostile home environments, and persistent failure at more normative mainstream endeavors may each serve a catalytic function.

Greenberg (1996) uses the construct of "criminal career" because for some individuals, crime becomes a "sequence of time-ordered occupational positions," with initiation, evolution, rewards and eventual cessation that may parallel phases in the development of a more conventional occupation. The onset of criminal conduct, changes in the specific types and/or seriousness of the crimes that are committed, and the status and prestige advantages afforded by criminal and (especially) aggressive behavior may mimic involvement in activities that most people associate with the world of work (Greenberg, 1996). Research concerning how criminal conduct may be commenced and maintained, terminated or escalated, suggests that efforts to prevent and treat both delinquency and youthful offending should be introduced as *early in*

childhood as possible (Loeber & Farrington, 1998; Farrington, 1996; Wilson, 1998).

Public perception of juvenile crime

Juvenile crime alarms citizens and social service personnel alike. High levels of fear (Flanagan & Longmire, 1996) have been generated by the dire predictions regarding the juvenile "superpredators" that stalk our neighborhoods. This relatively recent social construct "superpredator" (Bennett, DiIulio, & Walters, 1996) depicts a band of *"brutally remorseless"* juveniles, preying on their neighborhoods with vicious violence, sexual assault, gangs and lethal poisons (drugs and guns). But there is an enormous gap between this media hyperbole about "superpredators" and the reality of juvenile problem behavior and criminal involvement. In contrast to the above depiction, adolescent antisocial behavior is generally *affective and impulsive,* and frequently stems from deep areas of unresolved emotion (anger, hostility, sadness, and insecurity)—not *predatory or instrumental,* as depicted above. Preditory behaviors are more characteristic of adult crime (Fox & Levin, 2001). Most importantly, the difficult emotions of antisocial adolescents sit upon bedrock of *maladaptive cognitions,* which stem from early exposure to antisocial families, violent neighborhoods and deviant peers. Conduct-disordered youth have often borne the effects of victimization at home and on the streets. The vast majority of adolescents do not engage in any type of behavior that would be (seriously) labeled as antisocial or criminal.

Criminal processing

The rate of juvenile arrest stands at about 5% (ages 10 to 17) for any crime, i.e., 1 in 20 juveniles is arrested at some time during their childhood; and of those, only 9% are arrested for violent crime. *The majority of criminal offenders today are adolescents* (Moffitt et al., 2002); thus teenagers are responsible for a large component of the total crime in American society. This observation has generated considerable concern, as growth in the number of children (under age five) continues to accelerate (U.S. Dept of Commerce, 1995). Analysis of age trends in California projected a potential growth spurt in the adolescent age group to 15% of the population by 2010.

Minority overrepresentation in statistics on crime

Over the next several decades, growth in the number of youth is projected to be high among minority youth in the juvenile justice system (Glicken & Sechrest, 2003). An important segment of those who are overrepresented are the poor. In 1970, the most likely person to be found under the poverty line was an elder. Since then, a major shift in the structure of society has made this person more likely to be a child (Regoli & Hewitt, 1994). Disproportionate among the poor, as well as in criminal justice statistics, are minority subcultures; many are adolescents of African American, Hispanic American, Native American and Asian American descent. *Table 5.1* shows a racial comparison in projected age percentages of youth who will be under the age of 18 in the year 2010.

This spurt in the number of children reflects what is being called the "baby boomerang," i.e., offspring of the "baby boomers." The net effect will be to bring the number of children under age ten to 39 million children in 2010.

In analyzing the disproportionate representation of ethnic minorities in our country's courts and criminal justice system, it is important to consider that correlation does not imply causation. Although minorities may represent a higher percentage of violent perpetrators than population demographics would predict, this correlation is the result of a huge array of social and personal circumstances that *are associated with race, not the effect of race itself* (Fox & Levin, 2001).

When considering research on the incidence of problem behavior among adolescents from cultural minorities, it is important to consider the tendency for minority individuals to be disproportionately arrested (versus reprimanded) and sentenced more harshly than are other juveniles who commit similar offenses (Feld, 1997). African American adolescents are arrested for minor offenses about seven times more often than are European American adolescents engaging in the same crimes, and are more than twice as likely to be committed into juvenile correctional facilities than are European American youth who have engaged in the same level of criminal activity (Steinberg, 1999). These social consequences render a situation "so that official statistics may artificially inflate the proportion of crimes committed by poor,

minority youth" (Steinberg, 1999, p. 415). Indeed, self-report data across a wide range of American subcultures reveal that ethnic differences in rates of delinquent behavior as well as serious crime are quite a bit smaller than generally reported (Steinberg, 1999). In fact, the major area in which differences in prevalence of crime involvement appears is across *socioeconomic class* (rather than ethnicity), and due to the disproportionate number of minority adolescents living in impoverished conditions, they are overrepresented in regularly reported statistics on crime (Steinberg, 1999). Thus, the disproportionate representation of racial and ethnic minority adolescents in official crime statistics may stem from at least two sources:

- Higher levels of arrest in these groups (rather than higher levels of delinquent participation); and

- Over-representation of racial and ethnic minority adolescents living under conditions of poverty and community breakdown (Steinberg, 1999; Cernkovich, Giordano, & Rudolph, 2000; Linsky, Bachman, & Straus, 1995).

Not all studies indicate imbalance in the representation of ethnic groups in the judicial system. A study of 2,251 Denver City and County court probation youth referred to the *Treatment Alternative to Street Crime* AOD evaluation services compared the ethnic representation of this group with the ethnic representation in that county's school district (Wanberg, 2004). The probation youth were referred for evaluation for possible AOD problems. *Table 5.2* shows that ethnic representation in the probation system is very similar to the ethnic distribution in the Denver public school system.

However, studies of committed juvenile offenders *do indicate* ethnic imbalance. For example, a study of 437 committed juvenile offenders from the City and County of Denver incarcerated at one of the major institutions for committed offenders indicated that 31.1, 13.3, and 50.1% were African American,

Table 5.1 Projected Percentage of Each Racial Population Who Will Be Under Age 18 in 2010	
European American	6.2%
African American	13.9%
Hispanic Latino	30.0%

Source: U.S. Dept of Commerce, 1995, reported in Glicken & Sechrist, 2003

Table 5.2 Ethnicity of Juveniles in Public Schools vs. Probation Referrals to AOD Treatment

Ethnic Group	Denver Probation TASC referrals	Denver Public Schools Fall 1997	Denver Public Schools Fall 2000
African American	21.2	20.9	20.3
European American	19.9	23.4	22.0
Hispanic American	53.7	51.1	53.1
Other Groupings	25.2	4.6	4.6

European American and Hispanic American, respectively (1994-1996). When comparing this breakdown to the Denver Public Schools representation, African Americans are over-represented and European Americans under-represented. A study of a much smaller sample from the same institution representing referrals from Denver City and County indicated 25.0, 17.2 and 53.1% were African American, European American and Hispanic American, respectively.

Thus, at the probation end of a system, ethnicity is representative; at the other end of the system representing more severe offenders, representation is not congruent with the population at large, at least when using ethnic groupings in the school system.

Relationship of deviancy with risk factors

Using the Adolescent Self-Assessment Profile (ASAP: Wanberg, 1991, 1998) and several large samples of AOD clinical referrals and juvenile offenders, Wanberg (2000) found substantial correlations between deviancy and other salient risk factor scales. The most robust and hardy correlations were found between the Deviancy and AOD Disruption Scales which ranged from .52 to .63; with the Family Disruption Scale, the correlations ranged from .35 to .40; with School Adjustment, .35 to .40; with Psychological Symptoms, .41 to .44; and with peer Influence, .40 to .45. These correlations indicate that the interactions between deviancy and criminal conduct and the other major risk factors in adolescnce is very significant and substantial.

ADOLESCENCE AND DEVIANT SUBCULTURE

Mechanisms of deviant peer association

Most theories designed to explain the effects of deviant peer associations during adolescence take a *social learning perspective*. Sutherland (1947), for example, proposed that criminal skills are learned through association with peers, family and friends who've engaged in such behavior. In this view, criminal skills are acquired and antisocial peers, family and friends provide productive avenues for "training."

Crucial to this mechanism is the development of positive expectations about the aftermath of antisocial and criminal behavior. Teens observe that antisocial/criminal behaviors carried out by others around them can generate positive consequences—shoplifting, involvement with drugs and alcohol have their own "rewards." Observing that theft, substance use and even violence *may bring positive outcomes* to their users (material possessions, avenues of recreation, power) may lead an adolescent to expect similar outcomes for him- or herself. They may find that they receive more attention and more respect from others, when they "act out." This proposal is known as *differential association theory* (Sutherland, 1947).

More recently, Akers (2000) refined the above into *differential reinforcement theory*. This model proposes that reinforcement contingencies are the crucial aspect in the acquisition of criminal behavior. Mere association with antisocial peers is, in and of itself, not enough to bring about the widespread changes in behavior that we see in severe juvenile problem behavior. Rather, an interaction between observation and imitation, rewards for delinquent compliance (and punishments for "holding out"), and antisocial attitude development is necessary to bring about such a transition (Akers, 2000). All of these factors act in concert to produce a learning environment that is conducive to adolescent identification with the deviant subculture.

Some teens adopt a *negative identity*, choosing their delinquent peers as a reference group by which to define themselves, as well as guide their choice of attitudes and behavior. Anderson (1999) describes the *"code of the street"* as a "set of informal rules governing interpersonal public behavior, including violence. The rules prescribe both a *proper comportment and a proper way to respond if challenged"* (p. 33). Fagan and Wilkinson (1998) have indicated that exposure to successful violent exchanges in this context may induce internalization of the street code as a defensive posture. In this "subculture of violence," individuals may reward others for their aggressive/antisocial behavior and punish acts of kindness. Taunts and dares produce many aggressive and antisocial acts, which may be used to express defiance against the "system," camaraderie with the peer group, or just to "save face." Fox and Levin (2001) note the importance of receiving "respect" in this environment. "For inner-city youth the 'American Dream,' appearing absolutely unattainable, can be little more than a cruel nightmare."

Alienated from mainstream society, minority youngsters often obey the *code of the streets* in which *respect is the fundamental* and most vital commodity of daily life. In order to earn respect and then guard against losing it, ". . . a youngster must comport himself at all times in a manner showing that he's ready and willing to be violent . . . (B)eing disrespected is a fate worse than being murdered" (p. 78). Thus antisocial, aggressive, and violent behaviors are used for purposes of *self-image protection*. This type of self-presentation (Anderson, 1999) may help the adolescent to establish identity, self-respect, and a sense of personal "honor" (Anderson, 1999; Bynum & Weiner, 2002). This atmosphere of fear, violence and respect is graphically depicted in Anderson's (1999) theory concerning the *code of the street*.

Greenberg (1996) examines the *contemporary social construction* of the adolescent to explain their disproportionate participation in criminal conduct within the U.S. and Europe. He asserts that increases in juvenile crime can be explained by examining radical shifts in the position of adolescents in industrial societies during the twentieth century. Greenberg cites several factors that may be triggered in response to the relatively role-less situation of adolescents today, e.g.,

increasing anomie due to exclusion from the job market and "masculine status anxiety."

Fox and Levin (2001) explain the general effects of *group processes* on children and adolescents, which compel them to behave differently, and in some cases more viciously, than they would on their own (without peer influences). Group leaders (especially gang leaders) may provide strong pressure through a variety of means for others to engage in antisocial behavior along with them.

A group leader may feel good that others are willing to follow his lead even into areas of behavior that are cruel and vicious. At the same time, the followers can feel good about the praise they receive from the leader (and other group members) in joining along. In group settings, so-called mob psychology can sweep participants into committing even horrible crimes that no one in the group really wants to do. In situations of a "shared misunderstanding," each group member wrongfully believes that everyone else but him actually desires to commit an offense. Concerned about their reputation among friends, they all participate (Fox & Levin, 2001, p. 78).

Finally, assimilation into such a delinquent peer group deprives the adolescent of opportunities for exposure to non-offending individuals. This *isolates them* from more conventional avenues for attaining what they want and need (Sutherland, 1947). Delinquent peer groups often stereotype the rest of their (law-abiding) age cohort as "clueless" and naíve. This further isolates them from contact with more conventional norms for behavior (Akers, 2000). Thus, social learning explanations of adolescent problem behavior offer five very powerful mechanisms whereby deviant peers influence their friends and acquaintances:

- Association and consequent imitation;

- Punishment and reward;

- Attitude formation and maintenance;

- Development of self-concept (Glicken & Sechrist, 2003)

- Isolation from more adaptive, constructive skills and role models

Differentiating pro-social and antisocial patterns:

Fox and Levin (2001) summarize the many factors that may separate some adolescents from more conventional (prosocial) modes of behavior as follows:

- Behavioral interference and frustration;

- Relative deprivation and economic need;

- Minimal levels of social bonding to conventional individuals, attitudes and institutions,

- Repeated head trauma;

- Various types of personality disorder (e.g., a lack of moral restraint and empathy);

- Poor skills for everyday social functioning; or

- Growing up in a subculture of violence further isolates these adolescents from prosocial alternatives and styles of responding.

Gang membership and deviant identity

In an historic analysis of social structure and criminal behavior (Merton, 1957), delinquency and gang involvement were conceptualized as "innovative" behaviors, designed to *bridge the disparity* between American values of achievement and success and the deprivations of poverty. This notion assumes that individuals who become involved in these types of behavior accept the cultural value placed on material acquisition but find themselves without the means to achieve it. In the absence of perceived legal channels, they may resort to illegal strategies such as gang involvement and criminal conduct as a means to attain wealth. In impoverished environments that offer little

institutional support for the development of economic opportunity, this innovative strategy may become street crime (including property offense and violence), gang activity, and drug trafficking (Merton, 1957). Fox and Levin (2001) enumerate various functions that may be served by gangs:

- Self protection;

- Alternative family;

- Sense of belonging, especially to something "important," bigger than themselves;

- Sources of praise and excitement;

- Camaraderie (especially when participating in acts with multiple perpetrators); and

- Financial rewards (through criminal conduct).

In addition, participation in gangs may serve as a form of apprenticeship to the world of drugs, as well as providing an "alternative socializing mechanism" (Fox & Levin, 2001).

A longitudinal study of 808 Seattle students by the *Seattle Social Development Project* (SSDP) shows a strong correlation beween delinquency and gang membership (OJJDP, 2004). As shown in *Figure 5.1*, youth between the ages of 13 and 18 who belonged to a gang were much more likely to be involved in delinquent behaviors; drug selling (9% for non-gang youth and

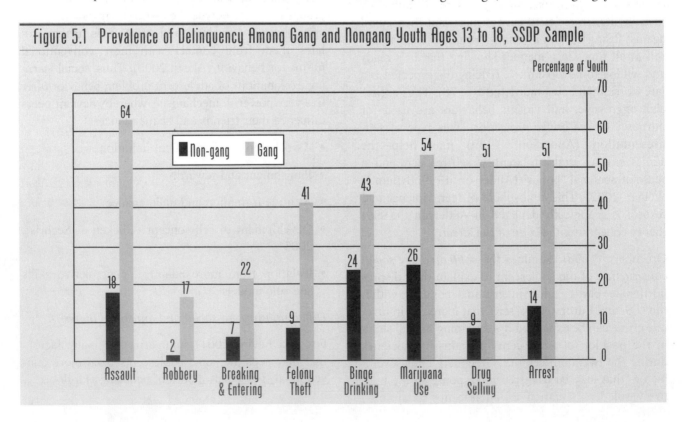

Figure 5.1   Prevalence of Delinquency Among Gang and Nongang Youth Ages 13 to 18, SSDP Sample

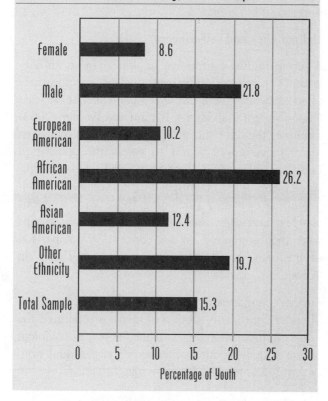

Figure 5.2 Percentage of Youth Ages 13 to 18 Who Joined a Gang, SSDP Sample

Category	Percentage
Female	8.6
Male	21.8
European American	10.2
African American	26.2
Asian American	12.4
Other Ethnicity	19.7
Total Sample	15.3

Percentage of Youth

51% for gang members) and assault (18% for non-gang members and 64% for gang members) were the most disparate categories.

As shown in *Figure 5.4*, gang membership is culturally diverse; however, this Seattle study showed the rate to be highest among African American youth, with 26.2% of African Americans reporting having joined a gang (OJJDP, 2004). The study also showed that the risk of joining a gang peaks at the age of 15, when most students are transitioning to high school.

CORRELATES OF JUVENILE DELINQUENCY AND CRIME

School discipline referrals and delinquency

School discipline referrals are useful in identifying teens who are at risk for delinquency. Sprague et al., (2001) found a positive relationship between school behaviors (measured by number of school discipline referrals and teacher nominations) and later referrals to juvenile authorities for illegal activities. Loeber and Farrington (1998) showed an association between frequent school discipline referrals and juvenile offending in community settings. Sugai, Sprague, Horner, and Walker (2000) found that a small

minority of elementary school students (6-9%) accounted for more than 50% of school discipline referrals and a sizeable majority (near all) of the serious behaviors recorded in the school setting (fighting, assault, weapons violations, property destruction). Early discipline problems such as these are strongly correlated with later adjustment problems and problem behaviors in adolescence (Tobin, Sagai, & Colvin, 2002; Walker, Colvin, & Ramsey, 1995).

Sprague et al. (2001) caution that school discipline referrals alone cannot identify specific individuals who will actually perpetuate criminal offenses at a later date. The development of major adjustment problems among youth is a complex process (Greenberg, Domitrovich, & Bumbarger, 1999); violent and antisocial behaviors are multiply determined (Loeber & Farrington, 1998). Rather, Sprague and colleagues (2001) propose assessment using a multiple gating approach, which combines information from several distinct sources in order to identify high risk. Four levels of assessment were used:

- Teacher nominations and referrals regarding students' antisocial behavior;

- Teacher ratings of student study skills, social skills as well as aggressiveness (threatening behaviors, bullying, possession of weapons), disruption/opposition-defiance, truancy, vandalism, etc.;

- School archival records;

- Public safety/criminal corrections records, e.g., police contacts, arrests, offenses, etc.

Sprague et al. (2001) found that those students who were nominated by their teachers as being at risk for adjustment problems shared both a number of discipline problems and negative scores on standardized behavioral assessments. More than 1/3 could be characterized as "early starters," i.e., they experienced their first contact with law enforcement *before the age of twelve*. Further investigation into the relationship between school and community-based problem behaviors identifies 3 subsets of students: 1) students who offend in the community but not at school; 2) students who experience frequent trouble at school but not in the broader community; and 3) students who offend in both school and community settings (Sprague et al., 2001).

Teachers can serve as useful and reliable sources of information in identifying youth at risk for adjustment problems while they are in school and in the larger community (Loeber et al., 2000). Sprague et al. (2001) advise that adding such school-derived information to other sources regarding child and adolescent adjustment will enhance detection of problem behaviors early in their trajectory. At present, however, few regions are utilizing such combined sources of information.

Deviant peers, substance abuse and juvenile delinquency

Fergusson and Horwood (1996) found an association between childhood conduct problems and adolescent delinquency. A 21-year longitudinal study of adolescents aged 14 to 21 years (that assessed psychosocial development, health and antisocial behavior) found that *deviant peer association* was significantly correlated with nicotine dependence, alcohol abuse, cannabis abuse, property crime, and violent crime (Fergusson, Swain-Campbell, & Horwood, 2002). A 3-year longitudinal study examined the relevance of two social process explanations to explain the correlations between deviant peer affiliation, drug use and delinquent behavior, combining the social control and differential association perspectives in their analysis (Erickson, Crosnoe, & Dornbusch, 2000). They found that decreased involvement in adolescent substance use and crime was explained by:

- Reduced affiliation with deviant peers (differential association), and by

- Reduced vulnerability to negative peer impact (social control).

Greater effect of peer deviance was found for friends' *substance use* than for friends' delinquency, and the effect of deviant peers was stronger among males compared to females (Erickson, Crosnoe, & Dornbusch, 2000). In the case of early onset of criminal conduct, *conviction* is *strongly correlated* with offending later in adolescence, although future convictions for violent offenses are more difficult to predict (Elander, Simonoff, Pickles, Holmshaw, & Rutter, 2000).

Juvenile problem behavior and gender development

Female juvenile offenders constitute the *largest growing segment* of the juvenile population (Acoca, 1998). In the past decade, the increase in girls' arrests for almost every type of offense is greater than the rate of increase of boys' arrests (Snyder, 1997). This includes arrests for violent crime, where research has long revealed far lower rates among females than males. Snyder (1997) reports that 723,000 girls younger than age 18 were arrested in 1996 alone. Thirty-one per-

cent of juvenile offenders are female. The phenomenon of delinquent girlhood as well as differences in developmental pathways to male and female offending is explored in *Chapter 6*.

Delinquency and self-concept

A recent finding (surprising to some) is that an adolescent's participation in the deviant subculture is often associated with *enhanced self-concept*, at least among violent individuals. Bynum and Weiner (2002) examined the self-concepts of urban African American males (aged 13-19 years) to assess the correlation between *violent delinquency* and *self-concept*. Adolescents were classified into *non-offenders, non-assaultive offenders* (including those with weapons charges) and *assaultive offenders*. The three groups were then compared on self-concept. A comparison of the mean total self-concept scores is shown in *Table 5.3*.

Further comparisons examined self-concept across offender types. This section of analysis separated the non-assaultive offending category above into violent (those with weapons possessions charges) and non-violent types. Results are shown in *Table 5.4*.

The common theme in the above research is that *assaultive offenders* score *statistically higher* on mean self-concept than *non-assaultive offenders*, and on a par with (or perhaps higher than) the non-offending group. Self-concept was measured using a combination of the *Adolescent Life Survey* (Bynum & Weiner, 2002) and the *Tennessee Self-concept Scale* (Fitts & Warren, 1996). These results make sense in the context of Anderson's (1999) *code of the streets* theory.

It seems clear that, at least within the case of violent offending, formation of a violent/delinquent self-concept may insulate an adolescent from negative self-examination. Perhaps violent delinquents grow so comfortable with this identity, that it is regarded as a normative and expected aspect of social interaction. Successful use of violent behavior provides reinforcement of these acts by delinquent peers and sometimes family. Violence becomes a "fixed strategy, completely consistent and entrenched within the youth's total personality. His view of himself as a violent person is internalized and is highly regarded as a way of effectively dealing with the outside world." (Bynum & Weiner, 2002, p. 483). Bynum & Weiner (2002) conclude: "violent assaultive delinquent youth . . . appear to be comfortable with their identity as assaultively violent individuals (p. 479).

Table 5.3 Comparison of Mean Self-Concept Score Across Offense Category

Non-offenders	Non-assaultive offenders	Assaultive offenders
50.6	45.9	53.2

Note: No statistically significant differences were found between assaultive offenders and non-offenders
Source: Bynum & Weiner, 2002

Table 5.4 Mean Total Self-Concept Scores Among Violent Youth

Non-assaultive violent offenders	Assaultive violent offenders
(weapons possessions charges only)	(physical assault charges)
44.1	53.2

Source: Bynum & Weiner, 2002

This collective construction of reality by adolescents and their peers provides the socializing environment for much of their development. Given the context that these constructions create and the troubled lives that many have lived at home, for some adolescents, aggressive and delinquent behavior is the "best" means of insuring survival in a hostile world. Given the research on self-concept presented above, delinquent behavior appears to be "more than a front-stage performance . . . it appears to be a total reality for these youth (Bynum & Weiner, 2002, p. 484).

THEORIES OF ADOLESCENT CRIME

Various theories of crime and violence have been proposed in the literature (for a review, see Hawkins, 1996). This section focuses on some of the initiating and maintaining mechanisms operative in the criminal career of an adolescent. Consideration of these elements may lead to more effective assessment, treatment planning and service delivery. Our eclectic approach assumes that each of the following theories bears merit and can contribute to the development of an overall platform for successful intervention.

General strain theory:

Focuses on the general level of stress and strain in an adolescent's life, identifying the origins of pent-up resentment and anger, as well as fears of violence within the community and family (Agnew, 1992;

1997). Disappointments in an adolescent's life, as well as feelings of relative deprivation and depression are factored in the etiology of criminal and aggressive behavior (Fox & Levin, 2001). This model seeks to identify destructive social relationships and conditions within the teen's life (Fox & Levin, 2001) that may be sources of child abuse, peer rejection, and school failure, as well as other aversive stimuli that may trigger an aggressive response. Additional elements of strain are the absence or disruption of conventional ties that may keep an adolescent bonded to normative behavior. These include death of a loved one, parental divorce, or continuous moving between homes and schools that may interfere with social ties.

In support of *General Strain* theory, many studies have linked the emergence of childhood aggression to early child abuse and neglect (Reiss & Rith, 1993; Widom, 1999; McCord, 1999; Heide, 1999). Busch (2001) compared two groups of adolescents, matched for age, race, sex and socioeconomics, who had engaged in criminal behavior—one group had perpetrated homicide while the other engaged in only non-violent crimes. Busch found that the violent perpetrators were more likely to come from violent families and to have learning disabilities and serious academic problems. Additional factors in the lives of (especially violent) juvenile offenders may be seen to contribute to an overall strain. Violent youngsters are more likely to suffer severe emotional, physical and sexual abuse, come from impoverished conditions, experience poor medical care and nutrition (including prenatally) and have severe substance abuse issues (Heide, 1999; Fox & Levin, 2001).

Relative deprivation:

Explains crime and violent behavior on the basis of adolescents' discernment of inequality between their own outcomes and those of others. This sense of relative deprivation *vis-a-vis* peers and other associations (such as media idols) rests upon the adolescent's perception that these other people *obtain more rewards, have more money, receive better educational opportunities and therefore receive better grades (etc.), because of "who they are" or "who they know"* (Fox & Levin, 2001). This type of belief system (which portrays others as favored and self as denied) may turn the adolescent to a life of crime due to a perceived insurmountable barrier between them and the achievement of their goals through legal means. This gulf between achievement, hopes and aims may underlie some of the increased risk among those adolescents living in poverty.

Social control theory:

Focuses on the *lack of conventional social bonds* that may underlie most adolescents' adherence to social norms and traditions (Fox & Levin, 2001). In the absence of such social bonds, or the presence of such ties to antisocial individuals, adolescents may fail to develop either external or internal controls on their behavior, which may keep them in sync with the ethics of mainstream culture. *Social Control* theory therefore asserts that it is *social connection* to more conservative and conforming individuals that may immunize most adolescents from engaging in crime or aggression. Those adolescents who lack these conventional social bonds, failing to receive such inoculation, become vulnerable to influences of the deviant subculture (Fox & Levin, 2001).

Differential association theory:

Social Control theory (as previously discussed) is closely allied with *Differential Association* theory (Sutherland, 1947), which proposes that criminal behavior is derived through *associations with significant others* who engage in crime. Friends and family with whom the adolescent is associated may provide a *training ground* wherein the adolescent learns thoughts, emotional reactions and behaviors associated with the criminal life. Experimentation with petty crime such as shoplifting may soon reinforce these beliefs, providing them with desired resources. "Hanging out" and identifying with those who possess

and/or market drugs may follow, introducing the adolescent to more dangerous climates and behaviors, such as the drug culture, association with guns (Heide, 1999) and the use of violence. Becoming further entrenched into this deviant subculture separates the adolescent from more conventional individuals who display more normative kinds of behavior, thus insulating them from social controls on aggression and criminality. These youth may encounter *hostile rejection* from conventional peers who reject this criminal lifestyle and its associated ideology. Street values may begin to dominate the adolescent's consciousness, as he or she adopts the attitudes and responses of criminal associates (Fox & Levin, 2001; Sutherland, 1947).

Observations in support of this hypothesis stem from research that compares adolescents who have engaged in serious (violent) vs. relatively non-serious delinquency. These studies reveal that the violent youngsters are more likely to have experienced low levels of parental supervision, high levels of exposure to violent media, separation from conventional peers and intense ties to delinquent peers, and to have participated in gang activities (Fox & Levin, 2001). Such context-dependent factors that may spur an adolescent's decisions toward criminal conduct are then interpreted through the particular filters of the adolescent subculture (Fagan, 2000), which may leave adolescents feeling that they have little to lose by engaging in antisocial aggressive behavior (Heide, 1999).

Social learning theory:

Focuses on the profound influence of *social norms* on the propensity toward criminality and aggression. (Bandura, Fox, & Levin, 2001). Cross-cultural literature provides empirical support for this approach. Both the incidence and specific form of violence vary enormously from culture to culture, with some (especially traditional - indigenous) cultures displaying little or no violence at all (Fox & Levin, 2001). Members of the *Santa Marta* culture, for example, resolve conflicts by each party selecting a stick to bang against a rock or tree until it breaks. The first party's stick to break is designated the winner. Members of the *Inuit of Alaska* and Canada resolve contests by making up malicious songs about their competitors. Cultures such as the *Kwakiuti Indians* exhibit a tradition known as "potlatch." Material possessions are believed to convey vulnerability to one's enemies. In the attempt to conquer members of an enemy society, therefore, rather than use physical force, individuals in this culture give away or destroy their own material possessions in order to promote spiritual protection.(Boring, 1939; Fox & Levin, 2001). Similar creative responses to conflict are found among the *Arapesh* of New Guinea, the *pygmies* of the Ituri rainforest, the *Lepchas* of Sikkim, and the *Australian Aborigines*. Among individuals from these cultures, we find few expressions of anger or rage and a sparse military vocabulary. Further, these are cultures where murder is nearly unknown. Such wide cultural variation would not be expected if indeed the propensity toward violence were an inborn trait of human nature.

Other support for the impact of social influence on criminality and aggression is found in statistics on violence. In contrast, California, Texas, Alaska, and New York exhibit a disproportionately high percentage of mass murders. In the south, murders are more likely to stem from arguments between persons who know each other well, especially when the *honor or reputation* of one is threatened by another. More than in other areas of the country, it is considered normative and appropriate in the South to use what is perceived as defensive violence in such instances (Wolfgang & Ferracuti, 1967). Further analysis reveals that men are generally more violent than women; young people tend to be more violent than elders; and the murder rate in this country has been observed to vary over time and across generations (Fox & Levin, 2001).

These cultural observations are significant to the task of understanding adolescent criminality and violence for several reasons. Widespread cultural variation in conflict resolution strategies support the importance of *social learning and social norms* in the formation and development of aggressive behavior (as previously emphasized in *Differential Association, Social Control and General Strain* theories). These observations may be important in rehabilitation, as teens who are involved in crime and violence are influenced profoundly by the social norms of the deviant subculture, which tell them that such behavior is innate, inevitable and the "only way" to resolve dilemmas within their peer communities. Exposure to the wide range of behaviors utilized within traditional and contemporary culture to solve conflict, combined with education to build respect for the longevity and endurance of these cultures, may expand the adolescent's *perception of options* for their own behavior.

The finding that the members of some societies apparently express no violent behavior at all may be the most persuasive argument that aggression is largely learned. In the absence of evidence that these and other peaceful groups are genetically abnormal or that

they differ in some other relevant biological way, it becomes difficult to accept the proposition that aggression is a necessary and inevitable element of our biological makeup. Unless violence is universal, it is difficult to argue that it is instinctual (Fox & Levin, p. 24).

Social Learning theory takes the position that most forms of aggression require the use of specific skills and techniques that must be *acquired from the environment* and practiced in perfecting their use. Simply stated, children are quick to learn that the use of aggression "works," by observing parental and peer behavior, images in the media, and direct responses to their own use of aggression. Processes of operant conditioning as well as complex modeling influences are clearly involved. Many researchers (e.g., Eron, Huesmann, & Zelli, 1991; Pepler & Rubin, 1991) have identified social influence factors that encourage and support the development of criminality and violence. For example, *significant others* as well as *images from the mass media* can provide powerful role models for aggressive behavior. A vast research literature on the effects of televised violence supports this supposition (Fox & Levin, 2001). Such role models may influence the development of even the most serious acts of violence. For example, homicide rates in the U.S. tend to rise by approximately 13% in the immediate aftermath of televised prizefights, with larger increases following more heavily publicized events (Phillips, 1983). These observations, combined with principles of differential association (Sutherland, 1947) and social control (Fox & Levin, 2001) support the contention that the different role models found in an adolescent's personally chosen reference group (whether deviant or conventional) may have a profound influence on the likelihood of any particular adolescent engaging in crime, even serious acts of criminal violence.

Differential Reinforcement theory, an important component of social learning theory, places key focus on the *environmental contingencies* that determine whether aggressive behavior is rewarded or punished. The peer group is important in influencing these environmental consequences - reinforcing those behaviors that are consistent with the group's worldview. Members from the subculture of violence are frequently found to reinforce aggression with status and other types of rewards, and may even punish (with intimidation and/or outright violence) law-abiding response tendencies (Akers, 2000). In support of these processes of social learning, many studies have linked parental response to the aggressive behavior of their children, especially sons, to the development of later aggressive behavior (Reiss & Rith, 1993; Widom, 1999; McCord, 1999).

In synthesizing the various theories of criminality and violence presented above, it becomes clear that much criminal and aggressive behavior may stem from distinct psychological mechanisms involved in deviant peer socialization. *Table 5.5* summarizes social influences on the development of adolescent crime and violence.

DEVELOPMENTAL ASPECTS OF ADOLESCENT CRIME

A variety of developmental theories have been used to explain continuity of criminal conduct from childhood and adolescence into adulthood, as well as its frequent desistance in the early adult years. These theories include analysis of transitions in the biological, cognitive and moral realms, as well as personality factors and the importance of changing social roles (Adams, 1997).

Biological influences: neurotransmitters and hormones

There is mounting evidence that, in some instances, a propensity toward the use of violence may involve biological factors (Elliott, 2000). The ability to *use and restrain* aggressive behavior involves a complex association of neural pathways that connect the cerebral cortex to the midbrain and limbic system, which serve as the brain's "alarm system" (Niehoff, 1999, Elliott, 2000). Neurotransmitters serve to activate these brain structures in the regulation of aggression; hence *any brain damage* that occurs within these neural networks can produce impulsive behavior (Elliott, 2000). Most notably, variation in levels of the neurotransmitter *serotonin* is associated with shifts in levels of

aggressive behavior. Research into the efficacy of pharmaceutical intervention (e.g., Prozac) is rapidly underway (Fox & Levin, 2001), although medication is generally advised for use *alongside* more conventional therapeutic interventions (not as a substitute for them) (Niehoff, 1999).

Research has also revealed that, in some cases, the behavior of severely aggressive boys may be influenced by *lower than normal* levels of the stress hormone, *cortisol* (McBurnett, Lahey, Rathouz, & Loeber, 2000). Cortisol has been implicated in normal reactions to threatening situations and appears to play a role in regulating the fear response (Niehoff, 1999). A longitudinal study of seriously aggressive, antisocial males, who had variously engaged in violent assault, theft, weapons possession and rape, revealed lower than normal levels of cortisol in saliva readings (McBurnett et al., 2000), perhaps suggesting that disruption in normal levels of fear may underlie the brazenness that accompanies the use of violence and criminal conduct (Fox & Levin, 2001).

Other researchers suggest that aggressive behavior may be associated with *high levels of testosterone*, though a direct one-to-one relationship between testosterone and aggression has been generally ruled out. Research has demonstrated the existence of a bi-directional feedback loop between hormones and behavior, with associations between higher levels of aggression among those with higher levels of testosterone, as well as increases in circulating levels of testosterone following aggressive activity. While the correlations found in this research may be suggestive, "there is little evidence yet of a strong effect of testosterone on the propensity to commit criminal violence" (Fox & Levin, 2001, p. 17).

Table 5.5 Summary of Social Influences on Development of Adolescent Crime and Violence

- Direct reinforcements for engaging in aggressive behavior

- Imitation through observation of others' criminal behavior and its consequences

- Development of expectancies for success or failure in the viewer of such behaviors

- Absence of more normative social control connections for curtailing the use of such behaviors

- Development of an ideology that may legitimate the use of crime and force, due to perceived inequities in the social environment which favor others and deny the self

- Learning a set of attitudes and values that comprise a generalized alternative worldview that may support and maintain criminality and violence

If the findings about testosterone, cortisol, or some other important hormone can be generalized, then at least some violent children - even those who grow up in a healthy, non-threatening family - may have a biological predisposition that makes them less likely to fear the possible consequences of their antisocial behavior and difficult to treat with counseling or therapy (Fox and Levin, 2001, p. 17).

Various other types of biological influences may be operating in the development of early onset aggressiveness, including possible genetic, hormonal, and/or neurological processes (Elliott, 2000), as well as pathological brain reactions that may be caused by substance use and abuse (Glicken & Sechrist, 2003).

A bio/psycho/social synthesis

As it is difficult to separate the interactions of these factors from other, more socially-generated processes, Fox and Levin (2001) advocate using a bio/psycho/social synthesis to understand the phenomena that may underlie criminal aggressiveness and homicidal behavior. Using a social interactionist approach, Reiss & Roth (1993) assert: "(r)esearch strongly suggests that violence arises from interactions among an individual's psychosocial development, their neurological and hormonal differences, and social processes." Similarly, Fagan (2000) argues that an adolescent's decision to engage in criminal behavior reflects a complex interaction between personality and other psychological factors, social cues, the behavior of significant others (including witnesses), the presence of weapons (Scott, 1999) and elements of social control operating in the social situation. Other researchers have also provided empirical support for interacting biological, psychological and environmental factors involved in the dynamics of adolescent aggression and other antisocial behavior (e.g., Steiner, Williams, Benton-Hardy, Kohler & Duxbury, 1997). It is important to keep in mind, therefore, that no one theory alone can explain, or predict, the phenomena of teen crime and violence—"Risk factors (identified in these theories) represent predispositions, not predestination" (Fox & Levin, 2001, p. 79).

TRANSIENT VERSUS STABLE PATTERNS OF DELINQUENCY AND CRIME

Two categories, "early-onset persistors" (life-course persistent - LCP) and "late-onset desisters" (adolescent limited—AL) have been used to describe involvement in juvenile crime and other forms of anti-social behavior. This bifurcated classification, also referred to as "early starters" vs. "late starters" combines both approximate age of onset and probable course of development (Moffitt, 1993; Patterson & Yoerger, 1993; 2002; Patterson, Reid & Dishion, 1992; Patterson, 1996). AL and LCP represent readily distinguishable clusters of personal characteristics and social correlates that suggest different underlying causes and patterns of problem behavior (Moffitt, et al., 2002; Rutter, 1997; Rutter, Giller & Hagell, 1998). It is notable that early- and late-onset adolescent substance abusers have also been identified (Sommers & Baskin, 1991). Understanding more about these etiologies may enhance service delivery by developing differentiated strategies for prevention, intervention and treatment designed for specific subgroups of juvenile offenders (Chung et al., 2002).

Evidence for the validity of this typological scheme of antisocial behavior can be found in similarities across various studies of adolescent problem behaviors:

- Approximately 5% of boys are labeled "very difficult to manage" by parents and caretakers before they enter school (McGee, Partridge, Williams, & Silva, 1991);

- Approximately 4 to 9% of boys are diagnosed with conduct disorder in the elementary school years (Costello, 1989);

- First arrest during childhood (pre-adolescence) occurs in the lives of 6% of boys;

- Convictions for violent crime occur in young men at a rate of approximately 3 to 6%;

- Using self-report data, approximately 4% of males report steady utilization of serious violence during adolescence; and

- When first arrest occurs between the ages of 7 to 11, there is a high probability of an elongated criminal career that lasts into adulthood; and conviction for a violent offense at this time predicts a later diagnosis of psychopathic antisocial personality disorder (Moffitt et al. 2002).

When considering the prevalence of antisocial personality disorder in the general population, there are approximately 4-5% of adult men with this diagnosis (Moffitt et al., 2002). "A substantial body of longitudinal research consistently points to a relatively small group of males who display high rates of antisocial behavior across time and in diverse situations." (Moffitt et al., 2002, p. 15).

Problem behaviors in youth who show early symptoms of antisocial behavior (before age 12, "early onset") generally *escalate* from childhood through adolescence into serious delinquency and criminal offense. Although few children display this pattern (Moffitt, 1993; Moffitt et al., 2002), *those who do commit more than half of all juvenile offenses* (Chung, et al., 2002). They are also at high risk for continuing into a lifetime of adult crime (Patterson, 1996; Moffit, 1997; Moffit et al., 2002).

Conversely, other youth (*late-onset desisters* - AL), do not begin to display antisocial characteristics until adolescence - after age 12 (Moffitt, 1993), hence the term: "*late starters*" (Patterson et al., 1992). Although very similar to *early-onset* individuals in the specific kinds and frequencies of delinquent activities during adolescence, these individuals often cease, or lessen, such activity during late adolescence or early adulthood (Moffitt, 1993). Some youth may persist in adjustment problems and minor levels of criminal activity (primarily property offenses) into adulthood (through age 26), perhaps due to prolonged adolescence in contemporary American society, or to consequences of previous criminal activity (Moffitt et al., 2002). Although property offenses may continue, adolescence-limited individuals generally do not continue into a lifetime of serious adult offending as do life-course persistent (LCP) individuals (Fergusson, Horwood, & Nagin, 2000; Patterson & Yoerger, 1997). For this reason, Moffitt et al. (2002) and others have referred to this category of antisocial behavior as "*adolescence-limited*" (AL). Fergusson, Lynskey, and Horwood (1996) found that *late-onset offenders* appeared to be intermediate in profile between *non-offenders* and *early-onset* groups.

Additional support for the distinction between LCP and AL patterns of antisocial behavior comes from a variety of sources. Significant correlations between LCP patterns of antisocial behavior and several biological, psychological and social factors are not found in the lives of AL offenders (Moffitt et al., 2002). Rutter and colleagues found that *early-onset* LCP offending is often correlated with *hyperactivity and attention deficits* not found among AL individuals, suggesting a genetic component in LCP not present in AL offending (Rutter, 1997; Rutter et al., 1998). Correspondingly, Silberg et al. (1996) indicate that *late-onset offending* is more closely correlated with *environmental and social factors* (Silberg et al., 1996). Other factors associated with LCP patterns of antisocial behavior include *neurological problems*

(which may underlie cognitive deficits); "*under-controlled" temperament; psychopathic personality traits; and the use of violence.* None of these elements is correlated with *late-onset* offending (Moffitt et al., 2002).

Furthermore, follow-up studies have revealed a *worsening in the severity* of antisocial behaviors, as well as increasing problems in mental health and overall social functioning in *early-onset* LCP offenders during young adulthood (age 26 years). These problems, combined with substance abuse, substance-related criminal conduct, violent crime and the use of violence against women and children, are all observed in early-onset offenders during early adulthood. In contrast, *late-onset* offending tends to become less severe with time (e.g., property offenses), or stop altogether in young adulthood, and while correlated with impulsivity, mental health problems and substance dependence, it is not associated with the breakdowns in general social functioning characteristic of the LCP trajectory (Moffitt, Caspi, Harrington, & Milne, 2002). These salient differences between LCP and AL patterns of adolescent delinquency provide empirical support for the usefulness of a bifurcated categorization.

Relationships between age and crime

Antisocial behavior (both situational and sporadic) is common among both male and female adolescents, while chronic and stable antisocial behavior which begins in childhood is quite rare (5-8%) and found mostly in males (Moffitt et al., 2002). Police records show that crime rates peak at age 17 and drop in young adulthood. As shown in *Figure 5.3*, this pattern represents rates of offending among the AL group, while the LCP group maintains fairly consistent levels of delinquent activity across age (Moffitt et al., 2002). The bulk of adolescent crime in the peak, therefore, is committed by the AL group; their delinquency starts after the LCP individuals and generally ceases, while LCP offending continues. Self-reports from adolescents placed in the AL category reveal that their actual rates of delinquent activity *far exceed* the official arrest statistics, so much so that participation in antisocial and delinquent activity can be labeled "normative" for this group at this age (Elliott, Ageton, Huizinga, Knowles, & Canter, 1983). As the majority of criminal offenders are adolescents (Moffitt et al, 2002), this accounts for a large component of total criminal activity.

With regard to the LCP trajectory, it is noted that relying on official records often neglects the lower end

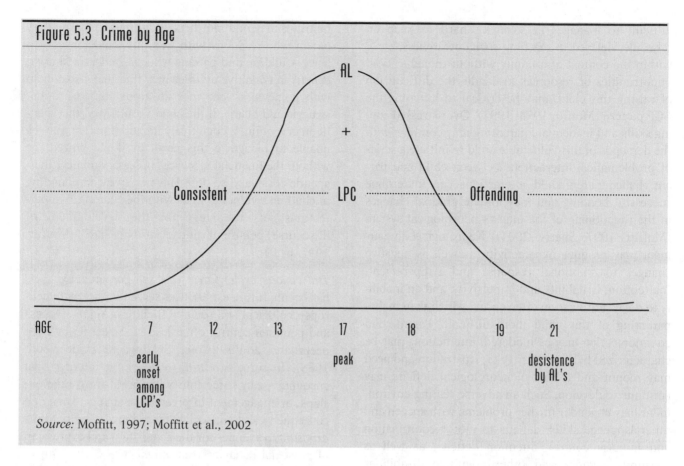

Figure 5.3 Crime by Age

Source: Moffitt, 1997; Moffitt et al., 2002

(earlier ages) of the age-crime curve (Moffitt et al., 2002). This has caused some inconsistency in the literature regarding what age actually constitutes "early-onset." As *age of first police arrest* is often used as the criterion for placement into these two categories, "early" is sometimes defined as mid-adolescence, whereas the onset of antisocial behavior (e.g., childhood conduct disorder) generally emerges earlier in the LCP group. Using reports from teachers and developmental psychologists, as well as official crime records, Moffitt et al. (2002) report that characteristics of antisocial behavior generally emerge by age 7 for LCP individuals, and escalate rapidly through age 17 and beyond. These individuals represent a small portion of the general population, yet account for the lion's share of crime that occurs overall, except during adolescence, when their crime is "masked" by the high incidence committed by the AL group.

Bio/psycho/social factors in "life-course-persistent" patterns of juvenile delinquency

Research on patterns of early child development validates the construct of "life-course-persistent" offending. Temperament in the first few years of life predicts convictions for violent assault later on (Henry, Moffitt, Caspi & Silva, 1994). Poor language skills, correlated with low self-control, hyperactivity, impulsivity and other symptoms of attention-deficit disorder are associated with early onset of aggressiveness and antisocial behavior in childhood (Moffitt, 1997). An interaction between a child's *cognitive abilities* and *family problems* predicts aggressiveness during adolescence (Moffitt, 1990). Cognitive deficits that stem from neuropsychological impairments are highly correlated with antisocial behavior (Moffitt, 1993). This latter association between neuropsychological impairment and cognitive deficits is very strong and manifests in two basic realms of cognitive function:

- *Verbal*: including abilities such as listening, reading, expressive speech and writing, memory and problem solving (Moffitt, 1993); and

- *Behavioral*: including inattention, impulsivity, aggression and poor judgment (Price, Daffner, Stowe & Mesulam, 1990).

These processes tend to be robust across socio-economic class, race, and academic achievement (Lynam, Moffitt & Stouthamer-Loeber, 1993).

Family Influences: It appears that a combination of factors must co-occur in order to create a pattern of "life-course-persistent" offending. An infant who is difficult to manage (i.e., colicky, hard to keep on schedule, delayed in reaching social awareness, etc.), within the context of a family without the education, opportunities or resources to handle the difficult job of raising this child, may be critical to initiating the LCP pattern (Moffitt, 1994, 1997). Over-stressed coping skills and inadequate parenting may combine with the demands of this vulnerable child to initiate a series of problematical interactions between child and parent. Failed parent-child interactions can undermine successful bonding and may initiate gradual changes in the functioning of the infant's neurological system (Moffitt, 1997; Sperry, 2003). Neurological impairment may produce hyperactivity, as well as negative changes to emotional response and temperament. Inattention, irritability and impulsivity, and an inability to delay gratification often ensue, which then makes parenting of this child more difficult. Parent-child communication may be hindered, interactions may be characterized by power struggles, frustration and need may mount and a host of neurological deficits may continue to develop. Such an adverse rearing environment may engender further problems with speech and other language skills, deficits to motor coordination and impulse control, attention deficits, as well as learning, memory and other cognitive disabilities (Moffitt, 1997). It has been found that irritable infants may elicit a negative parent-child environment (van den Boom & Hoeksma, 1994). In the above scenario, caretaker reactions may exacerbate the child's problems.

Factors such as economic disadvantage (associated with poor prenatal nutrition, maternal stress), parental distress (depression, mental illness) or parental deviance (drug and alcohol abuse, criminal behavior) often underlie the development of neuropsychological impairment in the child. The very situations that play a causative role in the development of neuropsychological difficulties also leave the parents of these children less capable of giving them what they need. Thus, parental behaviors, as well as their socio-economic conditions, frequently make a considerable contribution to the seriousness of the criminogenic environment in which the child grows. Severe antisocial behavior may be passed across generations in this manner (Huesmann, Eron, Lefkowitz, & Walder, 1984).

Plomin, Chipuer & Loehlin (1990) found that when parent and child are of similar temperament, a self-perpetuating cycle of destructive interactions might ensue. For example, a hyperactive child who throws tantrums may find him/herself disciplined by an angry parent who responds with shouting, coercion or violence. Children and parents who *share developmental deficits* in cognitive abilities may find that "extra help with homework" becomes an arena for frustration, struggle and blame. If the child should need therapeutic intervention, a cognitively impaired parent may be unable to recognize this need, or if recognized, be without the financial resources necessary to meet therapeutic costs, and so on. "This perverse compounding of children's vulnerabilities with their families' imperfections sets the stage for the development of life-course persistent antisocial behavior" (Moffitt, 1997, p. 19).

The vicious cycle: Once this self-perpetuating cycle has begun, future experiences serve to exacerbate neuropsychological and social difficulties. Aggressiveness and poor self-control often leads to rejection by both peers and adults (Coie, Belding, & Underwood, 1988). In turn, *expecting rejection* in interpersonal encounters can segue into withdrawal from relationships, or engagement in preemptive strikes. Thus, the consequences of antisocial and criminal activity *limits exposure* to avenues for the acquisition and expression of prosocial behaviors that might help LCP youth to find their way out of this downward spiral (Moffitt, 1997).

Poor communication skills, as well as failing to learn conventional social skills, sets the child up for disappointing and frustrating interpersonal encounters at home, in school and beyond (Moffitt, 1997). The child becomes burdened by a limited response repertoire, which is characterized by a distinctive lack of non-assertive, prosocial alternatives, further limiting avenues of change. This restricted response repertoire of LCP individuals leads to further accumulation of problems as the individual becomes ensnared in a deviant lifestyle by crime's consequences (Moffitt, 1997). Stigmas and labels further exacerbate the process. Aggressive children with *only antisocial behaviors* in their repertoire tend to *change less over time* than do children who engage in antisocial behavior yet have learned some prosocial behaviors in addition (Vitaro, Gagnon, & Tremblay, 1990). Moffitt (1997) asserts LCPs "miss out on opportunities to acquire and practice prosocial alternatives at each stage of development;" they become "ensnared by the consequences of their antisocial behavior" (p. 23).

Following these individuals from childhood through adolescence and into young adulthood shows:

- It is very difficult to recoup the necessary cognitive and social skills that these processes elicit (Moffitt, 1997);

- Failure to attain these basic skills restricts both the range of opportunities and the rewards likely to be obtained from legitimate work;

- A high probability of continuity into the "underground economy" is a likely result (Farrington, Gallagher, Morley, Ledger & West, 1986).

This closing of the "doors of opportunity" (Moffitt, 1997) may be exacerbated by other hazards that stem from faulty judgment along the life course, e.g., teenage parenthood, substance abuse, school dropout, disability, injury or AIDS, scars and other alterations to the body (such as massive tattooing and piercing), poor or nonexistent work history, time spent incarcerated, etc. These "snares" (Moffitt, 1997) further restrict access to normative lifetime experiences (such as finding lucrative employment, comfortable marriages, higher education, a healthy peer group, etc.) that might propel an individual out of life-course-persistent offending. Thus, from early childhood, the life of a "life-course-persistent" juvenile offender is characterized by a series of *narrowing options*.

Early onset offending is predicted by association with antisocial family members (Farrington & Hawkins, 1991) and peers, as well as by social isolation and depression (Loeber, 1991). High rates of school absence and low verbal IQ separate those who continue their participation in problem behavior vs. those who stopped these behaviors in adolescence ("persisters"/"desisters"). Participation and persistence in problem behaviors were more often associated with poor school adjustment and disruptive behavior (Loeber, 1991).

Bio/psycho/social factors in "adolescent limited" patterns of juvenile delinquency

There are many more adolescents on the AL pathway than on the LCP pathway (Moffitt, Caspi, Harrington & Milne, 2002). LCP problem behavior is often associated with *some other type of pathology*, such as a cognitive deficit, difficult temperament or hyperactivity. The etiology of adolescence-limited individuals differs markedly from the above pattern. First, most individuals involved in problem behavior during adolescence fall into the AL pattern. Many teens "try this lifestyle on" as part of their developmental process.

This problem behavior begins and ends during adolescence and represents a near "normative adjustment"

to the "maturity gap" (Moffitt et al., 2002). The onset of problem behavior generally can be traced to puberty and involves "otherwise healthy youngsters" who "experience dysphoria" during the "roleless years" of adolescence. Moffitt and colleagues suggest that it may be normative during this time for adolescents to "romanticize" the criminal lifestyle and *imitate their LCP peers* as a way to establish independence from family and other social institutions. Associated benefits such as praise and recognition from peers further makes this lifestyle appealing. Since the early development of AL individuals is relatively untroubled, most are able to cease participation in problem behaviors as they assume adult roles and responsibilities. Such vast differences in the etiologies of LCP and AL groups provide insight into designing effective individual-based treatment interventions.

When considering evidence for an "adolescence-limited" trajectory of antisocial behavior (which actually accounts for the bulk of adolescent offending), Moffitt and colleagues (2002) cite the observation that while *33% of males are arrested at some time in their lives* for a serious criminal offense, *fully 80% have documented contact with the criminal justice system* for a minor offense. These minor offenses, however, occur almost exclusively during adolescence, mostly between the ages of 11 and 15 years, as predicted by the "adolescence-limited" trajectory (Moffitt, Lynam & Silva, 1994). Self-report data reveals that it is statistically normative to engage in some forms of delinquent activity during adolescence (Moffitt et al., 1994). This "tidal wave of adolescent onset" (Moffitt et al., 2002, p. 15) has been uncovered on a global scale, including England, the U.S. and New Zealand, among others.

Meta-analysis reveals a prevalence rate of 5% for the "life-course-persistent" pattern, and 33% for the "adolescence-limited" trajectory. While this latter group displays virtually the *same levels* of delinquent activity as the LCPs in terms of the kind, frequency, and number of contacts with juvenile justice during adolescence, they are noteworthy for *having no history* of antisocial behavior in childhood. Another difference from the LCP group is that AL adolescents display occasional periods during which there is no criminal activity, a situation rare among LCPs. These adolescents also manifest little to no consistency in antisocial behavior across situations (Moffitt, 2002). For example, AL youth may be found to engage in minor property offenses such as vandalism, while still maintaining decent performance at school; or involvement with drug offenses (either through use or sales) may be found without other forms of concomitant criminal activity at all.

For delinquents whose criminal activity is confined to the adolescent years, the causal factors may be proximal - specific to the period of adolescent development - and theory must account for the discontinuity in their lives. By contrast, for persons whose adolescent delinquency is merely one inflection in a continuous lifelong antisocial course, a theory of antisocial behavior must locate its causal factors early in their childhoods and must explain the continuity in their troubled lives. If the causal theories are correct, and the causes and correlates of delinquency differ for the two groups, then research that fails to analyze them separately is predestined to generate attenuated findings about both groups (Moffitt et al., 2002, p. 17).

Alternative proposals for categorizing adolescent offenders

Based on the investigation of 808 5th-grade students from the *Seattle Social Development Project* (SSDP), a longitudinal study of youth living in high crime areas (Battin, Hill, Abbott, Catalano, & Hawkins, 1998), Chung et al., 2002) found evidence for five developmental trajectories:

- *Nonoffenders*—individuals who displayed no offending (24% of sample);

- *Late onsetters*—individuals who did not display delinquent activity until after age 13, and whose offending was generally of low seriousness (14.4% of sample);

- *Desisters*—individuals who engaged in low serious offending at age 13, but who had stopped their offending by age 21 (35.3% of sample);

- *Escalators*—individuals who engaged in low offending at age 13, and whose offending had increased to much higher levels by age 21 (19.3%);

- *Chronic offenders*—individuals whose offending behavior was both serious and occurred at high levels throughout adolescence and into young adulthood (7% of sample).

Some researchers assert that typological systems (such as the one described above) are not useful (e.g., Gottfredson & Hirschi, 1990). These researchers argue that a more general theory of offending that applies to all individuals involved in problem behavior would be more efficient, i.e., addressing a general lack of impulse control in treating offenders of all ages would be adequate and effective. This lumping of all offenders into a single diagnostic category has received some empirical support, as there are some factors that appear to predict offending (vs. non-offending) across trajectory groups (Chung, et al., 2002). These homogeneous risk factors include *affiliation with delinquent peers* and the *ratio of risk vs. protective factors* (Fergusson et al., 2000; Patterson & Yoerger, 1997). Differences in the development of delinquent behavior would then be predicted by the *degree of exposure to these risk and protective factors* (e.g., moderate vs. severe family-related risk factors).

Recidivism: the continuity of criminal behavior over time

A sizeable portion of adolescent offenders, *who in all likelihood do not experience the positive building blocks of human development,* continue offending behavior into young adulthood (Sampson & Laub, 1997). Factors that may place an adolescent at risk for longer-term offending seem to include *cumulative* (socioeconomic and other) *disadvantage* over time. Sampson and Laub (1997), by focusing on accumulation of risk as well as on the labeling processes that result from initial involvement in criminal behavior, have developed a general theory to explain stability of criminal careers during adolescence and into young adulthood. This theory identifies direct causal influences of cumulative disadvantage and early antisocial behavior, as well as social responses (labeling, stigma etc.) to that behavior, on the stability of an adolescent's criminal conduct. The model emphasizes the importance of these social elements in prolonging an adolescent's criminal career over the many individual differences that may also be operating to influence stability and change (Goffman, 1963; Sampson & Laub, 1997).

In examining recidivism rates among adolescents who had been arrested for delinquency and who received treatment within a juvenile corrections setting, Feder (2001) investigated the *psychosocial* and *cognitive predictor variables* associated with recidivism. Re-arrest status at one-year follow-up from discharge yielded two groups of subjects: those with re-arrest status (*n*=14) and those without (*n*=15). A variety of factors did not discriminate between adolescents on the basis of recidivism. These included race and number of biological parents living at home. Age at first arrest did not differentiate, in contrast to predictions from theory regarding early vs. late-onset offending (Moffitt, 1993; Patterson, Reid, & Dishion, 1992). There was, however, a relationship between *early age of entry* into the corrections setting and recidivism. Although total number of prior arrests was not found to differentiate likelihood of recidivism, the *number of prior arrests for drug-related offenses* was found to differentiate quite well. Findings are summarized in *Table 5.6*.

Risk for recidivism has also been explored in a 2-year follow-up study of adolescent offenders (Benda, Flynn, & Toombs, 2001). These researchers screened for factors that predict adolescent recidivism as well as adolescent entry into the adult correctional system. *Prior incarceration* proved to be the best predictor of these variables. Consistent with Moffitt and colleagues' (Moffitt, 1993; Moffitt et al., 2002) theory of "*life-course-persistent*" offending, early onset of problem behavior was also a prominent predictor. Following these, the major factors found to predict recidivism were: *gang involvement, age of first involvement with alcohol/drug use, elevated psychopathic deviant (MMPI pd) scores,* and *substance abuse*. In addition to the above, various scales and subscales correlated with probability of recidivism, such as the *denial subscale* and *social subscale* of the *Jesness Inventory* (Jesness, 1991).

Support for these two deviancy patterns is found in studies of 22 variables of the *Adolescent Self-Assessment Profile* measuring deviancy and criminal conduct across several large samples of juvenile offender and adolescent AOD clinical samples (Wanberg, 2004). Common factor and principal components analyses have identified two hardy and reliable factors: *minor deviancy and major deviancy*. The former is descriptive of the adolescence-limited (AL) pattern and the latter descriptive of the life-

course-persistent pattern. The correlation between these two patterns is .62, indicating that they overlap, yet they represent a significant percentage of independent variance. Most important is that *minor deviancy* scale scores do not significantly differ across six age categories, whereas *major deviancy* scale scores do show significant increase at the 18-year-old age category compared with the age categories of 13 through 17. These findings, represented in *Figure 5.4*, suggest that *major deviancy* not only persists but increases at the 18-year category. It can be noted that there is an increase in the *minor deviancy* scale scores at the 18-age category; however, it is not statistically significant.

TRENDS IN JUVENILE VIOLENCE

Prevalence and types of juvenile violence

The prevalence and rate of violent crime have experienced many ups and downs over the last half a century. However, observation of longer term trends (from 1971-1997), shows an increase of 97.8% in the violent crime rate overall, despite the fact that there was an overall decrease in the murder rate in 1998 to its lowest level in three decades (Glicken & Sechrist, 2003). Statistics were gathered using the *National Crime Victimization Survey of the Bureau of Justice Statistics* (NCVS) (1998) which reveals *self-reported victimization* by violent crime, as well as the *FBI Uniform Crime Reports* - crimes known to the police. Previous studies have attempted to conceptualize juvenile crime into two broad levels of severity, or *seri-*

Table 5.6 Predictor Variables for Recidivism in Juvenile Delinquency in Adolescents Aged 13-17 Years

Variables that differentiate adolescents on the basis of recidivism

- *Academic factors*, e.g., lower IQ scores (i.e., reduced cognitive ability, especially in the domains of Picture Arrangement, Coding and Vocabulary)

- *Offense history*, e.g., greater number of prior arrests for drug-related offenses

Variables that failed to differentiate adolescents on the basis of recidivism

- *Demographic characteristics*, e.g., race

- *Family characteristics*, e.g., the number of biological parents at home

- *Offense history*, e.g., first arrest, total number of prior arrests for any crime

Source: Feder (2001)

Figure 5.4   Comparison of Deviancy Patterns

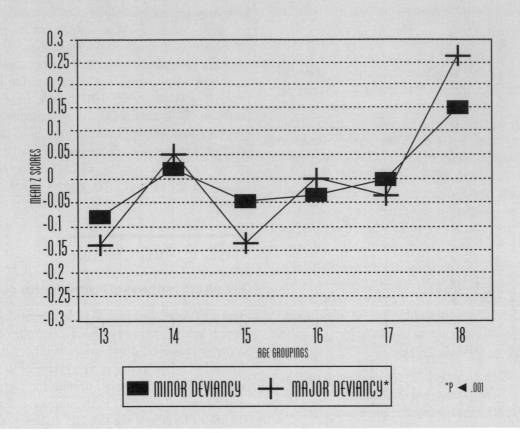

ousness of offense. The *Office of Juvenile Justice and Delinquency Prevention* (OJJDP) (Stahl, 1999) developed an offense hierarchy, delineated on the basis of offense severity (combining both extent of violence and seriousness of the crime). In addition to *status offenses*, which are considered offenses due to juvenile status, e.g., runaway or truancy, three tiers were identified:

- *Crimes against persons*—e.g., aggravated assault, murder, attempted murder, and sexual assault;

- *Crimes against property*—e.g., theft, arson, breaking and entering, and vandalism; and

- *Substance-related offenses*—e.g., possession, consumption, and or distribution of drugs or alcohol.

Characteristics of serious adolescent crime have been explored (Flowers, 2002). A comparison of Norwegian adolescent psychiatric in-patients who had committed violent vs. non-violent crimes identified distinct differences in the criminal careers of these two groups. Individuals predisposed toward the commission of *violent crime only* are relatively rare, as most violent criminals engage in a broader spectrum of criminal acts. The finding that most violent perpetrators engaged in both violent and non-violent crimes suggests that the pathways of development into violent offending may be imbedded in a more general criminal pathway (Kjelsberg, 2002).

Juvenile victims of crime

Although individuals under the age of 18 constitute only 10% of the general population, they account for 25% of *crime victims* (Steinberg, 1999). Victimization (especially violent victimization) has serious consequences, both for overall mental health and the likelihood of engaging in serious problem behavior. African Americans and Latino Americans living in inner-city environments experience the highest rates of victimization (Hutson, Anglin, & Pratts, 1994). In these environments, gang violence and violent victimization are a common threat in everyday life (Steinberg, 1999).

Assault: Juveniles (between ages 12 and 24) are at the highest risk for rape, robbery and aggravated assault in American society. Those aged 12 to 17 years are more likely than their older counterparts to experience simple assault, while those aged 18-24 were more likely than their younger counterparts to experience serious assault. The perpetrators of *serious violent assault* against juveniles were an *acquaintance* (18%), *a relative* (11%), *a friend* (34%) or *a stranger* (36%) (Snyder & Sickmund, 1999). Other types of crime committed against juveniles are kidnapping (21%), aggravated assault (4%), simple assault (4%) and robbery (2%). Thirty-seven percent of these victims were younger than age 7, and 47% of these victims were female (Snyder & Sickmund, 1999). The use of drugs among high school students placed them at greater risk for violent victimization than those who did not use.

Assault of juveniles under age 12 constitutes 5.5% of all reported violent crime. Sexual assault is, by far, the major form of assault experienced by juveniles under age 12, constituting 32% of all reported assaults of juveniles. In fact, OJJDP reports that 33% of sexual assault victims are under the age of 12. Females constitute 96% of all adult sexual assault victims and 92% of those experiencing sexual assault between the ages of 12 and 17, *but 26% of those sexually assaulted under age 12 are male* (Snyder & Sickmund, 1999). Juvenile offenders perpetrate a sizeable portion of the sexual assault of juveniles. The vast majority of these assaults are perpetrated by juveniles known to the victimized children. Juvenile perpetrators constitute a significant proportion (47%) of those who commit sexual assault against young children who are family members (Snyder & Sickmund, 1999).

Murder: Murder is one of the leading causes of death among youth. *Table 5.7* presents statistics regarding child mortality at each age range.

A significant percentage (26%) of juvenile homicides are perpetrated by another juvenile. Juveniles are indicted in 13% of homicides of children under age 6; 5% of these perpetrators were the child's teenaged parent; 18% were another family member (Snyder & Sickmund, 1999). *The perpetrators in 40% of juvenile homicides were family members.* Family members are more than twice as likely to be implicated in the murder of a juvenile female as of a male (Snyder & Sickmund, 1999). This latter statistic is especially important given the high rates of physical abuse of females within the family and emphasizes the potential lethality of this abuse.

Sixty-three percent of the murders committed by juveniles were of adolescents aged 15 and above. These *older victims* are more likely to be *killed by peers* and other acquaintances rather than family. There are no gender trends among murdered children (under the age of 13). Gender emerges as a significant factor at about age 14, when the percentage of male victims goes up. By age 15, the ratio of *male to female* juvenile homicide victims reaches *3 to 1*; by age 17, this figure rises to *4 to 1*. Overall, females accounted for 29% of murdered juveniles from 1990 to 1997. In 1997, 47% of juvenile murders were of black victims, a rate five times that of white juveniles. (Snyder & Sickmund, 1999).

Adolescent victimization is important to consider because victims of violent crime are more likely to report symptoms of posttraumatic stress disorder, depression, and academic difficulties, and are more likely to themselves engage in aggressive and antisocial behavior (Steinberg, 1999). So victimization by violence must be listed as another *prominent risk factor* for problem behavior.

Risks and predictors for adolescent violence

Adolescents constitute around 20% of all those arrested for a violent offense (Scott, 1999). In a literature review covering studies of violent crime over the life span, Laub and Lauritsen (1995), concluded that

Table 5.7 Ranking of Child Murder of Juveniles by Age

Age	Homicide
1-4 years	4th leading cause of death
5-14 years	3rd leading cause of death
15-24 years	2nd leading cause of death

11% of all homicide victims in 1997 were under the age of 18

Source: National Center for Health Statistics, 1997

socio-cultural sources of violent behavior were the most influential in explaining adolescent outcome with regard to violence. Predictors of aggressive anti-social behavior in adolescence encompass a wide range of such factors, including:

- Early emergence of aggression during childhood (Dahlberg & Potter, 2001);

- Family violence (Scott, 1999);

- Association with deviant peers in adolescence (Dahlberg & Potter, 2001);

- Gun possession (Scherzer & Pinderhughes, 2002); and

- Having a close friend or relative who was a victim of violence (Scherzer & Pinderhughes, 2002).

Just a small portion of the juvenile population accounts for the bulk of serious delinquency, including violence (Glicken & Sechrist, 2003). Prediction of exactly which individuals will become involved in criminal behavior is a difficult task (Bilchik, 1999). Based on a a meta-analysis of 66 longitudinal studies that examined non-incarcerated youth, the *Office of Juvenile Justice and Delinquency Prevention* (Hawkins, Herrenkohl, Farrington et al., 2000), identified five areas of risk for juvenile violence.

- *Individual factors;* including medical, physical and psychological;

- *Family factors;* including child abuse, parental involvement with substance abuse, criminal conduct and/or violence, poor bonding;

- *School factors*; including school failure, absenteeism, dropout;

- *Peer-related factors*; deviant peers, gang membership;

- *Community and neighborhood factors*; socioeco-

nomics, availability of weapons, drugs and alcohol, community violence and racial prejudice.

In this meta-analysis, age group was found to interact with type of risk factor in reaching the best prediction (Hawkins et al., 2000). *Table 5.8* shows the interaction between age and type of risk factor as predictors of juvenile violence.

Other correlates of juvenile violence that hold across age are: gender (males engage in violence at a much higher rate than females); socioeconomic status of family; and antisocial parents. Having divorced parents was a poor predictor of later violence (OJJDP—Hawkins et al., 2000).

Some researchers emphasize biological factors in the etiology of adolescent aggression (e.g., Bell, 2000; Tupin, 2000). These authors assert that a biopsychosocial analysis includes such phenomena as family violence, child and adolescent physical and sexual abuse, and sexual violence (Bell, 2000). As pathways to violence likely involve a wide array of biochemical, psychosocial and environmental factors, interventions of short duration are unlikely to be effective (Dahlberg & Potter, 2001). For a comprehensive review of the longitudinal research on reliable predictors of juvenile violence and serious crime, see Lipsey and Derzon (1998).

Teens and firearms

Gun possession is a major risk factor for adolescent violence (Scherzer & Pinderhughes, 2002). Firearms bring a more serious element to adolescent violence, and are frequently implicated in juvenile homicide. It is estimated that there are over *225 million handguns* alone in the U.S., approximately one for every American citizen. Firearm possession and use has been found to escalate throughout adolescence, accounting for approximately 80% of the murders committed by older adolescents. This has led to a widespread call for reductions in the availability of

Table 5.8 Interaction of Age and Type of Risk Factor for Best Predictors of Juvenile Violence	
Age at 1st Offense	**Best Predictor of Juvenile Violence**
6–11	Offense of any kind
11–16	Substance abuse
12–14	Lack of social ties and involvement with antisocial peers

Source: Hawkins et al., 2000

guns to adolescents as part of preventative programming (Kashani, Jones, Bumby, & Thomas, 1999; Scherzer & Pinderhughes, 2002).

Ready availability of guns to teens has been attributed to several causes, outbreak in sales and use of crack during the mid-1980s being a principal factor. To service the market in drug trafficking, "juveniles were recruited, they were armed with guns . . . guns that were diffused into the larger community of juveniles" (Glicken & Sechrest, 2003, p.6). This mixing of drugs and guns, which continued to grow through 1995, accompanied a twofold increase in the incidence of gun-related murders by teens (Blumstein, 1995) over that time.

Characteristics of teen homicide

Studies that investigate the development of homicide among juveniles have found several predictors of such violent behavior, among them the early emergence of aggression in childhood and association with deviant peers in adolescence (Dahlberg & Potter, 2001). Longitudinal studies show that children who display aggressive behavior at age 8 are more likely than other children to engage in criminal behavior and violence later on in their lives (Reiss & Roth, 1993).

The majority of adolescents who kill choose victims who are *close to their own age*, often involving senseless acts that seek revenge, status or social influence. The reasons for murder cited by adolescent perpetrators generally vary from those cited by adults, focusing around the desire to obtain a desired object, defend against a perceived insult, avenge against a romantic altercation or "just for the hell of it" (Fox & Levin, 2001). It is not uncommon to hear that a peer was murdered because of jealousy over the victim's popularity, that a store merchant was killed because of the refusal to yield up free merchandise, or that a teen participated in a group killing because their friends were doing it (Fox & Levin, 2001, p. 78). In fact, adolescents are far *more likely to kill in groups* (2 or more individuals) than to act alone. Thus, group process and peer influences appear to play a much more significant role in teen murder than in homicide committed by adults (Fox & Levin, 2001). Finally, teen homicide is generally impulsive and affective, rather than instrumental, as we frequently find in adults. *Table 5.9* presents characteristics of adolescent homicide.

Differences in age between victim and perpetrator of homicide do occur, but generally fall into one of the following scenarios. Approximately 175 parents are murdered by their children (under the age of 25) each year (Fox & Levin, 2001). Heide (2001) explains that this type of murder generally occurs in response to long-standing *physical or sexual abuse* at the hands of parents, and frequently is an act of self-defense. Another scenario that may trigger parricide by young people is the *defense of a significant other*, such as a sibling or mother who is being attacked by an abusive father. Infanticide also occurs by adolescent perpetrators, although this constitutes a very small proportion of the overall statistics on child murder within the family. Generally, infanticide at the hands of an adolescent perpetrator occurs when young and otherwise at-risk teen mothers or their boyfriends are *unable to cope* with the stress and strain of a newborn. Often, these attacks occur in a fit of anger and desperation, and only accidentally lead to fatal injury to the child (Fox & Levin, 2001).

Table 5.9 Characteristics of Adolescent Homicide (Higher than Average % of Perpetrators ◀ Age 18)

- Gang-related murders (34% of all gang-related homicides)

- Murders with multiple offenders

- Murders with strong peer influences

- Affective and impulsive murders (vs. premeditated acts that aim toward a particular incentive)

- Gun-related homicide (77% of teen murder - Snyder & Sickmund, 1999).

- Arson-related homicide

Source: Fox & Levin, 2001

Adolescents and mass murder: School shootings and other catastrophic episodes

Studies of adolescents (aged 11 to 19 years) who have perpetuated mass murder (at least 3 victims slain in a single event) have revealed some interesting insights into the more general phenomena of teen murder (Meloy, Hempel, Mohandie, Shiva, & Gray, 2001). These adolescent perpetrators seemed to share a number of characteristics that are consistent with the above-described theories of adolescent crime. For example, most of these adolescents were unpopular with their peers; over 50% had experienced bullying at the hands of another. Most kept pretty much to themselves and were "loners" who used alcohol and drugs to self-medicate. Brooding on fantasies of violence was common and frequently shared with others. Depression was commonplace, although only 23% had received a psychiatric diagnosis, and only 6% were considered impaired at the time of the murders (Meloy et al., 2001). A history of antisocial behavior and aggressiveness, however, was the usual pattern, even including verbal threats of intent before the homicidal incident. Motivations expressed by these individuals generally included some type of personal failure, either in social relationship or academically.

Three types of adolescent mass murderers were identified (Meloy, Hempel, Mohandie, Shiva, & Gray, 2001):

- Family annihilator

- Classroom avenger

- Criminal opportunist

Several indicators of stress and strain in the juvenile's life (experiences with bullying, failure at school, etc.), absence of conventional socializing agents (peer rejection), social triggers (e.g., romantic or school difficulties) are characteristic of violent adolescents.

Mai and Alpert (2000) evaluate the role of gender norms and interactions in the etiology of school-based mass murder (e.g., Columbine High School). They hypothesize that gender norms which socialize males to be independent, rugged individualists, who show no signs of stress, strain or weakness (all sources of shame) may have had a significant influence on the perpetrators' developmental process. This extreme act of violence, then, may be seen in the context of social image promotion and bravado (Mai & Alpert, 2000). Surely, the interaction of multiple factors suggests a complex relationship between clinical and sociocultu-ral factors that underlie the development of teen homicide (Meloy et al., 2001).

Though several theories of adolescent criminality have been discussed, it is unlikely that any one will be sufficient to explain the broad spectrum of youth violence and homicide (Kashani, Jones, Bumby, & Thomas, 1999). "It is likely that all of these notions have some merit - not to understand all kinds of murder, but perhaps some discrete subset." (Fox & Levin, 2001, p.27). For example, biological factors such as head trauma or environmental toxins should be explored as potential causative agents in abrupt and uncharacteristic outbreaks of homicidal mania, but they will offer little to explain the processes involved in serious gang murder, which is likely to be more closely tied to social learning and socioeconomic processes (Fox & Levin, 2001). Cold, calculated acts of premeditation require still different causal explanations, perhaps invoking antisocial psychopathology. Due to the complexities involved in explaining adolescent violence, Kashani et al. (1999) suggest using a "multidimensional psychosocial framework" which takes into consideration the full range of risk factors elaborated in *Chapter 1*, in order to achieve more reliable and effective treatment results.

Finally, in order to understand the most extreme form of antisocial behavior, violent homicide, we must analyze the factors that pull an individual *away from behavioral conventions* in the mainstream, as well as those that pull them *toward a criminal lifestyle*. Although there are many psychosocial factors that undoubtedly contribute to deviant behavior and violent criminal conduct, the construct of *personal responsibility* remains essential across prevention, treatment and rehabilitative domains.

[While a] diseased brain, poor parenting, maltreatment, drug side-effect, running with a bad crowd, exposure to harmful media, poor opportunities, bad days, bad breaks are all valuable notions, . . . none alone is generally sufficient to drive a person to kill . . . While our options and opportunities in life are impacted by a host of advantages and disadvantages, virtually all of us have some degree of free will. . . . By nature of heredity and nurture of environment, some individuals are more prone to violence than others, yet free will still exists. The will to kill, though governed by numerous internal and external forces, still includes choice and human decision making, and thus accountability and culpability (Fox & Levin, 2001. p. 28).

In a report to the U.S. Attorney General on youth violence Fox, 1997 concludes: "There are actually two crime trends in America: one for the young, one for the mature, which are moving in opposite directions." Glicken and Sechrest (2003) cite easy access to dangerous drugs and firearms as culprits in producing the cycles of adolescent problem behavior observed today. From the mid-1980s to mid-1990s, we witnessed steady inclines in rates of adolescent gun use, as well as a twofold increase in the number of adolescent perpetrators who used guns in the commission of murder (Blumstein, 1995). Currently, guns are the weapons utilized in 80% of murders committed by adolescents (Fox & Levin, 2001).

As frightening as these statistics may be, analysis of trends in adolescent problem behavior among youth looks better if we restrict ourselves to the last 10 years - here there is some cause for optimism. Recent studies show that while increases in juvenile crime originated in the late 1980s and peaked in 1994, there has been a steady decline in FBI juvenile arrest statistics between 1994-1998 (Snyder 1999). Extreme acts of violence by adolescents dropped 33% between 1993 and 1997 (Snyder & Sickmund, 1999), and arrests of adolescents for violent crime dropped 19% over this same time period (Glicken & Sechrist, 2003). However, Bilchik (1999) reports that arrests of juveniles for violent crime are still 49% higher than in 1988.

Personal and social responsibility for violent adolescent behavior

In order to understand even the most extreme form of antisocial behavior, violent homicide, we should analyze the factors that pull an individual away from mainstream society, as well as those that pull them toward a criminal lifestyle. While the overall rate of violent crime has decreased in America, and during the past decade, adolescents seem to have reduced their degree of involvement in violent criminal activity, the rate of adolescents involved in violent criminal activities is still nearly 50% higher than it was in 1988. The following points summarize pertinent elements of adolescent involvement in violent crime:

- Adolescents make up a significant portion of both violent and nonviolent crime;

- Violence among youth has become more normative;

- Urban areas of the U.S. appear to present a criminogenic environment for adolescents;

- Adolescents are not only the perpetrators of violent crime, they are also the most frequently victimized;

- Consequences of adolescent antisocial behavior are getting more serious;

- The increase in seriousness is associated with easy access to guns in American society;

- African American males (and females) are disproportionately victimized and arrested for violent criminal activity.

Sociocultural factors associated with adolescent violence include:

- The urban context;

- Experiences with violent trauma;

- Sociocultural experiences and conditions;

- Gender;

- Availability of handguns.

Table 5.10 presents a summary of trends in juvenile violence. Although there are many psychosocial factors that undoubtedly contribute to deviant behavior and violent criminal conduct, the construct of personal responsibility is essential across prevention, treatment and rehabilitation domains.

IMPLICATIONS FOR TREATMENT AND POLICY: A DEVELOPMENTAL PERSPECTIVE ON JUVENILE JUSTICE

Life-course-persistent adolescent offenders tend to develop a behavioral repertoire fraught with antisocial behaviors to the exclusion of prosocial development. Due to various factors (individual, familial and social), these individuals start their offending careers early in life, and as a consequence become deprived of opportunities to acquire and practice prosocial skills at each stage of development. The downward spiral of narrowing options for pursuing a more normative lifestyle propels them into a life of crime.

Due to fact that LCP offenders experience *extreme entrenchment* of multiple and severe life adjustment problems, in a host of personal-interactional and economic domains, Moffitt (1997) "anticipates disappointing outcomes when such persons are thrust into new situations that purportedly offer the chance to turn over a new leaf." . . . "Opportunities for

Table 5.10   Summary of Trends in Juvenile Violence

Violent Crime

- 80% of all violent acts are committed in the urban areas of 50 major U.S. cities (Glicken & Sechrist, 2003);

- Approximately 20% of violent crimes involved adolescents, especially during the 1990s (Fraser, 1996);

- Adolescents between ages 16 and 17 were responsible for 48% of all juvenile arrests, and 51% of the violent crimes (Bilchik, 1999 - National Report Series of the OJJDP);

- The state of California reported a 7% increase in the number of violent crimes committed by juveniles while at school (1998-1999), and an 11% increase in the number of alcohol and drug-related crimes (Glicken & Sechrist, 2003);

- From 1988-1992, juvenile arrest for rape rose 17%; 50% for robbery; and 49% for aggravated assault (Howell, 1995).

Aggravated Assault

- Arrests of adolescents for aggravated assault in 1999 rose nearly 70% above rates in 1983 (U.S. Surgeon General, 2001);

- A longitudinal study of adolescent self-reports found that 14% of children aged 12 (18% of 12-year-old males) had engaged in some form of assault. Seven percent (13% males) carried a handgun (Puzzanchera, 2000);

- Despite a backdrop of stability in assault rates among individuals of all ages, the severity of such incidents has steadily worsened, particularly among younger victims and offenders (Fagan, 1997);

- It is estimated that for every 10 adolescents who engage in violent behavior (with potentially lethal or serious consequences), only one is arrested in any given year (Glicken & Sechrist, 2003).

Juvenile Violence & Homicide

- There has been an increase in juvenile perpetration of violent murder; the vast majority are gun homicides (*National Crime Victimization Survey of the Bureau of Justice Statistics*,1998);

- Homicide offenses by persons age 25 or older has lessened steadily through the 1980s and 1990s (Fox & Zawitz, 2000). However, a rise in the homicide rate over this same period occurred among juveniles, especially adolescents. The extent of murder committed by adolescents increased threefold from 1985-1993, from 9.8 to 30.2 per 100,000, before a more recent decline (Fox & Levin, 2001; Glicken & Sechrist, 2003);

- The number of adolescents arrested for murder increased 168% between 1984-1993, while weapons violations increased by 126% (Fraser, 1996).

Violence and juvenile victimization

- Juveniles between the ages of 16 and 24 are more likely to be victimized by violence than any other age group (Glicken & Sechrist, 2003);

- The number of children under 5 who are victims of homicide is growing in proportion to their increase in the population. In these cases, the perpetrators of these crimes are most frequently the child's parents (Glicken & Sechrist, 2003);

- The number of juvenile murder victims increased by 82% between 1984-1994 (Snyder et al. 1996);

- African American adolescent males experience a disproportionately high rate of victimization by violent crime. They are also involved in a disproportionate number of arrests for such crime (Bynum & Weiner, 2002).

change will often be actively transformed by LCPs into opportunities for continuity: residential corrections programs provide a chance to learn from criminal peers, a new job furnishes a new opportunity to steal, and a new romantic partner provides a new victim for assaul." (p. 23).

Despite such pessimistic predictions, yet keeping these cautionary warnings in mind, the platform presented in this manual seeks to provide these individuals with opportunities to develop, practice and maintain the skills and developmental milestones that they have missed, in order to make available options for reintegration into society with the skills needed for them to realistically function in positive ways. We must provide *education and opportunity* for these individuals to observe, practice and come to appreciate the rewards of more conventional forms of behavior. In order to do this, basic redress of major cognitive, affective and neuropsychological deficits must be provided to re-open opportunities for rewarding social interaction. Experience with the rewards of human contact and compassion, along with necessary skills building in order to provide realistic options for success in legitimate avenues of life, may provide these individuals with the impetus and desire for a crime-free existence.

There is a need for enhanced services to treat a large population of high-risk adolescents (Glicken & Sechrist, 2003). Not only do they commit a significant component of antisocial and criminal behaviors but they also have a higher recidivism rate than their adult counterparts (Glicken & Sechrist, 2003). "The need to identify and respond appropriately to this (high risk) category of youthful offender has, in turn, led to a . . . sense of urgency to develop and implement specially-designed intensive programs, the goals of which include the closely supervised reentry of this subpopulation back into the host community, accompanied by sufficient services and support to ensure a reasonable level of community protection and public safety" (Glicken & Sechrist, 2003, p. 25).

CHAPTER REVIEW

Chapter 5 tackles the phenomena of adolescent crime, delinquency and violence. It begins by describing the characteristics of juvenile delinquency—including reference to adolescent motivations for crime, recidivism, juvenile delinquency and criminal careers. It then discusses major correlates of juvenile participation in crime, such as school discipline referrals,

association with deviant peers, and substance abuse, followed by public perceptions of juvenile crime. *Chapter 5* then overviews a wide range of theories of juvenile delinquency and crime, including *General Strain, Relative Deprivation, Social Control, Differential Association, and Social Learning.* Developmental aspects and pathways to adolescent offending are then discussed.

Biological influences on juvenile crime are addressed, stressing the need for a bio/psycho/social synthesis integrating multiple factors into a comprehensive evaluation of adolescent delinquency. Trends in juvenile violence are explored, such as offense seriousness, characteristics and types of teen homicide, including mass murder and school shootings. *Chapter 5* addresses reasons for the elevated rates of minority participation in crime, tracing this to the dynamics of poverty and hopelessness that many of these youth endure. Adolescent crime and personal responsibility are considered, followed by implications for treatment, policy and juvenile justice.

By illustrating some of the ways in which the lives of adolescent offenders have been impacted by their more general experiences as children and teens (e.g., attention deficits and learning disabilities, mental illness, traumatic violence, racism and sexism, troubled relationships with parents and peers, social stigmas, etc.), it becomes clear that these experiences require specific focus in the development of effective programming for problem juveniles. While these experiences may be associated with vulnerability for antisocial behavior, criminal conduct and substance abuse, they may also provide the adolescent with a reservoir of survival skills that can be modified using cognitive-behavioral interventions and a *strength-based orientation* for building a better life. Helping adolescents to understand and recognize their own strengths and abilities can contribute much toward improving self-esteem, self-awareness and recognition of personal rights and responsibilities that can propel them out of high-risk situations (such as deviant peer associations and the subculture of violence) and into those that facilitate them in reaching their goals.

Adolescent problem behaviors such as drug abuse and criminal conduct are associated with multiple childhood antecedents including low motivation toward success and achievement, minimal attachment to positive role models or institutions, and normalized images of crime and violence. A major tenet of *PSD-C*, however, is that across the entire continuum of criminal conduct, from minimal rule breaking to violent crime, positive change is, first and foremost, tied to recognizing that we are personally responsible for our actions. We can become healthy and productive community members by learning to control our thoughts, feelings, and behavior.

Gender and Adolescent Problem Behavior

6

Chapter Six:
Gender and Adolescent Problem Behavior

Chapter Outline

Adolescent Girls and Delinquency
- The scope of female juvenile delinquency

The Nature of Female Offense
- Girls and status offense
- Different patterns of criminal offense by gender
- Gender and adolescent murder

Gender Comparisons Across Risk and Drug Involvement

Risk Factors and Correlates of Juvenile Offending Among Females
- Family of origin
- Teen pregnancy
- School failure, teen pregnancy and delinquency
- Age of onset of delinquency in girls

Gender Norms and Sexual Violation
- Adolescent dating and sexuality
- Girls and relationality
- Early and late maturation: Taunts and sexual harassment
- Suppression of female voice vs. emergence of male entitlement

Sexual Assault During Childhood
- Prevalence of abuse
- Juvenile perpetrators of sexual abuse
- Adolescent sex offenders
- Sex offense and recidivism

Experiences with Violent Trauma in Childhood: A Major Route for Girls into Criminal Conduct
- Psychological and behavioral consequences of violent trauma in adolescence
- School failure and type of abuse
- Progression from juvenile to adult offending among females

Female Gang Participation

Trauma Within the Juvenile Justice System
- Adolescent female detention
- Mistreatment, abuse and neglect
- Housing, nutrition and healthcare

Implications for Treatment & Policy: A Gender-Focused Treatment Platform

Chapter Review

Chapter Objectives

- To describe rates of female participation in adolescent crime and delinquency;
- To describe relationships between gender norms and sexual abuse;
- To investigate gender differences in the nature of adolescent crime;
- To investigate gender differences in the nature of adolescent substance abuse;
- To investigate primary risk factors that predict entry of adolescent girls into the juvenile justice system;
- To discuss the incidence of sexual assault of females during childhood;
- To explore the role of violent trauma as a dominant factor in female juvenile offending;
- To identify some of the consequences of abuse in adolescence;
- To describe common characteristics found in the developmental trajectory from juvenile to adult offending among females;
- To discuss the phenomenon of female involvement in gangs;
- To examine the consequences of inadequate treatment and rehabilitative services within the juvenile justice system; and
- To describe essential factors for a gender-focused treatment platform.

INTRODUCTION

Although there are many similarities across male and female juvenile justice clients, treatment personnel can improve relapse and recidivism prevention outcomes by developing an awareness of gender differences in: (a) risk and resiliency factors that mediate substance abuse and criminal conduct; (b) patterns of substance abuse and crime; (c) exposures to violence and sexual assault; (d) gender schema that affect dating and teenage pregnancy; (e) gang participation; (f) trauma within the juvenile justice system. The purpose of this chapter is to increase awareness of gender differences with the goal of developing more appropriate strategies for addressing the needs of *both male and female* youthful offenders. As the rate of female offenses and involvement in the criminal justice system has seen steep inclines during the past decade, this chapter highlights important factors that improve treatment focus for female clients. However, insights gained from gender comparisons will elucidate essential treatment issues germane to both sexes.

ADOLESCENT GIRLS AND DELINQUENCY

Specific focus must aim at addressing those social patterns that perpetuate (class) and racial discrimination, as well as sexism. Thus, adequately redressing the roots of female offending requires that the physical, cognitive, emotional and spiritual needs of females be addressed, and that these needs be analyzed within an environmental and sociocultural context that recognizes the strengths and survival of girls and women.

- Covington, 1998, p. 1

The scope of female juvenile delinquency

Female juvenile offenders constitute the largest growing segment of the juvenile justice population (Acoca, 1998). In the past decade, girls have been arrested for almost every type of offense at a greater annual growth rate than boys (Snyder, 1997). This includes arrests for violent crime, where research has long revealed far lower rates among females than males. Snyder reports that 723,000 girls younger than age 18 were arrested in 1996 alone. Thirty-one percent of juvenile offenders are female.

Males are more likely to be re-arrested than females (46% of males vs. 27% of females) (Snyder &

Sickmund, 1999). Males and females differ in the seriousness of their crimes as well. Only 16% of females had been arrested for a serious offense, vs. 42% of males; *Chronic offending* (more than 4 referrals) occurred in 52% of male criminal justice careers vs. 19% of females (Snyder & Sickmund, 1999). Females and males, however, enter the criminal justice system at about the same age of 14. Those who come into contact with criminal justice earlier ("early onset offenders") are more likely to engage in serious offenses and to be chronic offenders (Snyder & Sickmund, 1999).

THE NATURE OF FEMALE ADOLESCENT OFFENSE

Girls and status offense

Girls constitute the largest percentage of arrests for *status offenses* (Acoca, 1998; Covington, 1998; Snyder & Sickmund, 1999; Belknap, Dunn, & Holsinger, 1997). Status offenses constitute "acts that would not be offenses if committed by adults, such as promiscuity, truancy, or running away" (Covington, 1998, p. 3). Most runaways are teenage girls (58%), who are between 16-17 years old (68%). Children may also find themselves on the streets because they have been "thrown away" by their parents or guardians; this term refers to "a child who was told to leave home, or whose caretaker refused to let come home . . . or whose caretaker made no effort to recover the child when the child ran away, or who was abandoned" (Snyder & Sickmund, 1999, p.38). Status offenses and "throwaway" status are frequently associated with *physical and sexual abuse* in the home and elsewhere (Covington, 1998). A full 70% of street girls have run from violence or other types of abuse at home (Chesney-Lind & Shelden, 1998). Most importantly, 29% of girls on the streets find themselves *without a familiar or safe place to stay*, and are therefore forced into unsafe housing arrangements that may set them up for further violent assault and other destructive experiences, such as sexual exploitation (Covington, 1998).

Upon discovery by the juvenile justice system, female "runaways" (and other juvenile offenders) are generally returned to the *same environments* where they were initially victimized, with minimal (if any) resources devoted to correcting or preventing re-occurrence of violent trauma. Caught in a degenerating spiral of abuse and detention, these girls may develop a sense of inevitability concerning victimization and abuse.

Many do not develop an awareness that they have the *right to protect themselves* or their bodily integrity; *substance abuse is often used to self-medicate* feelings that stem from continued abuse; and a *downward spiral of abuse, recidivism, and incarceration* may ensue (Acoca, 1998). Acoca accents the many "missed opportunities" to enhance the "developmental potential not only of this generation of girls but of future generations" (p. 563); i.e., a high percentage of female juveniles have children or are pregnant at the time of contact with the criminal justice system; therefore, the developmental needs of the next generation is compromised as well.

Different patterns of criminal offense by gender

Compared to their female counterparts, *male adolescents* tend to be involved more frequently and intensely in *crime and violence* (Snyder & Sickmund, 1999). However, using self-report surveys, Scherzer & Pinderhughes (2002) did not find gender differences in overall exposure to violence or in perpetration, although they report differences in the chosen types of criminal or violent activity. While females participate in most of the same kinds of delinquent behavior as males, percentages of participation in particular delinquent acts vary significantly by sex (Covington, 1998). Overall, female juvenile offending (including violence) more closely mirrors the patterns of adult female crime. While female offenses generally occur in the realm of *property crime,* males are far more likely to participate in *violent crime* (Covington, 1998; Snyder & Sickmund, 1999; Milkman, Wanberg & Gagliardi, 2002). *Table 6.1* shows the variation of self-reported criminal behaviors by sex.

Arrest ratios hold generally constant across race and ethnicity, especially for females. Five percent of White, 6% of Black and 7% of Hispanic female juveniles have ever been arrested (in contrast to slightly larger variations among males, at a rate of 9% of White, 13% Black and 12% Hispanic) (Snyder & Sickmund, 1999). *Violent assault* is more prevalent among males. Male juveniles tend to *fight more* than females (46% vs. 26%) at all grade levels. Males are also *more likely to carry weapons* to school (13% vs. 4% of females). Fifty percent of juveniles *commit their crimes with other juveniles or adults,* at twice the rate for adults, a pattern that holds true among both *male and female* juvenile offenders (Snyder & Sickmund, 1999).

Gender and adolescent murder

About 130 female juveniles perpetrate murder yearly, constituting only a small fraction (7%) of the total number of homicides committed by juveniles in any year. While the rate of male murder rose steadily from 1980-1997, more than tripling, the figure for females remained stable from 1980 through 1997. Males are *more likely to use firearms* when killing (73% vs. 14% who used a knife), while 32% of females used a knife

Table 6.1 - Variation in Self-Reported Criminal Behaviors by Sex

Kind of behavior	Self-reported incidence of offense types	
	% female	% male
Carrying a handgun	3	16
Gang participation	3	6
Purposeful property destruction	20	37
Theft of item >$50	3	7
Motor theft	1	2
Drug sales	5	9
Sold hard drugs	2	3
Assault	12	23
Arrest	≅ 5	≅ 10

Source: Snyder & Sickmund, 1999

and 41% used a firearm in carrying out their murder (Snyder & Sickmund, 1999).

Males and females tend to murder different victims. For example, *39% of females who killed*, murdered a *family member*, while only 15% killed a stranger. By contrast, *37% of males who killed*, murdered a *stranger*, and only 9% of male juveniles killed a family member. Age of victim was also significantly different for male and female homicide perpetrators. While only 1% of male murderers were involved in the murder of a child less than 6 years of age, 18% of female juvenile killers murdered *children* in this age range. However, it is important to remember that, because males kill at such a higher rate than females overall, approximately equal numbers of juvenile males and females are responsible for killing young children (Snyder & Sickmund, 1999).

Although the majority of murdered juveniles are male, females account for approximately 29% of murdered juveniles. Family members are more than *twice as likely* to be implicated in the *murder of a juvenile female* than of a male (Snyder & Sickmund, 1999). This latter statistic is especially important given the high rates of physical abuse of females within the family, and emphasizes the potential lethality of this abuse.

GENDER COMPARISONS ACROSS RISK AND DRUG INVOLVEMENT

Using the scales of the *Adolescent Self-Assessment Profile* (ASAP) (Wanberg, 1991, 1998), Wanberg (2004) studied gender differences in two large samples of adolescents:

- 3,262 youth admitted to statewide AOD treatment facilities in Colorado, 31.9 percent of whom are female;

- 2,502 youth processed through *Denver County Probation* and screened for referral to *Treatment Alternatives to Street Crime* (TASC) for AOD evaluation, 20.4 percent of whom are female.

The ASAP provides reliable and valid measures of the six major risk-resiliency factors: (a) *family adjustment*; (b) *mental health*; (c) *peer associations*; (d) *school adjustment*; (e) *deviancy-criminal conduct*; and (f) *AOD involvement*. The ASAP also measures involvement in the major drug categories: alcohol; marijuana; amphetamines; hallucinogens; inhalants; and other drugs including heroin, tranquilizers and barbiturates.

Figures 6.1 and 6.2 provide a comparison between males and females within these two samples across the six major risk-resiliency factors. Although the gender differences (effect size) are more pronounced in the treatment sample, the differences are similar. First, across both samples, females indicate *greater problem endorsement* in the *family adjustment, mental health,* and *AOD disruption* areas and males report more involvement in *deviancy* and *criminal conduct*. In the *Treatment Sample*, males indicate greater problems in *school adjustment* and more involvement in *negative peer influence*. These two differences are not found in the probation sample.

Figures 6.3 and 6.4 provide gender comparisons across six major AOD categories. Good comparison congruencies are found across the two samples on these six ASAP scales. Across both samples, female adolescents indicate higher involvement in *amphetamine-type drugs*; and *males* indicate higher involvement in *marijuana*. No gender differences were found on the *Inhalant and Other Drug Scales. Males in the Treatment* group score higher on *Alcohol Involvement* and *females in the Probation group* indicated greater involvement in *cocaine* than the male group. One clear discrepancy was found: *males in the Treatment* group scored higher on the *Hallucinogen Scale* whereas *females in the Probation* group scored higher on the *Hallucinogen Scale*.

What do these findings mean with respect to gender differences and, more specifically, treatment focus? First, the trend reported in the literature that female AOD clients and *female judicial clients* report greater adjustment problems in the area of *mental health and family* is certainly corroborated in these findings. This provides cogent support for greater treatment focus for females in these two adjustment problem areas. On the specific mental health scales on the ASAP, *female adolescents* in both samples report more *anxiety-depression and a greater history of self-harm thinking and behavior*. As well, females in both samples have higher scores on the scale that measures the *use of drugs to change and alter psychological moods such as anxiety and depression*.

With respect to family problems, the issue may not be that the problems of families as reported on by males are any less than those reported on by females. The issue, most likely, is that *girls are more sensitive to,*

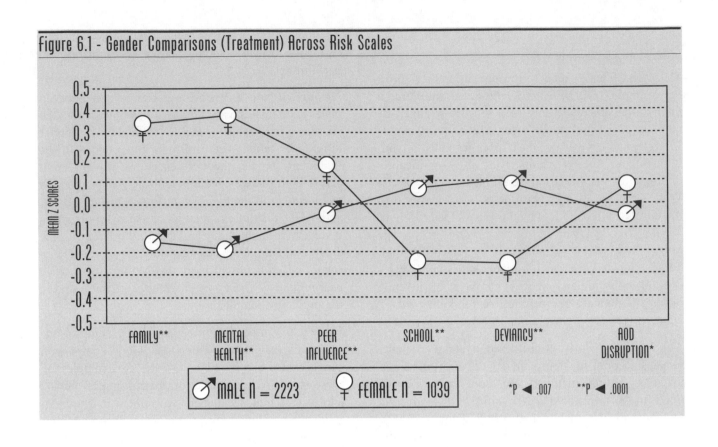

Figure 6.1 - Gender Comparisons (Treatment) Across Risk Scales

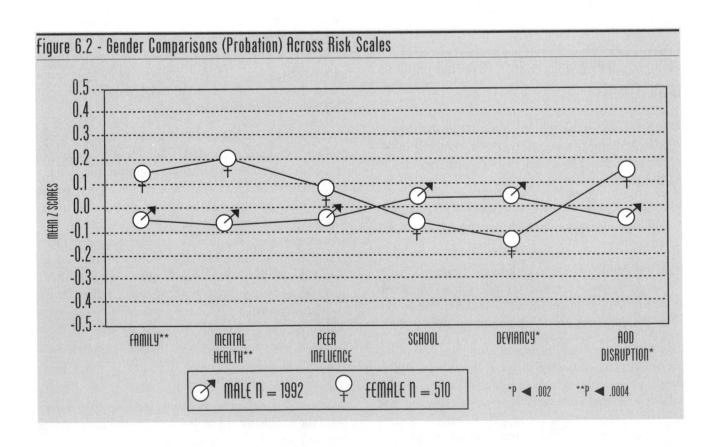

Figure 6.2 - Gender Comparisons (Probation) Across Risk Scales

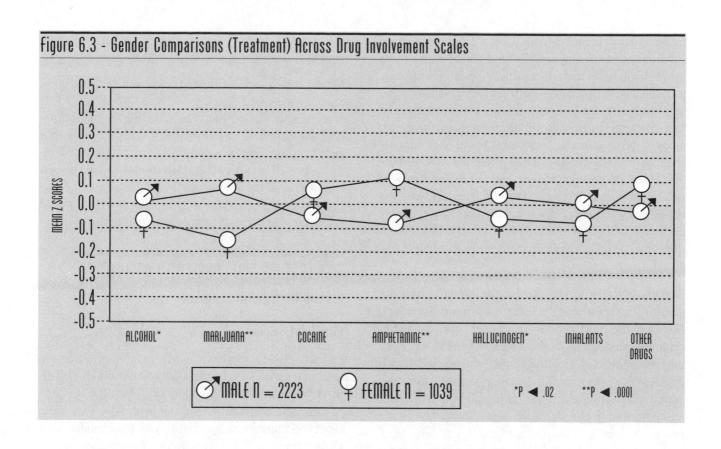

Figure 6.3 - Gender Comparisons (Treatment) Across Drug Involvement Scales

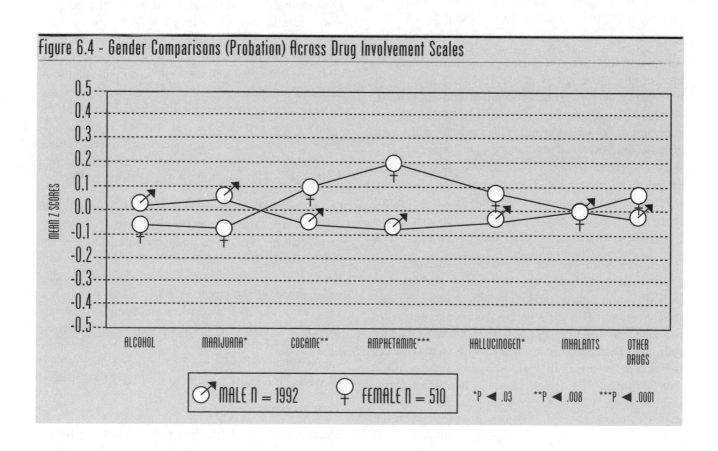

Figure 6.4 - Gender Comparisons (Probation) Across Drug Involvement Scales

more tuned-in to and probably *more impacted by family problems* than males. The tendency of males to be more involved in *activities outside of the family* may provide a buffer for males with respect to sensitivity to and being affected by family disruption problems. The fact that the magnitude of differences in these two areas is greater in the treatment group may support the idea that *the major referral issues for AOD female treatment adolescent clients are family and mental health problems*. With the *Probation* group, whereas these gender differences are apparent, the primary issue would most likely be deviancy and criminal conduct and AOD involvement for both males and females.

Across both samples, *male adolescents* indicate *greater involvement in deviancy and criminal conduct*. Boys are into more serious, or at least more extensive, criminal conduct in both samples. Female deviancy may be more tied into the family and mental health problems, whereas male deviancy is more tied into community acting out. Thus, although both males and females need focus in these areas, certainly in the *Probation* group, boys may need a different kind (e.g., more intensive) of judicial intervention and supervision than do girls. Further studies of these data indicate that girls in the *Treatment* group have lower scores on deviancy than girls in the *Probation* group.

An important finding in these data is that the magnitude of effect size is less in the *Probation* group and that there is no difference between girls and boys with respect to *negative peer influence and school adjustment* in the *Probation* group. This suggests that when girls become involved in deviancy and criminal conduct, they have similar risk-resiliency characteristics to those of male probation clients. This certainly points out that girls in the *Probation* group will need more focus in the area of acting-out behavior and involvement in antisocial behavioral patterns.

Differences with respect to AOD involvement are apparent in these data. Most important is that females in both samples have statistically higher scores on the *AOD Symptom-Disruption* scale. This is mainly due to the fact that females report having more AOD use symptoms that are more associated with mental health issues. For example, they score higher on the AOD *Psychophysical Disruption* subscale than males. With respect to treatment, these findings clearly indicate that a focus on changing patterns that lead to AOD use disruption are just as important, if not more important, among females as among males. Further, closer scrutiny is needed with females with respect to

the impact of direct and indirect (withdrawal) psychophysical symptoms related to AOD use.

More subtle gender differences are noted when comparing the two groups across specific AOD involvement. *Females* tend to score higher on *cocaine and amphetamine* use than males. This suggests that girls may be using stimulant drugs to mitigate depression. As well, the use of amphetamines to lose weight is more prevalent among girls. Certainly, greater focus on monitoring and *managing marijuana abuse* would be required with *treatment of male clients*.

RISK FACTORS AND CORRELATES OF JUVENILE OFFENDING AMONG FEMALES

Family of origin

Pollock (1998) reports on the results of extensive interviews with *female offenders* concerning their family environments during childhood. These women had begun their criminal activity as juveniles. Two basic family patterns emerged: (a) disappointment and intimidation; and (b) overburdened parents.

Disappointment and intimidation: Many of these girls came from homes where they felt little love or affection. They sensed that they had been a "disappointment" to their parents, who were strict disciplinarians, controlling the family through the use of fear and intimidation. Use of severe punishment was not uncommon in these families, and neglect of the child's needs and perspectives was the rule (Pollock, 1998). "Far from being *insulators against* delinquency, these families are *instigators of* delinquency, addiction and criminality" (Pollock, 1998, p. 52).

Overburdened Parent: The second pattern that emerged from these interviews involved an "overburdened parent." Forced to hold several jobs to feed the family, these parents were *unable to spend time* with their children, often leaving them alone, with other relatives or on the street. AOD use was generally *a way of life*, and loss of relatives and friends to murder and gang-related activities was common. Girls in these families were likely to run away, often with the motivation of helping to relieve the burden on their parents who had "too many mouths to feed" (Pollock, 1998).

Teen pregnancy

Major correlates of problem behavior among female juvenile offenders are *early-onset and promiscuous sexuality and teen pregnancy*. Rates of teenage pregnancy vary with racial/ethnic group. Two-thirds of all juveniles who give birth are European American; however, as shown in *Table 6.2*, birth rates are more than twice as high per 1,000 Hispanic, African American or Native American females ages 15 to 17.

Thirty-two percent of the teenage births are to *unmarried females*. This percentage of unmarried juvenile mothers is significantly higher than it was a generation ago. In fact, *juvenile mothers gave birth to 8% of all of the infants born in the U.S. in 1996*. Of this set of juvenile mothers, 6% were 10 to 14 years of age (Snyder & Sickmund, 1999).

Major vulnerability factors that place juveniles at risk for teen pregnancy are:

- Early school failure;

- Early behavioral problems;

- Family dysfunction; and

- Poverty

(Snyder & Sickmund, 1999).

These four conditions also place girls at greater risk for criminal behavior.

School failure, teen pregnancy and delinquency

A pattern of school failure is frequently found among female juvenile offenders. According to the *National Council on Crime and Delinquency* (NCCD), 92% of the delinquent girls in the study experienced at least one school failure, and 85% reported one to three (Acoca, 1998). The incidence is nearly absolute:

- Being left back in school;

- Expelled from classes;

- Placed in remedial classes; and

- Other forms of disciplinary action.

All are features that are common to the school experi-

Table 6.2 - Rates of Birth/1000 Females Ages 15-17

Hispanic American	69
African American	65
Native American	46
European American	28
Asian/Pacific Islander	15

Source: Acoca, 1998

ence of girls who become involved in delinquent acts. Chesney-Lind and Sheldon (1998) found that school failure is a major predictor of delinquency in girls; the strength of this correlation is higher among girls than among boys.

Age of onset of delinquency in girls

The age at which boys first display antisocial behavior generally *precedes* that of girls. This delay in the development of overt problem behaviors among girls may result in a *failure to provide timely services* for girls who are experiencing high risk in adolescence (Silverthorn & Frick, 1999).

GENDER NORMS AND SEXUAL VIOLATION

Adolescent dating and sexuality

Once a child enters adolescence, a host of *physical and psychological demands* are placed upon him or her by the prevailing culture (Crawford & Unger, 2004; Messner, 2003). These demands, most frequently related to gender, include gender norms and expectations, gender roles, media images and a complex system of gender meanings (Bem, 1996; Baca-Zinn et al., 2000; Pollack, 2003; Gilligan, 1980). Within this context, girls and boys begin to date. Rigid standards of attractiveness and lavish scripts of sexuality flourish in the teen environment, through both print and video imagery (Crawford & Unger, 2004). Research has found that powerful *gender expectations* at this time may set up situations whereby early childhood traumas can be rekindled in girls (Lewin, 1985; Saltzberg & Chrisler, 2003; Thompson, 2003; Bem & Bem, 1971; Litton-Fox, 1977). Lewin (1985) reports that the differences in dating expectations between boys and girls may combine to transpose a simple dating encounter into an occasion for date rape. Many *female offenders have reported date rape*: 29% reported rape, generally by their boyfriends, partners or dates (Acoca, 1998).

Males, frequently pressured into early sexual performance by *their peers* (Messner, 2003; Pollack, 2003) may enter a dating encounter with thoughts of "the score" and anticipation of boasting about his "manliness" to his friends. Girls, on the other hand, are *socialized to yield to the will and desires* of males (Bem, 1996; Litton-Fox, 1977), in the interests of her deep relational motivations. Combined with the suppression of voice that commonly occurs among females during adolescence (Gilligan, 1980), expectations that she will yield may supersede a girl's ability to speak out concerning her own wishes. Caught in an unfamiliar and highly gender-scripted situation, sexuality that invades a female's sense of bodily integrity may occur alongside a boy's [mis] perception of her willingness. Coercion is clearly at play, although it is as much coercion by the *internalization of gender scripting* as by the male's behavior in the scenario.

Girls and relationality

Many researchers have commented upon the positive aspects of a relational orientation for recovery in females (Covington, 2000; Gilligan, 1982; Bettridge & Favreau, 1995). There is professional consensus that *optimizing healthy relationality* is a key to successful recovery. However, it is also important to emphasize the many ways in which relationality may operate as a *risk factor* for women and girls. A relational orientation, unguided by boundaries, could propel females into relationships that undermine their ability to stay sober and crime-free. Unhealthy boundaries may contribute to poor decision-making about relationships, dating and otherwise, which, when placed in the context of male expectations for sexuality, may compromise sexual safety. Additional danger occurs when females find themselves without relational connections at all, or are faced with disrupted and unhealthy connections. This is associated with a wide range of physical and psychological difficulties, including increased risk for (usually non-fatal) suicide attempts (Bettridge & Favreau, 1995). In a study entitled "Suicidal behavior among adolescent females: The cry for connection," the importance of relational motivations for adolescent females is vividly expressed (Bettridge & Favreau, 1995).

Treatment with adolescent female offenders, therefore, is enhanced by including education regarding a girl's sexuality, her rights to bodily integrity, healthy boundary establishment, and the ways in which gender expectations can conspire to put her in bad situations. This aspect of empowerment is crucial in treatment with female offenders, for it may contribute to the restoration of self-respect, the development of a sense of safety (knowing she is better able to protect herself) and reductions in future trauma which undoubtedly will facilitate her recovery.

Early and late maturation: Taunts and sexual harassment

A history of trauma in the lives of female juvenile offenders may take many other forms, and occurs in a variety of contexts. Coincident with abuse in the family and/or the dating environment, females who offend often report *sexual harassment in their schools* and *on the streets* of their communities. High school girls report sexual harassment at school at the alarming rate of 81% (Sadker & Sadker, 1994). Girls who engage in fighting and other aggressive behavior cite frequent experiences with *threatening taunts and harassment* at bus stops, in schools and on the streets (Ford, 1998, in Acoca, 1998). Chronic experience with taunts and teasing is especially prevalent among girls who are either slow or fast in the maturation of their secondary sex characteristics (Pollock, 1998). For example, under-development or over-development of the breasts in adolescence makes girls especially vulnerable to this type of harassment from others.

Suppression of female voice vs. emergence of male entitlement

Social norms within adolescent subculture that teens be *independent of adult influence* frequently generalize into refusing assistance from adults as well. For girls, these norms are backed by more powerful forces, which may especially inhibit them from seeking assistance when dealing with trauma experience (Pollock, 1998). A general climate of disbelief and a "*conspiracy of silence*" (Butler, 1978) surrounds girls' reports of sexual abuse, especially incest (Butler, 1978). Accusations that she was somehow at fault for what happened to her are commonplace. These forces frequently cause girls to *suppress expression of their pain*, in service of more normative images of the "nice girl" who does not speak of such things, or make such accusations (Butler, 1978; Litton-Fox, 1977). Incipient rage may result, i.e., silencing of emotions (specifically rage) may motivate recourse to destructive outlets such as substance abuse, runaway and criminal offending (Girls Incorporated, 1996).

SEXUAL ASSAULT DURING CHILDHOOD

Prevalence of abuse

Although adolescent male offenders also report a high incidence of abuse, the prevalence of these experiences, especially *emotional* and *sexual abuse*, is *much higher in girls* than in boys (Acoca, 1998).

Girls in general report an exceedingly high incidence of violent trauma: *20% of girls in high school* report experiences with *physical and/or sexual abuse* of some kind. *Twelve percent* of high school girls report having experienced *sexual abuse* (compared to 5% of boys) and *17% of high school girls* report having experienced *physical abuse* (vs. 12% of high school boys) (Harris & Associates, 1997, reported in Acoca, 1998). "As prevalent as the various abuses of girls in the general United States population are, these abuses are *nearly universal* among girls in the juvenile justice system" (Acoca, 1998).

Physical assault of juveniles *under age* 12 constitutes 5.5% of all reported violent crime. Sexual assault is, by far, the major form of assault experienced by juveniles under age 12, constituting 32% of all reported assaults of juveniles. OJJDP reports that 33% of sexual assault victims are under the age of 12.

Current statistics suggest that females constitute 96% of all sexual assault victims, 92% of those experiencing a first sexual assault between the ages of 12 and 17; 26% per cent of those sexually assaulted under the age of 12 are male (Snyder & Sickmund, 1999).

Juvenile perpetrators of sexual assault

Among sexual assaults of juveniles, an age of victim by age of perpetrator interaction has been observed. Juvenile offenders perpetrate a sizeable portion of the sexual assault of other juveniles. Youth who are known to their victim perpetrate a large majority of these assaults. Statistics reveal (for all ages) that *47% of the perpetrators of sexual assault against children under age 12 are family members, 49% acquaintances, and just 4% are strangers* (Snyder & Sickmund, 1999). *Table 6.3* presents the percentage of perpetrators by age in the sexual assault of young people.

Other types of crime committed against juveniles are *kidnapping* (21%), *aggravated assault* (4%), *simple assault* (4%) and *robbery* (2%). Thirty-seven percent of these victims were younger than age 7, and 47% of these victims were female (Snyder & Sickmund, 1999). The use of drugs among high school students, (especially females), placed them at greater risk for (especially sexual) violent victimization than those who did not use. Sexual trauma plays a prominent role in the etiology of juvenile delinquency, especially among girls.

Adolescent sex offenders

Male juvenile sex offenders perpetuate a high percentage of the *most severe* sexual assaults. In a study that compared the sexual offense severity of incarcerated adult vs. adolescent male sex offenders, it was found that the sexual assaults *perpetrated by adolescents* were at least *as serious* (if not more so) than those carried out by adult rapists (Aylwin et al., 2000). This study found that adolescents tend to show less preference for a particular victim gender than do adults. Studies of adolescent sex offenders reveal that the most commonly found characteristics cluster in four domains:

- *Social skills and interaction*—including dating skills, emotional loneliness, and social competence;

- *Personal characteristics*—such as self-esteem and other personality factors;

- *Cognitive assessments*—including knowledge about sexuality, rape attitudes and beliefs; and

- *Delinquent behavior*—including drug and alcohol abuse (Beckett, 1999).

Adolescent sex offenders appear to differ in several ways from adolescents incarcerated for other serious types of crimes (Jonson-Reid & Way, 2001). For example, differences have been found in the incidence of childhood abuse and neglect across these two groups, with *sexual or physical abuse* occurring at a higher incidence than neglect among sexual offenders. Another significant difference was found with regard to the index of *serious emotional disturbance*, with sexual offenders receiving services for these difficulties at two times the rate of non-sexual serious offenders (Jonson-Reid & Way, 2001). Finally, these researchers found that sexual offenders tend to come into contact with the criminal justice system at *a later age* than non-sexual offenders (Jonson-Reid & Way, 2001). For further review of the dynamics of sexual violence from the perspective of the victim and the perpetrator see Bell (2000); Bloom, (2000); and Johnson, (2000).

Sex offense and recidivism

Hagan and Gust-Brey (2000) conducted a 10-year longitudinal study of *adolescent sexual perpetrators against children* to examine the incidence of recidivism for sexual offense. Upon release from a correctional treatment program, they found that while most of these individuals *did re-offend*, most were *not found to perpetrate another sexual assault*. Other studies have confirmed these results. Research on recidivism among adolescent sexual perpetrators (with victims of all ages) finds that, in general when re-offending does occur, it is much more likely to be *some other crime* or non-sexual violence, as opposed to a recurrent sexual offense (Beckett, 1999).

In an analysis of recidivism patterns among serious juvenile sex offenders, Minor (2002) found that re-

Table 6.3 - Percentage of Perpetrators by Age in the Sexual Assault of Juveniles

Age of victim	Perpetrator	Age of Perpetrator		
		under 12	12-17	0-17
<6	Family member	4.0	12.6	16.6
	Acquaintance	9.3	15.9	25.2
	Stranger	.3	.8	1.1
7-11	Family member	1.6	11.7	13.3
	Acquaintance	4.6	14.8	19.4
	Stranger	.4	1.1	1.5
12-17	Family member	.1	2.6	2.7
	Acquaintance	.5	19.6	20.1
	Stranger	0	1.5	1.5
∑ 0-17	Family member	5.7	26.9	32.6
	Acquaintance	14.4	50.3	64.7
	Stranger	.7	3.4	4.1

Source: Snyder & Sickmund, 1999

offense predictors vary for adolescent vs. adult sex offenders. Re-offending was defined as any parole violation, arrest or conviction since leaving a (corrections-based) sex offender program. Major factors that predicted an increased risk of re-offending include:

- Impulsiveness;
- Social interaction with young children;
- Early age at first offense; and
- Shorter duration of treatment.

Desistance from re-offense was predicted by:

- Victim sex, i.e., male;
- Personal experience with sexual abuse victimization; and
- "Multiple paraphilias."

Minor (2002) thus asserts the need for specific assessment and treatment procedures for adolescent sex offenders.

EXPERIENCES WITH VIOLENT TRAUMA IN CHILDHOOD: A MAJOR ROUTE FOR GIRLS INTO CRIMINAL CONDUCT

"[G]ender matters in the forces that propel women into criminal behavior" (Chesney-Lind, 2000). In developing a profile of the characteristics frequently found among female adolescent offenders, The National Council on Crime and Delinquency (NCCD, 1998) found that experiences with some form of violent trauma (emotional, physical or sexual abuse) was nearly universal in these girls. Ninety-two percent of female juvenile offenders report experience of one or more forms of violent trauma; many of these girls report having experienced these forms of abuse on many occasions.

Acoca, 1998

Another study conducted by the NCCD concerning adult female offenders also found an incidence of 92% of these women with a history of abuse (Acoca & Austin, 1996). *Table 6.4* shows a breakdown of abuse types as experienced by adolescent female offenders.

EMOTIONAL ABUSE includes incessant fear inducing, shouting and yelling, being forced into isolation, prevented from attending school or work, constant accusations of worthlessness and more. Witnessing domestic violence among members of the family is also included in emotional abuse. Emotional abuse was reported by 58% of adolescent female offenders (Acoca, 1998). Aggression and delinquency have been named as prominent among the consequences of this type of experience in childhood (Saunders, 1994).

PHYSICAL ABUSE was reported by 81% of the girls in the NCCD study (Acoca, 1998). Forty-five percent reported having been *burned or beaten* by the age of 13. This type of abuse generally occurred at the hands of boyfriends (20%), mothers (19%), and others (16%). Twenty-five percent reported being *shot or stabbed* at lease once in their lives. These crimes usually occurred outside of the girl's home. The *perpetrators were generally acquaintances* as well as gang members (36%), family members (8%), friends or neighbors (8%) and boyfriends (8%). Strangers accounted for 19% of the stabbing or shooting incidents (Acoca, 1998). From these statistics we infer

that, in addition to the high rates of violence these girls are experiencing inside their homes, the *communities in which these girls live* are also characterized by high rates of violence.

SEXUAL ABUSE was reported by 56% of the girls in the study (Acoca, 1998). Forty percent reported being *raped or sodomized*, 17% more than once. This type of assault also occurred most frequently between the ages of 12 and 15; the *greatest number occurred at age 13.* The perpetrators named in these assaults were *acquaintances* (28%), *boyfriends* (15%) and *dating partners* (14%), *family friends and neighbors* (14%) and strangers (15%). A third of the girls who reported sexual abuse reported that the molestation occurred at the age of five years on average. Molesters tended to be *friends or neighbors* (32%), *acquaintances* (31%), *stepfathers* (8%) and *strangers* (7%) (Acoca, 1998).

THROWN AWAY is a term used to describe the phenomenon of adolescent female offenders having been frequently *forced to leave* their homes, usually between the ages of 12 and 15 years. Mothers were the most frequent parent to initiate this expulsion (Acoca,

Table 6.4 - Types of Abuse Suffered by Adolescent Female Offenders

Type of Abuse	Percent of girl offenders who report this experience	Average Age of occurrence
Emotional abuse	88%	
Verbal threats of physical harm	46%	
Accusations of worthlessness	60%	
Physical +/or Sexual Abuse	81%	
beaten / burned	>45%	11-13 years
5 or more times	31%	
Shot / stabbed	25%	13-15 years
Sexual Abuse	>56%	
molested/fondled	>33%	5 years
rape or sodomy	40%	12-15 years
Forced to leave home	32%	12-15 years
Witnessed violent fights at home	58%	
Neglect (made wards of the state)	25%	12-14 years

Source: Acoca, 1998; Acoca & Dedel, 1998 - report from the NCCD study (1996).

1998). Often without options, many of these girls are forced to live on the streets, where they come into contact with the drug culture and other destructive elements of street life, such as prostitution and further sexual violence. As described above, these experiences frequently provide an inroad into criminal behavior in the interests of survival. Becoming affiliated with a powerful "pimp" or drug dealer may provide some form of protection in these environments. As a result of these and other contingencies, there appears an alarming rate of pregnancy and motherhood among young female offenders. Twenty-nine percent of the girls in the NCCD study reported at least one pregnancy, and 16% had experienced this pregnancy during confinement in a correctional facility (Acoca, 1998).

NEGLECT is another experience reported by young female offenders. Twenty-five percent of juvenile offenders had been made wards of the state due to parental neglect, 13 years being the most vulnerable age for this occurrence.

Acoca (1998) summarizes the findings of this NCCD study thusly:

Increasingly, violent victimization is being recognized as a major threat to the physical and psychological health of girls and ultimately that of their children. It is also identified as a primary precursor to involvement in the juvenile and, for a growing number of young women, the adult criminal justice system, p. 9.

Psychological and behavioral consequences of violent trauma in adolescence

Early experiences with emotional, physical and/or sexual assault are strongly associated with severe psychological disturbance among adolescent girls. Among these disturbances are *eating disorders, depression, suicidal ideation and attempts, risk taking and substance abuse* (Acoca, 1998). There is also a preponderance of *delinquent activity* (Belknap & Holsinger, 1998; Chesney-Lind & Sheldon, 1998; Owen & Bloom, 1997).

Among these behaviors can be found the use of *multiple drugs, participation in gangs, school failure, sex with many partners and early pregnancy.* These behaviors also show positive correlations with arrest and engagement with the juvenile justice system (Belknap & Holsinger, 1998; Chesney-Lind & Sheldon, 1998; Owen & Bloom, 1997).

Substance abuse: Interviews revealed that girls who had experienced some form of abuse deliberately used alcohol and other drugs as a means of self-medication (Acoca, 1998).

[On drugs] I like the feeling, I feel normal, like myself. When I'm sober I don't like it. On drugs I'm happy. Sober you think about everything. It sucks.

Interview with a 16-year-old girl (from Acoca, 1998)

Resonance is found in similar comments by a female adult offender.

Everyone keeps telling me that my substance abuse is a problem. It's not my problem; it's my solution.

(from Kerr, 1998).

When a young girl finds her solutions in substance abuse, she opens the door to learning deficits, poor coping abilities and deteriorating mental and physical health. As her life grows more desperate, the "solution" becomes a major source of problems in itself, which compounds the pain, rage and terror she may be feeling from other events in her life. *Multiple drug use,* prominent behavior among abused female delinquents, appears to be related to:

The number of emotional abuse experiences:

- 18 to 23% of girls who experienced one to three types of emotional abuse engaged in multiple use; and

- 43% of those who experienced four or more types of emotional abuse engaged in multiple use.

The number of sexual abuse experiences:

- 35% of girls who had experienced at least two types of sexual abuse used multiple drugs; and

- 21% of multiple drug users had not had these experiences.

The number of physical abuse experiences:

- Those who experienced at least three types of physical abuse were more likely to be multiple drug users.

School failure and abuse

School failure among girls is predicted by experiences with violent trauma in childhood (Acoca, 1998). The breakdown of school failure by abuse frequency and type, presented in *Table 6.5,* shows correlations between school failure and frequency of three types of abuse, e.g., approximately 55% of girls who had experienced one episode of sexual abuse is shown to have had 2 or more failures in school.

Progression from juvenile to adult offending among females

Violent trauma and *poverty* are viewed as the primary routes through which young girls enter a criminal lifestyle (Acoca, 1998, p. 568). A young girl's pathway into criminal conduct is described as having grown up in a home without the basics for survival. She engaged in street begging for food at age 10; by age 12 her profits had increased through the sale of crack cocaine. She gave the money to her mother to buy food for the family. The girl had repeatedly been the witness of violence in her home, fights between her parents, abuse of her brother and she, herself, had suffered child abuse, including beatings and stabbing

> *"I feel like I didn't have a childhood. After my stepfather abused me when I was nine, I didn't feel comfortable showing my body to anyone. [Now] I feel like a piece of meat. I want to be invisible."*
>
> Interview with a 17-year-old girl
> Acoca & Dedel (1998), p 568.

A major risk factor for female delinquency/adult crime, therefore, is *childhood victimization*, which is usually delivered at the hands of family or family friends (Acoca, 1998). Findings over the past two decades have consistently uncovered a common developmental pathway among female juvenile offenders: from *childhood emotional, sexual and physical abuse, to adolescent participation in criminal behavior, and eventual engagement with the juvenile justice system* (Belknap, Holsinger, & Dunn, 1997). The abuse histories of adolescent girls in corrections are very similar to those of adult women offenders (Covington, 1998). As female adolescent offenders grow older, their trajectory of development extends into the dynamics commonly found in the lives of women offenders (Milkman, Wanberg, & Gagliardi, 2004). With continuing cycles of *violent trauma, substance abuse and the effects of living in the drug culture and on the street*, women offenders, starting with delinquent behavior, later become enmeshed in a life of crime. Forty-six percent of women offenders report their *first arrest before the age of 18* (Acoca & Austin, 1996). During interviews, many report that abuse experiences in childhood were "the equivalent of first steps leading to offending as juveniles" (Acoca & Austin, 1996).

FEMALE GANG PARTICIPATION

Female adolescents constitute only a small fraction of all formal gang members. Estimates range from 7% (Pollock, 1998) through 10% (Snyder & Sickmund, 1999). Yet self-report data (NCCD, 1996) suggest higher rates of involvement—perhaps as high as 38% (Snyder & Sickmund, 1999). Forty-seven percent of female offenders report involvement with gang activity, and 71% of those report heavy involvement (Acoca, 1998). Self-reports regarding level of involvement in a gang, however, are difficult to interpret, due

Table 6.5 - School Failures and Types of Abuse

Emotional Abuse		Sexual Abuse		Physical Abuse	
#*		#		#	
0	30%**	0	45%	0	41%
1	50%	1	55%	1	49%
2	31%	2+	65%	2	59%
3	60%	3+	67%	4+	64%

* Number of abuse experiences

** Percentages represent female adolescents with two or more school failures

Source: Acoca, 1998

to phenomena such as peripheral contact and "wannabe's." Cepeda & Valdez (2003) found that within a sample of Mexican American gang members (ages 14 to 18), the *majority of females* who report gang association, do participate in the activities of male gangs (such as socializing on the street, and risk-taking), but are not formal gang members. A much smaller minority are actually female gang members themselves. Four risk factors were found to be associated with female gang involvement (Cepeda & Valdez, 2003):

• Sexual relations;

• "Partying";

• Substance use; and

• Crime involvement.

Negative effects of these risk factors appeared to be mediated by factors such as:

• The girl's particular relationship to the male gang (e.g., dating partner, friend, "tagalong");

• Socio-cultural features of their family and community (including family status); and

• Socio-economic conditions of their lives (Cepeda & Valdez, 2003).

These findings suggest that research into female gang participation should undergo an expansion of focus beyond a particular girl's individual problems, and into the broader socio-cultural context of the gang (Cepeda & Valdez, 2003).

The majority of girls who report gang involvement live in neighborhoods described as having active male gangs. Female gang participation tends to be concentrated in the smaller cities, where gang-related violence tends to be less violent and serious in general (Snyder & Sickmund, 1999). It appears that adolescent females engage in less frequent (and less severe) criminal activity than males when they are in a gang. Some indicators suggest that the presence of girls in gangs may even lessen the degree of violence among male gang members (Pollock, 1998). Other girls, however, have been reported to share the callous attitudes of males toward the "necessity" of violence "in the business" (Taylor, 1993).

Gangs often serve as surrogate families for their members, males and females alike. But the importance of support and protection derived from this "family" can be magnified when a *girl seeks asylum* from an abu-

sive or discordant home (Acoca, 1998; Pollock, 1998). The gang may appear to be a safe haven away from the harshness of her former experiences. Acoca (1998) indicates that the major reason that girls tend to join gangs is to gain "protection from harm" (p. 573). A large percentage of the girls who join gangs have suffered violent trauma (Acoca, 1998). Gang membership is found at a rate of 50% in girls who have experienced 2 forms of physical abuse, and in 63% of those who have experienced three or more types (vs. 35% who report no experience with physical abuse at all) (Acoca, 1998).

My people protect me. Older gang members want me to do good.

Interview with a 15-year-old girl

They were everything after my family. A lot of people join because they don't fit anywhere else. It's a place for people to belong if they aren't strong. You have protection [but] it does put you in danger.

Interview with a 14-year-old girl
(both quotes in Acoca, 1998)

Interviews with African, Jamaican and Hispanic American girls investigated their perceptions of the motivations and risk factors for female gang involvement (Walker-Barnes & Mason, 2001). Urban females (aged 12 to 17 years) listed as primary reasons for female gang involvement:

• Peer pressure;

• Protection from crime, family violence, other gangs, etc.;

• Family environments characterized by a lack of warmth and parental conflict;

• A source of thrills and excitement; and

• An entré into money-making opportunities;

• A source of respect (Walker-Barnes & Mason, 2001).

As discussed in previous chapters, male motivation for gang participation is more likely to center around the establishment of *status and dominance*, the acquisition of both monetary and territorial resources, and protection of personal and group honor (Horowitz, 1983).

Girls may enter the world of gangs by joining a predominantly male gang or through the formation of "girl gangs." Interviews with females in girl gangs from Detroit (Taylor, 1993) provide insight into the girls' perception of their own behavior. Generally, girls use gangs as a place to "hang out," a place where they can gather together with peers to socialize and dance. Their attitudes toward men are very independent—they feel that males are "nice to have around, but not necessary."

But girls do frequently perceive their gangs as "posses"—the equivalent of other criminal organizations. Living a crime-free life, in their expressed opinions, was "for jerks and honkies" (Taylor, 1993).

Researchers who have explored the qualitative differences in the nature of male and female gang involvement have similarly concluded that the actual nature of gang participation among girls *differs markedly* from media images that portray girls in gangs as similar to their male counterparts (Chesney-Lind, Shelden & Joe, 1996; Chesney-Lind, 1993; Joe & Chesney-Lind, 1995; Campbell, 1991). From motivations for entry, through specific types of criminal engagement, most adolescent females differ from males with regards to gang participation. This research counters the media's all-too-frequent tendency to depict girls in gangs as engaging in masculine types of violent delinquency and criminal conduct (Chesney-Lind et al., 1996; Cepeda & Valdez, 2003; Pollock, 1998; Walker-Barnes & Mason, 2001; Chesney-Lind, 1993; Joe & Chesney-Lind, 1995; Gilligan, 1982).

Four types of adolescent gangs have been identified:

- *Scavenger gangs* who sporadically engage in crime if the opportunity arises;

- *Territorial gangs* who exert control over a certain area with boundaries;

- *Commercial gangs* who engage in the supply (and sometimes manufacture) of a product (usually drugs) to sell for profit;

- *Corporate gangs* who are as organized as any criminal syndicate, are prominent players in the drug trade and make large sums of money for these activities. Individuals in corporate gangs are least likely to abuse substances.

Females participate in all four types of gangs (Pollock, 1998). Girls' participation in gangs generally mirrors the behavior of boys, with a major exception being the *serious violence and criminal activity* generally per-

petuated by male gang members only. Although fighting, hostility and conflict often characterize gang environments, girls who are involved in gangs have often learned to expect these behaviors as normative ways of resolving conflict (as they may never have experienced anything else). This latter point refers to the experience of many females throughout the criminal justice system, as well as those females who suffer violent abuse in their homes at the hands of abusive partners (Pollack, 1998). Another difference between male and female gang participation emerges when we look at age. Females tend to join gangs at a *later age* than do males. One study found that a third of girl gang members were older than 26 years of age (Pollock, 1998).

TRAUMA WITHIN THE JUVENILE JUSTICE SYSTEM

Adolescent female detention

In general, adolescent female offenders commit much less serious crimes than their male counterparts (Acoca, 1998). For example, girls constitute the largest percentage of arrests for status offenses; yet many of these girls end up in correctional facilities. In 1995, the *U.S. Department of Justice* issued a report (*Human Rights Watch*, 1995) to prevent status offenders from being "held in secure confinement" (Acoca, 1998, p.575). Nevertheless, these girls, as well as others who have engaged in offenses of low severity, are confined in the same type of juvenile detention facilities as boys who commit much more serious crimes, and are forced to undergo the same types of security measures as male juveniles, despite their lower security risk. What's more, these females are frequently deprived of the same privileges for exercise and recreation as their male counterparts possess. As girls are generally less violent than boys, they are more often housed in overcrowded rooms than are males, in rooms with poor ventilation (Acoca, 1998) and little space to call their own. These factors increase the likelihood of generating physical and psychological difficulties.

An increasing number of female adolescent offenders are being confined in adult correctional facilities (Acoca, 1998). The *Bureau of Justice Statistics* (1995) reported that 7,000 girls were incarcerated in U.S. jails in 1991. Among these detainees were girls who had experienced a history of abuse and neglect, as well as clinical depression. No special programming is provided for juveniles in adult correctional facilities, and what educational resources are available are generally geared to an adult level, which may render them difficult to understand for the average juvenile offender (Acoca, 1998). It is no wonder that the rate of suicide among girls housed in adult facilities is 7.7 times higher than the rate for those housed in juvenile detention facilities (Chesney-Lind & Sheldon, 1998). Adult women in these correctional facilities express fear for the girls' safety (Acoca, 1998).

Mistreatment, abuse and neglect

The *National Council on Crime and Delinquency* (Acoca & Dedel, 1998) also investigated the nature of girls' experiences within the juvenile justice system. Databases, case files and interviews with the girls were scrutinized to ascertain prominent risk factors (and other needs that might arise) for this population within the juvenile justice system itself. These investigations revealed that the procedures used in the juvenile justice system involve few, if any, considerations of the special needs of female juveniles, despite the fact that this group constitutes the largest growing proportion of the juvenile justice population (Acoca, 1998).

While investigation into the use and extent of physically harsh treatment of girls in the juvenile justice system was not the intent of the original study, many girls did report incidents of emotional, physical and sexual mistreatment that had occurred there (Acoca, 1998). In fact, some of the interviewers observed such behavior during the study.

[A] guy slammed a girl against the wall.
Interview with a 16-year old woman
(Acoca, 1998, p. 578)

These episodes often rekindled memories of past abuse, fueling feelings of confusion, sorrow and rage that may have been associated with a girl's entry into problem behavior in the first place. Adolescent girls may suffer "multiple additional violations" (Acoca, 1998) once they are involved with the juvenile detention system. Girls in juvenile detention report that staff use debasing comments and name-calling (such as "sluts" and "hookers"), loud shouts, threats of physical harm, and swear words to enforce compliance and produce silence.

Staff call us bad names, very disrespectful, fuck this, fuck that. If we talk back we go to the box. My teacher threatened to "kick my ass" because I complained about not being called on for 20 minutes.

Interview with a 17-year-old female
(Acoca & Dedel, 1998)

Girls who attempt to file grievances about abuses or inappropriate touching are frequently responded to with further intimidation. The girls report these incidents to be sexually demeaning, anxiety-producing and damaging to feelings of self-worth (Acoca, 1998).

Juvenile females also report instances of sexual trauma within the juvenile justice system (Acoca, 1998). Chesney-Lind and Sheldon (1998) report that males are frequently involved and thus may observe strip searches, showers and gynecological exams, as well as use mace during routine procedures (Acoca, 1998). Body cavity inspection may be demanded at any time—whenever a rule has been broken, or the detainee is visited from someone outside the correctional setting (Acoca, 1998). These are just a few of the invasive procedures that may increase the burden of trauma, shame and depression among female juvenile offenders. Many of the girls have become used to being treated in this manner.

I'm real used to doing that.
Interview with a female detainee
(Acoca, 1998, p. 579)

Experiences such as these seem to exacerbate the girls' already-present "perception, born for many with their experiences of sexual violation at home and in the streets, that they did not have the right or the power to protect their physical boundaries (Acoca, 1998, p. 579). The *Human Rights Watch* report (1996) adds: ". . . these women (who are victimized while incarcerated) have little awareness of their rights. (They do not) realize what rape (is), let alone sexual harassment" (quoted in Acoca, 1998, p. 579).

Acoca (1998) reports an absence of standardized methods for gathering data about the more serious abuses that may occur in the juvenile justice system. She asserts that these experiences within the juvenile justice system may compound injuries that female juveniles have experienced during earlier life experiences, and thereby undermine the potential for girls to benefit from juvenile correctional procedures. Further degeneration of mental health (such as PTSD symptoms), increased engagement with substance abuse (due to attempts at self-medication) and a lowering of self efficacy (regarding the ability to protect herself) may all contribute to higher rates of recidivism among female adolescent offenders. Acoca (1998) asserts:

Reported victimizations are included here not to castigate the majority of juvenile justice and correctional professionals who are dedicated to preserving public safety while maintaining the civil and personal rights of girls but as harbingers of a serious growing crisis within the entire juvenile justice system. As the population of juveniles in custody expands and public pressure to punish rather than habilitate mounts, it is in the nation's as well as the children's best interests to ensure that these facilities protect the youth in their charge from harm (Acoca, 1998, p. 574).

Housing, nutrition and health care

Currently, housing, feeding, health care and other important areas in correctional settings for juvenile offenders are not carefully monitored (Acoca, 1998; U.S. Dept. of Justice, 1995). *The U.S. Dept of Justice Human Rights Watch* (1995) reported that "[t]here is no general monitoring of the conditions in which adjudicated delinquents are confined" (Acoca, 1998, p. 575). Clothing that is unclean, loosely fitting or simply doesn't fit at all is common fare for girls in juvenile facilities. Inadequate hygiene and personal care products were named as responsible for a high incidence of head lice, scabies and dry or damaged skin among young female offenders. Besides being uncomfortable, these factors may contribute to *deteriorating psychological effects*, such as the low self-esteem and feelings of worthlessness that are frequently found among female offenders (Acoca, 1998).

Few gender-specific policies have been introduced into the procedures and practices of the juvenile justice system (Acoca, 1998). A large percentage of female adult and juvenile detainees are under the direct supervision of a *predominately male* staff. Under these circumstances, the specific health and emotional needs of female adolescent offenders are likely to be overlooked. Adequate health screening, food, hygiene and living space are essential to this population, who frequently enter the juvenile justice system with deteriorating health and a high probability of pregnancy or motherhood (Acoca, 1998). Twenty-nine percent of the girls in the NCCD study experienced pregnancy, 16% while confined in a correctional facility (Acoca, 1998). Yet, the NCCD study found that gynecological exams may be administered without proper procedures (Acoca, 1998). Further damage, both psychological and medical, can be found in correctional practices which utilize restraint as a form of punishment. Twenty-nine percent of pregnant teens in juvenile facilities reported being restrained during pregnancy, often leaving them in fear of falling and hurting their baby, or of being unable to obtain adequate medical attention should that be necessary (Acoca, 1998).

IMPLICATIONS FOR TREATMENT AND POLICY: A GENDER-FOCUSED TREATMENT PLATFORM

Feminist scholarship has elaborated numerous ways in which the lives of adolescent girls and women are affected by common social behaviors, beliefs and misunderstandings about gender. These include: social stereotypes and their associated stigmas; dynamics of relationship with men; experiences with violence; racism; and demands, e.g., care-giving, children, etc. (Covington, 2001; Pollack, 1998; Bem, 1996; Denmark et al., 1998). Having illustrated some of the ways in which the lives of girls are impacted by their more general experiences as females, we are confident that specific focus in the development of *gender-specific programming will improve treatment outcomes for adolescent female offenders* (CSAT, ; Covington, 2001; Pollack, 1998; Acoca, 1998).

An integrated treatment strategy for juvenile and adult female offenders includes *education on how female experience is affected by cultural constructions of gender*. Educating girls concerning the social position of women in society can help to *depersonalize responsibility* for many of the traumas they've experienced (such as sexual assault and battering). Effective treatment helps female clients arm themselves with emotional and cognitive reserves to aid in coping with *high-risk thoughts and situations*. There is a corresponding emphasis on teaching more effective responses to gender-normative situations, such as adolescent dating, perceived dependency needs, and career planning, etc. (Covington, 2001; Pollack, 1998; Bem, 1996).

The provision of *transitional services* for adolescent females (in order to prepare them for healthy living upon exit from the correctional system and/or substance abuse services) is a necessary feature of effective treatment. Successful transition to independent living is crucial in effecting reasonable expectation of successful (crime and substance-free) recovery within the community. Sample treatment options that may be initiated before release and sustained thereafter include:

- Modeling challenges to negative thinking, thought stopping;

- Generating alternative courses of action when likely difficult situations arise;

- On-site visits to community agencies;

- Aid in securing safe and affordable housing; and

- Aid in securing child care systems.

In conclusion to her comprehensive review of the conditions for girls in juvenile correctional facilities, Acoca (1998) asserts that the goals of the juvenile justice system would be more effectively addressed by incorporating the following gender-specific policies:

- Alternatives to incarceration for female adolescent offenders and their children;

- Specific education addressing issues of healthy boundary setting and relationality, the strengths and pitfalls of a relational orientation;

- Specific focus on helping the female client develop a sense of entitlement and voice, so she can express her needs and rights in an effective manner;

- Specific educational strategies designed to disrupt the generational cycle of child abuse, including parenting skills development, child care services and family systems support;

- Maternal health services, including prenatal care when needed; and

- Competency-based educational programming to provide training in coping and life skills.

These preparatory and after-care services are designed to address the following *milestones for comfortable and responsible living within the mainstream of society.*

Maintenance of Self Development: Helping girls recognize and place into practice (on a regular basis) a number of self-care and self-management activities may serve to enhance body awareness and increase self-respect and esteem. Inner and external forces that mitigate against utilizing these activities should be explored to provide realistic expectation of continued use.

Development of Healthy Relationships: Helping an adolescent girl to identify characteristics of high-risk relationships includes recognizing unreasonable and counter-productive demands and expectations from others as well as ways in which social scripts for the behavior of men and women may set girls up for recidivism, relapse, and potential re-entry into correctional services.

Ability to Utilize Community Resources: This component aims at helping girls to utilize the strengths of a relational orientation to aid in developing personal contacts and community resources that facilitate effective coping with the difficulties she is likely to encounter (e.g., support in resisting relapse, help and training in child care, job skills development etc., and finding safe/affordable housing, if return to the parental home is neither possible nor productive.

Finally, *The National Report on Juvenile Offenders* (1999) estimates that "allowing one youth to leave high school for a life of crime and drug abuse costs society $1.7 to $2.3 million. Saving the lives, hearts and minds of America's youth through early intervention and prevention programs is a cost-effective way to reduce crime in our country.

CHAPTER REVIEW

Many of the special needs of teenage girls who become involved in mental health and correctional services stem from the social position of females in society, reflecting their *unequal status and power* in relationships with men and in the general social hierarchy that confers male privilege and female subordination (Crawford & Unger, 2000; Miller & Stiver, 1997).

Female juvenile offenders are the largest growing segment of the juvenile justice population. Currently, 31% of juvenile offenders are female. Although males are generally arrested for more serious offenses, females are increasingly involved in violent crime. Those who come into contact with the criminal justice system *before the age of 14* (early onset offenders) are more likely to engage in serious offenses and to become chronic offenders. Girls constitute the largest percentage of status offenses, which would not be offenses if committed by adults, such as promiscuity, truancy or running away. Although most "runaways" are teenage girls between 16 and 17 years of age, many teenage females find themselves on the street because they have been "thrown away" by their parents. Status offenses and throwaways are often associated with *physical and/or sexual abuse* in the home or elsewhere. Unfortunately, female runaways are generally returned to the same environments that spawned their initial victimization. Many discover substance abuse as a means to *self-medicate* uncomfortable feeling states that stem from abuse. A downward spiral of abuse, recidivism and incarceration may ensue. The problem becomes multigenerational in that many juvenile females are pregnant at the time they enter the juvenile justice system.

Although females participate in the same kinds of delinquent behavior as do males, percentages of participation in particular delinquent acts vary by sex. While female offenses generally occur in the realm of property crime, males are far more likely to participate in *violent offenses*, including assault. Fifty percent of both males and females tend to commit their crimes *with other juveniles* or adults, which is more than twice the rate of collaboration found in the adult population. Males are far more likely to commit murder and more likely to use firearms (73% male vs. 41% female) as opposed to knives (32% females vs. 14% males) when trying to kill. While males are more likely than females to kill strangers, females are more likely to murder family members including children less than six years of age. As victims, females account for 29% of juveniles who are murdered, and are more than twice as likely than males to be murdered by a family member.

Studies of family relationships among female juvenile offenders reveal two basic dysfunctional patterns; *disappointment and intimidation*; and *overburdened parents*. Other major correlates of problem behaviors among female juvenile offenders are *early and promiscuous sexual activity and teen pregnancy*. These are positively correlated with *early school failure, behavioral problems, family dysfunction and poverty*. These four factors also place girls at risk for greater criminal conduct. Female offenders frequently report incidents of date rape, probably mediated by gender norms and differences in dating expectations between males and females (males are motivated to "score"; girls are socialized to yield to the will and desires of males). Along with abuse in the family and/or the dating environment, females who offend often report *sexual harassment at school and in their communities*. Female juvenile offenders appear to be socialized to suppress expression of pain concerning sexual abuse, probably contributing to underlying anger, which may become manifest in running away, substance abuse and criminal behavior.

Girls in general report an exceedingly high incidence of violent trauma. Twenty percent of girls in high school report some kind of physical and/or sexual abuse and these kinds of experiences are *nearly universal* among girls in the juvenile justice system. Current statistics suggest that females constitute 96% *of all sexual assault victims*, and 92% of those who were assaulted experienced their first sexual assault between the ages of 12 and 17. A large majority of perpetrators are *known to their victims*, i.e., 47% of sexual perpetrators are family members and 47% are acquaintances. The use of drugs among high school students put them at even greater risk for victimization including sexual and/or physical assault. Teenage males, many of whom have suffered sexual and physical abuse themselves, with consequent severe emotional disturbance, perpetrate a high percentage of the most severe sexual assaults against female adolescents. Male sex offenders tend to come into contact with the criminal justice system at a later age than non-sex offenders.

Trauma resultant from physical and/or sexual abuse plays a prominent role in the etiology of juvenile delinquency, especially among girls. Although interdependent, distinctions can be made between emotional, physical and sexual abuse, neglect, and abandonment. Early experiences with emotional, physical or sexual assault are strongly associated with *severe emotional and behavioral disturbance* including school failure, delinquency, gang affiliation, promiscuity, early pregnancy, eating disorders, depression, suicidal ideation and attempts, risk taking and multiple substance abuse. These behaviors are also positively correlated with arrest and engagement with the juvenile justice system. The two most important factors related to females entering a criminal lifestyle are *violent trauma and poverty*. Research over the past two decades consistently points to a *common developmental pathway* from juvenile to adult crime among female offenders: childhood emotional, sexual and physical abuse; adolescent participation in criminal behavior; engagement in the criminal justice system; return to the atmosphere of victimization; and further involvement and victimization within criminal justice settings.

Gangs often serve as *surrogate families* for their members, the "benefits" of which are magnified when a young female seeks asylum from an abusive or neglectful home. While the main reasons stated for gang membership among adolescent females are "peer pressure" and "protection from harm," males tend to be motivated by establishment of status, material acquisition, territorial resources and protection of personal or group honor. Self-report among female offenders regarding gang affiliation tends to be high (40%-70%); however, there is evidence that a considerably smaller percentage is actually gang members themselves. Factors that appear to be associated with female gang involvement are: *multiple sex partners, high levels of substance abuse in the context of peer activities* (i.e., heavy partying), and *criminal involvement*.

According to *The National Council on Crime and Delinquency,* there are *currently few, if any, considerations of the special needs of female adolescent offenders,* despite the fact that this group constitutes the largest growing proportion of the juvenile justice population. Clothing that is unclean or poorly fitting is common, as well as inadequate hygiene, a general lack of personal care products, improper gynecological exams and the use of restraint as a form of punishment. A large number of female adult and juvenile detainees are under the direct supervision of predominately male staff. As in adult settings, many girls report incidents of emotional, physical and sexual mistreatment while under the auspices of criminal justice supervision. These episodes *rekindle memories of past abuse,* which provided fuel for entry into criminal activity to begin with. Additional traumatic experiences within the juvenile justice system may undermine the potential for teenage girls to benefit from juvenile correctional procedures. Further *degeneration of mental health* (e.g., PTSD symptoms, increased substance abuse, and a lowering of self-efficacy regarding the ability to protect oneself) may *contribute to higher rates of recidivism* among female adolescent offenders.

The goals of the juvenile justice system would be more effectively addressed with institution of gender specific policies to encompass: providing alternatives to incarceration for female adolescent offenders and their children; delivering education and coping skills training regarding a girl's sexuality, healthy emotional and physical boundaries, and ways that gender expectations can lead to sexual compromise; educational strategies designed to interrupt the transgenerational cycle of child abuse including parenting skills, child care services and family systems support; and maternal health services including prenatal care when indicated.

The therapeutic atmosphere should be specifically orchestrated to meet the *health and safety needs* of young females. *Cognitive restructuring* and *social skills training,* targeted at critical issues such as childhood victimization and neglect, poverty, female oppression and parenting competence, are the mainstay of successful treatment services. Effective counselors and support personnel *model healthy alternatives to negative thinking and teach skills to avoid high-risk situations* that might result in substance abuse, sexual or physical victimization or criminal conduct. The capacity of females to form *relationships and strong commitments* to female advocates, family

members and children is a resiliency factor that motivates and fosters successful community reintegration, predicated upon adequate preparation and *provision for aftercare services.*

In summary, this chapter has taken us through the juvenile justice system as female adolescent offenders may experience it. Special notice has been paid to the specific needs of girl offenders as *adolescents,* as well as to areas of continuity between the problems of girl and adult women offenders as *women.* A specific trajectory of development from childhood experience with violent trauma to substance abuse and criminal activity has been identified. Various forms of criminal offense have been investigated, including participation in gangs and the drug culture. Correlates of criminal offense during adolescence, such as school failure, destructive dating norms, teen pregnancy, and poor mental and physical health have been identified. Finally, inadequate conditions within the juvenile justice system have been discussed, and treatment recommendations for female-specific programming have been made.

Youth Culture and Diversity

7

Chapter Seven:
Youth Culture and Diversity

Chapter Outline

Defining Culture and the Importance of Cultural Awareness

- Adolescence and identity formation
- Ethnic and racial identity

Adolescent Subcultures

- Violence-based subcultures
- Music-based subcultures
- Thrill-based subcultures
- Anti-authority-based subcultures

Cultural Competence

- Mindfulness
- Resources for teaching tolerance

Chapter Review

Chapter Objectives

- To define culture in a broad sense, beyond race and ethnicity;

- To show how developing cultural proficiency can lead to improved treatment outcomes;

- To explain how adolescent development is related to identity exploration and formation;

- To examine different types of racial and ethnic identity;

- To discuss similarities and differences between prominent adolescent subcultures;

- To present factors that contribute to cultural proficiency; and

- To show how counselors can develop skills to better understand an array of adolescent subcultures in the service of promoting positive identification with the treatment process.

DEFINING CULTURE AND THE IMPORTANCE OF CULTURAL AWARENESS

The term "culture" is often used to refer to *common characteristics that exist among a subgroup* of the general population, including beliefs, values, behaviors, communication patterns, art, language, and religion. Though we generally equate culture with ethnicity and race, many other subgroups of the population can be described as having culture. Age affiliation, gender identification, and socioeconomic standing can often group people into different subgroups and cultures. Included in this articulation of culture (beyond ethnicity and race) are subgroups often found among adolescents, subcultures that can affect how they interact with each other and the larger society in general. Although ethnicity and race often play a large part in an adolescent's identity, teenagers generally *group themselves with peers* who have similar beliefs and attitudes. Similarities can include music and clothes, common interests in sports and activities, and general similarities in attitudes and beliefs concerning drug use and criminal behavior. For our purposes, the word culture will be used as a metaphor for any cohesive and on-going community of people who participate in defining norms of criminal and AOD behaviors for each other. In addition to discussing groups that are traditionally defined as cultures (e.g., African American, Hispanic/Latino American, European American, Native American), this chapter will discuss the interaction of adolescent subcultures with AOD and criminal behaviors.

Cultural awareness has gained increasing importance in services and counseling in recent years. With the current emphasis on *cultural sensitivity*, the need for service providers to demonstrate cultural competence has also increased. A *strength based perspective* (building upon the positive behaviors and values that are fundamental for each culture) to create skills and beliefs that maximize positive outcomes concerning relapse and recidivism has become the major movement in counseling (Banks, 1991). In order for a counselor or youth advocate to use this strength based perspective, the service provider must move through a "transformational process of cultural competence" (Guajardo-Lucero, 2000), which involves movement from *cultural awareness* through *cultural sensitivity* to *cultural valuing*. The most important part of the transformation is for the provider to take a look at his or her own prejudices and stereotypes in order to counsel with *mindfulness*, i.e., to be aware of cultural

factors on both sides of the counseling equation (counselor and client) that might affect treatment outcomes.

As much as we would like to believe that we live in a world free from stereotypes and prejudices, every person is socialized with certain *ethnocentricities* and *expectations* for people who are unlike themselves. This often can lead to misunderstandings and confusion for the people involved when they are of different cultures (or subcultures for the purpose of this chapter). Different beliefs, language, and even body language, can confuse and frustrate the situation, and unconscious prejudices often lead to the confusion. The idea of *mindfulness* is for the provider to become aware of the prejudices that make up his or her schemata of the world, and then move forward to have an open acceptance for other cultures on the basis of their individuality. *Mindfulness* can be especially important when dealing with adolescents with criminal and AOD difficulties, most of whom are often confused, isolated from, and disillusioned with their external worlds. In order for a counselor to successfully treat a troubled adolescent, the adolescent needs to feel that he or she is validated and appreciated as an individual and a valued member of a group (the treatment facility or class). The adolescent needs to feel as if he or she is able to develop self-efficacy, that is, their sense of *capability and aspiration* needed to carry on a drug and crime free life outside of the treatment program (Bandura, 1986, 1989). Without an understanding of the role played by culture in driving an adolescent's substance abuse and delinquent activities, the counselor will be unable to develop the necessary treatment alliance to collaboratively (with the client) develop and implement an effective treatment plan.

The most important part of any treatment program for adolescents who manifest co-existing problems in substance abuse and delinquency is to develop *resiliency* and the ability to *succeed against relapse and recidivism*. By becoming educated in the general subcultures of adolescents, as well as the need behind the subcultures, and becoming aware of our own prejudices and cultural blind spots, we are more prepared to help adolescents with the most difficult part of any treatment—how to *integrate drug and crime free ideals* into an identity that, up to this point, has normalized, if not idealized, both criminal conduct and AOD behavior.

Adolescence and identity formation

Adolescence can be a very confusing and trying time, even for youth who are at low-risk. It is a time when parents are no longer the center of the world, and freedom increases. Vagueness, confusion, and discontinuity of identity due to a change in their roles from childhood to adulthood often occurs (Steinberg, 1985). Identity achievement *can* occur during these formative years, but developing a mature and socially responsible sense of purpose, self-concept and social role, is rare in the general population and almost never seen in treatment settings. Rather, adolescents in treatment facilities and in the court system often experience *identity diffusion or moratorium. Diffusion* occurs when confusion about what identity to assume arises and the adolescent becomes *apathetic to finding an identity* at all, while *moratorium* is considered a sort of time-out while the adolescent tries on *several different identities* without settling on any one (Erikson, 1968). Due to the external and internal pressures to form an identity, often with minimal support (family, school, etc.), the adolescent may begin to assume a *negative identity* that can tie the youth to criminal and AOD behavior.

While most adolescents go through some identity confusion and development, ethnic adolescents (i.e., race or culture different from mainstream society) struggle with difficulties on several levels (Ting-Toomey, 1998). The *primary identity*, which comprises our main cultural, ethnic, gender, and personal identity, contains unchangeable aspects. The *situational identity* (role, relational, etc.), however, contains aspects of the identity that are assumed for different areas of expectation (Ting-Toomey, 1998). While operating on separate spheres, the two areas of identity are interacting and confounding with each other. Confusion concerning ethnic and gender identity can also be confounded with confusion of role or relational identity. For example, if an adolescent is unsure about the expectations of manhood according to his ethnic culture, this may contribute to role confusion about how to relate to females in dating or other social situations. This may become a source of frustration to the individual which may become manifest in destructive or violent acts against people and/or society.

Ethnic and racial identity

When interacting with an adolescent of ethnic background, an important consideration is the *intensity* of which the adolescent identifies with their ethnicity. A racial identity model is useful for understanding a continuum of ethnic and/or racial identification along with different levels of sophistication of how the self is integrated into mainstream culture (Helms & Cook, 1999). This model consists of five statuses, each strati representing *assessments* of the ethnic/racial self and others. Although by no means static or segregated, the following categories give some idea of the different levels of ethnic/racial identification:

Conformity: consists of an ethnic/racial identity that assumes subordination due to social pressure and acceptance of hierarchy. For adolescents operating on this level, identity separation from the ethnic/racial culture is often expected and desired.

Dissonance: occurs when the individual becomes confused about social hierarchies and their own perceived role within the social stratum.

Immersion-emersion: arrives with a feeling of anger and a sense of rage at the dominating culture, followed by a mistrust of most cultures outside of one's own.

Internalization: begins the process of perceiving individuals instead of groups.

Integrative awareness: is the final stage in which the individual is *internally defined* and recognizes that all hierarchy and stereotypes are unfair, not just to ethnic/racial minorities. The strength and qualities of the individual's ethnic/racial identity will define how the individual deals with perceived cultural differences and misinterpretations. To assume that all adolescents of the same ethnic/racial background are operating on the same level and from the same culture is to undermine treatment before it has begun.

Personal identification and self-naming from the adolescent's point of view are important aspects to consider during treatment, whether the adolescent is from a different ethnic or racial background or not. In defining one's own identity, an adolescent's naming of his or her self becomes an important and integral part of his or her identity. To assume two youths that dress alike or listen to the same music identify themselves in the same way is detrimental to the treatment. Just as there are different intensities to ethnic/racial identity (Phinney, 1996), there are also different intensities concerning other adolescent subcultures. In this chapter we have broken the subcultures into four main groups; however, we are by no means declaring that all adolescents identify at the same level and in the same groups. The purpose is to *show the similarities* between the groups in order for a group therapy with multiple cultures and subcultures to empower and aid self efficacy within the individual adolescent client.

ADOLESCENT SUBCULTURES

As stated earlier, adolescence is a time of confusion and identity liquification of sorts. A feeling of belonging and approval may be very important for an adolescent during this time of uncertainty (Jensen, 1985). It is also during this time that peers begin to have an increasing influence over the individual in comparison to the family or childhood support system. During *identity diffusion or moratorium*, the needs of an adolescent are sometimes not met by the support system or larger society, which in turn allows for a subculture to form. Subcultures form in response to the larger society, yet cannot be totally different from the culture in which they are immersed, otherwise it would be termed a counter-culture (Wolfgang & Ferracuti, 1967). While a subculture responds and often reacts to the larger culture, it still contains some major values in common with the larger society.

Merton's (1968) *Strain Theory* uses four stages to define how an adolescent may identify and act in accordance with the norms of a subculture, including: (a) Innovation; (b) Ritualism; (c) Retreatism; and (d) Rebellion.

While mainstream society and the media often portray adolescent subculture as *rebellion*, that is not necessarily the case. Merton (1968) claims that conformity to the larger society implies acceptance to societal goals (*materialism*) and the means to attain the goals (*hard work*).

The *innovative stage* is likely to *subscribe to the goals* of the larger society, but is *not inclined to use the accepted means*. For example, a teenager who may be described as "innovative" may resort to violence in order to attain material success.

Ritualism, on the other hand, is opposite in that the individual *rejects the goals* yet often *accepts the means*. A person who is in ritualism may have a job for years but will never try for the promotion to further the societal goal.

Retreatism is when the individual *rejects both the goal and the means*.

Rebellion is rejection of both with a desire for a new social order.

In the quest to avoid relapse and recidivism, it is important for treatment providers to recognize the individual differences between clients while emphasizing *similarities of beliefs and values* in order to form a cohesive group. Due to the *influence of peers*, a cohesive group that focuses on similarities can become very beneficial in aiding the provider through the development of a positive attitude toward strategies and goals for effective treatment.

Violence-based subcultures

Although similar in many aspects, different subcultures often have different values and ideologies on which the group is based. Some of the most frequently thought of and media portrayed subcultures are those that surround *violence*. Included in these groups are *street gangs and racial pride groups* (such as the skinheads). These subcultures often use in-group ideology to separate themselves from the larger society, to a greater extent than other subcultures. Group identity becomes more important than the individual identity as the adolescent becomes more drawn into the subculture.

The most frequently used reason for a youth to join a violent street gang is *poverty* (Baron & Hartnagel, 1998). While economic disadvantage is found to be a consistent predictor of gang involvement, poverty is merely one element of a complicated and often convoluted purpose for an adolescent to become involved in a violent subgroup. The use of violence in a subculture involves *learned behavior* and a process of differential learning, association, or identification (Wolfgang & Ferracuti, 1967). Inclination for an adolescent to become involved in a violent subculture usually begins to form early in childhood as the youth is socialized into *accepting violence as normal*.

Vigil (1988) divides the identity of gang members into four components of self:

- *Ideal self*—what a person idolizes and wants to be;

- *Feared self*—what the youth does not want to be;

- *Claimed self*—the facade the adolescent wishes others to see; and

- *Real self*—what the youth believes he really is.

The adolescent strives for his other *real self* to as closely resemble the *ideal self* as possible. For a youth who has grown up in a poverty stricken, mother-centered household, where the father is either transient or absent, the *older male gang member* most closely represents the *ideal strong male figure* who the youth is searching for (Vigil, 1988). Due to a lack of parental supervision, possible feelings of abandonment, and a failure to succeed to societal norms, the adolescent is fragile and easily recruited by an older gang member.

Not only does the youth become closer to the ideal self with group affiliation, the adolescent moves further away from the *feared self* (unprotected and ignorant on the streets). The *feared self*, the *ideal* or *claimed self*, and the *real self* are constantly at war in the mind of the adolescent who is prone to gang membership. Isolation from most forms of socialization and an interpretation that school, sports, and other group activities have failed, the youth is inclined to join a group that represents *protection, safety, and comradarie with an underlying understanding*. The older males who the youth looks up to have similar life experiences, as well as a similar home life, and yet still manage to be feared and looked up to as strong males. The group also serves to allow the *release of aggression and anger*.

Abandonment, or perceived abandonment, is usually followed with anger, aggression, and violence later in the adolescent's development as the identity continues to struggle with formation without strong adult examples. Since the use of violence in a violence-based subculture is not necessarily viewed as illicit conduct, i.e., it is *normative*, the adolescent does not have to deal with the feelings of guilt that are socially associated with aggression (Wolfgang & Ferracuti, 1967). Unlike mainstream social expectations of anger and conflict management, gangs often participate in violence for and with each other, suggesting certain *normative expectations* of violence (Baron & Hartnagle, 1998). These expectations not only allow the youth to release anger and frustration in learned behaviors, but they allow the adolescent to develop a *claimed self* that is admired and looked up to within the group identity.

Members are often aware of the excessiveness of violence, but because violence was learned in the home and on the street at such an early age, it becomes a natural and expected part of everyday life. That is not to say that violence-based subcultures should and do express violence in all situations (Wolfgang & Ferracuti, 1967). Social functioning would become impossible if that were the case. Rather, violence-based groups are to be found in the *innovation typology* of Merton's *Strain Theory* (1968). Due to unstable home lives and poor economic means, the gang ideology tends to subscribe to society's goals of *materialism and power*, yet they reject the acceptable means to attain them. Power is attained by fear and violence, and money/materialism is often obtained through aggression or illegal commerce (selling drugs).

Keeping in mind the difference of intensity in violence identities (some adolescents permanently immerse themselves in gang identity; others are merely transient or experimenters), the environment of gang membership usually leads towards identity diffusion of the individual. *Group identity* can become more important than individual identity, and the *group role* may begin to overtake every aspect of his or her life. The closer the *real self* comes to the *ideal self*, the more the group decides and dictates the actions for the individual (Vigil, 1988).

Music-based subcultures

Music is not merely noise that separates and blocks out unwanted thoughts and ideas. For an adolescent, music may provide an *escape from life* as well as offering a connection to other adolescents. In essence, music can help define an adolescent in a time of *moratorium or confusion* (Fowler, 1994). Not only does music help define an individual identity, but music can also define youth as a *separate entity* from the adults, parents and society, setting up an autonomous aspect to the identity. Music becomes a means to produce *one's own culture* in a reaction and a struggle to define itself (adolescence) against the main culture. The assertion of these subcultures becomes almost cyclical in *appearance, acceptance, rejection, and reformation*.

As the subcultures appear, they begin to gain a more widespread acceptance due to media and a general agreement about the values found in the normative youth population. As the larger culture begins to accept the subculture and validate the subculture's views and beliefs, the subculture in turn rejects the acceptance of the parent culture. The point of the subculture's existence is a reaction against the larger society. Once accepted, the reason for existence becomes imaginary and adolescents struggle to reform into a new subculture, insisting on being *marginalized* and separate from the larger society.

In itself, this cyclical moratorium from society is not harmful to the adolescent and can allow the youth time to decide on his or her own value system. However, normalization of AOD and criminal behavior can cause problems for an adolescent, his or her family, the community and society at large. As parents become less dominant, other role models begin to be idolized and admired by the individual. The adolescent is likely to find risk behavior and AOD use (acceptably portrayed in the media) displayed by the new role model, allowing for normalization of AOD abuse and other patterns of deviant behavior to occur,

(DuRant et al., 1997). Rap, metal, rock and other genres often have drugs and risky behaviors lyrically exhibited, while some subcultures have sprung up almost as a support system for drug use (raves). Adolescents who are in the *innovative stage* (Merton, 1968) witness musicians speak their mind and receive an amazingly large amount of money allowing for a life of excess.

Outside of AOD use, there is another unhealthy aspect within the subculture of music. Unlike rave scenes, which often base themselves around acceptance and love (in association with the overwhelming use of MDMA), some music subcultures thrive on topics of *homicide, suicide, and violence*. Listeners of music based on violent topics are more likely to have remarried or unmarried parents and more likely to be white males in urban public schools (Wass, Miller, & Stevenson, 1989). In addition, there is a strong correlation between a preference for *music with destructive scenes* and *antisocial or destructive behavior* (Wass, Miller, & Redditt, 1991).

Thrill-based subcultures

Sensation seeking appears to be a biologically based trait with the individual preferring experiences or stimuli with *high-arousal potential* (Zuckerman, 1988). Thus, sensation seekers are more inclined to do things that increase the *perceived risk* of the situation. Adolescents in general tend to display risk behavior, but youth who are inclined to belong to the thrill-based subcultures *thrive on the uncertainty and intensity* that are associated with activities that most people consider terrifying. Although some actions and risks the adolescent may choose are accepted and sometimes take place in sanctioned areas (such as a sanctioned drag race), thrill seekers are particularly drawn to stimulation and/or mood altering effects of a variety of drugs.

A *low threshold of boredom* may cause the adolescent to search out means to relieve perceived mental boredom. Because of this low threshold, a *personality T* (thrill seeker) is more likely to begin experimenting and using drugs earlier in life, as well as using a variety of different drugs at higher levels (Zuckerman, 1979, 1983, 1994). Falling into *conformity* or *ritualism* (Merton, 1968) the adolescent who is a *T personality* is not trying to rebel against society's *goal of materialism* or *means of hard work*; rather, the individual is merely trying to meet the needs of high levels of sensation. The lack of "real-world" experience causes the adolescent with a *Type-T* personality to have

difficulty in channeling the risk seeking into productive, creative outlets, causing delinquency and criminal behavior to occur.

Anti-authority-based subcultures

Almost all subcultures have some authority issues. The need for an identity to separate itself from authority and authority figures (e.g., parents) often is one main reason for the formation of a subculture. Identifying with their peers and developing self-concepts that are separate from the larger culture through clothing, attitude, and action are the essence of adolescent subcultures. There is, however, a group of subcultures that base their ideology around the complete rejection of the larger culture. Found in Merton's (1968) fourth typology (*rebellion*), these adolescents not only reject the materialistic goal of society and the means (hard work), but the desire to *establish a new social* order is present.

Poverty does not play too much of a role in the development of these subcultures, as most of the adolescents inclined to spend a moratorium in these identities begin in a fairly comfortable socioeconomic standing. Without the fear for survival that is frequently found in street youth (Vigil, 1988), an individual may have the free time and thought to turn attention towards *reform and revolution*. Often the identity begins to form as a reaction against the parents, both of whom work in order to gain material goods. For some adults, owning objects contributes to a sense of well-being or quality of life.

As a reaction against the parental identity, the adolescent moves against what seems important to the parents. With the development of group identity, and an increase in world knowledge, a dissatisfaction and frustration with the larger culture begins to appear. Similar to the *immersion-emersion* of the paradigm for racial/ethnic identity, the youth becomes angry about the seemingly shallowness and triviality of the larger society. Just as the music-based subcultures react against society only to be accepted by it, these subcultures often dress and act in ways that physically separate them from the larger society (an example of rejection through dress can be found in the *punk and gothic* subcultures). Because a subculture is apart but also a part of the larger society (Wolfgang & Ferracuti, 1967), the adolescents in these subcultures often begin having value confusion. While dressing and acting as a completely separate entity than the larger society, these adolescents are likely to complain about being judged for their appearance and actions, not for their identity. The desire to be accepted into the larger society while acting apart and out of the larger society often brings the moratorium to an end.

Referring back to *strength and intensity of identity*, there are some groups within the anti-authority-based subcultures that truly try to become countercultures. Power struggles and the belief that *revolution and anarchy* can be the only answer to the problems of their identity confusion, this subculture can spawn some difficult adolescents to help and treat. Especially in the technologically advanced world, these adolescents are often not discovered until serious crimes or harm has occurred.

CULTURAL COMPETENCE

Similar to the goals of mainstream society toward acceptance of different ethnicities and cultural identities, *cultural competence* is extremely valuable in treating adolescents. Due to the *identity diffusion, moratorium, and exploration* that occur during adolescence, youth often align themselves with a peer group that reflects their own values and beliefs about the larger society. The fragility of an adolescent's identity often leads to avoidance of criticism while encouraging a *reaction to and rejection of* the subculture to which they belong.

In order to successfully treat adolescents, understanding the scale of cultural competence and its utilization can be very helpful (Cross, et al., 1989). There are six steps along a continuum of expertise in dealing with cultural diversity, including: (a) Destructiveness; (b) Incapacity; (c) Blindness; (e) Pre-competence; (f) Competence; and (g) Proficiency.

Destructiveness: This occurs when the governing body, organization, or person has discriminatory or exclusionary policies. Relegating another culture to a lower rung of the social ladder, and subsequently treating them as inferior, is predominating in this extreme of cultural incompetence. It is hoped that this is rarely occurring in treatment settings.

Incapacity: Although not as discriminatory as *cultural destructiveness*, this category often has negative attitudes towards another culture or group of people. Paternalism, or the belief that one group is responsible for another because of the other's supposed inferiority of either mind or body, is often found in this stage.

Blindness: This is the most often occurring category in the continuum of competence. In this stage, culture is considered irrelevant or neutral, not playing any part in the interaction among people. This belief can also be incredibly damaging in treatment settings, as it can lead to misunderstanding and confusion between people. Culture is something that exists for everyone, and there isn't any way to neutralize culture.

Pre-Competence: This step is marked by a realization that there are inadequacies in the organization or policy, but it is often a newly awakened realization without the motivation to change the organization.

Cultural Competence: This stage is when a person and/or the agency that they represent is aware of the dynamic of culture, and how culture can and does affect interactions between groups of people. At this point, growth and change can occur, as well as trust and understanding between different cultures. The presence of culturally preferred service models can be found in this stage as well.

Cultural Proficiency: This final stage means that the agency or individual has gained the ability to not only assess their own culture, but celebrate diversity in other cultures as well. Proficiency is marked by continual learning and growth in cross-cultural arenas. Idealistically all provider services would be found in this stage.

Mindfulness

In servicing and treating cross-culturally, we must look at our own *schemata and beliefs* concerning cultures outside of our own. While it is true that everyone perceives the world ethnocentrically, there is a large difference between *mindful awareness* of the world and *mindless acceptance* of the world. *Mindfulness* is a concept that encourages individuals to tune into their own *socialized mental scripts and preconceived expectations* (Langer, 1989, 1997). Included in the idea of mindfulness is the *readiness to shift one's frame of reference*, the *motivation to use different ideologies and categories* to understand cultural differences, and the *willingness to experiment with different ways of problem solving and decision making*. There are three elements to mindfully accepting another's cultural identity:

UNDERSTANDING

RESPECTING

SUPPORTING

When a person feels they have been *understood, respected* and *supported* regarding their cultural identity, the individual experiences a high sense of *identity satisfaction*. If the individual has not experienced the above three, there will be a low sense of satisfaction (Ting-Toomey, 1998).

Mindfulness can play an integral part of group treatment. Individuals tend to see their group identity in a positive light, allowing for *esteem and empowerment* in their identities. By empowering the adolescent in their individual identities, the provider allows for the client to be more open to developing an *in-group identity* with the treatment program. In-group identity refers to the *emotional attachments and shared fate* that the individual attaches to the selected subculture (the treatment group), while an out-group identity will lead to an *emotionally detached and distrustful identity* (Ting-Toomey, 1998). As adolescent therapy and treatment centers around promoting resiliency and avoidance of relapse and recidivism, an in-group identity is ideal. In order to achieve the ideal, the adolescent needs to feel his or her individual and subculture identities are *respected, understood, and supported*.

Resources for teaching tolerance

Teaching Tolerance (2004), published by the *Southern Poverty Law Center*, mailed free of charge to educators, is a semiannual journal whose *raison d'être* is to:

. . .Promote respect, acceptance and appreciation of the rich diversity of our world's cultures, our forms of expression and ways of being human . . . Tolerance is harmony in difference. (Declaration on Principles of Tolerance, UNESCO)

Writing for Change, a set of 50 activities to help students expel racism and sexism from the written word, can be downloaded for free at www.teachingtolerance.org/writing. The program is offered in partnership with the Oregon State University, *Difference, Power and Discrimination Program*.

Table 7.1 provides a list of videos available through *Teaching Tolerance* that may be used to enhance presentations on issues of racism, sexism or other destructive forms of stereotyping.

CHAPTER REVIEW

The normative AOD and criminal behavior found in some adolescent subcultures can be disconcerting and problematic unless dealt with in a manner that does not jeopardize the identity of the adolescent. If the adolescent client acquires a feeling of rejection or disrespect concerning the identity already formed, whether it is a *diffusion or moratorium*, the individual is likely to reject the treatment. The struggle therefore becomes how to help the adolescent avoid relapse and

---

Table 7.1 Videotapes and Teaching Tools

GLBTQ: The Survival Guide for Queer and Questioning Teens: Frank discussion directed to teens about homophobia, coming out, sexuality, religion and other topics. Grades 7-12. *Free Spirit Publishing*: 800-735-7323/ www.freespirit.com

Being Gay: Coming Out in the 21st Century: Includes a brief history and explanation of gay and lesbian issues and sexual orientations, myths, stereotypes and personal stories. Includes a 15-page teachers guide. Grades 9-12. *Films for the Humanities & Sciences*: 800-257-5126/ www.films.com

Rhythm, Rhyme and Life: Spoken Word and the Oral Tradition: Explores contemporary African American spoken word art forms, including poetry, storytelling and hip-hop music. Grades 6-12. *Teaching for Change*: 800-763-9131/ www.teachingforchange.org

The Roots of Prejudice and Intolerance and Overcoming Prejudice and Promoting Tolerance. Two 25-minute videos define terms such as prejudice, bigotry, stereotypes and tolerance and acts of intolerance through historical footage and first person accounts. Grades 9-12. *Jaguar Education*: 877-524-8200/ www.jaguared.com

The Hate Comes Home. CD Rom and Discussion Guide is an interactive movie about a fictional hate crime at school. Can be used as a teacher-led instructional tool over a 1-2 week period or as a self-paced activity for students. Grades 9-12. *Anti-Defamation League*: 212-885-7951/ www.adl.org

recidivism while allowing the identity to form around the adolescent's current needs and what he or she is comfortable with.

It is important to develop an awareness of *different subcultures* within the therapy group, as well as to strive for *cultural proficiency*. An adolescent who feels respected and understood as an individual, will be more inclined to develop an *in-group identity*. When the in-group identity has formed, the provider will have the most probability of success in imparting enduring treatment effects upon the adolescent.

While this chapter has described differences between some of the subcultures formed during adolescence, a more important focus is on the *similarities between subcultures*. While subcultures are seemingly based on different values, the adolescents who belong to them often have a great deal in common. Adolescence is frequently a very confusing and fluid time. Undesirable emotional states can occur within this period of growth, causing discomfort in the individual's identity. If a teenager does not have a strong support system to help him or her through this confusion, he or she may turn to drugs, thrill-seeking and risk-taking, give up or diffuse responsibility to others, or overload themselves with music or frenetic activities (Adams, 1997). The provider's responsibility becomes one of giving a safe environment using *mindfulness* to increase the chance for an *in-group identity* so the adolescent client has an opportunity to discover consistencies between his or her beliefs and standards and those of the mainstream. As well, adolescent clients become more adept at recognizing that inconsistencies are a part of human nature, and learn the virtue of having tolerance for others' views. In essence, the key against relapse and recidivism is *empowerment and self-efficacy* in the face of an identity influenced by multiple pressures and expectations from peer, media, family, community and social influences.

Perspectives On The Assessment

Chapter Eight:
Perspectives On The Assessment

Chapter Outline

Overview

Objectives of Screening and Assessment

**The Structure and Content of Assessment:
Data Sources and Report Subjectivity**

- Other-report data
- Self-report data

**Valuing Client Self-Disclosure When Discerning
Veridicality or the "True" Picture**

**Convergent Validation and the Process Model
of Assessment**

**Self-Report Data as a Valid Estimate of the
"True Condition"**

**Guidelines for Using Psychometric
Assessment Instruments**

- Psychometric, self-report methods
- Interview-based assessment instruments

**Determining Inclusion into a Substance
Abuse Category**

- Baseline: "any use"
- Minimum symptom criteria
- Problem severity continuum
- The threshold or stage model
- Drug specificity, pattern and setting
- Impaired Control Cycle (ICC)
- Self-selection
- The relationship identifier (RI)
- Standardized self-report psychometric approaches
- Two factor combination threshold model
- Multiple criteria model
- The problem with using DSM-IV criteria with adolescents
- Interpreting findings and error risk
- Levels of service model

The Process and Structure of Assessment

- Preliminary or preparatory screening
- Differential screening

- Comprehensive assessment: a multiple-risk and multidimensional approach
- Change and outcome assessment: treatment process and closure
- Short and long-term outcome assessment

**Special Focus Areas for Juvenile Justice
System Clients**

- Community responsibility: deviancy and criminal behavior
- Mental health and personality assessment
- Attention deficit and hyperactivity disorder (ADHD)
- Post-traumatic stress disorders (PTSD)
- Anxiety, depression and self-harm threat

Chapter Review

Chapter Objectives

- To provide a theoretical framework for the assessment of juvenile justice clients;
- To discuss the goals and objectives of screening and assessment and the key sources of data;
- To present the convergent validation model for establishing a valid information base using self and other report data;
- To present guidelines related to the use of assessment instruments
- To describe basic approaches for determining whether to include an adolescent in one or more diagnostic categories;
- To discuss the problems in the use of the DSM-IV in assessment decisions;
- To outline the various levels of assessment, including preliminary screening, differential screening, comprehensive assessment and process and outcome evaluation;
- To present an annotated reference list of instruments that can be used at the various levels of assessment; and
- To outline risk-resiliency factors for comprehensive assessment of juvenile justice/substance abusing clients.

OVERVIEW

It is common practice for jurisdictions, agencies and institutions servicing the juvenile offender to have some form of screening for alcohol or other drug (AOD) use problems to determine the need for further assessment and appropriate intervention placement. It is also common practice for intervention and treatment agencies to do in-depth or comprehensive assessment to determine the more specific needs of the client and to develop an individualized treatment plan (ITP). What is not common practice is for treatment agencies to do routine and consistent treatment process and outcome assessment. This chapter will focus on these assessment components.

Much of the information gathered in assessment relies on self-report from the individual adolescent. Yet, it is often believed, particularly among juvenile justice workers and evaluators that these self-reports are not reliable and are often not to be trusted. However, most would agree that assessment, particularly initial screening, is not only important, but essential in the process of developing an effective intervention and treatment placement plan for the substance abusing juvenile offender. Thus, how do we approach assessment so as to resolve the dilemma between this importance and the problem of report veridicality?

This chapter provides a theoretical framework and model for the assessment of juvenile justice system (JJS) youth with substance abuse issues. The dilemma between the importance of establishing a valid information base for placement and intervention planning and the problem of report veridicality will be addressed through the presentation of the convergent validation model. The various levels of assessment will be discussed, including preliminary screening, differential screening, comprehensive assessment and process and outcome evaluation. The specific areas of assessment, or risk-resiliency assessment factors, that need to be addressed in comprehensive assessment will also be outlined and discussed. This chapter will provide some guidelines as to specific evaluation instruments that can be used at the various levels of assessment.

This chapter will address the more general theory and approaches to the assessment of the juvenile offender with substance abuse issues. *Chapter 14, Operational Guidelines and Procedures for Program Delivery*, provides specific assessment guidelines along with a case presentation utilizing the Adolescent Self-Assessment Profile, and other assessment instruments available for PSD-C providers. *Chapter 14* also reviews legal and ethical issues regarding assessment and treatment.

OBJECTIVES OF SCREENING AND ASSESSMENT

The goal of screening in the juvenile justice system (JJS) is to identify youth who may be in need of a more comprehensive or in-depth assessment for substance use and life adjustment problems. The goal of comprehensive assessment is to identify the extent and severity of problems and strengths of the JJS client, to match the problems with intervention and treatment services, and to evaluate the changes and progress the client makes in treatment. These goals of screening and assessment have a number of common objectives.

- *To provide clients the opportunity to disclose information about themselves.* This objective, which begins with screening but continues throughout treatment and follow-up, is essential in that it defines how clients see themselves at any point of assessment and provides a baseline of the client's willingness to self-disclose along these points of assessment.

- *To give other individuals associated with the client an opportunity to disclose how they see the client.* "Other individuals" include persons who have both direct and indirect contact with the client. The former might be a parent; the latter might be a UA laboratory report.

- *To discern the level of openness or defensiveness of the client at the time of assessment.* This is important at screening and at the comprehensive level of assessment. The level of openness to disclose will have a direct bearing on the client's motivation to engage in change.

- *To use self-report and other-report to estimate the "true" condition of the client.* We never know how veridical or valid the information is with respect to this "true" condition. We only estimate this condition. Our estimate at screening will not be as veridical as our estimate at the more in-depth level of assessment. This estimate is ongoing and converging.

- *To make a summary assessment of the client's condition or situation that provides decision guidelines.* This will include the degree and level of problems in the various domains of assessment, a diagnosis and a statement as to client typology.

- *To make a referral and disposition decision.* At screening, the decision might be referral for comprehensive assessment or treatment. At the comprehensive level, the task is to match presenting problems with appropriate treatment resources. Matching is based on the specific problem areas that need to be addressed and the level of severity of these problems.

- *To evaluate treatment process and outcome.* Assessment continues throughout treatment and includes progress and outcome evaluations. It is often difficult to do short-term outcome (three to six months post discharge), but, clients can be easily evaluated for process changes during treatment. These are good predictors of short and long-term outcomes (Wanberg & Horn, 1983; Horn, Wanberg and Foster, 1990).

THE STRUCTURE AND CONTENT OF ASSESSMENT: DATA SOURCES AND REPORT SUBJECTIVITY

We can view assessment from the perspective of *structure and content.* Structure involves the sources of data and the manner in which we collect that data. The substance of the data is its content.

There are two sources of data: *other-report* and *self-report*, as well as different ways to structure the collection of data from these two sources.

Other-report data

Other-report data is a broad catch of information collateral to the client's self-report. All other-report data are subjective. In fact, they are *double-subjective.* Information the evaluator gets from the client, collaterals or official records is subjective. The evaluator's interpretation of the information is subjective, making the evaluator's final impressions or ratings double-subjective. In addition to being double-subjective, there are other problems with other-report data:

- Evaluators often do not agree about the presence or absence of a certain condition;

- The same evaluator on different occasions may reach different conclusions; and

- The evaluator may not be consistent in asking the same questions or may be biased or make a judgment on the basis of only a few items or symptoms.

Rater, or other-report data, *can* be made more objective, however, when standardized criteria are used to rate information provided by the client or collaterals.

Other-report data is sorted into three categories:

- Third parties who have some familiarity with the client;

- Official documentation such as laboratory report or legal records; and

- The ratings of interview data taken from the client.

Third party other-report data include collateral information from evaluation specialists, treatment professionals, probation officers, family members and peers, the school, child welfare and social services systems, religious leaders, mental health systems, judicial supervisors and reports and employers. When family members are involved in assessment, several important guidelines should be followed:

- Consent for family involvement, the consent age dependent on federal and state laws determining confidentiality;

- Definition of parameters for information disclosure to the family (McLellan & Dembo, 1993);

- An experienced evaluator in family work who can discern what information is needed in order to facilitate client services;

- Determination if family involvement will be helpful or harmful. Involvement of a parent actively using drugs or involved in criminal conduct may be detrimental to assessment and treatment.

Official documentation data include urine analysis results, criminal records and records of past treatment. These data are subjective and subject to error, distortion, misreporting and under-representation. A juvenile's record may not fully disclose the extent or nature of criminal conduct involvement. A final charge or conviction may be different from the original charge following plea-bargaining. The official record rarely reflects the extent of criminal activity. Using the same specimen, laboratory reports will differ as to THC nanogram levels. In spite of these problems, this source of data is essential when assessing a client's condition and treatment needs.

Interpretations or ratings of interview data by the evaluator are considered to be other-report data. It is common to conduct interview approaches in unstructured, semi-structured or structured formats.

- In the *unstructured interview*, the evaluator explores various topics not guided by specific standardized questions. The *unstructured interview summary* is in narrative and descriptive form. Psychosocial histories are typically placed in narrative-descriptive summary formats.

- In the *semi-structured interview,* specific questions guide the interviewer to explore various topics. The questions are not necessarily standardized nor consistently asked from client to client or interviewer to interviewer. The evaluator will interview around a set of criteria and then rate the client as to what criteria the client fits, such as when making a diagnosis using the DSM-IV. Structured data summaries or rater scales can be used with a semi-structured interview.

- The *structured interview format* is guided by a specific set of questions used in a standardized format and the answers are formal with standardized rating responses or scales. Structured rater summaries can be in the form of "item" data where the evaluator selects a specific answer to the question posed to the client. Or, structured rater summaries can be in the form of rater scales, which will include several individual items or questions to rate the client in a specific problem area. These rater scales can be submitted to psychometric scrutiny (e.g., scale reliability) and are amenable to summary profile outputs.

Structured ratings of clients should include all additional information at the evaluator's dispose. This would include collateral as well as official documentation.

Self-report data

Self-report data are also subjective. There are two ways to collect self-report data: Interview (narrative) and *psychometric test data.* Interview data recorded as verbatim (exactly what the client reports or says) is classified as self-report. However, the data become *other-report* when the interviewer makes an assessment statement or completes a rating scale around these data.

Self-report data become most meaningful and more objective when they are based on the principles of psychometric measurement. This approach reduces the subjectivity of self-report data and makes them more reliable and veridical (valid) with respect to the "true" condition of the client. Self-report data based on psychometric instruments are more objective than other-report data for several reasons.

- The questions and answers are in a standardized format and each subject is asked the same questions and is provided with the same response options.

- They are built on a multiple variable measurement approach where one area is measured by several questions, reducing the risk of error being made by asking only one question about the area.

- The results are usually interpreted in relationship to a normative sample where the client's peers are used as the normative basis upon which to interpret the results or scores.

- Such data are not double-subjective.

The subjectivity of self-report can also be reduced when trust and rapport are developed with the client. This enhances the veridicality (the hypothetical valid or true picture) of the client's self-disclosure.

Self-report information should be viewed from two perspectives: the specific content of the data that are used in estimating the client's "true" condition, and the changes in the reporting of this condition over time. The content of self-report and other-report data is most relevant when viewed within the process of change. Information taken at any one point of testing should never be taken as fixed and final. Any point in testing only provides us with an estimate of the client's condition and gives us guidelines for treatment needs at that point. From this perspective, the process of assessment is just as important as the structure and content of assessment.

VALUING CLIENT SELF-DISCLOSURE WHEN DISCERNING VERIDICALITY OR THE "TRUE PICTURE"

As noted, AOD evaluators and workers tend to distrust the "so-called" validity of client self-report, particularly those in the juvenile and adult justice systems. Evaluators are quick to conclude that clients are "lying" or "into denial" when they judge that the self-report does not reflect their "true" condition. However, when we see assessment as a process, we view all self-report as a valid representation of where the client is at a particular time. If we think the client is not accurately reporting his or her "real condition," we should view this within the framework of *self-defensiveness,* rather than denial.

This perspective views self-report as a baseline measure of the client's willingness to disclose his or her problems or conditions at the time of testing. Self-report tells us the degree of openness of this self-disclosure and "where the client is" at testing. The discernment of the validity or veridicality of the report revolves around this baseline self-reported perception and the level of defensiveness related to reporting this perception. What we are discerning, first and foremost, is the client's level of defensiveness and then the veridicality of the client's self-report as to the "true" condition of the client. This discernment is part of the overall task of the evaluator.

CONVERGENT VALIDATION AND THE PROCESS MODEL OF ASSESSMENT

Discerning the veridicality of self-report with respect to the client's "true" condition requires the utilization of other-report data. Both sources of data are essential in providing an estimate of the "true" condition. We can hypothesize about this condition. Our data then test the hypothesis.

Most importantly, self-report is essential in that it represents the client's current *willingness to report what he or she perceives to be going on*. This is where intervention and the change process begin: with the client's self-perception, or the willingness to disclose information around that self-perception. If self-report is not veridical with what is going on in the client's life, and if treatment is working, later self-reports will reflect a change in the reporting of self-perception. The first indication of treatment efficacy is found in the client's increase of self-disclosure and openness in treatment.

The convergent validation model (Wanberg & Horn, 1987; Wanberg, 1992, 1998, 2000) utilizes self-report *and* other-report as valid representations of where the client is at the time of assessment. Within this model, every client self-report is valid. If our objective is to measure where the client is and to get the best representation of how willing the client is to report his/her self-perceptions at the time of testing, then whatever the client tells us is valid. We conclude that this is a valid representation of at least the willingness to report that perception. Even a "slap-dash" responding to test items is valid—not in terms of content, but in terms of the client's response state at the time of testing.

We can only estimate the client's "true" condition through the use of other-report and self-report data. If there is a discrepancy between the self-report and collateral information and the client is defensive around self-disclosure, then the report is valid, in that we have an estimate of that discrepancy. This discrepancy is an assessment of the client's defensiveness and willingness to self-disclose and to engage in intervention and treatment services. This discrepancy becomes the basis for where treatment begins. Within this model, a *self-report is never invalid* as some self-report inventories indicate.

Figure 8.1 provides a graphic representation of this model. The vertical vector (A) represents the "true" or veridical condition of the client in a certain area of assessment, e.g., substance use involvement. Vector B represents the other-report source of data and vector C the self-report source of data. The magnitude of the angle (B-C) between vectors B and C is the theoretical estimate of the level of defensiveness or the willingness of the client to self-disclose. The magnitude of the angle between vector A and vector B represents the veridicality (validity) of the estimate of the client's "true" condition in the area of involvement in drug use using the other-report source of data. The B-C set of vectors would indicate a client who is relatively open to self-disclosure, whose self-report is discerned to be congruent with other-report data and both sources of data are good estimates of the client's "true" condition (vector A). The D-E set of vectors represents a very defensive client who's self-report is quite discriminate from the other report, but the other-report is also discerned to be not a good estimate of the client's "true" condition.

Convergent validation takes all sources of information to converge on key issues in assessment. These include the level of self-disclosure or defensiveness, degree of motivation for services and for change, evidence and degree of problems in specific areas of life adjustment, and the resiliency and strengths of the person being evaluated. This approach is also called the multiple-condition (Wanberg & Horn, 1987) or the multiple assessment approach (McLellan & Dembo, 1993; Winters, 1999, 2003).

The convergent validation approach prevents getting caught up in the question of whether the client is "lying," "under-reporting," "denying," or "falsifying." The initial goals are to discern the client's level of willingness to disclose, the discrepancy between self-report and other-report, and a valid representation of the problems and conditions the client is *willing to report* at the time of evaluation. This current condition of disclosure can then be used as a baseline for comparing problem-disclosure in ongoing assessment.

Figure 8.1   The Convergent Validation Model

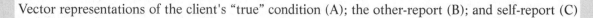

Vector representations of the client's "true" condition (A); the other-report (B); and self-report (C)

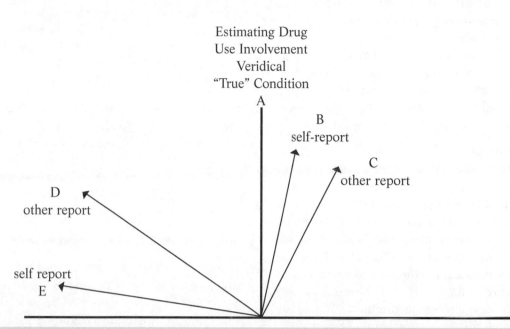

B-C   angle is the degree of discrepancy between self-report and other-report for this client and represents a measure of defensiveness—considered to be low discrepancy and thus low defensiveness.

B-C   average represents the estimate of A or "true condition" and for this client is a good estimate of the 1 "true condition."

D-E   angle is degree of discrepancy between self-report and other-report for this—considered to be high discrepancy and thus high defensiveness.

D-E   average angle represents estimate of A and is a poor estimate of the "true condition" for client.

SELF-REPORT DATA AS A VALID ESTIMATE OF THE "TRUE CONDITION"

Even though the convergent validation holds that all self-report is valid, the issue of how well any self-report at any given time represents a good estimate of the client's true condition has been a focus of much debate (Babor, Stephens & Marlatt, 1987; Watson, et al., 1984; Winters, 2001).

Winters (2001), citing a number of sources, indicates that there is support for the validity of self-report in giving us a good estimate of the client's true condition (Brown et al., 1998; Maisto, Connors & Allen, 1995; Shafer et al., 1993; Winters et al., 1991). This support comes from the findings that there is general consistency of disclosure over time, that large portions of clinical samples disclose the use of illegal drugs, that generally, there is a low rate of "faking bad" among self-report samples, that clinical samples tend to report a much higher prevalence of use and abuse than do normal samples, and there is good convergence between self-reports and other-reports.

GUIDELINES FOR USING PSYCHOMETRIC ASSESSMENT INSTRUMENTS

There are a number of important guidelines that should be followed when using self-report and interview-based psychometric methods or instruments.

Psychometric, self-report methods

Following are important guidelines to be followed when using psychometrically-based, self-report instruments.

- Psychometric instruments should demonstrate construct validity, which "refers to all the evidence, and sound theory derived from evidence, that can be brought to bear in interpretation of the measurements of a scale" (Horn, Wanberg & Foster, 1990; Wanberg, 1997). It is important to distinguish between the *validity of a test and the validity of the results of the testing of an individual subject*. The latter is seen as a valid representation of where the client is at the time of testing and based on the level of defensiveness. It is an estimate of the client's true condition. Clients open to self-disclosure and in a more advanced stage of change will provide a more veridical view of the client's "true condition."

- The test instructions *should be read* to the client. The most basic instructions prompt the respondent to: "answer each question as honestly as possible"; "answer questions as to how you see yourself"; "give only one answer to each question unless otherwise specified"; "answer all questions;" "the results will be treated within the confidentiality guidelines of the laws of your State and the Federal Guidelines of confidentiality"; "the results will be used to help develop services and treatments most appropriate for you"; and "the results of your testing will be shared with you."

- The methods of test administration *should be standardized*. For the interview method, the question and response choices should be read exactly as they are in the test booklet; the client should have a copy of the test booklet and read each question along with the evaluator. The client marks the answers on the answer sheet.

- The *reading level* of clients should be evaluated by asking them to read the first three or four questions.

- The evaluator should understand *what the test measures* and whether it fits with the evaluator's goals. Simple screening instruments should only be used to determine need for differential screening. Screening for treatment referral should be done with a differential screening instrument. A screening instrument should not be used for comprehensive assessment.

- The *test norms should be appropriate* for the group of clients being evaluated (Eyde et al., 1988). With some samples, it is helpful to have a set of norms representing the client's peers and another representing a group involved in services for which the client is being evaluated. For example, when evaluating judicial clients, it is helpful for the test to be normed on judicial clients as well as having a clini-

cal sample with which to assess the client's scores regarding need for treatment.

- When using computerized scoring, the *evaluator should have knowledge of the test* itself, and not just what the interpretive report says about any particular client. Computerized scoring may give a standardized interpretation of the test, based on its norms, but will not provide the more idiosyncratic nuances of each individual client.

- Clients should *receive feedback* as to how they compare with their peers, their level of defensiveness and how their results compare with the evaluator's estimate of the client's "true condition." This feedback is an essential part of the treatment process (Winters, 2001) and supports the partnership model of treatment (Wanberg & Milkman, 2004).

Interview-based assessment instruments

There are several instruments that can be used to structure the interview process. Some are other-report psychometric instruments that narrate the findings and score the instrument resulting in a scale score with a normative basis for interpretation.

Semi-structured approaches without instrumentation require higher clinical skill level and training (Winters, 2001), since their query method is not standardized or structured. Structured interview based instruments may not require as skilled of administrator, but requires the same level of evaluation expertise in interpreting the findings.

DETERMINING INCLUSION INTO A SUBSTANCE ABUSE CATEGORY

In screening, evaluators must determine whether there is sufficient evidence to show that the client has a substance abuse problem. In comprehensive assessment, the questions addressed are the degree and type of substance abuse and the life-adjustment problems that the client is experiencing.

Several models may be used to address the inclusion question and increase the probability of identifying juvenile justice clients with AOD use problems. These models depend on other-report and self-report data collected during screening and assessment. We will review some of these inclusion approaches.

Baseline: "any use"

This approach argues that "any use" of alcohol or illegal drugs by a minor poses an immediate problem of breaking the law and thus constitutes a drug use problem. Equating use with abuse in adolescents may be impractical (Winters, 2001). A majority of adolescents experiment with alcohol or other psychoactive substances; thus a broad-band inclusive criteria approach is not practical and gets in the way of identifying those who need early intervention or treatment services.

The "any use" criteria may have validity from a multiple-risk assessment perspective. Any or minimal use of substances, along with problems of family, emotional, school adjustment, or deviancy, may put the adolescent at high risk for using substances to manage these problem areas. "Any use," although not constituting dependence or abuse, may result in collateral problems. Any use may be so disturbing to the adolescent's parents that this in itself constitutes a problem. A juvenile probationer who takes one or two drinks is violating probation.

Minimum symptom criteria

The minimal symptom approach uses a set of diagnostic criteria and requires a certain number of these criteria be met for inclusion into the category of AOD problems, abuse or dependence.

The most common minimum symptom criteria are found in the Diagnostic and Statistical Manual of Mental Disorders IV (DSM-IV) (American Psychiatric Association, 1994). The DSM criteria go beyond screening utility and are used to provide substance use disorder diagnoses. The DSM-IV criteria and diagnosis do not represent a comprehensive or in-depth assessment.

The *DSM-IV* classifies substance use disorders into two groups: substance abuse and substance dependence. Tables 8.1 and 8.2 provide the minimum symptoms that must be met for a diagnosis of substance abuse or substance dependence.

Problem severity continuum

Winters (1999, 2001) suggests a drug use problem severity continuum involving several categories that are below the threshold of abuse and dependence. The continuum includes these categories:

- Abstinence;

- Experimental, recreational or minimal use;

- Early abuse with the emergence of negative consequences;

- Abuse involving regular and frequent use over a period of time with more notable negative consequences;

- Dependence involving regular, life-style, use and repeated negative consequences and indication of increased tolerance;

- Decision to discontinue use and maintain abstinence or involvement in a repeated cycle of abstinence and relapse.

Research does not support a continuum model. Numerous studies (e.g., Wanberg, 1998; Horn & Wanberg, 1969; Horn, Wanberg & Foster, 1990; Wanberg & Horn, 1987) show that various symptoms arising from AOD use form different dimensions that are independent and that one dimension or factor could have both symptoms of abuse and dependence as described in the DSM-IV.

The threshold or stage model

This approach establishes a threshold (Winters, 2001) of symptoms that indicate AOD problem inclusion. This is similar to a "stage" model, where the first stage, "early abuse," represents inclusion. The problem of this approach is determining which criteria define the threshold or "early abuse stage."

Drug specificity, pattern and setting

The type and nature of drug use can determine referral for further assessment or treatment. An adolescent's occasional use of alcohol may not trigger a referral unless there are signs of disruption or problems. An "occasional" use of cocaine or heroin would trigger a referral, even if there are no pathognomonic signs. Occasional use of alcohol in younger adolescents can trigger assessment or intervention, whereas a similar use pattern in older adolescents may require more discriminatory assessment before triggering referral. Prolonged use of substances, a large single episode intake or use in specific settings such as driving or at school would signal a referral need.

Impaired Control Cycle (ICC)

The ICC (Wanberg, 1974, 1990; Wanberg & Milkman, 1998) can be useful in identifying the presence of AOD problems in the adolescent. Impaired control occurs when negative consequences result from use (problems with parents, going to school

Table 8.1 Diagnostic and Statistical Manual - IV Criteria for Substance Abuse

A. A maladaptive pattern of substance use leading to clinically significant impairment or distress, as manifested by one (or more) of the following, occurring within a 12 month period:

- Recurrent substance use resulting in a failure to fulfill major role obligations at work, school, or home (e.g., repeated absences or poor work performance related to substance use; substance-related absences, suspensions, or expulsions from school; neglect of children or household)

- Recurrent substance use in situations in which it is physically hazardous (e.g., driving an automobile or operating a machine when impaired by substance use)

- Recurrent substance use despite legal problems (e.g., arrests for substance-related disorderly conduct)

- Continued substance use despite having persistent or recurrent social or interpersonal problems caused or exacerbated by the effects of the substance (e.g., arguments with spouse about consequences of intoxication, physical fights)

B. The symptoms have never met the criteria for Substance Dependence for this class of substance

Table 8.2 Diagnostic and Statistical Manual - IV Criteria for Substance Dependence

A maladaptive pattern of substance use, leading to clinically significant impairment or distress, as manifested by three (or more) of the following, occurring at any time in the same 12-month period.

1. Tolerance, as defined by either of the following:
   - a need for markedly increased amounts of the substance to achieve intoxication or desired effect
   - markedly diminished effect with continued use of the same amount of the substance

2. Withdrawal, as manifested by either of the following:
   - the characteristic withdrawal syndrome for the substance
   - the same (or a closely related) substance is taken to relieve or avoid withdrawal symptoms

3. The substance is often taken in larger amounts or over a longer period than was intended

4. There is a persistent desire or unsuccessful efforts to cut down or control substance use

5. A great deal of time is spent in activities necessary to obtain the substance, or use the substance

6. Important social, occupational, or recreational activities are given up or reduced because of substance use

7. The substance use is continued despite knowledge of having a persistent or recurrent physical or psychological problem that is likely to have been caused or exacerbated by the substance

Specify if:

With Physiological Dependence: evidence of tolerance or withdrawal (either item 1 or 2 is present)

Without Physiological Dependence: no evidence of tolerance or withdrawal (neither item 1 or 2 is present)

intoxicated, committing a crime when high on a drug, etc.). The cycle begins when drugs are used to manage problems that result from their use and continues when the individual continues to use drugs to solve the problems that come from drug use. If one defines a drug use problem on the basis of the occurrence of negative consequences resulting from drug use, then all persons who develop a disruptive effect from drug use meet the criteria for inclusion. This would include the adolescent arrested for alcohol possession.

Self-selection

This involves the adolescent being aware of having AOD use problems and acknowledges the need for help. Self-selection is enhanced when there is emotional concern about the disruptive quality of drug use. Self-selection is less frequently among adolescents. It is common for adolescents to openly admit to AOD use and use symptoms, but less common for them to admit that such use is a problem. If an adolescent with AOD use symptoms self-selects into treatment, these two factors alone are sufficient for referral.

The relationship identifier (RI)

An RI is a person who forges a link between some life-role performance problem(s) and substance use. The RI concludes that the undesirable behaviors of the user are a direct consequence of the use of drugs, although the life-role disruptions may be other than drug use. A school counselor who links academic failure and drug use is an RI. Sometimes the adolescent user accepts the RI's analysis and requests treatment. Others are more resistive and reject the RI's linkage. Until the adolescent makes a link between the use of drugs and life disruption problems, the user is likely to resist referral.

Standardized self-report psychometric approaches

Standardized self-report instruments are essential components of the convergent validation approach. The basic problem with psychometric measures has to do with which symptoms and how many should be counted or what score to use on a scale as the cut value in determining AOD problem inclusion. Clinical experience in the use of a scale or external criterion validity studies of the scale will help in determining appropriate cutoff values.

Two factor combination threshold model

Research suggests that there are two relatively independent, though correlated factors, around substance use (Wanberg, 1991, 2000):

- The degree of AOD involvement, both in terms of frequency, amount and drug type;

- The extent of negative consequences.

An example of a psychometric test that uses the two-factor model is the *Substance Use Survey* - SUS (Wanberg, 1991; 2000). These two factors can be used in combination with the threshold approach. A threshold can be determined for each factor or for the combination of both factors. An adolescent who reports having been intoxicated on alcohol 10 times in a lifetime would trigger a referral. An adolescent reporting a combined alcohol use of more than 10 times with marijuana use more than 25 times and who disclosed having had two or three salient disruptive symptoms more than two or three times would clearly indicate need for referral and intervention.

A combination threshold for these factors that indicate a history of involvement and a history of disruption provides a sound basis upon which to make referral for comprehensive assessment or treatment. Many adolescents will reach a combination threshold to warrant referral but not meet the DSM abuse or dependence criteria.

Multiple criteria model

Integrating the above inclusion approaches, it is suggested that one or more of the following criteria can trigger inclusion and referral for comprehensive assessment or treatment for AOD problems. This integrated approach is congruent with the convergent validation model.

- *Self-selection:* that the adolescent user admits to having problems associated with AOD use and needs intervention.

- *Relationship identifier:* one or more persons forges the link between life-role disruptions and the use of drugs.

- *Fitting the impaired control cycle:* there is a negative-consequence cycle indicating disruption of life functions follows from the use of drugs and subsequently results in the further use of drugs.

- *Utilization of a self-report psychometric instrument* which measures AOD use involvement and negative consequences.

The problem with using DSM-IV criteria with adolescents

Is the DSM IV, which is the standard for defining abuse and dependence, the answer to the problem of discernment of AOD use problems in adolescence, and more specifically, juvenile offenders? The diagnostic utility of the DSM IV criteria for determining whether an adolescent is in need of AOD treatment services has been called to question (e.g., see Martin & Winters, 1998; Wanberg, 1992; Winters, 2003). The DSM IV distinctions often do not consider the special case of adolescents (Winters, 2001).

- Adolescents often pose social and psychological problems resulting from AOD use without meeting the *DSM-IV* dependence criteria of a compulsive pattern of use or compulsive pattern of seeking drugs despite the presence of severe and disruptive consequences.

- The traditional diagnosis of dependence and abuse is limited for adolescents in that any use is illegal and thus is considered problematic. All adolescent drug users fit the "illegal use" criteria, but most will not fit the abuse or dependence criteria.

- Most adolescents who are assessed as needing intervention and treatment services do not fit the DSM-IV abuse let alone dependence criteria. There is a low prevalence of some *DSM IV* criteria among clinical samples of adolescent drug users (Winters, 2001). Very few adolescents in clinical samples have medically related withdrawal symptoms. Tolerance, which is an important component of the dependence criteria, has low specificity among adolescent drinkers because the development of tolerance seems to be a normal process to most adolescent drinkers (Winters, 2001). As well, tolerance seems to be prevalent in adolescent drinkers who do not show other signs of alcohol dependence as described by the DSM-IV (Martin et al., 1995).

- Judicial and clinical samples of adolescents will often display a pattern of rather extensive involvement in one or many drugs without the accompaniment of disruptive symptoms (Wanberg, 1998). For some drugs, what might be perceived as a problem from use by the clinician, such as hallucinations from using LSD, is perceived by the user as a benefit or purpose of use.

- The DSM-IV implies that alcohol abuse precedes alcohol dependence. With many adolescents, abuse symptoms often do not precede the onset of dependence symptoms; and many report one or two dependence symptoms but no abuse symptoms and thus will not meet the traditional criteria for dependence or abuse (Martin, et al., 1996; Winters, 2001).

- There are many adolescents who fit one or two of the dependence criteria but no abuse symptoms and thus do not qualify for any diagnosis. These are youth who "fall between the cracks" relative to the DSM-IV criteria. Others have labeled these "diagnostic orphans" (Harrison et al., 1998; Hasin & Paykin, 1998, 1995) who showed AOD *involvement* at the level similar to adolescents with alcohol abuse and higher than regular AOD users without an AOD diagnosis.

- Finally, there is sound evidence that AOD use and misuse patterns are multidimensional, and that, with adolescents and adults, it is best not to conceptualize these patterns across a continuum of abuse to dependence (e.g., Horn, Wanberg & Foster, 1990; Wanberg & Horn, 1987). A multidimensional model holds that there are independent patterns of AOD use problems. Many of these independent factors have both abuse and dependence symptoms, as defined by the DSM-IV.

Interpreting findings and error risk

There are several ways in which self-report and other-report data can be interpreted. Some psychometric self-report instruments only provide a profile output, and the evaluator interprets the meaning of the scale scores, usually with the help of the instrument's user's guide or manual. Some instruments provide cutoff values relative to various scales or relative to scale configuration. If a score falls in a certain range, this might suggest adjustment problems in certain domains of assessment, e.g., AOD use problems.

Regardless of the method interpreting the results, the final assessment or diagnosis is done by the evaluator or clinician. An instrument should never determine final assessment or diagnosis. The interpretative computer summaries must always state "there is indication," or "the results suggest," rather than have the summary provide a firm diagnostic statement.

The type of error risk must be considered when making judgments about findings. This is of particular concern with adolescents for whom criteria for making an assessment statement or diagnosis, such as the DSM IV, do not always fit. There are two kinds of errors that we define when interpreting clinical data.

The first is a *false negative* which is made when it is concluded that there is no problem when in fact there is. This error can be avoided by making the criteria for inclusion less stringent. For example, when using a psychometric scale, we will lower the inclusion cutoff score so that we will include more individuals who show symptoms. The false negative is a critical error, since it may cause us to fail to provide assessment or services for those who really need it.

When we reduce the false negative risk, we increase the risk of the second type of error, a *false positive*. This is concluding that there is a problem when there is not. In order to avoid this error, we may set more stringent inclusion criteria. This may mean that we require more symptoms or a higher cutoff value before we conclude that the individual fits the disorder.

Determining the level of risk that we will assume may be based on economic consideration, practice liability, client welfare or inconvenience. In the medical arena, to lower the false negative risk may mean that more patients will receive an expensive diagnostic procedure. However, to raise the false negative risk may increase medical liability in that patients who have the medical disorder will not receive the necessary diagnostic procedure to confirm diagnosis.

Most medical patients are willing to decrease the false negative risk, even though it means additional testing and expensive diagnostic procedures when it is not necessary. In behavioral health assessment, where the presence of a disorder is most often not life-threatening, this imposition may be unacceptable. A client who is diagnosed as having alcohol dependence, but in fact, does not, may find this to be adverse and detrimental.

One resolution to this dilemma is to have two levels of screening: preliminary and differential. We set criteria that will decrease the risk of a false negative at the level of initial or preliminary screening, and then increase the criteria at the differential level of screening where the decision for treatment referral is usually made. The "net" is initially large which increases the catch, and where the cost of assessment is less. At the differential screening, the criteria can be made more stringent, since the risk of false negatives was decreased at the initial screening. If proper screening has been done at the first two stages (preliminary and differential), the risk of false positives is minimized.

Levels of service model

It has been a recent practice to identify three categories of service related to AOD use: *prevention, intervention, and treatment* (Wanberg, 1990). This model was developed, in part, to address the problem of the false-negative assessment error. This model assures that all adolescents suspected of some AOD use will receive at least the minimum level of service - prevention.

It has been generally understood that *prevention* services are for individuals who have not established a pattern of AOD use, whose AOD use has been minimal, if not at all, and who may indicate an increased risk for developing a use or abuse pattern because of having a disruptive family, being involved in deviant

behavior, or experiencing social or psychological adjustment problems.

Intervention usually refers to a level of service for individuals who have established some pattern of AOD use, but who do not indicate signs and symptoms of AOD use disruptions. Such individuals have developed a pattern of use and also indicate risk in the areas of family, school, mental health, or deviant behavior.

Treatment service level is seen as appropriate for individuals whose use pattern has begun to cause at least some disruptive effects on life functioning. The pattern of use is clear and there are identifiable symptoms resulting from this use pattern.

When screening for these three levels of service those clients who fit the drug use problem category should be sorted out. These clients would fall within the treatment services category, or at least, fall in the category of needing further assessment for possible treatment services. If there is need to differentiate individuals on the basis of the levels of service, those clients who do not fall into the drug use problem category should be further evaluated for intervention or prevention services.

THE PROCESS AND STRUCTURE OF ASSESSMENT

There are six components of assessment. Most substance using and abusing juvenile offenders will cycle through these components if they enter some treatment or intervention process such as:

- Preliminary screening or pre-screening;

- Differential screening;

- Comprehensive, in-depth and differential assessment;

- Change and outcome assessment: treatment progress and process

- Change and outcome assessment: At treatment closure; and/or

- Change and outcome assessment: Short and long-term.

Figure 8.2 provides a schematic description of these components and the process of assessment. Each of these areas will be discussed.

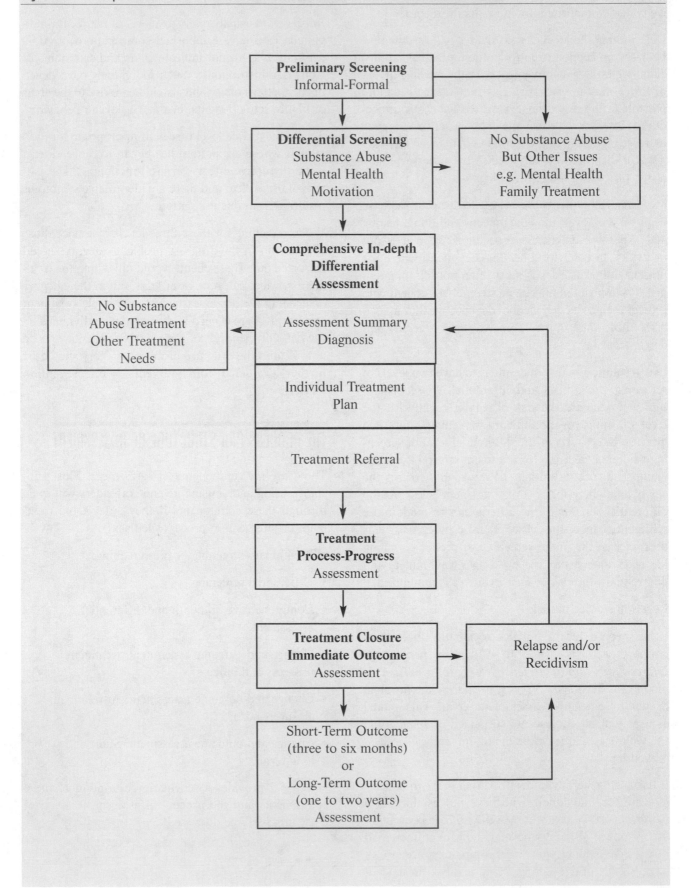

Preliminary or preparatory screening

Preliminary screening sets the stage for differential screening and provides a basis for prevention and early intervention. For JJS youth, this screening is done mainly in the AOD use area, because an adolescent who shows possible AOD use problems most likely will indicate problems in other areas, viz., the multiple-risk theory. Early intervention can be effective in preventing later, more serious problems associated with AOD use.

Preliminary screening occurs within the family, in schools, other community organizations, social services, welfare systems and health service organizations. Most often, this screening takes place within juvenile justice agencies, including municipal and district courts, probation, detention centers, correctional institutions and case management and parole departments.

Preliminary screening may be informal or formal. Informal preliminary screening is a "red flag" process and the "red flag" may not necessarily be an obvious AOD problem. Following are some of the indicators that will become triggers for either formal preliminary or differential screening (McClellan & Dembo, 1993; Wanberg, 1998; Winters, 1999).

- Sudden or marked changes in behavior, including aggressive behavior, depression, personal hygiene, abnormal sleep patterns, argumentation and agitation.

- Involvement in negative peer relationships or AOD using peers.

- Positive drug monitoring testing.

- Involvement in deviant and criminal conduct including running away from home or homelessness.

- Changes in or poor work or school performance.

- Indication of obvious AOD involvement such as alcohol on the breath, possession of drug paraphernalia, behavior suggesting drug intoxication such as staggering, "spaciness," etc.

- Increased conflict with parents and family.

- Parental alcohol or other drug abuse.

- Physical symptoms or changes in physical health.

- Being a victim of physical or sexual abuse.

- Involvement in high-risk sexual behaviors.

- Involvement in the juvenile justice or mental health system.

Informal detection may trigger a referral to a school counselor, nurse, probation officer or a welfare worker for a formalized preliminary screening. These personnel may do a more formal interview and administer a short preliminary screening instrument. Examples of these instruments are provided in *Table 8.3*. The results of the formal preliminary screening may trigger a more formal, differential screening process.

Differential screening

Preliminary and differential screening is often merged. In some systems, the preliminary screening is informal, and triggers a formal, differential screening process. Differential screening is done by human service workers or certified addiction counselors trained in the use of a differential screening instrument and interviewing.

Juveniles justice system (JJS) clients, particularly those in residential facilities, should receive differential screening (McLellan & Dembo, 1993; Winters, 1999) that include:

- Degree of drug use involvement;

- Degree of disruption from drug use;

- Mental health issues;

- Level of acknowledgement of having an AOD problem and willingness to be involved in intervention; and

- Willingness to self-disclose or level of defensiveness.

Differential screening may also include screening for family, school and deviancy problems.

Youth in juvenile justice residential facilities should also be observed and assessed for drug intoxication and withdrawal, suicidal thinking and intent, medical problems and threat of harm to others. This assessment should be completed within 24 hours of admission (McLellan & Dembo, 1993; Winters, 1999).

Differential screening often assesses for high-risk behavior that implicates sexually transmitted diseases (STDs). This includes history of sexual activity, where there is sexual promiscuity and a history of intravenous drug use. This assessment must comply with Federal and State confidentiality policies and laws regarding disclosure of STD and HIV information.

Differential screening will use other-report and self-report data. Other-report data may include results from drug monitoring. Such monitoring should not be used for forensic purposes and should always be conducted with the knowledge and consent of the adolescent (McClellan and Dembo, 1993; Winters, 1999).

Within the framework of the convergent validation model, a self-report, psychometrically based differential screening instrument should be used. Table 8.4 provides a list of these instruments commonly used with juvenile offenders. Table 8.5 provides a list of interview-based instruments that can be used in both differential screening and comprehensive assessment.

Comprehensive assessment: a multiple-risk and multidimensional approach

Studies by Wanberg, and Horn and Associates (e.g., Wanberg, 1992, 1998; Horn & Wanberg, 1969; Horn, Wanberg & Foster, 1990; Wanberg, Horn & Foster, 1977; Wanberg & Horn, 1987) provide cogent evidence supporting a multiple-risk or multidimensional model of assessment. This model holds that there are a number of distinctly different and independent dimensions associated with AOD use problems, criminal conduct and other problems associated with AOD misuse. The origins, expressions and continuation of criminal conduct and substance abuse are multidimensional and effective assessment will identify the multiple conditions that support and contribute to substance abuse and criminal conduct.

The multidimensional or multiple-construct model of assessment was applied to substance using and abusing adolescents during the 1980s. During this period, the concepts of risk, resiliency and protective factors emerged (Hawkins, Catalano & Miller, 1992; Hawkins, Lishner & Catalano, 1985; Newcomb, Maddahian & Bentler, 1986; Wanberg, Tjaden, Embree & Garrett, 1986; Wanberg, 1992, 1998). The risk factor model is a multidimensional model of assessment.

Support for this approach is found in the study of risk-resiliency factors in adolescents and more specifically, JJS youth. Studies by Wanberg (1992, 1998) provide multivariate validity for the multiple-risk theory. Using large samples of adolescents referred to AOD treatment and in the juvenile justice system, six independent and hardy factors were identified among 90 variables that describe problem conditions in adolescents across various life-functioning domains.

Assessment of adolescent substance use clients is built around this set of core risk factors:

- Family disruption;
- Mental health symptoms;
- Negative peer influence;
- School adjustment problems;
- Deviancy and criminal conduct; and
- Substance use involvement and negative consequences.

In programs where the cognitive-behavioral model is a major platform for treatment, comprehensive assessment should also involve the assessment of two cognitive structures and processes that are important in the development and continuation of substance abuse in adolescents (see Wanberg & Milkman, 2004).

- *Expectancies from use.* This pertains to the expected benefits of use and defensiveness against what might be the negative consequences from use. The strength of outcome expectancies are powerful determinants of why adolescents continue use. At the same time, these expectancies can conflict with the negative consequences of use. It is this conflict that can become the basis for the motivation to change. Adolescents have four benefit expectancies of substance use (Petraitis, Flay & Miller, 1995; Henly & Winters, 1988; Wanberg, 1992, 1998): social, mental, excitement and mood management.

- *Appraisals from the benefits of use.* The adolescent appraises the benefits of use and concludes that there is value for use. This becomes a powerful reinforcer for the continuation of use. The appraised benefits of use are also: social, mental, excitement and mood management (Petraitis et al., 1995; Wanberg, 1998).

The literature refers to this phase of evaluation as in-depth, comprehensive, multidimensional or multiple-condition assessment. We will use the term comprehensive assessment in this chapter. Comprehensive assessment explores all of the relevant domains of information that provide an intelligent understanding of the problem conditions in the adolescent offender's life. *Figure 8.3* provides a structure that outlines the seven major risk-resiliency domains to be explored in comprehensive assessment along with the specific factors to be assessed within each of these domains.

Figure 8.3 Conceptual Framework for Comprehensive and In-Depth Assessment of Juvenile Justice Clients

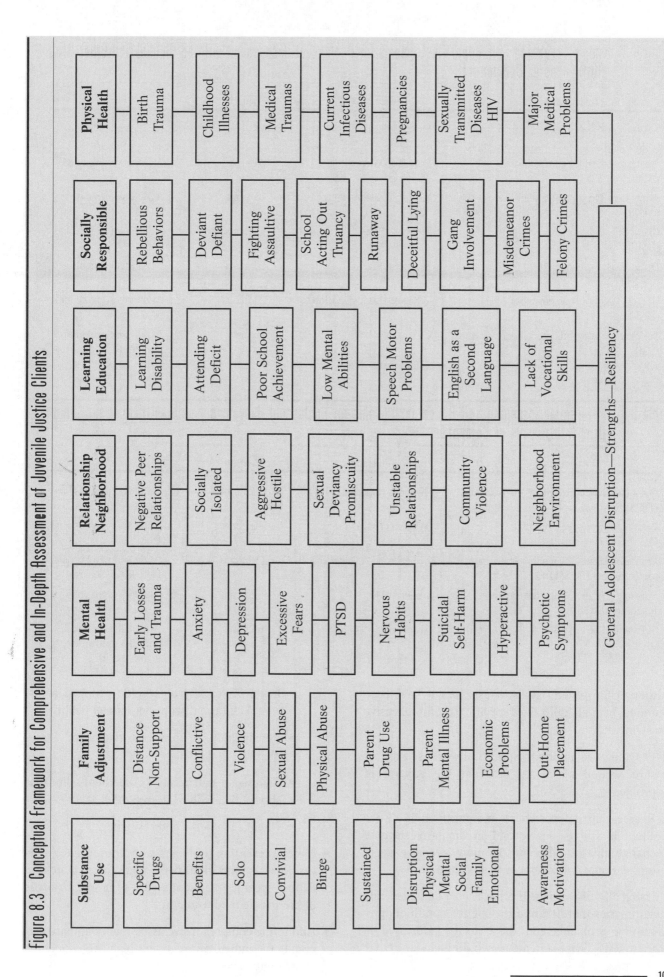

Table 8.3   Simple Screening Self-Report Instruments for Adolescent Assessment with an Alcohol and Other Drug (AOD) Focus or Component

Instrument	Author/source	Length	Focus
Adolescent Alcohol Involvement Scale (AAIS)	Mayer & Filstead (1979)	14 items	Alcohol Involvement
Adolescent Drinking Index (ADI)	Harrell & Wirtz (1985)	24 items	Alcohol Involvement
Adolescent Drug Involvement Scale (ADIS)	Moberg & Hahn (1991)	13 items	AOD involvement
Client Substance Index - Short (CSI-S)	Thomas (1990)	15 items	AOD involvement
Drug Abuse Screening Test (DAST)	Skinner (1982)	20 items	AOD involvement
Rutgers Alcohol Problem Index (RAPI)	White & Labouvie (1989)	23 items	AOD involvement and psychosocial
Simple Screening Inventory (SSI)	CSAT (1994)	16 items	AOD involvement and symptoms

Table 8.4   Differential Screening Self-Report Instruments for Adolescent Assessment with an Alcohol and Other Drug (AOD) Focus or Component

Instrument	Author/source	Length	Focus
Drug Use Screen Inventory-Revised (DUSI-R)	Tarter & Hegedus (1991)	159 items	AOD and psychosocial factors - 10 scales
Personal Experience Screening Questionnaire (PESQ)	Winters (1992)	40 items	AOD and psychosocial factors - 3 scales
Problem Oriented Screening Instrument for Teenagers (POSIT)	Gruenewald & Klitzner (1991)	139 items	AOD and psychosocial factors - 10 scales
Substance Abuse Subtle Screening Inventory (SASSI)	Miller (1990)	81 items	AOD involvement - 8 scales
Substance Use Survey (SUS)	Wanberg (1991, 2000)	64 items	AOD (lifetime and 6 months) motivation, mental health

Although the general goals of assessment have been outlined, here are objectives specific to comprehensive assessment:

- Providing an in-depth opportunity for self-disclosure around all of the relevant life adjustment problems;

- Reassessing defensiveness and motivation. If the client is still defensive and in an early stage of change, this would point to a more intensive use of motivational enhancement techniques;

- Using all self-report and other-report data, generate summaries that describe the client's condition, presenting problems and those to be addressed in treatment. These statements would include:

  - Level of severity of specific problem areas, e.g., AOD use disruption, mental health;

  - Revalidation of previous diagnostic statements;

  - Significant collaterals in the client's life that should be involved in treatment;

  - Client's strengths and resiliency.

- Match presenting problems with appropriate interventions in the treatment plan. The matching defines specific treatment services for specific areas of life-problem adjustment.

- Add to the comprehensive assessment database and update the individual treatment plan. Assessment is an ongoing process.

Comprehensive assessment is generally built upon these steps.

- *Initial informal interview* to build rapport, describe purpose of evaluation, explain client's rights, acquire consents and describe how the evaluation information will be used.

- *Formal interview* using a structured interview instrument (see *Table 8.5*) and/or an interview guide or structure such as the one provided in *Figure 8.3*.

- *Documentation* of information and observations of client's response to the interview and interactions with collaterals.

- *Administer a self-report psychometric instrument.* Table 8.6 provides a number of comprehensive, in-depth self-report instruments that meet this objective.

- *Client-generated summary profile or self-portrait* that provides opportunity for self-rating across the major risk-resiliency areas.

- *Written report* that summarizes the relevant problem areas, client strengths and provides the basis for the individual treatment plan (ITP). The report structure should clearly delineate the data, assessment and treatment plan components.

- *Feedback to the client* helps to build a partnership of change between the client and the treatment provider and makes the evaluation process the first and integral step of treatment.

- The *individual treatment plan* (ITP) that:

  - Defines the problems to be addressed in treatment;

  - Identifies the changes needed in thoughts and action;

  - Specifies the resources and tools to be used to address the needed changes and the objectives of treatment;

  - Records the time frame in which the problems are worked on and updated as the client progresses in treatment;

  - Is done in a partnership between client and counselor or provider;

  - The client should have his/her own ITP.

  - Assessment is ongoing, with regular evaluations of the client's progress and change.

Change and outcome assessment: treatment process and closure

Using both self-report and other-report data, there are three dimensions of change that can be evaluated in JJS clients progressing through treatment and at treatment closure:

- Changes in the level of self-disclosure and defensiveness;

- Acknowledgement of problems, motivation to change; and

- Changes in problem thinking and problem behavior, including AOD use problems, antisocial behavior, mental health problems, school adjustment, and relationship with family.

These assessments can be done at various points along the treatment progress and at discharge from treatment.

Changes in self-disclosure. If we assume that self-disclosure leads to self-awareness and self-awareness leads to change, then assessment in the change in willingness to disclose is important. There are two ways to assess this change. First, retesting on parts or all of the differential screening instrument or intake instruments will assess for changes in self-disclosure. Clients who are very defensive initially will indicate higher scores on scales measuring AOD use and disruption, criminal conduct and other areas of life adjustment. Any of the differential screening or comprehensive assessment instruments in *Tables 8.4 and 8.6* can be used for retest to assess changes in willingness to self disclose. Clients who are very self-disclosing in screening and intake will not show significant increases in their scores, but often show some decrease in their scores.

Second, a retest on scales designed to measure defensiveness will also provide a measure of change in willingness to self-disclose. Those low on defensiveness at intake will often show some increase in their defensiveness scores.

Problem acknowledgement and motivation for treatment is important in differential screening, in-depth assessment and in the assessment of treatment progress. People go through stages when making changes (DiClemente, 2003; DiClemente & Velasquez, 2002; Connors, Donovan & DiClemente, 2001; Wanberg & Milkman, 1998). Although there are several measurable dimensions of change, the two most salient ones are: readiness to change indicated mainly

Table 8.5 Differential Screening and In-Depth Structured Interview-Based Instruments for Adolescent Assessment with an Alcohol and Other Drug (AOD) Focus or Component

Instrument	Author/source	Length	Focus
Adolescent Diagnostic Interview (ADI)	Winters & Henly (1993)	Interview Varies	AOD involvement and psychosocial factors
Adolescent Drug Abuse Diagnoses (ADAD)	Friedman & Utada (1989)	150 items	AOD involvement and psychosocial
Adolescent Problem Severity Index (APSI)	Metzger, Kushner & McLellan (1991)	Varies	Multiple AOD and psychosocial areas
Comprehensive Addiction Severity Index for Adolescents (CASI-A)	Meyers (1996)	Varies	AOD involvement and psychosocial factors
Comprehensive Assessment and Treatment Outcome Research (CATOR)	Hoffman (1995)	Varies	Multiple AOD and psychosocial areas
Rating Adolescent- Adult Problems Scales (RAAPS)	Wanberg (1999)	46 items	AOD and psychosocial factors - 8 scales
Teen-Addiction Severity Index (T-ASI)	Kaminer, Bukstein & Tarter (1991)	133 items	AOD and psychosocial
Youth Level of Service/Case Management Inventory (YLS-CMI)	Hoge & Andrews (2003)	72-items	AOD, psychosocial and criminal conduct

Table 8.6 Differential In-Depth Assessment Instruments for Adolescent Assessment with an Alcohol and Other Drug (AOD) Focus or Component

Instrument	Author/source	Length	Focus-Description
Alcohol Expectancy Questionnaire - Adolescent (AEQ-A)	Christiansen, Goldman & Inn (1982)	90 items	Alcohol outcome expectancies - 6 scales
Alcohol Use Inventory (AUI)	Horn, Wanberg & Foster (1990)	228 items	Differential alcohol use patterns - 24 scales
Adolescent Self-Assessment Profile - II (ASAP-II)	Wanberg (1992, 1998)	262 items	Multiple AOD and life-adjustment risk factors - 35 scales
Chemical Dependency Assessment Profile (CDAP)	Harrell, Honaker & Davis (1991)	232 items	Differential AOD and psychosocial - 10 scales
Personal Experience Inventory (PEI)	Winters & Henly (1989)	276 items	AOD involvement and psychosocial factors - 22 scales

by the acknowledgement of problems and need for help; and taking action to change (Wanberg & Milkman, 1993). *Table 8.7* provides some examples of instruments that can be used with adolescents to measure acknowledgement of problems and motivation to change.

Changes in problem thinking and problem behavior. The test-retest method can be used to assess changes in problem behaviors. The most common method is to measure the individual's involvement in problem behavior in the six months prior to entering treatment, and then at six month intervals following treatment admission and at treatment discharge. For the JJS

client, this kind of assessment is typically done in the areas of substance use and criminal conduct, the latter often utilizing a measurement of prosocial attitudes and behaviors. If this method is used while the client is in treatment, and the client leaves treatment prior to the six months, then the assessment can be done at discharge.

Another approach to assessing change is to do repeated assessments monthly, using both client self-report and provider ratings. Using the Treatment Response Questionnaire (TRQ: Wanberg, 1996a), Wanberg (2003) found that incarcerated juvenile clients show steady improvement across several dimensions of

Table 8.7   Instruments for Assessing Treatment Progress and Change, During Treatment, at Discharge or at Post-Discharge.

Instrument	Author/source	Focus/description
Substance Use Survey (SUS)	Wanberg (1992, 2000)	Two six-month AOD involvement and disruption scales
Stages of Change and Readiness Treatment Eagerness Scale (SOCRATES)	Miller (1994)	Measures five stages of and change bases on Prochaska/DiClemente model
Adolescent Self-Assessment Questionnaire (ASAQ)	Wanberg & Milkman (1993)	Six primary scales and two broad scales measuring acknowledgement of need to change, readiness and action stages
Social Response Questionnaire (SRQ)	Wanberg (1997)	Three prosocial factors that are dynamic and can be retested at six month intervals
Colorado Youth Offender-Level of Supervision Inventory-Dynamic (CYO-LSI-Dynamic)	Colorado Judicial Branch (1995)	Retest of dynamic risk factor to determine changes in over all risk for criminal conduct
Treatment Response Questionnaire (TRQ)	Wanberg (1996a)	Assessment ratings, completed monthly by provider to measure changes in treatment involvement, problem thinking and problem behavior
Client Monthly Treatment Response Questionnaire (CMTRQ)	Wanberg (2001)	Self-report assessment completed monthly by client to measure changes in treatment involvement, problem thinking and problem behavior and self-improvement ratings
Client Manager Assessment Questionnaire	Wanberg (1996b)	Six-month post-incarceration discharge ratings by case supervisor as to adjustment in community
Follow-up Assessment Questionnaire (FAQ)	Wanberg (1996c)	Multiple scales measuring post-discharge outcome adjustment in the six major risk-factor areas

change for the first three or four months, and then showed a steady decline in improvement until the seventh or eighth month. At that point, clients began to show a steady increase in positive changes in thinking and behavior, treatment motivation and cooperativeness.

Short and long-term outcome assessment

Short-term follow-up refers to three to six months post-discharge; and long term refers to one year or longer follow-up. There are three ways to do these outcome assessments for JJS clients:

- Evaluating electronic tracking data which usually includes time in supervision, AOD treatment received in the community, recidivism and relapse information;

- Rater data taken from the client's judicial supervisor, e.g., probation or parole workers;

- Client community follow-up interviews.

All of these methods have their problems. Community follow-up assessment of clients following discharge from treatment services or judicial supervision is one of the most difficult tasks of the entire assessment process. The longer the time period between discharge and follow-up, the more difficult it is to locate clients. The find rate for judicial clients at six-month post-supervision discharge ranges from 20 to 70 percent.

Using a combination of all three of the outcome methods, valid and reliable information about JJS client outcomes can be acquired.

In doing treatment process and outcome assessment, it is important to remember that real or "true" change is always confounded by the increased willingness to self-disclose. If one looks for a reduction of AOD symptoms after starting treatment, one often finds an increase in acknowledgement of these symptoms due to an increased willingness to disclose. Although this may make the client look worse, it is actually a sign of treatment progress.

Table 8.7 provides a list of instruments that can be used for assessing treatment progress and change, during treatment, at discharge or at post-discharge.

SPECIAL FOCUS AREAS FOR JUVENILE JUSTICE SYSTEM CLIENTS

The seven broad domains of the risk-resiliency assessment areas in *Figure 8.3* define the basic focus in comprehensive differential assessment. Each of these broad domains is defined by specific areas or assessment. There are several of these areas that need special attention since they represent significant co-occurring difficulties often found in juvenile justice clients. These specialty areas of assessment are summarized.

Community responsibility: deviancy and criminal behavior

The general assessment domain of Social Responsibility (see *Figure 8.3*) has a number of specific factors that, when assessed, provide the evaluator with a good understanding of the extent to which the client is involved in deviancy and criminal conduct. These domains range from rebellious and oppositional-defiant behaviors to serious misdemeanor and felony crimes. School acting out and truancy are also important areas of antisocial and conduct problems. These areas of school adjustment are different from, though certainly correlated with, poor school achievement. Many adolescents with learning problems and difficulty in school achievement do not have school acting out, truancy and conduct disorder problems.

The most common social responsibility problems are *conduct disorder and oppositional defiant disorder*, which were discussed in *Chapter 2*. Although the DSM-IV (APA: 1994, 2000) provides the guidelines for assessing and diagnosing these areas, instruments designed to measure deviancy and criminal conduct among adolescents are also helpful in discerning the extent of these conditions. As noted in *Chapter 2*, there is a strong and robust correlation between conduct disorder and patterns of criminal conduct in adolescents.

Comprehensive personality and self-attitude inventories include scales that measure antisocial and conduct problems. Two of the most commonly used comprehensive personality inventories are: *MMPI-A* (Butcher et al., 1992); and the *Millon Adolescent Clinical Inventory* (MACI: Millon, Millon & Davis, 1999). These are referenced in *Table 8.8*.

There are a number of instruments that provided specific measurements of the client's involvement in deviancy and criminal conduct. These instruments are listed in *Table 8.8*. There are two rather distinct genres of instruments in this area: those that measure personality patterns; and those that focus on problem behavior and life-adjustment problems. The *Jesness Inventory* (2004) is an example of measuring personality types and patterns. The deviancy scale in the *Adolescent Self-Assessment Profile-II* (ASAP-II: Wanberg, 1998) is an example of measuring specific deviant and criminal conduct behaviors and acts. Some instruments combine the personality-self attitude measures with specific behavioral measurements.

Another component of community responsibility assessment is risk taking. Risk-taking is often involved in problem behavior and in adolescent criminal conduct (Jessor & Jessor, 1977). There are several inventories that are used to assess risk-taking listed in *Table 8.8*, including the *Multi-Problem Behavioral Checklist* (MPBI: Jessor & Jessor, 1977) and the *Screening for Pregnancy-Risk Drinking* (Russell, Martier & Sokol, 1994).

Mental health and personality assessment

Some of the most important co-occurring disorders are in the area of mental health. *Figure 8.3* provides some of the most salient mental health areas that need to be evaluated during comprehensive assessment. Table 8.9 provides a list of some of the instruments used in this area of assessment.

The comprehensive personality and self-attitude inventories provide assessment across the broad range of mental health and personality problems (e.g., *MMPI-A*: Butcher, et al., 1992; *Millon Adolescent Clinical Inventory*: Millon, Millon & Davis, 1999).

Table 8.8   Instruments That Assess Juvenile Delinquency and Criminal Conduct

Instrument	Author/source	Focus/description
Minnesota Multiphasic Personality Inventory-Adolescent (MMPI-A)	Butcher et al. (1992)	Assesses adolescent mood adjustment, conduct disorder and personality patterns.
Millon Adolescent Clinical Inventory (MACI)	Millon, Millon & Davis (1999)	Measures different personality patterns, adolescent expressed concerns and clinical syndromes (Ages 13-19)
Adolescent Self-Assessment Profile II (ASAP II)	Wanberg (1992, 1998).	One General Scale and two sub-scales Profile measuring minor and major deviancy and criminal conduct
Youth Level of Service/Case Management Inventory (YLS/CMI)	Hoge & Andrews (2003)	Risk-needs assessment and case management planning and surveys youth's attributes and life situation, and risk of reoffending
Hare Psychopathy Checklist: Youth Version (PCL;YV)	Hare & Kossan (2003)	Identify potential patterns of deviancy and antisocial acts.
Jesness Inventory-Revised (JI-R)	Jesness (2003)	Provides measures of personality subtypes relevant to adolescent deviancy and criminal conduct
The Risk Calibration Measure (RCM)	Fischoff & Halpern (1989)	Measures risking-taking and the propensity for problem behavior and criminal conduct.
The Multi-Problem Behavioral Checklist (MPBI)	Jessor & Jessor (1977)	Assess adolescent risk taking.
Screening for Pregnancy-Risk Drinking	Russell, Martier & Sokol (1994)	Screens for pregnancy risks related to the use of alcohol.

Following is a summary of the most salient areas that are usually assessed through these tests and inventories.

Personality patterns and disorders, including:

- deviant and antisocial patterns including conduct problems, non-conformity, oppositional-defiant, violence-aggression, impulsive;

- withdrawal and avoidant patterns including introversion, submissive, inhibited, dependent, passive-aggressive, over-conforming, schizoid;

- expressive-extroversion including histrionic and dramatic, narcissistic, aggressive, egocentric;

- obsessive-compulsive; and

- borderline personality.

Mood and affective problems and disruptions, including:

- anxiety, stress and tension;

- depression, sadness, grief, suicidal thinking;

- anger, resentment and hostility;

- guilt, self-devaluation, self-demeaning; and

- mood swings, bipolar.

Somatic, including:

- hypochondriasis;

- anorexia and other eating disorders;

- elimination disorders; and

- disturbed thinking and psychosis.

Mental and cognitive functioning and abilities including:

- low intellectual abilities;

- motor skills problems;

- learning disabilities;

- communication disorders, e.g., stuttering; and

- attention-deficit and hyperactivity.

Many instruments designed to do differential and comprehensive assessment provide a general measure of mood adjustment and psychological problems, as is the case with some of the instruments in *Table 8.6*. This is the case with the *ASAP-II*, which provides a general measure of mood adjustment and

Table 8.9   Instruments That Assess Adolescent Mental and Behavioral Adjustment Problems

Instrument	Author/source	Focus/description
Minnesota Multiphasic Personality Inventory-Adolescent (MMPI-A)	Butcher et al., (1992)	Mood adjustment, conduct disorder and personality patterns.
Millon Adolescent Clinical Inventory (MACI)	Millon, Millon & Davis (1999)	Different personality patterns, expressed concerns and clinical syndromes
Adolescent Self-Assessment Profile II (ASAP-II)	Wanberg (1992).	One General Scale and three subscales measuring anxiety-depression, self harm and impulsivity-anger
Conners' Rating Scales-Revised (CRS-R) (Parents and Teacher Rating Forms)	Conners (1997)	Assessment childhood and adolescent ADHD problems
Conners-Wells Adolescent Self-Report Scales (CASS)	Conners & Wells (1997)	Self-report of problem behaviors in youth, including family, mood, conduct, cognitive, ADHD issues
Conners' ADHD/DSM-IV Scales (CADS)	Conners (1997)	Measures ADHD and consists of the CADS-Parent, CADS-Teacher and CADS-A which is self-report
AD/HD Comprehensive Teacher's Rating Scale, Second Edition (ACTeRS)	Ullmann, Sleator & Sprague (1998)	Used to identify attention disorder with or without hyperactivity.
Children's Depression Inventory (CDI)	Kovacs (1992)	Self-report, parent and teacher rated evaluating presence of severe depression symptoms and patterned after the Beck Depression Inventory
Beck Depression Inventory-II	Beck & Steer (1987)	Assessment of levels of depression with adolescents and adults
Trauma Symptom Checklist	Briere & Runtz (1989)	Symptoms resulting from trauma exposure
Trauma History Questionnaire	Greene (1995)	Degree of exposure to trauma events

psychological problems along with three specific, but narrow mood adjustment scales.

We will briefly review three specific mental health areas that should be targeted for more focused assessment with some JJS clients. These areas are considered to be co-occurring problems with the substance abuse and criminal conduct.

Attention deficit hyperactivity disorder

The characteristics and guidelines for diagnosing ADHD and its relationship with deviancy and criminal conduct in adolescents were thoroughly discussed in Chapter 2. With respect to assessment, the most important consideration is that the general ADHD disorder is usually separated into two separate conditions: hyperactivity and attending deficits. Although there are relatively strong correlations between these two conditions and adolescent criminal conduct, hyperactivity seems to be more associated with deviancy and conduct problems, and attending deficits seem to be more associated with school adjustment problems.

There are a number of assessment instruments that can be used to measure ADHD. These are summarized in Table 8.9. The *Conners' ADHD/DSM-IV Scales* (Conners, 1997) and the *ACTeRS* are two of the most commonly used in the screening and assessment of ADHD.

Post-traumatic stress disorders (PTSD)

As discussed in Chapter 2, post-traumatic stress is an individual's response of intense fear, helplessness and horror based on having experienced a threat to one's own life or physical integrity. Assessment of post-traumatic stress disorders (PTSD) is most commonly based on the criteria defined in the DSM-IV (American Psychiatric Association, 1994).

It is standard procedure to assess the extent and type of traumatic events to which the client has been exposed. The most salient are: physical and sexual abuse, exposure to and victim of violence and violent crimes, accidents and natural disasters. This type of exposure coupled with the key symptoms spelled out in Chapter 2 would generate a hypothesis that the client may have diagnosable PTSD.

Elevated scores on mental health and psychological symptom scales, specific big-face items that measure exposure to traumatic events (e.g., self-report of being sexually abused) and interview data indicating extent and impact of such exposure will help the evaluator determine whether referral for more specialized assessment in this area is needed. *Table 8.9* provides a list of instruments that measure trauma and post-traumatic stress symptoms.

Anxiety, depression and self-harm threat

These are salient areas of assessment for JJS clients at the screening, comprehensive and treatment process levels. Counselors should be vigilant of the changes in mood of clients, particularly depression and those of a hypomanic nature. As well, pathological ideations accompanying these mood changes should be a continual focus of assessment, such as thoughts of harm to self or others.

Certainly, the comprehensive personality inventories (MMPI-A and Millon Adolescent) provide measures of anxiety and depression. Most differential assessment inventories, such as the ASAP-II (Wanberg, 1998) and the PEI (Winters & Henly, 1989) provide measures of anxiety and depression.

Specific assessment of depression is also needed at times. It this case, the *Beck Depression Inventory* (Beck & Steer, 1987) and the *Children's Depression Inventory* (Kovacs, 1992) are very helpful. These instruments can be used to monitor changes in mood over the course of treatment.

CHAPTER REVIEW

This chapter provides a theoretical framework and model for the assessment of juvenile justice system (JJS) youth with substance abuse issues. The objectives of screening and assessment are outlined and the data sources for assessment are identified. One of the most important parts of this chapter is the presentation of the convergent validation model that helps resolve the problem of JJS workers' distrust of juvenile offender self-reports. Within the convergent validation perspective, self-report is a valid representation of the client's willingness to self-disclose at particular assessment points. It tells the evaluator where the client is at the time of assessment and the client's level of openness (or defensiveness). This is where we start treatment, where the client sees him/herself at the time of assessment. The degree of discrepancy

between self-report and other report provides insight into the level of defensiveness and the degree to which the data estimate the "true" conditions of the client.

This chapter also outlines criteria for determining inclusion of the client into the category of substance use problems along with guidelines for the use of evaluation instruments. The various levels of assessment are discussed, including preliminary screening, differential screening, comprehensive assessment and process and outcome evaluation. Also presented are the specific areas of assessment or risk-resiliency assessment factors that need to be addressed in comprehensive assessment. Descriptions of instruments that can be used at the various levels of assessment are provided. The assessment of co-occurring disorders and problems are also discussed, including deviancy and criminal conduct, ADHD, PTSD, and anxiety, depression and self-harm.

The general theme of this chapter is that assessment is a process and occurs throughout all contacts with clients. The content of any particular point of assessment is mainly relevant within the context of the process of assessment and change.

SECTION II: THE TREATMENT PLATFORM FOR ADOLESCENT SERVICE DELIVERY

Progress is impossible without change, and those who cannot change their minds cannot change anything.

Foundations of Cognitive-Behavioral Therapy

9

Chapter Nine:
Foundations of Cognitive-Behavioral Therapy

Chapter Outline

Historical Roots of Cognitive-Behavioral Therapy

Contemporary CBT: Integrating Cognitive and Behavioral Principles and Approaches

Underlying Principles of Cognitive-Behavioral Therapy

Therapeutic Focal Points in CBT

- Cognitive focus

- Behavioral focus

- Self-efficacy in substance abuse and juvenile justice treatment

What Works in Psychotherapy: Empirical Support for the Use of CBT

Chapter Review

Chapter Objectives

- To explain the historical roots of cognitive-behavioral therapy and the integration of cognitive and behavioral approaches to treatment;

- To describe the underlying principles and therapeutic focal points in CBT;

- To discuss empirical evidence that supports a client centered and cognitive behavioral approach to treatment.

HISTORICAL ROOTS OF COGNITIVE-BEHAVIORAL THERAPY

Because cognitive-behavioral treatment (CBT) is basic to intervention and treatment for many adolescent problems, this chapter reviews both the historical background and contemporary principles of CBT. Research conducted during the past two decades has left little doubt that CBT, built on a solid foundation of therapeutic support and client-therapist alliance, is the treatment of choice for a broad range of social problem behaviors. Regarding treatment within specific subpopulations, e.g., adolescents, basic cognitive-behavioral blueprints are enhanced to match cultural differences and special areas of treatment focus. The purpose of this chapter is to provide a comprehensive description of the theoretical and research basis for CBT, setting the groundwork for *Chapter 10*, which discusses basic strategies for a comprehensive treatment approach, of which CBT is an essential component. *Chapter 11* presents an overview of how CBT and other fundamental treatment strategies are *adapted for adolescents* to achieve optimal treatment benefits.

Since *Pathways to Self-Discovery and Change (PSD-C)* is based on the theory and practice of cognitive-behavioral approaches, we first present the historical roots of this model and show how the two paths of behavioral therapy and cognitive therapy have merged.

The development of behavioral therapies of the late 1950s and 1960s provided the evolutionary foundation of the behavior component of cognitive-behavioral therapy. Franks and Wilson (1973) note that behavioral therapy has a long past but a short history. This long past is found in the work of the behaviorists and learning theorists in the first half of this century (Glass and Arnkoff, 1992). Pavlov's work in classical conditioning (Pavlov, 1927), the behaviorism of Watson (1913) and the operant conditioning models of Skinner (1938) in the early part of this century provided the theoretical foundations of behavioral therapy.

During this same period work in the psychology of learning by Thorndike (1931), Guthrie (1935), Hull (1943) and Mowrer (1947) also added to the theoretical grounding of behavioral therapy. As these theories emerged, so did the number of efforts to apply them clinically (Glass and Arnkoff, 1992). Most noteworthy was Dunlap's (1932) use of "negative practice"

involving the *repetition of undesirable behavior* such as tics, Mowrers' (Mowrer & Mowrer, 1938) "bell and pad" method of treating bed-wetting, Jacobson's (1938) method of *progressive relaxation* and Salter's (1949) method of directly practicing a behavior in a particular situation.

Emerging methods such as systematic desensitization (Wolpe, 1958) to manage anxiety and the applications of contingency reinforcement (Skinner, 1953) in behavioral management spelled the beginning of modern behavioral therapy in the 1950s and 1960s. Eysenck (1960) was the first to use the term "behavioral therapy" in a book title; he along with Rachman founded the *Journal of Behavioral Research and Therapy*. Behavioral therapy gained a strong foothold in psychology with the introduction of the concepts and applications of modeling (Bandura, 1969), anxiety management through flooding, behavioral self-control and self-monitoring (Goldiamond, 1965; Kanfer, 1970) and social skills training (Lange and Jakubowski, 1976) which is an important component of contemporary cognitive-behavioral therapy.

The historical roots of the cognitive component of cognitive-behavioral therapy (CBT) are found in the literature of philosophy and psychology and in the studies on self-change (Arnkoff & Glass, 1992). The concept that *our view of the world shapes the reality that we experience* is found in Greek thinking and in Plato's concept of *ideal forms* (Leahy, 1996). Plato saw these forms as existing within the mind and represent what is real in the world. Seventeenth and 18th century philosophers built their view of the world around the idea that the mind determines reality. This is particularly found in Descartes' concept, "I think, therefore I am," and Kant's idea that the *mind makes nature* (Collingwood, 1949).

Arnkoff and Glass (1992) note the difference of opinions as to whether cognitive therapy evolved within modern behavioral therapy or whether it emerged as a new and independent movement. Whichever the case, it seems fair to conclude that the cognitive approach was a reaction to the more narrow view of behavioral psychology which did not attend to, and even rejected, the importance of internal mediating cognitive responses and processes, e.g., attribution, problem solving, expectancy, etc. Bandura's classic work *Principles of Behavioral Modification* (1969) challenged the traditional view of non-mediational behavioral psychology. Bandura (1969, 1977a) stressed the importance of internal mental processes in the regulation and modification of behavior.

Arnkoff and Glass (1992) view modern cognitive restructuring therapies as emerging in the mid-1950s with the work of Ellis (Ellis & Harper, 1961) and his development of *Rational-Emotive Therapy* (RET), which he presented in his book *Guide to Rational Living* (1961). The work of Ellis is seen as an important precursor to the work of Beck (1963, 1964) who is commonly seen as the founder and developer of cognitive therapy emerging out of his work with depression at the University of Pennsylvania in the early 1960s (Arnkoff and Glass, 1992; Beck, 1995; Leahy, 1996). Leahy (1996) attributes Kelly (1955) for his development of *cognitive constructs* as "the early founder of cognitive therapy" (p.11). Beck (1996) made it clear that he borrowed from Kelly's cognitive constructs when he first applied "the concept of *negative cognitive schemas* to explain the 'thinking disorder' of depression . . ." (p. 1). The work of Kelly and Piaget (Kelly, 1955) in their study of the structure of thinking provided a firm foundation for the development of the cognitive restructuring therapies.

Following the work of Beck (1963, 1970, 1976) in applying the cognitive model to the treatment of depression, other cognitive restructuring therapies began to emerge. These different forms of cognitive therapy began to blend the elements of behavioral therapy with cognitive-restructuring therapy. Thus, as Dobson and Dozois (2001) note, the earliest of the CBTs emerged in the early 1960's (e.g., Ellis, 1962). The first major texts on cognitive-behavioral modification did not appear until the 1970s (Kendall & Holland, 1979; Mahoney, 1974; Meichenbaum, 1974).

Meichenbaum (1975, 1977) was instrumental in developing *self-instructional training, stress inoculation and coping skills training.* His approach had a strong influence from behavioral therapy. Goldfried et al. (1974) implemented systematic rational restructuring, which teaches the individual to *modify internal sentences* (thoughts) and then to practice the rational reanalysis of these thoughts through *role-playing and behavioral rehearsal.* Cautela (1966; Cautela & Kearney; 1990) conceived *covert sensitization* (1966) as a method for cognitive-behavioral change. *Problem solving* therapies and training became prominent features of cognitive behavioral treatment (Shure & Spivack, 1978; Spivack & Shure, 1974; D'Zurilla & Goldfried, 1971). The coping skills and stress inoculation training approaches were developed to help clients deal with problem and stressful situations

(Meichenbaum, 1977, 1985). The stress inoculation method involves teaching the individual coping skills and then practicing these skills when deliberately exposed to a stressful situation.

Although *behavioral therapies and cognitive restructuring* approaches seemed to develop in parallel paths, over time, the two approaches merged into what we now call *cognitive-behavioral therapy.* As Arnkoff and Glass (1992) note, "the line distinguishing behavior therapy from cognitive therapy has become blurred, to the point that cognitive-behavioral is a widely accepted term" (p. 667). The behavioral component is of crucial importance particularly in the treatment of children (Arnkoff and Glass, 1992) but also in the treatment of alcohol and other drug abuse problems and of criminal conduct. Alan Marlatt has noted (personal communication, 1995): "Cognitive therapy à la Ellis and Beck has over the years become progressively more behavioral and that behavioral therapy à la Bandura, Goldfried, Kanfer, Mahoney, Michenbaum, etc., has over the years become progressively more cognitive . . . together creating contemporary CBT."

CONTEMPORARY CBT: INTEGRATING COGNITIVE AND BEHAVIORAL PRINCIPLES AND APPROACHES

Contemporary behavior therapy places the focus on *current determinants* of behavior with an emphasis on *overt behavior change* guided by *specific treatment objectives* (Kazdin, 1978). It involves the application of principles that come from learning theory, social and experimental psychology. It involves environmental change and social interaction using approaches that enhance self-control (Franks & Wilson, 1973). It is further characterized by a focus on client responsibility and the therapeutic relationship (Franks & Barbrack, 1983). The common intervention approaches used in behavioral therapy are *coping and social skills training, contingency management, modeling, anxiety reduction and relaxation methods, self-management methods and behavioral rehearsal* (Glass & Arnkoff, 1992).

The underlying principle of contemporary cognitive therapy is that disturbances in behaviors, emotions and thought can be modified or changed by *altering the cognitive processes* (Hollen & Beck, 1986). In simplistic terms, "cognitive therapy is based on the simple idea that your thoughts and attitudes—and not external events—create your moods" (Burns, 1989, p. xiii). The fundamental idea of the cognitive model of emotion as outlined by Beck et al. (1975) is that "... emotions are experienced as a result of the way in which events are interpreted or appraised. It is the meaning of the event that triggers emotions rather than the events themselves" (Salkovskis, 1996a, p. 48).

The role of the cognitive therapist is to help the individual see alternative ways of thinking about and appraising a situation, to check the relative merits and accuracy of the alternatives against past, present, and future experiences, and then help the individual "identify any obstacles to thinking and acting in this new, more helpful way" (Salkovskis, 1996a, p. 49). The goal is not to convince the individual that his or her view of the situation is wrong, right, negative, and irrational, but rather to help the person discover other ways of looking at the situation.

Yet, this does not necessarily mean a straightforward cause and effect (thinking being the cause, and emotions and action the results). Cognitive psychology *assumes interplay* between thought, emotion and action. As Freeman and colleagues (1990) note, "the cognitive model is not simply that 'thoughts cause feelings and actions' " (p. 6). Emotions and moods can change cognitive processes. Actions can have an influence on how one sees a particular situation. Emotions can arouse behaviors. There are a number of studies to indicate how moods and emotions influence cognition, e.g., memory, perception (Freeman, et al., 1990).

The common intervention approaches used in cognitive therapy are (Leahy, 1996; Kendal & Bemis, 1983; Arnkoff & Glass, 1992):

- Restructuring cognitive distortions found in negative schemas, maladaptive assumptions and automatic thoughts

- Self-instructional training

- Problem solving skills development

- Coping skills

- Relaxation therapy

- Modeling and role playing strategies

- Thought stopping

- Covert conditioning

Contemporary CBT, then, is an integration of the key components of behavioral and cognitive therapy. Even though prominent publications have titles designated as "Cognitive Therapy," (e.g., J. Beck, 1995; Leahy, 1996; Salkovskis, 1996b), the descriptions of the methods and approaches of cognitive therapy in these texts clearly integrate the behavioral therapy counterpart. In 1983, Kendall and Bemis argued that behavioral influences were predominant in the practice of cognitive therapy. Even though there appears to have been an evolutionary merging of the two approaches over the past 20 to 25 years, there has been some resistance to integration, particularly from behavior therapists (Arnkoff & Glass, 1992). However, during the 1990s, there was a strong movement towards the integration of all forms of contemporary psychotherapy (Arnkoff & Glass, 1992; Goldfried, 1995).

Our review of the literature shows that the combining element of cognitive and behavioral approaches is found in the principle of self-reinforcement. This concept simply states that cognitive and behavioral changes reinforce each other. When cognitive change leads to changes in action and behavior, there occurs a sense of well being (positive outcome) which strengthens the change in thought structures that led to changes in action. In turn, the changes in thinking, reinforced by the changes in behavior, further strengthen those behavioral changes. It is not just the reinforcement of the behavior that strengthens the behavior; it is the reinforcement of the thought structures leading to the behavior that strengthens the behavior. This self-reinforcing feedback process is a key principle, which becomes the basis for helping clients understand the process and maintenance of change and is the basis for the cognitive-behavioral approach to change in this work—*Pathways to Self-Discovery and Change*.

UNDERLYING PRINCIPLES OF COGNITIVE-BEHAVIORAL THERAPY

The underlying principle of *Pathways to Self-Discovery and Change* is that both cognitive and behavioral approaches bring combined strengths to the implementation of effective education and treatment for teenage substance abuse, delinquency and crime. There are many forms and variations of CBT. Mahoney and Lyddon (1988) note that CBT is a generic term that refers to more than 20 approaches within this tradition. Yet, there are some basic principles shared across many of these variations in CBT (Arnkoff & Glass, 1992; Beck, 1995; Clark & Steer, 1996; Dobson & Block, 1988; Dobson & Dozois, 2001; Dryden & Ellis, 2001; Ellis, 1962, 1975; Freeman et al., 1990 Kendall & Bemis, 1983; Kendall & Hollon, 1979; Mahoney & Arnkoff, 1978; Wanberg

& Milkman, 1998, 2004). Some of these principles are premised on behavior therapy, others on cognitive therapy. All are important in the understanding and effective implementation of CBT.

Cognitive structures, activities and processes mediate learning and behavior: This mediation concept is at the core of CBT (Mahoney, 1974; Dobson & Dozois, 2001) and applies to affective and behavioral disturbances. Disturbances in behavior and emotion are a result of disturbances in mental activities - thinking, perceiving, and feeling. Thus, behavioral outcomes are a direct result of these cognitive activities.

People respond to their mental interpretation of the environment: CBT approaches examine the idiosyncratic meaning and interpretations the individual assigns to these external events or the environment in order to understand the resulting emotional and behavioral responses to these events (Neenan & Dryden, 2001). Individuals are actively involved in the construction of their realities and the role of the therapist is to "see" the world through the eyes of the client (Neenan & Dryden, 2001).

Individuals can monitor and control their cognitive structures and activities: Individuals can know about, get in touch with, monitor and control their cognitive structures and activities. As Dobson and Dozois (2001) state, ". . . clients are architects of their own misfortune, and they therefore have control over their thoughts and actions" (p. 28). Many CB theorists see self-monitoring and control as premised on the construct of *self-efficacy.* Since Bandura's introduction of this concept in social learning theory (Bandura, 1977b), this has become a prominent emphasis with many CB therapists. It is an important focus in the application of CB approaches for treating substance abusing clients.

An important corollary to this proposition is that an *accurate assessment* of cognitive structures and activities is an essential step to changing thinking in order to change behavior. Cognitive-behavioral theories often categorize mental structures into thoughts, attitudes and beliefs. For example, one category of thought is expectations. We take a drink because we expect the drink to relax us. When it does, not only is the behavior of drinking reinforced, the expectancy (cognitive structure) is also reinforced. Both self-assessment and professional assessment are possible in this monitoring process. Part of this assessment involves the identification of underlying functional and dysfunctional beliefs.

Individuals can alter or change their cognitive world, which leads to changes in behavior: Not only can we change our thoughts, we can alter our underlying beliefs. This was an early proposition of CBT in the work of Ellis. This proposition implies specific methods and techniques can be used to change thinking and beliefs. The methods fall under the rubric of cognitive restructuring. An elaborate cataloguing of such methods is found in the work of McMullin (2000). Self-control is increased when the individual discovers that thinking can be changed, and this thinking can lead to more positive outcomes. Most important, as a result of changes in cognition, changes in behavior follow.

Thoughts that lead to behavioral outcomes are strengthened: Changes in behavior are reinforced through the strengthening of thoughts that lead to those behaviors. Regardless of the outcomes of certain actions or behaviors, the thoughts and underlying beliefs that lead to those behaviors may be strengthened. This self-reinforcement process is an essential determinant of maintaining maladaptive behaviors or maintaining positive changes in behavior.

A traditional view of behavioral reinforcement holds that if a behavioral outcome is negative, the behavior should have less probability of repeating itself. However, common experience often belies this axiom. Why do people repeat behaviors that lead to negative outcomes, e.g., punishment, pain? One main reason is that the outcomes strengthen the thoughts and underlying beliefs that lead to those behaviors.

For example, an argument with a peer may produce thoughts of "being disrespected," or "not being treated fairly." The core belief leading to these thoughts might encompass, "life sucks; people can't be trusted; they'll turn on you." This may lead to feelings of anger and getting high with available, like-minded associates. After drinking and smoking marijuana on the street, the youth is arrested on a minor in possession charge. This event leads to further thoughts that "I'm being treated unfairly," reinforcing the underlying belief that "life sucks." Unless efforts are made to change these automatic thoughts and the underlying core beliefs related to these thoughts, then the person will continue to engage in behaviors that lead to negative outcomes and continue to strengthen the thoughts leading to those outcomes.

Outcomes can be improved by learning skills and behaviors that lead to positive outcomes: Behaviors are strengthened or reinforced when they result in certain consequences, contingencies or outcomes. This is the basis for the social-interpersonal skills component of cognitive-behavioral therapy and change. Self-control can be enhanced through learning and practicing skills that lead to better problem solving, more positive communication with others, and resolving conflicts in a more positive manner. Thus, when these behaviors lead to positive outcomes, these behaviors are strengthened. Behaviors get reinforced not only when they result in positive outcomes but when they are efficacious in avoiding negative outcomes. Positive and negative reinforcement are the underlying principles of behavioral therapy.

Distortions in thinking and beliefs lead to disturbances in emotions and behavior: Using an information-processing model, Beck (1976) holds that *information-processing errors or distortions* occur when individuals experience or encounter stressful events. During these stressful and threatening situations, our thinking can become rigid and distorted (Weishaar, 1996). Our information-processing skills and abilities become faulty resulting in errors or distortions in thinking (Neenan & Dryden, 2001). Identifying and *changing thinking errors or distortions* have become salient components of cognitive therapy (e.g., Beck, 1976; Burns, 1980; DeRubeis, Tang & Beck, 2001; Ellis, 1984; Ellis & Harper, 1975; Freeman, et al., 1990; Wanberg & Milkman, 1998, 2004). These sources provide long lists of thinking errors that include *catastrophizing, all or nothing thinking, magnifying, blaming, procrastinating, jumping to conclusions, etc.*

Identification of the cognitive structures underlying maladaptive feelings and behaviors is ongoing: Self-assessment is the process of identifying thoughts that lead to certain behaviors and outcomes and attitudes and beliefs that underlie those thoughts. This is an integral component of learning and change and does not stop at intake. It is ongoing and continuous. Assessment is mainly for the benefit of the client. The provider is continually providing feedback to the client with respect to findings and interpretation of this ongoing assessment.

CBT is problem and solution (goal) oriented: In the CBT approach, clients are asked to *identify specific problems* that bring them into treatment. Intervention and treatment are then focused on solving those problems. The basis of these problems and the solutions sought are built around *identifying the cognitive structures* that generate the problems and then to *change*

those structures so as to provide favorable and adaptive outcomes and solutions. Although all therapeutic approaches attempt to identify the referring and focal problem(s) of the client, CBT makes a specific effort to see the cause and solutions to these problems at the cognitive as well as behavioral levels.

CBT is a structured and usually time-limited therapy: Sessions are most always structured, with this structure determined by focal problems and focal solutions. During sessions, clients review homework, do worksheets, exercises, and role-playing and practice the various skills that are used in managing cognitive and behavioral problems. However, time is also provided for *unstructured sharing and self-disclosing* to allow for the expression of thoughts and emotions or to share experiences the client had between sessions. Yet, material emerging from these unstructured periods is used as "grist for the mill" in the CBT process.

Sessions are usually *time-limited* (Beck, 1995; Dobson & Dozois, 2001). This is a clear distinction from the more traditional unstructured therapies such as client-centered, psychoanalytic or psychodynamic approaches. Guidelines for the number of therapy sessions usually fall in the 5-15 session range. For clients who have more ingrained thinking and behavioral problems, e.g., character pathologies, substance abuse, it is recommended that treatment be protracted for as long as one year.

CBT providers go beyond the traditional role of counselor and therapist: Counselors and treatment providers fulfill the roles of evaluator, educator, teacher, consultant coach, as well as traditional therapist, in understanding disturbed and maladaptive thought processes and in developing, with the client, life-response changes. CBT approaches ". . . are by nature explicitly or implicitly educative" (Dobson & Dozois, 2001, p. 28). For example, clients are taught the CBT change model and a rationale is usually provided for the specific CBT interventions that are used.

The provider and client work as partners in solving client problems: An important component of CBT approaches is that the counselors or treatment providers and the client work together in a partnership or team in evaluating, assessing and developing solutions to problems. Beck (1979) calls this *collaborative empiricism*, which involves the process of "reality-testing clients' thoughts, assumptions and beliefs" (Neenan & Dryden, 2001, p. 11). These cognitions are viewed as hypotheses that clients develop about reality.

Therapy involves the process of the client collecting information to test these hypotheses. For example, a client's cognitive response (thoughts) to an interaction with mother is that "she is nosey." However, through cognitive restructuring, this thought is changed to "maybe she is just concerned." This hypothesis is tested through the application of effective communication skills (social skills building), and the client discovers that mother's responses *are* based on concern and caring. Thus, rather than experiencing anger the next time that mother offers advice, he acts on the underlying assumption that "mother cares and she may have some good advice" and this anger is replaced with reciprocal feelings of love and warmth.

The development of therapeutic alliance: Through the implementation of the partnership model and application of collaborative empiricism, a therapeutic alliance between the therapist and client is forged. Most CB (cognitive-behavioral) therapists construct that alliance through the application of the Rogerian (1951, 1959, 1980) principles of *empathy, genuineness, respect, warmth and unconditional positive regard.*

Early approaches to CBT saw therapeutic alliance and the therapeutic relationship as vehicles through which the CBT approach was applied. Now, most CBT theorists view the therapeutic relationship as a method for change *in and of itself* (Blackburn & Twaddle, 1996) and as an important and essential part of CBT (Beck, 1979; Arnkoff & Glass, 1992). Thus, building rapport and trust with the client, applying motivational methods and techniques in the therapeutic process and building an environment to maximize self-disclosure have become important factors in the evolution of CBT (Miller & Rollnick, 1991; Beck, et. al., 1993).

Between session application: One of the most important components of CBT is to practice the skills learned in therapy between sessions. Informal and formal homework is an ongoing ingredient of CBT. Many therapists use formal and structured worksheets as part of the homework. An important CBT homework construct is the thinking report and the rethinking report (Wanberg & Milkman, 1998; 2004).

There is a reciprocal interaction of thoughts, emotions and behaviors: An individual's thoughts, emotions and behaviors interact and affect each other. Neenan and Dryden (2001) note that the CBT model is not based just on the linear process whereby thinking leads to emotions and actions. Emotions and moods can lead to certain thoughts. Actions can influence how one thinks or feels. Emotions can lead to certain actions. Yet, the change model as utilized in most CBT approaches and the one used in this work is premised on the idea that we start with identifying the thinking, and the underlying beliefs, that lead to certain emotional and behavioral outcomes. In order to prevent dysfunctional emotional and behavior outcomes, we then make efforts to change the thinking and the underlying beliefs so as to increase the probability of more favorable and functional emotional and behavioral outcomes.

Greenberger and Padesky (1995) suggest that *the environment* and the *individual's physiological responses* are equally important components in this reciprocal or interactive process. External (or internal) events are important in bringing on certain thoughts based on the individual's beliefs and attitudes (Wanberg & Milkman, 1998, 2004). As well, initial physiological responses (e.g., rapid heart beat, urges or cravings) to these events or to thoughts, emotions and behaviors are also important focuses in the change processes. Greenberger and Padesky conclude that change in any one of the five components—the *environment, thoughts, attitudes/beliefs, emotions and behavior*—can have impact on the other four.

CBT initially places emphasis on the here and now: CBT focuses on thoughts and underlying beliefs that emerge out of *here and now events* in the client's life. It is problem and solution focused and self-discovery and change are based on the client's existential experiences. It is recognized that the thought habits and underlying beliefs have their roots in past experiences. Yet, the restructuring of these thoughts, the changing of these beliefs and the efforts to help clients build effective skills in managing interpersonal relationships are based on current life experiences. Past experiences and memories are dealt with as they are relevant in understanding and changing current dysfunctional thoughts, emotions and actions.

Enhancing client therapeutic independence: Most CB therapists and theorists agree that the ultimate goal of therapy is to build *self-direction* and *therapeutic independence.* In essence, this means that the client becomes a self-therapist (Neenan & Dryden, 2001). "Cognitive therapy . . . aims to teach the patient to be her own therapist" (J. Beck, 1995, p. 7). As clients increase self-control through inculcating the skills of cognitive restructuring and effective interpersonal management, the client becomes more and more his or her own therapist. Clients not only solve problems in therapy, they learn the process of problem solving and establishing self-control. The ultimate goal of the CBT therapist is based on the "teaching to fish" metaphor: Give *a person a fish, and you can feed him/her for a day; teach the person to fish and s/he can feed him/herself for a lifetime.*

THERAPEUTIC FOCAL POINTS IN CBT

CBT uses two basic approaches in bringing about change: (a) *restructuring of cognitive events* so as to bring about adaptive and positive outcomes; (b) *social and interpersonal skills training* to enhance adaptive interactions and positive outcomes. These two approaches are built on the two pathways of reinforcement: (a) *strengthening of the thoughts* that lead to that behavior; (b) *strengthening behavior* due to the consequence (reinforcement) or outcome of that behavior. The former has it roots in cognitive therapy; the latter has it roots in behavioral therapy. Together, they form the essential platform of cognitive-behavioral therapy.

Cognitive focus

Early cognitive therapy (CT) theorists and practitioners focused on key cognitive events or structures and processes (e.g., Beck, 1976; Beck et al., 1978; Burns, 1989; Ellis & Harper, 1975). These are:

• Automatic thoughts and automatic thinking

• Underlying assumptions

• Underlying core beliefs

These elements of cognition are the main targets of cognitive therapy (Neenan & Dryden, 2001). Early theorists also identified the important automatic thoughts that the cognitive therapist should focus on: *expectations* and *appraisals*, traditionally referred to as *automatic* (e.g., Beck, 1976, 1996; J. Beck, 1995; Freeman et al., 1990) because they seem to occur "without thought," or "automatically" as a response to external events. Wanberg and Milkman (1998, 2004) call these *thought habits* in order to help clients understand that thinking habits, which become the focus of change, are similar to our behavioral habits which also become the focus of change.

Underlying assumptions and core beliefs are often seen as *schemas* that structure our thinking. In fact Beck (1996) sees the "basic systems" of personality - cognitive (or information processing), affective, behavioral, and motivational - as composed of structures labeled schemas' (p. 4). Schema-focused

therapy (McGinn & Young, 1996) is part of the "new paradigms for treating patients with character pathology" (p. 182). It is "designed to extend Beck's original model of cognitive therapy and to specifically address the needs of patients with long-standing character disorders" (p. 182). It integrates cognitive, behavioral, experimental and interpersonal techniques, using a "schema" as the unifying element.

Seligman, Walker and Rosenhan (2001) categorize the mental or cognitive processes that are the main focus of cognitive therapy into *short-term and long-term* mental processes. They identify the short-term cognitive processes that become the focus of treatment as and *attributions*. The long-term processes are *beliefs*. Although Seligman et al., refer to these as processes, they are also referred to in the literature as schemas, constructs, concepts, cognitive events and structures.

Expectations, appraisals and attributions are mental events (automatic thoughts) that often come quickly and without deliberate thought and are the *short-term processes* in the Seligman et al. model. *Expectancies* are mental expectations that particular behaviors, e.g., drinking alcohol, will bring certain outcomes, e.g., pleasure. Bandura (1977a, 1981) distinguishes between *outcome expectations* and *efficacy expectations*. Outcome expectancies represent the individual's judgment about whether the performance of a particular behavior will produce a particular outcome. Or, it is knowledge of what to do and what will be obtained. If that behavior does fulfill the expectation, then the behavior is reinforced.

Efficacy expectation refers to the individual's assessment of his or her ability to successfully execute a particular behavior. Bandura sees this as a person's belief that he or she can carry out a certain course of action to get a certain outcome. If a person believes that he or she can perform a particular behavior, then most likely that individual will engage in that behavior. If the behavior is performed successfully, this reinforces the efficacy expectation. This concept is of particular importance in the treatment of the substance abuser. Helping the client develop the skill of coping *with anxiety* in ways other than AOD use, will build the efficacy expectation that he or she can handle stress-inducing situations in ways other than drinking or using drugs.

Appraisals represent cognitive events that lead to action and feelings (Rosenhan & Seligman, 1995; Seligman et al., 2001). This is the cognitive process that continually evaluates the *value and meaning* of what we are experiencing and our responses to those experiences. Often, these cognitive appraisals become distorted and result in thinking errors. As noted above, identifying and changing thinking errors or distortions have become salient components of cognitive therapy. For example, an appraisal of the depressed person who experiences rejection might be "I'm no good." This would also be classified as a *thinking error* or an error in logic. Beck holds that such appraisals, or automatic thoughts, usually precede and cause emotions. The appraisal that "he's taking advantage of me" usually leads to the emotion of anger.

Attributions are the individual's explanation of why things happen or the explanation of outcomes of certain behaviors. An important part of attribution theory is where the individual sees the source of his or her life problems or successes or one's *locus of control* (Rotter, 1966). This locus of control might be *internal* ("I'm responsible for the crime I committed") or *external* ("If they would have locked their car doors, I wouldn't have ripped off their stereo"). Attributions can be *global* or *specific* (Abramson, Seligman, & Teasdale, 1978). "I got drunk because life is just not fair" is a global attribution whereas a specific attribution would be, "I got drunk because my father yelled at me."

Long-term cognitive processes (Seligman et al., 2001) are less available to our consciousness. These mental processes are more durable and stable and they help determine the short-term mental processes that are in our conscious state. "One of these long-term cognitive processes is belief" (Seligman, et al., p. 114).

Beliefs are ideas that we use to judge or evaluate external situations or events. They are the personal "truths" from which we explain the world. Changing underlying core beliefs is a primary focus of cognitive therapy. For example, it is one of the primary target areas in *Rational Emotive Therapy* (Ellis, 1962, 1975), e.g., "In order to be happy, I must be in love." *Irrational beliefs* underlie and mediate our short-term cognitive processes - *expectations, attributions and appraisals* (Seligman et al., 2001). J. Beck's (1995) cognitive model introduces an intermediary layer of cognitive constructs that she calls *intermediate beliefs* distinguished from *core beliefs*. She labels the intermediate beliefs as *rules, attitudes and assumptions*. The core and intermediate beliefs are constructs that people use to make sense of their environment and organize their experience in a coherent way in order to function adaptively (J. Beck, 1995, p 16; Rosen, 1988).

Freeman and his colleagues (1990) suggest that cognitive therapy should focus on four major areas to bring about change in maladaptive and dysfunctional cognition and behavior:

- Automatic thoughts
- Underlying assumptions and beliefs
- Cognitive distortions
- Influence of emotions and mood on cognition

Most cognitive approaches see the process of treatment as starting with helping the client to first identify *automatic thoughts and cognitive distortions* and then addressing the *long-term underlying assumptions, intermediate and core beliefs* that are associated with the automatic thoughts and which lead to dysfunctional emotional and behavioral responses and outcomes (e.g., J Beck, 1995; 1990; Leahy, 1997).

Cognitive restructuring (CR) is the main method and technique used to change the above described short-term and long-term cognitive processes. *Self-talk* is seen as a generic CR method and includes *thought stopping, planting positive thoughts, countering, shifting the view, exaggerating the thought,* etc. (see McMullin, 2000, for a resource in CR techniques). Other examples of cognitive restructuring approaches are: *relaxation training* (Jacobson, 1938), *self inoculation training* (Meichenbaum, 1985, 1993a), *self-instructional training* (Meichenbaum, 1975), *problem solving skills* (D'Zurilla & Goldfried, 1971; D'Zurilla & Nezu, 2001), *mood-management training* (Beck, 1976; Monti et al., 1995), *critical reasoning* (Ross et al., 1986) and *managing and changing negative thoughts* (Beck, 1976; Wanberg & Milkman, 1998, 2004).

There are also a number of specific cognitive restructuring focuses that are relevant in treating crime and substance-abusing clients. These include managing *cravings and urges, critical reasoning and managing high-risk thinking in preventing relapse and/or recidivism.*

Behavioral focus

Coping and *social skills training* (CSST) evolved over the last two decades of the 20th century to become an essential component of cognitive-behavioral therapy (Monti, et al., 1995). It emerged out of social learning theory (Bandura, 1977a) and has solid empirical support from outcome research (Monti et al., 1989, 1995). Its premise is that clients with maladaptive thinking and behavioral patterns do not have adequate skills for facing daily living issues and problems.

There are a number of specific areas in which interpersonal and social skills building focus. These include *communication skills, assertiveness training, interpersonal problem solving skills, skills in building and maintaining intimate relationships, conflict resolution and managing aggression and violence* (Wanberg & Milkman, 1998).

Self-efficacy in substance abuse and juvenile justice treatment

The importance of *self-efficacy* (SE) in CBT is stressed by most authorities in the field. Bandura (1977b) sees SE as the unifying construct of the social-cognitive framework of therapy and SE has a primary role in his conceptual scheme. Self-efficacy is a cognitive construct that relates to and strengthens self-control (Bandura, 1978). Wilson and O'Leary, in their *Principles of Behavioral Therapy* (1980) identified SE as a key concept in the overall theory of behavioral change. "Efficacy expectations play a major part in the initiation, generalization, and maintenance of coping behavior" (p. 269). Goldfried (1995) sees the facilitation of SE and the client's perceived sense of *self-mastery and competence* as a key focus in treatment and devotes an entire chapter to this focus. Thus, the importance of this cognitive construct in CBT and self-management therapies is well established (e.g., above references; Freeman, et al., 1990; Maisto, Carey & Bradizza, 1999; Rokke & Rehm, 2001, etc.).

Within the area of the intervention and treatment of juvenile justice and substance use problems, *SE is viewed as a major focal construct.* Marlatt identifies four cognitive constructs as most salient in the intervention and treatment of individuals who have alcohol or other drug use problems. These are: *self-efficacy, outcome expectancies, attributions and decisions* (Marlatt, 1985b) Self-efficacy is a critical link in his relapse prevention model. Self-efficacy plays a major role in determining and strengthening behaviors in many different domains, e.g., success, academic achievement, managing anxiety and stress. It is considered to be one of the most important determinants of self-control over substance abuse problems and preventing relapse (Marlatt, Baer & Quigley, 1995).

Self-efficacy is defined as "a perception or judgment of one's capability to execute a particular course of action required to deal effectively with an impending situation" (Abrams & Niaura, 1987, p. 134). It is

"perceived control." It refers to the *belief that one is able to execute successfully the behavior required to produce a particular outcome* and pertains to the strength of ones convictions about personal effectiveness (Sarason & Sarason, 1995). Efficacy expectations have a major effect on whether a person initiates a coping behavior and how much effort will be put towards implementing that behavior (Bandura, 1982). SE is reinforced if the person copes successfully over time (Dimeff & Marlatt, 1995).

Bandura distinguishes SE, defined as *perceived performance competency in specific situations* from the constructs of self-esteem and self-concept, the latter which refers more to global constructs of self-image (Bandura 1977, 1981, 1982). Marlatt (1985a) also concludes that SE is not a global, cross-situational construct like self-esteem or locus of control. It refers to expectations or judgments people make about their capacity to cope with *situation-specific events.* Marlatt views SE as a state measure and not a trait measure such as self-esteem (Marlatt, 1985a).

Bandura argues that perceived self-efficacy is a major determinant of whether a person initiates a certain action or behavior and whether that person is motivated to extend that behavior. He holds that effective psychosocial interventions are *successful* because they *alter a person's expectation of self-efficacy* (Bandura, 1977b). Connors, Donovan & DiClemente (2001) indicate that helping clients increase their sense of self-efficacy is of particular importance during the *action stage* of change. Increasing the client's perceived SE involves focusing on the clients' success, strengthening positive decisions and helping clients make intrinsic attributions as to their source of change.

A number of studies indicate that SE has a significant relationship to alcohol use patterns. Hays and Ellickson (1990) found that in non-clinical samples adolescents with *higher levels of SE* were able to more effectively resist the use of alcohol, marijuana and tobacco. Adults in non-clinical samples who scored low on SE had higher levels of alcohol consumption (Young , Oei, & Crook, 1991). In clinical samples, longer-term abstainers reported higher levels of SE than either the active abusers or recently detoxed clients (Miller, Ross, Emerson, & todt, 1989).

WHAT WORKS IN PSYCHOTHERAPY: EMPIRICAL SUPPORT FOR THE USE OF CBT

Research with respect to the effectiveness and outcomes of psychotherapy and psychosocial oriented therapies has indicated that there is a *general positive treatment effect*. Summaries of meta-analyses of outcome studies conclude that "psychotherapy is effective at helping people achieve their goals and overcome their psychopathologies at a rate that is faster and more substantial than change that results from the client's natural healing process and supportive elements in the environment" (Lambert & Bergin, 1992). For example, the meta-analysis of 475 studies by Smith, Glass and Miller (1980) provided evidence for the efficacy of psychotherapy and concluded that those who had received psychotherapy were better off than 80 percent of those who did not.

Several findings are evident in the growing body of research literature regarding the outcome of psychosocial oriented therapies. One rather robust finding is that *no one clinical approach seems to be superior over another* (Lambert & Bergin, 1992) and those different therapeutic approaches, e.g., behavioral, psychodynamic, client-centered, "appear to secure comparable outcomes" (Garfield, 1992, p. 349). Differences in outcome between various forms of treatment are simply not as pronounced as might be expected (Lambert & Bergin, 1992) and "other purportedly unique features of a system may be relatively inconsequential" (Strupp & Howard, 1992, p. 313). These findings are supported by the *American Psychological Association's* special issue on outcome research (VandenBos, 1986) and other research studies by Nathan (Nathan & Gorman, 1998; Nathan, Gorman & Salkind, 1999).

This general finding of no-difference in outcome across diverse therapies leads us to the following hypotheses (Lambert & Bergin, 1992): 1) Different therapies can achieve similar goals through different processes; 2) Different outcomes do occur but these are not detected by current research strategies; or 3) Different therapies embody common factors that are curative but not emphasized by the theory of change central to a particular school.

Research literature supports the third conjecture that the *common features* of psychosocial therapies may be the *major contributor* to the effectiveness of treatment (Frank, 1992, p. 393). This conclusion is supported by

a long history of research on the efficacy and effectiveness of psychological oriented therapies. The early work of Rogers and Dymond (1954) on the efficacy of client-centered therapy supports this conclusion. The research of Truax and Carkhuff (1967) on the effectiveness of the paraprofessional in effecting change in clients certainly supports the common factors theory. The *Vanderbilt Study* (Strupp & Hadley, 1979) which found comparable outcomes among analytically-oriented therapists, experientially-oriented therapists and college professors is but another example of support for the common factors theory. Regardless of the theoretical orientation or even the type of disorder being treated, the common features or factors findings in psychosocial therapies is robust (Arkowitz, 1992; Elkin, 1986; Garfield, 1992; Glass & Arnkoff, 1988).

But what are these common features? Two of these common features that have been identified with psychotherapy efficacy are:

- Counselor personal characteristics; and

- Counselor/therapist-client relationship

Most relevant to this chapter, is that common factors of psychotherapy effectiveness have been identified across the various therapies (Lambert & Bergin, 1992). These elements are *grounded in cognitive-behavioral approaches*, and include the teaching and training of intrapersonal and interpersonal skills, the development of self-efficacy through training in self-help skills and overall skill development. Cognitive and cognitive-behavioral therapies are often seen as a basis for psychotherapy integration (Alford & Norcross, 1991; Arkowitz, 1992; Beck, 1991; Goldfried, 1995).

Another trend that has emerged out of the efforts to evaluate the efficacy of psychosocial therapies in the last part of the 20th century has been the development of empirically designed research to discern the efficacy of specific therapeutic interventions for specific kinds of psychosocial disorders (Lyddon & Jones, 2001). Particularly relevant to this work, *Pathways to Self-Discovery and Change*, is the development of a cadre of literature that supports cognitive-behavioral treatment for those with a history of substance use problems and a history of criminal conduct and character pathology.

Support for the use of CBT with individuals with a substance abuse history is robust (e.g., Beck, 1993; Nathan, Gorman & Salkind, 1999; Wanberg & Milkman, 1998; 2004). "One of the most promising types of psychological therapies available for alcohol substance disorder is cognitive-behavioral therapy" which includes enhancing the individual's cognitive and interpersonal skills in coping with everyday life circumstances (Nathan et al., 1999, p. 80).

There is also robust support for the use of CBT approaches to effect change with individuals with personality disorders (Cottraux & Blackburn, 2001), character pathology (McGinn & Young, 1996) and a history of criminal conduct (Andrews and Bonta, 1994; Wanberg & Milkman, 1998, 2004). The combination of these two bodies of literature provide the basis for using cognitive-behavioral approaches in the education and intervention of individuals with problems in substance abuse and juvenile justice.

CHAPTER REVIEW

This chapter explains the historical roots and major constructs that define contemporary cognitive behavioral treatment (CBT) approaches. The chapter shows how behavioral and cognitive approaches have merged to form the primary psychotherapeutic model for achieving positive outcomes in treatment for substance abuse and character pathology. A comprehensive description of the basic principles of cognitive-behavioral therapy is followed by an introductory discussion of the major focal points of CBT: *cognitive restructuring and social skills training.*

Core Strategies for Delinquency, Crime and Substance Abuse Treatment

10

Chapter Ten:
Core Strategies for Delinquency, Crime and Substance Abuse Treatment

Chapter Outline

Integrating Education and Therapy in the CBT Model

Seven Core Strategies in the Education and Treatment Process

- Multidimensional screening and assessment facilitates the treatment process

- Facilitating the cyclic process of growth and change for individuals and the treatment group

- Facilitating clients and the treatment group through stages of change

- Motivational enhancement and building the treatment alliance

- Cognitive–behavioral model for change: underlying assumptions and processes

- Cognitive restructuring—a primary method of changing maladaptive cognitive structures

- Relapse and recidivism prevention

- Using CBT approaches in developing moral and community responsibility

Chapter Review

Chapter Objectives

- To show how education and treatment are integrated in the CBT model for growth and change;

- To delineate core strategies in the CBT education and treatment process;

- To explain the use of cognitive restructuring as a primary model for changing maladaptive thoughts, feelings and actions;

- To present a schema of the CBT model for learning and change;

- To describe how Marlatt's Relapse Prevention Model has evolved as a useful strategy for preventing relapse and recidivism;

- To discuss the importance of building moral and social responsibility in juvenile justice clients; and

- To show how treatment effectiveness is improved through developing judicial and therapeutic partnerships.

INTEGRATING EDUCATION AND THERAPY IN THE CBT MODEL

Defining psychotherapy, counseling and education: Lang (1990) sees psychotherapy as "a relationship and interaction between an individual with an emotionally founded problem who is seeking help.... and an expert who is capable of assisting him or her in effecting its resolution . . .." (p. 3). He defines the core dimension of psychotherapy as the object relationship between the patient and therapist and the interpersonal interaction that unfolds on the basis of this relatedness (p. 219). Bateman, Brown & Pedder (2000) see psychotherapy as "a conversation that involves listening to and talking with those in trouble with the aim of helping them understand and resolve their predicament" (p. xiii).

Jerome Frank, who provided some of the earlier definitions of psychotherapy, considers the core of all psychotherapy approaches as a process through which a *socially sanctioned healer works to help individuals to overcome psychological stress and disability through a method or procedure that is based on a theory of the sufferer's difficulties and a theory of the methods to alleviate them*. Thus, he sees five features common to all forms of psychotherapy (Frank, 1963, 1974): (a) a trusting and emotionally charged relationship between client and therapist; (b) a therapist who is genuinely concerned about the sufferer's welfare and is committed to bring about some kind of change that is seen as desirable; (c) a conceptual framework that explains what has happened and what will happen; (d) a procedure or method that the therapist and patient follow for the purpose of bringing about changing and/or restoring health; and (e) the theory approaches, and outcome are linked to the dominant world view of the client's culture.

These definitions have several factors in common. There is a trusting and working relationship, a provider who has concern and empathy for the client's pain and welfare, a theory of psychological and behavioral problems, a method of how to approach those problems, a client who presents with a unique set of problems, and an expectation of change found within the context of a set of cultural and societal values.

In *Pathways to Self-Discovery and Change*, psychotherapy (therapist) and counseling (counselor) have similar meanings and, essentially, are used synonymously. However, there has been a long-standing discussion about whether psychotherapy and counseling are synonymous. The term psychotherapy was first used in the late 1880s (Efran & Clarfield, 1992) when at the time, psychological problems came to the forefront in medicine ("psyche" meaning mind, and "therapeia" meaning treatment). Carl Rogers began using counseling in the 1930s in order to "side-step" the legal restriction that only medical doctors were allowed legally to practice psychotherapy (Dryden & Mytton, 1999).

Most experts in the field see the two as having the same or similar processes and methods. Dryden & Mytton (1999) view the two as having the same meaning. Both refer to helping individuals with personal or relationship problems directed at effecting personal and emotional changes so as to improve personal functioning. Both definitions refer to a process of bringing about self-improvement and change.

Patterson (1966) made an effort to look at their differences and similarities and concluded that there is no essential difference between the two in terms of the process, methods or techniques, the goals or expected outcomes, the relationship between the client and therapist or the clients involved. The one distinction he makes is that counseling sometimes refers to work with *less disturbed clients or clients* with special change needs and psychotherapy may refer to work with *the more seriously disturbed* persons. Ivey & Simek-Downing (1980) also saw this as a noteworthy distinction: counseling directed at assisting "normal people" to achieve their goals or to function more effectively and psychotherapy as a longer-term process concerned with the implementation of personality change.

George and Cristiani (1981) concluded from their literature review that the distinction is more on a continuum, with counseling directed more at aiding growth, focusing on the present, aimed at helping individuals function adequately in appropriate roles, more supportive, situational, problem-solving and short term; whereas psychotherapy is *more reconstructive*, analytical, focuses on past and present, directed at more severe emotional problems and at change in basic character and personality (p. 8).

Given that the differences between psychotherapy and counseling seem to lie on a continuum, we treat the two as synonymous. In addition, we use the term therapy to refer to the counseling-psychotherapy continuum, and, as noted above, synonymous with treatment. Although the literature shows only minor differences between these two approaches, Patterson (1966) makes a clear distinction between counseling or psychotherapy and *education*. He states that counseling and psychotherapy deal with the *affective realm*—attitudes, feelings, and emotions, and not simply ideals (p. 3). Teaching or education is viewed as being concerned with the *rational, non-ego-involved, solution of problems*. "Where there are no affective elements involved, then the process is not counseling, but is probably teaching, information giving, or an intellectual discussion" (p. 3). More specifically, Patterson clearly states that counseling and psychotherapy are not just giving of information, advice, suggestions or recommendations, although counseling may involve these activities. He sees them as influencing and facilitating voluntary behavior change. In our work with juvenile justice clients, there is a strong focus on integrating education and psychotherapy, i.e., clients learn basic facts about how thought and behavior patterns are acquired, the process of change and the damaging effects of lifestyles built around delinquency and substance abuse. In this sense the treatment provider takes on the dual role of therapist-educator (DeMuro, 1997).

SEVEN CORE STRATEGIES IN THE EDUCATION AND TREATMENT PROCESS

We have identified seven core strategies for education and treatment of adolescents with concurrent criminal justice and substance abuse problems:

Multidimensional screening and assessment facilitates the treatment process

Client screening and assessment are based on a convergent validation model and lead to a multidimensional assessment of the client's condition. *Chapter 8* provides theoretical and research perspectives on screening and assessment along with the basic concepts of the convergent validation model. *Chapter 14* presents the operational design for the use of specific methods for PSD-C screening and in-depth assessment.

Facilitating the cyclic process of growth and change for individuals and the treatment group

Most approaches to therapy identify the process of treatment as one of personal growth and change. Building on the concepts of learning and change found in Lewin's steps of learning (Ham, 1957; Lewin, 1935, 1936, 1951) and Werner's *Orthogenetic*

Principle (1957), a process and structure for change in treatment was developed by Wanberg (1974, 1983; 1990; Wanberg & Milkman, 1998, 2004). This process of growth and change model is seen as an essential foundation of the PSD-C education and treatment platform.

Kurt Lewin conceptualized growth and change as being the same and saw the learning process as involving three response phases: *undifferentiated* or global; *differentiation*; and *integration*. The first response phase is a global or undifferentiated response to a situation, a set of stimuli or a situation that expects change and growth. This response can be observed in all living organisms. It occurs in a rapid, undifferentiated multiplication of cells in the first stages of a new organism; it can be observed in an infant child whose whole body responds to a stimulus. *Resistance and tension* are also identified in this stage of growth.

The second response phase of growth occurs when the individual units of the organism begin to *differentiate* among each other. Different sizes and shapes of cells begin to emerge; now the infant can reach out with his arms without the rest of the body moving. Lewin describes this stage as the *differentiated phase* of growth and change. "Ambivalence" about existence is resolved and organism identity is defined.

The third, integrative response phase of growth occurs when the various units begin to *show purpose* and functional integration. Now the elongated cells of the plant carry water and minerals to the flat leaf cells responsible for photosynthesis. The infant's reach now is for food, which she successfully places in her mouth.

Werner, in his *Orthogenetic Principle*, conceptualizes growth and change taking place in a very similar manner. "Wherever development occurs it proceeds from a state of relative globality and lack of differentiation to a state of increased differentiation, articulation, and hierarchic integration" (Werner, 1957, p. 126).

Utilizing the concepts of the process of growth and change provided by Lewin and Werner's *Orthogenetic Principle*, Wanberg (1983, 1990; Wanberg & Milkman, 1998, 2004) developed a cyclical or spiral model to explain the process of therapeutic change and a counseling skill structure to facilitate change. This is illustrated in *Figure 10.1*. The value of this model for growth and change is that it occurs over the course of learning and treatment; or it occurs within any one segment of learning and change. It is not a lin-

Figure 10.1   The Cyclical Process of Growth and Change in Treatment

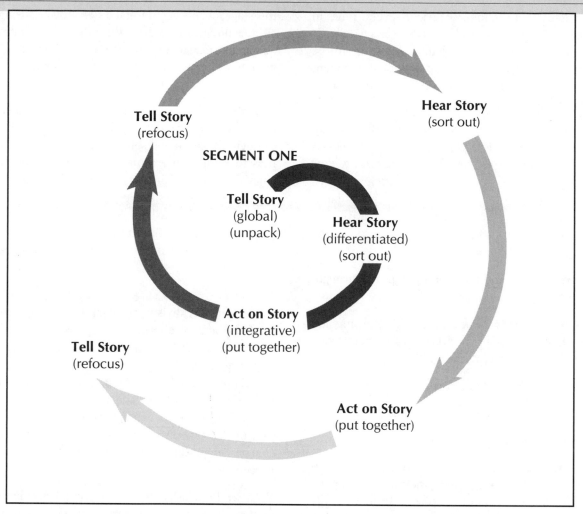

ear model that describes change in a stepwise fashion. Rather, it describes change as spiral in nature, and the model is applied to each individual growth experience.

Within the framework of PSD-C, this process takes place for the client and the treatment group as a whole. First, there is the global, undifferentiated phase of unpacking. The client globally responds to the treatment with an undifferentiated response. In a short time clients begin hearing information and sharing parts of their story. There is always a *global*, *undifferentiated*, and even confused response to all of the new events at certain points of dealing with their treatment/judicial episode.

Second, there is *the sorting out* phase. With an arrest, for example, the client understands the charges, gets legal, paralegal, or parental advice, and begins to sort out various responses that can be made. As clients experience PSD-C education and treatment, they hear specific information about AOD use, about delinquency, receive feedback about their own story, and begin to

label and identify thoughts, feelings and emotions.

Third, there is the *acting on the story* and integrating the events. With respect to judicial sanctioning process, the client receives legal council, the responses of family members, peers and significant others are integrated, and life is reorganized with certain decision responses. The client enters PSD-C (a new event that takes him through the three phases again). Now, as a consequence of getting feedback, understanding and learning cognitive and relationship coping skills, these skills are applied, substance abuse and delinquency are prevented, community access is restored, and irresponsible thinking and errors in logic are replaced so as to lead to more positive outcomes.

Thus, the phasic-spiral learning and change process occurs with both micro and macro life events. It is a process that occurs within the client's education and treatment experiences. These phases of *unpacking* (client receives information or client telling story), sorting out (client hearing story) and *integrating* (client acting on his story) may: (a) occur around one topic or issue in a session; (b) occur several times in the course of one session; (c) occur over several sessions around one theme, problem or topic; or (d) be descriptive of the client's or group's total treatment experience, e.g., over the entire CBT (cognitive-behavioral treatment) program.

The spiral concept illustrates that the client/group never returns to the same place, *but each cycle moves the treatment entity further away from the baseline conditions that brought them into treatment.* Thus, the client may relapse or the group may regress, but if therapeutic intervention and change is effective, disruption does not take the client back to the pre-treatment level of morbidity.

Facilitating clients and the treatment group through stages of change

When clients experience the process of learning and change, they go through specific stages. In our model, we identify three stages of change:

- WHAT—*Challenge to Change*,

- HOW— *Commitment to Change*, and

- NOW—*Ownership of Change*.

These stages integrate the more traditional stages developed by Prochaska and associates (Connors, Donovan & DiClemente, 2001; Prochaska & DiClemente, 1992; Prochaska, DiClemente & Norcross, 1992). The six stages of this transtheoretical model of how people change are briefly reviewed. These are congruent with the cyclic process of growth and change discussed above.

Precontemplation: Clients are resistive, do not process information about their problems, and give little or no thought or energy to self-evaluation or serious change in their behavior. Clients in the *contemplative* stage give some thought to change, but take little action to change. Clients are ambivalent about change but *are* more open to consciousness-raising techniques such as information feedback and interpretations and are more likely to respond to educational procedures. There is an increased self-evaluation, awareness of problems and a greater openness as to how these problems impact others. If the ambivalence about change is resolved, this stage becomes a turning point for the client.

Determination or preparation: As clients move into the determination or preparation for change (or treat-

ment) stage they continue to increase the use of cognitive, affective and evaluative processes of change. In this stage, clients begin to take steps toward using specific techniques to reduce their use of substances or delinquent maneuvers and to control their unique situations with methods other than using substances or committing deviant acts.

Action: A sense of self-direction and self-liberation begins to develop. There is greater internalization of self-determination and self-regulation and more openness to using reinforcement tools and techniques to change behavior. There is an increased reliance on support and understanding from significant others and helping relationships. The development of alternative responses to internal and external triggers for substance use and deviance is an important part of this stage.

Maintenance: This stage involves the prevention of relapse [and recidivism] through the development and reinforcement of alternative responses. Strategies to reinforce established changes and stimulus control (e.g., urge to drink when with friends) are used. There is a commitment to therapy and to receiving support from significant others and a continued practice of established skills to manage potential relapse are a part of this phase. Self takes on a greater value and change supporters are an important part of this process.

Relapse: Prochaska and Diclemente (1992) have postulated *relapse* [and recidivism] as a sixth stage where the individual begins to engage in behaviors and thinking that indicate a process of relapse or where the individual relapses into the full pattern of use. In this model, relapse is recognized as normal in the recovery process, i.e., "each slip brings you closer to recovery." Rather than inviting clients to relapse, the aforementioned phrase may simply prevent patients and staff from demoralization when unsteadiness or backsliding occurs.

Motivational enhancement and building treatment alliance

Most youth who enter treatment in response to judicial or other pressures initially present with a considerable degree of *defensiveness and resistance* to involvement with PSD-C intervention. Developing a working relationship with adolescent clients requires adroit and culturally sensitive utilization of the skills of motivational enhancement and therapeutic alliance building. This core strategy for PSD-C involves the utilization of motivational enhancement skills and building a working intervention relationship with clients. As presented in *Chapter 6*, developing sensitivity to adolescent subcultures and diversity within the treatment population is critical to motivational enhancement. There is a great deal of research evidence supporting the efficacy of motivational enhancement as an important component in building the therapist-client relationship and implementing treatment readiness and change in substance abuse clients (e.g., Miller & Rollnick, 1991, 2002; Project Match Group, 1997).

The necessity for the use of motivational enhancement methods is found in *client resistance and ambivalence*. Most teenagers with AOD and delinquency problems display ambivalence about changing their lives or at least, changing the behavior patterns that lead to such problems. Resolving ambivalence and resistance to these patterns, and helping clients to develop an internal sense of readiness, openness and responsiveness to treatment are primary objectives of the early phases of any intervention program. Some of the important elements of building the intervention relationship and enhancing motivation for involvement in education and therapy are explored.

Therapeutic Stance: The therapeutic stance underlying the building of the intervention relationship and motivating clients to change is based on the core elements of the client-centered therapeutic relationship: *warmth, empathy, genuineness and positive regard* (Rogers, 1951, 1957). There is a long research history supporting the finding that the degree of empathy shown by counselors during treatment is a significant predictor of treatment efficacy. Style of relating becomes apparent early in the intervention encounter and can impact retention, even in one introductory session. With respect to AOD clients, Miller and Rollnick (1991) showed that successful therapy is predicated upon counselors providing clients with three critical conditions: *accurate empathy, non-possessive warmth; and genuineness.*

Therapeutic Alliance: Therapeutic alliance builds on, but goes beyond the core elements of the therapeutic stance that underlie motivation enhancement. Therapeutic alliance involves a *collaborative relationship, affective bonding, rapport building, and a mutual understanding and sharing of the intervention goals* between the client and the therapeutic educator—referred to as the provider in most of this work (Bordin, 1979; Conners et al., 1997; Raue, Goldfried & Barkham, 1997).

One of the robust predictors of treatment retention and outcome is the relationship between the client and the provider, regardless of the therapeutic orientation or treatment approach (Bachelor, 1991, 1995; Barber, et al., 2001; Connors, et al., 1997; Gaston, 1990; Hartley & Strupp, 1983; Harvorth & Symonds, 1991; Krupnick et al., 1996; Martin, Garske & Davis, 2000; Raue & Goldfriend, 1994; Raue et al., 1997; Zuroff et al., 2000). Results from these various studies also indicate that client ratings of therapeutic alliance are more predictive of outcome than therapist ratings; therapeutic alliance scores tend to be higher for cognitive-behavioral sessions than for sessions conducted under a psychodynamic-interpersonal orientation; that the efficacy of therapeutic alliance is found across various therapeutic approaches and modalities; and that the positive therapeutic alliance from the early part of treatment predicts positive outcome in psychotherapy.

Using therapeutic confrontation in managing resistance and ambivalence: Developing a positive relationship and building rapport and trust with the client depends on how client resistance, defensiveness and ambivalence are managed. This management is of particular importance in the early stages of intervention. Traditional methods of confrontational therapy and coercive intervention in managing resistance and "denial"—previously touted as the treatment choice for substance abuse—often results in increasing client resistance and defensiveness. Bill Wilson, one of the co-founders of *Alcoholics Anonymous*, held that intervention works best on the basis of attraction and support. Wilson advocated that alcoholics be treated with an approach that "would contain no basis for contention or argument . . . Most of us sense that real tolerance of other people's shortcoming and viewpoints, and a respect for their opinions are attitudes which make us more helpful to others" (Alcoholics Anonymous, 1976, pp. 19-20).

The most effective way to manage client resistance, defensiveness and ambivalence is to **first** encourage the client to *share thoughts and feelings of resistance and defensiveness* and **second**, to use reflective-acceptance skills to help clients hear their resistance. These are the two basic steps of the therapeutic change process as described above, and represent the elements of reflective or therapeutic feedback (Wanberg, 1974, 1983, 1990; Wanberg & Milkman, 1998). These are the key components in Miller and Rollnick's motivational interviewing model (Miller & Rollnick, 1991, 2002). This involves providing the environment of acceptance for clients to share their thoughts and feelings and then reflecting the client's specific statements of anger, resistance and ambivalence. Miller's (1983; Miller and Rollnick, 2001) clinical principles of *avoid argumentation, develop discrepancy* and *roll with resistance* underlie the reflective-feedback approach in dealing with client resistance and defensiveness.

Expanding the knowledge base: Providing information on the causes and consequences of AOD abuse, delinquency and crime are necessary to the informed decision making process basic to the CBT platform. The first phase of the treatment process focuses on preparing clients for making a commitment to change by providing them with accurate, unbiased information concerning the multiple risk factors to which they are exposed. The educational component of treatment provides clients with a social learning perspective on substance abuse and crime, as well as explanation of how self-disclosure, openness to feedback and taking responsibility for thoughts and feelings can result in positive treatment outcomes.

Enhancing interest in change: Motivational strategies are based on the compensatory attribution model of treatment (Brickman et al., 1982), which sees the client as having the power to influence change and focuses on building client *self-efficacy and personal responsibility* in the change process. Motivation is a state of readiness and openness or eagerness to participate in a change process. Miller et al. (1995) have summarized the research on what motivates clients to change. Their work on *Motivational Enhancement Therapy* (MET) highlights the effectiveness of relatively brief treatment for problem drinkers. The elements that the authors consider necessary to induce change are summarized by the acronym FRAMES:

Feedback: provide objective information on degree and types of personal risk impairment

Responsibility: emphasis on personal responsibility for change

Advice: Clarify, model and affirm constructive thoughts and behaviors

Menu: provide a spectrum of alternative change options

Empathy: Clients perceive that the therapist understands the situational, emotional, cognitive and behavioral influences that impact his or her life

Self-efficacy: Therapist and treatment milieu provide reinforcement and positive feedback when client demonstrates personal empowerment and optimism about healthy life choices

Therapeutic interventions containing some or all of these motivational elements have been demonstrated to be effective in initiating treatment and in reducing long-term alcohol use, alcohol-related problems, and health consequences of drinking (Miller et al., 1995).

An important focus in enhancing motivation and interest for change in adolescent clients is that of developing "a more enlightened view of their self-interest and recognize that it is in their own best interest to anticipate the [short and] long-term consequences of their actions . . . " (Freeman et al., 1990, p. 229). This model is designed to help juvenile offenders to control impulsivity long enough to perceive the consequences of substance abuse and delinquency as *not as rewarding* as the long term consequences of prosocial behavior. In essence, motivation is enhanced by helping teenagers take a short and long-term view of their self interest. This can only be done when the counselor takes a *collaborative approach to treatment* (a key component of CBT) and a trust-based working relationship has been developed. These two objectives of treatment—*building a collaborative relationship and helping the client take short as well as long-term view of self-interest*—are primary focuses in the PSD-C education and treatment sessions.

Cognitive-behavioral model for change: underlying assumptions and processes

The primary cognitive-behavioral (CB) assumption underlying AOD misuse and delinquency: Cognitive structures and processes operate in such a manner so as to prevent self-control over the use of substances and responsible behavior in the community. AOD abuse and delinquency are consequences of the individual's cognitive organization and cognitive processes through which these structures are expressed. The CB approach to education and treatment is to modify and change the *proximal* or *short-term* structures (thought habits or automatic thoughts), e.g., outcome expectancies that lead to substance abuse and delinquency, and then moves to working on changing the *distal* or *long-term* structures, e.g., beliefs. This change process involves:

- Identifying the thought habits or automatic thoughts that lead to substance abuse outcomes and delinquent acts.

- Changing thought habits or proximal structures to ones that lead to self-control and adaptive prosocial outcomes.

- Changing proximal structures to help the client identify the more distal and ingrained structures of attitudes and beliefs that reinforce the thought habits or proximal structures that lead to substance use problems and delinquent actions.

- Challenging old beliefs and transforming and replacing these beliefs and assumptions into a belief system that generates and strengthens thought habits or proximal structures that lead to self-control and prosocial outcomes.

- Clients practice these changes, with counselor and group support, so that both the behaviors and cognitive changes are reinforced.

The PSD-C education and treatment protocol is built on three levels of cognitive structures: *(a) proximal; (b) intermediate; and (c) distal.* This model utilizes a combination of Seligman et al. (2001) and J. Beck (1995) and builds on the work of A. Beck (1995) and Bandura (1977). In PSD-C cognitive structures are referred to as *thought habits* and often referred to in the literature as automatic thoughts. Seligman et al. (2001) refer to these as short-term, more surface cognitive processes. We draw upon Bandura's work (1977) to expand them to five essential proximal structures.

Proximal Structures

Outcome expectancies: the individual's judgment about whether the performance of a particular behavior will lead to a certain outcome. It is the knowledge of what to do and what will result. If the behavior, and the outcome expectancy thoughts are fulfilled, both the thoughts and behavior are reinforced. Example: "If I smoke weed, I'll have more fun."

Efficacy expectations: the individual's assessment of his or her ability to successfully execute a particular behavior. This is the belief that one can carry out a certain course of action to achieve a certain outcome. If there is the belief that one can perform a particular behavior, then most likely one will engage in that behavior. If the behavior is performed successfully, this reinforces the efficacy expectation. Example: "If I carry out this robbery with my friends, I'll look cool, and gain respect from the gang – I know I can pull it off."

Appraisals: proximal structures that evaluate the value and meaning of what we are experiencing and our responses to those experiences. Appraisals can trigger powerful emotions which culminate in negative actions. These can become distorted resulting in thinking errors. Examples: "This guy just put me down in front of my friends" (appraisal); " I'm so angry" (emotional response); "He's gonna pay big time" (decision /outcome expectation).

Attributions: explanations of why things happen or the explanations of outcomes. It might be internalized, "I'm responsible for the vandalism"; or externalized, "The reason I got busted is the cops were after me."

Decisions: structures that actually lead to the behavior that can result in good or bad outcomes. This is an important component of Marlatt's (1985a) relapse prevention model, and represents the individual's conscious choice to take a certain action. It provides the basis of the underlying philosophy of freedom of choice in change and in self-determination and self-control.

Intermediate Structures

Intermediary or mediating structures: J. Beck (1995) refers to these as intermediate beliefs. We refer to these as go-between or mediating structures. They mediate between the underlying core beliefs and the thought habits or automatic thoughts. They line us up with our inside world or the outside world. Some important intermediary structures noted in the literature are *attitudes, values and rules.*

Attitudes: orient us for or against a situation, object or person. Attitudes cause us to line up our thoughts and feelings, positively or negatively, to something or someone outside ourselves. Or, they line us up for or against ourselves. They are usually affectively based with a powerful emotional charge. Examples: "School sucks," or " Cops will try to screw you over" or " Pot is good or else it wouldn't be here to smoke."

Values: guiding principles of our life. They determine the goals toward which we strive, e.g., family security, mature love, wisdom, salvation, an exciting life, comfort, prosperity, and social contribution. If we assign great value to money, then we will line ourselves up in a positive way with certain activities that bring financial reward. Material values might become manifest as an affiliation with a gang or scheme to manufacture or distribute drugs.

Rules: also line us up with the outside world and ourselves. If we have an internal rule that "I will not steal," that rule will determine how we associate our-selves with people and with systems. The person who has a strict rule of "never cheating," will point out to her friend that she shouldn't flirt or have sex with other guys because that would not be fair to her boyfriend. Rules are important in mediating core beliefs into thought habits or proximal structures. For example, a core belief that "I am an honest person," will translate into a rule of "I will never cheat on someone," leading to the automatic thought: "I need to tell my boyfriend that the guy over there is putting the moves on me."

Distal Structures

Core beliefs and assumptions: concepts that are used to judge or evaluate ourselves, situations, people, and the world. Beliefs bond us to ourselves or to the out-side world. We see these as the "truth," or a "conviction." Core beliefs are usually 100 percent and they are deeply ingrained. There are two kinds of core beliefs or assumptions that become the focus in CB treatment of delinquency and crime.

Beliefs about self: bond us to our sense of self. They include the core beliefs of self-importance and self-value. Examples of these beliefs about self are: "I'm a good person," "I feel I can handle life's problems," "I've made a positive contribution," "I can't handle life," or "I'm worthless."

Beliefs about the world: bond us to the outside world. They involve basic assumptions about how we see and perceive the world. Some examples of core beliefs are: "the sacredness of life" "right to make choices" "people are created equal" "my people are victims" "people from other cultures will try to hurt me." These beliefs are medi-ated by attitudes, rules and values and surface into automatic thoughts.

Figure 10.2 provides a schematic structure for these three levels of cognitive structures. Certainly, there are other cognitive structures that could be added to these levels. For example, a core belief that one should "treat others with respect" may be mediated by the rule of being "courteous," and an automatic thought of "I'm sorry when one makes a mistake or offends someone." Note that in *Figure 10.2,* the base of the pyramid is rep-resented by the core beliefs about self and the world, which are mediated by the *intermediary structures* to surface in *thought habits and automatic thoughts.*

Cognitive processes underlie the expression of cognitive structures: these are important cognitive process-es that operate in such a manner as to allow the expression and manifestation of the cognitive structures above.

Automatic thinking: produces a thinking pattern or thought habit that leads to the mental reactions already formed inside our heads (proximal structures). This is a response to the events that we experience. Automatic thinking leads us to form an opinion about an appraisal and outcome expectancy: "I need a drink and a drink will relax me."

Decision making: a cognitive process that allows the expression of the decision structure.

Cognitive distorting: a process where our reaction to the outside world leads to thought habits that are errors in judgment about what we are experiencing. "I can't handle things," is an appraisal that may be an error in thinking and needs changing to "I'll try to handle things."

Underlying assuming: the operational process through which attitudes, rules, values and core beliefs get expressed. Thought habits or automatic thoughts are manifestations of the process of underlying assuming.

Interaction of thoughts, emotion and behaviors: can lead to emotions and behaviors. However, emotions can lead to behaviors and thoughts; and behaviors can lead to thoughts and emotions. Our starting point in change is with our thoughts. However, we may have to label the emotion first in order to work back to the thought habit that leads to the feelings and outcome behaviors, e.g., " I recognize feeling angry . . . now I understand that the thought of being disrespected is fueling my anger."

The five cognitive processes above that underlie the expression of the core cognitive structures are noted in the three-dimensional pyramid of *Figure 10.2.*

Cognitive restructuring—a primary method of changing maladaptive cognitive structures

As discussed above, there are two traditional focuses in CB learning and change: *cognitive restructuring* and *social skills training.* Cognitive restructuring involves helping clients develop skills to alter the short term and long term structures that determine feelings and actions. Sometimes we call this intrapersonal skill building. Some of the specific methods that are used in changing both the proximal and distal maladaptive cognitive structures are:

- Self-talk

- Thought stopping

- Thought replacement

Figure 10.2 Model of Cognitive Structures and Processes

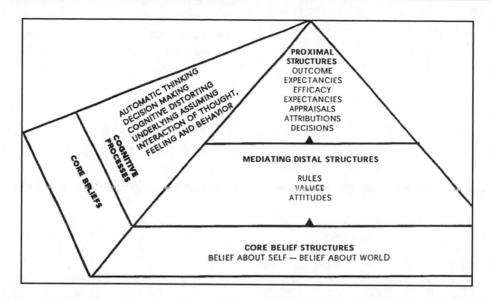

- Changing negative thinking

- Managing guilt, anger, stress

The second focus involved in CB learning and change is on interpersonal and social skills that enhance self-efficacy and lead to positive outcomes. This is the interpersonal restructuring component of CB treatment. This approach focuses on enhancing self-efficacy in interpersonal and social interactions. The specific focus areas of interpersonal or social skills training are:

- Communication skills

- Problem solving skills

- Conflict resolution skills

- Building life-style balances

The cognitive-behavioral (CB) assumption underlying AOD misuse and delinquent behavior is that cognitive structures and processes operate in such a manner so as to prevent self-control over the use of substances and responsible behavior in the community. AOD abuse and delinquency are a consequence of the individual's cognitive organization and cognitive processes through which these structures are expressed.

Schema for cognitive-behavioral learning and change: Most CB models assume that our thinking can lead to certain emotions that result in certain behavioral outcomes. Some theorists see emotions and feelings as the consequence or outcome that pre-

cede the behavior. The basic model in the PSD-C protocol is that thinking leads to emotions, and these emotions are representations of self-control or lack of self-control. Thus, the automatic thought, "He's cheating me," leads to feelings of "I'm damn mad about that." The next logical consequence is a behavioral response. The CB model identifies a number of core emotions that result from thought habits coming out of intermediary and core beliefs. These are usually anger, guilt, depression or sadness.

The CB change model assumes that patterns of AOD misuse and patterns of delinquency are determined by the individual's *cognitive structures and processes* that lead to emotions and feelings and result in overt AOD misuse and delinquent acts. Thus, the PSD-C education and treatment curriculum is directed at changing the thinking and underlying beliefs resulting in a change in feeling and subsequently bringing about change in behavior.

Based on core beliefs, external events or inside memories and feelings lead to automatic thoughts about self and about the world. A primary focus is to help the client recognize those automatic thoughts and the errors and distortions in thinking associated with those thoughts, and to change the core beliefs and intermediary attitudes, values and rules that underlie the automatic thoughts and thinking distortions. The key guiding principle of PSD-C education and treatment is that we can have control over our thoughts and feelings—we can change and choose our thoughts and our beliefs. *Cognitive restructuring and interper-*

sonal *skill* development are the vehicles through which change is achieved.

Automatic thoughts, which are based on core beliefs and attitudes, lead to overt behaviors. The CBT model holds that individuals make conscious choice of their behavioral responses to external events and to their internal thoughts and feelings. Coping and social skills training provide the key interventions in helping clients learn to choose adaptive behaviors to manage outside events and internal feelings. The coping actions we choose and the outcomes of those actions reinforce (strengthen) internal thoughts, underlying beliefs and the mediating assumptions that lead to certain outcomes. When the outcomes are positive, they strengthen the cognitive structures leading to the outcomes and reinforce the behavior responses.

Figure 10.3 provides the basic CB schema for the process of learning and change used in PSD-C. This is the *model for change*, not the model for explaining the process of how cognitive structures move from core beliefs to automatic thoughts. *Figure 10.3* depicts the two pathways of learning and reinforcement. When the certain automatic thoughts (based on underlying beliefs and mediated by attitudes, rules and values) lead to certain behaviors, those behaviors can result in positive actions or negative actions. If the action results in a positive outcome, then that behavior gets reinforced (strengthened), as indicated by the return

arrow from positive outcome back to adaptive positive action (upper right corner of *Figure 10.3*). Note that there is no comparable return arrow in the lower right of *Figure 10.3*, from negative outcomes back to negative maladaptive action. There are return arrows leading back to automatic thoughts from both positive outcomes and negative outcomes. This implies that the automatic thoughts and underlying beliefs can get reinforced (strengthened), whatever the outcome.

TREATMENT PROVIDERS WILL NOTE that the principles illustrated in *Figure 10.3* are presented in a simplified and artistically enhanced format in the *Participant's Workbook for Pathways to Self-Discovery and Change*. The schema is used as the primary visual tool for illustrating the logic and therapeutic process of the CBT paradigm for learning and change.

An example related to substance abuse and delinquency is used to illustrate the paradigm for change as shown in *Figure 10.3*. A teenage client had a fight with his father (backed up by his mother) about being forbidden to go to an overnight party. On the way home from school he thinks (automatic thought—*expectation*), "I'll stop off and have a joint with my friends. Make me feel better." Some more automatic thoughts—*appraisals*: "He doesn't care about what I want, nobody cares." Beneath these thoughts and feelings are the long held beliefs that "life isn't fair" and

Figure 10.3 Cognitive-Behavioral Process of Learning and Change: How Thoughts and Behaviors Are Strengthened

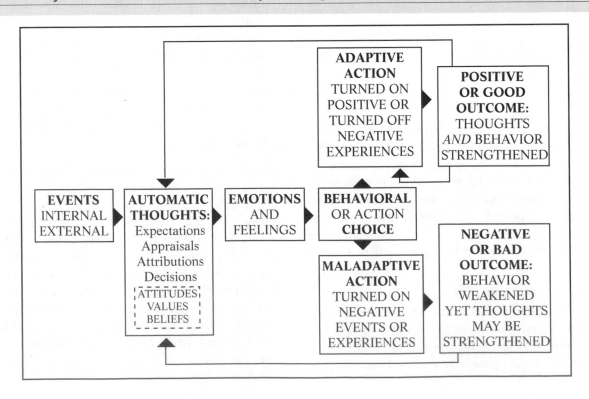

"not being cared about." From these *beliefs* there developed an underlying *attitude*: "To hell with it, the hell with everybody, screw it." This leads to a feeling of discouragement. He then has another automatic thought—*decision*: "I'll just stay here (at a friend's house) with my 'real' friends, where I'm cared about," (*appraisal*) and he has more marijuana and starts to consume alcohol. Automatic thought—*expectation*: "I'm not going home now because I'll just get caught being high, then I'll be in deep s...t." He continues to feel bad and sorry for himself and drinks more. He thinks, "I shouldn't be doing this," but the *underlying beliefs* of "life isn't fair and not being cared about" and the *underlying attitude* of "screw it," lead to the automatic thoughts—*appraisals*: "I feel really good, it's party time and I don't give a damn what my dad says. . . anyway, I don't care." *Expectation*: "I won't get busted." But his father figures out where he is, calls the police, he gets busted, is thrown in jail and charged with possession of an illegal drug. This event merely strengthens or reinforces this maladaptive thought pattern and strengthens his original thought of "nobody cares." It also strengthens the *attitude* of "screw it," and the underlying beliefs, of "life isn't fair and no one has really cared about me."

Relapse and recidivism prevention

PSD-C intervention is about preventing relapse and recidivism prevention. Clients, in partnership with their counselors, set their own relapse and recidivism goals. These goals are continually reevaluated, and the skills for achieving them are continually learned and practiced, as clients proceed through the program. The model for relapse and recidivism is based on Marlatt's model of RP (1985a). This model is presented in a simplified and artistically enhanced format in the *Participant's Workbook for Pathways to Self-Discovery and Change*.

Overview of Marlatt's Relapse Prevention model: Relapse prevention (RP) is a CBT self-management program "that combines behavioral skill training procedures with cognitive intervention techniques to assist individuals in maintaining desired behavioral changes" (Marlatt & Barrett, 1994, p. 285). Clients are taught new coping responses (e.g., alternatives to addictive behavior); they learn to modify maladaptive beliefs and expectancies concerning their behavior; they learn to change personal habits and lifestyles. The Marlatt RP model has been used as adjuncts to treatment programs and also as a stand-alone program for cessation and maintenance phases (Dimeff & Marlatt, 1995). A stand-alone Marlatt RP program is summarized in Dimeff & Marlatt (1995).

In the Marlatt model, presented in *Figure 10.4*, relapse is defined "as any violation of a self-imposed rule regarding a particular behavior" (Dimeff & Marlatt, 1995). The model stresses that relapse must be reframed from the traditional "all-or-nothing" view to the view that it is a transitional process in which slips or lapses may or may not result in a full return to the level of the pretreatment substance use pattern. A single occurrence is different from a full-blown relapse (Dimeff & Marlatt, 1995).

As a person develops control over the behavior targeted for change, there is an *increase in self-control and self-efficacy* in the context of previously high-risk (HR) situations. The self-efficacy is strengthened over time. Self-control becomes challenged when the person encounters an HR situation—a situation where the person's sense of self-control is threatened. HR situations can be external or internal cues that can set off relapse. If the person copes effectively with the HR situation, self-control and self-efficacy increases. If coping is ineffective, self-efficacy decreases. The first step in Marlatt's RP model is to help the client identify HR situations. The second step is to help the client build coping and problem solving skills to deal with HR situations without returning to the use of substances.

Another important component of the Marlatt RP model is to help the client deal with a lapse so that it does not lead to a full-blown relapse. The model uses the *rule violation effect* (RVE) to explain how lapses can lead to full relapse and help the client manage lapses or slips (Curry & Marlatt, 1987; Dimeff & Marlatt, 1995; Marlatt & Gordon, 1985). RVE is the result of violating the individual's rule to change target behaviors and will be discussed in more detail below. When RVE refers specifically to abstinence, it is appropriate to use the expression *abstinence violation effect* (AVE), a term used earlier in the Marlatt model.

Finally, the *Marlatt Relapse Prevention* (RP) model focuses on helping the client to deal with life-style imbalances that occur between the individual's perceived external demands or "shoulds" and perceived desires or "wants." Strong imbalances in the direction of "shoulds" may lead to strong feelings of being deprived and resulting desire to indulge (even to the point of a craving or urge). The goal is to help the client build a balanced life-style that ultimately helps the client deal with HR situations that can lead to relapse. The Marlatt RP model has developed *global intervention* procedures aimed at helping the client to

Figure 10.4 Marlatt's Cognitive-Behavioral Model of the Relapse Process

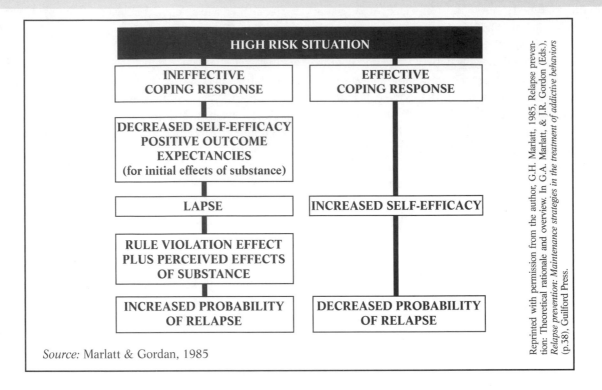

Source: Marlatt & Gordan, 1985

build a balanced life-style. This includes developing coping skills to effectively manage factors that are precursors to high-risk situations and relapse (Dimeff & Marlatt, 1995).

The PSD-C Relapse/Recidivism Prevention Model for Delinquency, Crime and Substance Abuse: Wanberg and Milkman (1998; 2004) have presented evidence of the robust relationship between AOD use and abuse and criminal conduct and have successfully adapted the Marlatt model for relapse prevention to encompass recidivism prevention as well. AOD misuse and juvenile delinquency are strongly related. In PSD-C we apply the Marlatt model for relapse prevention to preventing relapse and recidivism in juvenile justice clients. The elements of the Marlatt model that we have enhanced are briefly reviewed.

We want the clients to see that the relapse and recidivism (RR) are *gradual processes of erosion* and that the first steps in the erosion process are to engage in **high risk (HR) thinking** (I'll get drunk) and being exposed to **high risk situations** (hanging out with gang members). Thoughts about AOD use that would lead to further AOD use problems and thoughts about committing delinquent acts are initial steps of RR. Relapse begins with HR thinking which leads to use or a use pattern that leads to problem use. Recidivism begins when the individual engages in HR thoughts

that lead to delinquent behaviors. Thus, RR refers to lapsing back to thoughts, feelings and actions that lead to delinquency and/or AOD use problems. Thus, RR does not simply mean that the person has engaged in committing a crime or has engaged in a pattern of AOD abuse.

It is important to distinguish between *lapse and relapse* as applied to substance abuse and deviant behaviors. A lapse may be any drinking/drugging or engaging in a pattern that could lead to further substance abuse problems. We ask clients to use *abstinence and lawfulness* as their relapse and recidivism prevention goals. In the PSD-C model, we accept the client's lapse and relapse patterns and work with these in the education and treatment process. We interpret the initial stages of relapse and recidivism as engaging in thoughts and actions that lead to delinquency or substance abuse and we apply the *zero tolerance* approach. This is not to say that if a juvenile does re-offend, we "write him or her off." We work with changing the client's thinking and behavior leading to negative or antisocial behavior. However, we are obligated to deal with the rule violations from both therapeutic and correctional perspectives. This approach is further discussed below.

Another important modification of the Marlatt model is that we have expanded the concept of high-risk situations to high-risk exposures. Since high-risk exposures lead to recidivism and relapse, it is important for juvenile justice and/or adolescent substance abusing clients to clearly understand what are these high-risk exposures. *Figure 10.5* provides the pathways for relapse and recidivism as it is applied to adolescent substance abuse and delinquency. Relapse and recidivism (RR) occurs in steps. Individuals can be in RR before they use a substance or before engaging in delinquent acts. The following definitions are provided to clarify the meaning of terms in the RR prevention model.

High-Risk Exposures: situations, thoughts, feelings, attitudes and beliefs that threaten the sense of control, thereby increasing the risk for RR.

Self-Efficacy or Self-Mastery: clients' judgments about how well they are coping with the high-risk exposures and whether they have succeeded or failed when exposed to similar high-risk exposures. If clients have learned skills of managing the high risk exposures, they will develop strong coping responses and

increased sense of self-mastery and self-efficacy. Relapse and recidivism most likely will be prevented.

Expected Outcome: what clients expect the outcome to be. They may expect drinking to have a particular desired effect, e.g., makes you feel good. However, "expected effects" may be quite different from "real effects." When the prospect of AOD use is hooked in with a short-term positive outcome of AOD use, the probability of relapse and recidivism increases. Or, clients may think that AOD use is necessary, will solve their immediate problem of gaining confidence, or keep them in good standing with a deviant subgroup.

Rule Violation-Effect: the clients' reaction resulting from lapsing into a pattern where problem AOD use or deviant activity can result. They have violated the rules of "abstinence and lawfulness." They may take an initial risk of having minimal use of alcohol and/or another drug. Clients have seen themselves as not engaging in delinquency or drug abuse. Now they have violated those rules. They experience a lot of inner conflict. To solve this conflict, they are likely to return to their old view of themselves—acceptance of deviant

Figure 10.5 Cognitive-Behavioral Model for Relapse and Recidivism

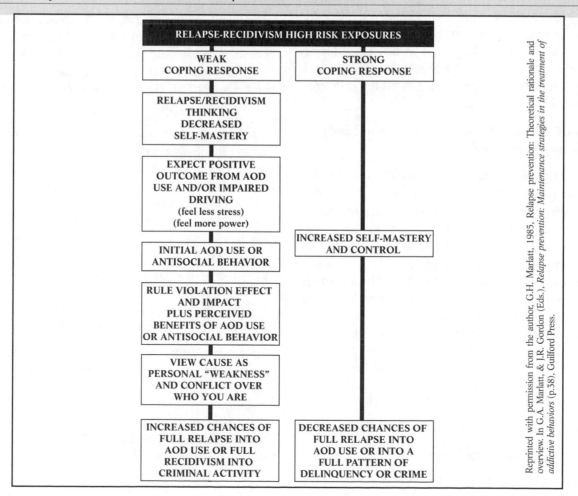

Reprinted with permission from the author, G.H. Marlatt, 1985, Relapse prevention: Theoretical rationale and overview. In G.A. Marlatt, & J.R. Gordon (Eds.), *Relapse prevention: Maintenance strategies in the treatment of addictive behaviors* (p.38), Guilford Press.

identity or engaging in the old patterns of drinking or drug abuse. The strength of this rule violation will depend on: 1) how much conflict and guilt they experience in their RR; 2) how much they blame their own personal weaknesses for the cause of the RR behavior.

Self-Attribution or Self-Credit: is most important when clients find themselves engaging in relapse or recidivism behavior. If they believe that the initial relapse is due to personal "weakness," then they set themselves up for continuing the relapse/recidivism episode. This is because they believe they have lost total control or it is beyond their control. If they credit strength to themselves by stopping at the point of initial relapse (engaging in thinking or action which leads to AOD abuse or criminal activity) or stopping at initial recidivism (seeking out the company of deviant associates) then it is unlikely that they will go into a full relapse/recidivism.

Figure 10.6 provides the pathways to preventing relapse and recidivism. In *Figure 10.6*, in the left column, the high-risk exposures and pathways leading to RR are reiterated. In the right column, adaptive and management responses to these high-risk exposures are provided. Note that the rule violation effect, decreased self-efficacy and weak coping responses are critical to leading to full recidivism and relapse. The connecting arrows indicate that at any point in the path, the client can manage the high-risk exposures and get on the track of prevention or on the path leading to recidivism and relapse.

Using CBT approaches in developing moral and community responsibility

For effective treatment of substance abuse and delinquency, the traditional CB focuses of developing self-control through cognitive restructuring and social and interpersonal skill development are not sufficient. In the education and treatment of juvenile offenders, a *third focus* is essential: developing skills to enhance moral responsibility to the community. This approach is based on the idea that cognitive processes and structures are organized and operate in such a manner as to prevent prosocial and morally responsible behavior in the community. The PSD-C model involves the restructuring of clients' relationship with society and the community. Here are some specific CBT themes through which we address moral responsibility.

- Managing aggression and preventing violence

- Moral development and reasoning

- Understanding and practicing empathy

- Critical reasoning

- Focusing on prosocial activities and behaviors

- Developing prosocial attitudes about emotional and physical intimacy

- Role modeling and mentoring

Developing a partnership between the therapeutic and correctional (sanctioning) approaches and systems: Our review of the literature in this and our previous work (Wanberg & Milkman, 1998, 2004) clearly indicated that sanctioning and punishment alone is not effective methods to prevent recidivism. We also indicated that treatment and intervention alone is not as effective as when intervention is integrated with the sanctioning process. The PSD-C model integrates the efforts of the sanctioning and judicial system with the efforts of the education and treatment system.

There are some traditional differences between the treatment of AOD abuse and intervention and treatment of criminal conduct or juvenile delinquency. First, alcohol or marijuana abuse by teenagers, in and of itself, usually does not involve the juvenile justice system.

Treatment outcomes for AOD abuse can tolerate relapse. Such treatment or education is usually psychotherapeutic and it is *client-centered* in that treatment starts with client and family goals, needs and expectations. The healing expectations come from the client and family.

The education and treatment of juvenile justice clients always involves sanctions: treatment and sanctioning are almost always integrated. The client's referral to education and treatment is considered part of the judicial sentence. There is "zero tolerance" for returning to illegal activities. Recidivism is not tolerated and when occurring, the provider must engage the correctional and judicial process. Treatment of juvenile delinquency is *society-centered*, it is correctional and parenting with a focus on behavior that violates society. The change expectations, at least initially, come from society—from outside the youthful offender.

Thus, when addressing juvenile recidivism, the focus must be on cognitive, affective and pre-recidivism behavior with these elements being considered as leading to recidivism (thinking about AOD abuse or delinquent acts; becoming involved in high risk situations; or high risk thinking that leads to substance abuse and delinquency).

Figure 10.6 Steps and Pathways for Relapse and Recidivism Prevention

PATHWAY TO RELAPSE/RECIDIVISM HIGH RISK EXPOSURES	PATHWAY TO PREVENTION HIGH RISK EXPOSURES
HIGH-RISK SITUATIONS Family, dating or peer conflicts. Problems at school. Socialize with AOD abusing friends. Attend drinking/drug parties. Friends pressure you to use.	**MANAGE HIGH-RISK SITUATIONS** Use skills to manage relationship conflicts. Avoid high risk situations. Use support groups, straight friends, family, counselor. Use refusal skills.
HIGH-RISK THINKING No one really cares. Being unfairly treated. Some AOD will help. Not fair, can't use. I don't fit in when I don't drink. A little bit would feel good.	**MANAGE HIGH-RISK THINKING** Use cognitive skills to change thinking: self-talk; shifting the view; positive thought arming; change errors in thinking.
HIGH-RISK FEELINGS Happy over getting a car. Feeling down and depressed. Angry at friend, dating partner or parent. I'm feeling stressed. Angry at everybody. Feeling lonely.	**MANAGE HIGH-RISK FEELINGS** Use active sharing. Change depressed thoughts. Use relaxations skills. Use anger management skills. Use assertiveness skills to express emotion.
ATTITUDES AND BELIEFS The world is not fair. Nothing ever works out. I feel better when I drink/drug. Everybody drinks and smokes dope.	**CHANGE ATTITUDES AND BELIEFS** Know your core beliefs. Get feedback from others on your attitudes. Change your beliefs by changing what you say to yourself.
RECIDIVISM/RELAPSE PATTERN Expect positive outcomes from drinking/using drugs. Rule violation effect. Decrease self-mastery or self-efficacy. Weak coping responses. Begin more frequent or daily use.	**R&R PREVENTION AND CONTROL** Clearly know negative outcomes of delinquency, crime or AOD use. Increase in self-mastery or self-efficacy leading to increase in self-esteem. Strong coping responses. More harmony with self, others.
RECIDIVISM FULL RELAPSE Harmful and disruptive results from AOD abuse. Increased delinquency or crime.	**TAKE OWNERSHIP OF CHANGE** RR Prevention goals are strengthened. Decrease chance of recidivism/relapse.

Adapted with permission from the author, G.H. Marlatt, 1985, Relapse prevention: Theoretical rationale and overview. In G.A. Marlatt, & J.R. Gordon (Eds.), Relapse prevention: Maintenance strategies in the treatment of addictive behaviors (p.38), Guilford Press.

The feedback or confrontational process is also different. The provider in the correctional role states, "I confront you with me, I represent the external world you have violated and I confront you with the values and laws of society and I expect you to change." The provider or therapist represents society in the intervention process and is the clients' "victim" as is any other member of society who is potentially impacted by delinquent acts. The provider has the clear role of helping to administer the judicial sentence. The intervention referral and the sentence are clearly linked.

In effect, the provider in the therapeutic role states: "I confront you with you, I confront you with what you say you want and need and the contradictions in your thinking, emotions and behavior that violate your own needs and goals." The provider, in the therapeutic role, always works towards helping clients achieve their agenda and assume responsibility for their own behavior.

What is most important in this integration process is that the provider always responds to the correctional process within the framework of the therapeutic role.

For example, if the client violates his or her terms of probation, such as AOD abuse, the provider first manages this situation from a therapeutic stance. The provider works with the client's thoughts, underlying beliefs and emotions that led to that behavior, and helps the client identify the triggers that led to that behavior. However, the provider has the final judicial obligation of engaging and informing the juvenile justice system in sanctioning or correcting the behavior that violates the judicial status of the client. This is done from a therapeutic perspective, and if there is a therapeutic alliance, then the client will take responsibility to engage and inform the judicial system around his or her infraction.

CHAPTER REVIEW

This chapter defines the meanings and distinctions between education, counseling and psychotherapy and then shows how PSD-C utilizes a psychoeducational model, combining therapeutic and didactic approaches to the process of learning and change. Core elements of the education and treatment platform are presented, followed by a comprehensive discussion of the underlying principles of the cognitive-behavioral model for growth and change. Analyses of methods to achieve cognitive restructuring are followed by discussion of how behavioral outcomes create and sustain old or new pathways to emotion and behavior. A schema is presented as a conceptual tool for understanding the CBT process of growth and change. The cognitive-behavioral blueprint for relapse and recidivism prevention is explained, elucidating the primary targets of change in the PSD-C treatment program. The chapter concludes with a discussion of a beneficial partnership between the therapeutic and correctional (sanctioning) approaches in achieving optimal treatment outcomes with teenagers who are involved with juvenile delinquency and substance abuse.

Cognitive-Behavioral Perspectives on Adolescent Treatment

11

Chapter Eleven: Cognitive-Behavioral Perspectives on Adolescent Treatment

Chapter Outline

Treatment Efficacy with Juvenile Justice Clients: Past and Present

Evidence for a Cognitive-Behavioral Approach to Adolescent Treatment

- Motivations for juvenile delinquency and crime

- Cognitive tendencies associated with adolescent participation in problem behavior and crime

Key Features of Cognitive-Behavioral Treatment for Adolescents

- Basic treatment assumptions

- Cultural and developmental factors

- A continuum of care in relapse and recidivism prevention

Summary of Cognitive-Behavioral Principles Targeted at Delinquency, Crime and Substance Abuse

Chapter Review

Chapter Objectives

- To present an historical perspective on treatment outcomes for adolescents with substance abuse and juvenile justice problems;

- To explain the strong relationship between faulty cognition and adolescent involvement in a range of social problem behaviors;

- To present key features of effective cognitive-behavioral treatment for teenage clients;

- To describe common features of the CBT approach in relationship to juvenile justice clients

TREATMENT EFFICACY WITH JUVENILE JUSTICE CLIENTS: PAST AND PRESENT

As early as 1920, the effort to treat 743 narcotic-addicted adolescents in a segregated unit at the *Worth Street Clinic* in New York City was declared a failure. Contemporary evaluation researchers typically deem earlier adolescent drug and alcohol treatment programs as largely unsuccessful. The lack of positive treatment outcomes may be attributed to multiple factors—if treatment is begun too late, if the program being utilized is intended for use with adults, or simply because long-term negative consequences rarely influence a teen's behavior (Dennis, Dawud-Noursi, Muck & McDermeit, 2003).

In addition, many teenagers are court ordered, rather than having personally sought treatment (Dennis et al., 2003). Dennis et al. also note that *few formal*, affordable, community-based programs for adolescents exist, even less having been produced in a format from which they can be replicated, such as published manuals.

Based on information provided to the federal government through the *Treatment Episode Data Set* (TEDS) by public treatment programs, the *Office of Applied Studies* (OAS) and the *University of Michigan* have assessed *changes in adolescent treatment programs* between 1992 and 1998. These records show that the number of adolescent admissions between 1992 and 1998 grew by 53% and that the primary substance for which the adolescent was admitted *changed from alcohol to marijuana*. Program modalities remained mostly outpatient throughout the six years, but there was a *154% increase in admissions to intensive outpatient programs and a 104% increase in admissions to hospital-based programs*. Several factors, however, may limit the validity of these findings (Dennis et al., 2003).

- Reporting is voluntary for clients as well as for some states;

- Data are based on admissions information and not on outcome information;

- Some programs do not report or report too late; and

- These statistics do not include information from private programs, those operated by other federal agencies, or treatment provided by individual therapists

Dennis et al. (2003) report that in the early 1970s *The Drug Abuse Reporting Program* (DARP) studied existing community-based programs for *teens using narcotics*. The research design included follow-up interviews three years later with 587 of the originally treated 5,405 adolescents. The study showed that following methadone maintenance, treatment in therapeutic communities, treatment in outpatient or detoxification centers (for a median length of two months), *all types of programs reduced opiate use, however, alcohol use went up slightly, and marijuana use remained the same or increased*.

In the late 1970s and early 1980s, *The Treatment Outcome Prospective Study* (TOPS) looked at *community-based treatment* programs for adolescents using any types of drugs. Interviews were conducted 1 year after discharge with 256 of the 1,042 adolescents originally treated either in a therapeutic community or outpatient treatment. Residential treatment (median stay of approximately three months) showed a *25% to 50% reduction in daily marijuana use, alcohol use, or other drug related problems*. Outpatient programs with a median length of three months showed only a *25% or less reduction in use*; several subgroups (e.g., 18-19 year olds in treatment for less than three months and 12-17 year olds in treatment for more than three months) had actually *increased* their rates of drug use (Dennis et al., 2003).

From the late 1980s to the early 1990s, the *Services Research Outcome Study* (SROS) gathered data at five years post-discharge from 156 treated adolescents who had abused various illicit drugs (68% marijuana, 80% alcohol, 20% cocaine and 2% opiates). Forty-eight percent went back into treatment one or more times in the five years after the initial treatment (65% of those initially receiving less than a week of treatment were readmitted; 40% of those receiving six months or more returned to treatment). Even though these findings were based on a relatively small sample, the results were alarming. Further, from five years before treatment to five years after treatment, substance use (five or more times in the past year) increased from 68% to 70% for marijuana, 80% to 92% for alcohol, 20% to 29% for cocaine and 2% to 7% for heroin (Dennis et al., 2003).

Continuing into the 1990s, the *National Treatment Improvement Evaluation Study* (NTIES) reviewed *community-based treatment programs* that had received grants to enhance their treatment programs. Based on intake and *one-year post-discharge* interviews with 236 adolescents after a median program length of two months, it was found that for *residential treatment, marijuana use* (five or more times in the past year) *declined from 97% to 72%, cocaine decreased from 52% to 30%* and *alcohol intoxication from 52% to 45%. Outpatient treatment* results showed a *drop in marijuana use* from 77% to 69%, *no change in cocaine use (13%) and an increase in alcohol intoxication from 32% to 37%* (Dennis et al., 2003).

From the mid to late 1990s *The Drug Abuse Treatment Outcome Studies of Adolescents* (DATOS-A) studied existing community-based treatments (which typically were *adult models* with minimum modifications made for adolescent presentation) for any kind of substance use. Adolescents from the age of 11 to 19 who were admitted to *long-term residential care, short-term residential care, and/or outpatient treatment programs* were studied. *Post-discharge* interviews were conducted at 12 months with 1,785 of the 3,382 adolescents who were originally admitted to long-term residential (727), short-term residential (613) and/or outpatient treatment (445). From the year before treatment to the year after, the *rates of marijuana use decreased* from *91% to 68%, heavy alcohol use* from *34% to 20%*, but *cocaine use rose* from *17% to 19%* (Dennis et al., 2003).

From the above studies, it is obvious that results are mixed: " . . . adolescent treatment research still is many years from demonstrating that its emerging models will be effective and cost-effective in practice" (Dennis et al., 2003, p.19). The methodological shortcomings of these early evaluations including *small sample sizes spread across a variety of programs, undefined modalities, short treatment time and only 50-70% follow-up rates*, limit their value, but still point to the conclusion that effective treatment programs *geared specifically for adolescents* is a field in desperate need of development.

EVIDENCE FOR A COGNITIVE-BEHAVIORAL APPROACH TO ADOLESCENT TREATMENT

Although outcome data regarding the efficacy of treatment across a range of treatment modalities (e.g., long-term residential care, short-term residential care, and/or outpatient treatment programs), shows mixed results, there is strong support for the use of cognitive-behavioral treatment techniques with the adolescent substance abusing population. Botvin, Baker, Dusenbury & Tortu (1990) report the successful

reduction of adolescent drug use through cognitive-behavioral intervention. Epstein, Griffin, & Botvin (2001) found that higher levels of *general competence* predicted greater *refusal assertiveness*, which was in turn linked to lower levels of alcohol use. These authors stress the importance of targeting *decision-making skills, generalized self-efficacy and refusal assertiveness* in adolescent alcohol programs.

Other researchers have stressed the importance of *improving adaptive skills* through treatment geared toward reducing delinquent behavior (e.g., Calhoun, Glaser, & Bartolomucci, 2001). These researchers urge that therapy should target the *specific environmental context* in which the adolescent lives. Programs like the *Benjamin E. Mays Institute Mentoring Program* (BEMI) for black male adolescents utilize a *cultural strengths* and *pride-based perspective* to buffer negative images of "Black manhood" that may have been internalized by young black males (Gordon, 2000). BEMI has produced positive changes in the *identity development, academic performance, and academic identification* of African American adolescents when compared to non-mentored males attending a regular public school program. Through involvement in the BEMI program (which focuses on such *cognitive patterns as identity formation*), cognitive development as indicated by academic performance and understanding of racial socialization helped African American males in their search for identity and ethnic commitment. What's more, these adolescents expressed stronger commitment to conventional institutions in both the home and the academic environment (Gordon, 2000).

Motivations for juvenile delinquency and crime

Lopez & Emmer (2000) examined the motivations, emotions and cognitions that drive adolescent males to commit antisocial or illegal acts. Several delinquency/crime contexts emerged, many of which were supported by specific cognitive tendencies. Examining adolescent offender's perspectives on their own behavior, Lopez and Emmer (2000) identified distinct trends in adolescent definition, interpretation, and justification for illegal conduct (Lopez & Emmer, 2000). Interviews conducted with 24 adolescent males (aged 14 to 20 yrs) revealed the following crime contexts.

- *Emotion-driven violent assault*: includes with a strong affective component, related to revenge, resentment, jealousy, etc.

- *Belief-driven violent assault*: encompasses a strong cognitive component, related to perceived injustice, restoration of equity or fairness, rights to self-protection (or the protection of others), etc.

- *Mixed-motive mixed-crime contexts* – includes a combination of the above (Lopez & Emmer, 2000).

Previously, Lopez (2000) reported on additional crime contexts to bring the total number to six.

- *Emotion driven/property theft*

- *Reward driven/drug dealing*

- *Reward driven/property theft*

Biering (2002) found gender differences have been found in teenagers' explanations for their involvement in violent crime. Adolescent girls attributed their violent acts to *violations of trust* in once valued relationships; males explained their violence on the basis of perceived *obstacles to attainment of a goal* or desired outcome.

Cognitive tendencies associated with adolescent participation in problem behavior and crime

The hostile world syndrome: Fox & Levin (2001), investigating the effects of media violence on the cognitive functioning of children and adolescents find that media may contribute to the development of a "false view of social reality," characterized by *higher rates of perceived threat*, violence and victimization than actually are the case. Heavy viewers of media also tend to exaggerate the number of people who are white and male, and underrate the extent of poverty, contributing to *distortions in their understanding of social dynamics* such as racism and socioeconomic inequality. Because issues of gender, race, socioeconomics and degree of threat are all implicated in predicting the readiness to aggress or commit crimes, these distorted perceptions may play a central role in some adolescent antisocial behavior.

To the extent that these faulty perceptions contribute to the "is-ought" discrepancy (i.e., perceived differences between how the adolescent sees the world and how the adolescent believes the world should be) they may contribute to a propensity for antisocial behavior. Media representations may also affect *estimates of relative deprivation*, potentially influencing the dynamics of rage, frustration and the need to restore justice. This "mean world view" or "hostile world syndrome" may also contribute to feelings of fear and intimidation – for many children and adolescents overestimate the probability that they will become victims. As a countermeasure, some become perpetrators (Fox & Levin, 2001).

Risky cognitions and the subculture of violence: As previously noted, *deviant peer associations* may have a profound effect on the development of adolescent cognition and identity formation. In this context, antisocial skills may be acquired and deviant tendencies may be supported and developed. Modification of several key *cognitive patterns* has been identified as central to effective intervention with adolescents.

- POSITIVE EXPECTANCIES about the aftermath of antisocial and criminal behavior (including more attention, more respect, monetary rewards, etc.).

- NEGATIVE IDENTITY – choosing delinquent peers as a reference group by which to define themselves, and to guide their attitudes and behavior.

- NEGATIVE STEREOTYPING OF THE OUTSIDER - may cause a perception of others who are not deviant as "clueless" or "uncool," thus generating a sequence of judgments that further isolates them from more conventional norms for behavior (Akers, 2000).

- ASSOCIATION OF VIOLENCE WITH GAINING RESPECT - Fox & Levin (2001) note how many juveniles conduct themselves in a manner that conveys a willingness to use violence in interpersonal conflict. They note that many juveniles consider "losing face" in these contests as a "fate worse than death."

These cognitive and social learning perspectives help to explain deviant peer associations, which typically occur before the onset of actual delinquent behavior. Hence, *cognitive interventions* that *occur early* in an adolescent's development may function to inoculate the individual from many of these effects.

Risky cognitions and driving while intoxicated: As discussed in Chapter 3, Substance Abuse and Adolescent Problem Behavior, risky cognitions are central to the decision to drink and drive. Teenagers who drink and drive are subject to multiple thinking errors or distorted cognitions. Firstly, in making the fateful decision to drink and drive, teenagers often *fail to acknowledge* that they are impaired and *reject the possibility* that anything bad (arrest, an accident, etc.) could happen to them. There is often a *failure to realize* how intoxicated they are and a lack of understanding that they will be impaired while driving. Because they *lack information* about the effects of alcohol, teenagers who drink and drive do not understand how much and what kinds of alcoholic beverages will have intoxicating effects. A general *lack of empathy* for the potential suffering of others permits acceptance of the "calculated risk" associated with drunk driving. Because they have driven after drinking before (without being caught), *they think they can do it again*. Finally, some teenagers find comfort in the belief that drinking and driving will allow them to *feel free from rules or societal norms*.

Negative Identity: Identification with a deviant subculture may have the effect of producing *self-labels* in terms of delinquency and crime (Bynum & Weiner, 2002). When such a *negative self-concept* is established, the development of pride, righteousness and justification in association with acts of violence and other acts of crime is frequently observed. Deeply entrenched yet largely cognitive, such labeling of the self can be at the root of subsequent delinquent behavior. In contrast to Reckless's (1967) *Containment Theory*, which predicts that positive self-concept may insulate an adolescent from delinquency and crime, Bynum & Weiner (2002) investigated the relationship between *self-concept and violent behavior* among a group of urban African-American adolescent males. The researchers found several "benefits" to the formation of a negative or deviant identity:

- Negative identity is often associated with positive self-regard;

- Positive self-regard derived from a deviant identity may foster the development of juvenile delinquency rather than deter it;

- Violent adolescents possessed *higher self-concept scores* than non-violent adolescents;

- Violent adolescents have generally accepted delinquency as appropriate behavior for themselves; and

- Violent offenders appear to be comfortable with this negative identity (Bynum & Weiner, 2002).

Masculinity and violence: Male adolescent offenders were interviewed regarding their violent criminal offenses in order to assess some of the basic thought patterns and motivations at the root of their decision to commit crime (Lopez & Emmer, 2000). Using a *Belief Driven/Violent Assault* crime context, adolescents' answers were analyzed in terms of crime motive, offense type, crime context (such as honor and vigilante crimes) and the thoughts and beliefs that support crime (cognition). A major factor that emerged was *adherence to traditional male values* (Lopez & Emmer, 2000). Alongside this "hyper-masculinity" orientation, was a belief system that supported the use of aggression in an inter-personal context. These underlying cognitive factors supported motivations/decisions to use violence in such contexts as self defense, protection of others and promotion of their gang (Lopez & Emmer, 2000). The authors conclude that *beliefs associated with the male gender role* appear to generate and support many of the cognitive and affective tendencies that attend acts of violence.

Social competence:

Social competence has been demonstrated to provide a direct protective buffer against alcohol use among adolescents. The particular competency skills associated with reduced drinking behaviors are *social confidence, assertiveness, communication skills and self-management techniques* (Griffin, Epstein, Botvin & Spoth, 2001; Epstein, Griffin & Botvin, 2001). As previously described in *Chapter 3, Substance Abuse and Adolescent Problem Behavior*, in a study named, "*Wadda ya mean, I can't drive?*" the level of threat to competence was evaluated as a factor in the effectiveness of interventions designed to prevent drunk driving. The study found that as the perceived level of threat to competence increased, evaluated effectiveness of the intervention technique decreased. The study implies that treatment outcomes may be improved by addressing some of the *underlying cognitions relating to perceived competence* (such as low self-esteem, the use of bravado to mask self-doubt, etc.) that may contribute to increased resistance to intervention (Shore & Compton, 1998).

As adolescent use of drugs and alcohol often attend their engagement in illegal behavior, it is useful to investigate some of the cognitions that support this use. Expectancies of substance use have emerged as a primary mediating factor in predicting both substance use and social competence among adolescents. Adolescents with low levels of social competence may turn to substance use because of perceived social benefits. Griffin et al. (2001) cite some of the perceived social benefits of alcohol and cigarette use as "having more friends" . . . "looking grown up and cool" . . . and "having more fun." Education aimed toward *enhancing interpersonal skills and adolescent social competence* may thereby inoculate youth against entry into substance use and abuse (and attendant delinquent behavior), by providing more constructive alternatives for gaining peer acceptance (Griffin et al., 2001).

Empathy development:

Broom (2000) conducted empirical assessment of issues regarding the relationship between juvenile delinquency and cognitive and affective empathy development. Citing previous research which found that *juveniles who engage in criminal conduct have lower empathy levels* than those who do not (e.g., Cohen & Strayer, 1996; Ellis, 1982; Marcus & Gray, 1998), Broom sought to identify specific factors that may be operating in this relationship. Levels of empathy in youth from four juvenile correctional facilities were obtained using the *Interpersonal Reactivity Index* (IRI). Levels of empathy were found to be below average, supporting previous assertions about this relationship. In addition, empathy levels were related to several other factors, including IQ and offense type. *Disability status* was also related to empathy level. Juveniles who suffered no identified disability (such as emotional/behavioral disorders or learning disabilities) scored lower on empathy than those that did (Broom, 2000). Age was not related to empathy status.

Interestingly, empathy levels were also related to the specific stage of treatment in a re-socialization program, indicating that *cognitive interventions regarding empathy* may be successful in enhancing such ability. Juveniles who had reached higher levels in Phases of Re-Socialization, an educational program that focuses on empathy development (*Texas Youth Commission*), showed enhanced empathy development. While Broom recognizes the need for further research on these complex issues, consistency with previous research (Broom, 2002) indicates an *important role for empathy development* and the reduction of youth crime. Cognitive-behavioral and affective programs that address empathic deficits in their early phases of development may prevent or reduce the incidence of juvenile participation in crime.

KEY FEATURES OF COGNITIVE-BEHAVIORAL TREATMENT FOR ADOLESCENTS

The cognitive-behavioral approach utilizes specific perspectives and techniques to create positive, productive and overt behavioral change with a *focus on rapport, trust and respect in the therapeutic alliance* (Beck et al., 1993; Miller & Rollnick, 1991, 2002). It also insists on client responsibility (Franks & Barbach, 1983). Utilizing these factors in treatment may help an adolescent to increase self-respect and self-efficacy,

and foster the skills of self-management. The final goals of cognitive-behavioral treatment are to help individuals develop an alternative perception of their environment and their behavioral options; to assess the merit of these alternatives against former self-defeating behavior patterns (such as substance abuse and criminal conduct); and to identify future obstacles to utilizing such a new approach to life (Salkovskis, 1996b).

Basic treatment assumptions

As outlined in *Chapter 9— Foundations of Cognitive-Behavioral Therapy and Chapter 10—Core Strategies for Delinquency, Crime and Substance Abuse Treatment*, the basic assumptions necessary to accomplish these therapeutic objectives are as follows.

- Behavioral disturbances can be altered by targeting the cognitive processes which underlie them (Hollen & Beck, 1986).

- Thoughts and attitudes underlie mood and emotion (Burns, 1989).

- The meaning of events, as interpreted and appraised by the person experiencing them, are what trigger emotion and behavior, not the events themselves (Salkovskis, 1996).

Cultural and developmental factors

It is essential that new ways of thinking are relevant to the adolescent subculture, and to the socioeconomic and socio-cultural realities of the adolescents' lives. In addition, gender considerations are essential as are the circumstances of each adolescent's personal life situations.

Gender considerations: The principles of cognitive-behavioral therapy have been found to apply similarly among males and females (CSAT, 1999). With specific regard to adolescent girls, however, the importance of *social constructs of gender* in creating different experiences, varying cognitive and emotional tendencies, and limited behavioral options, must be fully recognized in order to provide treatment that is gender-relevant. As previously described in *Chapter 6, Gender and Adolescent Problem Behavior*, a large percentage of female juvenile justice clients have been diagnosed with *post-traumatic stress disorder* as a result of a rape or other abuse experience (GAINS Center, 1997). This is just the tip of an enormous iceberg of profoundly destructive experiences that girls and women have had to endure. With specific regard to adolescent girls' emotion and evaluation of self-worth, *gender schema* may become so internalized that it develops primacy (Crawford & Unger, 2000). This may involve acceptance of *male entitlement to privilege* (which fosters female submission) and *caring for others* (especially men, children, and parents) at the expense of self-care.

Negative self-evaluation, low self-esteem, feelings of powerlessness and desperation are often the result. Unfortunately, these evaluations and feelings are all too often (seemingly) validated by life experiences within a sexist environment, the reactions of others who hold unrealistic expectations about her obligations as a female, and her own counter-productive thinking. The complex feedback loop between experience, thought, feeling and behavior may introduce a self-perpetuating cycle of self-destructive behavior and worsening life circumstance.

Sociocultural factors: The methods of cognitive-behavioral treatment can be generally effective in helping adolescents to overcome negative and difficult life experiences. However it is essential that *treatment is directly related and placed within contexts that are relevant to the juvenile's sociocultural experience.* Thus, issues of race and ethnicity, including racial discrimination and institutional racism, must be factored in when developing appropriate interventions that have relevance to the real life experiences and opportunities among adolescents from racial and ethnic communities. Finally, factors such as the socioeconomic circumstances, level of physical and/or psychological ability, disability, or diagnosis, sexual orientation, religion, etc. must also be considered in facilitating alternative patterns of thinking, feeling and acting.

On a more personal level, the constructivist approach advocated by Arnkoff & Glass (1992), Mahoney (1990) and others necessitates that treatment be directed toward the subjective reality of the client. Thus, it is imperative that we understand as thoroughly as possible, the life conditions experienced by at-risk adolescents in order to appreciate how that reality has undermined the development of adaptive thought, feeling and behavior.

A continuum of care in relapse and recidivism prevention

In order to prevent relapse and recidivism, adolescents need an environment with *support structures in place* to help them accomplish their goals. This is especially problematic, as most adolescents upon release from criminal justice programming re-enter the very situa-

tions and environments that initiated problem behavior in the first place. That is, they enter environments that may be abusive, which do not provide respect for their uniqueness as human beings, and afford little power to determine the conditions of their own lives or to earn their own money through legitimate means. An indifferent social response to their plight may mitigate against what gains they have made in treatment.

In order to succeed at the re-entry process, adolescents must be fortified to deal with realistic components of their life situations, through *explicit identification of problems and exploration of options* prior to release from treatment. Secondly, once beyond the supportive structure of a facilitating treatment environment, adolescents must be provided with somewhere to go for *support and re-kindling* of what they have learned. Such aftercare, as an integral part of the treatment process, can help adolescents to deal with these experiences in an on-going manner, gradually substituting more productive responses as they go along. Support structures in the community that provide adolescents with alternative places to "hang out" and meet new friends, with a drop-in counselor to talk to in times of need, and with opportunities to practice their newly developing cognitive abilities are essential. The adolescent who has been involved in problem behavior must be informed of, and taught how to use these community resources.

SUMMARY OF COGNITIVE-BEHAVIORAL PRINCIPLES TARGETED AT DELINQUENCY, CRIME AND SUBSTANCE ABUSE

This section cannot address the experiences of all adolescents in substance abuse and/or correctional treatment placements, but rather is aimed toward identifying some of the more prominent patterns that are found in their lives. Our discussion follows the cognitive-behavioral principles developed in *Criminal Conduct and Substance Abuse Treatment: The Provider's Guide* (Wanberg & Milkman, 1998, 2004).

Adolescents are actively involved in the construction of their realities:

These realities are constructed from a constellation of factors operating in the lives of adolescents, such as:

• Social constructs, stigmas and stereotypes regarding the meaning of "adolescence";

• Feelings of powerlessness in relationship to the adult world;

- Frequent experience with authoritarian treatment from adults (including abuse and violation) vs. respect and courtesy, etc.

Adolescents respond to their cognitive assessment and interpretation of the environment, rather than to the environment itself: Once adolescents have experienced poverty, sex or race discrimination, disrespect, physical or sexual violence, the burden of single parenting, etc., the meaning of their world, their trust in its responsiveness to them, and their perception of their own needs and desires may be profoundly altered. A common route taken by many an adolescent in response to such experience is to strike out and fend for themselves in a seemingly hostile world (see "The hostile world syndrome," described in *Chapter 7, Youth Culture and Diversity*). In this way, attraction to the deviant subculture, and initiation into substance abuse, promiscuous sexuality, gangs and criminal conduct can be seen as attempts (albeit maladaptive ones) to survive and find belonging under harsh conditions.

Feelings, thoughts and behaviors are interactive and interrelated: As this process continues, and becomes repetitive, the adolescent may increasingly fail to perceive alternative behaviors that could be employed, or alternative environments in which they could spend their time. They are likely to return to environments that are familiar to them (such as the street corner or other teen meeting places), despite the fact that these situations may encourage criminal conduct and be abusive in themselves. The sense of control that is fostered by choosing one's own environment and friends may provide a compelling alternative to stifling environments experienced at home. However, they also may foster the development of substance abuse, criminal conduct and other self-destructive behaviors in teens that would otherwise have little inclination to engage in them.

Disturbances in emotion and behavior are the result of disturbances in thought and perceptual processes: Gradually, chronic disturbances in emotions and behavior may develop from a failure to perceive alternatives to expectations of the inevitability of violence and crime. Negative self-identities may be supported by fleeting feelings of "well-being" (as a result of successful criminal behavior), and distorted outcome expectancies deepen for similar results in the future. Automatic thoughts may include heightened threat perception and the need to strike back (Niehoff, 1999).

A juvenile's psychological and emotional problems frequently rest within attitudes, expectancies and attributions: Adolescents may develop attitudes and beliefs that depict people who "submit" to society's dictates as "naïve losers" who don't know how to defend themselves against degradation. Ironically, these same adolescents generally do not perceive the connection between self-degradation and their own substance abuse and/or criminal conduct. Rather, outcome expectancies often develop that maintain the perception that the use of substances and engagement in criminal conduct bring about positive outcome, satisfaction and reward. External attributions underlie rationalizations and justifications, which may further support a downward spiral. Some teens come to believe that they "have been driven into" (rather than chosen) crime and other problem conduct, and that without substance abuse, criminal conduct, and/or other problem behavior, they would not survive.

Emphasis on identifying and changing dysfunctional thoughts and beliefs: The cognitive-behavioral approach helps the adolescent who has engaged in problem behavior and crime to see that while many of their problems may initially be traced to adverse life experiences, they now need to situate the cause of their difficulties in their own *maladaptive responses to these experiences.* This involves helping adolescents to understand that problem behavior, substance abuse, delinquency and criminal conduct conspire to deepen their difficulties rather than resolve them. Caution and care, rather than blame and confrontation, can help ease an adolescent into increased feelings of responsibility and self-efficacy. Enhanced self-efficacy may help adolescents to perceive and believe in the possibility of overcoming their problems through more constructive means than they have used in the past.

An educational as much as a therapeutic process: Counselors and treatment providers fulfill the functions of evaluation, education, consultation, coaching and support. They may also serve as role models, who demonstrate effective means of coping with stress and social interaction. In these ways, they may help adolescents to understand how they engage in counter-productive thought patterns, which may underlie self-destructive response to the environment. Adolescents must be encouraged to see their problem behavior, substance use and abuse and illegal behavior in the context of maladaptive response.

Studies on the effectiveness of treatment for adolescent delinquency, crime and substance abuse show mixed results. A plethora of methodological shortcomings include small sample sizes, undefined modalities, short treatment time and poor follow-up rates. There is consensus that treatment programs *geared specifically for adolescents* are in desperate need of development.

At present, there is strong support for the use of cognitive-behavioral techniques in treatment of adolescent juvenile justice clients who typically manifest both substance abuse and antisocial behavior patterns. Improved skills in decision-making and refusal assertiveness are seen as important targets for adolescent treatment programs. Some researchers stress interventions targeted at the specific environmental context in which the adolescent lives, e.g., providing adult mentors to counter negative images of "Black manhood."

Motivations for adolescent crime have been categorized according to qualitatively different appraisals for their delinquent or criminal acts (e.g., *emotion vs. belief* driven violent assault; or *emotion vs. reward* driven theft. Studies of gender differences in explanation for commission of crime show that females tend to explain their violent acts as reactions to violations of trust while males tend to view their violence as the result of perceived obstacles to the attainment of specific goals.

Certain cognitive tendencies or schemas have been identified as foundational to juvenile participation in illegal acts: the hostile world syndrome; risky cognitions involving positive outcome expectancies about the rewards associated with drugs or crime; defining outsiders as "losers"; association of violence with respect; distorted ideas about the safety of impaired driving; and perceived benefits of association with a deviant peer group. For some adolescents, the formation of a negative identity (i.e., taking pride in the commission of delinquent or violent acts) actually serves to bolster self-esteem. In some instances of violent/belief driven crime, beliefs associated with male gender role, e.g., self-defense, protection of others, and promotion of the gang are essential cognitive elements of the decision to commit violent crimes. Alcohol and drugs, which often play a role in illegal behavior, are perceived by some teenagers as augmenting social competence (e.g., "having more friends" or "being cool"). Deficits in the capacity for empathy are associated with juveniles who engage in criminal conduct. Cognitive-behavioral interventions that address empathic deficits may prevent or reduce the incidence of juvenile participation in crime.

With a *focus on rapport, trust and respect in the therapeutic alliance*, the cognitive-behavioral approach utilizes specific perspectives and techniques to create positive, productive and overt behavioral change. The basic assumptions necessary to accomplish therapeutic objectives are: behavioral disturbances can be altered by targeting the cognitive processes that underlie them; thoughts and attitudes underlie mood and emotion; the meaning of events, as interpreted by the person experiencing them, are what trigger emotion and behavior, not the events themselves.

Within this broad framework, cultural and developmental considerations call for adaptations to fit adolescent need. With regard to femininity, an adolescent girl's gender schema may become so internalized that it develops primacy in her emotions and evaluation of self-worth. This may involve acceptance of *male entitlement to privilege* (which fosters female submission) and *caring for others* (especially men, children, and parents) at the expense of self-care. It is essential that treatment is related to contexts that are relevant to the juvenile's sociocultural experience. As treatment providers, we strive to understand the life conditions experienced by at-risk adolescents (including factors pertaining to gender, race, ethnicity, poverty and handicap) in order to appreciate how that reality has undermined the development of adaptive thought, feeling and behavior.

Effective utilization of CBT for adolescents is predicated upon keen awareness of how the basic principles of CBT are operational in teenage culture. The fact that teens are actively involved in the construction of their realities is affected by adult and cultural stereotypes of "adolescence," feelings of powerlessness in relationship to the adult world, and frequent experiences with authoritarian figures. Attraction to a deviant subculture, and initiation into substance abuse, promiscuous sexuality, gangs and criminal conduct can be seen as attempts (albeit maladaptive ones) to survive, given their cognitive assessment of living in a harsh and punishing environment. As alienation and social problem behaviors become repetitive, the adolescent may increasingly fail to perceive behavioral alternatives that could be employed. Negative self-identities may be supported by fleeting feelings of "well-being" (as a result of successful criminal behavior). Some teens come to believe that they "have been driven into" (rather than chosen) crime and other problem behaviors, and that these patterns are necessary for survival. Support, concern and accurate information, rather than blame and confrontation, can move an adolescent into increased personal responsibility and self-efficacy. Counselors and treatment providers fulfill the functions of evaluation, education, consultation, coaching and support. They may also serve as role models, who demonstrate positive coping skills for dealing with adversity and challenge throughout the life trajectory.

Most adolescents upon release from criminal justice programming re-enter the very situations and environments that initiated problem behavior in the first place. Prior to release from structured treatment settings, clients should have a firm grasp on *identification of problems* connected with restored community living and exploration of *constructive options*. Beyond the supportive structure of a facilitating treatment environment, adolescents must be provided with somewhere to go for *support and rekindling* of what they have learned.

Treatment Systems and Modalities

12

Chapter Twelve:
Treatment Systems and Modalities

Chapter Outline

Individual Approaches to Treatment

- Brief interventions and motivational enhancement

- Motivational intervention

- Problem-solving skills training

Family Systems Theory and Family Therapies

- Family Systems Therapy

- Behavioral Therapy for adolescents and families

- Multidimensional Family Therapy

- Functional Family Therapy

- Multisystemic Therapy

Residential Treatment

Chapter Review

Chapter Objectives

- To outline essential principles of individual therapy with adolescent substance abusing offenders;

- To present the conceptual framework for family systems theory and family therapies;

- To describe the evolution of therapeutic communities for adolescent substance abusing juvenile justice clients.

There is ample evidence that faulty cognitions play a central role in adolescent substance abuse, criminal conduct and acts of violence. The cognitive-behavioral model for self-discovery and change has emerged as the major theoretical perspective guiding the treatment of adolescent substance abusing offenders. A variety of treatment systems have risen to meet the challenge of providing services to a broad range of juvenile justice clients who manifest differences in:

• Levels of family support;

• Severity of substance abuse, criminal conduct and mental disorder;

• Demographic factors (such as age, gender, race, socioeconomic background, ethnicity);

• Learning styles and cognitive abilities.

This section, although not exhaustive of all promising approaches, reviews a spectrum of evidence-based treatment systems and modalities for treatment of adolescent substance abuse, delinquency and crime.

INDIVIDUAL APPROACHES TO TREATMENT

Brief interventions and motivational enhancement

Smith and Anderson (2001) discuss the importance of motivational strategies when working with adolescents. Most teens do not correlate their drinking or drug taking with problem behaviors, nor do they relate to the long-term negative effects of drinking or drugging. Thus, motivation to change is limited. A 1983 study by Prochaska & Di Clemente (Smith & Anderson, 2001) showed that 49% of 10th and 11th grade drinkers were in the *precontemplation stage*, i.e., the person is not considering that there might be a problem or that change is possible. Monti, Barnett, O'Leary and Colby (2001) concur and encourage the use of *brief interventions* when the "window of opportunity" arises, namely in medical settings such as the emergency room. A motivational intervention that is nonjudgmental in nature and delivered in an *empathic style* has been found effective for heavy drinking adults who reported long-term changes in their drinking habits (Monti, et al., 2001).

It is important to note that *brief interventions* are not simply traditional treatments done in a short period of time. They are, instead, based on the integrated system of *motivational enhancement therapy* (MET) (Miller, Zweben, DiClemente, & Rychtarik, 1992), remem-

bered by the six-element acronym – FRAMES (Bien, Miller, & Tonigan, 1993; Miller & Sanchez, 1993):

FEEDBACK given within a 2-3 hour time period

RESPONSIBILITY for change given to the client

ADVICE or direction given for change

MENU that offers change options

EMPATHIC nature of the therapist

SELF-EFFICACY regarding the possibility of change is emphasized

Motivational intervention

The protocol developed by Monti et al. (2001) focuses on alcohol consumption and risky behavior, particularly drinking and driving. This *Motivational Intervention* (MI) approach is designed to be modified as appropriate for each teen and his or her interest in changing. The sessions are 30-45 minutes in length and are mostly used in the emergency room after a teen has been brought in due to an automobile accident, overdose, assault, or simply intoxication. After time is allowed for alcohol or drug levels to diminish, a mini-mental exam is administered to ensure the teen can understand and can give consent to participate.

The counselor's *initial goal* is to engage the adolescent and to gather information concerning the person's drinking habits. The teen is encouraged to talk about how his or her actions *caused the consequence* of being in the hospital and how he or she could have avoided being there. Monti et al. (2001) emphasize the importance of the counselor being empathic, concerned, non-authoritarian and nonjudgmental in style in order to establish rapport and limit the adolescent's predictable defensive stance.

The *second goal* of MI is to attempt to motivate the adolescent. In order to increase the teenagers' awareness of their patterns of destructive behavior, three steps are taken:

• Personalized and comparative feedback based on *assessment instruments*;

• Provide *educational information* concerning alcohol and its effects;

• Ask teenager to *describe his or her possible future* should he or she decide to change or not.

Adolescent alcohol abusers are encouraged to think about the negative outcomes if the decision is to continue drinking behavior. When the teen's drinking patterns are seen to interfere with his or her goals and aspirations for the future, a motivating force is more likely to occur (Monti, et al., 2001).

According to Monti and colleagues (2001), *all brief interventions must end with a plan for the teenagers' next steps*. For some, this initial intervention will have been sufficient for change, whether it is abstinence or moderation. Others may make a commitment to enter a treatment program. For either course, a well-established set of guidelines should be developed and outlined. In addition to goal setting, these should include the anticipation of barriers to success, such as peer pressure to drive after drinking. The adolescent should be made to feel *capable and confident* about being successful in implementing the plan. Reinforcement of the motivation process can be made via future contact between the counselor and the teen. Monti et al. indicate that even minimal continued contact will increase engagement in on-going treatment.

Monti et al. (2001) make a number of suggestions concerning the characteristics of successful therapists:

- Training in behavioral theory, with a minimum master's degree in a mental health discipline;

- Experience in clinical settings, with specific training in the unique needs of adolescents;

- Good interpersonal skills enabling them to connect with the teen;

- Appropriate role modeling for teens.

Outcome studies of the MI protocol show that "when introduced . . . *at a teachable moment* [MI] is particularly effective in reducing harmful behaviors such as drinking and driving, alcohol-related injuries, alcohol-related problems, and traffic violations among older adolescents and drunkenness and driving after drinking among younger adolescents" (Monti, et al., 2001, p. 179). The researchers acknowledge that MI has less impact on actual drinking and recommend "booster sessions" to increase the teens' interest in reducing alcohol intake as well as combining MI with other types of adolescent treatment programs.

Problem-solving skills training (PSST)

PSST is based on the idea that juvenile justice clients often exhibit disruptive behaviors that are representative of *cognitive deficits and distortions*, which can lead to aggression and violence (Kendall & Braswell 1985). Youth usually work on an *individual basis* with a licensed therapist to learn appropriate skills to use in interpersonal situations. PSST training may consist of up to 20 weekly sessions, each lasting 40-50 minutes. Pro-social solutions are fostered through *modeling, role-playing, coaching, practice and direct reinforcement* (Brunk, 2000). The model has been used extensively with adolescents who show disruptive, aggressive, and delinquent behavior. PSST is reported to show positive behavior changes at home, at school, and in the community, and these gains are evident up to one year later (Kazdin, 2001).

PSST programs share several common characteristics. The primary focus of treatment is on the *thought processes* rather than on the behavioral acts that result, teaching adolescents a *step-by-step* approach to *solving problems* (Webster-Stratton & Herbert, 1994).

First, emphasis is on how children approach situations, primarily focusing on the *thought processes* that dictate their behavior. By altering the way in which the youth perceives his or her environment, responses and reactions become less aggressive (Brunk, 2000). In essence children are trained to *think before they act*.

Second, youth are taught to use a *step-by-step approach* to solve interpersonal problems. Personal statements are used to directly confront the problem.

Third, treatments usually employ a wide range of games, academic activities and stories to relate problems to real-world situations.

Fourth, therapists play an active role in all phases of treatment. Finally, treatment involves several different procedures including modeling and practice, role-playing, and reinforcement.

PSST aims to provide adolescents with several life improving techniques (Spivack, Platt, & Shure, 1976):

- *Alternative Solution Thinking:* The ability to generate different options that can solve problems in interpersonal situations.

- *Means-End Thinking:* Awareness of the necessary intermediate steps toward achieving a particular goal. The focus of this technique is to recognize the obstacles involved in solving a problem and the step-by-step process necessary to solve the problem.

- *Consequential Thinking:* The ability to identify what might happen as a direct result of acting in a particular way or choosing a particular solution.

How will the remedy affect oneself and others?

- *Causal Thinking:* The ability to relate one event to another over time and to understand why one event led to a particular action.

- *Sensitivity to Interpersonal Problems:* The ability to perceive a problem when it exists and to identify the interpersonal aspects of the confrontation that may emerge.

Problems are a natural and inevitable part of life and it is in everyone's best interest to learn better ways of solving them. Ineffective strategies for managing problems can contribute to the continuation of interpersonal difficulties. *Table 12.1* outlines seven PSST guiding principles as a structured process to coach the client through what may seem an insurmountable problem (Bedell and Lennox, 1997).

Five Step Model for Problem Solving:

- Stop! What is the problem?

- What are some plans?

- What is the best plan?

- Do the plan.

- Did my plan work?

Decision-Making Problem-Solving:

- State decision to be made very clearly

- List Pros and Cons

- Weigh pros and cons on a scale of (1 to 5)

- Add up numbers for pros and cons separately

- The choice achieving the highest weighting should be the one selected

Table 12.1 Getting Principles for Problem Solving

Problems are natural and should be accepted as an inevitable part of life:
  Accepting problems helps people to be more open and less "defensive" about them.

Think before jumping to a solution:
  Once a problem is recognized, the individual will frequently act on the first solution
  he or she comes up with; however, many times the first reaction to a problem may not be the
  best way to solve it.

Most problems can be solved:
  Most people will view a particular problem as unsolvable. Many times they will give
  up before trying because the problem seems too complex and there is an exaggerated
  sense of difficulty. However, using a structured means for dissecting the problem will
  generally get results.

Take responsibility for your problems:
  Do not blame others for a problem that only you can solve. Encouraging teenagers to recognize
  their contribution to their own life events creates a sense of ownership and facilitates
  problem resolution.

State what you can do, not what you can't do:
  Make sure the solution is within the realm of possibility. Do not make promises to
  yourself or others that are unrealistic and unachievable.

The behavior must be legal and socially acceptable:
  Creating new solutions to solving a problem must fall within societal norms; otherwise
  new problems will arise from the solutions.

Solutions must be within your power and ability:
  Solutions that try to remedy a problem using techniques beyond your ability are doomed to
  failure. Only implement solutions that can be used now with current knowledge and skills.

Source: Braswell & Bloomquist (p. 300, 1991) provide three basic paradigms for effective problem solving.

Means-End Problem-solving:

- What is my goal?

- What steps do I need to reach my goal?

- Did my plan work? Did I reach my goal?

FAMILY SYSTEMS THEORY AND FAMILY THERAPIES

Family Systems Therapy

Having its roots in the 1930's, *Family Systems Theory* (FST) is based on the recognition that individuals are an interconnected and interdependent part of the family system. Familial relationships influence human behavior, emotion, values and attitudes, and as such, can be instrumental in both the cause and the correction of problem behaviors in teens. It has been shown that change in family functioning is linked to change in problem behaviors of the adolescent. There is sufficient agreement that family dynamics affect the emotional health of members of the family unit and therefore a disturbed family system may not protect against substance abuse among the children in that unit (Center for Substance Abse Treatment, 1999).

Family-Based Therapy, Family-Centered Therapy, or *Family Therapy* may differ in specific treatment techniques, yet all are geared toward creating family change. Building upon the basic tenant of FST, that a family is seen as an "organism" that continuously changes, family therapy is thought to be an effective tool in treating problem behaviors in teens (TIP 32). If part of the "organism" changes, interaction within the organism changes, thereby creating a wave of behavioral change.

The initial use of family therapy for teens exhibiting problem behaviors was based on a belief of causality—that certain parental practices actually *encouraged* the problem behaviors. This approach developed to focus on how *family dynamics increase or decrease risk and protective factors*. Most recently, family therapy has taken on a *multidimensional* approach to include all family members as well as the adolescent's peers. As family therapy has developed, it has expanded its reach to incorporate other aspects of the adolescent's life, seeking to embrace community institutions including the juvenile justice system, youth organizations, public health clinics, and schools (Center for Substance Abse Treatment, 1999).

It is important to note that not all family units need to make major changes. In the case of solid family functioning, therapy would be more *educational or supportive* in nature and may revolve around relapse prevention strategies.

The *initial goal* when utilizing family therapy with problem teens is to *engage the client*. As is widely accepted, it is extremely difficult to convince an adolescent of the need for treatment for drug use or criminal activity. Coercion by parents or the criminal justice system is typically the reason for teen treatment, hence the family therapist's first assignment is to utilize therapeutic tools based on FST to overcome resistance to participation; only then can intervention begin. Current practice indicates use of *Motivational Enhancement* techniques as indicated in the FRAMES acronym above (Bien, Miller & Tonigan, 1993; Miller and Sanchez, 1993) during the initial phases of client engagement, problem recognition, and developing a commitment to change.

The family therapist examines underlying causes of dysfunctional interactions and assists the family members in creating a new context in which to act in more adaptive ways. Simply put, *problem solving and negotiating skills* (both integral components of the cognitive-behavioral approach) are taught and the concepts of empathy and compromise are encouraged. The idea behind and the value of "I" statements is also explained and examples are shown. Family members are also asked to participate in *reflective listening assignments* (TIP 32).

Parenting techniques are also addressed. The typical problems that arise in families may be exacerbated by extreme parenting styles such as being too permissive, too lenient or simply inconsistent. Family therapists assist parents in developing *appropriate and consistent parenting* practices within the home, e.g., limit setting, family obligations, consequences, etc. They also help parents who are "at the end of their rope" in regaining the motivation for guiding the adolescent and in rebuilding emotional relationships within the family.

Behavioral Therapy for adolescents and families

This model, which has shown treatment efficacy for adolescent substance abuse, incorporates the principle that unwanted behavior can be changed by *clear demonstration of the desired behavior* and *consistent reward* of incremental steps toward achieving it (Azrin et al., 1996). Therapeutic activities include fulfilling specific assignments, rehearsing desired behaviors, and recording and reviewing progress, with praise and privileges given for meeting assigned goals. Urine samples are collected regularly to monitor drug use. The therapy aims to equip the patient to gain three types of control:

- *Stimulus Control* – helps clients avoid situations associated with drug use and learn to spend more time in activities incompatible with drug use;

- *Urge Control* – helps clients recognize and change thoughts, feelings and plans that lead to drug use;

- *Social Control* - involves family members and other people important in helping clients.

A parent or significant other attends treatment sessions when possible and *assists with therapy assignments and reinforcing desired behavior*. Research findings show increased abstinence and prolonged abstinence after treatment ends. Other areas of improvement include: employment/school attendance, family relationships, depression, institutionalization, and alcohol abuse. Such favorable results are attributed largely to family members in therapy and rewarding drug abstinence as verified by urine analysis (NIDA, 1999).

Multidimensional Family Therapy

As noted earlier, most family systems therapies utilized today are multidimensional in approach, i.e., they include peers, school and community to assist in the change process. *Multidimentional Family Therapy* (MDFT) (Rowe et al., 2003) is based on adolescent and family development theories and on research concerning the formation of drug use and problem behavior. MDFT is a multi-component, stage-oriented therapy utilizing an organized approach of step-by-step phases, each building upon one another to effect change.

Multisystemic assessment is a critical first step. All aspects of the adolescent's life are reviewed with family members, extended relatives, teachers, school personnel, and friends of the family. Therapists using the MDFT model utilize the "picture" of the adolescent's life as the foundation for building a trusting relationship with him or her as well as a way to assist the adolescent in developing his or her sense of self. As the authors explain, an adolescent's sense of self is profoundly influenced by the complex interrelationships among the teen, family and peers (Rowe et al., 2003). Since problems in *identity development* have

been linked to drug use and problem behaviors in youth, it is important to assist struggling adolescents in identifying what type of person they could be as opposed to the type they are. During this critical time of developing a sense of self, the teen is vulnerable to negative influences, hence the need for the therapist to be his or her advocate and supporter in renewing or creating a positive sense of self.

MDFT recognizes the importance of *peer interactions* in teen development (Rowe et al., 2003). As teens begin to spend less time with family and more time with friends, this influence becomes greater, especially for those teens with rejecting or absent parents. Just as children who come from a nurturing and supportive home seek positive peer relationships, those raised by neglectful or abusive parents seek out negative or aggressive friends. Not only can positive peer relationships serve as protection from negative behavior, they allow for a healthy expression of emotions, thereby eliminating an additional risk factor for drug or alcohol use. Adolescents in MDFT are encouraged to explore how their *friends may be negatively impacting* their lives. Parents are encouraged to learn more about their child's friends and their activities. Peers can also be brought into therapy sessions.

MDFT is an *outpatient family-based drug abuse treatment* for teenagers. MDFT views adolescent drug use in terms of a network of influences (i.e., individual, family, peer, community) and suggests that reducing unwanted behavior and increasing desireable behavior occur in multiple ways in different settings. Treatment includes *individual and family sessions* held in the *clinic*, in the *home*, or with family members at the *family court, school, or other community locations*. During initial sessions the teenager and therapist focus on important developmental tasks such as *decision making, negotiation and problem solving skills*. Teenagers acquire skills in communicating their thoughts and feelings to deal with life stressors and vocational skills. Parallel sessions are held with family members. Parents examine their particular parenting style, learning to distinguish *influence* from *control* and to have a positive and developmentally appropriate influence on their child (NIDA, 1999). Rowe et al. (2003) conclude that due to the significant changes taking place in the development of young adolescents, this time in life is ideal for positive influences to have great impact.

Functional Family Therapy (FFT)

FFT, a short-term intervention with an average of 8 to 12 one-hour sessions and up to 30 hours for more difficult situations, is designed for *conduct-disordered* youth between the ages of 11 and 18 (Alexander & Sexton et al., 1999). The program has been successfully utilized in programs grounded in diversion, probation, and treatment alternatives to incarceration, and reentry from high-security, severely restrictive institutional settings. Outcome data suggest that FFT can *reduce recidivism* between 25% and 60% (Alexander et al. 1999). A major goal of FFT is to improve family communication and supportiveness while *decreasing intense negativity* often experienced in conflictive family situations. Other goals include helping family members adopt positive solutions to family problems, and developing positive behavior change and parenting strategies. FFT has shown positive effects in multi-ethnic, multicultural contexts with pre-adolescents and adolescents diagnosed with conduct disorders, violent acting out and substance abuse (Sexton & Alexander, 2000). FFT is multisystemic in that it focuses on multiple domains and systems in which adolescents and their families live including the treatment system and the therapist as major components (Sexton & Alexander).

FFT is comprised of *three specific and sequential intervention phases* each with distinct goals and assessment objectives (Sexton & Alexander, 2000). The intervention involves a strong cognitive component, which is integrated into systematic skill training in *family communication, parenting skills, and conflict management skills* (James, 1999). Each phase is guided by core principles that help the therapist adjust and adapt the goals of the phase to the unique characteristics of the family (Sexton & Alexander).

Engagement and Motivation: Utilizing the *cognitive techniques of reattribution* and *reframing*, participants develop a sense of *hope, purpose, empowerment and entitlement* (Sexton & Alexander, 2000). These strategies help the family to decrease their resistance to change, improving relationships between family members, increasing trust in the therapist's judgment and their approach to treatment and create a lessening of negativity towards other individuals and their life situation.

Behavior Change: Applies individualized and developmentally appropriate techniques such as *communication training, specific tasks and technical aids, basic parenting skills, contracting and response-cost techniques* (Alexander et al., 1999).

Generalization: Aims to improve a family's ability to affect the multiple systems in which it is embedded, e.g., *school, court system, community*, with the ultimate goal of *transitioning the family* from therapist-care to *self-care* (Sexton & Alexander, 2000). The individual functional family needs take precedence. Maintenance and preventing relapse are the focus.

Assessment is ongoing and generally based on a combination of the following principles:

- Focus should be on family interaction and the resultant behavior problems;

- Risk and protective factors should be identified through clinical and formal assessment;

- Assessment should take into consideration the adolescent's full spectrum of cognitive and developmental abilities;

- Assessment of family functioning is the most helpful way to identify treatment options.

Multisystemic Therapy (MST)

MST is an intensive family and community based treatment that targets juvenile offenders (ages 12 to 17) and their families. Because of the *chronic and serious nature* of their *substance abuse or violence* these youth are usually *at-risk for out of home placement*. The "typical" MST youth is 14-16 years of age; has multiple arrests; lives in a single parent home; has major problems at school or does not attend; has deep involvement with delinquent peers; and abuses substances (marijuana, alcohol, cocaine). Therapists carry small caseloads (usually 4-6 families) and are available on a need basis (24 hours per day, 7 days a week). The therapist usually functions within a team of 4-6 practitioners who regularly participate in case conference consultations. Treatment is short term, usually 4-5 months in duration. There is daily contact with family members and therapy sessions are usually conducted at times convenient to the family, *directly in their home* (Henggeler, Pickrel, Brondino, & Crouch, 1996; Henggeler, Schoenwald, Borduin, Rowland, & Cunningham, 1998).

MST addresses the multiple factors associated with heightened antisocial behavior patterns. These include characteristics of the:

- *Adolescent* (e.g., favorable attitudes toward drug use and crime);

- *Family* (e.g., poor discipline, family conflict, parental drug abuse);

- *Peers* (e.g., positive attitudes toward drug use and crime);

- *School* (e.g., dropout, poor performance); and

- *Neighborhood* (e.g., criminal subculture).

As described below, *nine principles form the core of MST.* Each principle is flexible and fluid in its orchestration.

I. The primary purpose of assessment is to understand the fit between the identified problems and their broader systemic context (Henggeler et al., 1998).

The *focus of MST* is the *correct diagnosis of behavioral problems with subsequent matching of treatment objectives.* The goal is to **match the treatment model(s) to the multiple systems** within the child's life, i.e., peer, school, social, etc. Thus, the MST therapist attempts to determine how each factor, singularly or in combination, increases or decreases the probability of youth problem behaviors (Hengggler, et al.; p. 24, 1998). Several steps are taken to develop a correct fit assessment between the apparent problem behaviors and future treatment models within the child's life, e.g., *Method, Hypothesis Development and Hypothesis Testing* (Henggeler et al., 1998).

Fit assessment proceeds in an inductive manner, systematically examining the *strengths and needs of each system* and their relationship to identified problems (Henggeler et al., 1998; p.24). The list of possible problems is narrowed to several key areas or transactions, i.e., prominent problems that become known through in-depth investigation. The factors associated with the problem behavior are then examined across multiple settings allowing the therapist to acquire a comprehensive plan for integrating treatment approaches (Henggeler et al., 1998).

One focus of MST assessment is obtaining information regarding the child's **current psychological state** by interviewing known *family members, associates and school personnel.* By **integrating information received from multiple sources** the therapist is able to define a direction for future treatments and objectives. A *measurable hypothesis* is then developed to match the *initial assessments and subsequent treatment plans.* The hypothesis is then **vigorously tested**, measured and modified if necessary (Henggeler et al., 1998). *MST is a continuous process that reinvents itself as new problems arise or old objectives are met.*

II. Therapeutic contacts emphasize the positive and use systemic strengths as levers for change (Henggeler et al., p. 28, 1998).

In order to have a successful outcome it is imperative for the **youth's family to be directly engaged in treatment.** However, engaging the family means it will be necessary to have sincere cooperation and collaboration from each member. If this is achieved the youth develops multiple positive influences, or strengths, as a daily reminder of targets for change (Henggeler, et al.; 1998).

Several steps are taken to insure development and maintenance of the "strength" focus:

- *All participants* in the child's treatment use no pejorative language in verbal and written form;

- Teach and use techniques of *reframing*;

- Use *positive reinforcement* liberally;

- Incorporate and maintain a *problem-solving stance*;

- Provide *hope*; and

- Find and *emphasize* what the *family does well*

Each child has his/her own "strengths." These can be found in the youth's individual characteristics, or within peer, social or familial groups.

III. Interventions are designed to promote responsible behavior and decrease irresponsible behavior among family members (Henggeler et al., 1998).

It is important for *both parents and children* to achieve *positive outcomes* with regard to their behaviors. According to Henggeler et al. (1998), *parents have* **fundamental responsibilities** such as *support, guidance, nurturance, protection and discipline.* Yet they have an even *greater responsibility* to **proactively address** *factors that inhibit parental responsibilities,* take the initiative to delegate parental functions if necessary and taking the time to understand where aversive feelings about the child are originating from (Henggeler et al., 1998).

In order to promote responsible behavior with children Henggeler et al. (1998) contend that *reinforcement theories* such as those proposed by social theorists work well:

- Contingencies articulated clearly;

- Understanding rationality of rules;

- Tangible reinforcers for positive action;

- Aversive discipline;

- Minor transgressions equal minor sanctions; and

- Physical discipline should be discouraged.

IV. Interventions are present focused and action oriented, targeting specific and well-defined problems (Henggeler et al., 1998).

Emphasis is placed on *changing current circumstances. Little relevance is placed on past events* unless those events are directly effecting the youth's current situation. Action is of *utmost importance* when using MST. The brevity of MST requires that family members work intensely to solve long-standing problems (Henggeler et al., 1998). Thus, *swift and consistent action* is required to enable the family and key players in the social ecology to meet their treatment goals (Henggeler, 1998, p. 35).

Two types of specific treatment goals are used in MST—overarching goals and intermediate goals. It is imperative that both types are clearly defined, and target specific areas for improvement. *Overarching goals* represent *long-term objectives* defined by the family. *Intermediate goals* are *small day-to-day projects* usually initiated by the therapist.

V. Interventions target sequences of behavior within and between multiple systems that maintain the identified problems (Henggeler, et al.; 1998).

Interventions will vary from family to family. Every family is unique and as such requires its *own specific treatment model*. One of the defining features of MST, and a characteristic that differentiates it from the vast majority of models, is the *significant attention devoted to transactions between systems that are associated with identified problems* (Henggeler et al., 1998, p. 36). It is the belief of MST that importance must be placed on the interrelationship of all variables that create aversive behavior.

VI. Interventions are developmentally appropriate and fit the developmental needs of the youth (Henggeler et al.; 1998).

Children and their caregivers have *different* attitudes, beliefs, needs and desires at different points in their lives. Particular care must be given to *creating effective goals* and transactions that reflect the current developmental stage of all parties involved in treatment. A twenty-year-old single parent with a *ten-year-old child using drugs* will have *very different needs* than *forty year old* parents who have a seventeen year old *refusing to attend school. Every MST treatment is uniquely designed to fit the specific needs of the individual participants.*

VII. Interventions are designed to require daily or weekly effort by family members (Henggeler et al.1998).

If *all participants* in the treatment program are required to complete daily and weekly tasks the momentum of treatment continues and builds as time passes. Constant effort provides several advantages:

- Problems are resolved in a timely manner;

- Noncompliance of treatment goals becomes apparent;

- Goals can be assessed on a regular basis and adjusted accordingly;

- Feedback is continually produced; and

- Families become stronger as more tasks are accomplished.

VIII. Intervention *effectiveness is evaluated continuously from multiple perspectives with providers assuming accountability for overcoming barriers to successful outcomes* (Henggeler et al., 1998).

Constant evaluation of treatment objectives enables the therapist to determine what is working and what is not. MST is structured in a fashion that gives *multiple perspectives from multiple sources* on any given task. The objectives and tasks can continuously be *restructured and revised* depending on the amount of progression or regression experienced. The therapist then has the ability to mold the treatment to the individual.

IX. Interventions are designed to promote treatment generalization and long-term maintenance of therapeutic change by empowering caregivers to address family members' needs across multiple systemic contexts (Henggeler et al., 1998, p. 40, 1998).

Ensuring that treatment gains **will generalize** and be maintained *when treatment ends* is a critical and continuous thrust of MST interventions (Henggeler, p. 40, 1998). The ultimate goals of MST:

- Emphasize development of *skills that family members* will use to navigate their social ecology;

- Develop the capacity of family members to *negotiate current and future problems*;

- Delivery *primarily by caregivers*, with therapists playing primarily supportive and consultative roles;

- Accentuate and *build family strengths and competencies*;

- Make abundant use of *protective and resiliency factors* available in the natural environment.

(Henggeler et al., 1998, p. 41).

By participating in intense treatment in natural environments (homes, schools, and neighborhood settings) most youths and families complete a full course of treatment. MST significantly reduces adolescent drug use during treatment and for at least 6 months after treatment. For serious juvenile offenders, evaluations of MST have demonstrated:

- Reductions of 25-70% in long-term rates of re-arrest;

- Reductions of 47-64% in out of home placements;

- Extensive improvements in family functioning;

- Decreased mental health problems for serious juvenile offenders.

(Henggeler, Mihalic, Rone, Thomas, & Timmons-Mitchell, 1998)

The benefits of reduced numbers of incarcerations and out-of-home placements along with improved family and mental health functioning are viewed as cost saving in comparison to usual mental health and criminal justice services. These considerations may offset the expenditure of $4,500 per youth for the provision of this intensive service and maintaining the clinician's low caseloads (Blueprints for Violence Prevention, 2001). *Figure 12.1* below shows the MST conceptual model for goal setting, problem prioritization, intervention, and on-going evaluation.

RESIDENTIAL TREATMENT

Therapeutic Communities (TC) were originally used in 1958 when it was found that psychiatry and general medicine were not successful in treating substance use disorders. An early member of *Alcoholics Anonymous*, Chuck Dederich, founded the first TC to provide a substance-free environment where adult users could use the *principles of AA* as well as the *social learning model*. TCs differ from AA in one important aspect: rather than giving the power to a higher being, TCs maintain that the *individual is responsible for* his or her current situation and ultimately for change in behavior. The *community* itself *acts as therapist and teacher*. The highly structured environment and modeling by others become the basis for motivation to change. Treatment in a TC tends to

last one year to 18 months; however, budget constraints have led some programs to attempt a 6-month treatment protocol.

Although the core principles of promoting a healthy lifestyle and identifying areas for change remain, modifications have been made to the original adult model to include specific services for youth such as education and family support services. As Dennis, Dawud-Noursi, Muck, & McDerrmeit (2003) point out, there is increased emphasis on recreation, less confrontation, more supervision and evaluation, more assessment for psychological disorders, greater family involvement, more psychotropic medications used, and, of course, an integration of academics into the treatment program.

Residents in TC programs progress through developmental phases. Each phase prepares the individual for the next one and provides additional responsibilities and privileges. To advance, one must show *responsibility, self-awareness, and consideration* for others. While adults in TCs advance to the stage of helping manage the operation of the TC, adolescents continue to be "parented" by staff members.

As with most adolescent treatment therapies, TCs originally viewed families as the primary "cause" of the adolescent's problems and therefore the environment of the TC was that of a safe-haven, away from parents and other family members. Contemporary TC programs, however, recognize the *importance of family systems theory* and include family counseling, parent support groups and family education.

Specific issues of adolescence that are dealt with by TC therapists are *self-image, guilt, and sexuality*. Self-images are often *engrained in street culture and gang influence*. Adolescents are taught to understand how negative images are destructive, to determine their own self-image and that of others, and how to develop and monitor a new self-image.

A favorite mantra of TC therapists is "guilt kills." That is, negative behavior produces guilt, which produces more negative behavior to escape the guilty feelings. Through confessions made in "guilt" therapy sessions, encounter groups or seminars, the teens acknowledge past misdeeds and make a commitment to changing their behavior and hence envision a better future.

The period of adolescence is a time when feelings surrounding sexuality are intensified. *House rules* regarding sexual conduct, sex education seminars and *one-on-one counseling sessions* are utilized by TC

Figure 12.1 Conceptual Model of the MST Treatment Process

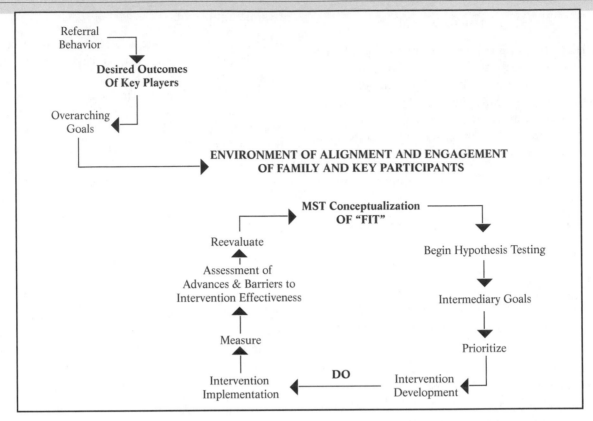

therapists to deal with issues of *strong sexual impulses, sexual identity adjustment, and possible previous sexual abuse*. In addition, the long-term stay of these adolescents assists in allowing them to understand and practice safe sex.

In a recent outcome study of 150 TC "graduates" (SAMHSA, TIP 32), 31% showed that there was a significant reduction in the extent or frequency of substance use as well as significant reductions in violent crimes, drug sales and property crimes. An earlier study also showed that the length of stay is a critical factor, with adolescents requiring longer treatment period than adults.

CHAPTER REVIEW

The cognitive behavioral model has emerged as the preeminent theoretical framework for treating adolescent substance abusing offenders. Individual treatment usually includes some facet of *motivational enhancement*, a set of principles that promote client engagement, including willingness to discuss relevant treatment issues and developing a plan for continued therapeutic engagement. A major focus of most cognitive–behavioral treatments is *"problem solving,"* which is an

especially important tool for dealing with interpersonal conflict. *Problem Solving Skills Training* (PSST) provides the framework for teaching a step-by-step approach to negotiate difficult interpersonal situations. Pro-social solutions are fostered through modeling, role-playing, coaching, practice and direct reinforcement.

An array of family therapy models have emerged to improve the odds for youth who are poorly supervised, enmeshed in chronic family distress, or are at risk for out-of-home placement. The basic premise of the family systems approach is that improvement in the dynamics of the family will result in increased resiliency for all involved. In *behavioral treatments for adolescents and their families*, a parent or significant other attends treatment sessions when possible and assists with therapy assignments and reinforcing desired behavior.

Most recently, family therapy has taken on a multi-factorial approach to include the adolescent's peers, school and community to assist in the change process. In *Multidimensional Family Therapy* (MFT) adolescents explore how their peers may be negatively affecting their lives and learn in communication, problem solving, negotiation and decision-making. Parallel sessions are held with family members where parents examine their particular parenting style, learning to distinguish *influence from control* and to have a positive and developmentally appropriate influence on their child.

Functional Family Therapy (FFT) is a short-term intervention (8-12 one-hour sessions) designed for youth between the ages of 11 and 18 who are involved in the continuum of criminal justice settings. The three-phase intervention involves a *strong cognitive component*, which is integrated into systematic skill training in family communication, parenting skills, and conflict management skills. The initial focus of FFT is engagement and motivational enhancement of family members, followed by training in individualized and developmentally appropriate techniques such as communication skills and basic parenting skills. A generalization phase aims to improve a family's ability to affect the multiple systems in which it is embedded.

Multisystemic Therapy (MST) is specifically designed for juvenile offenders who manifest *chronic and serious patterns* of substance abuse or violence. These youth are usually at-risk for out-of-home placement. While treatment is short, usually 4-5 months in duration, the program is very intense with therapists available on a 24-hour basis, 7 days each week. Nine principles form the core of MST with continuous assessment designed to identify behavioral problems with subsequent matching of treatment objectives. It is viewed as imperative that the youth's family is directly engaged in treatment, with total collaboration and cooperation from each member. All participants in the treatment program are required to complete daily and weekly tasks to ensure that the momentum of treatment continues and builds as time passes. Empowering caregivers to address family members' needs across multiple systemic contexts promotes long-term maintenance of treatment objectives.

In the domain of residential treatment the *therapeutic community* (TC) is explored as a highly structured long-term treatment approach (6-18 months) where the community itself acts as *therapist and teacher.* Modifications to the original adult model include specific services for youth such *as education and family support* services. There is increased emphasis on recreation, less confrontation, more supervision and evaluation, more assessment for psychological disorders, greater family involvement, more psychotropic medications used, and an integration of academics into the treatment program.

Exemplary Treatment Programs

Chapter Thirteen:
Exemplary Treatment Programs

Chapter Outline

Exemplary Youth Treatment Programs

- Teen Substance Abuse Treatment Program, Maricopa County, Arizona

- Chestnut Health Systems' Bloomington Outpatient and Intensive Outpatient Program for Adolescent Substance Abusers, McLean County, Illinois

- Epoch Counseling Center—Group-Based Outpatient Adolescent Substance Abuse Treatment Program, Baltimore County, Maryland

- La Cañada Adolescent Treatment Program, Arizona

- Phoenix Academy, Los Angeles, California

Nationally Recognized Programs

- Thinking for a Change (T4C) - Integrated Cognitive Behavior Change Program

- Motivational Enhancement Therapy/Cognitive Behavioral Therapy (MET/CBT5)

Chapter Review

Chapter Objectives

- To familiarize counselors and providers with a variety of existing youth treatment programs that are considered by national experts to be exemplary;

- To emphasize the importance of developing and (utilizing) youth-focused programs rather than placing youth in programs geared toward adults; and

- To encourage efficacy studies of the programs currently in use.

EXEMPLARY YOUTH TREATMENT PROGRAMS

In conjunction with the *National Institute on Alcohol Abuse and Alcoholism* (NIAAA), The *Center for Substance Abuse Treatment* (CSAT) has taken measures in the United States to identify and develop *effective models of adolescent treatment programs*. The *Adolescent Treatment Model* (ATM) funds the manualization and empirical evaluation of those programs thought to be exemplary in their efforts to treat adolescents (Dennis et al., 2003). The ATM program aim is to achieve the following goals:

- To identify existing, *potentially exemplary models* of treatment for adolescents;

- To collaborate with providers to *formalize the models* and disseminate manuals for replication;

- To determine *how the model has been tested* and the services received by adolescents;

- To evaluate the *effectiveness, cost, and cost-effectiveness* of the models;

- To ensure that the models and study findings are disseminated.

Below are summaries of *five of the ten* ATM model programs currently under study. Adolescents in these programs are mostly Caucasian males with *marijuana, alcohol, and criminal justice system involvement* (Dennis et al., 2003). The five programs outlined below represent differing theoretical perspectives as the basis for their treatment protocols including *cognitive-behavioral therapy, family systems theory, group therapy, social learning theory, and multidisciplinary approaches*.

Following the five ATM models are descriptions of two additional model programs currently in use, *Thinking for a Change (T4C)* and *Motivational Enhancement Therapy and Cognitive Behavioral Therapy for Adolescent Cannabis Users*.

Teen Substance Abuse Treatment Program (TSAT)

This cognitive-behavioral treatment (CBT) program for adolescent substance users, is also based on family systems theory (FST), and was developed in 1997 in Maricopa County, Arizona (Stevens et al., 2003). The program is a 3-month intensive (i.e., 9 or more hours per week) outpatient program for 12 to 17 year-olds and their families. Extensions can be granted based on individual needs. The primary referral source for TSAT clients is the juvenile probation system.

The TSAT program consists of three components including:

- In-home family and individual counseling;

- Teen group therapy; and

- Multi-family group.

All participants receive all three forms of treatment. Treatment goals of the program are:

- Reduced or eliminated substance use;

- Improved decision making;

- Improved family functioning;

- Reduced or eliminated criminal involvement; and

- Reduced out-of-home placement.

Stevens et al. (2003) point out that outcome studies have shown that *cognitive-behavioral approaches* to the treatment of substance abuse by adults are indeed effective. While *few studies* have been geared toward CBT of adolescents, an obvious consequence of the few number of adolescent programs in existence, it is widely thought to be a "promising approach." Consisting of a number of methods or techniques, CBT can be used in both *individual and group therapy* as well as in *family settings*, with the goal being to "change the adaptive behaviors of clients so that they have a new repertoire of skills enabling them to function without the use of drugs" (Steven et al., p. 41). Stevens also notes the critical nature of relapse prevention, which is an important aspect of CBT and TSAT.

Utilizing FST, staff, clients and family members of the adolescent (who was accepted into the program because of significant substance abuse problems or being alcohol or drug dependent) are engaged in the program and work together to strengthen good decision-making skills and appropriate behavior of all family members. FST assumes that the family and larger social system has been instrumental in the development of substance use. TSAT counselors therefore treat the entire family, addressing family structure, interactions, and patterns, assisting the family in identifying dysfunction and restructuring the system (Stevens, et al., 2003).

In-home program: The in-home program combines CBT and FST with techniques to encourage the clients to become aware of their feelings and motives behind their behaviors. Stevens et al. (2003) report that successful treatment begins with an agreement among the counselor, the adolescent, and the family members regarding their goals in therapy.

In-home sessions are adaptable to whichever family members are in attendance. For the first month, there are six hours per week of counseling; then, four hours for the second, and two hours for the final month. Counselors must also be alert to drug use by family members and make treatment referrals. Or, as appropriate, and depending on the openness of the drug-involved family members, counselors may bring multi-generational drug use issues directly into the sessions. Parenting skills may also be taught to help parents regain authority in the family unit. The program also assists the family in seeking any and all community service support (e.g., food stamps, child support, medical assistance, support groups, etc.).

Teen group: A group session for the adolescents is held three times a week for three hours. It was found that the highest rate of attendance was at groups held from 3:00 until 6:00. Communication and transportation problems are often solved by TSAT staff members who arrange to pick up their clients from school.

The primary approach is, again, teaching cognitive-behavioral techniques to create behavior change. Stevens et al. (2003) report that there is considerable flexibility in the use of worksheets, readings, movies, etc. so the provider can give attention to group dynamics and address specific needs of the individuals in the group.

Multifamily group: Once per month, a three-hour group meeting is held which takes the place of the teen group, but rescheduled for 6:00 to 9:00 p.m. A potluck dinner is served. Here, family members share their current progress, solutions, support and resources. One goal of this forum is to decrease the amount of isolation and stigma due to the family involvement in substance abuse. Discussions take place concerning coping skills, effective discipline techniques, communication, values, cooperation and trust. On occasion, art or talent shows are set up (Stevens, et al., 2003).

Drug use testing: A local drug testing facility handles testing of TSAT clients once per week, with the day chosen randomly. Results are shared with probation or the case manager, the teen, and his or her family. Relapses are used as a learning experience regarding triggers and subsequent behaviors. Discharge is not typical for relapses, but anyone suspected of being under the influence during the group is taken to the testing site at that time. Teens who refuse testing are taken home.

Evaluation An in-depth, comprehensive evaluation design has been implemented for the treatment outcome study, including baseline assessment, follow-up assessments at 3, 6, 9, and 12 months. Clients are paid $25 for all follow-up assessments. Assessment tools include Global Appraisal of Individual Needs, Hispanic acculturation scale, HIV/AIDS knowledge and risk assessment, environmental street inventory, adolescent relapse coping questionnaire, and a cognitive functioning questionnaire to assess problem solving, abstract reasoning, and knowledge and concepts of disease. Prior to the implementation of this study, findings showed that adolescents in the TSAT program were able to reduce drug use and related negative behaviors.

Chestnut Health Systems' Bloomington Outpatient and Intensive Outpatient Program for Adolescent Substance Abusers (CHS)

In existence since 1985 in McLean County, Illinois, this program is based on a "blended therapeutic approach" (Godley, Risberg, Adams & Sodetz, 2003). The theoretical basis for this program includes four approaches including: (a) Rogerian (unconditional positive regard, acceptance, building rapport and empowerment); (b) behavioral (skill-building, behavior modification and habit control); (c) cognitive (changing thinking patterns via reframing and cognitive restructuring); and (d) reality (understanding choices and their consequences).

Sixty-three percent of youths (under age 21) who are admitted are in an outpatient setting. Care for outpatient adolescents ranges from one to eight hours per week and inpatient from nine to twelve hours per week. The components of the program include:

- Use of the Global Appraisal of Individual Needs assessment and interviews with parents, probation officers, counselors, and school officials.

- Individualized treatment plans based on the above;

- Cognitive-behavioral based group sessions therapy sessions;

- Family Night program and a limited number of family counseling sessions;

- Transportation;

- Psychiatric services;

- Hepatitis B and C, HIV and TB prevention, testing, and counseling;

- Random urine tests; and

- Onsite GED classes.

Most of the treatment occurs in group settings, however, individual sessions are also conducted in order to determine and review the progress of the Master Treatment Plan (MTP). MTPs are highly variable and address emotional/behavioral issues, relapse potential and recovery environment (Godley, et al., 2003).

The types of groups include:

Orientation: Broken into two types, orientation groups can either be for those who have little or no prior experience in substance abuse treatment or groups designed for adolescents who are particularly resistant to treatment. The former type of orientation groups are to assist the adolescents in how to behave, how to bring up issues and how to confront or support their peers. The 12-step process is also introduced. Orientation groups for resistant teens are intended to assist the adolescents in recognizing the consequences of their problem behavior.

Drug education: These group discussions revolve around the behavioral and emotional effects of chemical use. Useful tools include videos, games and written assignments.

Relapse prevention: Problem situations and triggers are discussed and relapse prevention and survival plans are designed.

Life skills: Health issues such as hepatitis, AIDS and HIV are discussed as are fundamental skills such as job hunting, budgeting, etc. These groups utilize outside speakers and role-playing.

Self-esteem: Coping strategies are taught using videos, role-playing, art therapy, and guided-visualization.

Leisure education: Recreational activities are used to assist the teens in positive social activities, self-awareness, positive risk taking, appropriate self-disclosure, cooperation and teamwork, communication and stress management.

Emotions/Communication: Skills taught in this group are to build an assertive, expressive, open-minded communication style and to communicate a "recovery image."

Working recovery/decision making: Maintaining recovery is the goal of these sessions. Support groups such as AA/NA are introduced. A recovery plan is implemented.

Art therapy: Self-expression is encouraged in a creative environment where teens can continue their recovery efforts.

Counseling: These groups allow for discussion of personal issues where peers can present feedback and relate their own experiences. Gender specific groups are offered.

Family sessions are also conducted, in keeping with the program's recognition of the critical role that families play in recovery. Beginning with family members only, the session addresses topics such as drug education, relapse signs, denial, coping, enabling, detachment, and parenting skills. When the adolescents join the session, topics depend on the specific needs of the families, allowing for sharing, feedback, and problem solving.

Godley et al. (2003) find this program's strengths to include: the comprehensiveness of the assessment process; the individualization of the treatment process; the therapeutic approach which is based on established theories; the use of master's level therapists who are trained in social work or psychology; the regular clinical supervision these therapists receive; the program's emphasis on family involvement; and regular contact with collaterals.

In contrast, Godley et al. (2003) question the use of discharge status as the indicator of treatment success. While 56% of 41 clients were discharged "as planned" (meaning that the adolescent had met most or all of the MTP objectives), superior outcomes were not found at a 90-day follow-up. The in-depth outcome studies being funded by CSAT will provide needed knowledge concerning the efficacy of this model and whether or not replication of this model is warranted.

Epoch Counseling Center—Group-Based Outpatient Adolescent Substance Abuse Treatment Program

The basis of this ATM program, conducted in Baltimore County, Maryland, is two-fold: to develop and evaluate a group-based program and to evaluate how the addition of a motivational interview at the beginning of the program would impact engagement, retention, and outcome. The Center's adolescent program is based on social learning theory (to explain why substance abuse was initiated) and conditioning theory (to explain why it continues) (Battjes et al., 2003).

Battjes et al. (2003) cite research to support the belief that drug use is a learned behavior "that is affected by an interaction between adolescents' perceptions of their social environment and the pharmacological properties of the substances used" (p. 84). Modeling is also important in directing one's beliefs about alcohol as shown by research indicating that even children with little or no drinking experience have beliefs about the effects of alcohol. Through exposure to alcohol use by significant people in the child's life, adolescent drinking behavior is formed, and drinking begins earlier in life when the child believes that alcohol use is a positive behavior (Battjes et al., 2003).

In this program, Skinner's operant conditioning theory is the basis for why adolescents continue drug and alcohol use and is explained by the adolescent being rewarded by positive outcomes. Classical conditioning theory explains how, with continued use, adolescents associate certain cues with the substances themselves. When exposed to those cues, cravings, and even withdrawal-like symptoms can be experienced; the adolescent therefore uses the substance to alleviate these aversive symptoms and feelings (Battjes et al., 2003).

Drug and alcohol use is also believed to be influenced by lack of parental supervision and permissive parenting. Because the children of less authoritative parents are not punished, they receive little negative consequences for their deviant behaviors. Adolescents with poor family relationships may avoid being at home, thereby increasing their opportunity to associate with deviant peers and therefore increase the number of cues associated with substance use (Battjes et al., 2003).

The Epoch program attempts to teach adolescents a variety of skills to assist them in disassociating the learned cues from the use of substances. Relaxation exercises, assertiveness training, anger management and self-esteem lessons focus on the psychological and emotional factors associated with relapse. Battjes et al. (2003) also report that the Epoch treatment program is directed toward family interactions and helps to reduce conflict and teaches parenting skills and strategies to assist parents in helping their adolescent remain drug or alcohol free.

As Battjes et al. (2003) note, client motivation is integral to treatment engagement and outcome, therefore the Epoch program is exploring the effects of a method to increase readiness to change. Since evidence has been shown of its effectiveness with alcoholic adults including drug-dependent women in hospital emergency department settings, marijuana users, heroin addicts in methadone maintenance, and drug-abusing probationers in a treatment community, it is thought that similar induction methods should be valuable when treating adolescents. Indeed, long-term positive effects have been found after brief motivational interviews with incoming college freshmen related to their drinking habits. In addition, short-term reductions in drinking were also shown in intoxicated teenage emergency room patients when they received a 45-minute motivational intervention (Battjes et al.).

After an initial intake assessment that utilizes a number of assessment tools, approximately 50% of the adolescents (most of whom are referrals from the Department of Juvenile Justice) receive a motivational interview lasting 75 minutes. Within this time period, two treatment phases are administered. The first is one in which information is gathered from the client: problems associated with substance use, how decisions about substance use are arrived upon, and the client's future plans. Throughout this phase, the client is encouraged to make a commitment to begin or continue change as the counselor utilizes techniques such as reflective listening, "rolling with resistance," and structured feedback (Battjes et al., 2003).

The second phase of the motivational interview focuses on developing a plan of action: how will change be achieved? Having utilized a change plan worksheet through this process, the counselor can then use this product of the client's statements and plans toward the goal of having the client make a formal commitment to abstinence.

The remaining clients, as a control group for research purposes, receive a 60-75 minute counseling session that focuses on the upcoming treatment program. Rather than attempting engagement and motivation to change, the counselors describe the treatment process including the counseling relationship and different treatment modalities, and elicit feedback from the adolescent concerning his or her expectations, concerns and thoughts about the treatment (Battjes, et al., 2003).

The client and the counselor then design a treatment plan. This "work-in-progress" will outline the short and long-term objectives including issues that relate to abstinence such as school, job, legal problems, family, communication skills and anger management (Battjes et al., 2003). Actual treatment programs at Epoch are flexible, semi-structured, 20 weeks in length, and clients attend at least one 75 minute group session each week. Two phases are outlined:

Phase I: Drug Education

- Physical, psychological and behavioral effects of substances

- Progression of substance use

- Relapse

- Family influence

Phase II: Skills Building/Relapse Prevention

- Goals Group I

  - Coping with stress

  - Coping with hurdles in recovery

  - Managing thoughts about using

- Process Group I

  - Self-esteem

  - Outside speaker: STDs/NIV

  - Assertiveness: Relationships

- Process Group II

- Goals Group II

  - Assertiveness: Drink/drug refusal

  - Anger

- Process Group III

  - Physical Health

  - Increasing pleasurable activities

Clients are required to attend at least three individual counseling sessions: the initial session which focuses on the treatment plan, a second session at week thirteen to update the plan, and a final session to develop a recovery plan when out of treatment. Four family sessions are also required to address familial issues that may be affecting the client's substance use. Educational support groups for parents are also offered, with a requirement that four are attended throughout the adolescent's treatment. Topics include:

- Enabling

- Communication patterns

- Stages of addiction

- Parenting styles

- Understanding adolescence

- Limit setting

- Anger management

- Maintaining recovery after treatment

- Single parenting

- Codependency and boundary issues

- Discussion of video: "Seven Worst Things Parents Do"

- Breaking destructive patterns

The Epoch adolescent treatment program is seen by Battjes et al. (2003) as a comprehensive and feasible program that can be implemented in community based facilities. Should outcome studies show significant value in the first motivational interview that was added to the program, this intervention technique may help improve services provided for adolescents throughout the country.

La Cañada Adolescent Treatment Program

Serving ethnically diverse adolescents in five southern counties of Arizona, La Cañada began in 1996 and provides a residential, step-down treatment program for substance abusers. Approximately 87% of the clients have been referred by juvenile county courts. Other health care agencies, families, and adolescents themselves make up the remaining 13% of referrals (Stevens et al., 2003).

The philosophy of the program, according to Stevens et al. (2003), is a combination of traditional psychiatric approaches and systems theory. Family dysfunction is seen as the cornerstone for problem behaviors among adolescents, therefore family involvement in therapy is an important aspect of the La Cañada program. Clients live in a supportive, yet structured environment that addresses problems and fosters growth in all aspects of daily living, including personal care, social development, interpersonal behavior and recreation.

A treatment plan is developed through negotiation among the counselor, family, and adolescent, with abstinence being the goal. This plan is in force throughout a 30-day residential program and two aftercare phases of treatment. With slots for six males and three females, La Cañada's admissions occur on an ongoing basis, as openings occur, providing clients a time away from family and school. This allows the now clear-headed adolescent time for self-exploration in a safe and drug-free environment, one that allows family problems to be addressed as well as physical, emotional and social issues. The process of increasing the adolescent's sense of pride becomes the basis for his or her motivation to continue recovery after the residential portion of treatment (Stevens et al., 2003).

Treatment within the residential phase includes one hour per week of individual therapy, one hour of family therapy, five hours of group therapy, three hours of psycho educational groups and four hours of case management. Individual therapy is designed to offer the adolescent a safe place to discuss sensitive issues such as sexual abuse, trauma, sexual orientation and sensitive family matters.

Phoenix Academy

Located in Los Angeles and established in 1987 by Phoenix House, this nonprofit program is a modified therapeutic community with an on-site public school. Housing the treatment center is a building that rests on 15 acres in a middle-class residential neighborhood, and is surrounded by parks and recreational facilities. The four dormitory areas can house up to 150 adolescents. Ninety percent of clients are referred from Juvenile Probation, five percent from the Department of Children and Family Services and five percent from the Department of Mental health, self-referrals, or other agencies. Clients range from 13 to 17.5 years, must be able to function voluntarily in an open, community environment, must speak English, and must have already undergone detoxification if necessary (Morral et al., 2003).

As purported by therapeutic community theory, this model takes a holistic view of substance abuse, that being that it is "the outward manifestation of a broad set of personal and developmental problems" (Morral et al., 2003, p. 216). Rather than focusing on physiological dependence or behavioral, cognitive, or emotional problems, the Phoenix Academy's philosophy is that change requires a commitment to help oneself as well as others.

The consequences of behavior is one of the first lessons learned at Phoenix Academy, hence compliance with rules is rewarded with status promotions and privileges. Deviations from acceptable behavior are met with disciplinary actions. These consequences are known throughout the community and residents learn from their own behaviors as well as by witnessing the consequences of others' behavior. As social learning theory prescribes, members of the community will adopt behavior that they have observed to elicit rewards and privileges and avoid behavior that results in punishment or negative outcomes.

Other than those items deemed to be basic necessities such as food, sleep, clean clothing, hygiene and education, nothing is offered the resident without having been earned. As the client meets the goals of each phase of the program, privileges such as access to personal property, free time, assignment to a more desirable room, or permission for special trips, are granted. Sanctions for violation of house rules lead to the removal of a privilege.

Residents are assigned to groups or "clans," each with six to fifteen members and a leader who is the primary counselor. Tasks are assigned to increase responsibility, with advancement in the community based on performance as well as achieving treatment goals. A variety of meetings take place within the community including daily meetings such as "family gatherings" where attendance is taken, new residents are assimilated and the community itself is affirmed as the teacher and healer. Other meetings include:

- Seminars to address core concepts of the Phoenix Academy;

- Workshops to address topics relevant to treatment and recovery;

- Tutorials are experiential groups that focus on a life theme;

- Peer support groups give residents a forum for receiving support from others at the same stage of change;

- Peer process groups are discussion forums for residents, reactions to previous program activities;

- Encounter groups utilize confrontation by peers to address negative attitudes and behavior; and

- Marathons which are extended therapeutic groups held just a few times a year to work through major issues in a cathartic manner.

Individual counseling sessions are held at least once a week, always after clients have home visits, after encounter groups if the youth was confronted, following a crisis, or whenever the adolescent requests it. As opposed to the more confrontational aspect of peer group interactions, counselors play a more supportive role when counseling the residents.

Family therapy includes a two-hour parent orientation meeting, family assessment, parent education semi nars and informal, unstructured social visit. Family recreation occurs every six to eight weeks for four hours. Family therapists work individually with the resident if family involvement does not exist. Vocational counselors assist residents with educational and career goals and pre-employment counseling.

The program begins with an orientation and stabilization process where residents learn the philosophy, concepts, and rules of the community. Gradually, they begin to participate in a wider range of activities as they become fully engaged in the treatment process and are in compliance with program rules. During months six through nine, the goal is for the internalization of values and a motivation for drug-free living. A reentry process occurs during months nine through twelve. Here, residents are prepared for the transition back to their own communities. Aftercare continues for another twelve months where the youths may enter another program or may continue to be involved in he Phoenix Academy case management, weekly group meetings or overnight visits.

Currently, Phoenix Academy is part of an outcome study comparing it to six other ethnically diverse community treatment settings. Approaches of the other sites include cognitive-behavioral therapy; reality therapy; peer culture and consensual decision making; and group processes and self-governance. Two sites listed no specific philosophy.

While Morral et al. (2003) report that there is considerable anecdotal evidence of the effectiveness of the Phoenix Academy's approach, few rigorous studies such as the one currently being conducted have been previously carried out. Precise statistical methods are being utilized to determine the efficacy of this community-based treatment method.

NATIONALLY RECOGNIZED PROGRAMS

Thinking for a Change (T4C)—
Integrated Cognitive Behavior Change Program

Originally designed for adult offenders, T4C (Bush, Glick, & Taymans, 1997) has been adapted for use with teenage populations. The program consists of 22 lessons with the capacity to extend the program indefinitely. An additional 10 lessons are recommended to explore the self-evaluations done in the 22nd lesson. Groups meet one to two hours weekly. Although facilitators need not have specific credentials or education level, they should be caring, like to teach, understand group processes and interpersonal

interactions, be able to control an offender group, had have been trained in a three-to-five day T4C implementation plan with two master trainers. The lesson format is predicated on the students' attainment of the abilities to understand, learn and perform cognitive skills. Each lesson is organized according to the following scheme:

- Homework review;

- Summary and rationale for the lesson - specific scripts are provided for facilitators;

- Definition of words and concepts - group members read aloud from the text;

- Modeling—facilitators demonstrate how to use the skill being learned. They break out of their role throughout the modeling exercise in order to explain the cognitive processes going on;

- Skits—group members act out real-life examples to utilize the skill being taught. The stage is appropriately set with props, arrangements, and set description. The facilitators interrupt the skit at any time when the skill steps are not being followed;

- Feedback—group members respond with ideas on how else to handle the situation;

- Overheads—provided in the manual; and

- Handouts—with homework assignments provided in the manual;

Motivational Enhancement Therapy/Cognitive Behavioral Therapy

This program is based on *Motivational Interviewing: Preparing People to Change Addictive Behavior*; (Miller, Rollnick 1991).

This outpatient program is designed for treatment of cannabis abuse or dependence and associated problems in youth age 14 to18. It encourages, but does not demand abstinence. The program is not suggested for poly-substance dependence, including heavy drinking and is not recommended for patients with mental disorders that would impair full participation, nor is it intended for in-patient use. The treatment protocol offers the following five presentation options depending on the level of client involvement and family participation.

Motivational Enhancement Therapy/Cognitive Behavioral Therapy (MET/CBT5): This session treatment includes two individual motivational enhancement sessions designed to help develop and support the client's belief that he or she can change. Counselors utilize the motivational interviewing skills of expressing empathy, developing discrepancy, avoiding argumentation, rolling with resistance, and supporting self-efficacy. Three cognitive-behavioral group sessions are designed to restructure thinking and behavior patterns follow.

MET/CBT5+CBT7: Above with seven additional CB sessions to cover additional coping skills topics.

FSN: Family Support Network: MET5+CBT7 plus additional family intervention (home visits, parent education, aftercare);

ACRA: Adolescent Community Reinforcement Approach—12 individual sessions with parents, caregiver, or concerned others. To learn coping skills within the adolescent's environment. Attempt to change environmental contingencies.

CHAPTER REVIEW

Outlined in this chapter are youth programs that are currently utilized in the United States. They are considered by many, including the *National Institute on Alcohol Abuse and Alcoholism* and the *Center for Substance Abuse Treatment,* to be exemplary models. Outcome studies are currently underway to confirm the efficacy of these programs. The consistent thought throughout is that effective treatment for youth must be geared toward their express needs through peer, family, and individual involvement.

SECTION III: PROGRAM IMPLEMENTATION

We are not in a position in which we have nothing to work with. We already have capacities, talents, direction, missions, callings.

—Abraham H. Maslow

Operational Guidelines and Procedures for Program Delivery

14

Chapter Fourteen:
Operational Guidelines and Procedures for Program Delivery

Chapter Outline

Overview

Characteristics of the Effective Juvenile Justice Treatment Counselor

- Counselor as person
- The technical dimension
- The philosophical – knowledge dimension

The Process and Structure of Program Delivery

- The process of learning and growth
- Facilitating the process of growth and change
- Reflective therapeutic confrontation in managing resistance and ambivalence

Ethical and Legal Considerations in Screening and Assessment

Client Participation Guidelines and Ground Rules

Program Structure and Delivery Guidelines

- Time-frame structure and presentation
- Group delivery format
- Orientation
- Judicial terms and structures

Intake and Admission Methods and Procedures

Principles of Effective Group Management and Leadership

- Methods of group facilitation
- Depersonalizing the leadership authority

Operational Model for Assessment

- Case description
- Differential screen
- Comprehensive assessment
- Treatment process assessment
- Long-term outcome

Chapter Review

Chapter Objectives

- To outline the basic elements, guidelines and procedures for effective program delivery;
- To delineate the characteristics of effective juvenile justice treatment providers;
- To clarify the importance of establishing a balance between correctional and therapeutic roles in the counseling relationship;
- To examine the process of growth and change in treatment as related to the stage of change model and adolescent development;
- To summarize ethical and legal issues for assessment and treatment;
- To delineate the program structure and delivery options;
- To outline intake and admission procedures;
- To present an operational model for the assessment process; and
- To discuss group leadership in the context of manual guided therapy.

CHAPTER OVERVIEW

The purpose of this chapter is to outline the basic elements, guidelines and procedures for effective delivery of *Pathways to Self-Discovery and Change* (*PSD-C*). The characteristics of effective juvenile justice system (JJS) providers are presented including the importance of establishing a balance between the correctional and therapeutic roles and the counselor-client relationship. The process of growth in treatment and the stages that adolescents go through when making changes are discussed. Ethical and legal issues related to the assessment and treatment of alcohol and other drug (AOD) treatment clients are summarized. The program structure and delivery options are discussed and guidelines and procedures for intake and admission are outlined. An operational model of the assessment process is presented, using a case-study approach. The chapter concludes with a discussion of effective group leadership within the framework of a manual-guided treatment approach.

CHARACTERISTICS OF THE EFFECTIVE JUVENILE JUSTICE TREATMENT COUNSELOR

Research over the years has shown that psychosocial therapies have been effective at helping people solve their psychological and emotional problems at a rate faster than that resulting from the client's natural health process and supportive elements in the environment (Lambert & Bergin, 1992). This research has also shown that different therapeutic approaches, e.g., behavioral, psychodynamic, client-centered, "appear to secure comparable outcomes" (Garfield, 1992, p. 349). With both adolescent and adult clients, what is also evident is that the common features of psychosocial therapies may be the major contributors to the effectiveness of treatment (Frank, 1992, p. 393). One set of common features is the treatment provider and the provider's relationship with the client. These include the counselor's personal characteristics, technical skills and philosophical orientation. *Figure 14.1* provides an outline of these characteristics.

Counselor as person

Core dimensions and characteristics of an effective therapist or counselor have been identified (e.g., Rogers, Gendlan, Kiesler & Truax, 1967; Truax & Carkhuff, 1967; Carkhuff & Berenson, 1977; Berenson & Carkhuff, 1967; Carkhuff, 1969;

Carkhuff, 1971; Truax & Mitchell, 1971; Rogers, 1957; Wanberg & Milkman, 1998, 2004). These are the traits of warmth, genuineness, respect and empathy. Such traits translate into an approach of empathic understanding and genuineness, a caring relationship, congruence in presentation, a positive regard and respect for clients, and a concreteness or specificity of expression. It is commonly agreed that these are basic to an effective helping relationship and in producing the desired change in clients. With juvenile and adult offenders, Andrews and Bonta (2003) emphasize the core characteristics of caring, genuineness and empathy.

Rogers (1957) concluded that communicating genuine warmth and accurate empathy alone are sufficient in producing constructive changes in clients. Miller and Rollnick (2002) conclude "the therapeutic skill of reflective listening or accurate empathy, as described by Carl Rogers, to be the foundation on which clinical skillfulness in motivational interviewing is built" (p. 37).

Whether these traits can be learned or whether they are natural to the individual is debatable. However, each of these traits is observable and measurable. Thus, most experts in the field of counseling would also say *trainable*.

Each juvenile justice (JJ) counselor or provider also has a set of values, beliefs, personal experiences, social role orientation, unresolved personal conflicts and personal biases that impact on treatment (Wanberg & Milkman, 1998). An effective counselor will have full awareness of these personal features and how they can contribute to or hinder the delivery of effective counseling to the adolescent client. Biases towards different cultures, different offender types, and representative groups within the society can influence the process of counseling. Adolescents in general and JJ clients in particular are quick to detect these biases. Counselors with unresolved personal issues may find these issues getting in the way of being client-oriented and objective.

Self-disclosure is the skill through which the counselor's personal features and experiences are utilized in treatment (Wanberg, 1990; Wanberg & Milkman, 1998). Self-disclosure is the sharing of experiences, ideas and beliefs that are personal and unique to the counselor. It can enhance the opening up process, increase treatment communication, and help the client feel more at ease knowing that the counselor has real and human experiences.

Figure 14.1   Profile of the Juvenile Justice Provider and Counselor

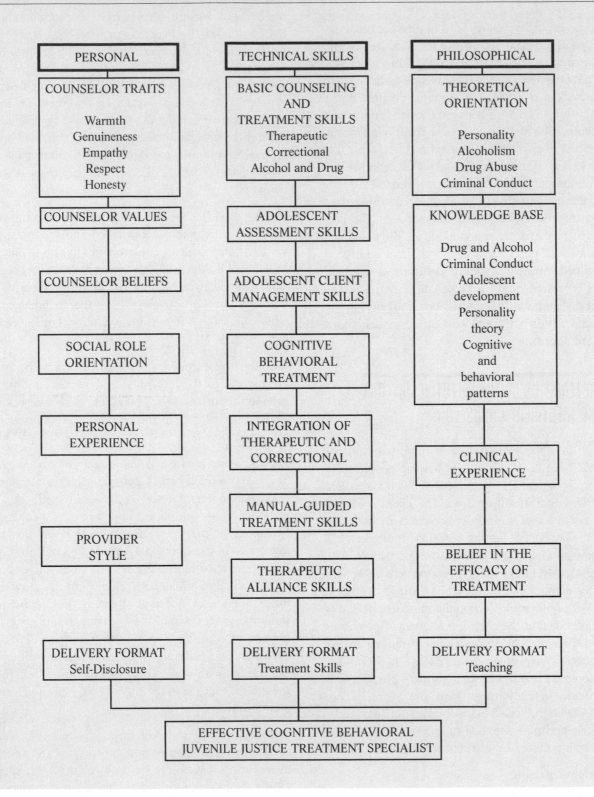

Evidence that self-disclosure is working is noted when, following self-disclosure, clients: (a) share at a deeper and more personal level; (b) utilize some of the personal approaches that the counselor has used in his/her own problem-solving; (c) expresses acceptance of inner feelings and problems; and (d) feel better understood, more supported and then continue to share personal material at a deeper level.

Self-disclosure can also present barriers in treatment (Wanberg, 1990). It can slow down or stop opening up and sharing. If the counselor indicates having been through a particular experience, clients may internally reflect that "there is no reason to go on; the counselor already knows what we've been through." It may cause clients to lose confidence in the counselor. Clients may begin to focus more on the counselor's issues. Self-disclosure may cause the counselor to lose concentration on the client's agenda and affect. It may inhibit clients from seeing the counselor as competent. Counselor self-disclosure of past antisocial experiences could reinforce procriminal and antisocial behavior in the JJ client. A rule of thumb is that self-disclosure is *only indicated* when it is of benefit to the client.

The technical dimension

The second dimension that defines the effective JJ provider or counselor is the area of technical skills. These skills are outlined in *Figure 14.1,* and include counseling, assessment, client management, cognitive-behavioral treatment and building a therapeutic relationship.

Basic counseling skills: A standard for the application of these skills is found in the practice of medical surgery. The skills, tools and instruments are precisely labeled and identified, and the surgeon clearly understands the process of surgery and knows under what conditions which skills should be applied. Imagine during surgery, you wake up and hear the surgeon say: "Gee, that's an interesting instrument. Don't know what it is, but I'll try it."

Applying the same standard to psychosocial treatment, we should have an awareness of the process of therapy and change, label our skills and tools, and then know when in the treatment and change process to apply those skills. We should have an idea of the results of using a particular skill. We would expect no less of our surgeon; our clients should expect no less of us. In psychosocial treatment, we may not always have the definitive knowledge of the process and the skills, as in medicine. Yet we should be grounded in the skills and process that bring around therapeutic and correctional change.

Elements of effective juvenile correctional counseling: There are some salient elements of effective correctional counseling that are relevant to JJ treatment providers (Andrews & Bonta, 2003; Nissen et al., 1999; Wanberg & Milkman, 1998).

- ESTABLISHING A HIGH QUALITY AND PRODUCTIVE INTERACTION AND RELATIONSHIP involves encouraging openness and free expression on the part of the juvenile offender within the context of mutually agreed upon boundaries and limits of physical and emotion expression. Productive interactions always involve limit setting on and disapproval of antisocial and procriminal behaviors.

- EFFECTIVE MODELING demonstrates anticriminal expressions (Andrews & Bonta, 2003, p. 314). Juvenile justice clients are sharp in picking of deviancy and antisocial characteristics and behaviors of other people. This provides justification for their antisocial and deviant behaviors. The juvenile justice counselor must be consistent and unerring in prosocial and high moral values. Providers reinforce criminal conduct when they fail to see their own antisocial attitudes, by using "street talk" to get close to clients, and by expressing cynicism regarding the justice system.

- EFFECTIVE POSITIVE REINFORCEMENT includes approval of prosocial and anticriminal expressions, pointing out the consequences of illegal activities for the client as well as the victim and community and rejecting rationalizations for criminal acts. The hazards of associating with other juvenile offenders in the community and benefits of positive peer associations are stressed. Effective positive reinforcement includes: reinforcing the clients' use of normative vocabulary, beliefs or styles of behavior; not attend to risk-taking talk; supporting taking responsibility for antisocial behaviors; reinforcing session attendance, and completion of homework assignments. The JJ counselor will capitalize on client strengths and assets (CSAT, 1999) and on opportunities to reinforce client changes. A continual reinforcement of abstinence from criminal and drug use behaviors should be an ongoing agenda for the juvenile justice counselor. Rewarding positive thoughts and behaviors requires use of a wide variety of reinforcers. The continuation of a positive and therapeutic counseling relationship may serve as the most powerful anticriminal reinforcer.

- EFFECTIVE SANCTIONING AND DISAPPROVAL. Criminal expressions, attitudes, values and beliefs and acts have characteristic language and thought patterns that may normalize and reinforce criminal conduct. Disapproval of the JJ clients, procriminal talk and expressions while at the same time demonstrating alternatives is a vigilant process. Often juvenile justice counselors express negative attitudes toward the law, police and courts, accept rule violations and disregard of the law, endorse strategies for exoneration and even identify with the adolescent offenders. JJ clients quickly sense these in providers. Effective disapproval and punishment occur within the context of a caring, genuine and empathic relationship. Reduced interest may be a successful disapproval approach. Andrews and Bonta (2003, p. 316) highlight several important components of high-level disapproval in youth correctional counseling. Each one of these can be reflected to indicate high-level approval responses in JJ counseling.

  - Strong, emphatic and immediate disapproval and nonsupport of antisocial statements and behavior (or approval of prosocial behavior).

  - Elaboration of the reason why the provider disapproves (or approves of prosocial behavior).

  - Expression of disapproval is sufficiently intense to distinguish it from the background levels of support, concern and interest that are normally offered.

  - Reduce the level of disapproval and introduce positive reinforcement when the JJ client shows prosocial attitudes and behaviors.

Delivery of cognitive-behavioral treatment: The JJ counselor is proficient in the delivery of the dimensions of cognitive-behavioral treatment: cognitive restructuring, interpersonal skills training and community responsibility and moral development training. The primary goal of these skills is to build self-efficacy in order to prevent relapse and recidivism.

Skills of assessment and case management and program delivery: The essential elements of effective assessment were covered in *Chapter 8.* Client management utilizes the basic counseling skills and integrates the therapeutic and correctional approaches. It is difficult for JJ providers trained in traditional counseling to make sanctioning and punishment an integral part of client management. Program delivery involves using effective group management and facilitation skills, to be discussed later.

Therapeutic relationship and alliance: One of the most prominent common factors identified as contributing to positive treatment outcomes is the counselor-client relationship or *therapeutic* alliance. Therapeutic alliance involves a collaborative relationship between therapist and JJ client, has an emotional bonding component, and a shared belief in the goals and tasks of treatment (Bordin, 1979; Connors et al., 1997; Greenson, 1967).

Research has clearly shown that provider-client relationship is central to therapeutic change and most experts in the field agree that therapeutic alliance and the therapeutic relationship significantly and consistently influence the outcome of treatment (e.g., Constantino, Castonguay, & Schut, 2002; Horvath, 1994; Lambert & Bergin, 1992; Strupp & Howard, 1992; Wampold, 2001). Gurman and Messer (2003) note that of the major research in the study of *empirically supported treatments*, is the effort to identify the characteristics and features of the *empirically supported relationships.* Research findings show that the influence of the therapist as person and the therapeutic relationship may be more powerful than any particular therapy method (Wampold, 2001).

The therapeutic alliance is central to all forms of verbal therapies (Lambert, 1983). It is essential in cognitive and behavioral therapies and a basic element of developing motivation in the treatment of the substance abuser (Miller & Rollnick, 2002).

What promotes an effective treatment relationship is trust and acceptance (George and Christiani, 1981; Miller & Rollnick, 2002). With adolescent clients, this is often a difficult task since their behaviors are often directed at rejecting closeness with and trust of adults. The key characteristics and elements of the therapeutic relationship are often difficult to actualize with adolescent clients. Here are some of these specific characteristics and elements (George & Christiani, 1981; Wanberg & Milkman, 1998, 2004).

- Explores emotions and feelings

- Is intense and promotes open sharing

- Involves and promotes growth and change: it is dynamic, changing

- It is private and confidential

- It is supportive

- Is based on honest, open and direct communication

- Promotes a release of tension

- Involves cognitive learning

- Involves operant conditioning and reinforcement

- Involves reality testing and limit setting

Manual guided or protocol treatment or operationalized models of treatment: Manual-driven treatment protocols have become a major innovation in psychosocial and correctional therapies over the past 10 years. One of the first comprehensive approaches to this method was Project Match (1993) where treatment was structured around three different theoretical approaches: motivational interviewing, cognitive-behavioral approaches, and the 12-step model. The scant research that has been done on provider satisfaction for this approach has indicated a variety of results: very positive (Najavits, et al., 2000); positive but tends to ignore the unique contributions of providers (Addis & Krasnow, 2000); positive and does allow therapist to address the unique needs of clients (Godley, et al., 2001); and very positive, but time to feel comfortable with protocol delivery, supervision more important on implementing the treatment than the manual themselves, and that without modification, the likelihood of using them again was low (Najavits, et al., 2004).

Integrating the correctional and therapeutic approaches: As stressed in several places in this Provider's Guide, effective Juvenile Justice treatment integrates the correctional and the therapeutic approaches. Providers must be able to facilitate sanctioning and punishment when necessary while at the same time utilizing the basic skills of psychosocial therapy and counseling. This is most difficult with counselors and therapists who were trained in doing traditional psychotherapy and counseling where sanctioning, moral development and punishment did not have a prominent role. The JJ provider is encumbered with the responsibility of helping to administer the judicial sanctioning and sentencing of the JJ client.

The philosophical-knowledge dimension

The philosophical perspective provides the JJ provider with a theoretical orientation and knowledge structure within which he or she practices the delivery of services to juvenile justice clients. The effective provider will have knowledge of personality theories, a theory of counseling and treatment, understanding of alcoholism and drug abuse and a perspective on the nature, etiology and development of criminal conduct.

Important areas of knowledge for the JJ counselor are the development stages and the psychological tasks of adolescents (Schulenberg, Maggs, Steinman, & Zucker, 2001). The major tasks of developing autonomy, identity, and social and personal competence become foundational in working with youth. Distinguishing between growth and change is essential (Bustamante, 2000). For example, in the adolescent's effort to develop autonomy, a certain amount of rebellion occurs. The juvenile justice counselor may get caught up in trying to change rebellious thoughts and behaviors that are important in achieving independence and autonomy. Distinguishing between normal growth behaviors and pathological behaviors in rebelling towards authority is essential. Treatment can be directed at 1) facilitating normal growth and development; and 2) facilitating change of pathological behaviors that impede normal development. The change effort must be structured within the normal developmental processes of adolescence.

Teaching and imparting knowledge is the primary skill through which the counselor brings to bear his or her knowledge and theoretical orientation on the treatment process. *Sections I and II of this Guide* have been devoted to providing theoretical and philosophical perspectives in the understanding, assessment and treatment of the adolescent, and more specifically, the adolescent offender.

THE PROCESS AND STRUCTURE OF PROGRAM DELIVERY

A conceptual framework for the implementation and delivery of Pathways to Self-Discovery and Change (PSD-C) is structured around a model of growth and learning and the stages of change. Implementing changes in the adolescent client is done within the framework of normal developmental learning and growth. As we noted above, it is important to distinguish between growth and change. We first look at a model that describes a normal process of learning and growth. Then, we describe a model or approach through which we implement change in the adolescent client, and more specifically, the JJ client, based on this model of growth and learning.

The process of learning and growth

The process of therapy and treatment can be illustrated through the use of the concepts of learning and growth in Lewin's steps of learning (Ham, 1957;

Lewin, 1935, 1936, 1951) and Werner's Orthogenetic Principle (1957). The Orthogenetic Principle conceptualizes development or growth proceeding from "....a state of relative globality and lack of differentiation to a state of increased differentiation, articulation, and hierarchic integration" (p. 126). It is through this process that the cognitive system develops and sustains itself (Delia, O'Keefe & O'Keefe, 1982). PSD-C uses these three response phases as the foundation for change in the treatment of juvenile justice clients (Wanberg and Milkman, 1998).

Undifferentiated or global response: The first phase of growth is *global response* to an internal or external set of stimuli or conditions. This response occurs in a rapid, undifferentiated multiplication of cells in the first stages of a new organism; it can be observed in an infant whose body makes a global response to a stimulus. The organism is *challenged*, even to the point of survival. In the *undifferentiated phase*, the juvenile justice client globally responds to legal problems, being put on probation, committed to an incarcerated setting, being sent to AOD or correctional treatment. There is always a global and often a confused response to all of the new events at certain points of dealing with the judicial process. The adolescent's global response to treatment is often more behavioral, moody, resistant to talking, acting confused, being openly defiant and even angry, showing restless behavior, and being unable (or unwilling) to focus on session topics. Resistance and tension are integral to this stage of growth. In treatment, the goal of this phase is *unpacking*, getting the clients to tell their story and giving clients information about their condition and problems. There begins to emerge a *commitment* to growth and identity.

Differentiation: The second response phase of growth and change occurs when the individual parts of the organism begin to differentiate among each other and become *sorted out*. Different sizes and shapes of cells emerge; the infant can reach out with his arms without the rest of the body moving. "Ambivalence" about existence is resolved and organism identity is defined. In treatment, adolescent clients receive feedback around their story, sort out and label thoughts and emotions, and begin to learn and practice skills that enhance normal growth and that change problem thinking and behavior. Restless behavior moves into verbal expression. They begin to get a sense of direction. There is a *commitment* to and an active participation in growth and in change.

Integration: The third response phase of growth occurs when the various units of the organism begin to show purpose and functional integration. The parts that were sorted out and differentiated are put together as a functional unit. The infant's reach now is for food, which she successfully places in her mouth. For JJ clients, being put on probation or being committed is accepted and seen as part of the process of rehabilitation and change. Life is put back together. The skills learned and practiced in the differentiation phase reach a higher state of mastery and self-efficacy. Freedom and privileges are restored, and irresponsible thinking and errors in logic are replaced so as to lead to more positive outcomes. This is the *putting together* phase of treatment where commitment has led to an *ownership* of growth and change.

This process of learning and growth in treatment is spiral, as illustrated in *Chapter 10*, Core Strategies for Delinquency, Crime and Substance Abuse Treatment, *Figure 10.1*. The process occurs over the course of learning and treatment; or it occurs within any one segment of learning and change. It occurs with both micro and macro life events. It occurs within the client's treatment experiences. The *unpacking, sorting out and putting together* may occur: (a) around one topic or issue in a session; (b) several times in the course of one session; (c) over several sessions around one theme, problem or topic; or (d) over the client's total treatment experience.

The spiral concept shows the client never returning to the same place, but each cycle moves the client further away from the baseline conditions that brought him or her into treatment. The client may relapse, but if therapeutic intervention and change is effective, the relapse does not take the client back to the pre-treatment level of morbidity.

Facilitating the process of growth and change

When clients experience the process of growth in treatment, they go through specific stages of change. We identify three stages of change: *Challenge to Change, Commitment to Change*, and *Ownership of Change* (Wanberg & Milkman, 1998). The model is integrated into the process and structure of therapeutic growth and change as described above. Our three stages integrate the six stages of the transtheoretical model of Prochaska and associates (Connors, Donovan & DiClemente, 2001; Prochaska & DiClemente, 1992): *precontemplative, contemplative, preparation, action, maintenance and relapse*. These three stages are discussed within the framework of the learning and growth model described above and in their application to the *PSD-C* treatment protocol.

Challenge to Change—The Global Response: An initial step in the change process is a challenge to make changes or improvements. That challenge comes in the normal process of the global phase of growth and also when problem behaviors have negative impact on others and the environment. Adolescents first meet this challenge to change when their behaviors result in the loss of freedom or privileges. The JJ client first meets this challenge when put on probation or incarcerated. In this phase of growth and stage of change, the approach is to facilitate self-disclosure around this challenge, to give them information to help them understand their position, and provide introductory skills to work through the challenge stage. JJ clients initially resist self-disclosing and accepting information. They are often unable to verbalize their thoughts and feelings. It is best to view this resistance as ambivalence in the growth and change process; an essential step that people go through when making changes. Other clients may openly share and spurt forth material that, at the most severe level of dysfunction, may be disconnected and uncontrolled. An underlying premise of this phase is that self-disclosure leads to self-awareness and self-awareness leads to change. Self-disclosure is enhanced through the use of client-centered counseling skills.

Phase I of **PSD-C** helps clients work through the global phase of intervention, and challenges them to listen to information relevant to AOD use, deviancy and criminal conduct. It also challenges them to *unpack or disclose* their own AOD use and criminal history and develop awareness of the need to change. The objectives of this phase are to:

- Build rapport and trust in the purpose of PSC-C and the providers so clients will openly share thoughts and feelings about self including the realities of their AOD use patterns and criminal history—to tell their story;

- Help clients develop a core knowledge base in the areas of AOD abuse, the process of cognitive-behavioral change, relapse and recidivism, and the interaction of their history of delinquency, crime and AOD abuse;

- Help clients develop an awareness of their own cognitive sets that lead to deviance and AOD abuse and motivate them to changes and shifts in these cognitive sets;

- Provide clients with the cognitive and behavioral concepts and tools of relapse and recidivism prevention and begin setting goals in this area.

The *counseling skills that facilitate the Challenge* stage are giving information through interactive and multisensory learning approaches, invitation to share skills (open questions and statements) and completion of worksheets that challenge clients to self-disclose. These skills help clients to share concerns and problems, lower defenses, and release cognitive and emotional material. This provides the basis for the next phase of growth, differentiation of feelings, thoughts and behaviors. It is a necessary step to cognitive-behavioral change.

Challenge begins with assessment, which challenges clients to self-disclose through formal, psychometric methods and structured interviews. Assessment occurs in each session as clients explore and share their past history and their current thoughts, beliefs, attitudes and emotions. The *undifferentiated* and *unpacking* phase of growth represents the pre-contemplative and contemplative stages of change in the Prochaska and associates model (2001).

At the end of PSD-C *Phase I*, clients do an in-depth assessment through completion of the *Self-Portrait (SP)* and *Plan for Change (PFC)*. This enhances awareness of life-situation problems, AOD abuse, cognitive schemas and behaviors associated with illegal activities, and identify their own unique cognitive and behavioral patterns. Successful completion of the SP and PFC indicates that the client has become committed to treatment and is therefore ready to move on to *Phase II: Commitment to Change.*

Commitment to Change—The Differentiation Response: Once JJ clients have learned some key concepts of AOD abuse, patterns of deviant behavior, and how people change, and once they begin to unpack the thoughts and feelings related to the treatment focus, there is an increase of commitment. This is enhanced when core beliefs and feelings are identified and issues and concerns are explored in greater depth to identify the targets of change and how change can take place. The feedback loop is the key process through which clients "hear and see" their story, their dilemmas, problems, dysfunctions and pathological responses to the world. This sets the stage for how to correct or change their thinking and responses that led to these problems. The defensive system opens up, allowing increased self-awareness and self-understanding. While the primary focus of Phase I is on helping clients to commit to change, the focus of Phase II is on facilitating use of the Tools for Change.

The *Commitment to Change* phase centers on taking action in making cognitive and behavioral changes. This is done through learning and using the skills (or tools) of change. These skills are listed in *Table 15.1, Skills for Self-Management, Responsible Living and Change*. Clients are engaged in specific coping and responsibility skills training experiences (e.g., intrapersonal, interpersonal and community responsibility skill development) to bring about shifts in cognitive schemas and behaviors. The principles and methods of preventing relapse and recidivism are continually practiced and clients use the SP and PFC as a guide to making changes and as a way to monitor and evaluate their changes.

The following are the more specific objectives of the differentiation phase of growth and the commitment stage of change.

- Through self-disclosure and intensive feedback, awareness, understanding and recognition is developed of high-risk patterns of thinking and behavior that trigger relapse and recidivism;

- Learn and demonstrate skills in cognitive self-control, managing relationships and community responsibility;

- The client commits to engaging in specific patterns of change so as to enhance self-efficacy in preventing relapse and recidivism and commit to changes that strengthen prosocial behaviors and AOD problem-free living.

The provider skills used in the *Commitment* stage include *feedback clarification* skills (reflection, paraphrasing, summarization, change clarification) and *reflective confrontation* (therapeutic and correctional). Through feedback clarification, clients hear their own story, sort out the feelings, thoughts and behaviors involved in dysfunctional and pathological responding and begin to develop a clear perspective of needed growth and change. This process increases self-awareness and self-understanding. Worksheets throughout the PSD-C curriculum provide opportunity for focused self-disclosure, group and provider feedback.

Providers increasingly use *reflective therapeutic* and *reflective correctional confrontational* skills in this phase of growth and stage of change. These skills can only be used after trust and rapport have been devel-

oped with the client. *Reflective therapeutic confrontation* confronts the client with the client, and gives the message that change is really up to the client. It challenges adolescent clients with the discrepancies and contradictions between their goals and expectations and actual behaviors. In this type of confrontation, the counselor is an advocate for the client's goals and expectations. *Reflective correctional confrontation* presents the client with the expectation of society and the community, and challenges the client with the discrepancies and contradictions between his/her thinking and the expectations and goals of society. In this sense, correctional confrontation is an advocate for community and society. PSD-C is designed to blend these two approaches in the treatment of the juvenile justice (JJ) client.

Assessment in this phase of treatment builds on the *Self Portrait (SP)* and the *Plan for Change (PFC)* developed at the end of *PSD-C Phase I*. The results of assessment are used in the feedback process to help clients sort out their own patterns of criminal behavior, AOD use, feelings, thoughts and emotions.

From the Prochaska et al. (2001) model, this phase represents the *determination* and the *action* stage of change. Clients resolve the ambivalence to committing to change and some changes have been made.

Ownership of Change —The Integration Response: In the integration phase of growth and the Ownership stage of change, the growth and changes that have been made are strengthened. Clients now put together the meaning of the intervention experience and *demonstrate consistency* in changes they have made. Although some of the change goals may still be those of some external system - the court, judicial client manager, juvenile justice system - what is important is consistent demonstration of change and that clients internalize the change and claim it to be theirs.

Evidence of these changes comes from client *self-reports*. These include statements of commitment and ownership of staying drug free, not committing crimes, no incident reports during incarceration, improved relationships with family, increased ability to handle stress, etc. Evidence of these changes was observed during *Phase I and II*. The difference between the *Commitment* and *Ownership* phase is that clients talk about "owning" these changes and the desire for these changes independent of expectations from external systems.

There is a consistent involvement and self-mastery in using skills that lead to self-control and positive outcomes. There is a demonstration of self-efficacy or self-mastery over thoughts and situations that are high risk for recidivism and relapse.

In the *Ownership* phase, intervention builds on the client's increased self-mastery in the change skills learned and practiced in PSD-C. Clients tie together various feelings, thoughts and behaviors that have emerged in the overall treatment experience. The counselor then reinforces and strengthens improvement and change in specific areas. Relapse and recidivism prevention (RP) training are continued. Clients are taught to utilize community resources and self-help groups in maintaining change. The following are the more specific objectives of this phase.

- Take ownership and demonstrate maintenance of change over time;

- Develop self-mastery around staying free of drug use and illegal conduct;

- Prevent cognitive recidivism and relapse from manifesting into overt conduct and behavior; and

- Utilize community support resources to maintain change;

- Provide role modeling for other clients who are engaged in the process of change.

The counselor skills that facilitate ownership are *change clarification* and *change reinforcement*. Changes that can be made are clarified, and when change is noted, it is strengthened through the use of change reinforcement skills. Through the reinforcement process, clients experience consistent cognitive, affective and behavioral changes, and begin to feel the strength of the maintenance of these changes. *Phase III* of *PSC-C* is designed to achieve this goal.

Important in this phase of treatment and stage of change is the concept of *attribution*. The most effective changes occur when clients attribute change to themselves (Kanfer, 1975, 1986; Marlatt, 1985b). The internalization of change is most apt to occur when feedback reinforcement skills are utilized in such a manner that clients feel that changes are due to their own efforts. Within the context of the Prochaska et al. (1992) model, this phase of treatment represents both the *action* and *maintenance* stages of change.

Reflective therapeutic confrontation in managing resistance and ambivalence

We distinguish *reflective therapeutic confrontation* from the *traditional methods of confrontational ther-*

apy and coersive intervention. These traditional methods—previously touted as the treatment choice for substance abuse— were employed to manage resistance and "denial"—often resulting (problematically) in increasing client resistance and defensiveness (Miller & Rollnick, 2002).

Adolescent resistance to treatment can be *passive-oppositional* or *overtly aggressive*. The resistance and defiance may be part of normal adolescent development; or they may be a pathological, abnormal, and even out-of-control behavioral response. The former can be dealt with through therapeutic skills; the latter may require behavioral management approaches such as using agency restraining procedures or law enforcement intervention. Therapeutic skills should always be used along with implementing these more extreme measures.

The *first step* in managing adolescent resistance and opposition to treatment involves creating an environment of acceptance for clients to share their thoughts and feelings and then reflecting the client's anger, resistance, opposition and ambivalence. This is done through the use of *reflective-acceptance skills*, which are based on *invitations to share* and *reflective feedback*. For most youth, resolution is achieved when they sense they are being heard. Often, just a few *reflective-acceptance* statements are needed. Sometimes it requires a series of reflective-interactive exchanges. If the resistance and opposition persist and the client is not resolved, then the *second step* is to use *problem-solving skills*. Resolving resistance and opposition may require solving some problem with the goal of making it a win-win for the client and provider and group. The *third* step is to *define and set limits and boundaries* within the framework of reflective-acceptance. Boundaries are determined by the rules and behavioral limits of the group and treatment program and by agency rules and policies.

Several guidelines are helpful when following these steps to manage adolescent resistance and opposition to treatment. *Avoid personalizing* the resistance and defiance. This results in making it a "personal battle." Do not debate or argue with the client but *roll with resistance* (Miller and Rollnick, 2002). Use the *rules and regulations* of the provider and agency when defining acceptable behaviors and behavioral consequences. This depersonalizes the reflective confrontation approach and "puts the onus" on the back of the agency or provider policies. Always strive to maintain rapport and a therapeutic alliance, regardless of the initial negative fallout that might come from setting limits and managing behavior. Finally, remember that an end product of this process is *modeling conflict resolution and problem solving.*

Figure 14.2 provides a conceptual framework for the implementation of PSD-C. It is within this framework that the treatment sessions are delivered with the goal of effecting change and growth in the client. This framework includes the following elements:

- The provider skills required to facilitate growth and change within the program phases;

- The assessment components which provide the necessary data base for treatment planning and client self-awareness;

- The treatment goals that guide the change process;

- The basic CB strategies used to bring about change which are the building stones for PSD treatment;

- The expected client experiences within the respective program phase.

ETHICAL AND LEGAL CONSIDERATIONS IN SCREENING AND ASSESSMENT

The key ethical issues involved in adolescent assessment and treatment are *informed consent, confidentiality, privacy rulings, record keeping and documentation of assessment, treatment process and outcomes.* Agencies will address these issues in their policies and procedures manuals and will have trained staff in adhering to ethical guidelines and legal requirements.

Of primary importance is *informing the client of the purpose and process of assessment,* how assessment information is utilized and the methods and approaches of treatment. The client has a right to receive feedback on the results of the assessment and the provider's perceived progress in treatment. Not only are ethical and legal purposes served, but assessment, intervention and treatment efficacy are enhanced when the client consents for assessment, knows the purpose of assessment and treatment and receives feedback on results.

Federal confidentiality guidelines require that *clients be notified as to their right of confidentiality and privacy* and that they receive a written summary of these guidelines. It is wise to have the client sign a copy of the guidelines to be included in the treatment file.

All assessments should be done within the guidelines of local, State and Federal laws regarding consent for evaluation and treatment, confidentiality and follow-up assessment and evaluations. The *Screening and Assessment of Alcohol-and Other Drug-Abusing Adolescents* (McLellan & Dembo, 1993) and *Screening and Assessing Adolescents for Substance Use Disorders* (Winters, 1999) provide a comprehensive review of the legal issues in assessment and treatment. This section briefly summarizes the most salient issues in this area.

FEDERAL LAW PROTECTING RIGHT TO PRIVACY: All programs that provide AOD evaluation, prevention, intervention or treatment services to adolescents must comply with Federal confidentiality regulations (42 U.S.C Section 290dd-2 and 42 Code of Federal Regulations [C.F.R] Part 2). These regulations apply to any agency that receives Federal assistance, directly or indirectly through state funding, and any agency that has tax-exempt status. The general rule *protects any information about an adolescent who has applied for or received any AOD related services, including evaluation, treatment and follow-up assessment.* The restrictions on disclosure apply to any information that would identify any adolescent as an AOD abuser, directly or implicitly. Information may be disclosed after the client has signed the proper consent form. In some states, parental consent may also be required. Disclosure made with written client consent must be accompanied by a written statement that the information disclosed is protected by Federal law and that re-disclosure is also regulated the Federal confidentiality regulations (42 C.F.R).

RULES ABOUT CONSENT: These guidelines are strict and clearly defined, and the consent form, at minimum, must include following elements:

- Program or agency's name, specific person or agency to receive the information and name of client, and purpose and amount of information to be released.

- The right to revoke consent at any time;

- Expiration of consent, which can be a date, an event (end of probation) or a condition (successful probation completion);

- Client signature, and if required by a particular State or jurisdiction, signature of parent, guardian or individual legally responsible for client;

- The disclosure must state that the information is

Figure 14.2   Conceptual framework for the Pathways to Self-Discovery and Change

INTERVENTION PHASES	CHALLENGE TO CHANGE	COMMITMENT TO CHANGE	TAKING OWNERSHIP OF CHANGE
CHANGE PROCESS	UNDIFFERENTIATED	DIFFERENTIATED	INTEGRATIVE
PSD-C PROTOCOL	Phase I - WHAT?	Phase II - HOW?	Phase III - NOW!
GOALS AND OBJECTIVES	Help client tell story. Unpack feelings, thoughts and problems.	Help client hear his or her story. Sorting, labeling, identifying feelings, thoughts.	Help client act on story. Putting together.
BASIC COUNSELING AND THERAPY SKILLS TO FACILITATE LEARNING, SELF-IMPROVEMENT AND CHANGE	Responding attentiveness Encouragers to share	⟶ ⟶	
	Learner-centered and interactive teaching Group sharing Multi-media presentation Interactive worksheets Rehash discussions	Paraphrasing Clarification Reflection of Behavior Feelings Thoughts Reflective Confrontation Therapeutic Correctional	⟶ ⟶ ⟶ ⟶ ⟶
		Learner-centered education Process-discussion groups Individualized services Interactive worksheets	Change clarification, confrontation: therapeutic correctional. Change Reinforcement: therapeutic correctional.
ASSESSMENT	SCREENING	IN-DEPTH	CHANGE MONITORING
TREATMENT AND CORRECTIONAL GOALS	Build trust, rapport Establish climate of caring Open sharing and self-disclosure Building AOD and CB change knowledge base Increase openness Decrease client resistance Client thinks about change	In-depth AOD, legal and life-situation assessment and develop treatment plan Get client to commit to change. Develop self-control, relationship and moral responsibility skills. Self-awareness	Establish measured pattern of change in AOD use/abuse, criminal conduct Establish self-regulation self-direction self-determination Address individual client problems. Reinforce changes Address relapse and recidivism.
BASIC TREATMENT METHODS AND APPROACHES	Self-evaluation Build knowledge Motivational enhancement skills Develop moral responsibility CB restructuring Recidivism and relapse prevention Skills rehearsal	⟶ ⟶ ⟶ ⟶	

protected by Federal and State law and that re-disclosure of the information is also protected by Federal and State law.

SEEKING INFORMATION AND COMMUNICATING INFORMATION ABOUT THE CLIENT: These endeavors fall under the *confidentiality and privacy rules* and require written consent under the above stated rules. Communication with collaterals, including parents, requires adherence to these rules. Federal regulations allow program directors to communicate with parents if 1) the director or a fiduciary of the program believes the adolescent, because of extreme AOD use or medical condition, is not able to rationally decide whether to consent to proper notification of parents or guardian, and 2) the release of information is necessary to manage a substantial threat to the well-being or life of the client or another person.

REPORTING CHILD ABUSE AND NEGLECT: Required by all U.S. jurisdictions and states. The definition of abuse and neglect, the process of reporting and the reporting requirements vary from state to state. Most state statutes define the report on the basis of "suspecting" child abuse and neglect and in all States, the reporting person is immune from prosecution. Federal rules are clear that the child abuse/neglect exception to confidentiality and privacy applies only to initial reporting and disclosure. The reporting agency or personnel may not respond to follow-up requests for information or even to subpoenas for additional information, even if the records are sought for use in civil or criminal proceedings resulting from the program's initial report (McLellan & Dembo, 1993; Winters, 1999), unless the adolescent consents or the court issues an order under subpart E of the regulations.

DUTY TO WARN OF THREAT OF HARM TO OTHERS OR SELF: Statutory in most states, following the Tarasoff versus Regents of the University of California, 17 Cal.3rd 425 ruling (1976). The basic rules and laws at the state level are that *if a client threatens to harm a specific person, the counselor, or the responsible person in the agency are required to inform the potential victim and law enforcement.* Counselors who determine a client to be of imminent danger to him/herself are also required to take action to protect the individual client. In both of these circumstances, the decision to report and protect should be approached therapeutically within the framework of the treatment objectives and the safety and welfare of the client, potential victims and community. Sometimes, these laws can be seen as in conflict with

the Federal guidelines. The Federal law states that when warning of threat to self or others, the agency or provider cannot reveal that the client is being treated for substance abuse. However, for programs that are exclusively AOD service oriented, this may set up a conflict between the state statutes regulating the duty to inform or warn and the Federal Law, since it may be difficult to not communicate that the client is a substance abuse treatment client. When providers in substance abuse programs exercise the duty to warn and protect requirement, providers should adhere to this Federal law.

Juvenile justice system agencies are obligated to follow the same confidentiality and privacy rules that other systems are required to follow. When a JJ client is referred by the court for evaluation as part of a court mandate, such as probation, parole, commitment, etc., a consent form or court order is required for release of information. However, the length of in-force time for the consent depends on the expected duration of treatment, what specific intervention or treatment information is needed in order to execute the supervision process, type of criminal proceedings and the date of final disposition. Revocability of the consent cannot take place once the client has agreed to the conditions of the court proceedings, e.g., treatment in lieu of incarceration. This allows the court to monitor the progress of the client. The consent form can state that the consent is irrevocable, however, the irrevocability cannot extend beyond the final disposition of the criminal proceedings. Thus, if the condition is that the client consents to release information as to treatment progress during the term of probation, which was in lieu of incarceration, the consent form can state the irrevocability of the consent through the probation time period.

DISCLOSURES NOT IDENTIFYING THE CLIENT: Allowed under Federal and state guidelines. These disclosures allow information about clients to be disclosed in aggregate formats, e.g., part of a database, as long as no specific client is identified. Internal agency management information systems (MIS) may have client-identifying information.

COURT ORDERED DISCLOSURES: May allow information to be released if the client and program are notified that there has been an application for such an order, and both have opportunity to make an oral or written statement to the court. Such a response is done in anonymity through giving a fictitious name so that the response itself does not violate the confidentiality of the client. The court must find good cause for such disclosure, there is a limit to such information that is disclosed and all efforts must be taken to protect the confidentiality of the client.

MEDICAL EMERGENCIES: May be disclosed only to medical personnel where there is an immediate threat to the individual or others. Such disclosures, according to Federal rules, cannot disclose that it is an alcohol or other drug treatment client. All states have statutes and rules that allow disclosure of information regarding the threat of suicide. Law enforcement can be engaged when protecting the client who is of imminent danger to self or others. Federal regulation holds that the individual cannot be identified as an AOD client.

THE HEALTH INSURANCE PORTABILITY AND ACCOUNTABILITY ACT (HIPAA): Went into effect in 2003 requiring all health care providers who do business with insurance carriers or transmit health information in electronic form to adhere to the privacy rules and regulations defined by that Act. Under HIPAA, only the minimal necessary information is to be disclosed when individually identifiable health information is disclosed for purposes such as:

- Pre-certification or pre-authorization for treatment;

- Completion of insurance claim forms and follow-up as necessary;

- Referrals to other professions or programs;

- Filing workers' compensation or disability claims, etc.

Release of the above or other client information requires written consent and/or authorization on the part of the client, depending on the type of information to be transmitted. HIPAA spells out the exceptions which include situations of: child abuse, neglect and endangerment; domestic violence and abuse; severe mental incapacitation, imminent threat to health or safety of self; imminent threat to the safety of others; serious injury or illness; or as legally or judicially required.

All agencies under the HIPAA ruling should have a summary of salient information about the HIPAA regulation and be directed at the HIPAA website, www.hhs.gov/ocr/hipaa. The client should be asked to sign the summary statement of *Notice of Privacy Rights* to verify that he/she had opportunity to read the summary.

CLIENT PARTICIPATION GUIDELINES AND GROUND RULES

The participation guidelines and ground rules are discussed in *Chapter 15* and in the orientation sessions (*Chapter 1*) or the *Participant's Workbook*. These are reviewed within the context of the therapeutic relationship using basic counseling and motivational interviewing skills.

PROGRAM STRUCTURE AND DELIVERY GUIDELINES

Pathways to Self-Discovery and Change (PSD-C) is divided into: three phases of treatment; 15 chapters; and 32 treatment sessions. *Phase I is comprised of five chapters and 10 sessions; Phase II, five chapters and 10 sessions; and Phase III five chapters and 12 sessions.* The various structures and delivery formats are presented below.

Time-frame structure and presentation

Various time-frame structures can be used in presenting PSD-C. Sessions may be conducted once a week, in which case, it would take 32 weeks to complete the program. Here are some other options:

- *Phase I* delivered in a two-session a week format over a period of five weeks and *Phases II and III* delivered once a week over a period of 22 weeks, with a total program delivery time of 25 weeks;

- *Phase I, II* and *III* delivered in a two-session a week format, with total delivery time of 15 weeks or four months;

- Other combinations of the above or a delivery format of three sessions a week in *Phase I* and two sessions a week in *Phases II and III.*

The time-frame delivery format will depend on the JJ client setting, and will be dictated by the jurisdictional norms with respect to length of time clients are on probation, incarcerated or on parole. Most judicial jurisdiction probation terms are a minimum of six months; most incarceration periods are a minimum of four to six months.

Group delivery format

PSD-C can be delivered in either a closed or open group format. The closed group involves admitting a group of clients at a particular point in time, and the same group of clients continues together through the

32 sessions. The open group format provides rolling admissions, where clients can enter the program at any time, but at the beginning of a PSD-C chapter.

A *closed group format* is often not practical for several reasons. If an agency has only one group, then clients have to wait for the next closed group to start to enter the program. Large agencies can have several PSD-C groups going, however, if even the time-frame format of two sessions a week is used, then for an agency with four groups operating concurrently, a client would still have to wait one month before entering a group.

An open group format usually is more practical. Clients can enter the program at certain break points, and the longest wait-time for entry would be two weeks. In this format, all clients would receive the orientation sessions, *Chapter 1*, before entering the open group. The entry points are at the beginning of a new Chapter. The open group format has the advantage in that the "old timers" in the group, who are usually committed to the program, help to manage the resistance of new members.

Group format combinations would involve conducting *Phase I* in closed group over a five week period, and then *Phases II and III* conducted in an open group format. Maximum wait time for entry for this format would be five weeks.

A *format of discrete groups for each phase* is recommended. This would mean that clients complete one phase before entering the next one. Providers may be tempted to integrate *Phases II and III* into one group. The is not recommended. Both the client and provider should make the decision in partnership as to whether a client proceeds on to the next Phase. Mutual or unilateral decisions might be made that a client would not proceed to *Phase II* because of unsuccessful, disruptive or incomplete participation in Phase I. This decision should be based on clinical judgment. However, with some jurisdictions, clients may only be eligible for one or two phases of PSD-C.

Orientation

Chapter 1, comprised of two treatment sessions, is the orientation to PSD-C. All clients are to have this initiation to treatment before they proceed with Chapters 2 through 15. If a closed group format is used, then clients receive the orientation at the beginning of the program. When an agency uses an open group format, the orientation session can be done either in an individual session or in an orientation group. An agency

or provider may conduct one or two orientation sessions a month to accommodate new clients into the program.

Judicial terms and structures

As noted above, the judicial rules, policies and statutes will impinge on the delivery of any manual-guided format. These conditions are the length of probation, commitment to incarceration or parole. Providers need to know the judicial terms under which clients are supervised, and will have to adapt PSD-C to those structures and terms.

INTAKE AND ADMISSION METHODS AND PROCEDURES

Programs of the *PSD-C* genre are usually offered as a stand-alone program within an agency, or as a program nested within a more comprehensive correctional program or system. Under the stand-alone condition, the client is admitted into *PSD-C* through the formal intake and admission procedures of the host agency. The host agency will have its own admission and intake forms and admission policies. In this case, the admission procedure will be more specific to *PSD-C* and the program rules, objectives, curriculum and structure will be carefully described to the client. The initial client referral begins the intake process. It is recommended that the referring agency complete the *Referral Summary (RES)* as shown in *Appendix A*.

Under the nested condition, the client will have been through the correctional agency or institution's formal admission and assessment process. The client may then be selected to enroll into *PSD-C*, as part of a comprehensive correctional program. In this case a second intake procedure should be conducted to orient the client to the *PSD-C* rules, guidelines, curriculum and structure.

In both the stand-alone and nested models, the provider responsible for delivering *PSD-C* should do a formal interview with the client. The provider makes sure all of the required admission forms have been completed and the client is oriented to *PSD-C*.

All clients should complete forms that meet the state and federal regulations of consent for treatment and release of confidential information. In addition to these forms, some states require full disclosure of the provider's credentials and treatment philosophy to clients and the legal requirements under which confidential information may be disclosed without written consent (e.g., child abuse, danger to self or others). Parents must sign a consent form to give permission for their child to be enrolled in treatment, if the client is under the legal age to make the decision independently. For example, in Colorado, a youth 15 or older may admit him/herself to treatment without parental consent.

The following forms will cover the legally required consents to meet Federal regulations and most state statutes.

- Referral Evaluation Summary

- Intake Personal Data Form

- Client Rights Statement

- Consent for Program Involvement

- The Health Insurance Portability and Accountability Act (HIPAA) disclosure form

- Intake Personal Data Form

- Parental Consent for Program Involvement

- Provider Full Disclosure Statement

- Notice of Federal Requirements Regarding Confidentiality

Samples of these forms are provided in *Appendix A*.

PRINCIPLES OF EFFECTIVE GROUP MANAGEMENT AND LEADERSHIP

The ranges of verbal and behavioral expressions of adolescent group members can be extreme. Effective management of the adolescent treatment group and adolescent behavior is essential for the successful delivery of the PSD-C protocol. Some basic guidelines and principles for effective group facilitation and management are reviewed.

Methods of group facilitation

There are three major approaches to group facilitation (Glassman, 1983; Wanberg & Milkman, 1998). The *first is facilitation in* the group. This approach focuses on individuals in the group and is doing individual counseling within a group setting. The vehicle for change is the personal experiences of individual group members.

A *second* method is to facilitate the interaction among individuals in the group or *facilitation with the group*.

Interpersonal interactions help individual clients to self-disclose and work on their problems and issues. The vehicle for change is the interaction the client experiences in the group.

The *third* involves seeing the group as an individual and is *facilitation* of the group. In this method, treatment of the client occurs through treatment of the group. The group "is the client," and the group is the vehicle for change and growth in the individual based on the idea that a healthy group produces healthy members. The same skills that are used in individual counseling are used with the group. The counselor invites the group to share and tell *its* story. The counselor reflects the group's feelings, thoughts, actions, gets the group to change and then reinforces that change. Development of group cohesion and trust becomes a primary focus. The group becomes a powerful initiator and reinforcer of the changes in its members. The group leader will look after the group to nurture it, protect it, and facilitate *its* growth.

Depersonalizing the leadership authority

Adolescents see the authority for controlling and sanctioning behavior as centered in the group leader or counselor. Because adolescence is a time of challenging and questioning authority, there will be a certain degree of rebellion towards the group leader. An effective approach is to allow the structure, rules and guidelines of the group or program to manage the group and the individual behaviors of group members. This centers the authority on the program rules and guidelines and helps to *depersonalize* (Bush & Bilodeau, 1993) the use of leader authority while maintaining group control.

The effectiveness of depersonalizing leadership authority is based on having well defined rules and limit setting on acceptable group behavior. Using therapeutic and correctional counseling skills, the leader communicates to the adolescent group that: 1) the behavior disrupts the task at hand; 2) the client has the choice whether or not to participate; and 3) there are consequences related to not fully participating in the group. With regard to rules, leaders will communicate that the intent is not to force clients to comply, but rather helping them to succeed.

Center the authority within the group: Depersonalization of leadership authority is facilitated by centering a certain degree of authority with the group itself. This is congruent with the "leadership of the group" model described above. The group leader facilitates group responsibility in developing positive behavioral responses in the group. There is a delicate balance between centering authority in the group and using leadership authority. Sometimes, the leader needs to exercise authority to control unacceptable behavior. Most often, the skilled adolescent group leader can get the group to manage and control the behavior of individual group members. This will not work if the group leader gets caught up in a power struggle with the group.

Center the authority within the group member: This involves placing the authority and responsibility with the individual group member on questions of appropriate behavior. The goal is to empower the adolescent by enhancing self-control through skill development. The therapeutic and correctional confrontation strategies involve stressing that the locus of control is always internal and the decision to change or not to change is always within the power of the client.

Keep the focus on the PSD-C themes and concepts: Providers can get caught up with process and interaction at the expense of not focusing curriculum content and theme. Strong process-oriented providers have to shift their therapeutic paradigm to effectively deliver protocol programs. The group does need time to process both the experiences with the group and the content.

Keep the focus on the steps of cognitive-behavioral change: Each group session should focus on cognitive-behavioral (CB) approaches to the process of self-discovery and change. Applying the CB methods and skills to preventing relapse and recidivism is a continual focus of the *PSD-C* program.

Collaborative relationship between provider and group members: Effective group management is directed at achieving cooperation between group members and the provider (Wanberg & Milkman, 1998). Adolescents typically take on the posture of "us or them," which must eventually be worked through to achieve this collaborative relationship. The collaborative relationship helps replace the patterns of hostility and social conflict with prosocial cooperation. Working through angry and hostile attitudes that block communication is a major task in adolescent group treatment.

These attitudes may be due to the perceived leader's authority as preventing freedom of expression.

Maximize individual involvement in the group process. Effective group leadership maximizes participation of group members while at the same time being sensitive to individual differences with respect to group comfort, feeling at ease, and ability to share. As group cohesion and trust builds, even the most "threat sensitive" group member will begin to feel a greater degree of comfort in sharing with the group.

A balance must be established between attention given to group members and attending to the group itself. Although the group leader may work with a single group member on a given exercise, all participants should be actively contemplating the lessons involved. The group may be asked to assist the leader in actively engaging its members.

OPERATIONAL MODEL FOR ASSESSMENT

Chapter 8 provided a comprehensive view of the content, structure and theoretical underpinnings of assessment of the juvenile justice client. We indicated that the process of assessment had several components: preliminary and differential screening, differential in-depth assessment, process and progress evaluation and short-term and long-term outcome. We now spell out a specific model based on those components and specific instruments to fulfill the objectives of the assessment components. The instrument profiles illustrate a client progressing through treatment in a juvenile justice system. The case profile for each instrument is presented. Some of the instruments are provided in Appendix B.

Case description

The case is an adolescent male who was placed on probation at the age of 15 for non-violent criminal acts, including trespassing. He violated his probation on several occasions and, at age 16, was sentenced to a state youth corrections institution, incarcerated for one year. He received the correctional treatment program at that institution along with a specialized AOD treatment program. Prior to being sentenced, he had gang involvement, was involved in selling drugs, and had received AOD and mental health services in the community. He had several arrests between ages 13 to 15. His overall response to treatment services was positive and cooperative. Results from the various instruments administered to this client are briefly reviewed.

Differential screen

Client was administered the *Substance Use Survey (SUS)* for differential screening following his sentencing. The SUS profile, *Figure 14.3*, indicated very high life-disruption from AOD use with primary drugs being marijuana and alcohol. He was not defensive, was open and cooperative, evinced low-moderate motivation, and indicated moderate levels of mental health and mood adjustment problems. The evaluator rated him high on AOD involvement and disruption and he was referred for an in-depth, comprehensive differential assessment, based on the *SUS results*. The *SUS*, along with the scoring guide, is included in *Appendix B*.

Comprehensive assessment

In the initial comprehensive assessment process, client was administered the *CYO-LSI (Figure 14.4), the Adolescent Self-Assessment Profile (ASAP) (Figure 14.5)* and a diagnostic interview. When the client was admitted to the specialized AOD treatment program, he was administered the *Adolescent Self-Assessment Questionnaire (ASAQ)*, which measures motivation and readiness for treatment and change *(Figure 14.6)*, and the *Social Response Questionnaire (SRQ)*, which provides measures of prosocial attitudes and behaviors *(Figure 14.7)*. The *ASAQ* and *SRQ* along with scoring procedures are shown in Appendix B.

The diagnostic interview indicated non-violent felony-type of criminal acts, gang involvement, and high range substance abuse problems. The intake *CYO-LSI (Figure 14.4)* indicated low criminal involvement, moderate AOD involvement and significant problems in the area of school, family and mood adjustment issues. Results from the *ASAP* indicated moderate to high mental health, school adjustment and deviancy problems. He has high scores on AOD disruption and dependence and falls in the drug dependent range based on the criteria of the DSM-IV. His ratings by his evaluator are in the moderate-to-high range on overall AOD and psychosocial problems. His *Global Disruption* score is high.

At intake into the specialized AOD program, he acknowledges needing help, having problems in psychosocial and community adjustment, indicated having made some changes in his life in the area of AOD use and abuse, and was high in readiness to change. Yet, he displays a sense of ambivalence about committing to no drug use. What is most significant is that this client showed minimal defensiveness and a high degree of openness to self-disclosure. Also important, his baseline scores on prosocial attitudes and behaviors were in the low to moderate range.

Overall, this client has a substantial history of AOD involvement, showed moderate commitment to using

drugs at the beginning of treatment, sees drug use as not really a serious problem, yet whose use has caused serious life-adjustment problems. He is an excellent candidate for more intensive AOD treatment and needed strong motivational enhancement work because of his past commitment to AOD use. The treatment plan targeted family problems, mental health, AOD problems, school adjustment and deviancy for intensive treatment focus with primary emphasis on cognitive-behavioral approaches.

Treatment process assessment

At six to seven months following admission into the specialized AOD program, the client was reassessed using the *ASAQ (Figure 14.8)*, *CYO-LSI (Figure 14.9)* and the *SRQ (Figure 14.10)*. His progress was monitored over his eight months in the specialized AOD program through the use of the *Treatment Response Questionnaire (TRQ; Figure 14.11)*, a monthly rating form completed by the client's primary provider (counselor). He showed significant changes in his scores on the CYO-LSI Dynamic Scale (score decreased from the 95th percentile to the 10th percentile). Overall, his CYO-LSI scores dropped, mainly on those scales where dynamic variables contribute to the measurement variance. His scores on the prosocial scales of the SRQ significantly increased and leveled out in the high medium range. Because this client had moderate to moderate-high scores on the ASAQ readiness for treatment and change scores at the beginning of treatment, he did not show marked and dramatic changes in these areas. As expected, he had a lower score on HELP ACKNOWLEDGEMENT - clients having received treatment see less of a need for help. He indicated having made more changes in the AOD use and abuse area; his ACTION score remained about the same. On the TRQ *(Figure 14.11)*, this client was initially rated as cooperative, willing to change, and making changes. However, his scores did show a clear monotonic increase across the eight months of treatment.

Long-term outcome

Two instruments were used to evaluate the client one year after returning to the community: The *Client Manager Assessment Questionnaire (CMAQ)*, completed by the client manager towards the end of a year of community supervision; and the *Follow-Up Assessment Questionnaire*, a self-report instrument completed in a face-to-face interview with the client in the community.

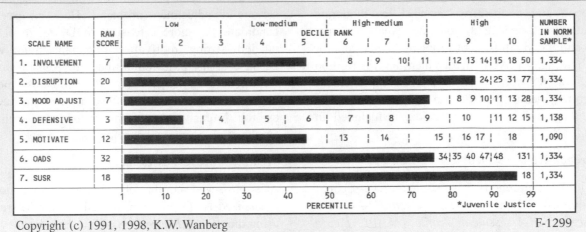

Figure 14.3   Substance Use Survey (SUS)—Intake Testing

SCALE NAME	RAW SCORE	Low			Low-medium		High-medium			High		NUMBER IN NORM SAMPLE*
		1	2	3	4	5	6	7	8	9	10	
1. INVOLVEMENT	7						8 9 10 11			12 13 14 15 18 50		1,334
2. DISRUPTION	20									24 25 31 77		1,334
3. MOOD ADJUST	7									8 9 10 11 13 28		1,334
4. DEFENSIVE	3			4	5	6	7	8	9	10	11 12 15	1,138
5. MOTIVATE	12					13	14		15	16 17 18		1,090
6. OADS	32									34 35 40 47 48 131		1,334
7. SUSR	18										18	1,334

DECILE RANK

PERCENTILE: 1 10 20 30 40 50 60 70 80 90 99

*Juvenile Justice

Copyright (c) 1991, 1998, K.W. Wanberg

F-1299

Figure 14.4   Colorado Youth Offender—Level of Service Inventory (CYO-LSI)—Intake Testing

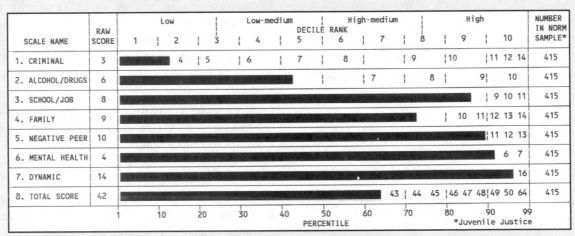

SCALE NAME	RAW SCORE	Low			Low-medium		High-medium			High		NUMBER IN NORM SAMPLE*
		1	2	3	4	5	6	7	8	9	10	
1. CRIMINAL	3	4 5		6	7	8		9	10	11 12 14		415
2. ALCOHOL/DRUGS	6				7		8		9 10			415
3. SCHOOL/JOB	8									9 10 11		415
4. FAMILY	9						10	11 12 13 14				415
5. NEGATIVE PEER	10								11 12 13			415
6. MENTAL HEALTH	4								6 7			415
7. DYNAMIC	14								16			415
8. TOTAL SCORE	42					43 44	45 46 47 48 49 50 64					415

DECILE RANK

PERCENTILE: 1 10 20 30 40 50 60 70 80 90 99

*Juvenile Justice

Note: The CYO-LSI profile was developed on a normative sample of incarcerated youth. The CYO-LSI is comparable to the Youth Level of Service/Case Management Inventory (YLS/CMI: Hoge Andrews, 1994). The YLS/CMI may be purchased from MHS, P.O. Box 950, North Tonawanda, N.Y. 14120-0950.

F0100

The *CMAQ* profile (*Figure 14.12*) indicates psychosocial adjustment ratings in the high-medium range with an overall general adjustment score bordering the high range. His relapse-recidivism score on the *CMAQ* was in the low-medium range. Overall, from the client manager's perspective, this client, who was living at home, was doing well, however, had experienced some lapses, and had a couple encounters with law enforcement.

His self-report scores on the *FAQ* indicated he was in the very low range of relapse, that he was committed to not using drugs in the present and future, that he had virtually no use in the three months and thirty days prior to the interview, but that, by self-report, he was still involved in some deviant conduct, though not enough to indicate full recidivism or to get him back into the legal system. He had very positive regard for treatment staff and rated the treatment program as very helpful. Most significant is that this client readily admitted to having significant, if not serious, psychosocial adjustment problems, mainly in the area of family and mood adjustment problems. These problems would need addressing for this client to move along in the rehabilitation and change process. However, overall, from the time of admission to the one-year follow-up (*Figure 14.13*), this client made very good progress, and was showing acceptable to good adjustment in the community.

Figure 14.5 Adolescent Self-Assessment Profile—II (ASAP II) Admission Testing

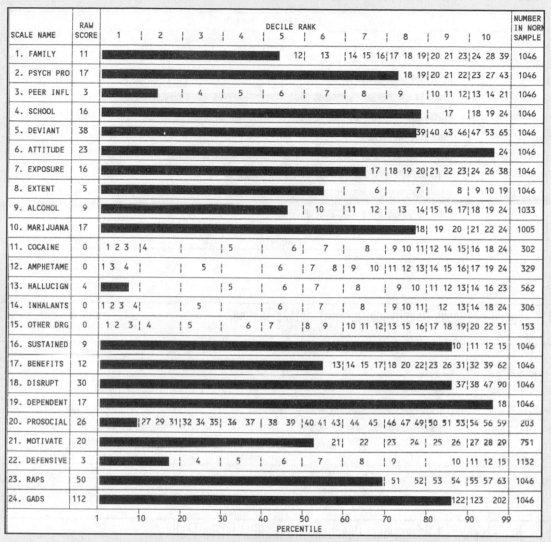

Normative Group: 1,046 juvenile offenders screened for needing alcohol or other drug intervention services and sentenced to a youth corrections institution.

Copyright (c) 1998, K.W. Wanberg

F0398

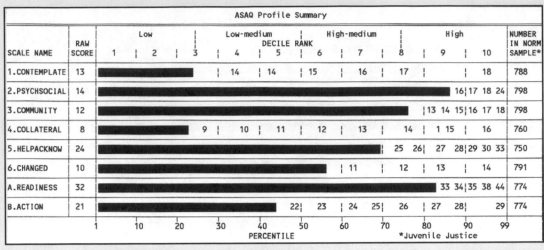

Figure 14.6 Adolescent Self-Assessment Questionnaire (ASAQ)—Intake Testing

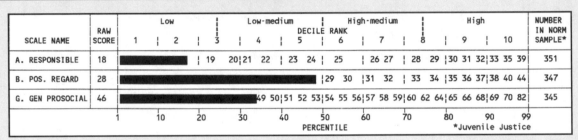

Figure 14.7 Social Response Questionnaire (SRQ)—Intake Testing

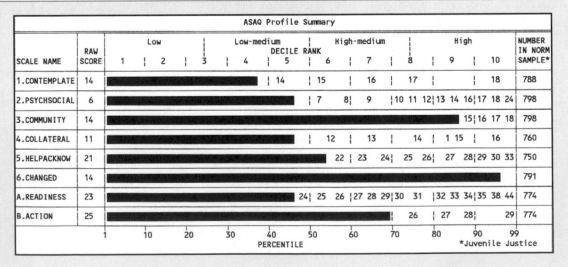

Figure 14.8 Adolescent Self-Assessment Questionnaire (ASAQ)—Intake Testing

Figure 14.9 Colorado Youth Offender—Level of Service Inventory (CYO-LSI)—Six Months Retest

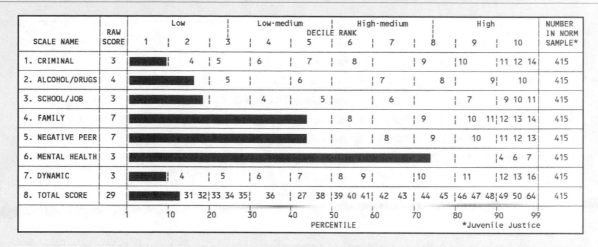

SCALE NAME	RAW SCORE	Low			Low-medium		High-medium			High			NUMBER IN NORM SAMPLE*
		DECILE RANK											
		1	2	3	4	5	6	7	8	9	10		
1. CRIMINAL	3	▓▓▓ 4	5	6	7	8		9	10	11 12 14			415
2. ALCOHOL/DRUGS	4	▓▓▓▓▓	5		6		7	8	9	10			415
3. SCHOOL/JOB	3	▓▓▓▓		4	5		6		7	9 10 11			415
4. FAMILY	7	▓▓▓▓▓▓▓▓▓▓▓			8		9	10	11 12 13 14				415
5. NEGATIVE PEER	7	▓▓▓▓▓▓▓▓▓▓▓			8	9	10	11 12 13					415
6. MENTAL HEALTH	3	▓▓▓▓▓▓▓▓▓▓▓▓▓▓▓							4 6 7				415
7. DYNAMIC	3	▓▓▓ 4	5	6	7	8 9	10	11	12 13 16				415
8. TOTAL SCORE	29	▓▓▓▓ 31 32 33 34 35	36	27	38 39 40 41	42 43	44	45 46 47 48 49 50 64					415

PERCENTILE 1 10 20 30 40 50 60 70 80 90 99

*Juvenile Justice

Figure 14.10 Social Response Questionnaire (SRQ)—Six Months Retest

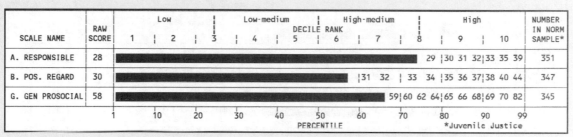

SCALE NAME	RAW SCORE	Low			Low-medium		High-medium			High			NUMBER IN NORM SAMPLE*
		DECILE RANK											
		1	2	3	4	5	6	7	8	9	10		
A. RESPONSIBLE	28	▓▓▓▓▓▓▓▓▓▓▓▓▓▓▓▓▓▓▓▓▓▓ 29	30 31 32 33 35 39										351
B. POS. REGARD	30	▓▓▓▓▓▓▓▓▓▓▓▓▓▓▓▓▓▓▓▓ 31	32	33	34 35 36 37 38 40 44								347
G. GEN PROSOCIAL	58	▓▓▓▓▓▓▓▓▓▓▓▓▓▓▓▓▓▓▓▓ 59 60 62 64 65 66 68 69 70 82											345

PERCENTILE 1 10 20 30 40 50 60 70 80 90 99

*Juvenile Justice

Copyright (c) 1997, 2002 K.W. Wanberg

Figure 14.11 Treatment Response Questionnaire (TRQ) Monthly Rating by Primary Counselor

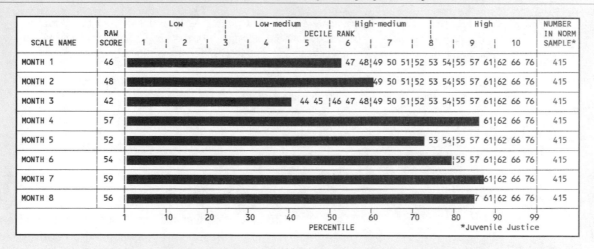

SCALE NAME	RAW SCORE	Low			Low-medium		High-medium			High			NUMBER IN NORM SAMPLE*
		DECILE RANK											
		1	2	3	4	5	6	7	8	9	10		
MONTH 1	46	▓▓▓▓▓▓▓▓▓▓▓▓▓▓▓▓▓ 47 48 49 50 51 52 53 54 55 57 61 62 66 76											415
MONTH 2	48	▓▓▓▓▓▓▓▓▓▓▓▓▓▓▓▓▓▓ 49 50 51 52 53 54 55 57 61 62 66 76											415
MONTH 3	42	▓▓▓▓▓▓▓▓▓▓▓▓▓ 44 45 46 47 48 49 50 51 52 53 54 55 57 61 62 66 76											415
MONTH 4	57	▓▓▓▓▓▓▓▓▓▓▓▓▓▓▓▓▓▓▓▓▓▓▓ 61 62 66 76											415
MONTH 5	52	▓▓▓▓▓▓▓▓▓▓▓▓▓▓▓▓▓▓▓▓▓ 53 54 55 57 61 62 66 76											415
MONTH 6	54	▓▓▓▓▓▓▓▓▓▓▓▓▓▓▓▓▓▓▓▓▓▓ 55 57 61 62 66 76											415
MONTH 7	59	▓▓▓▓▓▓▓▓▓▓▓▓▓▓▓▓▓▓▓▓▓▓▓▓ 61 62 66 76											415
MONTH 8	56	▓▓▓▓▓▓▓▓▓▓▓▓▓▓▓▓▓▓▓▓▓▓▓ 7 61 62 66 76											415

PERCENTILE 1 10 20 30 40 50 60 70 80 90 99

*Juvenile Justice

Figure 14.12   Client Manager Assessment Questionnaire (CMAQ) Six Months Post-Discharge

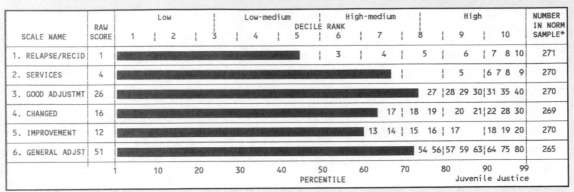

Copyright (c) 1996 K.W. Wanberg

F-129

Figure 14.13   Follow-Up Assessment Questionnaire (FAQ)—Six Months Post-Discharge Self-Report

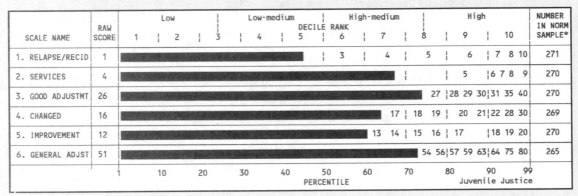

Copyright (c) 1996 K.W. Wanberg

F-1299

Note: The *SUS, ASAQ, TRQ, CMAQ,* instruments and *User's Guides* may be ordered from the *Center for Addiction Research and Evaluation (CARE)*, 5460 Ward Road, Suite 140, Arvada, CO 80002. These instruments may be used without cost when used with clients enrolled in *PSD-C.*

The *ASAP* instrument and *User's Guide* may be ordered from the *Center for Addiction Research and Evaluation (CARE)*, 5460 Ward Road, Suite 140, Arvada, CO 80002.

The *FAQ* instrument and *User's Guide* may be ordered from the *Center for Addiction Research and Evaluation (CARE)*, 5460 Ward Road, Suite 140, Arvada, CO 80002. This instrument may be used without cost when used with clients enrolled in *PSD-C.*

Chapter Review

This chapter outlined the basic elements, guidelines and procedures for effective delivery of *Pathways to Self-Discovery and Change (PSD-C)*. The characteristics of effective juvenile justice system (JJS) providers were presented including the importance of establishing a balance between the correctional and therapeutic roles and the counselor-client relationship. The process of growth in treatment and the stages that adolescents go through when making changes were discussed. Ethical and legal issues related to the assessment and treatment of alcohol and other drug (AOD) treatment clients were summarized. Program structure and delivery options were delineated along with guidelines and procedures for intake and admission. Principles of effective group leadership are discussed within the framework of a manual-guided treatment approach. The final section   used a case study approach to describe an operational model of the assessment process.

The Treatment Curriculum

Chapter Fifteen:
The Treatment Curriculum

Chapter Outline

Initiation of Treatment: Challenge to Change

Cognitive-Behavioral Skill Development: Commitment to Change

Cementing Gains: Ownership of Change

Getting Started

- Program orientation

Curriculum Description

Chapter 1: Building Trust and Motivation to Change

Chapter 2: Building a Knowledge Base

Chapter 3: Talking About Yourself and Listening to What Others Say

Chapter 4: Backsliding to Drugs and Crime

Chapter 5: Making a Commitment to Change

Chapter 6: Basic Communication Skills

Chapter 7: Avoiding Trouble and Playing Fair

Chapter 8: Responsibility to Others and the Community

Chapter 9: Zeroing in on Negative Thinking

Chapter 10: Handling Anger, Guilt, and Depression

Chapter 11: Overcoming Prejudice

Chapter 12: Exploring Individual Intimacy

Chapter 13: Problem Solving and Decision Making

Chapter 14: Lifestyle Balance

Chapter 15: Stability and Growth

Chapter Review

Chapter Objectives

- To provide guidelines for how to establish a safe and motivating environment for CBT with adolescent clients;

- To explain the three phases of the PSD-C curriculum;

- To present a summary and self-rating form for self-management skills;

- To outline tools and strategies for adolescent focused treatment delivery;

- To summarize guidelines for program orientation; and

- To provide a brief description of the content of each session.

INITIATION OF TREATMENT: CHALLENGE TO CHANGE

Many cognitive-behavioral treatment techniques (e.g., Beck, 1995; Clark & Steer, 1996; Leahy, 1997; Wanberg & Milkman, 1998, 2004) can be effectively utilized with adolescents involved in substance abuse, delinquency and crime. However, effective delivery requires an *adolescent focus* in order to best facilitate client engagement, cognitive restructuring and behavioral change. Establishment of *trust and rapport* are essential. Early responses to the treatment setting include *ambivalence, resistance,* and *anger*. Some simple procedures may by used to promote an atmosphere of safety and trust (CSAT, 1999).

- A WARM WELCOME, beginning with the initial intake counselor, and remaining consistent across treatment providers and correctional personnel, especially group leaders.

- ABSENCE OF BARRIERS in the treatment room, such as desks, podiums, speeches, etc.

- Conducting GROUP IN A CIRCLE or other configuration that promotes interaction among the teens in a positive and interdependent manner.

- Addressing the group with a CONVERSATIONAL STYLE, rather than one that is formal and authoritative.

- Using EVERYDAY LANGUAGE, avoiding use of psychological jargon.

- Working with youth to name their ensuing treatment experience in ways that are POSITIVE AND SELF-AFFIRMING.

A supportive ambiance communicates that the treatment program is designed to *help* adolescents *get their lives back on track*, and not merely a context for punishment. By treating adolescent offenders with respect, by *allowing them time to speak* about their lives and perceptions, and by attentive listening, the program conveys that the adolescent's life *matters*, and that treatment is designed to promote health, good judgment and constructive decision-making. Clients are encouraged to consider that active participation in the group can substantially *improve his or her life*, as well as *reducing the likelihood* of returning to the juvenile justice system and correctional facilities. Readiness to change is enhanced by providing the opportunity for teenagers to *meet and talk* with each other, hearing recurrent themes in the experiences, thoughts and feelings of others. Early camaraderie among group participants and treatment personnel sets the tone for deeper trust, support and willingness to share.

Clients express the emotions, defensive postures, and (sometimes distorted) perceptions formed in response to harsh life experiences. They may feel (often for the first time) that they have been heard. However, probing too deeply and especially too early into these memories and emotions and is *not* indicated. Allowing youth to share the general nature of their lives in a "getting-to-know-you," conversational fashion, enhances trust and rapport. Productive topics include *obstacles to recovery* and *apprehension* regarding lifestyle re-adjustment and change. Despite an environment that encourages openness and sharing, treatment providers promote *healthy boundaries* among participants, and are expected to model effective and *unambiguous* boundary setting.

The primary objective of program orientation is to *lower resistance*, drawing participants toward a state of *readiness* – into a treatment attitude that allows for openness to the possibility for change (i.e., from precontemplation to contemplation). These aims should not be pushed, however, as new clients will likely need time to test the limits of the treatment environment. There is ample time for therapeutic challenges and confrontations that facilitate the recovery/rehabilitative process, after trust and rapport have been established, i.e., roll with resistance (Miller and Rollnick, 2002). Optimization of early treatment is first and foremost predicated on provision of a *safe and supportive environment* in which self-disclosure is encouraged and healthy boundaries are maintained.

Trust and motivation are facililtated through straightforward discussion of PSD-C goals and objectives and its interactive style of education and treatment. Participants are *challenged to change* through learning *fundamental principles* of delinquency, crime, and substance abuse, causes, consequences and pathways to self-discovery and change. The *Challenge to Change* phase culminates for each member when he or she demonstrates an awareness of specific problem areas (*Self-Portrait*) and an operational *Plan for Change* (PFC).

COGNITIVE-BEHAVIORAL SKILL DEVELOPMENT: COMMITMENT TO CHANGE

Once treatment has been initiated and a sense of rapport is established, relevant cognitive-behavioral interventions are designed to provide teenagers with an arsenal of tools for cognitive restructuring and behavioral change. Through modeling, role-playing and behavioral rehearsal the PSD-C curriculum emphasizes enhancement of basic communication skills. These provide the foundation for within group interaction, which promotes skill building in the personal, interpersonal and societal domains.

As detailed in *Chapter 9, Foundations of Cognitive-Behavioral Treatment and Chapter 10, Core Strategies for Delinquency, Crime and Substance Abuse Treatment*, the basic cognitive restructuring techniques of *thought stopping, thought arming, and shifting the view* enable clients to choose their own interpretation or meaning of critical life events; recognize counter-productive thoughts, feelings and desires; and replace them with previously determined, and more productive, alternatives. A primary treatment focus is *accurate matching of outcome expectations with probable outcome* (Miller and Rollnick, 1991, 2002). Adolescents learn to evaluate the outcomes of their behaviors in order to develop a more accurate understanding of how their own self-interests are best served through self-regulation. For example, youth explore such questions as: "What situations lead you to think you are being disrespected?". . . " What are some other ways that you can view the meaning of those events?" or "What are the likely consequences when you take drugs to deal with your feelings?" . . . "What is likely to happen when you lose your temper?"

Social skills training is designed to provide clients with necessary life-management skills to foster a crime- and substance-free lifestyle. By developing *social skills proficiency*, teenagers are more likely to break the hold of negative identity, engender an internal locus of control, and derive positive outcomes from learning how to self-regulate thoughts, feelings and actions.

Through modeling, role-playing and behavioral rehearsal during the *Commitment to Change* phase, the PSD-C curriculum emphasizes the enhancement of basic communication skills. These provide the foundation for learning and practicing skills in the areas of refusal, negotiation, assertiveness, managing cravings and urges, empathy, changing negative thinking, preventing aggression and violence.

CEMENTING GAINS: OWNERSHIP OF CHANGE

Upon successful attainment of skill sets in the domains of *cognitive-restructuring, relating to others, and coping with feelings*, the *Ownership* phase addresses skills that sustain *problem-free living into the future*. Participants practice skills in the area of *social responsibility*. Of particular relevance is developing the understandings, skills and attitudes toward the formation of a positive self-identity, free of bigotry and stereotyping. This paves the way for appreciation of how emotional intimacy is the crucial forerunner of sexual intimacy, based on mutual concern, respect and commitment to one's partner. Successful community re-entry is facilitated by the attainment of skill proficiency in problem solving, decision-making, critical reasoning and lifestyle balance. Finally, participants develop strategies for establishing and sustaining healthy family relationships as well as planning for short and long-term goal attainment.

Changes in thought and behavior must be responded to with *internal* as well as external reward. Internal reward (*self-reinforcement*) is necessary in order to maintain positive treatment outcomes. Adolescents are encouraged to develop an *internal process* whereby they recognize the little steps that initiate change, feel a sense of accomplishment in making these small changes, and see how small changes become large as they accumulate over time. For example, helping an adolescent to realize mutually beneficial outcomes in resolving a peer conflict can build self-efficacy in the broad domain of stress management. With time, clients learn to check *newly acquired patterns of thought* against previous experience, and *identify obstacles* in their environments and in personal relationships that may prevent them from using these new alternatives (Salkovskis, 1996).

At this point, the aim of treatment is to develop an *expanded perception of options*, so teenage clients can see for themselves that behaviors such as unsafe sex, substance abuse and crime are self-destructive, and that *more constructive strategies* will take them beyond their current levels of functioning, enjoyment and self-actualization. Small cognitive and behavioral changes will reinforce one another, gradually increasing self-efficacy and an overall sense of well being.

Table 15.1 provides a checklist that treatment providers may use to teach *self-evaluation* of cognitive restructuring and social skills proficiency throughout the program.

GETTING STARTED

Treatment providers are well advised to develop an array of strategies and techniques for engaging juvenile justice clients in the educational and therapeutic aspects of each treatment session. The following techniques are suggested as tools for improving client interest and learning, group decorum and therapeutic gains.

BRAINSTORM – Ask the group to come up with as many solutions as possible to the various ethical and moral dilemmas, emotional behavioral problems or high-risk situations that are discussed throughout the PSD-C program.

SMALL GROUPS – Tackle interactive discussions in small group formats, which may be varied in number and pairing of participants, i.e., some discussions may be organized in dyads, others triads, and some may occur between four or more group members. Program facilitators should periodically re-arrange small group constellations so the same members are not always talking with one another.

ROLE PLAY – Adolescent clients enjoy active and direct involvement in learning experiences and therapeutic operations. Treatment providers may increase participation and the success of role-plays in the early phase of treatment by pre-scripting (on index cards) some of the responses required in a particular exercise, e.g., Joe is offered some alcohol and his initial response is: "Well I really shouldn't. . . but if nobody tells on me, I'm down for it."

MODELING – Treatment providers and facilitators are powerful models for how clients will conduct themselves both inside and outside of the formal treatment setting. Care should be taken to avoid striving for friendship with clients. Instead, the goal is to engender respect through establishing healthy boundaries and by being a role model for positive coping skills and self-management.

MULTISENSORY ACTIVITIES – Youth differ in terms of learning styles and degrees of attention to didactic and experiential techniques for modifying thoughts, feelings and behaviors. Individuals and the group as a whole will benefit through exposure to various sensory formats to accommodate diversity in learning styles and patterns of engagement, e.g., participating in a role-play of how different components of the neuron are affected when someone is under the influence of alcohol or drugs.

CAROUSEL BRAIN STORMING – Youth may rotate in small groups through several flip chart stations in the treatment environment to brainstorm solutions to designated problems associated with the lesson at hand.

CASE STUDIES – Interest in session content is heightened by presenting examples of how others have struggled with similar issues. Discussion is geared toward the positive and negative consequences attendant to their thoughts, feeling and actions. PSD-C features *illustrated case studies* designed as lead-ins to discussion of how the session content pertains directly to the clients in the current treatment group.

CURRENT EVENTS – High impact news topics can trigger a range of cognitive events, e.g., anger, sadness, anxiety, etc., that can form the basis for discussing how the cognitive-restructuring and social skills components of PSD-C may be utilized to improve outcomes in real-life situations.

REFLECTION BACK TO EARLIER LESSONS – Skill retention is enhanced by reflecting back to earlier lessons, showing how earlier lesson content and exercises are relevant to current session topics as well as how the increased repertoire of cognitive-behavioral skills is a process that involves building more advanced skills on earlier skill platforms.

Program orientation

Group facilitators follow the *Welcome Section* of the *Participant's Workbook* to lead clients through why they have been selected for this program and the basic ideas of *Pathways to Self-Discovery and Change*. *Table 15.2* presents an outline of topics covered during the program orientation.

The following sections of this chapter provide an overview of the entire PSD-C curriculum content.

Table 15.1 Skills for Self-Management, Responsible Living and Change

Put the date you started work on the skill and rate your mastery level. Update your level of mastery after each session. Make Good to Very Good your goal for each skill.

	Description of Skills	Date began Example of skill use	Poor	Fair	Good	Very Good
MENTAL	1. Cognitive behavioral map					
	2. Mental restructuring					
	3. Relaxation skills					
	4. Changing AOD use patterns					
	5. Preventing AOD problems					
	6. Managing urges/cravings					
	7. Change negative thinking					
	8. Change thinking errors					
	9. Managing stress/anxiety					
	10. Managing depression					
RELATIONSHIP	11. Anger management skills					
	12. Reading non-verbal cues					
	13. Active sharing skills					
	14. Active listening skills					
	15. Starting a conversation					
	16. Giving compliments/praise					
	17. Receiving compliments					
	18. Problem solving skills					
	19. Assertiveness skills					
	20. Close relations skills					
	21. Manage high risk exposures					
SOCIETY	22. Refusal skills					
	23. Preventing relapse					
	24. Lifestyle balance skills					
	25. Preventing recidivism					
	26. Prosocial skills					
	27. Strengthen moral character					
	28. Empathy skills					
	29. Conflict resolution skills					
	30. Negotiation skills					

Table 15.2   Outline of Orientation of Topics

WELCOME

WHY HAVE YOU BEEN SELECTED?

Past experiences with crime and substance abuse and willingness to explore options.

WHEN WE LEARN HOW TO CONTROL OUR THOUGHTS

We gain freedom and strength by learning how to control our own thoughts. Then we can change our feelings and actions.

WE DO NOT TELL YOU WHAT TO THINK OR DO

The main idea is to help you to understand how your thoughts and reactions decide your future.

WHEN YOU TAKE CONTROL OF YOUR THOUGHTS

Feel the power and excitement of self-improvement. Do positive things for yourself and move closer to your goals of freedom and success.

WHAT DO WE GET FROM DRUGS AND CRIME?

Crime and drugs are exciting. They give us a rush and prop up our courage. They help us get things we think we deserve. They set us apart from the crowd. THEY BRING NEGATIVE CONSEQUENCES.

THE GOALS OF THIS PROGRAM

To feel different. To be different without harming ourselves or others. To gain personal strength. To earn trust and gain respect. To invest in your positive future – WITHOUT USING DRUGS OR COMMITTING CRIMES.

HOW IS THIS PROGRAM DIFFERENT FROM OTHERS?

Designed to be of special interest to people in your situation. Stories of teenagers who have struggled with AOD abuse, delinquency and crime. Illustrations are artistic ways to explain the stories and make them come alive. Each session is designed to provide an exciting and meaningful experience through:

- Modeling
- Role-playing
- Action skits
- Practicing life-skills
- Small group discussions
- You select targets and means for change
- Feedback and advice
- Caring atmosphere
- Support for your efforts at self-improvement and change

PHASE I: WHAT? CHALLENGE TO CHANGE

Build trust and be open to sharing your story and hear others. Learn facts about how you came to rely on AOD and criminal activity. Be aware of how your thoughts play a role in AOD and criminal activity. Understand triggers for returning to AOD abuse, delinquency or crime. Develop a Self–Portrait and Plan for Change.

PHASE II: HOW? COMMITMENT TO CHANGE – USING TOOLS FOR CHANGE

Discover tools and learn skills to achieve Phase I commitments. Improve communication. Avoid trouble and play fair. Develop a sense of responsibility and concern for others. Change negative thinking. Handle feelings of anger, guilt and depression.

PHASE III: NOW – TAKING OWNERSHIP AND CALLING YOUR OWN SHOTS

Put knowledge from program into use in your own life situation. Overcome prejudice, understand intimacy, master problem solving and decision-making, maintain lifestyle balance, build family and community support, practice healthy leisure activities.

PROGRAM GUIDELINES

Abstinence: Be alcohol, drug and crime free.

Be on time and attend all groups.

Take an active part in the program.

CONFIDENTIALITY:

- What is said and heard in the group remains in the group
- True for counselors as well as participants
- EXCEPT if there is a question of harm to self or others
- EXCEPT if someone needs to be held accountable for child abuse

No eating or smoking in group

Counselor and agency decide on breaks and snacks

GROUP RULES

- No side conversations
- One person talks at a time
- No put downs or name-calling
- Use respectful language
- Be active and cooperative
- Be helpful to others
- Other (group brainstorms rules)

PHASE I: WHAT? CHALLENGE TO CHANGE— DECIDING WHAT TO CHANGE

CHAPTER 1: BUILDING TRUST AND MOTIVATION TO CHANGE

Cognitive-behavioral therapy is widely accepted as having promise for individual therapy and group rehabilitation of adolescents who manifest multiple behavioral problems (Kashani et al., 1999). In working with troubled youth, however, there are certain things to keep in mind:

- Adolescents in these programs are not here of their own volition; most have been court ordered (Dennis et al., 2003);

- The identity of the individual plays a large part in his or her willingness to try, as well as the identity the individual forms within the group;

- Peers have more influence on how an adolescent thinks and feels than an adult authority figure (e.g., counselors, parents, etc.).

The first chapter opens with the program orientation (see *Table 15.2 - outline of orientation topics*) including discussions about trust and group identity. In accordance with the therapeutic community principle of the treatment group as *therapist, teacher, and support system*, providers are encouraged to form a strong and trusting bond between group members. Participants discuss guidelines for the formation of a positive group identity. By using activities that progressively immerse the group in self-disclosure and openness to feedback, members begin to recognize each other as individuals that share similar ideas and goals. Development of an *in-group* identity begins in the first session and progresses through the entire program. Providers model "mindfulness" a principle that encourages awareness of our own mental scripts and preconceived expectations (Langer, 1989, 1997), taking care to avoid stereotyping and unsubstantiated generalizations. Willingness to share and openness to feedback are key elements of these introductory sessions. The first chapter sets the tone of the group, as the overture to a symphony foretells how future musical themes will unfold.

Session 1: Getting started

The first session is meant as a launching pad for the entire group. Acknowledgment that some or many group members may not want to be in the program, along with reviewing the guidelines and rules of the program, allow the individuals time to settle in, establish boundaries and develop peer camaraderie (i.e., peers vs. adults, similar backgrounds and reasons for being there). The session revolves more around group discussion and activities than the gaining of knowledge. This allows the group to become comfortable with each other, as well as gain some understanding of how each individual plays a part in the group identity. The activities of this session are designed to progressively allow the adolescent to share deeper aspects of themselves, while planting some ideas about integral parts of the program, e.g., "We can change and control our thoughts and feelings." THE REAL ME activity is not only engaging and fun, but guides members to recognize the existence of individual differences and unique personalities within the group. The TELEPHONE activity not only exhibits the idea of sharing, but also reinforces the knowledge of confidentiality within the group. At the end of every session a "Putting it Together" section pinpoints the important ideas, allowing participants to think about them on his or her own terms.

Session 2: The power of thought

The basic concepts behind cognitive-behavioral therapy (CBT) are introduced through the *six building blocks of change*.

- Our attitudes, beliefs and thinking patterns control us in everything we do

- Everyone likes to think they are in control

- No one likes changing

- We are confused and have mixed feelings about change

- We are responsible for bringing about change in our lives

- Keep the future in mind

The group learns how attitudes and beliefs affect our thoughts, and how thoughts can lead to feeling and action. Concrete examples and visual schema facilitate understanding of the cyclical occurrence of thoughts, feelings, and actions. *Figure 1, Pathways to Learning and Change* provides a visual map of how thoughts lead to feelings and actions and how positive or negative outcomes can strengthen patterns of thinking and acting. Participants discuss the value of the program in terms of long-term benefits as well as the importance of choice and personal responsibility required for successful treatment outcomes.

JEB

Jeb is a seventeen-year-old boy who is in jail for selling a controlled substance. Although Jeb has an above average intelligence, he is the eldest son of a single mother, which has resulted in spending most of his childhood unsupervised by adults. Consequently, he began smoking marijuana at the age of twelve. Since Jeb is logical and opportunistic, he sees the chance to make money and help his family through the business of selling drugs. Jeb constantly makes excuses and finds reasons for why selling drugs is not a negative thing. Jeb does not begin to *accept responsibility* for his actions until he is threatened with an adult sentence, and even then he believes that he could have gotten away with it if he had done something different. At the very base of Jeb's situation is his *belief and attitude* that he wasn't doing anything wrong.

Jeb not only participates in *reward-driven* drug dealing, but he also justifies his behavior and actions. His *expectations, appraisals, attributions* and *beliefs* about selling drugs profoundly affect him. For example his perceptions about the extent of people using and the relative harmlessness of smoking marijuana are false. Even if an adolescent does not have experience selling drugs, he or she will more than likely recognize (identify with) the common belief that "natural" drugs do not harm a person, at least not as much as synthetic drugs. The assertion that Jeb knows more than his mother, the belief that marijuana does not hurt anyone, and the thought that he was not hurting anyone by selling drugs are thoughts and attitudes that adolescents find familiar. Studying Jeb's story and what he could have done differently allows the group to look at their own thoughts and attitudes without feeling attacked by the program and/or provider.

CHAPTER 2: BUILDING A KNOWLEDGE BASE

Risky cognition is one of the most influential variables in the development of a deviant adolescent identity (e.g., little knowledge combined with positive outcome expectancies from AOD behavior and criminal conduct). While the provider's task is to counsel and lead the group towards *empowerment and self-efficacy*, education also plays an important role in preventing relapse and recidivism. While *Chapter 1* introduces the principles of cognitive-behavioral therapy (CBT), its primary focus is building *within-group trust and rapport* and a therapeutic alliance with the counselor and treatment agency.

Beginning with the concept that behavioral disturbances can be changed by targeting the *thought processes* behind them (Hollen & Beck, 1986), this chapter introduces how thoughts and attitudes underlie mood and emotions (Burns, 1989) and *how a person's interpretation of a situation*—not the situation itself—triggers emotions and thoughts (Salkovskis, 1996). Included in the education aspect of this chapter are the biological and mental effects of substance use, and how crime and AOD behavior work together, defeating positive outcomes for an individual.

Session 3: How thoughts and feelings affect behavior

After a review of the previous session's discussion on *thoughts, attitudes, and beliefs*, the group is introduced to the principles of the cognitive-behavioral model. Frequently, adolescents with behavioral difficulties suffer from an *external locus of control*. By introducing the idea that the individual's beliefs, attitudes, and thoughts about a situation actually control actions and feelings, adolescents hear the message that they can control what happens in their lives.

The group is introduced to the *concepts of learning* (i.e., how behavioral outcomes affect future responsibilities), and how certain expectations and behaviors can be learned and thus unlearned. By learning the *principles of learning and change*, the group develops the foundation for building social skills, competence, and self-efficacy later on in the program. In order to place abstract ideas into a context that is familiar, the activities of this session focus on developing an in-group identity (e.g., *Rules of our Group*). The role-plays and interpretation of *Jarrod's Story* act as a lead-in to discussion about each individual's experience with thoughts having power over feelings and actions. This discussion sets the stage for personal reflection on *thought-mood-action links*, as called for in the session worksheets. In addition to promoting increased understanding of the principles of learning, interactive group activities serve the dual purpose of strengthening peer relationships.

Session 4: Basic knowledge about drug abuse and addiction

Rather than thinking about the indirect and *withdrawal effects* of pleasure inducing drugs, users generally focus on the expected positive results, e.g., excitement or euphoria. Lack of information and a failure to realize how abuse can progress to addiction can lead to long-term harm. This session is mostly educational, progressing from last session's discussion of the *concepts of learning* to understanding how drugs and alcohol affect *mind, mood and behavior*. The lesson outlines how outcomes of use can lead to a cycle of addiction. An important component is the *drug test*, which is administered at the beginning of the session. The group is encouraged to recognize how *peer driven knowledge* differs from what really occurs in the mind and body. Facts can lead to informed thoughts and actions concerning drug use.

Session 5: Criminal conduct and the influence of drugs

With the progressive building and upward spiraling targeted throughout this curriculum, *Session 5* applies what was learned in *Sessions 3 and 4* to criminal activities. By this point, the group has become familiar with the interaction of thoughts, actions, and emotions relative to drugs. Now they can transfer this knowledge to other problem areas (i.e., delinquency and crime). The group takes on a more direct and individualized approach. Worksheets promote reflection on how each group member would successfully handle specific high-risk situations. Participants practice arming themselves with positive thoughts and actions in the face of triggers for substance abuse, delinquency and crime.

JARROD

Jarrod is a fifteen-year-old boy who suffers from role confusion. He is not sure where he fits in the outside social environment. Although this may be due to lack of parental support and lack of an adult male role model, it has more to do with ongoing depression coupled with deficits in social adaptability and lack of self-confidence. Jarrod's identity is easily swallowed by Mary's, allowing her to influence him to take drugs. Following along with the addiction cycle, specifically referred to as *Learning Concept 1: Turning on Positive Feelings*, Jarrod begins to spend considerable time with Mary and to take Ecstasy every weekend. Due to his errors in thinking (related to the effects of the drug), Jarrod drives while high, resulting in the death of Mary and another woman. This story exemplifies how drug use can turn into addiction without conscious choice, and how drug use can lead to criminal conduct, causing the situation to be worse than before drug use began.

CHAPTER 3: TALKING ABOUT YOURSELF AND LISTENING TO WHAT OTHERS SAY

While empowering youth to take charge of their lives is a theme that cuts across all content and exercises of the curriculum, social competence is emphasized within certain skill-building sessions. For some adolescents who lack effective communications skills, social competence is difficult to achieve in the face of unsatisfying interpersonal interactions and relationships. Effective communication is of vital importance in building trust, solving problems, negotiating, being assertive and attaining safe satisfaction of wants and needs.

Session 6: Learning communication skills

Continuing with the cognitive-behavioral principle that mental preparation precedes skill development and rehearsal (Meichenbaum & Novaco 1985), this session begins with a discussion of the two components of communication. *Self-oriented* communication consists of self-disclosure and receiving feedback; *other-oriented* communication entails asking open questions, active listening, and giving feedback. Activities allow for the practice of these basic communication skills. Participants are then introduced to methods of recognizing their own thought patterns through utilization of the three primary tools for change: *autobiography, journal writing, and thinking reports*. These enable us to take charge of our lives by recognizing how we have been influenced by our past and the connections between current thoughts, feelings, actions and resultant consequences.

Session 7: Sharing your story

After a review of how memories of neglect, mistreatment or negative role models can affect goals and choices, this session begins to take a more individual look. For the first time, participants are asked to *share something very personal* about themselves. Providers should advise the group about confidentiality guidelines and use caution to prevent re-traumatization from discussing emotionally charged events. The group is then directed to take one of several chances to do a check-up on themselves and their personal growth thus far into the curriculum. Participants re-examine their answers and current scores on inventories and questionnaires that they took at the beginning of the program. They have an opportunity for increased self-disclosure and honesty. Activities and worksheets emphasize that although adverse life experiences play a role in problems, it is the individual's own thoughts and responses to the experiences that perpetuate problems.

CYNTHIA

Cynthia is an example of a "throwaway" adolescent who left home due to excessive physical abuse and was never searched for by her parents. Due to the young age that she ran away, Cynthia has no work skills and very few social skills. Cynthia found a place to stay with the help of a prostitute, but has to sell her body in order to pay for the room and earn money for food. Cynthia thinks there is nothing of value in her except her sexuality. In the very essence of her prostitution, she plays into the male entitlement of sex, and continues her declining self-esteem and self-efficacy. The most important thing that Cynthia lacks is empowerment over herself and her environment.

CHAPTER 4: BACKSLIDING TO DRUGS AND CRIME

From a *strengths-based perspective*, it is important to *promote resiliency* in order to avoid relapse and recidivism. The prelude to relapse/recidivism prevention skills is education about the nature of high-risk situations as well as how thoughts and emotions can trigger substance abuse and crime. Self efficacy, in which the treatment goals become the goals of the individual, is predicated upon mastery of trials that will be faced in the real world, outside of treatment supervision. Recognition of *trigger thoughts and high-risk situations* continues the cognitive restructuring (Leahy, 1996) that is imperative for successful treatment outcomes. Becoming aware of the automatic thoughts that lead to AOD behavior, delinquency and crime is the first step. This chapter attempts to bring the group to a point of analyzing thought patterns in an effort to consider consequences and healthier alternatives to previously destructive actions. Toward establishing an *internal locus of control* (leading to a pro-social lifestyle) the curriculum stresses the importance of acknowledging *personal responsibility* for our actions, which are brought about by our thoughts and emotions, for which we also take personal responsibility.

Session 8: Identifying triggers and your high-risk situation

Session 8 is informational in that the group learns about how high-risk thoughts and situations act as triggers for problem behaviors. The relationship between *relapse* (returning to pre-treatment levels of

substance abuse) and *recidivism* (committing a crime) and the beliefs and thoughts that lead up to *violating an important rule*, is firmly established. The group studies elemental steps that can be taken to avoid *relapse and recidivism*, and how these safeguards are under the individual's control. The activities in this session focus on individually completed worksheets so each adolescent is able to comprehend how the relapse/recidivism information plays a role in his or her own situation.

Session 9: Learning how to avoid trouble

The last session of this chapter, *Backsliding to Drugs and Crime*, focuses mainly on how thoughts, emotions, and actions can play an important role in relapse and recidivism. This session begins with a discussion on the nature of *relapse/recidivism erosion*, and how individuals can recognize the onset of relapse/recidivism in their own lives. The intent of this session is to establish analytical observation of the adolescent's own thoughts and actions and development of the necessary skills to prevent relapse and recidivism. Emphasis is placed on the *rule violation effect* and *self-blame* because these elements hold the keys for progression from lapse to relapse and from impulse to full-blown acting out. Through self-knowledge and finely tuned relapse/recidivism prevention skills, the individual can successfully intervene in the relapse/recidivism process.

TYLER

Tyler is a seventeen-year-old male who is artistic and may suffer from clinical depression. Intelligent and excelling in his non-conformist identity, Tyler tends to hide from his problems and prefers isolation and withdrawal rather than being in the spotlight. At a social event Tyler finds himself in a high-risk situation for relapse to heroin. Instead of leaving, he chooses to participate in using. Tyler quickly finds himself confused, and begins the erosion to relapse. The step that most contributes to Tyler's relapse is the *Rule Violation Effect*, in which Tyler is unable to confront his relapse and still move on with his new identity.

CHAPTER 5: MAKING A COMMITMENT TO CHANGE

Up to this point, the group has learned about how beliefs, attitudes, and thoughts that underlie mood and emotions (Burns, 1989) can affect the emotions and choices that are made (Salkovskis, 1996). Most important is the notion that the *individual is responsible* for his or her actions (Franks & Barbach, 1983), as represented through an *internal locus of control*. Although it is unlikely that these concepts have been completely internalized, *Chapter 5* marks the conscious decision to move from *Phase I* which focuses on building trust and gaining knowledge about CBT, substances, communication, and relapse and recidivism prevention, to *Phase II*, which is learning how to use the *tools for change*, initially explored during *Phase I*. The group is encouraged to take responsibility for the situations they find themselves in (e.g., no longer blaming the courts, their family, neighborhood or police for their current situation), and to begin using self-awareness to start the change process.

Session 10: Developing your Plan For Change (PFC)

Although introduced in *Phase I*, cognitive restructuring begins to take a main focus. The group is introduced to the *stages of change model*, and then asked to individually fill out worksheets to help focus their specific desires, goals, and responsibilities. Beginning with self-rating and analysis for their stage of change in criminal thinking and conduct, the individual is then asked to list strengths and problems to work on throughout the rest of the program. A *Self-Portrait* (rating problem severity in exposure and disruption from substance abuse and crime, as well as current thoughts, attitudes, associates and life conditions that perpetuate risk) is developed, followed by a *Plan for Change*. Due to the amount of effort and time necessary, these self-evaluations are completed with the *Treatment Provider* in individual sessions. The session prepares individual group members for the next stage, which is using the tools learned in order to bring about change, empowerment, and self-efficacy. Successful completion of *Session 10* marks the movement of group participants from *Phase I – Challenge to Change* to *Phase II – Commitment to Change*.

MIKE

Mike is a sixteen-year-old male who does not exhibit any major mental issues. While claiming to enjoy drinking just to have fun, Mike's drinking is extensive and he exhibits strong symptoms for alcoholism (inability to stop, blacking-out, etc.). The story suggests a biological predilection toward addiction, and early influence from parents or family environment. Mike is at-risk, mostly due to early onset of substance (alcohol) use and his cognitive expectancies from alcohol. Mike's mother's excessive drinking also increases his risk behavior. A lack of other behavioral or affective problems lends to the idea that Mike suffers

primarily from a substance disorder. After considering the negative legal and relationship consequences that seem to be related to his drinking problem, Mike becomes committed to quitting.

PHASE II: HOW? CHALLENGE TO CHANGE— USING THE TOOLS FOR CHANGE

CHAPTER 6: BASIC COMMUNICATION SKILLS

The goal of *Chapter 6* is to refine and practice basic skills to avoid relapse and recidivism. Adolescents with deviant identities frequently have not had the socialization required to play a positive role in society. Due to *interpersonal skill deficits* the teenager falters in developing healthy relationships. Poor communication skills – such as *low levels of assertiveness and refusal*, are among the most prominent of risk factors for AOD and criminal conduct (Scheier et al., 1997). Through *social skills training* the adolescent can become more socially competent, as well as develop the necessary problem solving skills to avoid relapse or recidivism. In *Chapter 3*, the concept of communication was addressed, with a focus on what communication is and what it can do to help a person gain what is desired. *Chapter 6* takes the ideas learned in *Chapter 3* into a larger perspective, with more in-depth instruction and practice. By learning to use these skills, youth are better able to develop healthy, productive, and positive relationships with others, which can help them avoid relapse and recidivism. Being able to effectively communicate helps develop a higher sense of esteem and an increased identification with society at large. Acquiring assertiveness skills and being able to practice them in a safe environment is one more step toward social competence, which in turn protects from high-risk encounters in every-day life.

Session 11: Give and take with others

Opening with a review of skills that were covered in *Chapter 3*, this session offers activities for the practice of communication skills including *how to start a conversation* and *how to give and receive compliments*. Adolescents with low self-esteem may feel uncomfortable in situations with people they do not know. By becoming more comfortable with starting conversations, youths become more open to the outside environment and community. In addition, individuals with low self-esteem and negative identity have difficulty hearing positive comments about themselves and they often assume the other person is lying, making fun, or wants something from them. Learning to give and receive compliments in a safe environment can help the adolescent overcome distortions of self-concept.

Session 12: Assertive skills development

Peers can have powerful positive or negative influences on adolescents, especially youth who have *distorted self-concepts* in combination with peers who manifest *antisocial attitudes* (Ray & Ksir, 2002). An adolescent may not even realize that how they deal with daily situations can have a negative effect on them and can lead to AOD and criminal behavior. In this session, the group learns about ineffective ways to handle conflict, with *assertive techniques* being offered as a positive alternative. This directive instruction (Meichenbaum & Novaco, 1985; Arnkoff & Glass, 1992; Leahy, 1996) not only offers a positive alternative, but also provides a safe environment in which the adolescent can practice the newfound skill.

CRYSTAL

Crystal is a fourteen-year-old girl who does not know how to effectively communicate with her parents. Although *passive* with her friend, to the point of shoplifting to impress her, Crystal is *passive-aggressive* and *aggressive* with her parents. If Crystal had been more *assertive* with her friend, she would not have gotten in trouble for shoplifting. Crystal would benefit from learning how to improve communication with her parents in order to avoid fighting and blaming, and by becoming more assertive with her friends.

CHAPTER 7: AVOIDING TROUBLE AND PLAYING FAIR

The primary goals of this curriculum are to learn skills of how to *avoid high-risk situations* and to gain control over *high-risk thoughts and feelings*. Group participants not only learn to distinguish between *cravings and urges*, but how to attain need gratification without compromising their health and well being or having a negative impact on others, i.e., they learn and practice the skills of *negotiation*. By exploring alternative ways to cope with cravings and urges, the group begins to understand new ways of dealing with their lives. In short, the individual develops alternative means to satisfy needs and longings previously fulfilled through *deviant actions* and *negative peer associations*. Participants complete worksheets to match their former expectations of substance abuse and crime with probable outcomes. Up to this point, the expected outcomes from crime and AOD behaviors have been positive, but by realizing that probable outcomes for future goal attainment are negative, youth can break away from distorted outcome expectancies and begin a fresh start.

Session 13: Managing cravings and urges about crime and substances

Group members are taught how expected outcomes can lead to a *craving* (mental desire) or *urge* (physical movement) toward a need-gratifying object or experience. A review of high-risk situations and triggers (*Chapter 4*) moves the session into a discussion of appropriate tools for dealing with cravings and urges so as not to succumb to the desires. The important *cognitive restructuring* (Leahy, 1996) techniques of *thought stopping, shifting the view and positive thought arming* are reintroduced as effective and self-controlled methods to avoid relapse/recidivism. Participants make a plan that they feel most comfortable using in the case of cravings and urges, increasing his or her self-efficacy in dealing with high-risk situations. By confronting maladaptive automatic thoughts, the adolescent can effectively begin the process of self-control.

Session 14: How to bargain and when to say no

Problem solving techniques are something that most people pick up through the process of modeling. For an adolescent who has a negative identity, and often little if any social support, problem solving is a developmental step that may have been skipped altogether. Because of the program's cyclical and progressive nature, the *negotiation* session follows discreetly behind the *communication* sessions. By this point, group members know how to communicate effectively, as well as how to be *assertive* about what they want. Communication and assertion are not the only problem solving techniques needed, however. *Negotiation skills* can effectively allow the individual to gain what he or she desires through socially acceptable methods without having to resort to emotional or physical abuse or crime. Similarly, the ability to say "no" and stand up for one's self is a major step in avoiding relapse and recidivism. In order to recognize when to *negotiate* and when to say "no," group members learn to identify when a demand is unreasonable or counterproductive to what they are trying to achieve.

Anthony is a young male who lives in a neighborhood that is controlled by a gang. Having been raised only by his mother, Anthony grew up idolizing the older gang members in his neighborhood. Although he exhibits some signs of *Oppositional-Defiant Disorder,* the money and power that the gang represented became Anthony's *ideal self*—while his *feared self* is to be "a nobody" who is poor and without power. The gang offers Anthony a place in which he can commit crimes, vandalize, and act out with violence toward a society that hasn't offered him anything, i.e., his ideal-self (albeit deviant) suppresses his feared-self (Pulkkinen, Maennikkoe, & Nurmi, 2000). With the death of his friend, Anthony becomes confused and unsure whether to stay in the gang. He realizes that, although the gang offers him things that represent a strong male, the gang has also taken away someone who was very close to him. With the help of a counselor, Anthony is able to view the previously expected outcomes versus the probable outcomes of his gang involvement, and although the desire to remain in the gang is strong, his will to succeed is stronger.

CHAPTER 8: RESPONSIBILITY TO OTHERS AND THE COMMUNITY

Responsibility, self-awareness, and consideration for others are important aspects of any treatment that attempts to change the thoughts and behaviors of troubled youth. As explained by *social control theory* (Steinberg, 1999), it may not be the complete lack of bonds, but rather the bonding of the individual to *unconventional or negative values* and morals that leads to extensive AOD and illegal behavior. Although sometimes handicapped by the disadvantage of having been exposed to negative sets of morals and values, it is the individual's personal responsibility to accept or reject the thoughts and beliefs of others.

Broom (2000) reports that *increased empathy* can decrease juvenile participation in crime, possibly through a re-alignment with social values and ideals. Group members develop self-awareness of how and why they formulated ideas about the outside world, and then discover how *inner conflict* can arise from going against our own standards of right and wrong. Participants examine behavioral patterns formerly taken for granted and asked to consider rejecting some of the ideas they have always held to be truth. This chapter brings about a personal examination of morals

and values by presenting a series of moral dilemmas in which ill-considered personal choices (e.g., drugged or drunk driving) lead to potentially catastrophic outcomes.

Session 15: Understanding values and moral development

Development of morals and values occur early in a child's development, *becoming internalized* before the individual gains enough self-awareness to be knowledgeable about the impact and importance of what they have accepted. Unethical guidelines may be acquired in dysfunctional homes or from the streets. Worksheets are designed to facilitate exploration and differentiation between *morals, values and community standards* (norms), in order to clarify (and develop) *internal standards* for personal conduct. The basic principle of this session is that harm to yourself and others can be avoided by becoming aware of your personal values and morals, as well as community and cultural standards, thereby enabling self-discovery and change.

Session 16: Understanding and practicing empathy

By learning and practicing *empathy*, teenagers modify cognitive distortions and irrational beliefs about society (Ellis & Harper, 1961). Increasing the individual's understanding and acceptance of society's desires and needs allow for more positive experiences to occur. Activities and worksheets in this session are designed to teach the skill of immersing oneself in another person's experience (putting yourself in someone else's shoes). By challenging the group with *moral dilemmas* (i.e., situations in which one person's goals are harmful to another) participants practice viewing a situation from someone else's perspective. In tandem with communication and problem solving skills, a *capacity for empathy* helps to promote positive experiences with others and in the community, strengthening the capacity to achieve meaningful and caring relationships throughout life.

HUNTER

Hunter is a fifteen-year-old male who lives with his father. Exhibiting symptoms of *conduct disorder,* Hunter lives in a world of black and white with values and morals that have been set and solidified by his father. Hunter is egocentric with the strong negative identity of a loner and true believer in *Social Darwinism,* i.e., survival of the fittest. When Hunter meets a homeless girl, his values and morals come into question. Although not enough of a moral dilemma to change his beliefs, Hunter's interaction with the girl brings into question his value that homeless people are a waste to society. Although he does not end up changing his values and rather chooses to run away from the issue, Hunter has now begun to understand that not all things are black and white. He has entered a *contemplation stage* regarding his beliefs about those who are less fortunate than he is.

CHAPTER 9: ZEROING IN ON NEGATIVE THINKING

The development of self-esteem and self-efficacy may become negative and counterproductive in an adolescent who has been compromised due to outside influences and experiences. Self-defeating thought patterns, which can be found in thinking errors and distortions, often contribute to elevated risk (Jessor et al., 1998). This chapter takes specific negative thoughts and teaches participants the skills of how to recognize and change them in order to avoid negative *emotions, actions and dire consequences (see Table 15.1 - Skills for self-management, responsible living and change)*. In order to stop the cycle of AOD abuse and criminal behavior, group participants develop a sense of positive interaction with the world at large, which occurs when negative thoughts are replaced with alternative appraisals, expectations and attributions (short-term cognitive structures) as well as a revised set of beliefs, attitudes and values (long-term cognitive structures).

Session 17: Recognizing and changing negative thoughts

Recognition of different types of negative thoughts (i.e., *expecting the worst; self put downs; jumping to conclusions; self-blame; negative view of the world*) facilitates implementation of specific strategies for cognitive restructuring: *thought stopping, thought replacement* and *positive self-talk*. In this session, group members learn about the different types of negative thoughts, and through structured activities, they examine how *negative thinking causes problems* for themselves and others. Worksheets and activities focus on how negative thoughts have led to problems in the past and how these patterns can be modified through cognitive restructuring. Personal responsibility, resiliency, and having an internal locus of control are all emphasized, as is the means to control negative thinking. Through practicing alternatives to negative thinking, participants develop an *arsenal of positive cognitions*, which can be used outside formal treat-

ment settings. Relapse and recidivism are constant threats, and the more cognitive-behavioral alternatives available, the greater chance to remain drug and crime free.

Session 18: Errors in thinking

Although negative thoughts are specific cognitions that can lead to trouble and difficulty, *errors in thinking* are more general and pervasive patterns within the youth's identity. Some examples of negative thinking are: *blaming others, seeing things only your way, put things off until it is too late, etc.* They often present obstacles to change and allow us to participate in negative behavior. Other examples of distorted thinking are: "I had no choice" or "Everyone thinks the way I do." Activities and worksheets in this session ask participants to identify their *characteristic errors and thinking distortions* and to explore how they have led to problems in living. The session culminates in individual and group reflection on how thinking distortions and errors can be modified to achieve improved outcomes.

GAVIN

Gavin is a fourteen-year-old boy who exhibits signs of *Attention Deficit Disorder* as well as possible signs of *Oppositional-Defiant Disorder*. Given his *multiple personality problems*, he is at risk for delinquent behavior. Gavin continues to fall back on his thinking, which causes difficulties because his thought patterns are filled with errors and negativity, causing him to react destructively in some situations when there may not have been anything to react to. Interactions with his teacher and advisor suggest that Gavin is always on the defensive against adults, especially those who he perceives as having power or control over his life, lending to an external locus of control. Not only does Gavin fall into thinking errors when dealing with other people, he also tends to use an "entitlement trap" as an excuse for his actions.

CHAPTER 10: HANDLING ANGER, GUILT, AND DEPRESSION

Aggression and violence can be used as a defensive posture to *gain respect* and *avoid victimization* (Anderson, 1994, 1999). Although anger is a normal emotion, aggression and violence are often found in adolescents who have disorganized attachment patterns and a large amount of family distress. These can predict adolescent difficulty in anger management

(Thornberry et al., 1999). Social orientation and cognitive deficits can increase an adolescent's active involvement in violence (Jessor et al., 1998; Levitt & Lochner, 2001). In dealing with feelings that can lead to AOD abuse and criminal behavior, participants are taught that although anger is a natural reaction to *harsh life events*, using violence or aggression is neither acceptable nor healthy. Understanding aggression and violence, and the cycle that anger, depression, and guilt can form, allow the individual to restructure his or her own thoughts and actions. Strong and healthy social ties to the group and group identity can also provide a resiliency against violence and aggression (Fox & Levin, 2001). The prosocial spirit of some group leaders can facilitate a de-normalized perception of violence as an acceptable standard of conduct.

Session 19: Dealing with feelings

Anger, depression, and guilt often play a large part in the individual's choice of participation in AOD abuse, illegal or deviant behavior. Due to family distress, social modeling (in the case of gang members), and a pervasive sense of isolation and alienation from the larger society, troubled youth develop poor coping responses to negative feelings such as anger. Before learning the skills to avoid violence and aggression, participants learn that negative emotions are normal—everyone has them—and they are not something to ignore or avoid. By realizing that thoughts can lead to anger, and that *one can then control the thinking* that fuels anger, the adolescent takes a step towards a *healthy self-regulation*.

Session 20: Preventing aggression

In preventing aggression and violence, the group is asked to use all the interpersonal, intrapersonal and social responsibility skills that have previously been learned (See *Table 15.2*) in training (Wanberg and Milkman, 1998, 2004. All play an important role in avoiding violence and substance abuse. Group members practice a pledge to remain calm, then learn to use constructive problem solving, understanding how each individual plays an important part in every confrontation. Social skills developed throughout the curriculum foster an *internal locus of control*, allowing participants to access cognitive-behavioral alternatives to aggression and violence.

TRISTAN

Tristan is an eighteen-year-old boy who has anger problems as well as a substance abuse problem. The family distress that Tristan suffers makes dealing with his anger difficult, and by using alcohol and drugs to escape from the problems he has at home, Tristan lowers his self-control and reacts in anger and frustration in situations with his girlfriend. Suffering from guilt and depression, Tristan never deals with his angry emotions, allowing them to build up as negative thoughts in his head until they erupt once again. As modeled by his father, Tristan continues to use alcohol to deaden his feelings, until he is triggered by some event and is unable to control himself. His girlfriend breaks up with him, sending Tristan into a spiral of depression and guilt. Using alcohol to deaden his emotions, Tristan is merely allowing them to build up again. Although he does not want to deal with the issues, nor does he have the skills to deal with them, he is aware of the potential violence that runs under the surface.

PHASE III: NOW! OWNERSHIP OF CHANGE— CALLING THE SHOTS
CHAPTER 11: OVERCOMING PREJUDICE

Chapter 11 allows the group to internalize cognitive-behavioral tools gained through the previous ten chapters. Social competence is continually emphasized as the chapter moves the group through *cultural and gender awareness*. Individual group members closely observe and identify their self-description (Pullkinen, Maennikkoe, & Nurmi, 2000) and how it relates to their *ethnic, cultural, and gender identity*. With increased cultural and gender awareness, not only pertaining to within group diversity, but the society at large, individuals become more comfortable with their uniqueness and respectful of diversity in others. By identifying and breaking ethnic, racial and gender stereotypes, increased self-esteem, enhanced self-efficacy and improved relationships are likely to occur.

Session 21: Respecting others

The objectives of this session are to understand the meanings of *ethnicity, culture and diversity*; then to discover how stereotypes can become prejudices, taking personal inventory of how these principles apply to our own experience. The ultimate goal of this chapter is to develop competency in appreciating diversity and respecting others. Group activities invite participants to look at *Conner's Story* in relation to their own stereotypes and prejudices.

Session 22: Gender issues

Social scripts for behavior are defined by several factors, including parents, friends, and media. These preconceived role definitions can exert a negative influence on the behavior of adolescents who become harmfully involved in substance abuse, delinquency and crime. For example, without positive socialization, a teenager may view older (albeit violent) males as positive role models. Understanding and internalizing an *individual identity* (instead of a prescribed role) enables clients to develop enhanced cultural competence as well as staging improved self-efficacy derived from self-determination and improved relationships with others. Activities are designed to assist clients to discover their own gender scripts and to make modifications if stereotyping and prejudice interfere with meaningful and satisfying relationships.

CONNOR

Connor is a fifteen-year-old boy who lives with both parents in a city apartment. Similar to Hunter, his father has influenced, and to a great extent determined, Connor's values and morals. Connor has strong prejudices against other races that he comes in contact with every day, as well as strong ideas about gender roles. Although Connor's father is prejudiced because of his need for superiority and the thoughts of being threatened in his home and his work, Connor has prejudices due to lack of information. Connor finds an exception for his stereotypes in one of his friends, although he claims it is because his friend is smarter than "the others." Even his mother conforms to his father's concepts of gender role behavior. Connor has rigid guidelines for living, and when something does not go his way, his father has given him full permission to blame it on another race or gender.

CHAPTER 12: EXPLORING INDIVIDUAL INTIMACY

Identity formation during adolescence can be difficult. Within treatment settings, most teenagers, due to poor or non-existent role models and lack of social support, have already formed some elements of a *deviant identity*. Internal conflict (manifested by anxiety, depression, substance abuse, etc.) results from the incompatibility of an internalized set of conventional values (acquired through positive cultural models), offset by social roles and patterns of behavior that include illegal and dangerous actions. AOD abuse and criminal conduct are incorporated as components (albeit undesirable) of one's self-concept. Fortunately,

many adolescents *experiment with different social roles* before reaching an identity that is compatible with his or her beliefs and values. In the "adolescent limited" form of deviant identity teenagers move from alienation, impulsivity and immersion in illegal and dangerous pursuits to more traditional roles in family, work and community interactions. Effective treatment can expedite the process of *positive identity formation*, short-circuiting momentum toward "life-course persistent" patterns of delinquency and crime.

During adolescence, teenagers not only experiment within substance abuse and different standards of legal conduct, but also with closeness, intimacy, and sexuality. Our sense of self allows us to be attracted to people who apparently share our values, beliefs and sense of the world. A negative self-concept attracts deviant associates. However, in order to be genuinely close to another person we need to know *who we are and what we expect* from the world. The most important element in developing emotional intimacy is trust, which is predicated upon honest *communication and caring* for someone else.

Individuals who are at risk for drug abuse, delinquency and crime, are also at risk for other deviant behaviors such as early sexual activity (Ray & Ksir, 2002). While PSD-C *encourages sexual abstinence*, adolescents with problem behaviors are likely to already be sexually active. Education about sexual intimacy, pregnancy prevention, and sexually transmitted disease are viewed as protective factors in increasing the overall health of the adolescent.

This chapter includes four sessions. *Identity and Emotional Intimacy* develops an understanding of how *emotional intimacy* is built upon self-knowledge, trust and open communication, which is the necessary precursor to sexual intimacy. The next session on *Sexual Intimacy and Orientation* clarifies differences in *sexual orientation* and helps to define personal standards for intimacy and sexual conduct. Worksheets and activities are designed to explore participants' personal values about sex, clarifying essential differences between intimacy and abuse. The remaining sessions on *Safe Sex* and *STDs* and *HIV Prevention* are designed to provide important information about preventing pregnancy and protection from sexually transmitted disease.

Session 23: Identity and emotional intimacy

Before discussing sexuality, this chapter examines the formation of individual identity and interpersonal relationships. High-risk teenagers are often handicapped by *lack of exposure* to positive role models who manifest conventional patterns of thinking, emotional expression and behavior regarding close and intimate relationships. A negative peer group may emerge from a quest for *closeness and belonging* in the wake of an inability to develop healthy and supporting relationships. This session provides activities and worksheets designed to help teenagers examine how they may have experimented with the values and behavior patterns of different social groups in pursuit of closeness, intimacy and belonging. The defining characteristics of each participant's positive identity are discussed, followed by an exploration of how trust and intimacy can develop through improved channels of communication: *don't expect people to read your mind; don't let things build up; express your positive feelings; remember win-win*. The session concludes with reflection on the importance of maintaining a *balance between closeness and separateness*, particularly in our intimate relationships.

Session 24: Sexual intimacy and orientation

The purpose of this session is to educate the group and its members about intimacy concerning sex, and the nature of positive sexual relationships. Formation of individual values and standards of conduct enable adolescents to mature beyond a negative identity, which may include deviant or unsafe sexual activity. Promoting prosocial morals and values is particularly important for teens that have grown up according to "the code of the streets" as "runaways," "throw aways" or children of young mothers. In this session, participants learn to define sexual intimacy, as well as becoming clearer about their own sexual identity by learning distinctions between different sexual orientations. Adolescents who receive treatment in juvenile justice settings often have a dichotomous view of homosexual vs. heterosexual orientation, and do not understand the distinction between sexual activity and intimacy.

Session 25: Safe sex

In consideration of high correlations between early sexual activity, teen pregnancy and patterns of AOD abuse (Ray & Ksir, 2002), this session is devoted to education about birth control and pregnancy prevention. Lack of information can lead to life-long mistakes. Therefore, treatment is enhanced through increased understanding of how AOD abuse can trigger *poor impulse control* and a *false sense of intimacy*, which can culminate in *abuse and unsafe sexual activity*. A person who is concerned about his or her own health and the welfare of others is less likely to become involved in AOD abuse and unhealthy patterns of sexual behavior.

Session 26: STDs and HIV prevention

It is estimated that one in five people in the U.S. has a sexually transmitted disease with 25% of new cases found in teenagers. The concept that abstinence is the only sure prevention of STDs is emphasized throughout the chapter, but education about STDs can be beneficial for at-risk adolescents. This session focuses on the most prevalent diseases and infections, including symptom descriptions and possible treatments. Education is considered important and preventative; if an adolescent hasn't become sexually active, knowledge of these diseases can become the best enforcer of abstinence.

ALYSSA

Alyssa is a fifteen-year-old girl who is pushing the boundaries in order to find an identity for herself. Part peer pressure and part curiosity, Alyssa and her girlfriend kiss at a party in order to win a beer from older boys. This experimentation begins to confuse Alyssa as she views sexual orientation in black and white terms. Alyssa exhibits her lack of emotional maturity by claiming the biggest benefit of a relationship with another girl would be being able to share clothes. She also exhibits her lack of knowledge about pregnancy and sexually transmitted infections. Part of the reason for her confusion is that she is already emotionally intimate with her girlfriend, and thus the kiss had more meaning than an isolated act of "showing off." Her confusion over sexual identity is confounded by her thoughts about kissing a male with whom she does not have emotional intimacy.

CHAPTER 13: PROBLEM SOLVING AND DECISION MAKING

Because deficits in cognitive ability predict substance abuses and criminal involvement (Levitt & Lochner, 2001), this chapter focuses on further development of problem solving and decision-making skills. Training in problem solving can be beneficial in helping adolescents re-analyze their thought patterns in terms of usefulness and consequences. An adolescent who is involved in AOD or criminal behaviors generally reacts on impulse and urge instead of thinking through a situation. In order to avoid the most easily missed pitfalls of relapse and recidivism, the individual must be able to consciously think out decisions that include the pros and cons for every high-risk situation. In the case of juvenile justice clients, these steps are practiced and thoroughly rehearsed before leaving the safety of the treatment setting. In essence, the adolescent who makes a positive post-treatment adjustment has developed the skill to *think before reacting*.

Session 27: Problem solving

Similar to anger, problems may be repressed or ignored because the adolescent is unsure how to deal with them. In order to be effective in problem solving, clients first become aware of how to *recognize and define a problem*. Group members are guided through steps to problem solving (*problem definition and goals; facts about the problem; alternative solutions; best solution; evaluate results*) and then led through activities that call for dealing with a personal problem as well as practicing problem solving techniques. With an eye toward being part of a healthy community, group members are asked to focus on solutions that help everyone involved (win-win), not just the individual. An important concept to keep in mind is that AOD use prevents individuals from using problem solving techniques.

Session 28: Decision making

While problem solving helps individuals deal with situational conflicts, decision-making affects a larger and broader scheme of the adolescent's life. Problem behaviors mostly occur when an adolescent is unable to make decisions on his or her own because of low self-esteem or when pressured by peers. By learning and practicing critical thinking as well as how to recognize propaganda the adolescent can internalize a sense of self-control over his or her environment. Activities and worksheets are designed to build skills to resist propaganda while using effective problem solving and decision-making to make independent and healthy life choices.

JORDAN

Jordan is a fifteen-year-old boy who exhibits a lack of decision-making as well as an inability to solve problems to the benefit of the group. While at a friend's house, Jordan allows himself to be influenced by his friend's brother despite his insistence that he does not want to do the drug. Finally convinced that he should have fun while he is young, Jordan "caves in" and takes a hit of cocaine or methamphetamine. As the group of friends decides to go to a convenience store

in order to buy drinks, they encounter a fence in the way of their usual route. While Jordan paces back and forth, trying to decide what to do, the older boys decide to solve the problem by tearing down the fence. Because of the destruction of private property, Jordan and the rest of the group are arrested. While Jordan is waiting for his mom, he begins to question his own decision-making and problem solving abilities.

CHAPTER 14: LIFESTYLE BALANCE

As the program progresses towards completion, participants are asked to take more responsibility for their own actions and for their own rewards and enjoyments. Part of *taking ownership* of the changes that occurred through this program is the making of a plan to maintain skills developed during the three phases of treatment. At this point, graduating youth should have well begun the process of developing an internal locus of control (Rotter, 1966). Plans formulated through activities and worksheets are designed to strengthen capacities for positive self-efficacy, improved problem solving and enhanced decision-making in the face of interpersonal conflict, negative peer influence, changing self-image and uncomfortable feeling states —all predictable occurrences throughout the life trajectory.

Session 29: Staying strong without drugs or crime

Because adolescents are actively involved in the construction of their own realities, it is important for them to *internalize the reward process* and make their own plans to avoid relapse and recidivism. During this session, each participant is asked to create a *viable plan* to avoid drugs and crime. Each plan is developed by teenage clients who are verging on treatment termination, not by the provider. In designing their *own strategies*, youth become focused on *critical triggers*, e.g., high-risk thinking and high-risk situations that they are likely to encounter. The point of this session is to emphasize the individual's strengths in order to develop a balanced and lasting plan for change.

Session 30: Critical reasoning

In connection with preventing relapse and recidivism, this session focuses on cognitive restructuring tools that are meant to help the adolescent avoid *negative peer influence*. With *critical thinking* and *critical reasoning*, youth revisit the importance of applying the *techniques of cognitive restructuring, assertiveness, negotiation and problem solving skills* during conflicts with authority figures, family, peers or other members of their community.

Zach is a sixteen-year-old boy on probation who is struggling with his life while working to pay back damages he did to the neighbor's car and the owner of a tree. While exhibiting some signs of Oppositional-Defiant Disorder, Zach is more likely suffering from a lack in judgment and bad decision making. While he is trying to make good and get his life back on track, he does miss the feeling of being an AOD user. Zach's friend tries to lighten his mood by taking him to do something that Zach would get in trouble for if caught, and Zach shows good judgment by walking away. Although he is trying to move his life forward, his friends and girlfriend constantly remind Zach how much fun his life used to be before he was caught. Because of the lack of balance in Zach's life, with few interests outside of school and work, Zach is at high risk for relapsing into his past substance use or for committing crimes again.

CHAPTER 15: STABILITY AND GROWTH

Having learned the tools of change and practiced those tools in a safe environment, the purpose of this chapter is to prepare youth to transfer these skills to unsupervised community settings. In order to prevent relapse and recidivism, adolescents must be aware of the *challenges* they will face once out of the program and the available sources of support. Keeping in mind the *realistic life environment* of many treatment level youth (unhealthy family environments, lack of financial support, lack of education, etc.), a plan is developed whereby the teenage clients decide on healthy options. Self-efficacy gained throughout the program comes into full play as the individuals decide for themselves what they will do and where they are going in the future. The development of this plan is the final step before leaving the program and taking on the challenge to live an AOD and crime free life. Secure knowledge that *support is available* even after the program is finished is an important aspect in keeping the newly formed identity resilient and able to face the challenges of a healthy lifestyle.

Session 31: Building community support: family, friends, and fun time

A healthy support system is the *most important resiliency factor* in an adolescent's life. Too often, the family is not available for that support. In this session, group members are asked to view their current support system, discussing how and where to seek other

healthy sources of comfort and strength. By becoming aware of their own interests, teenagers can choose gratifying, safe and pleasurable activities, helping to avoid the leap from boredom to drug use, delinquency and crime. Group members take *The Personal Pleasure Inventory* to focus on positive activities, critical in avoiding substance abuse and crime. The focus of this session on the various self-selected domains that provide *healthy pleasure* sets a template for positive leisure and recreational pursuits.

Session 32: Planning for the future

Without a plan for maintaining treatment gains, the adolescent may exit, only to *recycle and regress* back into his or her old lifestyle. During this final session, youth who are transitioning out of court supervision develop a plan to overcome immediate desires in exchange for long-term goals. Goals are set by each graduating youth, therefore establishing pride in self-determination and ownership of personal responsibility in maintaining a comfortable and responsible lifestyle, free of substance abuse, delinquency and crime.

LUKE

Luke is a sixteen-year-old boy who is struggling with the loneliness, boredom, and depression that can come after giving up a previous life in order to create a new one. Because of a negative home life, Luke does not have the support of his family and therefore has to create one of his own. It is not until Luke develops outside interests, such as writing and joining a book club, that he begins to feel good about his decision to be clean and crime free. With the help of his counselor and a group friend, Luke is able to begin building a healthy life. Although Luke remains clean and crime free, he still suffers from depression and moments of loneliness for his friends from his past life. The constant struggle between his new identity and his old identity causes some difficulties, but with support and becoming involved in fulfilling activities, Luke can maintain a comfortable and responsible lifestyle.

CHAPTER REVIEW

This chapter begins with discussion of guidelines for how to establish an atmosphere of safety, trust and rapport in treatment settings designed for juvenile justice clients who have identified problems in the areas of delinquency, crime and substance abuse. The operational design of the treatment curriculum is presented as it moves clients through *Phase I:*

Challenge to Change, Phase II: Commitment to Change, and Phase III: Ownership of Change. Table 15.1 presents a summary of the cognitive-behavioral skills developed throughout the program in mental, relationship and social domains. The section on *Getting Started* describes an array of strategies for engaging youth in the treatment process, including role-playing, modeling and multi-sensory activities. *Table 15.2* presents a summary of orientation topics, which can be used as a checklist and presentation outline by providers as they initiate adolescent clients into the treatment process. The final section summarizes the rationale for each chapter in the *Participant's Workbook* with a *content description* for each treatment session. Chapter summaries include brief discussion of how the illustrated case examples are used to heighten program interest, clarify session content and enliven program participation.

REFERENCES

Abrams, D. B., & Niaura, R.S. (1987). Social learning therapy. In H.T. Blane & K.W. Leonard (Eds.), *Psychological theories of drinking and alcoholism* (pp. 131-178). New York: Guilford Press.

Acoca, L. (1998a). Defusing the time bomb: Understanding and meeting the growing healthcare needs of incarcerated women in America. *Crime & Delinquency, 44*(1), 49-69.

Acoca, L. (1998b). Outside/inside: The violation of American girls at home, on the streets, and in the juvenile justice system. *Crime and Delinquency, 44*(4), 561-589.

Acoca, L., & Austin, J. (1996). *The hidden crisis: Women in prison.* San Francisco: The National Council on Crime and Delinquency.

Acoca, L., & Dedel, K. (1998*). No place to hide: Understanding and meeting the needs of girls in the California juvenile justice system.* Washington, D.: The National Council on Crime and Delinquency.

Adams, K. (1997). Developmental aspects of adult crime. In T. P. Thornberry (Ed), *Advances in criminological theory: Vol. 7. Developmental theories of crime and delinquency.* (pp. 309-342). New Brunswick, NJ: Transaction Publishers.

Addis, M., & Krasnow, A. (2000). A national survey practicing psychologists' attitudes toward psychotherapy treatment manuals. *Journal of Consulting and Clinical Psychology, 68*, 331-339.

Adler, F. (1975). *Sisters in crime: The rise of the new female criminal.* New York: McGraw-Hill.

Agnew, R. (1984). Autonomy and Delinquency. *Sociological Perspectives, 27*, 219-40.

Agnew, R. (1992). Foundation for a general strain theory of crime and delinquency. *Criminology, 30.* 47-88.

Agnew, R. (1995). The contribution of social-psychological strain theory to the explanation of crime and delinquency. In: F. Adler & W. Laufer. (Eds), *Advances in criminological theory: Vol. 6. The legacy of anomie theory.* (pp. 113-137). New Brunswick, NJ: Transaction Publishers.

Agnew, R. (1997). Stability and change in crime over the life course: A strain theory explanation. In T. P. Thornberry (Ed.), *Advances in criminological theory: Vol. 7. Developmental theories of crime and delinquency* (pp. 101-132). New Brunswick, NJ: Transaction Publishers.

Agostinelli, G. (1994). Drinking and thinking: How does personal drinking affect judgments of prevalence and risk? *Journal of Studies on Alcohol, 55*(3), 327-337.

Akers, R. L. (2000). *Criminological theories: introduction, evaluation and application.* Los Angeles, CA: Roxbury Publishing.

Alcoholics Anonymous. (1976). *Alcoholics Anonymous: The story of how many thousands of men and women have recovered from alcoholism* (3rd ed.). New York: Alcoholics Anonymous World Series.

Alexander, M. J. (1996). Women with co-occurring addictive and mental disorders: An emerging profile of vulnerability. *American Journal of Orthopsychiatry, 66*(1), 61-70.

Alexander, J. F., & Sexton, T. L. (1999). Helping our youth: Clinical update. *Adolescent Disruptive Behavior Disorders, 1(5),* 1-8.

Alford, B., & Norcross, J.C. (1991). Cognitive therapy as an integrated therapy. *Journal of Psychotherapy Integration, 1,* 175-190.

Ambrosini, P.J., Metz, C., Prabucki, K., & Lee, J.C. (1989). Videotape reliability of the third revised addition of the K-SADS-III-R. *Journal of the American Academy of Child and Adolescent Psychiatry, 28*, 723-728.

Amen, D.G. (1998). *Change Your Brain Change Your Life.* New York: Random House.

American Psychiatric Association. (1991). *Diagnostic and statistical manual of mental disorders (Revised).* Washington, DC: American Psychiatric Association.

American Psychiatric Association. (1994). *Diagnostic and statistical manual of mental disorders (4th ed.).* Washington DC: American Psychiatric Association.

American Psychiatric Association. (2000). *Diagnostic and statistical manual of mental disorders (4th ed., text revision).* Washington DC: American Psychiatric Association.

Ames, G., Schmidt, D., Klee, L., & Saltz, R. (1996). Combining methods to identify new measures of women's drinking problems. Part I: The ethnographic stage. *Addictions, 91*(6), 829-844.

Anderson, E. (1994). Sex codes and family life among Northton's youth. In G. Handel & G. G. Whitchurch (Eds.), *The psychosocial interior of the family* (4th ed., pp. 585-608). New York: Aldine de Gruyter.

Anderson, E. (1999). *Code of the street: Decency, Violence and the Moral Life of the inner City.* New York: Norton.

Anderson, J. C., Williams, S. M., McGee, R., & Silva, P. A. (1987). DSM-III disorders in preadolescent children: Prevalence in a large sample from the general population. *Archives of General Psychiatry, 44*(1), 69-76.

Anderson, L. E., & Walsh, L. A. (1998). Prediction of adult criminal status from juvenile psychological assessment. *Criminal Justice and Behavior, 25*, 226-239.

Andrews, D. A., & Bonta, J. (1994). *The psychology of criminal conduct.* Cincinnati, OH: Anderson Publishing Co.

Andrews, D. A., & Bonta, J. (2003). *The psychology of criminal conduct* (3rd ed.). Cincinnati, OH: Anderson Publishing Co.

Anglin, M. D., & Perrochet, B. (1998). Drug Use and Crime: A Historical Review of Research Conducted by the UCLA Drug Abuse Research Center. *Substance Use and Misuse, 33,* 1871-1914.

Archer, R.P. (1992). *MMPI-A: Assessing adolescent psychopathology.* Hillsdale, NJ: Erlbaum.

Archer, R.P., Maruish, M., Imof, E.A., & Piotrowski, C. (1991). Psychological test usage with adolescent clients: 1990 survey findings. *Professional Psychology: Research and Practice, 22*, 247-252.

Arfaniarromo, A. (2001). Toward a psychosocial and sociocultural understanding of achievement motivation among Latino gang members in U.S. schools. *Journal of Instructional Psychology, 28*(3), 123-136.

Arkowitz, H. (1992). Integrative theories of therapy. In D.K. Freedheim (Ed.), *History of psychotherapy: A century of change* (pp. 261-304). Washington, DC: American Psychological Association.

Arnett, J. (1990). Drunk driving, sensation seeking, and egocentrism among adolescents. *Personality & Individual Differences, 11*(6), 541-546.

Arnett, J. (1992). Socialization and adolescent reckless behavior: A reply to Jessor. *Development Review, 12*, 391-409.

Arnkoff, D. B., & Glass, C. R. (1992). Cognitive therapy and psychotherapy integration. In D. K. Freedheim & H. J. Freudenberger (Eds.), *History of psychotherapy: A century of change.* Washington, DC: American Psychological Association.

Arroyo, C. G., & Zigler, E. (1995). Racial identity, academic achievement, and the Psychological well-being of economically disadvantaged adolescents. *Journal of Personality and Social Psychology, 69*(5), 903-914.

Arsenio, W. F., Cooperman, S., & Lover, A. (2000). Affective predictors of preschoolers' aggression and peer acceptance: Direct and indirect effects. *Developmental Psychology, 36*(4), 438-448.

Ary, D. V., Duncan, T. E., Biglan, A., Metzler, C. W., Noell, J. W., & Smolkowski, K. (1999*).* Development of adolescent problem behavior. *Journal of Abnormal Child Psychology, 27,* 141-150.

Asendorpf, J. B. (2000). A person-centered approach to personality and social relationships: Findings from the Berlin Relationship. In: L. R. Bergman, R. B. Cairns, L. G. Nilsson & L. Nystedt (Eds.), *Developmental science and the holistic approach* (pp. 281-298). Mahwah, NJ: Erlbaum.

Attkisson, C. C., & Zwick, R. (1982). The Client Satisfaction Questionnaire: Psychometric properties and correlations with service utilization and psychotherapy outcome. *Evaluation and Program Planning, 5*(3), 233-237.

Aylwin, A. S., Clelland, S. R., Kirkby, L., Reddon, J. R., Studer, L. H., & Johnston, J. (2000). Sexual offense severity and victim gender preference: A comparison of adolescent and adult sex offenders. *International Journal of Law & Psychiatry, 23*(2), 113-124.

Azrin, N. H., Acierno, R., Kogan, E., Donahue, B., Besalel, V., & McMahon, P. T. (1996). Follow-up results of supportive versus behavioral therapy for illicit drug abuse. *Behavioral Research and Therapy, 34*(1), 41-46.

Babor, T. F., Stephens, R. S., & Marlatt, G. A. (1987). Verbal report methods in clinical research on alcoholism: Response bias and its minimization. *Journal of Studies on Alcohol, 48*(5), 410-424.

Bachelor, K. A. (1991). Comparison and relationship to outcome of diverse dimensions of the helping alliance as seen by client and therapist. *Psychotherapy, 28,* 234-249.

Bachelor, K.A. (1995). Clients' perception of the therapeutic alliance: A qualitative analysis. *Journal of Counseling Psychology, 42*, 322-337.

Bachman, R., & Saltzman, L. E. (1995). *Violence against women: Estimates from the redesigned survey.* Washington, D.C.: U.S. Department of Justice, Bureau of Justice Statistics.

Bagley, C., & Pritchard, C. (1998). The billion dollar costs of troubled youth: Prospects for cost-effective prevention and treatment. *International Journal of Adolescence Youth, 7*, 211-225.

Bailey, S. L., Flewelling, R. L., & Rachal, J. V. (1992). The characteristics of inconsistencies in self-reports of alcohol and marijuana use in longitudinal study of adolescents. *Journal of Studies on Alcohol, 53*, 636-647.

Bandura, A. (1969). *Principles of behavior modification.* Oxford, England: Holt, Rinehart, & Winston.

Bandura, A. (1977a). Self-efficacy: Toward a unifying theory of behavioral change. *Psychological Review, 84*(2), 191-215.

Bandura, A. (1977b). *Social learning theory.* Oxford, England: Prentice-Hall.

Bandura, A. (1978). The self-system in reciprocal determinism. *American Psychologist, 33*, 344-358.

320

Bandura, A. (1982). Self efficacy mechanisms in human agency. *American Psychologist, 37,* 122-147.

Bandura, A. (1986). The explanatory and predictive scope of self-efficacy theory. *Journal of Social & Clinical Psychology, 4*(3), 359-373.

Bandura, A. (1989). Regulation of cognitive processes through perceived self-efficacy. *Developmental Psychology, 25*(5), 729-735.

Bandura, A., & Schunk, D. H. (1981). Cultivating competence, self-efficacy, and intrinsic interest through proximal self-motivation. *Journal of Personality & Social Psychology, 41*(1), 586-598.

Banks, J. A. (1991). Multicultural education: Its effects on students' racial and gender role attitudes. In J. P. Shauer (Ed.), *Handbook of research on social studies teaching and learning* (pp. 459-469). New York: Macmillan.

Barber, J.P., Connolly, M.B., Crits-Christopher, P., Gladis, L., & Siqueland, L. (2001). Alliance predicts patients' outcome beyond in-treatment change in symptoms. *Journal of Consulting and Clinical Psychology, 68,* 1027-1032.

Barbrack, C. R., & Franks, M. B. (1986). In S. Modgil & C. Modgil (Eds.), *Hans Eysenck: Consensus and controversy.* Brighton: Falmer.

Bardone, A., Moffitt, T., Caspi, A., Dickson, N., & Silva, P. (1996). Adult Mental Health and social outcomes of adolescent girls with depression and conduct disorder. *Development and Psychopathology, 8,* 811-829.

Barkley, R. A. (1998). *Attention-deficit hyperactivity disorder: A handbook for diagnosis and treatment* (2nd ed.). New York: Guilford Press.

Barkley, R. A., Edwards, G. H., & Robin, A. L. (1999). *Defiant teens: A clinician's manual for assessment and family intervention.* New York: Guilford Press.

Barnett, A., Blumstein, A., & Farrington, D. P. (1987). Probabilistic models of youthful criminal careers. *Criminology, 25,* 83-107.

Baron, R. M., & Kenny, D. A. (1986). The moderator-mediator variable distinction in social psychological research: Conceptual, strategic, and statistical considerations. *Journal of Personality and Social Psychology, 51,* 1173-1182.

Baron, S. W., & Hartnagel, T. F. (1998). Street youth and criminal violence. *Journal of Research in Crime & Delinquency, 35*(2), 166-192.

Bartlett, T. (2004). Ecstasy Agonistes. *The Journal of Higher Education,* (5), 1-25.

Basen-Engquist, K., Edmundson E., & Parcel, G. (1996). Structure of health risk behavior among high school students. *Journal of Consulting and Clinical Psychology. 64,* 764-775.

Bateman, A., Brown, D., & Pedder, J. (2000). *Introduction to psychotherapy: An outline of psychodynamic principles and practice (Third Edition).* London: Routledge.

Battin, S. R., Newcomb, M. D., Abbott, R. D., Hill, K. G., Catalano, R. F., Hawkins, J. D. (2000). Predictors of early high school dropout: A test of five theories. *Journal of Educational Psychology, 92*(3), 568-582.

Battjes, R. J., Sears, E. A., Katz, E. C., Kinlock, T. W., Gordon, M., & The Epoch Project Team. (2003). Evaluation of a group-based outpatient adolescent substance abuse treatment program. In S. J. Stevens & A. R. Morral (Eds.), *Adolescent substance abuse treatment in the United States.* (pp. 57-80). New York: Haworth Press.

Baumrind, D. (1991a). Parenting styles and adolescent development. In R. Lerner, A. Petersen, & J. Brooks (Eds.) *The Encyclopedia on Adolescence* (pp. 746-758). New York: Garland.

Baumrind, D. (1991b). The influence of parenting style on adolescent competence and substance use. *Journal of Early Adolescence, 11,* 56-95.

Bautista de Domanico, Y., Crawford, I., De Wolfe, A. S. (1994). Ethnic identity and self-concept in Mexican-American adolescents: Is bicultural identity related to stress or better adjustment? *Child and Youth Care Forum, 23*(3), 197-206.

Beck, A. T. (1963). Thinking and depression: I. Idiosyncratic content and cognitive distortions. *Archives of General Psychiatry, 9*(4), 324-333.

Beck, A. T. (1964). Thinking and depression: II. Theory and therapy. *Archives of General Psychiatry, 10*(6), 561-571.

Beck, A. T. (1970). Cognitive therapy: Nature and relation to behavior therapy. *Behavior Therapy, 1*(2), 184-200.

Beck, A. T. (1976). *Cognitive therapy and the emotional disorders.* Oxford, England: International Universities Press.

Beck, A. T. (1979). Schools of "thought." *American Psychologist, 34*(1), 93-98.

Beck, A. T. (1991). Cognitive as the integrative therapy. *Journal of Psychotherapy Integration, 1,* 191-198.

Beck, A. T. (1993). Cognitive approaches to stress in P. M. Lehrer& R. L. Woolfolk (Eds.). *Principles and practice of stress management,* Second edition. New York: Guilford Press.

Beck, A. T. (1995). Cognitive therapy: Past, present, and future. In M. J. Mahoney (Ed.), *Cognitive and constructive psychotherapies: Theory, research, and practice* (pp. 29-40). New York: Springer Publishing Co.

Beck, A. T. (1996). Beyond belief: A theory of modes, personality, and psychopathology. In P. M. Salkovskis (Ed.), *Frontiers of cognitive therapy* (pp. 1-25). New York: Guilford Press.

Beck, A. T., Beck, R., & Kovacs, M. (1975). Classification of suicidal behaviors: I. Quantifying intent and medical lethality. *American Journal of Psychiatry, 132*(3), 285-287.

Beck, A. T., & Rush, A. J. (1978). Cognitive approaches to depression and suicide. In G. Serban (Ed.), *Cognitive defects in the development of mental illness* (pp. 235-257). Oxford, England: Brunner/Mazel.

Beck, A. T., Wright, F., Newman, C., & Liese, B. (1993). *Cognitive therapy of substance abuse.* New York: Guilford Press.

Beck, J. S. (1995). *Cognitive therapy: Basics and beyond.* New York: Guilford Press.

Beck, J. S., & Steer, R. A. (1987). *Manual for the revised Beck Depression Inventory.* San Antonio, TX: The Psychological Corporation.

Becker, H.C., Hale, R.L. (1993). Repeated episodes of alcohol withdrawal potentiate the severity of subsequent withdrawal seizures: an animal model of alcohol withdrawal "kindling." *Alcoholism: Clinical and Experimental Research, 17*, 94-98.

Beckett, R. (1999). Evaluation of adolescent sexual abusers. In M. Erooga, & H. C. Masson (Eds), *Children and young people who sexually abuse others: challenges and responses* (pp. 204-224). London, Routledge.

Bedell, J. R. & Lennox, S. S. (1997). *Handbook for Communication & Problem-Solving Skills Training: A Cognitive-Behavioral Approach.* New York: John Wiley & Sons, Inc.

Belknap, J. (1996). *The invisible woman: Gender, crime and justice.* Belmont, CA: Wadsworth Publishing Company.

Belknap, J., & Holsinger, K. (1998). An overview of delinquent girls: How theory and practice have failed and the need for innovative changes. In R. T. Zaplin (Ed.), *Female crime and delinquency: Critical perspectives and effective interventions* (pp. 31-64*)*. Gaithersburg, MD: Aspen Publishers.

Belknap, J., Holsinger, K., & Dunn, M. (1997). Understanding incarcerated girls: The results of a focus group study. *The Prison Journal, 77*(4), 381-404.

Bell, Carl C., (Ed). (2000). *Psychiatric aspects of violence: Issues in prevention and treatment.* Series Title: New directions for mental health services, No. 86. San Francisco: Jossey-Bass.

Belson, W.A. (1975). *Juvenile theft: The Causal factors.* London: Harper and Row.

Bem, S. L. (1996). Transforming the debate on sexual inequality: From biological difference to institutionalized androcentrism. In J. C. Chrisler, C. Golden, & P. D. Rozee (Eds.), *Lectures on the psychology of women* (pp. 9-21*)*. New York: McGraw-Hill.

Bem, S. L., & Bem, D. (1971). Training the woman to know her place: The power of a nonconscious ideology. In M. H. Garskof (Ed.), *Roles women play: Readings toward women's liberation* (pp. 84-96). Belmont, CA: Brooks/Cole Publishing Company.

Benda, B. B., & Corwyn, R.F. (2000). A test of the validity of delinquency syndrome construct in a homogeneous sample. *Journal of Criminal Justice, 27,* 111-126.

Benda, B. B., Flynn C. R., & Toombs, N. J. (2001). Recidivism among adolescent serious offenders: Prediction of entry into the correctional system for adults. *Criminal Justice & Behavior, 28*(5), Oct pp. 588-613.

Benda, B. B., & Tollett, C. L. (1999). A study of recidivism of serious and persistent offenders among adolescents. *Journal of Criminal Justice, 27*, 111-126.

Bennett, W. J., DiIulio, J. & Walters, J. P. (1996*). Body Count: Moral Poverty and How to Win America's War against Crime and Drugs.* NY: Simon & Schuster.

Bensley, L. S., Spieker, S. J., Van Eeenwyk, J., & Schoder, J. (1999). Self-reported abuse history and adolescent health problems. II. Alcohol and drug use. *Journal of Adolescent Health, 24*(3), 173-180.

Bensley, L. S., Van Eeenwyk, J., Spieker, S. J., & Schoder, J. (1999). Self-reported abuse history and adolescent problem behaviors. I. Antisocial and suicidal behaviors. *Journal of Adolescent Health, 24*(3), 163-172.

Benson, P. L. (1998). *All Kids are Our Kids: What Communities Must do to Raise Caring and Responsible Children.* New York: Jossey Bass, Inc.

Benson, P. L., Leffert, N., Scales, P. C., & Blyth, D. A. (1998). Beyond the "village" rhetoric: Creating healthy communities for children and adolescents. *Applied Developmental Science, 2*(3), 138-159.

Berenson, B. G., & Carkhuff, R. R. (1967). *Sources of gain in counseling and psychotherapy.* New York: Holt, Rinehart & Winston.

Bergman, L. R. (2000). The application of a person-oriented approach: Types and clusters. In: L. R. Bergman, R. B. Cairns, L. G. Nilsson & L. Nystedt (Eds.), *Developmental science and the holistic approach.* Mahwah, NJ: Lawrence Erlbaum Associates.

Bergman, L. R., Cairns, R. B., Nilsson, L.G., & Nystedt, L., (Eds.) (2000). *Developmental science and the holistic approach.* Mahwah, NJ: Lawrence Erlbaum Associates.

Berkowitz, L. (1993). *Aggression: Its Causes, Consequences, and Control.* Philadelphia: Temple University Press.

Berman, M. O. (1990). Severe brain dysfunction: Alcoholic Korsakoff's syndrome. *Alcohol Health & Research World, 14*(2), 120-129.

Bernal, M. E., Saenz, D. S., Knight, G. P. (1991). Ethnic identity and adaptation of Mexican American youths in school settings. *Hispanic Journal of Behavioral Sciences, 13*(2), 135-154.

Bernstein, D. P., Fink, L., Handelsman, L., Foote, J., Lovejoy, M., & Wenzel, K., et al. (1994). Initial reliability and validity of a new retrospective measure of child abuse and neglect. *American Journal of Psychiatry, 151*(8), 1132-1136.

Bettridge, B. J., & Favreau, O. (1995). Suicidal behavior among adolescent females: The cry for connection. In S. S. Canetto, & D. Lester (Eds.), *Women and suicidal behavior. Focus on women* (pp. 109-119). New York: Springer Publishing.

Biederman, J., Mick, E., Faraone, S. V., Braaten, E., Doyle, A., & Spencer, T., et al. (2002). Influence of gender on attention deficit hyperactivity disorder in children referred to a psychiatric clinic. *American Journal of Psychiatry, 159*(1), 36-42.

Biederman, J., Newcorn, J., & Sprich, S. (1991). Comorbidity of ADHD with conduct depressive, anxiety, and other disorders. *American Journal of Psychiatry, 148*, 564-577.

Bien, T.H., Miller, W.R., & Tonigan, J.S. (1993). Brief interventions for alcohol problems: A review. *Addictions, 88,* 315-336.

Blackburn, I. M., & Twaddle, V. (1996). *Cognitive therapy in action: A practitioner's casebook.* London: Souvenir Press.

Blair, R. J. R., Colledge, E., Murray, L., & Mitchell, D. G. V. (2001). A selective impairment in the processing of sad and fearful expressions in children with psychopathic tendencies. *Journal of Abnormal Child Psychology, 29*(6), 491-498.

Bloom, B., Chesney-Lind, M., & Owen, B. (1994). *Women in California prisons: Hidden victims of the war on drugs.* San Francisco: Center on Juvenile and Criminal Justice.

Bloom, S. L. (2000). Sexual violence: The victim. In C. C. Bell (Ed), *New directions for mental health services: Vol. 86. Psychiatric aspects of violence: Issues in prevention and treatment* (pp. 63-71). Washington, DC: American Psychological Association.

Blum, K. (1991). *Alcohol and the Addictive Brain: New Hope for Alcoholics from Biogenic Research.* New York: Macmillan.

Blume, S. B. (1991). Sexuality and stigma: The alcoholic woman. *Alcohol Health and Research World, 15*(2), 139-146.

Blume, S. B. (1998). Addictive disorders in women. In R. J. Frames & S. I. Miller (Eds.), *Clinical Textbook of Addictive Disorders* (2nd ed., pp. 413-429). New York: Guilford Press.

Blume, S. B., & Russell, M. (1993). Alcohol and substance abuse in the practice of obstetrics and gynecology. In D. E. Stewart & N. L. Stotland (Eds.), *Psychological aspects of women's health care: The interface between psychiatry and obstetrics and gynecology* (pp. 391-409). Washington, DC: American Psychiatric Press.

Blumstein, A. (1995a). Violence by young people: Why the deadly nexus? *National Institute of Justice Journal, 229*, 2-9.

Blumstein, A. (1995b). Youth violence, guns, and the illicit drug industry. *Journal of Criminal Law and Criminology, 86*, 10-36.

Bolla, K.I., et. al. (2002). Dose-related neurocognitive effects of marijuana use. *Neurology, 59*(9), 337-1343.

Bond, N.W. (1979). Impairment of shuttlebox avoidance learning following repeated alcohol withdrawal episodes in rats. *Pharmaco Biochem Behav*, 11:589-591.

Bordin, E. S. (1979). The generalizability of the psychoanalytic concept of the working alliance. *Psychotherapy: Theory, Research and Practice, 16*, 252-260.

Boring, E. G., Langfeld, H. S., & Weld H.P. (1939). *Introduction to Psychology.* NewYork: Wiley.

Botvin, G. J. (1983). Prevention of adolescent substance abuse through the development of personal and social competence. In *Preventing adolescent drug abuse: Intervention strategies.* NIDA Research Monograph 47, Department of Health and Human Services, National Institute on Drug Abuse, 115-140.

Botvin, G. J. (1985). The Life Skills Training Program as a health promotion strategy: Theoretical issues and empirical findings. *Special Services in the Schools, 1*(3), 9-23.

Botvin, G. J., Baker, E., Dusenbury, L., Tortu, S., and Botvin, E. M. (1990). Preventing adolescent drug abuse through a multimodal cognitive-behavioral approach: Results of a three-year study. *Journal of Consulting and Clinical Psychology, 58*, 437-446

Botvin, G. J., Baker, E., Filazzola, A. D. & Botvin, E. M. (1990). A cognitive-behavioral approach to SA prevention: One-year follow-up. *Addictive Behaviors. 15*(1), 47-63.

Botvin, G. J., & Griffin, K. W. (2001). Life Skills Training: Theory, methods, and effectiveness of a drug abuse prevention approach. In E. F. Wagner & H. B. Waldron (Eds.), *Innovations in adolescent substance abuse interventions* (pp. 31-49). Amsterdam, Netherlands: Pergamon/Elsevier Science Inc.

Botvin, G. J., & Griffin, K. W. (2002). Life skills training as a primary prevention approach for adolescent drug abuse and other problem behaviors. *International Journal of Emergency Mental Health, 4*(1), 41-48.

Brack, C., Brack G., & Orr, D. (1994). Dimensions underlying problem behaviors, emotions and related psychosocial actors in early and middle adolescence. *Journal of Early Adolescence. 14*, 345-370.

Braswell, L. & Bloomquist, M. L. (1991). *Cognitive Behavioral Therapy with ADHD Children.* New York: Guilford Press.

Braun, S. (1996). *Buzz.* New York, Oxford: Oxford University Press.

Brennan, T. (1998). Institutional classification of females: Problems and some proposals for reform. In R. T. Zaplin (Ed.), *Female offenders: Critical perspectives and effective intervention* (pp. 179-204). Gaithersburg, MD: Aspen Publishers.

Brennan, T., & Austin, J. (1997, March). *Women in jail: Classification issues.* Washington, D.C.: U.S. Department of Justice, National Institute of Corrections.

Brestan, E. V., & Eyeberg, S. M. (1998). Effective psychosocial treatments of conduct-disordered children and adolescents: 29 years, 82 studies, and 5,272 kids. *Journal of Clinical Child Psychology, 27*(2), 180-189.

Brezina, T. (1999). Teenage violence toward parents as an adaptation to family strain: Evidence from a national survey of male adolescents. *Youth & Society, 30*, 416-444.

Brickman, P., Rabinowitz, V.C., Karuza, J., Coates, D., Cohn, E., & Kidder, L. (1982). Models of helping and coping. *American Psychologist, 37*, 368-384.

Briere, J., & Runtz, M. (1989). The Trauma Symptom Checklist (TSC-33): Early data on a new scale. *Journal of Interpersonal Violence, 4*(2), 151-163.

Broening, H.W., Morford, L.L., Inman-Wood, S.L., Fukumura, M., and Vorhees, C.V. (2001). 3,4-methyleneioxymethamphetamine (ecstasy)-induced learning and memory impairment depend on the age of exposure during early development. *Journal of Neuroscience, 21*(9), 3228-3235.

Brooks, C. M. (1996). The law's response to child abuse and neglect. In B. D. Sales, & D. W. Shuman (Eds), *Law, mental health, and mental disorder.* Pacific Grove, CA: Brooks/Cole.

Broom, E.W. (2000). An examination of factors related to the cognitive and affective. *Dissertation Abstracts International. 63 (02a)*, 554.

Brown, G. (1995). Borderline states, incest, and adolescence: Inpatient psychotherapy. In M. Sidoli, & G. Bovensiepen (Eds), *Incest fantasies & self destructive acts: Jungian and post-Jungian psychotherapy in adolescence* (pp. 281-296).

Brown, G. L., Ebert, M. H., Goyer, P. F., et al. (1982). Aggression suicide and serotonin: relationships to CSF amine metabolites. *American Journal of Psychiatry, 139*, 741-746.

Brown, M., Anton, R., Malcolm, R., & Ballenger, J. L. (1998). Alcohol detoxification and withdrawal seizures: clinical support for a kindling hypothesis. *Biological Psychiatry, 23*, 507-514.

Brown, S. A., Myers, M. G., Lippke, L., Tapert, S. F., Stewart, D. G., & Vik, P. W. (1998). Psychometric evaluation of the Customary Drinking and Drug Use Record (CDDR): A measure of adolescent alcohol and drug involvement. *Journal of Studies on Alcohol, 59*, 427-438.

Brownmiller, S. (1975). *Against our will: Men, women and rape.* New York: Simon and Schuster.

Brownstein, Henry H. (2000). *The social reality of violence and violent crime.* Boston, MA: Allyn & Bacon.

Brunk, M. (2000). Effective treatment of conduct disorder. *Juvenile Justice Fact Sheet.* Charlottesville, VA: Institute of Law, Psychiatry, & Public Policy, University of Virginia.

Budney, A.J., Hughes, J.R., Moore, B.A., & Novy, P.L. (2001). Marijuana abstinence effects in marijuana smokers maintained in their home environment. *Archives of General Psychiatry, 58*(10), 917-924.

Burns, D. D. (1980). *Feeling good: The new mood therapy.* New York: William Morrow.

Burns, D. D. (1989). *The feeling good handbook: Using the new mood therapy in everyday life.* New York: William Morrow.

Busch, K. G., Zagar, R., Hughes, J. R., & Arbit, J., et al. (1990). Adolescents who kill. *Journal of Clinical Psychology, 46*(4), 472-485.

Bush, J. M., & Bilodeau, B. C. (1993). *Options: A cognitive change program* (Prepared by J. M. Bush and B. C. Bilodeau for the National Institute of Corrections and the U.S. Department of the Navy). Washington, DC: National Institute of Corrections.

Bush, J., Glick, B., & Taymans, J. (1997). *Thinking for a change: Integrated cognitive behavior change program.* Washington, DC: National Institute of Corrections.

Bush-Baskette, S. (2000). The war on drugs and the incarceration of mothers. *Journal of Drug Issues, 30*(4), 919-928.

Bustamante, E. M. (2000). *Treating the disruptive adolescent: Finding the real self behind oppositional defiant disorders*. Northvale, NJ: Jason Aronson Inc.

Butcher, J. N., & Williams, C. L. (1992). *Essentials of MMPI-2 and MMPI-A interpretation*. Minneapolis: University of Minnesota Press.

Butcher, J. N., Williams, C. L., Graham, J. R., Archer, R. P., Tellegen, A., Ben-Porath, Y. S., & Kaemmer, B. (1992). *Minnesota Multiphasic Personality Inventory-Adolescent (MMPI-A)*. Minneapolis, MN: University of Minnesota Press.

Butler, S. (1978). *Conspiracy of silence: The trauma of incest*. San Francisco: New Glide Publications.

Bynum, Evita G., & Weiner, Ronald I. (2002). Self-concept and violent delinquency in urban African-American adolescent males. *Psychological Reports, 90*(2), 477-486.

Cabral, G.A. (1995). National Conference on Marijuana Use; Prevention, Treatment and Research. Arlington, VA.

Cabrera, S.S. (2001). An examination of the influence of acculturative stress on substance use and related maladaptive behavior among Latino youth. Dissertation Abstracts International: Section B: *The Sciences & Engineering*, 62(5-B), pp. 2532.

Cadet, J. L., Ordonez, S. V., & Ordonez, J. V. (1997). Methamphetamine induces apoptosis in immortalized neural cells: Protection by the proto-oncogene, b-cl-2. *Synapse, 25*, 176-184.

Calabrese, R. L., & Noboa, J. (1995). The choice for gang membership by Mexican-American adolescents. *High School Journal, 78*, 226-235.

Calhoun, G. B., Glaser, B. A., Barolomucci, D. L. (2001). The juvenile counseling and assessment model and program: A conceptualization and intervention for juvenile delinquency. *Journal of Counseling and Development, 79:2,* 131-141.

Camarena, M., Sarigiani, P. A., & Petersen, A. C. (1997). Adolescence, gender, and the development of mental health. In A. Lieblich, & R. Josselson (Eds.). *The narrative study of lives* (pp. 182-206). Thousand Oaks, CA: Sage Publications.

Campbell, A. (1991). *The girls in the gang* (2nd ed). Cambridge, MA: Basil Blackwell.

Campbell, A. (1993). *Men, women, and aggression.* New York: Basic Books.

Campbell, M., & Cueva, J. E. (1995). Psychopharmacology in child and adolescent psychiatry: A review of the past seven years: II. *Journal of the American Academy of Child & Adolescent Psychiatry, 34*(10), 1262-1272.

Capaldi, D. (1991). Co-occurrence of conduct problems and depressive symptoms in early adolescent boys, I: Familial factors and general adjustment at grade 6. *Development and Psychopathology, 3,* 277-300.

Carkhuff, R. (1969). *Helping in human relations* (Vols. 1 & 2). New York: Holt, Rinehart & Winston.

Carkhuff, R. (1971). *The development of human resources*. New York: Holt, Rinehart & Winston.

Carkhuff, R. R., & Berenson, B. G. (1977). *Beyond counseling and therapy* (2nd ed.). New York: Holt, Rinehart & Winston.

Cashel, M. L., Rogers, R., Sewell, K. W., & Holliman, N .B. (1998). Preliminary validation of the MMPI-A for a male delinquent sample: An investigation of clinical correlates and discriminate validity. *Journal of Personality Assessment, 7*, 49-69.

Caspi, A. (2000). The child is father of the man: Personality continuities from childhood to adulthood. *Journal of Personality & Social Psychology, 78*(1), 158-172.

Caspi, A., Henry, B., McGee, R. O., Moffitt, T. E., & Silva, P. A. (1995). Temperamental origins of child and adolescent behavior problems: From age 3 to age 15. *Child Development, 66*, 55-68.

Caspi, A., Lyman, D., Moffitt, T. E., & Silva, P. A. (1993). Unraveling girls' delinquency, biological, dispositional and contextual contributions to adolescent misbehavior. *Developmental Psychology, 29*, 19-34.

Castellanos, F. X., Elia, J., Kruesi, M. J., Gulotta, C. S., Mefford, I. N., Potter, W. Z., et al. (1995). Cerebrospinal fluid monoamine metabolites in boys with attention deficit hyperactivity disorder. *Psychiatry Research, 52*, 305-316.

Catalano, R. F., & Hawkins, J. D. (1996). The social development model: A theory of antisocial behavior. In J. D. Hawkins (Ed.), *Delinquency and crime: Current theories. Cambridge criminology series*. (pp. 149-197). Cambridge, England: Cambridge University Press.

Cautela, J. R. (1966). Treatment of compulsive behavior by covert sensitization. *Psychological Record, 16*(1), 33-41.

Cautela, J. R., & Kearney, A. J. (1990). Behavior analysis, cognitive therapy, and covert conditioning. *Journal of Behavior Therapy & Experimental Psychiatry, 21*(2), 83-90.

Center for Substance Abuse Treatment (1994). *Simple Screening Instrument for Outreach for Alcohol and Other Drug Use and Infectious Diseases.* (Department of Health and Human Services, Publication No. SMA 94-2094). Washington DC: US Government Printing Office.

Center for Substance Abuse Treatment (1999). *Treatment of Adolescents with Substance Use Disorders: Treatment Improvement Protocol (TIP) Series 32.* (Department of Health and Human Services, Publication No. SMA 99-3283). Washington, DC: US. Department of Health and Human Services.

Cepeda, A. & Valdez, A. (2003). Risk behaviors among young Mexican American gang-associated females: Sexual relations, partying, substance use, and crime. *Journal of Adolescent Research, 18*(1), 90-106.

Cernkovich, S. A., Giordano, P. C., & Rudolph, J. L. (2000). Race, crime and the American dream. *Journal of Research in Crime and Delinquency, 37,* 131-170.

Chang, L., Ernst, T., Speck, O., Patel, H., DeSilva, M., Leonida-Yee, M., et al. (2002). Perfusion NMI and computerized test abnormalities in abstinent methamphetamine users. *Psychiatry Research Neuroimaging, 114*(2), 65-79.

Chasnoff, I. (1997). Cocaine: Effects on the developing brain. Conference held in Washington D.C., Sept. 16-19.

Chesney-Lind, M. (1993). Girls, gangs and violence: Reinventing the liberated female crook. *Humanity and Society, 17,* 321-344.

Chesney-Lind, M. (1997). *The female offender: Girls, women and crime.* Thousand Oaks, CA: Sage Publications.

Chesney-Lind, M. (2000). Women and the criminal justice system: Gender matters. *Topics in Community Corrections, 5,* 7-10.

Chesney-Lind, M., & Sheldon, R.G. (1998). *Girls, delinquency, and juvenile justice* (2nd ed.). Belmont, CA: West/Wadsworth.

Chesney-Lind, M., Shelden, R. G., & Joe, K. A. (1996). Girls, delinquency, and gang membership. In C. R. Huff (Ed.), *Gangs in America* (2nd ed.) (pp. 185-204). Thousand Oaks, CA: Sage Publications.

Christiansen, B. A., Goldman, M. S., & Inn, A. (1982). The development of alcohol-related expectancies in adolescents: Separating pharmacological from social learning influences. *Journal of Consulting and Clinical Psychology, 20,* 336-344.

Chung, I., Hill, K. G., Hawkins, J. D., Gilchrist, L. D., & Nagin, D. S. (2002). Childhood predictors of offense trajectories. *Journal of Research in Crime & Delinquency, 39*(1), 60-90.

Cicchetti, D., & Rogosch, F. A. (1996). Equifinality and multifinality in developmental psychopathology. *Development and Psychopathology, 8*(4), 597-600.

Clark, D. A., & Steer, R. A. (1996). Empirical status of the cognitive model of anxiety and depression. In P. M. Salkovskis (Ed.), *Frontiers of cognitive therapy.* New York: Guilford Press.

Cohen, D., & Strayer, J. (1996). Empathy in conduct-disordered and comparison youth. *Developmental Psychology, 32*(6), 988-998.

Cohen, P., & Brook, J. S. (1995). The reciprocal influence of punishment and child behavior disorder. In J. McCord (Ed). *Coercion and punishment in long-term perspectives* (pp. 154-164). Cambridge, England: Cambridge University Press.

Coie, J. D., Belding, M., & Underwood, M. (1988). Aggression and peer rejection in childhood. In B. Laheny & A. Kazdin (Eds.), *Clinical Child Psychology* (pp. 125-58). New York, NY: Plenum Press.

Coie, J. D., & Dodge, K. A. (1997). Aggression and antisocial behavior. In W. Damon & N. Eisenberg (Eds.), *Handbook of child psychology, Vol. 3. Social, emotional, and personality development* (5th ed.) (pp. 779-862). New York: Wiley.

Colby, S..M., & O'Leary, T.A. (Eds.), *Adolescents, alcohol, & substance abuse: Reaching teens through brief interventions* (pp. 80-108). New York: Guilford Press.

Coll, C. G., Miller, J. B., Fields, J. P., & Matthews, B. (1997). The experiences of women in prison: Implications for services and prevention. *Women and Therapy, 20*(4), 11-28.

Collingwood, R.G. (1945). *The idea of nature.* London: Oxford University Press.

Colorado Judicial Branch (1995). *Colorado Young Offender-Level of Service Inventory (CYO-LSI) Scoring Manual.* Originating and Revised from: I. Shields, *Young Offender-Level of Service Inventory (YO-LSI) Scoring Manual* and from D. Andrews, D. Robinson, & R. D. Hoge, *Youth-Level of Service Inventory (Y-LSI).* Juvenile Standardized Assessment, State of Colorado, Interagency Steering Committee.

Conger, R. D., & Rueter, M. A. (1996). Siblings, parents, and peers: A longitudinal study of social influences in adolescent risk for alcohol use and abuse. In G. H. Brody (Ed.), *Advances in applied developmental psychology, Vol. 10. Sibling relationships: Their causes and consequences* (pp. 1-30). Westport, CT: Greenwood Publishing Group.

Connelly, C. D., & Straus, M. A. (1992). Mother's age and risk for physical abuse. *Child Abuse and Neglect, 16,* 709-718.

Conners, C. K. (1997). *Conners' Rating Scales-Revised (CRS-R).* Toronto, Ontario: Multi-Health Systems, Inc.

Conners, C. K., & Wells, K.C. (1997). *Conners-Wells Adolescent Self-Report Scales (CASS).* Toronto, Canada: MultiHealth Systems, Inc.

Connors, G. J., Carroll, K. M., DiClemente, C. C., Longabaugh, R., & Donovan, D. M. (1997). The therapeutic alliance and its relationship to alcoholism treatment participation and outcome. *Journal of Consulting and Clinical Psychology, 65,* 582-598.

Connors, G. J., Donovan, D. M., & DiClemente, C.C. (2001). *Substance abuse treatment and the stages of change.* New York: The Guilford Press.

Constantino, M. J., Castonguay, L. G., & Schut, A. J. (2002). Predicting the effect of cognitive therapy for depression: A study of unique and common factors. *Journal of Consulting and Clinical Psychology, 64,* 497-504.

Cook, E., Stein, M., & Krasowski, M. (1995). Association of ADD and the dopamine transporter gene. *American Journal of Human Genetics, 56,* 933-998.

Cordess, C. (1995). Breaking and entering in phantasy and fact. In J. Ellwood (Ed.), *Psychosis: Understanding and treatment* (pp. 133-146). Bristol, PA: Jessica Kingsley Publishers.

Corwyn, R. F., & Benda, B. B. (1999). Multiple contingency table analysis of the deviance syndrome: How much overlap is there? *Journal of Child & Adolescent Substance Abuse, 9,* 39-56.

Corwyn, R. F., & Benda, B. B. (2002). The relationship between use of alcohol, other drugs, and crime among adolescents: An argument for a delinquency syndrome. *Alcoholism Treatment Quarterly, 20*(2), 35-49.

Costa, F. M., Jessor R., & Turbin, M. S. (1999). Transition into adolescent problem drinking: The role of psychosocial risk and protective factors. *Journal of Studies on Alcohol, 60*(4), 480-490.

Costello, E. J. (1989). Developments in child psychiatric epidemiology. *Journal of the American Academy of Child and Adolescent Psychiatry, 28,* 836-41.

Costello, J. E. (1999). Prevalence and impact of parent-reported disabling mental health conditions among U.S. children: Comment. *Journal of the American Academy of Child & Adolescent Psychiatry, 38*(5), 610-613.

Costello, J. E., Angold, A., Burns, B. J., Erkanli, A., Stangl, D. K., & Tweed, D. L. (1996). The great smoky mountains study of youth: Functional impairment and serious emotional disturbance. *Archives of General Psychiatry, 53*(12), 1137-1143.

Cottraux, J., & Blackburn, I. (2001). Cognitive therapy. In W.J. Livesley (Ed.), *Handbook of personality disorders* (pp. 377-399). New York: Guilford Publications.

Covington, S. S. (1998). Women in prison: Approaches in the treatment of our most invisible population. *Women & Therapy, 21*(1), 141-155.

Covington, S. S. (2000a). Helping women recover: A comprehensive integrated treatment model. *Alcoholism Treatment Quarterly, 18*(3), 99-111.

Covington, S. S. (2000b). Helping women to recover: Creating gender-specific treatment for substance-abusing women and girls in community corrections. In M. McMahon, (Ed.), *Assessment to assistance: Programs for women in community corrections* (pp. 171-234). Lanham, MD: American Correctional Association.

Covington, S. S. (2001). Creating gender-responsive programs: The next step for women's services. *Corrections Today, 63*(1), 85-87.

Covington, S. S., & Surrey, J. L. (1997). The relational model of women's psychological development: Implications for substance abuse. In R. W. Wilsnack & S. C. Wilsnack (Eds.), *Gender and alcohol: Individual and social perspectives* (pp. 335-351). New Brunswick, N.J.: Rutgers Center of Alcohol Studies.

Crawford, M., & Unger, R. (2003). *Women and gender: A feminist psychology.* New York: McGraw-Hill.

Crick, F. (1995). *The Astonishing Hypothesis. The Scientific Search for the Soul.* New York: Simon and Schuster

Cross, T. L., Bazron, B. J., Isaacs, M. R., & Dennis, K. W. (1989). *Towards a culturally competent system of care: A monograph on effective services for minority children who are severely emotionally disturbed.* Washington, DC: Georgetown University Center for Child Health and Mental Health Policy, CASSP Technical Assistance Center.

Curry, S. G., & Marlatt, G. A.(1987). Building self-confidence, self-efficacy and self-control. In W.M. Cos (Ed.), *Treatment and prevention of alcohol problems: A resource manual* (pp. 117-138). New York: Academic Press.

Dacey, J., & Kenny, M. (1997). *Adolescent Development.* 2nd edition. Boston, MA: WCB McGraw Hill.

Dahlberg, L. L., & Potter, L. B. (2001). Youth violence: Developmental pathways and prevention challenges. *American Journal of Preventive Medicine, 20*(1), 3-14.

Davis, A. Y. (1981). *Women, race, & class.* New York: Vintage Books.

Dawson, J. M. (1994). *Murder in families* (Bureau of Justice Statistics Special Report). Washington, D.C.: U.S. Department of Justice, Bureau of Justice Statistics.

Dearwater, S. R., Coben, J. H., Campbell, J. C., Nah, G., Glass, N., & McLoughlin, E., et al. (1998). Prevalence of intimate partner abuse in women treated at community hospital emergency departments. *JAMA: Journal of the American Medical Association, 280*(5), 433-438.

DeBellis, M. D., Clark, D. B., Beers, S. R., Soloff, P. H., Boring, A. M., Hall, J., Kersh, A., & Keshaven, M. S. (2000). Hippocampal volume in adolescent-onset alcohol use disorders. *American Journal of Psychiatry, 157,* 737-744.

DeCourville, N. H. (1995). Testing the applicability of problem behavior theory to substance use in a longitudinal study. *Psychology of Addictive Behaviors. 9*(1), 53-66.

Delia, J. G., O'Keefe, B. J., & O'Keefe, D. J. (1982). The constructivist approach to communication. In F. E. X. Dance (Ed.), *Human communication theory: Comparative essays* (pp. 147-191). New York: Harper & Row.

Demark, F. L. (1998). Women and psychology. *American Psychologist, 53*(4), 465-473.

Dembo, R., Hughes, P., Jackson, L., & Mieczkowski, T. (1993). Crack cocaine dealing by adolescents in two public housing projects: A pilot study. *Human Organization, 52*(1), 89-96.

Dembo, R., Wothke, W., Seeberger, W., Shemwell, M., Pacheco, K., & Rollie, M. et al., (2002). Testing a longitudinal model of the relationships among high risk youths' drug sales, drug use and participation in index crimes. *Journal of Child & Adolescent Substance Abuse, 11*(3), 37-61.

DeMuro, S.A. (1997). *Development and validation of an instrument to measure DUI therapeutic educator style: Therapeutic educator countermeasures inventory.* Denver, CO: University of Denver Unpublished Doctoral Dissertation.

Dennis, M. L., Dawud-Noursi, S., Muck, R. D., & McDermeit, M. (2003). The need for developing and evaluating adolescent treatment models. In S. J. Stevens & A. R. Morral (Eds.), *Adolescent substance abuse treatment in the United States: Exemplary models from a national evaluation study* (pp. 3-34). Binghamton, NY: Haworth Press.

DeRubis, R. J., Tang, T. Z., & Beck, A. T. (2001). Cognitive therapy. In K. S. Dobson (Ed.), *Handbook of cognitive-behavioral therapies* (2nd ed.) (pp. 349-392). New York: Guilford Press.

DiClemente, C. C. (2003). *Addiction and change.* New York: The Guilford Press.

DiClemente, C. C., & Velasquez, M. M. (2002). Motivational interviewing and the stages of change. In W. R. Miller & S. Rollnick (Eds.), *Motivational interviewing, second edition: Preparing people for change* (pp. 201-216). New York: Guilford Press.

Dimeff, L.A. & Marlatt, G.A. (1995). Relapse prevention. In R.K. Hester & W.R. Miller (Eds.), *Handbook of alcoholism treatment approaches: Effective alternatives* pp. 176-194). Boston: Allyn & Bacon.

Dishion, T. J., Capaldi, D., Spracklen, K. M., & Li, F. (1995). Peer ecology of male adolescent drug use. *Development and Psychopathology, 7*, 803-824.

Ditton, P. M. (1999). *Mental health and treatment of inmates and probationers.* Washington DC: U.S. Department of Justice, Bureau of Justice Statistics.

Dobson, K. S., & Block, L. (1988). Historical and philosophical bases of the cognitive-behavioral therapies. In K. S. Dobson (Ed.), *Handbook of cognitive-behavioral therapies* (pp. 3-38). New York: Guilford Press.

Dobson, K. S., & Dozois, D. J. (2001). Historical and philosophical bases of the cognitive-behavioral therapies. In K. S. Dobson (Ed.), *Handbook of cognitive-behavioral therapies* (2nd ed.) (pp. 3-39). New York: Guilford Press.

Dodd, M. H. (1997). Social model of recovery: Origin, early features, changes and future. *Journal of Psychoactive Drugs, 29*(2), 133-139.

Donovan, D. M., Marlatt, G. A., & Salzberg, P. M. (1983). Drinking behavior, personality factors and high-risk driving: A review and theoretical formulation. *Journal of Studies on Alcohol, 44*(3), 395-428.

Donovan, J. E. (1999). Adolescent problem drinking: Stability of psychological and behavioral correlates across a generation. *Journal of Studies on Alcoholism. 60*(3), 352-361.

Donovan, J., Jessor, R., & Costa, F. (1991). Adolescent health behavior and conventionality-unconventionality: An extension of problem behavior theory. *Health Psychology, 10*, 52-61.

Downs, W. R., & Miller, B. A. (1998). Relationships between experiences of parental violence during childhood and women's psychiatric symptomatology. *Journal of Interpersonal Violence, 13*(4), 438-455.

Dryden, W., & Ellis, A. (2001). Rational emotive behavioral therapy. In K.S. Dobson (Ed.), *Handbook of cognitive-behavioral therapies,* Second Edition (pp.295-348). New York: Guilford.

Dryden, W., & Mytton, J. (1999). *Four approaches to counseling and psychotherapy.* New York: Routledge.

Duku, J., Fleming E., & Walsh, C.A. (1999). Slapping, spanking and lifetime psychiatric disorder in a community sample of Ontario residents. *Canadian Medical Association Journal, 7*, 805-809.

Duman, J.E., & Nilsen, W.J. (2003) *Abnormal child andaAdolescent psychology.* Boston: Allyn & Bacon.

Duncan, S. C., Duncan, T. E., Biglan, A., & Ary, D. (1998). Contributions of the social context of the development of adolescent substance use: A multivariate latent growth modeling approach. *Drug and Alcohol Dependence, 50*, 57-71.

Dunlap, K. (1932). *Habits: Their making and unmaking.* Oxford, England: Liveright.

DuPaul, G. J., & Barkley, R. A. (1993). Behavioral contributions to pharmacotherapy: The utility of behavioral methodology in medication treatment of children with Attention Deficit Hyperactivity Disorder. *Behavior Therapy, 24*(1), 47-65.

DuRant, R. H., Getts A., Cadenhead, C., & S. Emans, J. (1995). Exposure to violence and victimization and depression, hopelessness, and purpose in life among adolescents living in and around public housing. *Journal of Deviant Behavior in Pediatrics, 16*, 233-237.

DuRant, R. H., Rome, E. S., & Rich, M. (1997). Tobacco and alcohol use behaviors portrayed in music videos: A content analysis. *American Journal of Public Health, 87*(7), 1131-1135.

Durrant, J. E. (1999). Evaluating the success of Sweden's corporal punishment ban. *Child Abuse & Neglect, 23*, 435-448.

Durrant, J. E. (2000). Trends in youth crime and well-being since the abolition of corporal punishment in Sweden. *Youth & Society, 31*(4). 437-455.

Dusenbury, L. A., Botvin, G. J., & Diaz, T. (1994). Social influence predictors of alcohol use among New York Latino youth. *Addictive Behaviors, 19*(4), 363-372.

D'Zurilla, T. J., & Goldfried, M. R. (1971). Problem solving and behavior modification. *Journal of Abnormal Psychology, 78*(1), 107-126.

D'Zurilla, T. J. , & Nezu, A.M. (2001). Problem-solving therapies. In K.S. Dobson (ed). *Handbook of cognitive-behavioral therapies.* Second Edition. New York: The Guilford Press.

Efran, J. S. & Clarfield, L. E. (1992). Constructionist therapy: Sense and nonsense. In S. McNamee & K.J. Gergen (Eds.), *Therapy as social construction* (pp. 200-217). London, UK: Sage

Ehlers, A., & Clark, D. M. (2003). Early psychological interventions for adult survivors of trauma: A review. *Biological Psychiatry, 53*(9), 817-826.

Elander, J., Simonoff, E., Pickles, A., Holmshaw, J., & Rutter, M. (2000). A longitudinal study of adolescent and adult conviction rates among children referred to psychiatric services for behavioral or emotional problems. *Criminal Behavior & Mental Health, 10*(1), 40-59.

El-Bassel, N., Gilbert, L., Schilling, R. F., Ivanoff, A., Borne, D., & Safyer, S. F. (1996). Correlates of crack abuse among drug-using incarcerated women: Psychological trauma, social support, and coping behavior. *American Journal of Drug and Alcohol Abuse, 22*(1), 41-56.

Elkin, K. (1986). *NIMH treatment of depression collaborative research program.* Paper presented at the annual meeting of the Society for Psychotherapy Research, Wellesley, MA.

Elliott, D. M., & Briere, J. (1990). Predicting molestation history in professional women with the Trauma Symptom drug-using incarcerated women: Psychological trauma, social support, and coping behavior. *American Journal of Drug and Alcohol Abuse, 22*(1), 41-56.

Elliott, D. S. (1994). Serious violent offenders: Onset, developmental course, and termination--The American Society of Criminology 1993 Presidential Address. *Criminology, 32*, 1-21.

Elliott, D. S., Ageton, S. S., Huizinga, D., Knowles, B. A., & Canter, R. J. (1983*). The Prevalence and Incidence of Delinquent Behavior: 1976-1980.* (The National Youth Survey Report No. 26). Boulder, CO: Behavioral Research Institute.

Elliott, F. A. (2000). A neurological perspective of violent behavior. In D. H. Fishbein (Ed.), *The science, treatment, and prevention of antisocial behaviors: Application to the criminal justice system.* Kingston, NJ: Civic Research Institute.

Ellis, A. (1962). *Reason and emotion in psychotherapy.* Oxford, England: Lyle Stuart.

Ellis, A. (1984). Expanding the ABCs of RET. *Journal of Rational-Emotive Therapy, 2*(2), 20-24.

Ellis, A., & Harper, R. A. (1961). *A guide to rational living.* Oxford, England: Prentice-Hall.

Ellis, A., & Harper, R. A. (1975). *A new guide to rational living.* Oxford, England: Prentice-Hall.

Ellis, J. W. (1996). Voluntary admission and involuntary hospitalization of minors. In B. D. Sales & D. W. Shuman (Eds.), *Law, mental health, and mental disorder* (pp. 487-502). Pacific Grove, CA: Brooks/Cole Publishing.

Ellis, P. L. (1982). Empathy: A factor in antisocial behavior. *Journal of Abnormal Child Psychology, 10*(1), 123-133.

Ellison, C. G., & Sherkat D. E. (1993). Conservative Protestantism and support for corporal punishment. *American Sociological Review, 58*, 131-44.

Emler, N., & Reicher, S. (1995). *Adolescence and delinquency: The collective management of reputation.* Malden, MA: Blackwell Publishers.

Epstein, J. A., Botvin, G. J., Diaz, T., & Schinke, S. P. (1995). The role of social factors and individual characteristics in promoting alcohol use among inner-city minority youths. *Journal of Studies on Alcohol. 56*(1), 39-46.

Epstein, J. A., Griffin, K. W., & Botvin, G. J. (2001). Risk taking and refusal assertiveness in a longitudinal model of alcohol use among inner-city adolescents. *Prevention Science, 2*(3), 193-200.

Erickson, E. H. (1950). *Childhood and society.* New York: Norton.

Erickson, K. G., Crosnoe, R., & Dornbusch, S. M. (2000). A social process model of adolescent deviance: Combining social control and differential association perspectives. *Journal of Youth and Adolescence, 29*, 395-425.

Erickson, K., Crosnoe, R., & Dornbusch, S. M. (2000). A social process model of adolescent deviance: Combining social control and differential association perspectives. *Journal of Youth & Adolescence*, 29(4), 395-425.

Erikson, E. H. (1963). *Childhood and society* (2nd ed.). New York: Norton.

Erikson, E. H. (1968). *Identity: Youth and crisis*. Oxford, England: Norton.

Eron, L. D., Huesmann, L. R., & Zelli, A. (1991). The role of parental variables in the learning of aggression. In: D. Pepler & K. Rubin (Eds.), *The development and treatment of childhood aggression* (pp. 169-188). Hillsdale NJ: Erlbaum.

Eronen, M. (1995). Mental disorders and homicidal behavior in female subjects. *American Journal of Psychiatry, 152*(8), 1216-1218.

Esman, A. H., Flaherty, L. T., & Horowitz, H. A. (Eds.). (1998) *Adolescent psychiatry: Vol. 13. Developmental and clinical studies* (pp. 121-138). Chicago, IL: University of Chicago Press.

Evert, D.L., and Oscar-Berman, M. (1995). Alcohol-related cogitative impairments: An overview of how alcoholism may affect the workings of the brain. *Alcohol Health Resource World, 14*(2), 120-129.

Eyde, L. D., & Quaintance, M. K. (1988). Ethical issues and cases in the practice of personnel psychology. *Professional Psychology: Research & Practice, 19*(2), 148-154.

Eyde, L. D., Moreland, K. L., Robertson, G. J., Primoff, E. S., & Most, R. B. (1998). *Test user qualifications: A data-based approach to promoting good test use (Executive summary)*. Joint Committee on Testing Practices, Test User Qualifications Working Group. Washington, DC: American Psychological Association.

Eysenck, H. J. (1960). *Behaviour therapy and the neuroses: Readings in modern methods of treatment derived from learning theory*. New York: Pergamon Press.

Fagan, J. (2000). Contexts of choice by adolescents in criminal events. In T. Grisso & R. G. Schwartz (Eds.), *Youth on trial: A developmental perspective on juvenile justice* (pp. 371-401). Chicago: University of Chicago Press.

Fagan, J., & Wilkinson, D. L. (1998). Guns, youth violence, and social identity in inner cities. In M. Tonry & M.H. Moore (Eds.), *Youth Violence: Vol 24.* (pp. 105-188). Chicago, IL: University of Chicago Press.

Fagan, J. & Wilkinson, D. L. (1998). Social context and functions of adolescent violence. In D.S. Elliott, B.A. Hamburg, & K.R. Williams (Eds.) *Violence in American schools: A new perspective* (pp. 55-84). New York: Cambridge University Press.

Falck, R. S., Wang, J., Carlson, R.G., & Siegal, H. A. (2001). The epidemiology of physical attack and rape among crack-using women. *Violence and Victims, 16*(1), 79-89.

Falsetti, S. A., Resnick, H. S., Resick, P. A., & Kirkpatrick, D. G. (1993). The Modified PTSD Symptom Scale: A brief self-report measure of posttraumatic stress disorder. *The Behavior Therapist, 16*(6), 161-162.

Farabee, D., Shen, H., Hser, Y., Grella, C. E., & Anglin, M. D. (2001). The effect of drug treatment on criminal behavior among adolescents in DATOS-A [Special issue]. *Journal of Adolescent Research, 16*(6), 679-696.

Farrell, A. D. (1992). Relationship between drug use and other problem behaviors in urban adolescents. *Journal of Consulting and Clinical Psychology, 60*(5), 705-712.

Farrington, D. P. (1996). Criminological psychology: Individual and family factors in the explanation and prevention of offending. In C. R. Hollin (Ed.), *Working with offenders: Psychological practice in offender rehabilitation* (pp. 3-39). New York: Wiley and Sons.

Farrington, D. P. (1996). The explanation and prevention of youthful offending. In J. D. Hawkins (Ed.), *Cambridge criminology series. Delinquency and crime: Current theories* (pp. 68-148). New York: Cambridge University Press.

Farrington, D.P., B. Gallagher, L. Morley, R.J. Ledger, and D.J. West (1986). Unemployment, school leaving, and crime. *British Journal of Criminology 26*, 335-56.

Farrington, D. P., & Hawkins, J. D. (1991). Predicting participation, early onset and later persistence in officially recorded offending. *Criminal Behavior & Mental Health, 1*(1), 1-33.

Farrington, D. P., Loeber, R., Stouthamer-Loeber, M., Van Kammen, W., & Schmidt L. (1996). Self-reported delinquency and a combined delinquency seriousness scale based on boys, mothers, and teachers: Concurrent and predictive validity for African-Americans and Caucasians. *Criminology, 34*, 501-25.

Farrington, D. P., Loeber, R., & Van Kammen, W. B. (1990). Long-term criminal outcomes of hyperactivity-impulsivity-attention deficit and conduct problems in childhood. In L. N. Robins & M. Rutter (Eds.), *Straight a devious pathways from childhood to adulthood* (pp. 62-81). New York: Cambridge University Press.

Farrow, J. A. (1985). Drinking and driving behaviors of 16 to 19 year-olds. *Journal of Studies on Alcohol, 46*(5), 369-374.

Feder, A., & Brett, C. (2001).. Psychosocial and cognitive variables associated with recidivism in juvenile delinquency: A one-year follow up study of graduates from a level VI juvenile justice center. *Dissertation Abstracts International: Section B: The & Engineering*, Vol 61(9-B), pp. 4979.

Feigelman, S., Howard, D. E., Xiaoming, L., & Cross, S. I. (2000). Psychosocial and environmental correlates of violence perpetration among African-American urban youth. *Journal of Adolescent Health, 27*, 202-209.

Feld, B. C. (1998). The juvenile court. In M. H. Tonry (Ed.), *Handbook of crime and punishment* (pp. 509-541). London: Oxford University Press.

Felix-Ortiz, M., & Newcomb, M. D. (1999). Vulnerability for drug use among Latino adolescents. *Journal of Community Psychology, 27*(3), 257-280.

Fergusson, D. M., Horwood, L. J., & Nagin, D. S. (2000). Offending trajectories in a New Zealand birth cohort. *Criminology, 38*, 401-427.

Fergusson, D. M., Lynskey, M. T., & Horwood, L. J. (1996). Factors associated with continuity and changes in disruptive behavior patterns between childhood and adolescence. *Journal of Abnormal Child Psychology, 24*(5), 533-553.

Fergusson, D. M., Swain-Campbell, N. R., Horwood, L. J. (2002). Deviant peer affiliations, crime and substance use: A fixed effects regression analysis. *Journal of Abnormal Child Psychology, 30*(4), 419-430.

Fergusson, D. M., & Woodwood, L. J. (1996). The role of adolescent peer affiliations in the continuity between childhood behavioral adjustment and juvenile offending. *Journal of Abnormal Child Psychology, 24*, 205-221.

Fergusson, D. M., & Woodward, L. J. (1999). Maternal age and educational and psychosocial outcomes in early adulthood. *Journal of Child Psychology & Psychiatry & Allied Disciplines, 40*(3), 479-489.

Fergusson, D. M., Woodward, L. J., & Horwood, L. J. (1999). Childhood peer relationship problems and young people's involvement with deviant peers in adolescence. *Journal of Abnormal Child Psychology, 27*, 357-370.

Finch, J. J. (1993). *Cognitive-behavioral procedures with children & adolescents: A practical guide.* Boston, MA: Allyn & Bacon.

Finkelhor, D. (1984). *Child sexual abuse: New theory and research.* New York: Free Press.

Flanagan, T. J. & Longmire, D. R. (Eds.). (1996). Americans view crime and justice: A national public opinion survey. National Crime and Justice Survey (NCJS). Thousand Oaks, CA: Sage Publications.

Fletcher, B. R., Shaver, L. O., & Moon, D. G. (1993). *Women prisoners: A forgotten population.* Westport, CT: Praeger.

Flowers, R. B. (2002). *Kids who commit adult crimes: Serious criminality by juvenile offenders.* New York: Haworth Press, Inc.

Foa, E. B., Hearst-Ikeda, D., & Perry, K. J. (1995). Evaluation of a brief cognitive-behavioral program for the prevention of chronic PTSD in recent assault victims. *Journal of Consulting & Clinical Psychology, 63*(6), 948-955.

Fonagy, P., Target, M., Steele, M., & Steele, H. (1997). The development of violence and crime as it relates to security of attachment. In J. D. Osofsky (Ed.), *Children in a violent society* (pp. 150-177). New York: Guilford Press.

Fonagy, P., Target, M., Steele, M., Steele, H., Leigh, T., Levinson, A., & Kennedy, R. (1997b). Morality, disruptive behavior, borderline personality disorder, crime and their relationship to security of attachment. In L. Atkinson & K. J. Zucker (Eds.), *Attachment and psychopathology* (pp. 223-274). U.S. Department of Justice.

Forth, A. E., & Mailloux, D. L. (2000). Psychopathy in youth: What do we know? In C. B. Gacono (Ed.), *The clinical and forensic assessment of psychopathy: A practitioner's guide.* The LEA series in personality and clinical psychology (pp. 25-54). Trenton, NJ: Erlbaum Associates.

Fox, G. L. (1977). "Nice girl": Social control of women through a value construct. *Signs: Journal of Women in Culture and Society, 2*(4), 805-817.

Fox, J. A. (1997). Trends in Juvenile homicide; Report to the U.S. Attorney General. Retrieved 4-9-02 from the World Wide Web: <www.oip.usdoj.gov/gjs/labstract/tjvfox.htm>

Fox, J. A., & Levin, J. (2001). *The will to kill: Making sense of senseless murder.* Boston, MA: Allyn & Bacon.

Fox, J. A., & Zawitz, M. W. (March 2000). Homicide trends in the United States. Crime Data Brief. Washington, DC. Bureau of Justice Statistics, U.S. Department of Justice.

Frank, J. D. (1963). *Persuasion and healing: A comparative study of psychotherapy.* New York: Schocken Books.

Frank, J. D. (1974). Psychotherapy: Restoration of morale. *American Journal of Psychiatry, 131,* 271-274.

Frank, J. D. (1992). Historical development in research centers: The Johns Hopkins Psychotherapy Research Project. In D. K. Freedheim (Ed.), *History of psychotherapy: A century of change* (pp. 392-395). Washington, DC: American Psychological Association.

Franks, C. M., & Barbarck, C. R. (1983). Behavior therapy with Adults: An integrative perspective. In M. Hersen, A.E. Kazdin, & A. S. Bellack (Eds.), *Clinical psychology handbook* (pp.507-524). New York: Pergamon.

Franks, C. M., & Wilson, G. T. (1973). *Annual review of behavior therapy: Theory & practice 1973*. Oxford, England: Brunner/Mazel.

Franzek, E., & Beckmann, H. (1992). Sex differences and distinct subgroups in schizophrenia: A study of 54 chronic hospitalized schizophrenics. *Psychopathology, 25*(2), 90-99.

Fraser, M. W. (1996). Aggressive behavior in childhood and early adolescence: An ecological-developmental perspective on youth violence. *Social Work, 41*(4), 347-361.

Freeman, A. M., Pretzer, J. L., Fleming, B., & Simon, K. M. (1990). *Clinical applications of cognitive therapy*. New York: Plenum Press.

Freud, A. (1958). Adolescence. *Psychoanalytic Study of the Child, 13*, 255-278.

Freud, S. (1915). *Thoughts for the times on war and death*. In Standard Edition of the Complete Psychological Works of Sigmund Freud. (1957). London: Hogarth Press.

Frick, P. J. (1998). *Conduct disorders and severe antisocial behavior*. New York: Plenum Press.

Frick, P. J., Barry, C. T., & Bodin, S. D. (2000). Applying the concept of psychopathy to children: Implications for the assessment of antisocial youth. In C. B. Gacono (Ed.), *The clinical and forensic assessment of psychopathy: A practitioner's guide. The LEA series in personality and clinical psychology*. (pp. 3-24). Trenton, NJ: Erlbaum Associates.

Frick, P. J., Bodin, D. S., & Barry, C. T. (2000). Psychopathic traits and conduct problems in community and clinic-referred samples of children: Further development of the Psychopathy Screening Device. *Psychological Assessment, 12*(4), 382-393.

Frick, P. J., Christian, R. E., & Wooton, J. M. (1999). Age trends in association between parenting practices and conduct problems. *Behavior Modification, 23*(1), 106-128.

Frick, P. J., & Ellis, M. (1999). Callous-unemotional traits and subtypes of conduct disorder. *Clinical Child & Family Psychology Review, 2*(3), 149-168.

Friedman, A. S., & Utada, A. (1989). A method for diagnosing and planning the treatment of adolescent drug abusers: Adolescent Drug Abuse Diagnosis instrument. *Journal of Drug Education, 19, 285-312.*

Friedman, M., Glasser, M., Laufer, E., Laufer, M., Wohl, M. (1996). Attempted suicide and self-mutilation in adolescence: Some observations from a psychoanalytic research project. In J. T. Maltsberger & M. J. Goldblatt (Eds.), *Essential papers on suicide. Essential papers in psychoanalysis* (pp. 259-268). New York: New York University Press.

Frieze, I. H. (1983). Investigating the causes and consequences of marital rape. *Signs: Journal of Women in Culture and Society, 8*(3), 532-552.

GAINS Center. (1997). *Women's program compendium: A comprehensive guide to services for women with co-occurring disorders in the justice system*. Delmar, NY: The GAINS Center / Policy Research Associates, Inc.

Gallant, G. P. Keita, & R. Royak-Schaler (Eds.), *Health care for women: Psychological, social, and behavioral influences* (pp. 97-114). Washington, DC: American Psychological Association.

Gallucci, N.T. (1997). On the identification of patterns of substance abuse with the MMPI-A. *Psychological Assessment, 9*, 224-232.

Garfield, S. L. (1992). Major issues in psychotherapy research. In D. K. Freedheim (Ed.), *History of psychotherapy: A century of change* (pp. 335-359). Washington, DC: American Psychological Association.

Garmezy, N., Masten, A. S., & Tellegen, A. (1984). The study of stress and competence in children: A building block for developmental psychopathology. *Child Development, 55*(1), 97-111.

Gaston, L. (1990). The concept of the alliance and its role in psychotherapy: Theoretical and empirical considerations. *Psychotherapy, 27,* 143-153.

Ge, X., Best, K., Conger, R., & Simons, R. (1996). Parenting behavior and the occurrence and co-occurrence of adolescent depressive symptoms and conduct problems. *Developmental Psychology. 32*, 717-731.

Gebotys, R. J., & Dasgupta, B. (1987). Attribution of responsibility and crime seriousness. *Journal of Psychology, 121*(6). 607-613.

Geissinger, C. J., & Hill, M. M. (2000). *Vicarious trauma debriefing groups: Getting started*. Denver, CO: Colorado Organization for Victim Assistance.

George, R. L. (1990). *Counseling the chemically dependent: Theory and practice*. Englewood Cliffs, NJ: Prentice-Hall.

George, R. L., & Cristiani, T. S. (1981). *Theory, methods and processes of counseling and psychotherapy*. Englewood Cliffs, NJ: Prentice-Hall.

Gergen, M. M., & Davis, S. N. (Eds.) (1997). *Toward a new psychology of gender: A reader*. New York: Routledge.

Giedd, J., Blumenthal, J., Jeffries, N., Castillanos, F., Liu, H., Fijdenbos, A., Paus, T., Evans, A., Rapoport, J. (1999). Brain development during childhood and adolescence: a longitudinal MRI study. *Nature Neuroscience*, 2:861 863.

Gil, A. G., Tubman, J. G., Wagner, E. F., (2001). Substance abuse interventions with Latino adolescents: A cultural framework. In: E. F. Wagner, & H. B. Waldron, (Eds.), *Innovations in adolescent substance abuse interventions* (pp. 353-378). Amsterdam, Netherlands:Pergamon/Elsevier Science Inc.

Gilliard, D. K., & Beck, A. J. (1994). *Prisoners in 1993.* Washington, D.C.: U.S. Department of Justice, Bureau of Justice Statistics.

Gilligan, C. (1982). *In a different voice: Psychological theory and women's development.* Cambridge MA: Harvard University Press.

Girls Incorporated (1996). *Prevention and parity: Girls in juvenile justice.* Indianapolis, IN: Girls Incorporated National Resource Center.

Gjerde, P. F. (1995). Alternative pathways to chronic depressive symptoms in young adults: Gender differences in developmental trajectories. *Child Development, 66*(5), 1277-1300.

Glaser, B. A., Calhoun, G. B., & Petrocelli, J. V. (2002). Personality characteristics of male juvenile offenders by adjudicated offenses as indicated by the MMPI-A. *Criminal Justice & Behavior, 29*(2), 183-201.

Glass, C.R., & Arnkoff, D.B. (1988). Common and specific factors in client descriptions of and explanations for change. *Journal of Integrative and Eclectic Psychotherapy, 7,* 427-440.

Glass, C. R., & Arnkoff, D. B. (1992). Behavior therapy. In D. K. Freedheim & H. J. Freudenberger (Eds.), *History of psychotherapy: A century of change* (pp. 587-628). Washington, DC: American Psychological Association.

Glassman, S. (1983). In, with, and of the group: A perspective on group psychotherapy. *Small Group Behavior, 14,* 96-106.

Glicken, M. D., & Sechrist, D. K. (2003). *The role of helping professions in treating the victims and perpetrators of violence.* Boston, MA: Allyn & Bacon.

Godley, S. H., Risberg, R., Adams, L., & Sodetz, Al. (2003). Chestnut Health Systems' Bloomington outpatient and intensive outpatient program for adolescent substance abusers. In S. J. Stevens & A. R. Morral (Eds.), *Adolescent substance abuse treatment in the United States.* (pp. 57-80). New York: Haworth Press.

Godley, S., White, W., Diamond, G., Passetti, L., & Titus, J. (2001). Therapist reactions to manual-guided therapies for the treatment of adolescent marijuana users. *Clinical Psychology: Science and Practice, 8,* 405-417.

Goffman, E. (1963). *Stigma.* Englewood Cliffs, NJ: Prentice-Hall.

Goldfried, M. R. (1995). *From cognitive-behavior therapy to psychotherapy integration: An evolving view.* New York: Springer Publishing Co.

Goldfried, M. R., Decenteceo, E. T., & Weinberg, L. (1974). Systematic rational restructuring as a self-control technique. *Behavior Therapy, 5*(2), 247-254.

Goldiamond, I. (1965). Self-control procedures in personal behavior problems. *Psychological Reports, 17*(3), 851-868.

Goldman-Fraser, J. (1998). Cognitive influences on mother-infant interaction: A focus on substance-dependent women in treatment during pregnancy and postpartum. *Dissertation Abstracts International, 58*(12), 6844B. (UMI No. 9818337)

Goodman, L. A., Dutton, M. A., & Harris, M. (1995). Episodically homeless women with serious mental illness: Prevalence of physical and sexual assault. *American Journal of Orthopsychiatry, 65*(4), 468-478.

Gordon, L. R., (2000). *Existentia Africana: Understanding Africana existential thought.* New York: Routledge

Gorman, D. M. (1998). The irrelevance of evidence in the development of school-based drug prevention policy, 1986-1996 [Special issue]. *Evaluation Review, 22*(1), 118-146.

Gottfredson, M., & Hirschi, T. (1990). *A General Theory of Crime.* Stanford, CA.: Stanford University Press.

Grasmick, H. G., Bursik, R.J. Jr., & M'lou, K. (1991). Protestant fundamentalism and attitudes toward corporal punishment of children. *Violence and Victims, 6,* 282-98.

Greenberg, D. F. (Ed.). (1996a). *Criminal careers: Vol. 2. The international library of criminology, criminal justice and penology* (pp. 339-375). Brookfield, VT: Dartmouth Publishing.

Greenberg, D. F. (1996b). Delinquency and the age structure of society. In D. F. Greenberg (Ed.), *Criminal careers: Vol. 1. The international library of criminology, criminal justice and penology* (pp. 13-47). Brookfield, VT: Dartmouth Publishing.

Greenberg, M.T., Domitrovich, C., & Bumbarger, B. (1999). *Preventing mental disorders in school-age children: A review of the effectiveness of prevention programs.* U.S. Dept. of Health and Human Services. State College, PA: Pennsylvania State University, Prevention Research Center for the Promotion of Health and Human Development.

Greenberger, D., & Padesky, C. A. (1995). *Mind over mood: A cognitive therapy treatment manual for clients.* New York: Guilford Press.

Greene, B. (1995). Trauma History Questionnaire (adapted from the DSM-IV Field Trial High Magnitude Stressor Questionnaire). In B.H. Stamm & E. M. Varra (Eds.), *Measurement of stress, trauma, and adaptation* (pp. 366-369). Lutherville, MD: Sidron Press.

Greenhill, L. L. (1998). Attention-deficit/hyperactivity disorder. In T. B. Walsh (Ed.), *Child psychopharmacology* (pp. 29-64). Washington, DC: American Psychiatric Association.

Greenson, R. R. (1967). *Technique and practice of psychoanalysis.* New York: International University Press.

Gregoire, T. K., & Snively, C. A. (2001). The relationship of social support and economic self-sufficiency to substance abuse outcomes in a long-term recovery program for women. *Journal of Drug Education, 31*(3), 221-237.

Greven, P. (1991). *Spare the child: The religious roots of physical punishment and the psychological impact of physical abuse.* New York: Knopf.

Griffin, K. W., Botvin, G. J., Epstein, J. A., Doyle, M. M., & Diaz, T. (2000). Psychosocial and behavioral factors in early adolescence as predictors of heavy drinking among high school seniors. *Journal of Studies on Alcohol. 61*(4), Jul. pp. 603-606.

Griffin, K. W., Botvin, G. J., Scheier, L. M., Diaz, T., & Miller, N. L. (2000). Parenting practices as predictors of substance use, delinquency, and aggression among urban minority youth: Moderating effects of family structure and gender. *Psychology of Addictive Behaviors.* Vol 14(2), Jun. pp. 174-184.

Griffin, K. W., Epstein, J. A., Botvin G. J., & Spoth, R. L. (2001). Social competence and substance use among rural youth: Mediating role of social benefit expectancies of use. *Journal of Youth & Adolescence, 30*(4), 485-498.

Griffin, K. W., Scheier, L. M., Botvin, G. J., & Diaz, T. (2000). Ethnic and gender differences in psychosocial risk, protection, and adolescent alcohol use. *Prevention Science, 1*(4), 199-212.

Griffin, K. W., Scheier, L. M., Botvin, G. J., & Diaz, T. (2001). Protective role of personal competence skills in adolescent substance use: Psychological well-being as a mediating factor. *Psychology of Addictive Behaviors*, 15(3), 194-203.

Gruenewald, P. J., & Klitzner, M. (1991). Results of a preliminary POSIT analyses. In E. Radhert (Ed.). *Adolescent Assessment and Referral System Manual* (DHHS Publication No. ADM 91-1735). Rockville, MD: National Institute on Drug Abuse.

Guajardo-Lucero, M. (2000). *The Spirit of Culture: Applying Cultural Competency to Strength-Based Youth Development.* Denver, CO: Assets for Colorado Youth.

Gunnoe, M. L., & Mariner, C. L. (1997). Toward a Developmental-Contextual Model of the Effects of Parental Spanking on Children's Aggression. *Archives in Pediatric Adolescent Medicine, 151*, 768-775.

Gurman, A. S., & Messer, A. S. (2003). Contemporary issues in the theory and practice of psychotherapy: A framework for comparative study. In A.S. Gurman & S. B. Messer (Eds.), *Essential psychotherapies, Second Edition: Theory and practice (pp.1-23).* New York: The Guilford Press.

Guthrie, E. R. (1935). *Psychology of learning.* Oxford, England: Harper.

Haeuser, A. A. (1990). *Banning Parental Use of Physical Punishment: Success in Sweden.* Presented at the Eighth International Congress on Child Abuse and Neglect, Hamburg, Germany, 2-6 September.

Hagan, M. P., & Gust-Brey, K. L. (2000). A ten-year longitudinal study of adolescent perpetrators of sexual assault against children. *Journal of Offender Rehabilitation, 31*(1-2), 117-126.

Hall, G. S. (1916). *Adolescence (Vols. 1-2).* New York: Appleton.

Halligan, S. L., Michael, T., Clark, D. M., & Ehlers, A. (2003). Posttraumatic stress disorder following assault: The role of cognitive processing, trauma memory, and appraisals. *Journal of Consulting & Clinical Psychology, 71*(3), 419-431.

Halperin, J. M., Newcorn, J. H., Kopstein, I., McKay, K. E., Schwartz, S. T., Siever, L. J., & Sharma, V. (1997). Serotonin aggression, and parental psychopathology in children with attention-deficit hyperactivity disorder. *Journal of American Academy of Child and Adolescent Psychiatry, 36*, 10.

Ham, H. (1957). *Lecture on the concepts of Kurt Lewin's theory of growth and learning.* Denver, CO: Iliff School of Theology.

Haney, M., Ward, A.S., Comer, S.D., Foltin, R.W., & Fischman, M.W. (1999). Abstinence symptoms following smoked marijuana in humans. *Psychopharmacology, 141*, 395-404.

Hare, R. D., Hart, S. D., & Harpur, T. J. (1991). Psychopathy and the DSM-IV criteria for antisocial personality disorder. *Journal of Abnormal Psychology, 100*(3), 391-398.

Hare, R. D. & Kossan, D. S. (2003). *Hare Psychopathy Checklist: Youth Version (PCL:YV).* Toronto, Ontario, Canada: Multi-Health Systems.

Hare-Mustin, R.T., & Marecek, J. (Eds.). (1990). *Making a difference: Psychology and the construction of gender.* New Haven, CT: Yale University Press.

Harrell, A. V., & Wirtz, P. W. (1985). *The adolescent drinking index professional manual.* Odessa, FL: Psychological Assessment Resources.

Harrell, T. H., Honaker, L. M., & Davis, E. (1991). Cognitive and behavioral dimensions of dysfunction in alcohol and polydrug abusers. *Journal of Substance Abuse, 3*, 415-426.

Harrison, P. A., Asche, S.E. (2001). Adolescent treatment for substance use disorders: Outcomes and outcome predictors. *Journal of Child & Adolescent Substance Abuse, 11*(2), 1-18.

Harrison, P. A., Fulkerson, J. A., & Beebe, T. J. (1998). DSM-IV substance use disorder criteria for adolescents: A critical examination based on a statewide school survey. *American Journal of Psychiatry, 155*, 486-492.

Hartley, D., & Strupp, H. (1983). The therapeutic alliance: Its relationship to outcome in brief psychotherapy. In J. Mesling (Ed.), *Empirical studies of psychoanalytic theory.* Vol.1, pp. 1-38). Hillsdale, NJ: Erlbaum.

Hasin, D., & Paykin, A. (1998). Dependence symptoms but no diagnosis: Diagnostic orphans in a "community" sample. *Drug and Alcohol Dependence, 50*, 19-26.

Hawkins, J. D., Catalano, R. F., & Miller, J. Y. (1992). Risk and protective factors for alcohol and other drug problems in adolescence and early adulthood: Implications for substance abuse prevention. *Psychological Bulletin, 112*, 674-105.

Hawkins, J. D., Herrenkohl, T. I., Farrington, D. P., Brewer, D., Catalano, R. F., Harachi, T. W., & Cothern, L. (2000). *Predictors of Youth Violence.* Juvenile Justice Bulletin (April 2000). Rockville, MD: Office of Juvenile Justice and Delinquency Prevention.

Hawkins, J. D., Lishner, D. M., & Catalano, R. F. (1985). Childhood predictors and the prevention of adolescent substance abuse. In C. L. Jones & R. J. Battjes (Eds.) *Etiology of drug abuse: Implications for prevention* (pp. 75-125). Washington, D. C.: National Institute on Drug Abuse.

Hawkins, J. D., (Ed). (1996). Delinquency and crime: Current theories. Series Title*: Cambridge criminology series.* New York: Cambridge University Press.

Hawkins, J. D., Herrenkohl, T., Farrington, D. P., Brewer, D., Catalano, R. F., & Harachi, T. W. (1998). A review of predictors of youth violence. In R. Loeber & D. P. Farrington (Eds.), *Serious & violent juvenile offenders: Risk factors and successful interventions* (pp. 106-146). Thousand Oaks, CA: Sage Publications.

Hayes, R.D., & Ellickson, P.L. (1990). How generalizeable are adolescents' beliefs about pro-drug pressures and resistance self-efficacy? *Journal of Applied social Psychology, 20,* 321-340.

Heide, K. M. (1999). *Young killers: The challenge of juvenile homicide.* Thousand Oaks, CA: Sage Publications.

Helms, J. E., & Cook, D. A. (1999). *Using race and culture in counseling and psychotherapy: Theory and process.* Needham Heights, MA: Allyn & Bacon.

Hemenway, D., Prothrow-Stith, D., Bergstein, J., Adler, R., & Kennedey, B. (1996). Gun carrying among adolescents. *Law and Contemporary Problems 59*, 39-53

Henggeller, S. W., Cunningham, P. B., Pickrel, S. G., & Schoenwald, S. K. (1996). Multisystemic therapy: An effective violence prevention approach for serious juvenile offenders. *Journal of Adolescence, 19*(1), 47-61.

Henggeler, S. W., Mihalic, S. F., Rone, L., Thomas, C., & Timmons-Mitchell, J. (1998). *Blueprints for violence prevention: Multisystemic therapy.* Boulder: University of Colorado at Boulder, Center for the Study and Prevention of Violence, Blueprints Publications.

Henggeler, S.W., Pickrel, S.G., Brondino, M.J., & Crouch, J.L. (1996). Eliminating (almost) treatment dropout of substance abuse or dependent delinquents through home-based multisystemic therapy. *American Journal of Psychiatry, 153:* 427-428.

Henggeller, S. W., Schoenwald, S. K., Borduin, C. M., Rowland, M. D., & Cunningham, P. B. (1998). *Multisystemic treatment of antisocial behavior in children and adolescents.* NY: Guilford Press.

Henker, B., & Whalen, C. K. (1989). Hyperactivity and attention deficits. *American Psychologist, 44*(2), 216-223.

Henly, G. A., & Winters, K. C. (1988). Development of problem severity scales for the assessment of adolescent alcohol and drug abuse. *International Journal of the Addictions, 23*(1), 65-85.

Henry, B., Caspi, A., Moffitt, T., & Silva P. (1994). *Temperament and Family Predictors of Violent and Nonviolent Criminal Conviction: From Age 3 to Age 18.* Manuscript submitted for publication.

Henry, B., Feehan, M., McGee, R., Stanton, W., Moffitt, T., & Silva, P. (1993). The importance of conduct problems and depressive symptoms in predicting adolescent substance use. *Journal of Abnormal Child Psychology. 21*, 469-480.

Hibbs, E. D., & Jensen, P. S. (Eds.). (1996). *Psychosocial treatments for child and adolescent disorders: Empirically based strategies for clinical practice.* Kazdin: American Psychological Association.

Hidalgo, R. B., & Davidson, J. R. (2000). Selective serotonin reuptake inhibitors in post-traumatic stress disorder. *Journal of Psychopharmacology, 14*(1), 70-76.

Hinden, B., Compas, B., Howell D., & Achenbach, T. (1997). Covariation of the anxious-depressed syndrome during adolescence: Separating fact from artifact. *Journal of Consulting and Clinical Psychology, 65*, 6-14.

Hingson, R., Heeren, T., Levenson, S., Jamanka, A., & Voas, R. (2002). Age of drinking onset, driving after drinking, and involvement in alcohol related motor-vehicle crashes. *Accident Analysis & Prevention, 34*(1), 85-92.

Hinshaw, S. P., Klein, R. G., & Abikoff, H. (1998). Childhood attention deficit hyperactivity disorder: Nonpharmacological and combination treatments. In P. E. Nathan & J. M. Gorman (Eds.), *A guide to treatments that work* (pp. 26-41). London: Oxford University Press.

Hinshaw, S. P., Lahey, B. B., & Hart, E. L. (1993). Issues of taxonomy and comorbidity in the development of conduct disorder. *Development and Psychopathology, 5*, 31-49.

Hoffman, G. (1995). *Comprehensive Assessment and Treatment Outcome Research (CATOR).* St. Paul, MN: CATOR.

Hofmann, A. (1980). *LSD: My Problem Child.* New York: McGraw-Hill.

Hoge, R. D. (2001). *The juvenile offender: Theory, research and applications.* Series Title: Outreach scholarship series. Boston, MA: Kluwer Academic Press.

Hoge, R. D., & Andrews, D. A. (2003). *Youth Level of Service/Case Management Inventory (YLS/CMI).* North Tomawanda, NY: Multihealth Services.

Hohman, M. M., & Galt, D. H. (2001). Latinas in treatment: Comparisons of residents in a culturally specific recovery home with residents in non-specific recovery homes. *Journal of Ethnic and Cultural Diversity in Social Work, 9*(3-4), 93-109.

Hohman, M. M., McGaffigan, R. P., & Segars, L. (2000). Predictors of successful completion of a post-incarceration drug treatment program. *Journal of Addictions and Offender Counseling, 21*(1), 12-22.

Hollen, S., & Beck, A.T. (1986). Research on cognitive therapies. In S.L. Garfield & A.E. Bergin (Eds.), *Handbook of psychotherapy and behavior change.* (3rd ed., pp. 443-482). New York: Wiley.

Holmes, S. E., Slaughter, J. R., & Kashani, J. (2001). Risk factors in childhood that lead to the development of conduct disorder and antisocial personality disorder. *Child Psychiatry & Human Development, 31*(3), 183-193.

Horn, J. L., & Wanberg, K. W. (1969). Symptom patterns related to excessive use of alcohol. *Quarterly Journal of Studies on Alcohol, 30* (1-A), 35-58.

Horn, J. L., Wanberg, K. W., & Adams, G. (1982). Diagnosis of alcoholism. In E. M. Pattison (Ed.), *Selection of treatment for alcoholics.* New Brunswick, NJ: Rutgers Center of Alcohol Studies.

Horn, J. L., Wanberg, K. W., & Foster, F. M. (1990). *Guide to the Alcohol Use Inventory (AUI).* Minneapolis, MN: National Computer Systems.

Horowitz, R. (1983). *Honor and the American dream: Culture and identity in a Chicano community.* New Brunswick, NJ: Rutgers University Press.

Horvath, A. O. (1994). Research on the alliance. In A. O. Horvath & L. S. Greenberg (Eds.), *The working alliance: Theory, research, and practice* (pp. 259-286). New York: Wiley.

Howell, J.C., (Ed). (1995). *Guide for implementing the comprehensive strategy for serious, violent, and chronic juvenile offenders.* Washington, DC: Office of Juvenile Justice and Delinquency and Delinquency Prevention, Office of Justice Programs , U.S. Department of Justice.

Huesmann, L. R., Eron, L. D., Lefkowitz, M. M., & Walder, L. O. (1984). Stability of aggression over time and generations. *Developmental Psychology, 20*, 1120-1134.

Huizinga, D., & Jakob-Chien, C. (1998). The contemporaneous co-occurrence of serious and violent juvenile offending and other problem behaviors. In R. Loeber & D. P. Farrington (Eds.), *Serious & violent juvenile offenders: Risk factors and successful interventions* (pp. 47-67). Thousand Oaks, CA: Sage Publications.

Huling, T. (1991). *Breaking the silence.* Albany, NY: Correctional Association of New York.

Hull, C. L. (1943). *Principles of behavior: An introduction to behavior theory.* Oxford, England: Appleton-Century.

Hume, M.P., Kennedy, W.A., Patrick, C.J., & Partyka, D.J. (1996). Examination of the MMPI-A for the assessment of psychopathy in incarcerated adolescent male offenders. *International Journal of Offender Therapy and Comparative Criminology, 40*, 224-233.

Hutson, H., Anglin, D., & Pratts, M. (1994). Adolescents and children injured or killed in drive-by shootings in Los Angeles. *New England Journal of Medicine, 330*, 324-327.

Inciardi, J., Horowitz, R., & Potteiger, A. (1993). *Street kids, street drugs, street crime: An examination of drug use and serious delinquency in Miami.* Belmont, CA: Wadsworth Publishing Company.

Inciardi, J. A., & Saum, C. A. (1996). Legalization madness. *Public Interest, 123,* 72-83.

Ireland, T., & Widom, C. S. (1994). Childhood victimization and risk for alcohol and drug arrests. *International Journal of the Addictions, 29*(2), 235-274.

Ivey, A.E., & Simek-Downing, L. (1980). *Counseling and psychotherapy: Skills, theories, and practice.* Englewood Cliffs, NJ: Prentice-Hall, Inc., 1980.

Jacobson, E. (1938). *Progressive relaxation* (2nd ed.). Oxford, England: University of Chicago Press.

Jaffe, H. (2002, June). New coke. *Men's Health, 17,* 128.

James, J. B., Huser, L. J., & O'Toole, J. G. (1997). In search of resilience in adult survivors of childhood sexual abuse: Linking outlets for power motivation to psychological health. In A. Lieblich & R. Josselson (Eds.), *The narrative study of lives.* Thousand Oaks, CA: Sage Publications

Jensen, L. C. (1985). *Adolescence: Theories, research, application.* St Paul, MN: West Publishing Co.

Jesness, C. F. (1991). *The Jesness Inventory* (revised ed.). North Tonawanda, NY: Multi-Health Systems.

Jesness, C. F. (2003). *Jesness Inventory-Revised (JI-R)3.* Toronto, Ontario: Multi-Health Systems, Inc.

Jesness, C. F. (2004). *Jesness Inventory-Revised (JI-R).* Lutz, FL: Psychological Assessment Resources, Inc.

Jessor, R. (1987a). Problem-behavior theory, psychosocial development, and adolescent problem drinking. *British Journal of Addiction, 82*(4), 331-342.

Jessor, R. (1987b). Risky driving and adolescent problem behavior: An extension of problem-behavior theory. *Alcohol, Drugs & Driving, 3*(3), 1-11.

Jessor, R. (1993). Successful adolescent development among youth in high-risk settings. *American Psychologist, 82*(2), 117-126.

Jessor, R. *Problem-Behavior Theory and the Life Course in Adolescence: Epistemology in Action.* Presented at the First International Congress of Adolescentology, Assisi, Italy, October 22-24, 1993

Jessor, R. (1998). *New perspectives on adolescent risk behavior.* New York: Cambridge University Press.

Jessor, R., Donovan, J. E., Costa, F. (1996). Personality, perceived life chances, and adolescent behavior. In K. Hurrelmann & S. F. Hamilton (Eds.), *Social problems and social contexts in adolescence: Perspectives across boundaries* (pp. 219-233). New York: Aldine de Gruyter.

Jessor, R.,, & Jessor, S. L. (1977a). *The Multi-Problem Behavior Checklist (MPBI).*

Jessor, R., & Jessor, S. L. (1977b). *Problem behavior and psychosocial development: A longitudinal study of youth.* New York: Academic Press.

Jessor, R., Turbin, M. S., & Costa, F. M. (1998). Protective factors in adolescent health behavior. *Journal of Personality & Social Psychology, 75*(3), 788-800.

Jessor, R., Van Den Bos, J., Vanderryn, J., Costa, F. M., & Turban, M. S. (1995). Protective Factors in adolescent problem behavior: Moderator effects and developmental change. *Developmental Psychology. 31*(6), 923-933.

Jessor, R., Van Den Bos, J., Vanderryn, J., Costa, F. M. & Turin, M. S. (1997). Protective factors in adolescent problem behavior: Moderator effects and developmental change. In: Marlatt, G. Alan & Van Den Bos (Eds.). *Addictive Behaviors: Readings on etiology, prevention, and treatment* (pp. 239-264). Washington, DC: American Psychological Association.

Joe, K. A., & Chesney-Lind, M. (1995). Just every mother's angel: An analysis of gender and ethnic variations in youth gang membership. *Gender & Society, 9,* 408-431.

Johnson, B. R. (2000). Sexual violence: The perpetrator. In C. C. Bell (Ed.), *New directions for mental health services: Vol. 86. Psychiatric aspects of violence: Issues in prevention and treatment.* San Francisco: Jossey-Bass.

Johnson, J. G., Cohen, P., Smailes, E., Kasen, S., Oldham, J. M. & Skodol, A. E. (2000). Adolescent personality disorders associated with violence and criminal behavior during adolescence and early adulthood. *American Journal of Psychiatry, 157*(9), 1406-1412.

Johnston, L.D., O'Malley, P.M., & Bachman, J.G. (2002*). Monitoring the Future national results on adolescent drug use: Overview of key findings, 2001.* (NIH Publication No. 02-5105). Bethesda, MD: National Institute on Drug Abuse.

Jonson-Reid, M., & Way, I. (2001). Adolescent sexual offenders: Incidence of childhood maltreatment, serious emotional disturbance, and prior offenses. *American Journal of Orthopsychiatry, 71*(1), 120-130.

Juhasz, S. (in press). *A desire for women: Relational psychoanalysis, writing, and relationships between women.* New Brunswick, NJ: Rutgers Press.

Kalb, C. (2001). Alcoholism: Can this pill keep you from hitting the bottle? *Newsweek 11:12,* 48-51.

Kaminer, Y., Bukstein, O. G., & Tarter, R. E. (1991). The Teen Addiction Severity Index: Rationale and reliability. *International Journal of the Addictions, 26,* 219-226.

Kandel, D. (Nov. 1975). Stages in adolescent involvement in drug use. *Science, 190,* 912-914.

Kandel, D. B., & Jessor, R. U. (2002). The gateway hypothesis revisited. In D. B. Kandel (Ed.), *Stages and pathways of drug involvement: Examining the gateway hypothesis* (pp. 365-372). New York; Cambridge University Press.

Kandel, D., Raveis, V., & Davies, M. (1991). Suicidal ideation in adolescence: Depression, substance abuse and other risk factors. *Journal of Youth and Adolescence, 2*, 289-310.

Kandel, D. B., & Yamaguchi, K. (1993). From beer to crack: Developmental patterns of drug involvement. *American Journal of Public Health, 83*, 851-855.

Kandel, D. B., Yamaguchi, K., & Chen, K. (1992). Stages of progression in drug involvement from adolescence to adulthood: Further evidence for the gateway theory. *Journal of Studies on Alcohol, 53*, 447-457.

Kanfer, F. H. (1970). Self-monitoring: Methodological limitations and clinical applications. *Journal of Consulting & Clinical Psychology, 35*(2), 148-152.

Kanfer, F. H. (1975). Self-management methods: In F. H. Kanfer & A. P. Goldstein (Eds.), *Helping people change.* New York: Pergamon.

Kanfer, F. H. (1986). Implications of a self-regulation model of therapy for treatment of addictive behaviors. In W. R. Miller & N. Heather (Eds.), *Treating addictive behaviors: Processes of change.* New York: Plenum.

Kaplan, H. B. (1980). *Deviant behavior in defense of self.* New York: Academic Press.

Kaplan, H. B. (1995). Drugs, crime, and other deviant adaptations. In H. B. Kaplan (Ed.), *Drugs, crime, and other deviant adaptations: Longitudinal studies* (pp. 3-46). New York: Plenum Press.

Kaplan, H. B., & Damphousse, K. R. (1995). Self-attitudes and antisocial personality as moderators of the drug use-violence relationship. In H. B. Kaplan (Ed.), *Drugs, crime, and other deviant adaptations: Longitudinal studies. Longitudinal research in the social and behavioral sciences: An interdisciplinary series* (pp. 187-210). New York: Plenum Press.

Kapp, M. B. (1996). Treatment and refusal rights in mental health: Therapeutic justice and clinical accommodation. *American Journal of Orthopsychiatry*, 64, 223-233.

Kashani, J. H., & Allan, W. D. (1998). *The impact of family violence on children and adolescents.* Thousand Oaks, CA: Sage.

Kashani, J. H., Jones, M. R., & Bumby, K. M. (1999). Youth violence: Psychosocial risk factors, treatment, prevention, and recommendations. *Journal of Emotional & Behavioral Disorders, 7*(4), 200-210.

Kashani, J. H., Jones, M. R., Bumby, K. M., & Thomas, L. A. (2001). Youth violence: Psychosocial risk factors, treatment, prevention, and recommendations. In H. M. Walker & M. H. Epstein (Eds.), *Making schools safer and violence free: Critical issues, solutions, and recommended practices* (pp. 39-49). Austin, TX: PRO-ED, Inc.

Kassebaum, G., & Chandler, S. M. (1994). Polydrug use and self control among men and women in prisons. *Journal of Drug Education, 24*(4), 333-350.

Kassebaum, P. (1999). *Substance abuse treatment for women offenders: Guide to promising practices* (DHHS Publication No. SMA 99-3303). Washington, D.C.: U.S. Government Printing Office.

Katz, R.C., & Marquette, J. (1996). Psychosocial characteristics of young offenders. *International Journal of Offender Therapy and Comparative Criminology, 40*, 224-233.

Kazdin, A. E. (1978). Behavior therapy: Evolution and expansion. *Counseling Psychologist, 7*(3), 34-37.

Kazdin, A.E. (1987). *Conduct disorders in childhood and adolescence.* Beverly Hills, CA: Sage Publications.

Kazdin, A. E. (1996). *Conduct disorders in childhood and adolescence* (2nd ed.). Thousand Oaks, CA: Sage Publications.

Kazdin, A. E. (2001). *Behavior Modification in Applied Settings* (6th ed.). Belmont: Wadsworth/Thomson Learning.

Keeney, B. T., & Heide, K. M. (1994). Gender differences in serial murderers: A preliminary analysis. *Journal of Interpersonal Violence, 9*(3), 383-398.

Kelley, B. T., Thornberry, T. P., & Smith, C. A. (1997). *In the wake of childhood maltreatment.* Washington, DC: U.S. Department of Justice, OJJDP.

Kelly, G. A. (1955). *The psychology of personal constructs. Vol. 1: A theory of personality. Vol. 2: Clinical diagnosis and psychotherapy.* Oxford, England: W. W. Norton.

Kendall, P.C., & Braswell, L. (1985). *Cognitive-behavioral therapy for impulsive children.* New York: Guilford Press.

Kendall, P. C., & Bemis, K. M. (1983). Thought and action in psychotherapy: The cognitive-behavioral approaches. In M. Hersen, A. E. Kazdin, & A. S. Bellack (Eds.), *The clinical psychology handbook.* New York: Pergamon Press.

Kendall, P. C., & Hollon, S.D. (1979). *Cognitive behavioral interventions: Theory, research, and procedures.* New York: Academic Press.

Kerr, D. (1998). Substance abuse among female offenders: Efforts to treat substance-abusing women offenders must address underlying reasons for use. *Corrections Today, 60*(7), 114-120.

Kilpatrick, D. G., Acierno, R., Saunders, B., Resnick, H. S., Best, C. L., & Schnurr, P. P. (2000). Risk factors for adolescent substance abuse and dependence: Data from a national sample. *Journal of Consulting & Clinical Psychology, 68*(1), 19-30.

Kjelsberg, E. (1999). Adolescence-limited versus life-course-persistent criminal behaviour in adolescent psychiatric inpatients. *European Child and Adolescent Psychiatry, 8*, 276-282.

Kjelsberg, E. (2002a). DSM-IV conduct disorder symptoms in adolescents as markers of registered criminality. *European Child & Adolescent Psychiatry, 11*(1), 2-9.

Kjelsberg, E. (2002b). Pathways to violent and non-violent criminality in an adolescent psychiatric population. *Child Psychiatry & Human Development, 33*(1), 29-42.

Klepp, K. I., & Perry, C. L. (1990). Adolescents, drinking, and driving: Who does it and why? In R. J. Wilson & R. E. Mann (Eds.), *Drinking and driving: Advances in research and prevention* (pp.42-67). New York: Guilford Press.

Kluft, R. P., Bloom, S. L., & Kinzie, J. D. (2000). Treating traumatized patients and victims of violence. In C. C. Bell (Ed.), *New directions for mental health services: Vol. 86. Psychiatric aspects of violence: Issues in prevention and treatment* (pp. 79-102). San Francisco: Jossey-Bass.

Koss, M. P., Heiss, L., & Russo, N. F. (1994). The global health burden of rape. *Psychology of Women Quarterly, 18*(4), 509-537.

Kosterman, R., Hawkins, D. J., Guo, J., Catalano, R. F., & Abbott, R. D. (2000). The dynamics of alcohol and marijuana initiation: Patterns and predictors of first use. *American Journal of Public Health, 90*(3), 360-367.

Kouri, E.M.; Pope, H.G.; and Lukas, S.E. (1999). Changes in aggressive behavior during withdrawal from long-term marijuana use. *Psychopharamcology, 143*, 302-308.

Kovacs, M. (1992). *Children's Depression Inventory manual.* North Tonawanda, NY: Multi-Health Systems.

Krohn, M. D., Akers, R. L., Radosevich, M. J., & Lanza-Kaduce, L. (1982). Norm qualities and adolescent drinking and drug behavior: The effects of norm quality and reference group on using and abusing alcohol and marijuana. *Journal of Drug Issues, 12*(4), 343-359.\

Krupnick, J.L., Sotsky, S.M., Simmens, S., Moyer, J., Elkin, I., Watkins, J., & Pilkonis, P.A. (1996). The role of therapeutic alliance in psychotherapy and pharmacotherapy outcome: Findings in the National Institute of Mental Health Treatment of Depression Collaborative Research Program. *Journal of Consulting and Clinical Psychology, 64,* 532-539.

Kubota, M., Nakazaki, S., Hirai, S., et. al. (2001). Alcohol consumption and frontal lobe shrinkage: Study of 1432 non-alcoholic subjects. *Journal of Neurology, Neurosurgery and Psychiatry, 71*(1), 104-106.

Labouvie, E., Bates, M. E., & Pandina, R. J. (1997). Age of first use: Its reliability and predictive utility. *Journal of Studies on Alcohol Use, 58*, 638-643.

La Fond, J. Q. (1996). The impact of law on the delivery of involuntary mental health services. In B. D. Sales & D. W. Shuman (Eds.), *Law, mental health, and mental disorder.* Pacific Grove, CA: Brooks/Cole.

Lahey, B. B., McBurnett, K., Loeber, R., & Hart, E. L. (1995). Psychobiology. In G. P. Sholevar (Ed.), *Conduct disorders in children and adolescents* (pp. 27-57). Washington, DC: American Psychiatric Press.

Lambert, M. J., & Bergin, A. E. (1992). Achievements and limitations of psychotherapy research. In D. K. Freedheim (Ed.), *History of psychotherapy: A century of change* (pp. 360-390). Washington, DC: American Psychological Association.

Lang, R. (1990). *Psychotherapy: A basic text.* Northvale, NJ: Jason Aronson, Inc.

Langbehn, D. R., Cadoret, R. J., Yates, W. R., Troughton, E. P., & Stewart, M. A. (1998). Distinct contributions of conduct and oppositional defiant symptoms to adult antisocial behavior: Evidence from an adoption study. *Archives of General Psychiatry, 55*(9), 821-829.

Lange, A. J. (1976). *Responsible assertive behavior: Cognitive-behavioral procedures for trainers.* Champaign, IL: Research Press.

Lange, A.J., & Jakubowski, P. (1976). *Responsible assertive behavior.* Champaign, IL: Research Press.

Langer, E. J. (1989). Minding matters: The consequences of mindlessness-mindfulness. In L. Berkowitz (Ed.), *Advances in experimental social psychology, Vol. 22* (pp. 137-173). San Diego, CA: Academic Press.

Langer, E. J. (1997). *The power of mindful learning.* Reading, MA: Addison-Wesley.

Larzelere, R. A. (1994). Should the use of corporal punishment by parents be considered child abuse? Response. In M. Mason & E. Gambrill (Eds.), *Debating children's lives: Current controversies on children and adolescents* (pp. 217-218). Thousand Oaks, California: Sage Publications.

Laub, J. H., & Lauritsen, J. L. (1995). Violent criminal behavior over the life course: A review of the longitudinal and comparative research. In R. B. Ruback & N. A. Weiner (Eds.), *Interpersonal violent behaviors: Social and cultural aspects* (pp. 43-61). New York: Springer Publishing.

Laub, J. H., & Sampson, R. J. (1995). The long-term effect of punitive discipline. In J. McCord (Ed.), Coercion and punishment in long-term perspectives (pp. 247-258).

Laufer, M. E. (1995). Depression and self-hatred. In M. Laufer (Ed.), *The suicidal adolescent* (pp. 21-27).

Lawrence M. & Botvin, G. J. (1996). Purpose in life, cognitive efficacy, and general deviance as determinants of drug abuse in urban Black Youth. *Journal of Child & Adolescent Substance Abuse*. Vol 5(1). pp 1-26.

Lawson, C. (1992, August 6). Violence at home: 'They don't want anyone to know.' *The New York Times,* pp. C1-C7.

Lazarus, A. A. (1971). *Behavior therapy and beyond.* New York: McGraw-Hill.

Leahy, R. L. (1996). *Cognitive therapy: Basic principles and applications.* Northvale, NJ: Jason Aronson, Inc.

Leahy, R.L. (1997). Cognitive therapy interventions. In R.L. Leahy (Ed.), *Practicing cognitive therapy: A guide to interventions* (pp. 3-20). Northvale, NJ: Jason Aonson, Inc.

Lerner, B.G. (2001). BEAT IT!: Booster Efficacy Awareness Therapy Intervention Treatment. HIV prevention for severe mental ill alcohol/drug adult abusers (Immune deficiency). *Dissertation Abstracts International, 61*(10), 5570B. (UMI No. 9991530)

Levitt, P., Harvey, J. A., Friedman, E., Simansky, K., & Murphy, E. H. (1997). New evidence for neurotransmitter influences on brain development. *Trends in Neuroscience, 20*(6), 269-274.

Levitt, S. D., & Lochner, L. (2001). The determinants of juvenile crime. In J. Gruber (Ed.), *Risky behavior among youths: An economic analysis* (pp. 327-373). Chicago: University of Chicago Press.

Levy, K. S. C. (1997). The contribution of self concept in the etiology of adolescent delinquency. *Adolescence, 32*, 671-686.

Lewin, M. (1985). Unwanted intercourse: The difficulty of saying no. *Psychology of Women Quarterly, 9,* 184-192.

Lewis, C. C. (1988). Preventing traffic casualties among youth: What is our knowledge base? *Alcohol, Drugs & Driving, 4*(1), 1-7.

Lewis, D.C. (1997). The role of the generalist in the care of the substance-abusing patient. *Medical Clinics of North America, 81*(4), 831-843.

Lewin, K. (1935). *A dynamic theory of personality.* New York: McGraw-Hill.

Lewin, K. (1936). *Principles of topological psychology.* New York: McGraw-Hill.

Lewin, K. (1951). *Field theory in social science: Selected theoretical papers.* In D. Cartwright (Ed.). New York: Harper.

Lieblich, A., & Josselson, R., (Eds.). (1997). *The narrative study of lives.* Thousand Oaks, CA: Sage Publications.

Liechti, M. E., Gamma, A., & Vollenweider, F. X. (2001). Gender difference in the subjective effects of MDMA. *Psychopharmacology, 154*, 161-168.

Lightfoot, L. (1997). *What works in treating the correctional substance abuser?* Paper presented at the ICAA Fifth Annual Research Conference, Cleveland, OH.

Linehan, M. M., & Addis, M.E. (1990). *Screening for suicidal behaviors: The Suicidal Behaviors Questionnaire.* Unpublished manuscript. University of Washington, Seattle.

Linnoila, M., Virkkunen, M., Scheinin, M., Nuutila, A., Rimon, R., & Goodwin, F. K. (1983). Low cerebrospinal fluid 5-hydroxyindoleacetic acid concentration differentiates impulsive from nonimpulsive violent behavior. *Life Sciences, 33,* 2609-2614.

Linsky, A. S., Bachman, R., & Straus, M. A. (1995). *Stress, culture, & aggression.* New Haven, CT: Yale University Press.

Lipsey, M. W., & Derzon, J. H. (1998). Predictors of violent or serious delinquency in adolescence and early adulthood: a synthesis of longitudinal research. In R. Loeber & D. P. Farrington (Eds.), *Serious and violent juvenile offenders: Risk factors and successful interventions* (pp. 86-105). Thousand Oaks, CA: Sage.

Little, P. J., Kuhn, C. M., Wilson, W. A., & Schwartzwelder, H. S. (1996). Differential effects of alcohol in adolescent and adult rats. *Alcohol Clinical Experimental Research, 20,* 1341-1351.

Little, R. U., & Clontz, K. (1994). Young, drunk, dangerous and driving: Underage drinking and driving research findings. *Journal of Alcohol & Drug education, 39*(2), 37-49.

Litton-Fox, G. (1977). Nice girls: Social control of women through a value construct. *Signs: Journal of Women in Culture & Society, 2*(4), 805-817.

Litz, B. T., Gray, M. J., Bryant, R. A., & Adler, A. B. (2002). Early intervention for trauma: Current status and future directions. *Clinical Psychology, 9*(2), 112-134.

Loeber, R. (1991). Antisocial behavior: More enduring than changeable? *Journal of the American Academy of Child & Adolescent Psychiatry, 30*(3), 393-397.

Loeber, R. (1996). Developmental continuity, change, and pathways in male juvenile problem behaviors and delinquency. In J. D. Hawkins (Ed.), *Delinquency and Crime. Current theories. Cambridge criminology series* (pp. 1-27).

Loeber, R., Burke, J. D., Lahey, B. B., Winters, A., & Zera, M. (2000). Oppositional defiant and conduct disorder: a review of the past 10 years, part I. *Journal of the American Academy of Child and Adolescent Psychiatry, 39,* 1468-1484.

Loeber, R., Dishion, T. J. & Patterson, G. R. (1984). Multiple Gating: A multi-stage assessment procedure for identifying youths at risk for delinquency. *Journal of Research in Crime and Delinquency, 21*, 7-32.

Loeber, R., & Farrington, D. P. (1998). *Serious and violent juvenile offenders: Risk Factors and successful interventions.* Thousand Oaks, CA: Sage.

Loeber, R., Farrington, D. P., Stouthamer-Loeber, M., Moffitt, T. E. & Caspi, A. (2001). The development of male offending: Key findings from the first decade of the Pittsburgh Youth Study. In R. Bull (Ed.), *Children and the law: The essential readings. Essential readings in developmental psychology* (pp. 336-378). Malden, MA, US: Blackwell Publishers.

Loeber, R., Green, S. M., Keenan, K., & Lahey, B. B. (1995). Which boys will fare worse? Early predictors of the onset of conduct disorder in a six-year longitudinal study. *Journal of the American Academy of Child & Adolescent Psychiatry, 34*(4), 499-509.

Loeber, R, Green, S. M. Lahey, B. B., Frick, P. J. & McBurnett, K. (2000). Findings on disruptive behavior disorders from the first decade of developmental trends study. *Clinical Child and Family Psychology Review, 3*, 37-59.

Loeber, R., & Keenan, K. (1994). Interaction between conduct disorder and its comorbid conditions: Effects of age and gender. *Clinical Psychology Review, 14*(6), 497-523.

Loeber, R., Stouthamer-Loeber, M., & White, H. R. (1999). Developmental aspects of delinquency and internalizing problems and their association with persistent juvenile substance use between ages 7 and 18. *Journal of Clinical Child Psychology, 28*, 322-32.

Lopez, V. A. (2000). Adolescent male offenders' cognitions and emotions: A grounded theory study of delinquent crime contexts. *Dissertation Abstracts International Section A: Humanities & Social Sciences*, 61(1-A), 375.

Lopez, V. A., & Emmer, E. T. (2000). Adolescent male offenders: A grounded theory study of cognition, emotion, and delinquent crime contexts. *Criminal Justice & Behavior, 27*(3), 292-311.

Lorber, J. (1994). *Paradoxes of gender.* New Haven, CT: Yale University Press.

Losada-Paisey, G. (1998). Use of the MMPI-A to assess personality of juvenile male delinquents who are sex offenders and nonsex offenders. *Psychological Reports, 83*, 115-122.

Luborsky, L., Barbar, J. P., Siqueland, L., Johnson, S., Najavits, L. M., & Frank, A., et al. (1996). The Revised Helping Alliance Questionnaire (HAq-II): Psychometric properties. *Journal of Psychotherapy Practice and Research, 5*(3), 260-271.

Luster, T., & Small, S. (1995). Factors associated with sexual risk-taking behaviors among adolescence. *Journal of Marriage and Family. 56*, 622-632.

Lyddon, W.J., & Jones, J.V. (2001). Empirically supported treatments: An introduction. In W.J. Lyddon & J.V. Jones (Eds.), *Empirically supported cognitive therapies: Current and future applications.* New York: Springer Publishing Company.

Lynam, D. R. (1996). Early identification of chronic offenders: Who is the fledgling psychopath? *Psychological Bulletin, 120*(2), 209-234.

Lynam, D., Moffitt, T. E., & Stouthamer-Loeber, M. (1993). Explaining the relation between IQ and delinquency: Class, race, test motivation, school failure, or self-control? *Journal of Abnormal Psychology 102*, 187-96.

Lyons-Ruth, K. (1996). Attachment relationships among children with aggressive behavior problems: The role of disorganized early attachment patterns. *Journal of Consulting and Clinical Psychology, 64*, 64-73.

MacMillan, H. L., Boyle, M. H., Wong, M. Y., Duku, E. K., Fleming, J. E., & Walsh, C. A. (1999). Slapping, spanking and lifetime psychiatric disorder in a community sample of Ontario residents. *Canadian Medical Association Journal, 7*, 805-809.

Magnusson, D. (1996). The patterning of antisocial behavior and autonomic reactivity. In D. M. Stoff & R. B. Cairns (Eds.), *Aggression and violence: Genetic, neurobiological, and biosocial perspectives* (pp. 291-308). Mawah, NJ: Lawrence Erlbaum Associates.

Magnusson, D. (2000). The individual as the organizing principle in psychological inquiry: A holistic approach: In Bergman, Cairns, Nilsson & Nystedt (Eds.), *Developmental science and the holistic approach* (pp. 33-48). Mawah, NJ: Lawrence Erlbaum Associates.

Maguin, E., & Loeber, R. (1996). Academic performance and delinquency. In M. Tonry & D. P. Farrington (Eds.), *Crime and justice: Vol 20* (pp. 145-264). Chicago, IL: University of Chicago Press.

Mahoney, J. J. (1990). *Human change processes: Theoretical bases for psychotherapy.* New York: Basic Books.

Mahoney, M. J. (1974). *Cognitive and behavior modification.* Oxford, England: Ballinger.

Mahoney, M., & Arnkoff, D. (1978). Cognitive and self-control therapies. In S. Garfield & A. Bergin (Eds.), *Handbook of psychotherapy and behavioral change.* New York: John Wiley and Sons.

Mahoney, M. J., & Lyddon, W. J. (1988). Recent developments in cognitive approaches to counseling and psychotherapy. *Counseling Psychologist, 16*(2), 190-324.

Mai, R. Y., & Alpert, J. L. (2002). Separation and socialization: A feminist analysis of the school shootings at Columbine. In A. E. Hunter & C. Forden (Eds.), *Readings in the psychology of gender: Exploring our differences and commonalities* (pp. 227-243). Needham Heights, MA: Allyn & Bacon.

Maisto, S. A., Carey, K. B., & Bradizza, C. M. (1999). Social learning theory. In H. T. Blane & K. W. Leonard (Eds.), *Psychological theories of drinking and alcoholism* (pp. 305-345). New York: Guilford.

Maisto, S. A., Connors, G. J., & Allen, J. P. (1995). Contrasting self-report screens for alcohol problems: A review. *Alcoholism: Clinical and Experimental Research, 19*, 1510-1516.

Mandel, H. P. (1997). *Conduct disorder and under-achievement: Risk factors assessment, treatment, and prevention.* New York: John Wiley & Sons Inc.

Mann, C. R. (1995). Women of color and the criminal justice system. In B. R. Price & N. J. Sokoloff, (Eds.), *The criminal justice system and women: Offenders, victims, and workers* (2nd ed., pp. 118-135). New York: McGraw Hill.

Mannuzza, S., Klein, R. G., Bessler, A., & Malloy, P., & LaPadula. (1993). Adult outcome of hyperactive boys: Educational achievement, occupational rank, and psychiatric status. *Archives of General Psychiatry, 50*(7), 565-576.

Mansvelder, H. D., & McGehee, D. S. (2000). Long-term potentation of excitatory inputs to brain reward areas by nicotine. *Neuron, 27*(2), 349-357.

Mansvelder, H. D., & McGehee, D. S. (2002). Synaptic mechanisms underlie nicotine-induced excitability of brain reward systems. *Neuron, 33*(6), 905-919.

Marcus, R. F., & Gray, L. Jr. (1998). Close relationships of violent and nonviolent African American delinquents. *Violence & Victims, 13*(1), 31-46.

Markarian, M., & Franklin, J. (1998). Substance Abuse in Minority Populations. In R. J. Frances & S. I. Miller, (Eds.), *Clinical textbook of addictive disorders* (2nd ed., pp. 397-412). New York: Guilford Press.

Markwiese, B. J., Acheson, S. K., Levin, E. D., Wilson, W. A., & Swartzwelder, H. S. (1998). Differential effects of ethanol on memory in adolescent and adult rats. *Alcohol Clinical & Experimental Research, 22*, 416-421.

Marlatt, G.A. (1985a). Cognitive assessment and intervention procedures for relapse prevention. In G.A. Marlatt & J.R. Gordon (Eds.), *Relapse prevention: Maintenance strategies in the treatment of addictive behaviors* (pp. 201-279). New York: Guilford Press.

Marlatt, G.A. (1985b). Situational determinants of relapse and skill training intervention. In G.A. Marlatt & J.R. Gordon (Eds.), *Relapse prevention: Maintenance strategies in the treatment of addictive behaviors* (pp.71-124). New York: Guilford Press.

Marlatt, G.A., Baer, J.S., & Quigley, L.A. (1995). Self-efficacy and addictive behavior. In A. Bandura (Ed.), *Self-efficacy in changing societies.* New York: Cambridge University Press.

Marlatt, G.A., & Barrett, K.B. (1994). Relapse prevention. In M. Galentern & H. Kleber (Eds.), *The textbook of substance abuse treatment.* New York: American Psychiatric Press.

Marlatt, G.A., & Gordon, J.R. (1985). *Relapse prevention: Maintenance strategies in the treatment of addictive behaviors.* New York: Guilford Press.

Martin, C. S., & Winters, K. C. (1998). Diagnosis and assessment of alcohol use disorders among adolescents. *Alcohol Health and Research World, 22*, 95-106.

Martin, C. S., Kaczynski, N. A., Maisto, S. A., & Tarter, R. E. (1996). Polydrug use in adolescent drinkers with and without DSM-IV alcohol abuse and dependence. *Alcoholism: Clinical and Experimental Research, 20*, 1099-1108.

Martin, C. S., Kaczynski, N. A., Maisto, S. A., Bukstein, O. M., & Moss, H. B. (1995). Patterns of DSM-IV alcohol abuse and dependence symptoms in adolescent drinkers. *Journal of Studies on Alcohol, 56*, 672-680.

Martin, D. J., Garske, J. P., & Davis, M. K. (2000). Relation of the therapeutic alliance with outcome and other variables: A meta-analytic review. *Journal of Consulting and Clinical Psychology, 68*, 438-450.

Martin, S. J., & Morris, R. G. (2002). New life in an old idea: the synaptic plasticity and memory hypothesis revised. *Hippocampus, 12*, 609-636.

Maruna, S. (1997). Going straight: Desistance from crime and life narratives of reform. In A. Lieblich & R. Josselson (Eds.), *The narrative study of lives* (pp. 59-93).

Mason, D. A., & Frick, P. J. (1994). The heritability of antisocial behavior: A meta-analysis of twin and adoption studies. *Journal of Psychopathology and Behavioral Assessment, 16*(4), 301-23.

Matthys, W., Cuperus, J. M., & Van Engeland, H. (1999). Deficient social problem-solving in boys with ODD/CD, with ADHD, and with both disorders. *Journal of the American Academy of Child & Adolescent Psychiatry, 38*(3), 311-321.

Mauer, M., Potler, C., & Wolf, R. (1999). *Gender and justice: Women, drugs and sentencing policy.* Washington, DC: The Sentencing Project.

Mayer, J., & Filstead, W. J. (1979). The Adolescent Alcohol Involvement Scale. *Journal of Studies on Alcohol, 40*(3), 291-300.

Mayes, L. C., Bornstein, M. H., Katarzyna, C., & Granger, R. H. (1995). Information processing and developmental assessment in three-month-old infants exposed prenatally to cocaine. *Pediatrics, 95*, 539.

McBurnett, K., Lahey, B. B., Rathouz, P. J., & Loeber, R. (2000). Low salivary cortisol and persistent aggression in boys referred for disruptive behavior. *Archives of General Psychiatry, 57*, 21-27.

McCann, U. D., Szabo, Z., Scheffel, U., Dannals, R. F., & Ricaurte, G. A. (1998). Positron emission tomographic evidence of toxic effect of MDMA ("Ecstasy") on brain serotonin neurons in human beings. *The Lancet, 352*, Oct. 31.

McCord, J. (Ed.). (1995a). *Coercion and punishment in long-term perspectives*. Cambridge England: Cambridge University Press.

McCord, J. (1995b). Relationship between alcoholism and crime over the life course. In H. B. Kaplan (Ed.), *Drugs, crime, and other deviant adaptations: Longitudinal studies. Longitudinal research in the social and behavioral sciences: An interdisciplinary series* (pp. 129-141). New York: Springer.

McCord, J. (1999). Understanding childhood and subsequent crime. *Aggressive Behavior, 25*(4), 241-253.

McGee, R. F., Williams, S. M., & Silva, P. A. (1991). A twelve-year follow up to preschool hyperactive children. *Journal of the American Academy of Child and Adolescent Psychiatry, 30*, 224-32.

McGinn, L. K., & Young, J. E. (1996). Schema-focused therapy. In P. M. Salkovskis (Ed.), *Frontiers of cognitive therapy* (pp. 182-207). New York: Guilford Press.

McLellan, A. T., Alterman, A. I., Cacciola, J., Metzger, D., & O'Brian, C. P. (1992). A new measure of substance abuse treatment: Initial studies of the Treatment Services Review. *Journal of Nervous and Mental Disease, 180*(2), 101-110.

McLellan, T., & Dembo, R. (1993). *Screening and assessment of alcohol-and other drug-abusing adolescents: Treatment Improvement Protocol (TIP) Series*. Rockville, MD: U.S. Department of Health and Human Services, Public Health Service, Substance Abuse and Mental Health Services Administration, Center for Substance Abuse Treatment.

McMahon, M. (Ed.). (2000). *Assessment to assistance: Programs for women in community corrections*. Lanham, MD: American Correctional Association.

McMullin, R. E. (2000). *The new handbook of cognitive therapy techniques*. New York: W. W. Norton.

McNally, R. J., Bryant, R. A., & Ehlers, A. (2003). Does early psychological intervention promote recovery from posttraumatic stress? *Psychological Science in the Public Interest, 4*(2), 45 79.

McQuaide, S., & Ehrenreich, J. H. (1998). Women in prison: Approaches to understanding the lives of a forgotten population. *Affilia, 13*(2), 233-246.

Meichenbaum, D. (1974). *Cognitive behavior modification*. Morristown, NJ: General Learning Press.

Meichenbaum, D. (1975). Enhancing creativity by modifying what subjects say to themselves. *American Educational Research Journal, 12*(2), 129-145.

Meichenbaum, D. (1977). Dr. Ellis, please stand up. *Counseling Psychologist, 7*(1), 43-44.

Meichenbaum, D. (1985). *Stress inoculation training: A clinical guidebook*. Old Tappan, NJ: Allyan & Bacon.

Meichenbaum, D. (1993). Changing conceptions of cognitive behavior modification: Retrospect and prospect. *Journal of Consulting and Clinical Psychology, 61*, 292.304.

Meichenbaum, D., & Novaco, R. (1985). Stress inoculation: A preventative approach. *Issues in Mental Health Nursing, 7*(1-4), 419-435.

Meloy, J. R., Hempel, A. G., Mohandie, K., Shiva, A. A. & Gray, B. T. (2001). Offender and offense characteristics of a nonrandom sample of adolescent mass murderers. *Journal of the American Academy of Child & Adolescent Psychiatry, 40*(6), 719-728.

Merton, R. K. (1957). *Social theory and social structure* (Rev. Ed.). New York: Free Press.

Merton, R. K. (1968). Social structure and anomie. In N. J. Smelser (Ed.), *Theory of collective behavior* (pp. 185-214). New York: Free Press.

Mesrian, P. (1998). Analytical description of psychological constructs of women who drink alcohol during pregnancy. *Dissertation Abstracts International, 58*(10), 5633B.(UMI No. 9813153)

Metzger, D., Kushner, H., & McLellan, A. T. (1991). *Adolescent Problem Severity Index*. Philadelphia: University of Pennsylvania.

Meyers, (1996). *Comprehensive Adolescent Severity Inventory (CASI)*. Philadelphia: University of Pennsylvania, Treatment Research Institute.

Milkman, H., Wanberg, K., & Robinson, C. P. (1996). Project Self Discovery: Artistic Alternatives for High-Risk Youth [Monograph]. *Journal of Community Psychology*. Special issue.

Milkman, H. (2001 Mar/Apr). Better than dope. *Psychology Today, 34,* 32-38.

Milkman, H., & Sunderwirth, S. (1993). *Pathways to Pleasure.* New York: Lexington Books.

Miller, B. A., Downs, W. R., & Testa, M. (1993, September). Interrelationships between victimization experiences and women's alcohol use. In L. A. Pohorecky, J. Brick, and G. G. Milgram (Eds.), *Journal of Studies on Alcohol, Supplement No. 11: Alcohol and Aggression. Proceedings of the Symposium on Alcohol and Aggression held at the Center of Alcohol Studies, Rutgers University, October 8-9, 1992,* 109-117.

Miller, E. M. (1986). *Street woman.* Philadelphia: Temple University Press.

Miller, G. (1990). *The Substance Abuse Subtle Screening Inventory - Adolescent Version.* Bloomington, IN: Substance Abuse Subtle Screening Inventory Institute.

Miller, J. B., & Stiver, I. P. (1997). *The healing connection: How women form relationships in therapy and in life.* Boston: Beacon Press.

Miller, P.J., Ross, S. M., Emeerson, R.Y., & Todt, E.H. (1989). Self-efficacy in alcoholics: Clinical validation of the sitatuional confidence questionnaire. *Addictive Behaviors, 14,* 217-224.

Miller, W. R., Brown, J. M., Simpson, T. L., Handmaker, N. S., Bien, T. H., Luckie, L. F., Montgomery, H. A., Hester, R. K., & Tonigan, J. S. (1995). What works? A methodological analysis of the alcohol treatment outcome literature. In R. K. Hester & W. R. Miller (Eds.), *Handbook of alcoholism treatment approaches: Effective alternatives.* (2nd ed., pp. 12-44). New York: Allyn and Bacon.

Miller, W. R., & Rollnick, S. (1991). *Motivational interviewing: Preparing people to change addictive behavior.* New York: Guilford Press.

Miller, W. R., & Rollnick, S. (2002). *Motivational interviewing, second edition: Preparing people for change.* New York: Guilford Press.

Miller, W. R., & Sanchez, V. C. (1993). Motivating young adults for treatment and lifestyle change. In G. Howard (Ed.), *Issues in alcohol use and misuse by young adults* (pp. 55-81). Notre Dame, IN: University of Notre Dame Press.

Miller, W. R., & Tonigan, J. S. (1996) Assessing drinkers' motivation for change: The Stages of Change Readiness and Treatment Eagerness Scale (SOCRATES). *Psychology of Addictive Behaviors, 10(2),* 81-89.

Miller, W. R., Zweben, A., DiClemente, C. C., & Rychtarik, R. G. (1992). *Motivational Enhancement Therapy manual: A clinical research guide for therapists treating individuals with alcohol abuse and dependence.* Rockville, MD: National Institute on Alcohol Abuse and Alcoholism.

Millon, T., Millon, C., & Davis, R. (1999). *Millon Adolescent Clinical Inventory (MACI).* Bloomington, MN: Pearson Assessments.

Miner, M. H. (2002). Factors associated with recidivism in juveniles: An analysis of serious juvenile sex offenders. *Journal of Research in Crime & Delinquency, 39*(4), 421-436.

Moberg, D. P., & Hahn, L. (1991). The adolescent drug involvement scale. *Journal of Adolescent Chemical Dependency, 2,* 75-88.

Mocan, H. N., & Corman, H. (1998). An economic analysis of drug use and crime. *Journal of Drug Issues, 28*(3), 613-630.

Moffit, T. E., Lynam, D. R., & Silva, P. A. (1994). Neuropsychological tests predict persistent male delinquency. *Criminology, 32,* 101-124.

Moffitt, T. E. (1990). Juvenile delinquency and attention-deficit disorder: Developmental trajectories from Age 3 to 15. *Child Development, 61,* 893-910.

Moffitt, T. E. (1990b). The neuropsychology of delinquency: A critical review of theory and research. *Crime and Justice, 12,* 99-169.

Moffitt, T. E. (1991). Juvenile delinquency: Seed of a career in violent crime, just sowing wild oats – or both? Paper presented at the Science and Public Policy Seminars of the Federation of Behavioral, Psychological and Cognitive Sciences, Washington, DC.

Moffitt, T. E. (1993a). "Life-course–persistent" and "adolescence-limited" antisocial behavior: A developmental taxonomy. *Psychological Review, 100,* 674-701.

Moffitt, T. E. (1993b). The neuropsychology of conduct disorder. *Development and Psychopathology, 5,* 133-151.

Moffitt, T.E. (1994). Natural histories of delinquency. In H. J. Keerner & Weitekamp (Eds.), *Cross-national longitudinal research, human development and criminal behavior* (pp. 3-64). Dordrecht: Kluwer Academic Press.

Moffitt, T. E. (1997). Adolescence-limited and life-course-persistent offending: A complementary pair of developmental theories. In T. P. Thornberry (Ed.), *Advances in criminological theory: Vol. 7. Developmental theories of crime and delinquency* (pp. 11-54). New Brunswick, NJ: Transaction Publishers.

Moffitt, T. E., Caspi, A., Harrington, H., & Milne, B. J. (2002). Males on the life-course-persistent and adolescence-limited antisocial pathways: Follow-up at age 26 years. *Development & Psychopathology, 14*(1), 179-207.

Moffitt, T. E., Mednick, S. A., & Gabrielli, W. F. (1989). Predicting criminal violence: Descriptive data and predispositional factors. In D. Brizer & M. Crowner (Eds.), *Current Approaches to the Prediction of Violence* (pp. 13-34). New York: American Psychiatric Association Press.

Monti, P. M., Abrams, D. B., Kadden, R. M., & Cooney, N. L. (1989). *Treating alcohol dependence: A coping skills training guide.* New York: Guilford Press.

Monti, P. M., Barnett, N. P., O'Leary, T. A., & Colby, S. M., (2001). Motivational enhancement for alcohol-involved adolescents. In P. M. Monti, S. M. Colby, & T. A. O'Leary (Eds.), *Adolescents, alcohol, and substance abuse: Reaching teens through brief interventions* (pp. 145-182). New York: Guilford Press.

Monti, P. M., Rohsenow, D. J., Colby, S. M., & Abrams, D. B. (1995). Coping and social skills training. In R. K. Hester & W. R. Miller (Eds.), *Handbook of alcoholism treatment approaches: Effective alternatives* (pp.221-241). Boston: Allyn & Bacon.

Moore, J. M., Thompson-Pope, S. K., & Whited, R. M. (1996). MMPI-A profiles of adolescent boys with a history of fire setting. *Journal of Personality Assessment, 67,* 116-126.

Morral, R. (Ed.), *Adolescent substance abuse treatment in the United States: Exemplary models from a national evaluation study* (pp. 3-34). New York: Haworth Press.

Morris, R., Harrison, E., Knox, G., Tromanhauser, E., Marquis, D., & Watts, L. (1995). Health Risk behavioral survey from 39 juvenile correctional facilities in the U.S. *Journal of Adolescent Health, 17,* 334-344.

Moss, H. B., & Kirisci, L. (1995). Aggressivity in adolescent alcohol abusers: Relationship with conduct disorder. *Alcoholism: Clinical and Experimental Research, 19,* 642-646.

Mowrer, O. H. (1947). On the dual nature of learning: A re-interpretation of "conditioning" and "problem-solving." *Harvard Educational Review, 17,* 102-148.

Mowrer, O. H., & Mowrer, W. M. (1938). Enuresis: A method for its study and treatment. *American Journal of Orthopsychiatry, 8,* 436-459.

Moy, S., Duncan, G., Knapp, D., & Brease, G. (1998). Sensitivity to alcohol across development in rats: comparison to [3H] zolpidem binding. *Alcoholism: Clininical and Experimental Research, 22,* 1485-1492.

Murphy, L.L. (1995). National Conference on Marijuana Use: Prevention, Treatment, and Research. Arlington, VA.

Nagin, D., Farrington, D., & Moffitt, T. E. (1995). Life-course Trajectories of Different Types of Offenders. *Criminology, 33,* 111-139.

Nagin, D., & Land, K. (1993). Age, criminal careers, and population heterogeneity; Specification and estimation of a nonparametric mixed poisson model. *Criminology, 31,* 327-62.

Najavits, L. M., Weiss, R. D., & Liese, B. S. (1996). Group cognitive-behavioral therapy for women with PTSD and substance abuse disorder. *Journal of Substance Abuse Treatment, 13*(1), 13-22.

Najavits, L. M., Weiss, R. D., & Shaw, S. R. (1997). The link between substance abuse and posttraumatic stress disorder in women: A research review. *The American Journal on Addictions, 6*(4), 273-283.

Najavits, L. M. (1994a). *Didactic Questionnaire.* Unpublished measure, Harvard Medical School, Boston.

Najavits, L. M. (1994b). *End-of-Treatment Questionnaire.* Unpublished measure, Harvard Medical School, Boston.

Najavits, L. M., Ghinassi, F., Van Horn, A., Weiss, R. D., Siqueland, L., Frank, A., Thase, M. E., & Loborsky, L. (2004). Therapist satisfaction with four manual-based treatments on a national multisite trial: An exploratory study. *Psychotherapy, Theory, Research, Practice, Training, 41,* 26-37.

Najavits, L. M., Weiss, R. D., Shaw, S. R., & Dierberger, A. E. (2000). Psychotherapists' views of treatment manuals. *Professional Psychology: Research and Practice, 31,* 404-408.

Najavits, L. M., Weiss, R. D., Shaw, S. R., & Meunz, L. R. (1998). "Seeking safety": Outcome of a new cognitive-behavioral psychotherapy for women with posttraumatic stress disorder and substance dependence. *Journal of Traumatic Stress, 11*(3), 437-456.

Nathan, P. E., & Gorman, J. M. (Eds.) (1998) *A guide to treatments that work.* New York: Oxford University Press.

Nathan, P. E., Gorman, J. M., & Salkind, N. J. (1999). *Treating mental disorders: A guide to what works.* New York: Oxford University Press

National Center on Addiction and Substance Abuse at Columbia University (1998). *Behind bars: Substance abuse and America's prison population.* New York: Author.

National Conference on Marijuana Use: Prevention, Treatment, and Research (1995), July. Arlington, VA.

National Council on Alcoholism, Criteria Committee (1972). Criteria for the diagnosis of alcoholism. *Journal of Psychiatry, 129,* 127-135.

National Household Survey on Drug Abuse (1997). Rockville, MD: U.S. Department of Health and Human Services, Substance Abuse and Mental Health Services Administration.

National Institute on Alcohol Abuse and Alcoholism (2003). College Drinking. Changing the Culture. *Newsweek* Feb. 12, 2001.

Neenan, M., & Dryden, W. (2001). *Learning from errors in rational emotive behaviour therapy.* London, England: Whurr Publishers, Ltd.

Neumark-Sztainer, D., Story, M., French, S., Cassuto, N., Jacobs, J. D., & Resnick, M. (1996). Patterns of health-compromising behaviors among Minnesota adolescents: Sociodemographic variations. *American Journal of Public Health, 86*, 1599-1606.

Newcomb, M.D., Maddahian, E., & Bentler, P. M. (1986). Risk factors for drug use among adolescents: Concurrent and longitudinal analyses. *American Journal of Public Health, 76*, 525-531.

NIDA (1999). *Monitoring the Future Study.* University of Michigan Institute for Social Research.

NIDA (2000). Ecstasy. *Infofaxy, 1354-7.*

NIDA NOTES (2001). NIDA Conference Highlights Scientific Findings on MDMA/ECSTASY, 16(5)1-9.

NIDA, Research Report Series (1998). Methamphetamine Abuse and Addiction.

NIDA, Research Report Series (2002). Inhalant Abuse, Publication No. 00-3818.

Niehoff, D. (1999). *The biology of violence: How understanding the brain, behavior, and environment can break the vicious circle of aggression.* New York: Simon & Schuster.

Nissen, L. B., Vanderbury, J. D., Embree-Bever, J., & Mankey, J. (1999). *Strategies for Integrating Substance Abuse Treatment and the Juvenile Justice System: A Practice Guide.* Washington DC: Center for Substance Abuse Treatment, Denver Juvenile Justice Integrated Treatment Network, U. S. Department of Health and Human Services.

Offer, D. (1987). The mystery of adolescence. *Adolescent Psychiatry, 14,* 7-27.

Olds, J., & Milner, P. (1954). Positive reinforcement produced by electrical stimulation of septal area and other regions of rat brain. *Journal of Comparative & Physiological Psychology, 47,* 419-427.

Oliver, S. J., & Toner, B.B. (1990). The influence of gender role typing on the expression of depressive symptoms. *Sex Roles, 22*(11-12*),* 775-790.

Olson, S. L. (1992). Development of conduct problems and peer rejection in preschool children: A social systems analysis. *Journal of Abnormal Child Psychology, 20*, 327-350.

Ott, A., Andersen K., Dewey, M.. E., Letenneur, L., Brayne, C., Copeland, J. R., et al. (2004). Effect of smoking on global cognitive function in nondemented elderly. *Neurobiology, 62*, 920-924.

Owen, B., & Bloom, B. (1997). *Profiling the needs of young female offenders: A protocol and pilot study (Final report)* (NCJ 179988). Washington, D. C.: U. S. Department of Justice, National Institute of Justice.

Palacios, W. R., Urmann, C. F., Newel, R., & Hamilton, N. (1999). Developing a sociological framework for dually diagnosed women. *Journal of Substance Abuse Treatment, 17*(1-2), 91-102.

Palmgreen, P., Donohew, L., & Lorch, E. P. (1991). Sensation seeking, message sensation value, and drug use as mediators of PSA effectiveness. *Health Communication, 3*(4), 217-227.

Patterson, C. H. (1966). *Theories of counseling and psychotherapy.* New York: Harper & Row.

Patterson, G. R. (1995). Coercion as a basis for early age of onset for arrest. In J. McCord (Ed.), *Coercion and punishment in long-term perspectives* (pp. 81-105). New York: Cambridge University Press.

Patterson, G. R. (1996). Some characteristics of a developmental theory for early-onset delinquency. In M. F. Lenzenweger & J. J. Haugaard (Eds.), *Frontiers of developmental psychopathology* (pp. 81-124). New York: Oxford University Press.

Patterson, G. R. (1999). A proposal relating a theory of delinquency to societal rates of juvenile crime: Putting Humpty Dumpty together again. In M. J. Cox & J. Brooks-Gunn (Eds.), *Conflict and cohesion in families: Causes and consequences. The advances in family research series* (pp. 11-35). Mawah, NJ: Lawrence Erlbaum Associates.

Patterson, G. R., Reid, J. B., & Dishion, T. (1992). *Antisocial boys: A social interactional approach (Vol. 4).* Eugene, OR: Castalia Publishing Company.

Patterson, G. R., Reid, J. B., & Dishion, T. J. (1998). Antisocial boys. In J. M. Jenkins & K. Oatley (Eds.), *Human emotions: A reader* (pp. 330-336). Malden, MA: Blackwell Publishers.

Patterson, G. R., Reid, J. B., & Eddy, M. (2002) A brief history of the Oregon model. In J. B. Reid, G. P. Patterson, & J. Snyder (Eds.), *Antisocial behavior in children and adolescents: A developmental analysis and model for intervention.* Washington, DC: American Psychological Association.

Patterson, G. R., & Yoerger, K. (1993). Developmental models for delinquent behavior. In S. Hodgkins (Ed.), *Mental disorder and crime* (pp. 140-172). Thousand Oaks, CA: Sage Publications.

Patterson, G. R., & Yoerger, K. (1997). A developmental model for late-onset delinquency. In D. W. Osgood (Ed.), *Motivation and delinquency* (pp.119-177). Lincoln, NE: University of Nebraska Press.

Patterson, G. R., & Yoerger, K. (2002). A developmental model for early- and late-onset delinquency. In J. B. Reid & G. R. Patterson (Eds.), *Antisocial behavior in children and adolescents: A developmental analysis and model for intervention* (pp. 147-142). Washington, DC: American Psychological Association.

Pavlov, I. (1927). *Conditioned reflexes.* New York: Oxford University Press.

Pena, I. M., Megargee, E.L., & Brody, E. (1996). MMPI-A patterns of male juvenile delinquents. *Psychological Assessment, 8,* 388-397.

Pepler, D. & Rubin, K. (Eds.), *The development and treatment of childhood aggression.* Hillsdale NJ: Erlbaum.

Perlin, M. L. (1996). The insanity defense: Deconstructing the myths and reconstructing the jurisprudence. In B. D. Sales & D. W. Shuman (Eds.) *Law, mental health, and mental disorder.* Pacific Grove, CA: Brooks/Cole.

Petchers, M., & Singer, M. (1987). Perceived benefit of drinking scale: Approach to screening for adolescent alcohol use. *Journal of Pediatrics, 110,* 977-981.

Petraitis, J., Flay, B. R., & Miller, T. Q. (1995). Reviewing theories of adolescent substance use: Organizing pieces of the puzzle. *Psychological Bulletin, 117,* 67-86.

Pfefferbaum, A., Kim, K. O., Zirpursky, R. B., Mathalon, D. H., Lane, B., Ha, C.N., et. al. (1992). Brain gray and white matter volume loss accelerates with aging in chronic alcoholics: A quantitative study. *Alcoholism: Clinical and Experimental Research, 16*(6), 1078-1089.

Phillips, D. P. (1983). The Impact of Mass Media Violence on Homicide. *American Sociological Review, 48,* 560-568.

Phillips, S. D., & Harm, N. J. (1997). Women prisoners: A contextual framework. *Women and Therapy, 20*(4), 1-9.

Phinney, J. S. (1996). Understanding ethnic diversity: The role of ethnic identity. *American Behavioral Scientist, 40*(2), 143-152.

Piaget, J. (1952). *The origins of intelligence in children* (2nd E. M. Cook, Trans.). New York: International Universities Press. (Original work published 1952)

Pike, K. M., & Striegel-Moore, R. H. (1997). Disordered eating and eating disorders. In S. J. Gallant, G. P. Keita, & R. Royak-Schaler (Eds.), *Health care for women: Psychological, social, and behavioral influences* (pp. 97-114). Washington, DC: American Psychological Association.

Piquero, A. (2001). Testing Moffitt's neuropsychological variation hypothesis for the prediction of life-course persistent offending. *Psychology, Crime & Law, 7*(3), 193-215.

Plomin, B. H., Chipuer, M., & Loehlin J. C. (1990). Behavioral genetics and personality. In L. A. Pervin (Ed.), *Handbook of personality theory and research* (pp. 225-43). New York: Guilford Press.

Pobanz, M. S. (2001). Using protective factors to enhance the prediction of negative short-term outcomes of first-time juvenile offenders. *Dissertation Abstracts International Section A: Humanities & Social Sciences, Vol 62*(5-A), Dec pp. 1948.

Pollock, D. (2003). Pro-eating disorder websites: What should be the feminist response? *Feminism & Psychology, 13*(2), 246-251.

Pollock, J. M. (1998). *Counseling women in prison.* Thousand Oaks, CA: Sage Publications.

Pope, H. G. Jr., & Yurgelun, T. (1996). The residual cognitive effects of heavy marijuana use in college students. *Journal of the American Medical Association, 275*(7), 521-527.

Powers, S. I., Hauser, S. T., & Kilner, L. A. (1989). Adolescent mental health. *American Psychologist, 44*(2), 200-208.

Preski, S., & Shelton, D. (2001). The role of contextual, child and parent factors in predicting criminal outcomes in adolescence. *Issues in Mental Health Nursing, 22*(2), 197-205.

Price, B. H., Daffner, K. R., Stowe, R. M., & Mesulam, M. M. (1990). The comportmental learning disabilities of early frontal lobe damage. *Brain, 113,* 1383-1393.

Prochaska, J.O., & DiClemente, C. C. (1992). Stages of change in the modification of problem behavior. In M. Hersen, R. Eisler, & P.M. Miller (Eds.), *Progress in behavior modification* (pp. 184-214). Sycamore, IL: Sycamore Publishing.

Prochaska, J. O., DiClemente, C. C., & Norcross, J. C. (1992). In search of how people change: Application to addictive behaviors. *American Psychologist, 47(9),* 1102-1114.

Project MATCH Research Group (1993). Project MATCH: Rationale and methods for a multisite clinical trial matching patterns to alcoholism treatment. *Alcoholism: Clinical and Experimental Research, 17,* 1330-1345.

Project MATCH Research Group. (1997). Matching alcoholism treatments to client heterogeneity: Project MATCH posttreatment drinking outcomes. *Journal of Studies on Alcohol, 58,* 7-29.

Prothrow-Stith, D. B. (1995).The epidemic of youth violence in America: using public health prevention strategies to prevent violence. *Journal of Health Care for the Poor and Underserved, 6*, 95-101.

Pulkkinen, L., Maennikkoe, K., and Nurmi, J.E. (2000). Self-description and personality styles. In: L. R. Bergman, R. B. Cairns, L.-G. Nilsson & L. Nystedt, (Eds). *Developmental science and the holistic approach* (pp. 265-280). Mawah, NJ: Lawrence Erlbaum Associates.

Puzzanchera, C. M. (2000). *Self-reported delinquency by 12-year-olds, 1997*. OJJDP Fact Sheet. Washington, DC: Office of Juvenile Justice and Delinquency Prevention, U.S. Department of Justice.

RachBeisel, J., Scott, J., & Dixon, L. (1999). Co-occurring severe mental illness and substance abuse disorders: A review of recent research. *Psychiatric Services, 50*(11), 1427-1434.

Raue, P.J., Goldfried, M.R. (1994). The therapeutic alliance in cognitive-behavior therapy. In A.O. Horvath & L.S. Grenberg (Eds.), *The working alliance: Theory, research and practice* (pp. 131-152). New York: Wiley.

Raue, P.J., Goldfried, M.R., & Barkham, M. (1997). The therapeutic alliance in psychodynamic-interpersonal and cognitive-behavioral therapy. *Journal of Consulting and Clinical Psychology, 65,* 582-587.

Rawson, R. A., Shoptaw, S. J., Obert, J. L., & McCann, M. J. (1995). An intensive outpatient approach for cocaine abuse treatment: The Matrix model. *Journal of Substance Abuse Treatment, 12*(2), 117-127.

Ray, O, & Ksir, C. (2002). *Drugs, society, and human behavior* (9th ed.). New York:McGraw-Hill.

Reckless, W. C. (1967). *The crime problem* (4th ed.). New York: Appleton-Century-Crofts.

Reed, B. G., & Leavitt, M. E. (2000). Modified wraparound and women offenders in community corrections: Strategies, opportunities, and tensions. In M. McMahon, (Ed.) *Assessment to assistance: programs for women in community corrections* (pp. 1-106). Lanham, MD: American Correctional Association.

Regier, D.A., Farmer, M.E., Rae, D.S., Locke, B.Z., Keith, S.J., Judd, L.L., et al. (1990). Comorbidity of mental disorders with alcohol and other drug abuse. *JAMA: Journal of the American Medical Association, 264*(19), 2511-2518.

Reid, J.B., Patterson, G. R., & Snyder, James, (Eds). (2002). *Antisocial behavior in children and adolescents: A developmental analysis and model for intervention*. Washington, DC: American Psychological Association.

Reiss, A. J., Jr., & Roth, J. A. (Eds). (1993a). *Understanding and preventing violence: Panel on the understanding, and control of violent behavior.* Washington, DC: National Academy of Science.

Reiss, A. J., Jr., & Roth, J. A. (Eds.). (1993b). *Understanding and preventing violence, Vol. 1.* Washington, DC: National Academy Press.

Ricaurte, G. A., Yuau, J., McCann, U. D. (2000). (±)3,4-Methylenedioxymethamphetamine ('Ecstasy')-induced serotonin neurotoxicity: studies in animals. *Neuropsychobiology, 42*, 5-10.

Richie, B.E. (1996). *Compelled to crime: The gender entrapment of battered black women.* New York: Routledge.

Roberts, R. E., Attkisson, C. C., & Rosenblatt, A. (1998). Prevalence of psychopathology in children and adolescents. *American Journal of Psychiatry, 155*(6), 715-725.

Robins, L. N. (1966). *Deviant Children Grown Up.* Baltimore, MD: Williams and Wilkins.

Robins, L. N. (1978). Sturdy childhood predictors of adult antisocial behaviour: Replications from longitudinal studies. *Psychological Medicine, 8*(4), 611-622.

Robins, R., Caspi, J.O., Moffitt, T., & Stouthamer-Loeber, M. (1996). Resilient, overcontrolled and undercontrolled boys: Three replicable personality types. *Journal of Personality and Social Psychology, 70*, 157-171.

Rodgers, J., Buchanan, T., Scholey, A. B., Hoffernan, T. M., Ling, J., & Parrott, A. C. (2003). Patterns of drug use and the influence of gender on self-reports of memory ability in ecstasy users: a web-based study. *Journal of Psychopharmacology, 17*(4), 389-396.

Rodney, H. E., & Mupier, R. (2000). Comparing the behaviors and social environments of offending and non-offending African-American adolescents. In N. J. Pallone (Ed.), *Race, ethnicity, sexual orientation, violent crime: The realities and the myths* (pp. 65-80).

Rogers, C. R. (1951). *Client-centered therapy.* Oxford, England: Houghton Mifflin.

Rogers, C. R. (1957). The necessary and sufficient conditions of therapeutic personality change. *Journal of Consulting Psychology, 22*, 95-103.

Rogers, C. R. (1959). The essence of psychotherapy: A client-centered view. *Annals of Psychotherapy, 1*, 51-57.

Rogers, C. R. (1980). *A way of being.* Boston: Houghton Mifflin.

Rogers, C.R., & Dymond, R. (1954). *Psychotherapy and personality change.* Chicago: University of Chicago Press.

Rogers, C. R., Gendlin, E. T., Kiesler, D., & Truax, C. B. (1967). *The therapeutic relationship and its impact: A study of psychotherapy with schizophrenics.* Madison: University of Wisconsin Press.

Rokke, P. D., & Rehem, L. P. (2001). In K. S. Dobson (Ed.), *Handbook of cognitive-behavioral therapies, Second edition.* New York: Guilford Press.

Root, M. P. P. (1992). Reconstructing the impact of trauma on personality. In L. S. Brown & M. Ballou (Eds.), *Personality and psycholopathology: Feminist reappraisals* (pp. 229-265). New York: Guilford Press.

Rosen, H. (1988). The constructivist-development paradigm. In R.A. Dorfman (Ed.), *Paradigms of clinical social work* (pp. 317-355). New York: Brunner/Mazel.

Rosenblatt, J. A., Rosenblatt, A., & Biggs, E. E. (2000). Criminal behavior and emotional disorder: Comparing youth served by the mental health and juvenile justice systems. *Journal of Behavioral Health Services & Research, 27*(2), 227-237.

Rosenhan, D.L., & Seligman, M.E.P. (1995). *Abnormal psychology* (3rd ed.). New York: W.W. Norton.

Rotter, J. B. (1966). Generalized expectancies for internal versus external control of reinforcement. *Psychological Monographs, 80,* (1 Whole No. 609).

Routtenberg, A. (1978). The reward system of the brain. *Scientific American, 239*(5), 154-164.

Rowe, C., Parker-Sloat, E., Schwartz, S., Liddle, H. (2003). Family therapy for early adolescent substance abuse. In S. Stevens & A. Morral (Eds.), *Adolescent Substance Abuse Treatment in the United States* (pp. 105-132). New York: Haworth Press.

Russell, M., Martier, S. S., & Sokol, R. J. (1994). Screening for pregnancy-risk drinking. *Alcoholism: Clinical and Experimental Research, 18*(5), 1156-1161.

Rutter, M. (1990). Psychosocial resilience and protective mechanisms. In J. E. Rolf & A. S. Masten (Eds.), *Risk and protective factors in the development of psychopathology.* New York: Cambridge University Press.

Rutter, M. (1997). Nature-nurture integration: The example of antisocial behavior. *American Psychologist, 52*(4), 390-398.

Rutter, M., Giller, H., & Hagell, A. (1998). *Antisocial behavior by young people.* New York: Cambridge University Press.

Sadker, M., & Sadker, D. (1994). *Failing at fairness: How our schools cheat girls.* New York: Touchstone Books.

Saigh, P. A., Yasik, A. E., Sack, W. H., & Koplewicz, H. S. (1999). Child-adolescent posttraumatic stress disorder: Prevalence, risk factors, and comorbidity. In P. A. Saigh, & J. D. Bremner (Eds.), *Posttraumatic stress disorder: A comprehensive text* (pp. 18-43). New York: Allyn & Bacon.

Salkovskis, P.M. (1996a). The cognitive approach to anxiety: Threat beliefs, safety-seeking behavior, and the special case of health anxiety and obsessions.. In P.M. Salkovskis (Ed.), *Frontiers of cognitive therapy* (pp.48-74). New York: Guilford.

Salkovskis, P. M. (Ed.). (1996b). *Frontiers of cognitive therapy.* New York: Guilford Press.

Salter, A. (1949). *Conditioned reflex therapy, the direct approach to the reconstruction of personality.* Oxford, England: Creative Age Press.

Saltzberg, E. A., & Chrisler, J. C. (1995). Beauty is the beast: Psychological effects of the pursuit of the perfect female body. In E. Disch (Ed.), *Reconstructing Gender* (pp. 146-156). New York: McGraw-Hill.

Sampson, R. J., & Laub, J. H. (1993). *Crime in the making: Pathways and turning points through life.* Cambridge, MA: Harvard University Press.

Sampson, R. J., & Laub, J. H. (1997). A life course theory of cumulative disadvantage and the stability of delinquency. In T. P. Thornberry (Ed.), *Advances in criminological theory: Vol. 7. Developmental theories of crime and delinquency* (pp. 133-161). Sommerset, NJ: Transaction Publishers.

Sanders-Bush, E. (1994). Neurochemical evidence that hallucinogenic drugs are 5-HT2c receptor agonists: What next? In G. C. Lin, & R. A. Glennon (Eds.), *Hallucinogens: An update* (pp. 203-213). National Institute on Drug Research Monograph, No. 146 NIH Pub. No. 94-3872, Washington, D.C.

Sankey, M., & Huon, G. E. (1999a). An evaluation of a maximum security therapeutic community for psychopaths and other mentally disordered offenders. *Law and Human Behavior, 4,* 253-264.

Sankey, M., & Huon, G.E. (1999b). Offence seriousness in adolescent delinquent behavior. *Legal & Criminological Psychology,* Vol. 4 (Part 2), Sep. pp. 253-264.

Sarason, I.G., & Sarason, B.R. (1995). *Abnormal psychology: The problem of maladaptive behavior.* Englewood Cliffs, NJ: Prentice-Hall.

Saunders, D.G. (1994). Child custody decisions in families experiencing woman abuse. *Social Work, 39*(1), 51-59.

Schaffer, D., Fisher, P., Dulcan, M. K., Davies, M., Piacentini, J., Schwab-Stone, M. E., et al. (1996). The NIMH Diagnostic Interview Schedule for Children version 2.3(DISC-2.3): Description, acceptability, prevalence rates, and performance in the MECA study. *Journal of the American Academy of Child and Adolescent Psychiatry, 35*(7), 865-878.

Scheier, L. M., & Botvin, G. J. (1996). Purpose in life, cognitive efficacy, and general deviance as determinants of drug abuse in urban Black youth. *Journal of Child & Adolescent Substance Abuse, 5*(1), 1-26.

Scheier, L. M., & Botvin, G. J. (1997). Expectancies as mediators of the effects of social influences and alcohol knowledge on adolescent alcohol use: A prospective analysis. *Psychology of Addictive Behaviors, 11*(1), 48-64.

Scheier, L. M. & Botvin, G. J. (1998). Relations of social skills, personal competence, and adolescent alcohol use: A developmental exploratory study. *Journal of Early Adolescence, 18*(1), 77-114.

Schier, L. M., & Botvin, G. J. (2002). Influence of competence and alcohol use on self-esteem: Latent growth curve models using longitudinal data. In T. M. Brinthaupt & R. P. Lipka (Eds.), *Understanding early adolescent self and identity: Applications and interventions: SUNY Series, Studying the self* (pp. 225-264). Albany, NY: State University of New York Press.

Scheier, L. M., Botvin, G. J., Diaz, T., & Griffin, K. W. (1999). Social skills, competence, and drug refusal efficacy as predictors of adolescent alcohol use. *Journal of Drug Education, 29*(3), 251-278.

Scheier, L. M., Botvin, G. J., Diaz, T., & Ifill-Williams, M. (1997). Ethnic identity as a moderator of psychosocial risk and adolescent alcohol and marijuana use: Concurrent and longitudinal analyses. *Journal of Child & Adolescent Substance Abuse, 6*(1), 21-47.

Scheier, L. M., Botvin, G. J., & Griffin, K. W. (2000). Dynamic growth models of self esteem and adolescent alcohol use. *Journal of Early Adolescence, Special Issue: Self esteem in early Adolescence: Part II, 20*(2), 178-209.

Scheier, L. M., Botvin, G. J., & Miller, N. L. (1999). Life events, neighborhood stress, psychosocial functioning and alcohol use among urban minority youth. *Journal of Child & Adolescent Substance Abuse, 9*(1), 19-50.

Scheier, L. M., Miller, N. L., Ifill-Williams, M., & Botvin, G. J. (2001). Perceived Neighborhood risk as a predictor of drug use among urban ethnic minority adolescents: Moderating influences of psychosocial functioning. *Journal of Child and Adolescent Substance Abuse, 11*(2), 67-106.

Schenck, E. R., Lyman, R. D., Bodin, S. D. (2000). Ethical beliefs, attitudes, and professional practices of psychologists regarding parental use of corporal punishment: A survey. *Children's Services: Social Policy, Research, and Practice, 3*, 23-38.

Scherzer, T., & Pinderhughes, H. L. (2002). Violence and gender: Reports from an urban high school. *Violence & Victims, 17*(1), 57-72.

Schulenberg, J., Maggs, J. L., Steinman, K. J., & Zucker, R. (2001). Development matters: Taking the long view on substance abuse etiology and intervention during adolescence. In P. M. Monti, S. M. Coby, & T. A. O'Leary (Eds.), *Adolescents, alcohol and substance abuse: Reaching teens through brief interventions* (pp. 19-57). New York: The Guilford Press.

Scott, C. L. (1999). Juvenile violence. *Psychiatric Clinics of North America, 22*(1), 71-83.

Seligman, M. E. P., Walker, E., & Rosenhan, D. L. (2001). *Abnormal Psychology* (4th ed.). New York: W. W. Norton.

Sexton, T.L., Alexander, J.F. (December, 2000). Functional family therapy. *Office of Juvenile Justice & Delinquency Prevention, Juvenile Justice Bulletin,* 3-7.

Shafer, M. A., Ekstrand, M. L., Hilton, J., Keogh, J., Gee, L., DiGiorgio-Haag, L., et al. (1993). Relationship between sexual, drug use behaviors and occurrence of STDs among high risk male youth. *Sexually Transmitted Diseases, 20*, 307-313.

Shaffer, D., Fisher, P., & Dulcan, M. (1996). The NIMH Diagnostic Interview Schedule for children (DISC2.3): Description, acceptability, prevalences, and performance in the MECA study. *Journal of the American Academy of Child and Adolescent Psychiatry, 35*, 865-877.

Shastri, L. (2002). Episodic memory and cortio-hippocampal interactions. *Trends in Cognitive Sciences, 6*(4), 162-168.

Sheley, J. F., & Wright, J. D. (1995). *In the line of fire: Youth, guns and violence in urban America.* New York: Aldine.

Shope, J. T. (2002). Drinking-driving as a component of problem driving and problem behavior in young adults. *Journal of Studies on Alcohol, 63*(1), 24-33.

Shore, E. R., & Compton, K. L. (1998). Wadda ya mean, I can't drive?: Threat to competence as a factor in drunk driving intervention. *Journal of Prevention & Intervention in the Community, 17*(1-2), 45-53.

Shure, M. B., & Spivack, G. (1978). *Problem solving techniques in childrearing.* San Francisco, CA: Jossey-Bass.

Sickmund, M., Snyder, H. N., & Poe-Yamagata, E. (1997). *Juvenile offenders and victims: 1997 update on violence.* Washington, DC: Office of Juvenile Justice and Delinquency Prevention.

Sigvardsson, S., Bohman, M., & Cloninger, C. R. (1996, August). Replication of the Stockholm Adoption Study of Alcoholism: Confirmatory cross-fostering analysis. *Archives of General Psychiatry, 53*(8), 681-687.

Silberg, J. L., Rutter, M., & Meyer, J. (1996). Genetic and environmental differences on the covariation between hyperactivity and conduct disturbance in juvenile twins. *Journal of Child Psychology & Psychiatry & Allied Disciplines, 37*(7), 803-816.

Silveri, M., & Spear, L. (1998). Decreased sensitivity to hypnotic effects of alcohol early in ontogeny. *Alcoholism: Clinical and Experimental Research, 20,* 671-676.

Silverthorn, P., & Frick, P. J. (1999). Developmental pathways to antisocial behavior: The delayed-onset pathway in girls. *Development and Psychopathology, 11*, 101-126.

Simon, L. M. J. (1996). The legal processing of domestic violence cases. In B. D. Sales & D. W. Shuman (Eds.), *Law, mental health, and mental disorder* (pp. 440-463). Pacific Grove, CA: Brooks/Cole.

Simon, R.J. (1975). *Women and Crime.* Lexington, MA: Lexington Books.

Skinner, B. F. (1938). *The behavior of organisms: An experimental analysis.* Oxford, England: Appleton-Century.

Skinner, B. F. (1953). *Science and human behavior.* Oxford, England: Macmillan.

Skinner, H. A. (1982). The Drug Abuse Screening Test. *Addictive Behaviors, 7*, 363-371.

Smith, G. T., & Goldman, M. S. (1995). Alcohol expectancy theory and the identification of high-risk adolescents. In G. M. Boyd & J. Howard (Eds.), *Alcohol problems among adolescents: Current directions in prevention research* (pp. 85-104). Hillsdale, NJ: Lawrence Erlbaum Associates.

Smith, M. L., Glass, G. V., & Miller, T. I. (1980). *The benefits of psychotherapy.* Baltimore: Johns Hopkins University Press.

Smith, P. B., & Bond, M. H. (1998). *Social psychology: Across cultures* (2nd ed). Boston, MA: Allyn & Bacon.

Smith, P. K., & Myron-Wilson, R. (1998). Parenting and school bullying. *Clinical Child Psychology & Psychiatry, 3*(3), 405-417.

Smith, R.F. (2003). Animal models of peri-adolescent substance abuse. *Neurotox Teratol, 25*, 291-301.

Smith-Bell, M., & Winslade, W. J. (1996). Confidentiality in the psychotherapeutic relationship. In B. D. Sales & D. W. Shuman (Eds.), *Law, mental health, and mental disorder.* Pacific Grove, CA: Brooks/Cole.

Smith, G.T., and Anderson, K.G., (2001). Personality and learning factors combine to create risk for adolescent problem drinking: A model and suggestions for intervention In P. M. Monti, S. M. Colby, & T.A. O'Leary (Eds.), *Adolescents, alcohol, and substance abuse: Reaching teens through brief interventions* (pp. 109-141). New York: Guilford Press.

Snell, T. L. (1994, March). *Women in prison: Survey of state prison inmates, 1991* (BJS Special Report, NCJ 145321). Washington, DC: U. S. Department of Justice, Bureau of Justice Statistics.

Snow, R. W., & Cunningham, O. R. (1985). Age, machismo, and the drinking locations of drunken drivers: A research note. *Deviant Behavior, 6*(1), 57-66.

Snyder, H. N. (1997, November). Juvenile Arrests 1996 (NCJ 167578). *Juvenile Justice Bulletin, November 1997.* Washington, D. C.: U. S. Department of Justice, Office of Juvenile Justice and Delinquency (OJJDP).

Snyder, H. N., & Sickmund M. (1999). *Juvenile offenders and victims; 1999 national report.* Washington, DC: Office of Juvenile Justice and Delinquency Prevention. U.S. Department of Justice.

Snyder H. N., Sickmund, M., & Poe-Yamagata, E. (1996). *Juvenile offenders and victims: 1996 update on violence.* Washington, DC: Office of Juvenile Justice and Delinquency Prevention National Center for Juvenile Justice, U.S. Department of Justice.

Snyder, H. N. & Sigmund, M. (1995). *Juvenile offenders and victims; A focus on violence.* Washington, DC: Office of Juvenile and Delinquency Prevention, U.S. Department of Justice.

Sokol, R. J., Martier, S. S., & Ager, J. W. (1989). The T-ACE questions: Practical prenatal detection of risk-drinking. *American Journal of Obstetrics and Gynecology, 160*(4), 863-870.

Sommers, I., & Baskin, D. R. (1991). Assessing the appropriateness of the prescription of psychiatric medications in prison. *Journal of Nervous & Mental Disease, 179*(5), 267-273.

Sommers, I., & Baskin, D. R. (1992). Sex, race, age, and violent offending. *Violence & Victims, 7*(3), 191-201.

Sommers, I., & Baskin, D. R. (1993). The situational context of violent female offending. *Journal of Research in Crime & Delinquency, 30*(2), 136-162.

Spak, F., & Hallstrom, T. (1996). Screening for alcohol dependence and abuse in women: Description, validation, and psychometric properties of a new screening instrument, SWAG, in a population study. *Alcoholism: Clinical and Experimental Research, 20*(4), 723-731.

Spear, L. P. (2000). The adolescent brain and age-related behavioral manifestations. *Neuroscience & Biobehavioral Reviews, 24*(4), 417-463.

Spence, M. F. (1998). Risk-taking in adolescence: An exploration of basic constructs. *Dissertation Abstracts International, 58*(11-A), 4189.

Sperry, L. (2003). Commonalities between Adlerian psychotherapy and cognitive therapies: An Adlerian perspective. In R. E. Watts (Ed.), *Adlerian, cognitive, and constructivist therapies: An integrative dialogue* (pp. 59-70). New York: Springer Publishing.

351

Spivack, G., Platt, J., & Shure, M. (1976). *The problem-solving approach to adjustment.* San Francisco: Jossey-Bass.

Spivack, G., & Shure, M. B. (1974). *Social adjustment of young children.* San Francisco, CA: Jossey-Bass.

Sprague, J., Walker, H. M., Stieber, S., Simonsen, B., Nishioka, V., & Wagner, L. (2001). Exploring the relationship between school discipline referrals and delinquency. *Psychology in the Schools, 38*(2), 197-206.

Stacy, A. W., & Newcomb, M. D. (1995). Long-term social-psychological influences on deviant attitudes and criminal behavior. In H. B. Kaplan (Ed.), *Drugs, crime, and other deviant adaptations: Longitudinal studies. Longitudinal research in the social and behavioral sciences: An interdisciplinary series* (pp. 99-127). New York: Plenum Press.

Stacy, A. W., Bentler, P. M., & Flay, B. R. (1994). Attitudes and health behavior in diverse populations. *Health Psychology, 13*(1), 73-85.

Stahl, A. I. (1999). *Offenders in juvenile court. 1996.* Juvenile Justice Bulletin. Washington, DC: U.S. Department of Justice. Office of Juvenile Justice and Delinquency Prevention.

Stattin, H., Janson, H., Klackenberg-Larsson, I., & Magnusson, D. (1995). Corporal punishment in everyday life: An intergenerational perspective. In J. McCord (Ed.), *Coercion and punishment in long-term perspectives* (pp. 315-347). New York: Cambridge University Press.

Steele, C.T. (2000). Providing clinical treatment to substance abusing trauma survivors. *Alcoholism Treatment Quarterly, 18*(3), 71-81.

Stefan, S. (1996). Issues relating to women and ethnic minorities in mental health treatment and law. In B. D. Sales & D. W. Shuman (Eds.), *Law, mental health, and mental disorder.*

Steinberg, L. (1985). Early tempermental antecedents of adult Type A behaviors. *Developmental Psychology, 21*(6), 1171-1180.

Steinberg, L. (1999). *Adolescence* (5th ed.). Boston, MA: McGraw Hill.

Steiner, H., Williams, S. E., Benton-Hardy, L., Kohler, M., & Duxbury, E. (1997). Violent crime paths in incarcerated juveniles: Psychological, environmental, and biological factors. In A. Raine & P. A. Brennan (Eds.), *Biosocial bases of violence. NATO ASI series: Series A: Life sciences, Vol. 292.* (pp. 325-328). New York: Plenum Press.

Stevens, S. J., Estrada, B. D., Carter, T., Reinardy, L., Seitz, V., Swartz, T. (2003). The teen substance abuse treatment program: program design, treatment issues, and client characteristics. In S. J. Stevens & A. R. Morral (Eds.), *Adolescent substance abuse treatment in the United States.* (pp. 37-56). New York: Haworth Press.

Stewart, A. J. (1994). Toward a feminist strategy for studying women's lives. In C.E. Franz & A.J. Stewart (Eds.), *Women creating lives: Identities, resilience and resistance* (pp. 11-35). Boulder, CO: Westview Press.

Strassberg, Z., Dodge, K. A., Pettit, G. S., & Bates. J. E. (1994). Spanking in the home and children's subsequent aggression toward kindergarten peers. *Development and Psychopathology, 6*, 445-461.

Straus, M. A. (1991). Discipline and deviance: Physical punishment of children and violence and other crime in adulthood. *Social Problems, 38*, 101-23.

Straus, M. A. (2001). *Beating the devil out of them: Corporal punishment in American families and its effects on children.* New York: Transaction Publishers. xxv, 317

Straus, M. A., & Donnelly, D. (1993). Corporal punishment of teen age children in the United States. *Youth and Society, 24*, 419-42.

Straus, M. A., Gelles, R. J., & Steinmetz, S. K. (1980). *Behind closed doors: Violence in the American family.* Garden City, NY: Anchor Press/Doubleday.

Strauss, S. M., & Falkin, G. P. (2001). Social support systems of women offenders who use drugs: A focus on the mother-daughter relationship. *The American Journal of Drug and Alcohol Abuse, 27*(1), 65-89.

Strupp, H.H., & Hadley, S.W. (1979). Specific versus nonspecific factors in psychotherapy. *Archives of General Psychiatry, 36*, 1125-1136.

Strupp, H. H., & Howard, K. I. (1992). A brief history of psychotherapy research. In D. K. Freedheim (Ed.), *History of psychotherapy: A century of change* (pp. 309-334). Washington, DC: American Psychological Association.

Sugai, G., Sprague, J. R., Horner, R. H., & Walker, H. M. (2000). Preventing school violence: The use of office discipline referrals to assess and monitor school-wide discipline interventions. *Journal of Emotional & Behavioral Disorders, 8*(2), 94-101.

Sullivan, H. S. (1947). *Conceptions of modern psychiatry.* Washington, DC: William Alanson White Psychiatric Foundation.

Sunderwirth, S. G., & Milkman, H. (1991). Behavioral and neurochemical commonalities in addiction. *Contemporary Family Therapy, 13*(5), 422-433.

Sutherland, E. H. (1947). *Principles of Criminology.* 4th ed. Philadelphia, PA: JB Lippincott.

Swartzwelder, H. S., Wilson, W. A., & Toyyeb, M. I. (1995). Differential sensitivity to NMDA receptor-mediated synaptic potentials to ethanol in immature vs. mature hippocampus. *Alcoholism: Clinical and Experimental Research, 19*, 320-323.

Swisher, J. D. (1988). Problem-behavior theory and driving risk. *Alcohol, Drugs & Driving, 4*(3), 205-219.

Szatmari, P., Boyle, M. H., & Offord, D. R. (1989). ADDH and conduct disorder: Degree of diagnostic overlap and differences among correlates. *Journal of the American Academy of Child & Adolescent Psychiatry, 28*(6), 865-872.

Tarter, R. E., & Hegedus, A. M. (1991). Drug Use Screening Inventory: Its application in the evaluation and treatment of alcohol and other drug abuse. *Alcohol Health Research World 15(1)*: 65-75.

Taylor, C. (1993). *Girls, gangs, women and drugs.* East Lansing, MI: Michigan State University Press.

Teicher, M. H., Gallitano, A. L., Gelbard, H. A., & Evans, H. K. et al. (1991). Dopamine D-sub-1 autoreceptor function: Possible expression in developing rat prefrontal cortex and striatum. *Developmental Brain Research, 63*(1-2), 229-235.

Teplin, L. A., Abram, K. M., & McClelland, G. M. (1996). Prevalence of psychiatric disorders among incarcerated women: Pretrial jail detainees. *Archives of General Psychiatry 53*(6),505-512.

Teusch, R. (1997). Substance-abusing women and sexual abuse. In S. L. A. Straussner & E. Zelvin (Eds.), *Gender and addictions: Men and women in treatment* (pp. 97-122). Northvale, NJ: Jason Aronson.

Thomas, D. W. (1990). *Substance Abuse Screening Protocol for the Juvenile Courts.* Pittsburgh, PA: National Center for Juvenile Justice.

Thompson, R. A. (2003). Cheerleader weight standards. *Eating Disorders: The Journal of Treatment & Prevention, 11*(1), 87-90.

Thornberry, T. P. (1998). Membership in youth gangs and involvement in serious and violent offending. In R. Loeber & D. P. Farrington (Eds.), *Serious & violent juvenile offenders: Risk factors and successful interventions* (pp. 147-166). Thousand Oaks, CA: Sage Publications.

Thornberry, T. P., Krohn, M. D., Lizotte, A. J., & Chard-Wierschem, D. (1993). The roles of juvenile gangs in facilitating delinquent behavior. *Journal of Research in Crime and Delinquency, 30*, 55-87.

Thornberry, T. P., Lizotte, A. J., Krohn, M. D., Farnworth, M., et al. (1996). Delinquent peers, beliefs, and delinquent behavior: A longitudinal test of interactional theory. In D. F. Greenberg (Ed.), *Criminal careers, Vol. 2. The international library of criminology, criminal justice and penology* (pp. 339-375). Aldershot, England: Dartmouth.

Thornberry, T. P., Smith, C. A., Rivera, C., Huizinga, D., & Strouthamer-Loeber, M. (September 1999). *Family disruption and delinquency.* Juvenile Justice Bulletin, Office of Juvenile Justice and Delinquency Prevention, U.S. Department of Justice, Washington, DC.

Thorndike, E. L. (1931). *Human learning.* Oxford, England: Appleton-Century.

Ting-Toomey, S. (1998). *Communicating across cultures.* New York: Guilford.

Tobin, D.L., Holroyd, K. A., Reynolds, R. V., & Wigal, J. K. (1989). The hierarchical factor structure of the Coping Strategies Inventory. *Cognitive Therapy and Research, 13*(4), 343-361.

Tolan, P. H., & Loeber, R. (1993). Antisocial Behavior. In P. H. Tolan & B. J. Cohler (Eds.), *Handbook of clinical research and practice with adolescents* (pp. 307-331). New York: John Wiley.

Tor, P. B., & Sales, B. D. (1996). Guardianship for incapacitated persons. In B. D. Sales & D. W. Shuman (Eds.), *Law, mental health, and mental disorder* (pp. 202-218). Pacific Grove, CA: Brooks/Cole.

Toyer, E. A., & Weed, N. C. (1998). Concurrent validity of the MMPI-A in a counseling program for juvenile offenders. *Journal of Clinical Psychology, 54*, 395-399.

Tremblay, R. E. (1995). Kindergarten behavioral patterns, parental practices, and early adolescent antisocial behavior. In J. McCord (Ed.), *Coercion and punishment in long-term perspectives* (pp. 139-153). New York: Cambridge University Press.

Triplett, R. (1996). The growing threat: Gangs and juvenile offenders. In T. J. Flanagan & D. R. Longmire (Eds.), *Americans view crime and justice: A national public opinion survey* (pp. 137-150). Thousand Oaks, CA: Sage Publications.

Truax, C. B., & Carkhuff, R. R. (1967). *Toward effective counseling and psychotherapy.* Chicago: Aldine.

Truax, C. B., & Mitchell, K. M. (1971). Research on certain therapist interpersonal skills in relation to process and outcome. In A. E. Bergin & S. L. Garfield (Eds.), *Handbook of psychotherapy and behavioral change: An empirical analysis* (pp. 299-344). New York: John Wiley.

Ullmann, R. K., Sleator, E. K. & Sprague, R. L. (1998). *AD/HD Comprehensive Teacher's Rating Scale, Revised (ACTeRS).* Champaign, IL: MetriTech, Inc.

Uniform Crime Reports, 1990. Washington DC: U. S. Government Printing Office.

U. S. Department of Health and Human Services (2001a). *Cannabis Youth Treatment Series.* Rockville, MD: Substance Abuse and Mental Health Services Administration.

U. S. Department of Health and Human Services. (2001b). *Hallucinogens and Dissociative Drugs* (NIH Publication No. 01-4209). Rockville, MD.

U. S. Department of Health and Human Services, (2001c). *National Household Survey on Drug Abuse.* Rockville, MD: Substance Abuse and Mental Health Services Administration.

U. S. Department of Health and Human Services. (2001d). *Youth Violence: A Report of the Surgeon General.* Rockville, MD: US. Department of Health and Human Services, Centers for Disease Control and Prevention, National Center for Injury Prevention and Control; Substance Abuse and Mental Health Services Administration, Center for Mental Health Services; and National Institutes of Health, National Institute of Mental Health.

U. S. Department of Justice (1997). *Juvenile Arrests 1995.* Office of Justice Programs. Office of Juvenile Justice and Delinquency Prevention. Retrieved May 20, 2004 from http://www.ncjrs.org.

Utting, D. (1996). Tough on the causes of crime? Social bonding and delinquency prevention. In S. Kraemer & J. Roberts (Eds.), *The politics of attachment: Towards a secure society* (pp. 75-87).

Valente, C. M., Duszynski, K. R., Smoot, R. T., Ferentz, K. S., Levine, D. M., & Troisi, A. J. (1992). Physician estimates of substance abuse in Baltimore and Cumberland:1991. *Maryland Medical Journal, 41*(11), 973-978.

Van den Boom, D., & Howkam J. (1994). The effect of infant irritability on mother-infant interaction: A growth-curve analysis. *Developmental Psychology, 30,* 581-590.

VandenBox, G.R. (1986). Psychotherapy research: A special issue. *American Psychologist, 4:1,* 111-112.

Van Goozen, S. H. M., Matthys, W., Cohen-Kettenis, P. T., Westenberg, H., & Van Engeland, H. (1999). Plasma monoamine metabolites and aggression: Two studies of normal and oppositional defiant disorder children. *European Neuropsychopharmacology, 9*(1-2), 141-147.

Venezia, M. G. Juvenile offenders: Profiles and predictions. *Dissertation Abstracts International*: Section B: The Sciences & Engineering, Vol 61(12-B), 2001. pp. 6693.

Veysey, B. M., DeCou, K., & Prescott, L. (1998). Effective management of female jail detainees with histories of physical and sexual abuse. *American Jails, 12*(2), 50-54.

Vigil, J. D. (1988). Group processes and street identity: Adolescent Chicano gang members. *Ethos, 16*(4), 421-445.

Vitaro, F., Gagnon, C., & Tremblay, R. E. (1990). Predicting stable peer rejection from kindergarten to grade one. *Journal of Clinical Child Psychology, 19,* 257-64.

Volkow, N., Wang, G. J., & Doria, J. J. (1995). Monitoring the brain's response to alcohol with positron emission tomography. *Alcohol Health Research World, 19*(4), 296-299.

Walker, H. M., Block-Pedego, A., Todis, B., & Severson, H. (1991). *School Archival Records Search (SARS): User's Guide and technical manual.* Longmont, CO: Sopris West.

Walker, H. M., Colvin, G., & Ramsey, E. (1995). *Antisocial behavior in school: Strategies and best practices.* Belmont, CA: Brooks/Cole Publishing.

Walker H. M., & Severson, H. H. (1991). *Systematic Screening for Behavior Disorders (SSBD): Training manual.* Longmont, CO: Sopris West.

Walker, L. E. (1989). Psychology and violence against women. *American Psychologist, 44*(4), 695-702.

Walker-Barnes, C. J. (2000). Risk factors for gang involvement among ninth-grade students: A prospective investigation. *Dissertation Abstracts International*: Section B: The Sciences & Engineering, Vol 60(10-B), pp. 5236.

Walker-Barnes, C. J., & Mason, C. A. (2001). Perceptions of risk factors for female gang involvement among African American and Hispanic women. *Youth & Society, 32*(3), 303-336.

Wallner, M., Hanchar, H. J., & Olsen, R.W. (2002). Ethanol enhances alpha 4, beta 3, delta and alpha6, beta3, delta gamma-aminobutyric acid type A receptors at low concentrations known to affect humans. *Procedures of the National Academy of Sciences, 100*(25), 15218-15223.

Wampold, B. E. (2001). *The great psychotherapy debate: Models, methods and findings.* Mahwah, NJ: Erlbaum.

Wanberg, K. W. (1974). *Basic counseling skills manual.* Denver: Alcohol and Drug Abuse Division, Colorado Department of Health.

Wanberg, K. W. (1983). *Advanced counseling skills: The process and structure of therapeutic counseling, a client-oriented, therapist-directed model.* Denver: Alcohol and Drug Abuse Division, Colorado Department of Health.

Wanberg, K. W. (1990a). *Basic counseling skills manual.* Denver: Alcohol and Drug Abuse Division, Colorado Department of Health.

Wanberg, K. W. (1990b). *Basic counseling skills manual, Second Edition.* Denver: Alcohol and Drug Abuse Division, Colorado Department of Health.

Wanberg, K. W. (1991). *User's Guide to the Substance Use Survey (SUS).* Arvada, CO: Center for Addictions Research and Evaluation.

Wanberg, K. W. (1992). *A Guidebook to the Use of the Adolescent Self-Assessment Profile - ASAP.* Arvada, CO: Center for Addictions Research and Evaluation.

Wanberg, K. W. (1996a). *Treatment Assessment Questionnaire (TRQ).* Arvada, CO: Center for Addictions Research and Evaluation.

Wanberg, K. W. (1996b). *Client Manager Assessment Questionnaire (CMAQ).* Arvada, CO: Center for Addictions Research and Evaluation.

Wanberg, K. W. (1996c). *Follow-up Assessment Questionnaire (FAQ).* Arvada, CO: Center for Addictions Research and Evaluation.

Wanberg, K. W. (1997). *The Social Response Questionnaire (SRQ).* Arvada, CO: Center for Addictions Research and Evaluation.

Wanberg, K. W. (1998). *User's Guide to the Adolescent Self-Assessment Profile - II (ASAP-II).* Arvada, CO: Center for Addictions Research and Evaluation.

Wanberg, K. W. (1999). *Rating Adolescent Problems (RAP).* Arvada, CO: Center for Addictions Research and Evaluation.

Wanberg, K. W. (2000). *User's Guide to the Substance Use Survey (SUS): Differential Screening of Adolescent Alcohol and Other Drug Use Problems.* Arvada, CO: Center for Addictions Research and Evaluation.

Wanberg, K. W. (2001). *Client Monthly Treatment Response Questionnaire (CMTRQ).* Arvada, CO: Center for Addictions Research and Evaluation.

Wanberg, K. W. (2003). *Project evaluator's report: A comprehensive substance abuse treatment program for correctional populations-state juvenile justice population through the Colorado Division of Criminal Justice.* Arvada, CO: Center for Addictions Research and Evaluation.

Wanberg, K. W., & Horn, J. L. (1973). Alcoholism syndromes related to sociological classifications. *International Journal of the Addictions, 33,* 1076-1098.

Wanberg, K. W., & Horn, J. L. (1983). Assessment of alcohol use with multidimensional concepts and measures. *American Psychologist, 38,* 1055-1069.

Wanberg, K. W., & Horn, J. L. (1987). The assessment of multiple-conditions in persons with alcohol problems. In M. Cox (Ed.), *Treatment and prevention of alcohol problems: A resource manual.* New York: Academic Press.

Wanberg, K. W., Horn, J. L., & Foster, F. M. (1977). A differential assessment model for alcoholism: The scales of the Alcohol Use Inventory. *Journal of Studies on Alcohol, 38,* 512-543.

Wanberg, K. W., & Milkman, H. B. (1993). *User's guide for the Adolescent Self-Assessment Questionnaire (ASAQ).* Arvada, CO: Center for Addictions Research and Evaluation.

Wanberg, K. W., & Milkman, H. B. (1998). *Criminal conduct and substance abuse treatment: Strategies for self-improvement and change.* Thousand Oaks, CA: Sage Publications.

Wanberg, K. W. (2004). *Comparing three groups of adolescent substance abusers.* Arvada, CO: Center for Addictions Research and Evaluation.

Wanberg, K. W., & Milkman, H. B. (2004). *Criminal conduct and substance abuse treatment: Strategies for self-improvement and change* (2nd ed.). Thousand Oaks, CA: Sage Publications.

Wanberg, K. W., Tjaden, C.D., Embree, J., & Garrett, C. J. (1986). *A multiple construct approach for the assessment of drug use and deviant behavior among committed juvenile offenders.* Paper presented to the Annual International Differential Treatment Association, Estes Park, CO.

Warr M., & Statford, M. (1991). The Influence of Delinquent Peers: What they think or what they do. *Criminology, 29,* 851-66.

Wass, H., Miller, M. D., & Redditt, C. A. (1991). Adolescent and destructive themes in rock music: A follow up OMEGA. *Journal of Death and Dying, 23,* 199-206.

Wass, H., Miller, M. D., & Stevenson, R. G. (1989). Factors affecting adolescents' behavior and attitudes toward destructive rock lyrics. *Death Studies, 13*(3), 287-303.

Watkins, K.E., Shaner, A., & Sullivan, G. (1999). Addictions services: The role of gender in engaging the dually diagnosed in treatment. *Community Mental Health Journal, 35*(2), 115-126.

Watson, C., Tilleskjor, C., Hoodecheck-Show, E., Purcel, J., & Jacobs, L. (1984). Do alcoholics give valid self-reports? *Journal of Studies on Alcohol, 45,* 344-348.

Watson, J. B. (1913). Psychology as the behaviourist views it. *Psychological Review, 20*(2), 158-177.

Weaver, T. L., Kilpatrick, D. G., Resnick, H. S., Best, C. L., & Saunders, B. E. (1997). An examination of physical assault and childhood victimization histories within a national probability sample of women. In G. K. Kantor & J .L. Jasinski (Eds.), *Out of the darkness: Contemporary perspectives on family violence* (pp. 35-46). Thousand Oaks, CA: Sage Publications.

355

Webster-Stratton, C. & Herbert, M. (1994). *Troubled Families/Problem Children*. West Sussex: John Wiley & Sons, Ltd.

Weishaar, M. (1996). Developments in cognitive therapy. In W. Dryden (Ed.), *Developments in psychotherapy: Historical Perspectives* (pp. 188-212). Thousand Oaks, CA: Sage Publications.

Weiss, R. D., & Najavits, L. M. (1994). *Modified Weekly Self-Help Questionnaire.* Unpublished measure, Harvard Medical School, Boston.

Weissman, M. M., & Bothwell, S. (1976). Assessment of social adjustment by patient self-report. *Archives of General Psychiatry, 33*(9), 1111-1115.

Weissman, M. M., Prusoff, B. A., Thompson, W. D., Harding, P. S., & Myers, J. K. (1978). Social adjustment by self-report in a community sample and in psychiatric outpatients. *Journal of Nervous and Mental Disease, 166*(5), 317-326.

Welle, D., & Falkin, G. (2000). The everyday policing of women with romantic codefendants: an ethnographic perspective. *Women & Criminal Justice, 11*(2), 45-65.

Wellisch, J., Anglin, M. D., & Prendergast, M. L. (1993). Numbers and characteristics of drug-using women in the criminal justice system: Implications for treatment. *Journal of Drug Issues, 23*(1), 7-30.

Wells, J. K., Preusser, D. F., & Williams, A. F. (1992). Enforcing alcohol-impaired driving and seat belt use laws, Binghamton, NY. *Journal of Safety Research, 23*(2), 63-71.

Werner, H. (1957). The concept of development from a comparative and organismic point of view. In D. B. Harris (Ed.), *The concept of development* (pp. 125-146). Minneapolis: University of Minnesota Press.

Whitaker, M. S. (2000). Responding to women offenders: Equitable does not mean identical. *Topics in Community Corrections Annual Issue 2000: Responding to Women Offenders in the Community, 4-6.*

White, A. M. (2003). Substance use and adolescent brain development: An overview of recent findings with a focus on alcohol. *Youth Studies Australia, 22*, 39-45.

White, A. M., Matthews, D. B., & Best, P. J. (2002). Ethanol, memory, and hippocampal function: A review of recent findings. *Hippocampus, 10*, 88-93.

White, A., Truesdale, M., Bae, T., Ahmad, S., Wilson, W., Best, P., & Swartzwelder, H. S. (2002). Differential effects of alcohol on motor coordination in adolescent and adult rats. *Pharmacol Biochem Behav, 73*, 673-677.

White, H. R. (1992). Early problem behavior and. *Journal of Research in Crime and Delinquency, 29*, 412-429.

White, H. R. (1997). Alcohol, illicit drugs, and violence. In D. Stoff, J. Brieling & J. D. Maser (Eds.), *Handbook of antisocial behavior* (pp. 511-523). New York: John Wiley.

White, H. R. (1998). Acute and long-term effects of drug use on aggression from adolescence into adulthood. *Journal of Drug Issues, 28*, 837-58.

White, H. R., & Gorman, D. M. (2000). Dynamics of the drug-crime relationship. In G. LaFree (Ed.), *Criminical justice: Vol. 1. The nature of crime: Continuity and change* (pp. 151-218). Washington, DC: U.S. Department of Justice.

White, H. R., & Labouvie, E. W. (1989). Towards the assessment of adolescent problem drinking. *Journal of Studies on Alcohol, 50*, 30-37.

White, H. R., Loeber, R., Stouthamer-Loeber, M., & Farrington, D. P. (1999). Developmental associations between substance use and violence. *Development and Psychopathology, 11*, 785-803.

White, J., Moffitt, T. E., Earls, F., Robins, L. N., Silva, P. A (1990). How early can we tell? Preschool predictors of boys' conduct disorder and delinquency. *Criminology, 28*, 507-33.

White, H. R., Tice, P. C., Loeber, R., & Stouthamer-Loeber, M. (2002). Illegal acts committed by adolescents under the influence of alcohol and drugs. *Journal of Research in Crime & Delinquency, 39*(2), 131-152.

Widom, C. S. (1997). Child abuse neglect, and witnessing violence. In D. M. Stoff, J. Breiling, & J. D. Maser (Eds.), *Handbook of antisocial behavior* (pp. 159-70). New York: Wiley.

Widom, C. S. (1999). Childhood victimization and the development of personality disorders: Commentary. *Archives of General Psychiatry, 56*(7), 607-608.

Wiebe, R. P. (1996). The mental health implications of crime victims' rights. In B. D. Sales & D. W. Shuman (Eds.), *Law, mental health, and mental disorder.* Pacific Grove, CA: Brooks/Cole.

Wilke, D. J. (2001). Reconceptualizing recovery: Adding self-esteem to the mix. *Dissertation Abstracts International, 61*(12), 4950A. (UMI No. 9996821)

Williams, C., Epstein, J. A., Botvin, G., Schinke, S. P., & Diaz, T. (1998). Psychosocial determinants of alcohol use among minority youth living in public housing developments. *Journal of Developmental & Behavioral Pediatrics, 19*(3), 145-154.

Wilsnack, S. C. (1995). Alcohol use and alcohol problems in women. In A. L. Stanton & S. J. Gallant (Eds.), *Psychology of women's health: Progress and challenges in research and application* (pp. 381-443). Washington, DC: American Psychological Association.

Wilsnack, S. C., Vogeltanz, N. D., Klassen, A. D., & Harris, T. R. (1997). Childhood sexual abuse and women's sexual abuse: National survey findings. *Journal of Studies on Alcohol, 58*(3), 264-271.

Wilson, G.T., & O'Leary, K.D. (1980). *Principles of behavioral therapy.* Englewood Cliffs, NJ: Prentice-Hall, Inc.

Wilson, J. Q. (1998). Never too early. In R. Loeber & D. P. Farrington (Eds.), *Serious & violent juvenile offenders: Risk factors and successful interventions.* Thousand Oaks, CA: Sage Publications.

Wilson, M. K., & Anderson, S. C. (1997). Empowering female offenders: Removing barriers to community-based practice. *Affilia, 12*(3), 342-358.

Winick, B. J. (1996). Incompetency to proceed in the criminal process: Past, present, and future. In B. D. Sales & D. W. Shuman (Eds.), *Law, mental health, and mental disorder* (pp. 77-111). Pacific Grove, CA: Brooks/Cole.

Winters, K. C. (1992). Development of an adolescent alcohol and other drug abuse screening scale: Personal Experience Screening Questionnaire. *Addictive Behaviors, 17,* 479-490.

Winters, K. C. (1999). *Screening and assessing adolescents for substance use disorders.* Rockville, MD: U.S. Department of Health and Human Services, Public Health Service, Substance Abuse and Mental Health Services Administration, Center for Substance Abuse Treatment.

Winters, K. C. (2001). Assessing adolescent substance use problems and other areas of functioning: State of the art. In P. M. Monti & S. M. Colby (Eds.), *Adolescents, alcohol, and substance abuse: Reaching teens through brief interventions* (pp. 80-108). New York: Guilford Press.

Winters, K. C. (2003). Assessment of alcohol and other drug use behaviors among adolescents. In J. P. Allen & V. B. Wilson (Eds.), *Assessing alcohol problems: A Guide for clinicians and researches, Second Edition* (pp. 101-123). Bethesda, MD: National Institute on Alcohol Abuse and Alcoholism, U.S. Department of Health and Human Service.

Winters, K. C., Anderson, N., Bengston, P., Stinchfield, R.D., & Latimer, W. W. (2000). Development of a parent questionnaire for use in assessing adolescent drug abuse. *Journal of Psychoactive Drugs, 32,* 3-13.

Winters, K. C., & Henly, G. A. (1989). *Personal Experience Inventory (PEI) Test and Manual.* Los Angeles, CA: Western Psychological Services.

Winters, K. C., & Henly, G. A. (1993). *Adolescent diagnostic interview (ADI) manual.* Los Angeles, CA: Western Psychological Services.

Winters, K. C., Stinchfield, R. D., Henly, G. A., & Schwartz, R. H. (1991). Validity of adolescent self-report of alcohol and other drug involvement. *International Journal of Addictions, 25,* 1379-1395.

Wolfgang, M. E. & Ferracuti, F. (1967). *The Subculture of Violence: Towards an Integrated Theory of Criminology.* London: Tavistock Publishing.

Wolpe, J. (1958). *Psychotherapy by reciprocal inhibition.* Stanford, CA: Stanford University Press.

Woodward, L. J., & Fergusson, D. M. (1999). Childhood peer relationship problems and psychosocial adjustment in late adolescence. *Journal of Abnormal Child Psychology, 27,* 87-104.

Woodward, L. J., Fergusson, D. M., & Horwood, L. J. (2002). Deviant partner involvement and offending risk in early adulthood. *Journal of Child Psychology and Psychiatry, 43,* 177-190.

Wooton, J. M., Frick, P. J., Shelton, K. K., & Silverthorn, P. (1997). Ineffective parenting and childhood conduct problems: The moderating role of callous-unemotional traits. *Journal of Consulting & Clinical Psychology, 65*(2), 301-308.

Wu, P. & Kandel, D. B. (1995). The roles of mothers and fathers in intergenerational behavioral transmission: The case of smoking and delinquency. In: Kaplan, Howard B. (Ed), *Drugs, crime, and other deviant adaptations: Longitudinal studies.* Longitudinal research in the social and behavioral sciences: An interdisciplinary series. pp. 49-81. New York: Plenum Press.

Yarkin, K. L., Town, J.P., & Wallston, B. S. (1982). Blacks and women must try harder: Stimulus persons' race and sex attributions of causality. *Personality and Social Psychology Bulletin, 8*(1), 21-24.

Young, R. M., Oei, T. P. S., & Crook, G. .M. (1991). Development of drinking self-efficacy questionnaire. *Journal of Psychopathology and Behavioral Assessment, 13,* 1-15.

Zador, P. L., Krawchuk, S. A., & Voas, R. B. (2000). Alcohol-related relative risk of driver fatalities and driver involvement in fatal crashes in relation to driver age and gender: An update using 1996 data. *Journal of Studies on Alcohol, 61*(3), 387-395.

Zhang, L., Welte, J. W., Wieczorek, W. F. (1999). The influence of parental drinking and closeness on adolescent drinking. *Journal of Studies on Alcohol, 60*(2), 245-251.

Zhang, L., Wieczorek, W., & Welte, J. W. (1997). The impact of age of onset on substance use and delinquency. *Journal of Research in Crime and Delinquency, 34,* 253-268.

Zlotnick, C., Kohn, R., Peterson, J., & Pearlstein, T. (1998). Partner physical victimization in a national sample of American families: Relationship to psychological functioning, psychosocial factors, and gender. *Journal of Interpersonal Violence, 13*(1), 156-166.

Zucchi, Elaine C. 1996. *Risk factors and drug use in suburban adolescents.* Dissertation Abstracts International Section A: Humanities and Social Sciences, Vol 57(1-A) Jul. pp 0108.

Zuckerman, M. (1988). Behavior and biology: Research on sensation seeking and reactions to the media. In L. Donohew, & H. E. Sypher (Eds.), *Communication, social cognition, and affect* (pp. 173-194). Hillsdale, NJ: Lawrence Erlbaum Associates.

Zuckerman, M. (1983). Sensation seeking and sports. *Personality & Individual Differences, 4*(3), 285-292.

Zuckerman, M. (1994). *Behavioral expressions and biosocial bases of sensation seeking.* New York: Cambridge University Press.

Zuckerman, M. (1979). *Sensation seeking: Beyond the optimal level of arousal.* Hillsdale, NJ: Erlbaum.

Zuckerman, M., & Kuhlman, D. M. (2000). Personality and risk-taking: Common biosocial factors. *Journal of Personality, 68*(6), 999-1029.

Zuroff, D.C., Blatt, S. J., Sotsky, S. M., Krupnick, J. L., Martin, D. J., Sanislow, C. A., III, & Simmens, S. (2000). Relation of therapeutic alliance and perfectionism to outcome in brief outpatient treatment of depression. *Journal of Consulting and Clinical Psychology, 68(1),* 114-124.

INDEX

A

Abstinence, 230
Abstinence violation effect, 229
Acculturative stress:
  AOD abuse and, 80, 84
  delinquency/adolescent substance abuse and, 31
Acting out behaviors, 41, 118
  aggression, 41
  delinquency, 41
  See also Disruptive behavior disorders, diagnostic criteria and; Status offenses; Under-controlled syndrome
Acute stress disorder, 53
Aderall, 62, 63, 68, 83
AD/HD Comprehensive Teacher's Rating Scale, Second Edition (ACTeRS), 198
Adolescence:
  biological condition, 110
  cultural concept, 110
  defining, 3
  developmental-contextual view, 3
  stereotypes of, 242, 244
Adolescent Alcohol Involvement Scale (AAIS), 192
Adolescent Community Reinforcement Approach (ACRA), 270
Adolescent crime, 41
  public perception, 116, 141
  recidivism and, 115-116
  See also Adolescent crime, developmental aspects of; Adolescent crime, motivations for; Adolescent crime, theories of; Juvenile delinquency
Adolescent crime, developmental aspects of, 126-133, 141
  biological influences, 126-127
  bio/psycho/social synthesis, 127, 141
  See also Hormones, adolescent crime and; Neurotransmitters
Adolescent crime, motivations for, 115
  belief-driven, 115, 239
  emotion-driven, 115, 239
  emotion-driven/property theft, 115, 239
  mixed-motive mixed crime contexts, 115
  reward-driven/drug dealing, 115, 239
  reward-driven/property theft, 115, 239
Adolescent crime, theories of, 123-126, 141
  differential association theory, 124, 125, 141
  differential reinforcement theory, 126
  general strain theory, 123-124, 125, 141, 169-171
  relative deprivation theory, 124, 141
  social control theory, 8, 77, 124, 125, 141, 310
  social learning theory, 46, 56, 77, 83, 124-125, 141, 208, 213, 263
Adolescent Diagnostic Interview (ADI), 194
Adolescent Drinking Index (ADI), 192
Adolescent Drug Abuse Diagnoses (ADAD), 194
Adolescent Drug Involvement Scale (ADIS), 192
Adolescent girls, delinquency and, 145
  scope, 145
  See also Female adolescent offenses, nature of; Female juvenile offenders
Adolescent Life Survey, 122
Adolescent limited offenders, 12, 14, 27, 116, 127, 128, 133

age and crime, 128-129
  bio/psycho/social factors, 131-132
  environmental factors and, 128
  prevalence rate, 131
Adolescent offenders:
  "criminal career," 27
  proposals for categorizing, 132
  risk assessment, 27
  "teen culture," 27
  See also Adolescent limited offenders; Female juvenile offenders; Juvenile delinquency; Juvenile male offenders; Life-course persistent offenders
Adolescent problem behavior:
  mental health and, 11
  risk factors for development of, 32
  substance abuse and, 11-12
  See also Adolescent problem behavior, principles for understanding; Adolescent problem behavior, scope of; Adolescent problem behavior and crime, cognitive tendencies associated with; Adolescent problem behaviors; Problem behavior theory (PBT)
Adolescent problem behavior, principles for understanding, 6-8
  person-oriented perspective, 7, 11
  social learning perspective, 6-7, 11
  strength-based perspective, 7-8, 11, 12, 21, 307
Adolescent problem behavior, scope of, 21-23
  alcohol or other drugs, 21-22
  antecedents/correlates of adolescent drug abuse, 22
  delinquency and crime, 23
  gateway experiences, 22
  mental disorder, 23, 37
  parent and peer influences, 22
Adolescent problem behavior and crime, cognitive tendencies associated with, 239-241
  belief-driven/violent assault crime context, 240, 244
  empathy development, 241, 244
  hostile world syndrome, 239, 243, 244
  masculinity and violence, 240
  negative identity, 240
  risky cognitions and driving with intoxicated, 239-240, 244
  social competence, 240
Adolescent problem behaviors:
  correlations among, 8-9
  gender and, 9, 11, 12
  race/ethnicity and, 9, 11
  risk and resiliency factors, 26
  See also specific adolescent problem behaviors
Adolescent Problem Severity Index (APSI), 194
Adolescent relapse coping questionnaire, 264
Adolescent Self-Assessment Profile (ASSP), 23, 74, 82, 118, 133, 147, 177, 194, 291
Adolescent Self-Assessment Profile-II (ASAP-II), 196, 197, 198, 199
admission testing, 293
Adolescent Self-Assessment Questionnaire (ASAQ), 195, 291, 329, 335-338
  intake testing, 294
  scoring instructions, 339
Adolescent subcultures, 169-172

anti-authority, 12, 171-172
  music-based, 12, 170-171
  thrill-based, 12, 171, 174
  violence-based, 12, 169-170
  See also Gang members, identity of; Gang membership; Gangs; Racial pride groups
Adolescent Treatment Model (ATM), 14, 263, 265
  goals, 263
  treatment protocols, 263
  See also Chestnut Health System Bloomington Outpatient and Intensive Outpatient Program for Adolescent Substance Abusers (CHS); Epoch Counseling Center—Group-Based Outpatient Adolescent Substance Abuse Treatment Program; La Cañada Adolescent Treatment Program; Motivational Enhancement Therapy/Cognitive Behavioral Therapy (MET/CBT); Phoenix Academy; Teen Substance Abuse Treatment Program (TSAT); Thinking for a Change (T4C)
African Americans:
  adolescent drug use, 22
  alcohol and other drug (AOD) abuse, 80, 81, 82, 83-84
  overrepresentation in crime statistics, 117, 118
  gang membership, 121
  juveniles, 9
  juvenile victims of crime, 134
  teen pregnancy, 151
Age affiliation, 167
Alcohol, 92, 95-98, 110, 147
  adolescent brain and, 97-98, 110
  adolescent learning/memory and, 97-98, 110
  adolescent use, 12, 22, 37, 41, 61
  brain damage from, 95, 98, 110
  dopamine levels and, 93, 94
  health effects, 98
  male juvenile use of, 147
  memory impairment, 97
  neurotransmission and, 96-97
  prevalence of adolescent use, 61, 62
  problems related to, 95
  treatment for abuse of, 238
  withdrawal symptoms, 98
  See also Wernicke-Korsakoff Syndrome
Alcohol and other drug (AOD) abuse, American subcultures and, 80-82, 83-84
  African Americans, 80, 81, 82, 83-84
  disruption to ethnicity and, 82
  ethnic identity and, 80-81, 84
  ethnicity and, 82
  European Americans, 80, 81, 82, 83
  health-related knowledge, 80, 84
  Hispanic Americans, 80, 81, 82, 83
  peer/social influences, 80, 84
  psychosocial risk factors, 81
  See also Acculturative stress
Alcohol and other drug (AOD) involvement, 12
  age and disruption of, 75-76
  age and drug use prevalence, 74
  age and number of drugs used, 74
  gateway theory, 74, 75
  See also specific drugs
Alcohol Expectancy Questionnaire-Adolescent (AEQ-A), 194

Alcoholics:
  blackouts, 96
  brains, 95
  frontal lobe damage, 96
Alcoholics Anonymous, 223, 257
Alcohol poisoning, acute, 96
Alcohol Use Inventory (AUI), 194
All or nothing thinking, 209
Ambivalence, client, 223, 299
Amphetamines, 66, 92, 147
  adolescent use, 61
  dopamine levels and, 93, 94
  female juvenile offender use of, 147, 150
  prevalence of adolescent use, 62
Anger, 299, 312
  managing, 227
Antisocial attitudes, 309
Antisocial behavior, 41, 118, 128
  adolescence-limited, 46
  age and, 128-129
  definition, 41
  juvenile participation in, 3
  life-course persistent, 46
  neuropsychological deficits and, 46
  predictors of adolescent, 136
  self-image protection and, 119
Antisocial personality disorder, 46, 49, 56, 127
  adolescent conduct disorder and, 42, 43
Anxiety in adolescents, 41
  psychotherapeutic medication for, 55
  PTSD and, 51
Anxiety reduction methods, 206
Appraisals, 211, 212, 225, 228, 305
Assertive techniques, 309
Assessment and screening, multidimensional: treatment process and, 220
  See also Convergent validation model
Assessment and treatment, ethical and legal issues involved in PSD-C, 284, 286-287, 296
  confidentiality, 15, 284, 286, 306
  court-ordered disclosures, 286-287
  disclosures not identifying client, 286
  duty to warn of threat of harm to others/self, 286
  Health Insurance Portability and Accountability ACT (HIPAA), 287
  informed consent, 284, 286
  medical emergencies, 287
  privacy rulings, 284, 286
  record keeping and documentation of assessment, 284
  reporting child abuse and neglect, 286
  treatment process and outcomes, 284
Assessment findings, interpreting, 186
Assessment of juvenile justice substance abuse clients, 177-179
  objectives, 177-178
  operational approach, 15
  perspectives, 13
  See also Assessment of juvenile justice substance abuse clients, process and structure of; Psychometric assessment instruments, guidelines for using
Assessment of juvenile justice substance abuse clients, process and structure of, 187-196
  components, 187, 188
  differential screening, 177, 187, 189-190, 199
  preliminary/pre-screening, 177, 187, 189, 199
  See also Change and outcome assessment; Comprehensive/in-depth/differential assessment

Assumptions, 212
  underlying, 211, 212, 226
Attention deficit hyperactivity disorder (ADHD), 11, 21, 23, 37, 42, 47-49, 54, 56, 199, 311
  behavioral therapy, 49, 50, 56
  combined drug and behavioral therapy, 49, 50, 56
  criminal conduct and, 47
  development of conduct disorder and, 47
  drug therapy, 49, 50, 55, 56
  DSM-IV-TR diagnostic criteria, 47, 48
  prevalence, 47
  PTSD and, 51
  serotonin and, 45
  treatment, 47, 49, 50
  See also Aderall; Ritalin
Attitudes, 212, 225, 243
Attributions, 211, 212, 213, 225, 243, 283, 305
  global, 212
  specific, 212
Attribution theory, 212
Autobiography, 306
Automatic thinking, 211, 226
Automatic thoughts, 208, 211, 212, 226, 227, 228, 243, 307
  changing, 225
  identifying, 224
  See also Though habits

B

Barbiturates, 63, 147
Beck Depression Inventory II, 198, 199
Behavioral rehearsal, 206, 299
Behavioral self-control, anxiety management through, 205
Behavioral therapy, 4, 205, 206, 207, 208, 215
  beginning of modern, 205
  common intervention approaches, 206
  for adolescents and families, 252-253, 258
  therapeutic activities, 253
  underlying principles, 209
Behaviorism, 205
Behaviorists, 205. *See also names of specific behaviorists*
Behavior system, 21, 23, 37, 73
  conventional behavior structure, 23
  deviant lifestyle and, 24
  problem behavior structure, 23
Beliefs, 211, 212, 305
  about self, 226
  about world, 226
  altering underlying, 208
  intermediate, 212
  irrational, 212
  underlying, 212
  See also Core beliefs and assumptions
Benjamin E. Mays Institute Mentoring Program (BEMI), 238
Benzodiazepines, 63
Binge drinkers, adolescent: frequent, 72
  See also Binge drinking
Binge drinking, 61, 95
  dangers, 98
  deaths, 95, 110
  repeated, 98
  See also Binge drinkers
Bipolar mania, adolescent:
  psychotherapeutic medication for, 55
Brain, adolescent, 92-95

alcohol and, 97-98
  alcohol and learning/memory, 97-98
  alcohol neurotoxicity, 98
  brain development, 92-95
  development, 12
  drug abuse/risky behavior and, 95
  immaturity of frontal lobes, 95, 110
  substance abuse and, 12
  See also Brain, human
Brain, human, 87-92, 96
  adrenal glands, 89
  adrenaline, 89
  amygdala, 95, 97, 110
  axon, 87, 88
  cerebellum, 93, 97, 101
  cerebral cortex, 97, 101, 107, 108, 111
  corpus callosum, 93
  dendrites, 87, 88, 101
  endorphins, 92, 103, 110
  enkephalin, 90, 91-92, 103, 111
  frontal cortex, 98, 106, 111
  frontal lobes, 93, 96
  HPA axis, 89a
  hippocampus, 96, 97, 98, 101, 102, 105, 111
  hypothalamus, 89, 90, 91, 97
  locus ceruleus, 88, 97, 107, 108, 111
  neocortex, 93
  neurons, 87, 98, 106
  neurotransmission, 88-90, 96-97
  nucleus accumbens, 91, 92, 93, 100, 101, 104, 108, 110, 111
  pituitary gland, 89
  postsynaptic neuron, 88-89, 100
  prefrontal cortex, 93-94, 95
  presynaptic neuron, 88
  striatum, 98
  synapse, 87, 88
  synaptic homeostasis, 96
  synaptic junction, 87
  ventral tegmental area, 100, 108, 110
  See also Brain, adolescent; Neurotransmitters
Brainstorming, 301
Brief treatment interventions, 249. *See also* Motivational enhancement therapy

C

Carousel brainstorming, 301
Case studies, 301
Catastrophizing, 209
Center for Substance Abuse Treatment (CSAT), 14, 263, 270
Centers for Disease Control, 108, 109
Challenge to change (PSD-C Phase I), 15, 222, 280, 281, 282, 285, 299, 303
  assessment, 281
  counseling skills facilitating, 281
  focus, 282
  objectives, 281
  See also Plan for Change; Self-Portrait
Change and outcome assessment: changes in problem thinking/behavior, 194-195
  changes in self-disclosure, 187
  problem acknowledgment and motivation for treatment, 193-194
  self-report data, 187
  short and long-term, 187
  treatment process and closure, 187
  See also Other-report data; Self-report data
Change clarification, 283
Change reinforcement, 283

Chemical Dependency Assessment Profile (CDAP), 194
Chestnut Health System Bloomington Outpatient and Intensive Outpatient Program for Adolescent Substance Abusers (CHS), 264-265
  blended therapeutic approach, 264
  group setting, 265
  Master Treatment Plan, 265
  parent educational support groups, 267
  phases of treatment, 267
  program components, 264-265
  strengths of program, 265
  theoretical basis, 264
  types of groups, 265
Children's Depression Inventory (CDI), 198, 199
Cigarette smoking, 108-109
  adolescent and later marijuana use, 22, 61-62, 77, 83
  heart disease, 109, 110, 111
  lung cancer, 109, 110, 111
  prevalence, 62
  stroke and, 110
  mental function in elderly and, 109, 111
  See also Cigarette smoking, adolescent; Nicotine; Tobacco
Classical conditioning, 205
Classical conditioning theory, 266
Client-centered therapy, 214
  core elements, 210, 223
  See also Rogers, Carl
Client Manager Assessment Questionnaire (CMAQ), 195, 291, 292, 296
Client Monthly Treatment Response Questionnaire (CMTRQ), 195
Client Rights Statement, 289, 319, 323
Client self-disclosure, valuing, 179-180. *See also* Self-report data
Client Substance Index—Short (CSI-S), 192
Club drugs, adolescent use of, 62, 83, 104-105, 111
  GHB, 62, 64, 83
  Ketamine, 62, 64, 83
  PCP, 62, 64, 83
  PMA, 62, 83
  Rohypnol, 62, 63-64, 83
  See also Ecstacy (MDMA), adolescent use of
Coaching, 14
  problem-solving, 250, 258
Cocaine, 66, 90, 92, 99-101, 110
  adolescent use, 12, 22, 41, 77
  dopamine levels and, 93, 94, 100, 101
  female juvenile offender use of, 150
  health effects, 100-101, 110
  high, 100
  neuronal growth and, 101
  occasional use of, 183
  prevalence of adolescent use, 62
  treatment for abuse of, 238
  See also Crack cocaine
Cocaine psychosis, 79
Codeine, 62, 65, 83
"Code of the streets," 7, 28, 119, 314
Code of the streets theory, Anderson's, 122
Cognitive-behavioral interventions/approaches, 36, 279
Cognitive-behavioral model for change, underlying assumptions/processes, 224-226, 234
  distal structures, 224, 225, 226
  intermediate structures, 225-226
  proximal structures, 224, 225, 226
Cognitive-behavioral principles targeted at

delinquency/crime/substance abuse, 242-243
Cognitive-behavioral skill development, 300
Cognitive-behavioral therapists, 210
  ultimate goal, 211
Cognitive-behavioral therapy (CBT), 3, 5, 14, 205, 206, 209, 249, 258, 263, 304
  between-session application, 210
  contemporary, 206-207, 215
  empirical support for, 214-215
  here and now emphasis, 210
  historical roots, 205-206
  underlying principles, 207-211
  See also Cognitive behavioral therapy, focal points of
Cognitive behavioral therapy, focal points of, 211-213
  behavioral, 212-213
  cognitive, 211-212
  See also Substance abuse and juvenile justice treatment, self-efficacy in
Cognitive-behavioral treatment, 11, 13
  contemporary, 13
  foundations, 13
  PTSD and, 51-52, 53
  See also Cognitive-behavioral treatment for adolescents, key features of; Cognitive restructuring; Social skills training
Cognitive-behavioral treatment for adolescents, key features of, 241-242
  basic assumptions, 241
  client responsibility, 241
  constructivist approach, 242
  continuum of care in relapse/recidivism prevention, 242
  cultural/developmental factors, 241-242
  gender considerations, 241-242, 244
  race/ethnicity, 242
  rapport, 241, 244
  respect, 241, 244
  trust, 241, 244
Cognitive constructs, 206
Cognitive distorting, 226
Cognitive distortions, 212
Cognitive functioning questionnaire, 264
Cognitive responses and processes, internal mediating, 205
Cognitive restructuring, 13, 73, 206, 207, 208, 210, 211, 212, 215, 226-229, 234, 299, 307, 308, 309, 311
  specifically for criminal/substance-abusing clients, 212
  techniques, 299
  See also Coping skills training; Self-instructional training; Shifting the view; Stress inoculation training; Thought arming; Thought stopping
Cognitive therapist, 207
Cognitive therapy, 205-206, 207, 208, 211, 215
  common intervention approaches, 207
Collaborative empiricism, 209-210
Colorado Youth Offender—Level of Service Inventory (CYO-LSI), 291, 292, 295
Colorado Youth Offender-Level of Supervision Inventory-Dynamic (CYO-LSI-Dynamic), 195
Columbine High School shootings, 79, 138
Commitment to change (PSD-C Phase II), 15, 222, 280, 281-282, 285, 300, 303
  counseling skills facilitating, 282
  focus, 282
  specific objectives, 282
Communication:
  other-oriented, 306
  self-oriented, 306

Community-based treatment programs, adolescent, 237, 238
Comprehensive Addiction Severity Index for Adolescents (CASI-A), 194
Comprehensive Assessment and Treatment Outcome Research (CATOR), 194
Comprehensive/in-depth/differential assessment, 177, 187, 190-193, 199
  administer self-report psychometric instrument, 193
  appraisals from benefits of use, 190
  client-generated summary profile/self-portrait, 193
  conceptual framework, 191
  documentation, 193
  expectancies from use, 190
  feedback to client, 193
  formal interview, 193
  goal, 177
  initial informal interview, 193
  objectives specific to, 192
  written report, 193
  See also Individual treatment plan (ITP)
Conduct disorder, 11, 21, 23, 37, 41, 42-45, 49, 56, 129, 310
  ADHD and, 45, 47
  age and patterns of, 43
  antisocial personality disorder and, 46
  biological correlates, 45
  criminal behavior and, 45-46
  DSM-IV-TR diagnostic criteria, 43, 44, 45
  ODD and, 42, 45, 47
  psychosocial correlates, 43, 45
  PTSD and, 51
  treatment, 45, 46-47
  See also "Fledgling psychopath"
Conners' ADHD/DSM-IV Scales (CADS), 198
Conners' Rating Scales-Revised (CRS-R), 198
Conners-Wells Adolescent Self-Report Scales (CASS), 198
Consent for Program Involvement, 289, 319, 324
Consent for Release of Confidential Information, 319, 322
Containment theory, 28, 240
Contingency management, 206
Contingency reinforcement, 205
Convergent validation model, 13, 177, 180-181, 199, 220
Coping and social skills training (CSST), 206, 207, 212-213
Coping skills development, 73
Coping skills training, 228, 282
Core beliefs, underlying, 211
  changing, 212
Core beliefs and assumptions, 226, 227, 228
Corporal punishment:
  delinquency/adolescent substance abuse and, 30
  Swedish law prohibiting, 30
  Correctional and therapeutic approaches, integrating, 5, 279
Cortez, Hernan, 106
Counseling:
  defining, 219
  versus education, 220, 234
Counselor bias, 275
Counselor personal characteristics, 214
Counselors:
  as coaches, 243, 245
  as educators, 243, 245
  as evaluators, 243, 245

as role models, 14, 243, 245
characteristics of effective, 14
functions, 14
See also Juvenile justice treatment coun
selors, effective PSD-C
Countering, 212
Covert conditioning, 207
Covert sensitization, 206
Crack babies, 101
Crack cocaine, 100, 110
    aggressive behavior and, 79
    crime and, 77-78
    free basing, 100, 110
    paranoia and, 101
    prevalence of adolescent use, 62
    See also Cocaine psychosis
Cravings and urges:
    distinguishing between, 309
    managing, 212
Crime. See specific types of crime;
Adolescent crime; Juvenile delinquency
Crime aftermath, positive expectancies of,
239, 244-245
Crime statistics, overrepresentation of
minorities in, 116-118
    African American, 117, 118
    Asian American, 117
    Hispanic American, 117, 118
    Native American, 117
Criminal conduct and substance abuse treat-
ment
    cognitive-behavioral perspectives on, 13-
    14
    core strategies for, 13
    fundamental principles for, 5.
    See also Cognitive-behavioral therapy;
Correctional and therapeutic approaches,
integration of; Differential assessment;
Motivational enhancement; Multidimensional
assessment; Rapport building in therapeutic
alliance; Relapse and recidivism prevention;
Stages of change; Strength-based orientation
Cultural awareness, 167-169, 174, 312
    strength-based perspective, 167
Cultural competence, 172-173
Cultural diversity, dealing with, 172-173. See
also Cultural competence; Cultural proficien-
cy
Cultural proficiency, 12, 172, 174
Cultural sensitivity, 167
Cultural valuing, 167
Culture, defining, 167. See also Adolescent
subcultures
Cyclic (phasic-spiral) process of growth and
change in treatment, 220-222, 280
    integrating, 221, 280
    sorting out, 221, 280
    unpacking, 221, 280, 281
    value of model, 220-221
    See also Learning, Lewin's steps of;
Orthogenetic Principle, Werner's

D

Data collection:
    outcome, 15
    process, 15
Date rape, 12
    juvenile female offenders and, 151, 163
Decisions, 213, 225, 226
Dederich, Chuck, 257
Defensiveness, client, 222, 223
Delinquency syndrome, 77, 132
Depression in adolescents, 23, 41, 56, 312
    corporal punishment and, 30
    delinquency and substance abuse and, 28

in life-course persistent offenders, 131
    psychotherapeutic medication for, 54, 55
    PTSD and, 51, 57
    violent trauma in childhood and, 156,
163
Descartes, R., 205
Deviancy, risk factors and, 118
Deviant identity, 11, 14, 313
Deviant peer association, mechanisms of,
118-120
    differential association theory and, 118
    differentiating pro-social and antisocial
    patterns, 119-120
    differential reinforcement theory, 118-
    119
    social learning theory and, 118, 119
    See also Code of the streets; Subculture
    of violence
Deviant peer associations, 141
    as high-risk situation, 36
    delinquency and, 122
    delinquency/adolescent substance abuse
    and, 30, 37
    substance abuse and, 122
    See also Deviant peer association, mecha
    nisms of
Deviant subculture, adolescence and, 11,
13, 118-121. See also Deviant peer associa-
tion, mechanisms of; Gang membership
Dextromethorphan, 108, 111
Diagnostic Interview Schedule for Children,
23
Differential assessment, 5, 13, 15
Differential association theory, 118, 124,
125, 141
    drug-crime connection and, 77
Differential reinforcement theory, 118-119,
126
Direct reinforcement, 14, 250, 258
Disruptive behavior disorders, diagnostic
criteria and, 42-49, 56. See also specific dis-
ruptive behavior disorders
Dissociative drugs, 107-108, 111. See also
Ketamine; PCP
Distal structures, 23, 224, 225, 226
Distorted self-concepts, 309
Drinking behaviors, reduced:
    competency skills associated with, 240
Driving while intoxicated, adolescents, 8,
71-74
    alcohol-related accidents/fatalities, 71, 83
    BACs, 72, 83
    offender characteristics, 72
    prevalence, 72, 83
    See also Driving while intoxicated, causes
    of adolescent
Driving while intoxicated, causes of adoles-
cent, 72-74, 83
    attribution of responsibility, 73-74
    cognitive deficits, 73
    cognitive errors, 72, 83
    early drinking onset, 72-73
    life history/environmental factors, 72
    motivational biases in cognition, 74
    personality characteristics, 73
    risky cognitions, 74, 239-240, 244
    rite of passage, 74
    threat to perceived self-competence, 74
    See also Problem Behavior Theory;
    Sensation seeking
Drug Abuse Reporting Program (DARP),
237
Drug Abuse Screening Test (DAST), 192
Drug Abuse Treatment Outcome Studies of
Adolescents (DATOS-A), 238

Drug Abuse Warning Network, 62
Drug-crime connection, 77-79, 83
    crime in drug subculture, 79, 83
    need for money, 79, 83
    physiological effects of drugs, 79, 83
    prescription drugs, 79-80
    See also Crack cocaine; Delinquency syn
    drome; Drug-violence connection, adoles-
    cent
Drug Use Screen Inventory Revised (DUSI-
R), 192
Drug-violence connection, adolescent, 79-80
Drugs, commonly abused, 61, 63-67. See
also specific drugs
Drug threats, imminent, 61-62, 68-69. See
also specific drugs
Drug use, predictors of:
    peer variables, 22, 37
Drug use, racial differences in adolescent:
    African Americans, 22
    Anglo Americans, 22
    Hispanic Americans, 22
DSM-IV criteria, adolescents and, 13, 183,
185-186, 291
    conduct disorder, 43, 44, 45
    oppositional defiant disorder, 42, 43
    personality disorders, 49
    problem, 185-186
    substance abuse, 183, 184
    substance dependence, 183, 184

E

Eating disorders, 41
Ecstasy (MDMA), 90, 104-105, 111, 171
    adolescent use, 12, 61, 62, 66, 83
    brain damage, 105, 111
    effects on females versus males, 105
    health effects, 104-105, 111
    long-term memory difficulties, 104
    Parkinson's disease and, 105
    prevalence of adolescent use, 62
    See also Club drugs
Education:
    versus counseling/psychotherapy, 220,
    234
    See also Treatment of adolescents with
    criminal and substance abuse problems,
    core strategies in
Efficacy expectations, 225
Egocentrism, 27
Ego-diffusion, 21
Ego-identity, 21
Emotions and mood, cognition and, 212
Empathy, 210, 310
Empathy deficit:
    adolescent problem behavior and, 33
    conduct disorder and, 46
Empathy development, 241
Environment, perceived. See Perceived envi-
ronment system
Environmental street inventory, 264
Epoch Counseling Center—Group-Based
Outpatient Adolescent Substance Abuse
Treatment Program, 265-267
    client motivation in, 266
    long-term effects, 266
    modeling in, 266
    motivational interview, 266
    program basis, 265
    skills taught, 266
    social learning theory/conditioning theory
    approach, 265
Error risk, 186-187
Ethical issues, working with adolescents

and, 14, 284, 286-287
Ethnic adolescents:
    primary identity, 168
    situational identity, 168
Ethnic/racial identity, 168. *See also* Racial identity model
Expectancies, 211, 243. *See also* Outcome expectancies
Expectations, 208, 211, 212, 305
outcome versus efficacy, 211
Expected outcome, 231

f

Family-based therapy, 252. *See also* Family Systems Therapy (FST)
Family-centered therapy, 252. *See also* Family Systems Therapy (FST)
Family communication, importance of, 34
Family Support Network (FSN), 270
Family systems theory, 257, 263
Family systems therapy (FST), 252, 258
    concept of compromise, 252
    concept of empathy, 252
    initial goal, 252
    negotiating skills training, 252
    parenting techniques training, 252
    premise, 14
    problem-solving skills training, 252
    reflective listening assignments, 252
    using motivational enhancement techniques, 252
    See also Family-based therapy; Family-centered therapy; Family therapy
Family therapists, 252, 269
Family therapy, 252. *See also* Family systems therapy (FST)
Feedback clarification skills, 282
Female adolescent offense, nature of, 145-147
    girls and status offense, 145-146
    murder, 146-147
    patterns of criminal offense, 146
    property crime, 146
    See also Female juvenile murderers; Female juvenile offenders; Female juvenile offending, risk factors and correlates of
Female juvenile murderers, 146-147
    children as victims of, 147, 163
    common weapons used, 146
    type of victims, 147, 163
Female juvenile offenders, 9, 122
    age of entrance into criminal justice system, 145
    arrests, 122
    family problems, 147, 150
    mental health problems, 147, 150
    number of, 145, 162
    substance abuse, 147, 149, 150
    See also Female juvenile murderers
Female juvenile offending, risk factors and correlates of, 145, 150-151, 164
    age of delinquency onset, 151
    family disappointment/intimidation and, 150, 163
    family of origin, 150
    overburdened parents and, 150, 163
    school failure, 151, 163, 164
    teen pregnancy150-151, 163, 164
Female voice, suppression of, 152
Fentanyl, 65
Fight or flight response, 88
Firearms, teens and, 136-137
    drugs and, 137
    murder and, 139
"Fledgling psychopath," 46, 56

Flooding, anxiety management through, 205
Follow-up Assessment Questionnaire (FAQ), 195, 291, 292, 296
Full Disclosure Statement Sample, 319, 327
Functional family therapy (FFT), 4, 254, 259
    assessment, 254
    behavior change, 254
    conflict management skills, 254, 259
    engagement and motivation, 254, 259
    family communication, 254, 259
    for conduct disordered youth, 254, 259
    generalization, 254, 259
    major goal, 254
    outcome data, 254
    parenting skills, 254, 259
    phases of intervention, 254
    See also Reattribution techniques; Reframing techniques

G

Gang members, identity of:
    claimed self, 169, 170
    feared self, 169, 170
    ideal self, 169, 170
    real self, 169, 170
Gang membership, 169-170
    abandonment and, 170
    African American youth, 121
    culturally diverse, 121
    delinquency and, 120-121
    delinquency/adolescent substance abuse and, 31
    deviant identity and, 120-121
    perceived abandonment and, 170
    poverty and, 169
    See also Gang participation, female; Gangs
Gang participation, female, 145, 157-159, 163, 164
    gang type, 159
    mediating factors against, 158
    reasons, 158, 163
    risk factors, 158
    See also Gangs
Gang participation, male, 158
age, 159
    dominance and, 158
    status and, 158
Gangs, 169
    aggression release and, 170
    anger release and, 170
    "commercial," 159
    "corporate," 159
    functions, 120
    murder by, 138
    "scavenger," 159
    "territorial," 159
    See also Gang membership; Gang participation, female; Gang participation, male
Gateway substances, 37. *See also* Alcohol; Cigarette smoking; Marijuana
Gender affiliation, 167
Gender expectations, 151, 152
Gender-focused treatment platform, 161-162, 164
    ability to utilize community resources, 162
    cognitive restructuring, 164
    development of healthy relationships, 162
    maintenance of self development, 162
    sample treatment options, 161-162
    social skills training, 164
Gender identity, 168

Gender meanings, 151
Gender norms, 12. *See also* Gender norms, sexual violation and
Gender norms, sexual violation and, 145, 151-152
    adolescent dating/sexuality, 145, 151-152
    early maturation, 152
    female voice suppression, 152
    late maturation, 152
    girls and relationality, 152
    See also Date rape
Gender roles, 151
Gender scripting, internalization of, 152
Gender-specific programming, need for, 12
Global Assessment of Individual Needs, 264
Goth subculture, 171
Group identity, 170
Group management and leadership, effective PSD-C, 15, 296
    center authority within group, 289-290
    center authority within group member, 290
    depersonalizing leadership authority, 289-290
    facilitation in group, 289
    facilitation of group, 289
    facilitation with group, 289
    focus on cognitive-behavioral change steps, 290
    focus on PSD-C themes/concepts, 290
    group facilitation methods, 289
    maximize individual involvement, 290
    provider-member collaborative relationship, 290
Group role, 170
Group therapy, 263
Guilt, managing, 227, 312

H

Hallucinogenic drugs, 64-65, 106, 111, 147
    adolescent use, 12, 61
    mescaline, 106
    peyote, 106, 108, 111
    prevalence of adolescent use, 62
    psychedelic plants, 106, 108, 111
    summary of effects, 108
    See also LSD
Hare Psychopathy Checklist-Revised, 45
Hare Psychopathy Checklist: Youth Version (PCL, YV), 197
Harris, Eric, 79
Hashish, 63
Head trauma, delinquency/substance abuse and, 28
Health Insurance Portability and Accountability Act (HIPAA) disclosure form, 289, 319, 325
Heffter, A., 106
Heroin, 65, 92, 103, 110, 147
    dopamine levels and, 93, 94
    effects, 104
    hepatitis and, 104
    HIV/AIDS and, 104
    modes of administration, 104
    occasional use, 183
    prevalence of adolescent use, 62
    withdrawal symptoms, 104
High-risk encounters, 308
High-risk environments, 34
High-risk exposures, 231, 232
High-risk situations, 229, 230-231, 232, 307, 309, 315. *See also* High-risk exposures
High-risk thinking, 230, 232
    relapse/recidivism prevention and, 212

High-risk thoughts, 307, 309
High-risk youth, identification of, 25
Hispanic Acculturation Scale, 264
HIV/AIDS:
  heroin and, 104
  teenagers with, 22
HIV/AIDS knowledge, 314
  and risk assessment, 264
Hofmann, Albert, 106, 111
Homicide, teen, 12, 137, 141
  in groups, 137
  reasons cited, 137
  See also Female juvenile murderers;
  Infanticide, adolescent; Mass murderers,
  adolescent; Parricide, adolescent; School
  shootings
Hormones, adolescent crime and, 126-127
  cortisol, 126, 127
  testosterone, 126, 127
Hostile world syndrome, 239, 243, 244

I

Identity confusion, 21
Identity crisis, 21
Identity diffusion, 168, 169, 172, 174
Identity formation, adolescence and, 168,
313. *See also* Identity diffusion; Moratorium
Impaired Control Cycle (ICC), 183-184
Impulsiveness, adolescent pathological:
  psychotherapeutic medication for, 54
  Inclusion into substance abuse category,
  determining, 182-187
  baseline—"any use," 183
  drug pattern, 183
  drug setting, 183
  drug specificity, 183
  levels of service model, 187
  minimum symptom criteria, 183
  multiple criteria model, 185
  problem severity continuum, 183
  relationship identifier, 185
  self-selection, 185
  standardized self-report psychometric
  approaches, 185
  threshold/stage model, 183
  two factor combination threshold model,
  185
  See also DSM-IV criteria with adolescents; Impaired Control Cycle (ICC)
Individual treatment plan (ITP), 177, 193
Infanticide, adolescent, 137
Information-processing errors/distortions,
209
In-group identity, 12, 173, 174, 304
Inhalants, 67, 105-106, 111, 147
  adolescent use, 12, 22, 61
  brain and, 105-106
  brain damage, 105-106
  high, 106
  nitrates, 105
  prevalence of adolescent use, 62
  toluene, 105
Insomnia, adolescent:
  psychotherapeutic medication for, 54
Intake and admission methods/procedures,
PSD-C, 288-289
  filling out forms, 288-289
  formal client interview, 288
  initial client referral and, 288
  See also specific forms
Intake Personal Data Form, 289, 319, 321
Intermediate structures, 225-226
Internal Personal Data Form, 289
Interpersonal Reactivity Index (IRI), 33, 241
Intervention, National Institute of Justice

principles of, 10
Intervention services, 187
Intravenous drug use, adolescent, 22
  AIDS and, 22

J

Jesness Inventory (JI), 133, 196
Jesness Inventory-Revised (JI-R), 197
Journal writing, 306
Jumping to conclusions, 209
Juvenile arrests, 37, 78
  estimated number, 23
  estimated number for violence, 23
Juvenile correctional counseling, effective:
  basic counseling skills, 277
  cognitive-behavioral treatment delivery,
  278
  elements, 277-278
  high-quality/productive interaction and
  relationship, 277
  modeling, 277
  positive reinforcement, 277
  sanctioning and disapproval, 278
  See also Juvenile justice treatment counselor, effective PSD-C; Manual-driven
  treatment protocols
Juvenile delinquency:
  characteristics, 115-118, 141
  definition, 115
Juvenile delinquency, criminal careers and,
116
Juvenile delinquency and crime, correlates
of, 121-123, 141
  deviant peers, 122, 141
  gender development, 122
  school discipline referrals, 121-122, 141
  self-concept, 122-123
  substance abuse, 122, 141
Juvenile delinquency and crime, motivations
for, 238-239
  belief-driven, 238-239, 244
  emotion-driven, 238, 244
  mixed-motive, 239
  reward driven, 239, 244
  See also Adolescent crime, motivations
  for
Juvenile jurisdiction versus adult jurisdiction, 3
Juvenile justice, developmental perspective
on, 139, 140, 141-142. *See also* Life course-
persistent offenders
Juvenile justice system, trauma within, 12,
116, 145, 164
  adolescent female detention, 159-160
  adolescent females in adult facilities, 159
  deteriorating psychological effects, 161,
  164
  housing/nutrition/health care, 161, 164
  lack of age-appropriate educational
  resources, 160
  mental health issues, 159, 160
  mistreatment/abuse/neglect, 160-161
  pregnancy and, 161, 162
  restraint, 161, 164
  sexual, 160
Juvenile justice treatment counselor, effective PSD-C, 275-279, 296
  assessment and case management skills,
  278
  personal dimension, 275-277
  philosophical-knowledge dimension, 276,
  279
  profile of, 276
  technical skills dimension, 276, 277-279

See also Juvenile correctional counseling,
effective; Motivational interviewing;
Reflective listening; Therapeutic alliance
Juvenile male offenders:
  abused, 152
  chronic offending, 145
  firearms, 146
  re-arrest, 145
  seriousness of crime, 145
  violent assault by, 146
  violent crime participation, 146
Juvenile offenses, 115
  non-aggressive, 115
  See also specific types of crime; Gang
  membership; Juvenile delinquency; Status
  offenses
Juvenile violence, 115
  prevalence of, 133
  types, 134
  See also Juvenile violence, trends in;
  Violence, adolescent
Juvenile violence, trends in, 133-139, 140,
141
  juvenile victims of crime, 134-135
  prevalence of juvenile violence, 133
  risks/predictors, 135-136
  teen homicide, 137
  teen mass murder/school shootings, 138-
  139
  teens and firearms, 136-137
  types of juvenile violence, 134
  See also Violent adolescent behavior, personal responsibility for; Violent adolescent behavior, social responsibility for

K

Kant, I., 205
Ketamine, 107, 108, 111
  as "date rape drug," 108, 111
Kinkel, Kip, 79
La Cañada Adolescent Treatment Program,
267-268
  aftercare treatment, 267-268
  family involvement, 267
  negotiated treatment plan, 267
  philosophy, 267
  residential phase, 267, 268
  step-down, 267

L

Lapse:
  versus relapse, 230
Lawfulness, 230
Learning, Lewin's steps of, 279
  differentiated response, 219, 221
  global/undifferentiated response, 219,
  221
  integration response, 219, 221
  See also Cyclic (phasic-spiral) process of
  growth and change in treatment
Learning, psychology of, 205
Learning and change, cognitive-behavioral
process of, 228
Learning theorists, 205
Life-course persistent offenders, 12, 27,
115, 116, 127-133, 139, 141
  ADHD and, 128
  age and crime, 128-129
  aggressiveness-rejection cycle, 130-131
  antisocial family members and, 131
  antisocial peers, 131
  bio/psycho/social factors, 129-131
  cognitive abilities, 129
  depression, 131

economic disadvantage, 130
family influences, 130
life of narrowing options, 131
neurological problems, 128
parental deviance, 130
poor communication skills, 130
prevalence rate, 131
psychopathic personality traits, 128
social isolation, 131
under-controlled temperament, 128
use of violence, 128
Locus of control:
external, 70, 71, 212, 305
internal, 33, 70, 83, 212, 290, 307, 308, 311, 312
Long-term cognitive processes, 212
Long-term potentiation, 97
LSD, 64, 106-107, 108, 111
adolescent use, 22
effects, 107, 111
long-term effects, 107
Luvox, 79

M

Magical thought, 21
Magnifying, 209
Maladaptive cognitions, 116
Male deviancy, 150
Male juvenile murderers, 146-147
victims, 147
weapons, 146
See also Homicide, teen; Mass murderers, adolescent; School shootings
Male values, 240
Manual-driven treatment protocols, 15, 279, 296. *See also* Project Match
Manzie, Sam, 79
Marijuana, 63, 92, 101-103, 110, 147, 237
adolescent use, 12, 21-22, 37, 41, 61
chronic abuse effects, 101
cigarette smoking and adolescent use, 61
dopamine levels and, 93, 94
effects on brain, 101
effects on cognition, 102, 103, 110
endocrine system and, 102, 110
hallucinogenic effects, 101
immune system and, 102, 110
long-term health effects, 102, 110
male juvenile use of, 147, 150
prevalence of adolescent use, 62
respiratory illness and, 102, 110
THC, 101, 102, 110
treatment for abuse of, 238
withdrawal effects, 101-102
Masculine status anxiety, 119
Mass murderers, adolescent, 138-139
characteristics, 138
classroom avenger type, 138
criminal opportunist type, 138
family annihilator type, 138
See also School shootings
Mass murder:
states with highest rates, 125
teen, 138-139, 141
See also Mass murderers, adolescent; School shootings
Mean world view, 239
Mediation, 208
Mental health issues, scope of adolescent, 21, 37, 41-42, 55, 56-57
co-occurring disorders, 41-42, 56
externalizing disorders, 41, 56
internalizing disorders, 41, 56
See also specific mental health disorders; Substance disorders

Mescaline, 65
Methamphetamine, 66, 90, 92, 98-99
adolescent use, 12, 61, 68-69, 83
brain damage, 98
effects, 98
effects on brain, 68, 83
Huntington's chorea-like symptoms, 98
neurotoxic effects, 99
Parkinson's disease-like symptoms, 99
prevalence of adolescent use, 62
tardive dyskinesia-like symptoms, 98
Methamphetamine addiction, treatment for, 68-69
cognitive-behavioral, 68
family involvement, 69
group/individual participation, 68-69
Matrix Model, 68
relapse prevention and education, 69
structure, 69
therapist support, 68
12-step program, 69
Millon Adolescent Clinical Inventory (MACI), 196, 197, 198, 199
Mindfulness, counseling with, 167, 172-173, 174, 304
group treatment, 173
importance, 167
preconceived expectations and, 172
respecting, 173
socialized mental scripts and, 172
supporting, 173
understanding, 173
Minnesota Multiphasic Personality Inventory-Adolescent (MMPI-A), 196, 197, 198, 199
diagnosis and treatment planning using, 54, 57
Mob psychology, 119
Modeling, 14, 46, 56, 77, 205, 206, 207, 299, 301, 317
conflict resolution, 284
problem-solving, 250, 258, 284
Monitoring the Future (MTF) survey, 2003, 22, 61, 82
prevalence of 12th-grade drug use, 62
Mood management training, 212
Moral and community responsibility, CBT approaches and developing, 232-234
feedback/confrontational process, 233
specific themes, 232
therapeutic and correctional partnership, 232-234
Morals, 310
Moratorium, 168, 169, 170, 172, 174
Morphine, 65, 103, 110
dopamine levels and, 94
Motivational enhancement, 5, 14, 222-224
necessity for, 223
research efficacy, 223
Motivational Enhancement Therapy (MET), 224, 249, 258
Motivational Enhancement Therapy/Cognitive Behavioral Therapy (MET/CBT), 14, 263, 269-270
motivational interviewing, 270
outpatient, 269
treatment protocol, 269
Motivational Enhancement Therapy/Cognitive Behavioral Therapy (MET/CBT5+CBT7), 270
Motivational intervention (MI) approach, 249-250
counselor goals, 249-250
outcome studies, 250
successful therapist characteristics, 250

Motivational interviewing, 36, 37, 223-224, 275, 279
Motivational interviewing model, Miller and Rollnick's, 223-224
Motivational methods/techniques, therapeutic, 210
Multidimensional assessment, 5
Multidimensional family therapy (MDFT), 4, 253, 258-259
decision-making skills, 253
multisystemic assessment step, 253
negotiation skills, 253
parenting style, 253
problem-solving skills, 253
Multiple pathway theory, drug-crime connection and, 77, 83
Multi-Problem Behavioral Checklist (MPBC), 196, 197
Multisensory activities, 301, 317
Multisystemic therapy (MST), 4, 254-257, 259
benefits, 257
daily or weekly client effort, 256, 259
developmentally appropriate interventions, 256
evaluating effectiveness, 256
focus, 255
goals, 255, 256-257
interventions for responsible behavior, 255
length of treatment, 254, 259
positive/strength-focused therapeutic contacts, 255
present-focused/action-oriented interventions, 256
primary purpose
principles, 255-257, 259
promoting treatment generalization/long-term maintenance of therapeutic change, 256
typical adolescent client, 254, 259
Music:
connection to other adolescents, 170
escape from life, 170
homicide as topic, 171
producing one's own culture, 170
suicide as topic, 171
support system for drug abuse, 171
violence as topic, 171

N

National Conference on Marijuana Use, 102
National Council on Crime and Delinquency (NCCD), 151, 156, 160, 164
National Institute on Alcohol Abuse and Alcoholism (NIAAA), 14, 263, 270
National Institute on Drug Abuse, 61
National Treatment Improvement Evaluation Study (NTIES), 237
Native American juveniles, 9
Negative cognitive schemas, 206
Negative identity, 168, 239, 244
Negative practice, 205
Negative reinforcement, 46, 56, 209
Negative self-concept, 240. *See also* Self-concept
Negative self-evaluation, 242
Negative self-identities, 13, 243, 244
Negative self-image, 28
Negative thinking, changing, 227
Negative thoughts, 311
changing, 212
managing, 212
Negotiation skills, 309

Neurotransmitters, 87, 88, 89, 90, 96, 110
  adolescent crime and, 126
  dopamine, 90-92, 93, 104, 108, 110, 111
  GABA, 90, 91, 93, 96, 97-98, 103, 108,
  110, 111
  glutamate, 96, 108, 110
  NMDA, 96, 97
  norepinephrine, 88, 90
  serotonin, 90, 91, 104, 111, 126
  See also Reward Cascade
Nicotine, 41, 66, 109, 110, 111
  dopamine levels and, 93, 94, 108-109,
  111
  glutamate release and, 108, 111
  See also Cigarette smoking; Tobacco
Notice of Federal Requirements Regarding
Confidentiality, 289, 319, 328

O

Observational learning, 46, 56
Obsessive-compulsive disorder (OCD), ado-
lescent:
  psychotherapeutic medication for, 54, 55
Office of Juvenile Justice and Delinquency
Prevention, 134, 135, 136, 153
Omen formation, 51
Operant conditioning, 205
Operant conditioning theory, Skinner's, 266
Operational model for assessment, PSD-C
  comprehensive assessment, 291
  differential screen, 290-291
  long-term outcome, 291-292
  treatment process assessment, 291
Opiates, 65, 103-104, 110-111
  adolescent use, 12
  brain and, 103-104
  See also Heroin; Morphine
Oppositional defiant disorder (ODD), 11,
23, 37, 42, 56, 310, 311, 316
  conduct disorder and, 42, 45, 47
  DSM-IV-TR diagnostic criteria, 42, 43
  prevalence, 42
  PTSD and, 51
Orthogenetic Principle, Werner's, 220, 280
Other-report data, 178-179, 180, 186, 187
  double-subjective, 178
  official documentation, 178
  ratings of interview data, 178-179
  semi-structured interview, 179
  structured interview format, 179
  third-party, 178
  unstructured interview, 178-179
Outcome expectancies, 213, 224, 225
  distorted, 243
Outcome measures, 13
Out-group identity, 173
Outpatient treatment programs, adolescent,
237, 238. See also specific outpatient treatment programs
Outsider, negative stereotyping of, 239
Over-controlled syndrome, 41
Ownership of change (PSD-C Phase III), 15,
222, 280, 282-284, 285, 300, 303
  counseling skills facilitating, 283
  specific objectives, 283
Oxycontin, 62, 65, 83, 103, 110

P

Panic disorder, PTSD and, 51
Parental cigarette smoking, adolescent smok-
ing and, 29
Parental Consent for Program Involvement,
289, 319, 326
  Parental criminal conduct, delinquency/

adolescent substance abuse and, 29
Parental incarceration, delinquency/adoles-
cent substance abuse and, 29
Parental substance abuse, delinquency/ado-
lescent substance abuse and, 29
Parental supervision, degree of:
delinquency/adolescent substance abuse
and, 29
Parricide, adolescent, 137
Partnership for a Drug-Free America, 61
Pathways to Self-Discovery and Change
(PSD-C) program, 3, 141
  admission, 15
  curriculum, 14
  full disclosure statements, 15
  involvement consent, 15
  minimum symptom admission criteria, 10
  operational guidelines, 14-15
  orientation of topics, 303
  program implementation, 14-15
  program rationale, 3-4
  providers, 177
  psycho-educational model, 13
  purpose, 4
  rights notification, 15
  target populations, 10
  See also Pathways to Self-Discovery and
Change (PSD-C) program, effective delivery of; PSD-C orientation; PSD-C Phase
I; PSD-C Phase III; PSD-C Phase II;
Treatment curriculum, PSD-C
Pathways to Self-Discovery and
Change(PSD-C) program, effective delivery
of, 275, 296
  group management and leadership, 289-
290
  ethical and legal screening and assessment considerations, 284, 286-287
  intake and admission methods/proce-
dures, 288-289
  juvenile justice counselor, 275-279
  operational model for assessment, 290-
296
  See also PSD-C program process and
structure; PSD-C program structure and
delivery guidelines
Pavlov, I., 205
Paxil, 79
PCP, 107-108, 111
  rush, 108
Peer groups, 167
Perceived environment system, 21, 23, 37,
73
  deviant lifestyle and, 24
  distal structure, 23
  proximal structure, 23
Perfusion Nuclear Magnetic Imaging, 99
Personal Experience Inventory (PEI), 194,
199
Personal Experience Screening
Questionnaire (PESQ), 192
Personal identification, adolescent, 168
Personality disorders, 11, 49-50, 56
  criminal conduct and, 49-50
  DSM-IV diagnostic criteria, 49
  narcissistic, 49, 50, 56
  paranoid, 49, 50, 56
  passive-aggressive, 49-50, 56
  violent behavior and, 49-50, 56
Personality system, 21, 23, 37, 73
  deviant lifestyle and, 24
  motivational-instigation structure, 23
  personal belief structure, 23
  personal control structure, 23
Personal Pleasure Inventory, 316

Phases of Re-socialization program, 33, 241
Phobia in adolescents, 41
Phoenix Academy, 268-269
  aftercare, 269
  "clan," 268
  client referrals, 268
  effectiveness, 269
  family recreation, 269
  family therapy, 268-269
  holistic view of substance abuse, 268
  individual counseling, 268
  meetings, 268
  modified therapeutic community, 268
  outcome study, 269
  philosophy, 268
  social learning theory and, 268
Phoenix House, 268
Pizarro, Francisco, 99, 110
Plan for Change, 15, 281, 282, 299, 308
Plato, "ideal forms" of, 205
Positive reinforcement, 46, 56, 209
Positive thoughts, planting, 212
Post-traumatic stress disorder (PTSD), 11,
23, 37, 50-54, 56-57, 199, 241
  age and, 51
  associated problem behavior problems,
51, 57
  avoidance symptoms, 52
  depression and, 51, 57
  hyperarousal and, 52
  intrusive symptoms, 52
  parental reaction to traumatic event and,
50
  physical proximity to traumatic event
and, 50
  post-traumatic play and, 51
  post-traumatic reenactment and, 51
  precipitating traumatic events, 50
  substance abuse and, 51
  traumatic event severity and, 50
  treatment, 51-52
  See also Omen formation; Post-traumatic
stress disorder (PTSD), treatment for;
Time skew
Post-traumatic stress disorder (PTSD), treatment for, 51-52
  cognitive-behavioral, 51-52, 53-54, 57
  evaluation of efficacy, 53-54
  natural healing, 53
  psychological debriefing, 53
  psychotherapeutic medication, 54
Poverty, delinquency/adolescent substance
abuse and, 30-31
Practice, problem-solving, 250, 258
Prescription drug abuse, adolescent, 62-68,
83
  benzodiazepines, 62, 83
  opiates, 62, 83
  stimulants, 62, 83
  See also specific drugs; Aderall; Ritalin
Prescription drugs, crime/violence and, 79-
80
Prevention services, 187
Problem behavior theory, 8, 11, 21, 23-24,
73
  drug-crime connection and, 77, 83
  See also Behavior system; Perceived environment system; Personality system; Risk;
Risk factors, adolescent substance
abuse/delinquency
Problem Oriented Screening Instrument for
Teenagers (POSIT), 192
Problem solving, 258
  decision-making, 251-252
  5-step model for, 251

means-end, 252
Problem solving skills, 212, 283
  development, 207
Problem solving skills therapy (PSST), 14, 250-252, 258
  alternative solution thinking, 250
  causal thinking, 251
  common program characteristics, 250
  consequential thinking, 250
  fostering pro-social solutions, 250, 258
  guiding principles, 251
  life-improving techniques, 250-251
  means-end thinking, 250
  See also Coaching, problem-solving;
    Direct reinforcement; Modeling; Practice,
    problem-solving; Role-playing
Problem-solving therapies, 206
Process measures, 13
Process model of assessment, 180-181
Procrastinating, 209
Progressive relaxation, 205
Project Match, 279
Project on Human Development in Chicago
Neighborhoods, The, 51
Pro-social solutions, 14
Protection, definition of, 25
Provider Full Disclosure Statement, 289
Proximal structures, 23, 224-225, 226
Prozac, 79, 90, 91, 94, 126
Pryor, Richard, 100
PSD-C orientation, 301, 304
  primary objective, 299
PSD-C Phase I, 287, 288, 303, 304-308, 316-317
  Chapter 5: "Making a Commitment to
    Change," 307-308
  Chapter 4: "Backsliding to Drugs and
    Crime," 307
  Chapter 1: "Building Trust and Motivation
    to Change," 304-305
  Chapter 3: "Talking About Yourself and
    Listening to What Others Say," 306-307,
    308
  Chapter 2: "Building a Knowledge Base,"
    305-306
  Session 5: "Criminal Conduct and the
    Influence of Drugs," 306
  Session 4: "Basic Knowledge About Drug
    Abuse and Addiction," 305-306
  Session 1: "Getting Started," 304
  Session 3: "How Thoughts and Feelings
    Affect Behavior," 305
  Session 2: "Power of Thought," 304-305
PSD-C Phase III, 287, 288, 303, 312-317
  Chapter 11: "Overcoming Prejudice,"
    312-313
  Chapter 15: "Stability and Growth," 316
  Chapter 14: "Lifestyle Balance," 315-316
  Chapter 13: "Problem Solving and
    Decision Making," 314-315
  Chapter 12: "Exploring Individual
    Intimacy," 313-314
  Session 30: "Critical Reasoning," 315
  Session 31: "Building Community
    Support—Family, Friends, and Fun Time,"
    316
  Session 32: "Planning for the Future," 316
  Session 28: "Decision making," 315
  Session 25: "Safe Sex," 314
  Session 24: "Sexual Intimacy and
    Orientation," 314
  Session 29: "Staying Strong Without
    Drugs or Crime," 315
  Session 21: "Respecting Others," 312
  Session 27: "Problem Solving," 315

Session 26: "STD's and HIV Prevention,"
  314
Session 23: "Identity and Emotional
  Intimacy," 313-314
Session 22: "Gender Issues," 313
PSD-C Phase II, 287, 288, 303, 308-312,
  317
  Chapter 8: "Responsibility to Others and
    the Community," 310-311
  Chapter 9: "Zeroing in on Negative
    Thinking," 311
  Chapter 7: "Avoiding Trouble and
    Playing Fair," 309-310
  Chapter 6: "Basic Communication Skills,"
    308-309
  Chapter 10: "Handling Anger, Guilt, and
    Depression," 311-312
  Session 18: "Errors in Thinking," 311
  Session 11: "Give & Take with Others,"
    308-309
  Session 15: "Understanding Values &
    Moral Development," 310
  Session 14: "How to Bargain and When
    to Say No," 309-310
  Session 19: "Dealing with Feelings," 312
  Session 17: "Recognizing & Changing
    Negative Thoughts," 311
  Session 16: "Understanding & Practicing
    Empathy," 310-311
  Session 13: "Managing Cravings & Urges
    about Crime and Substances," 309
  Session 12: "Assertive Skills
    Development," 309
  Session 20: "Preventing Aggression," 312
PSD-C program process and structure, 279-
284
  facilitating growth and change process,
    280-283
  learning and growth process, 279-280
  PSD-C program structure and delivery
    guidelines, 287-288, 296
  group delivery format, 287-288
  judicial terms and structures, 288
  orientation, 288
  time-frame and presentation, 287-288
  See also PSD-C Phase I; PSD-C Phase III;
    PSD-C Phase II
Psychometric assessment instruments, guidelines for using, 181-182
  construct validity, 181-182
  interview-based, 182
  self-report methods, 181-182
  See also specific psychometric assessment
    instruments
Psychopathy Screening Device, 43
Psychotherapeutic medications for chil-
dren/adolescents, 54-55, 57. See also specific medications
Psychotherapy:
  common features of all types, 219
  core dimension, 219
  defining, 219
  versus education, 220, 234
Punk subculture, 171

R

Racial identity model, 168
Racial pride groups, 169
Rating Adolescent-Adult Problems Scales
(RAAPS), 194
Rational-Emotive Therapy, 206, 212
Reattribution techniques, 254
Recidivism, adolescent, 132-133
  age of first involvement with

alcohol/drugs, 133
cumulative disadvantage, 132
early age of entry into corrections setting,
  132-133
elevated psychopathic deviant scores, 133
gang involvement, 133
prior incarceration, 133
substance abuse, 133
violent offender, 12
  See also Life-course persistent offenders
Re-entry, community, 300
Referral Evaluation Summary (RES), 288,
  289, 319, 320
Reflective-acceptance skills, 283
Reflective confrontation, 282
Reflective correctional confrontational, 282
Reflective feedback, 283
Reflective listening, 275
Reflective therapeutic confrontation, 282
  managing resistance and ambivalence in,
    282, 283-284
Reframing techniques, 254
Reinforcement theories, 255-256
Relapse and recidivism, 307
Relapse and recidivism erosion, 307
Relapse and recidivism prevention, 5, 13,
  229-230, 283
  continuum of care in, 242
  empowerment and, 174
  importance of after care, 242
  self-efficacy and, 174
Relapse and recidivism rates, adolescent, 3
Relapse Prevention model, Marlatt's, 229-
230
  definition of relapse in, 229
  global intervention procedures for bal-
    anced life-style, 229-230
  See also Relapse/Recidivism Prevention
    Model for Delinquency, Crime, and
    Substance Abuse, PSD-C (cognitive-
    behavioral); Rule violation effect
Relapse/Recidivism Prevention Model for
Delinquency, Crime, and Substance Abuse,
PSD-C (cognitive-behavioral), 230-232,
234. See also Expected outcome; High-risk
exposures; Rule violation effect; Self-attribu-
tion; Self-efficacy
Relative deprivation theory, 124, 141
Relaxation methods, 206
Relaxation therapy, 207
Relaxation training, 212
Report veridicality problem, 177
Residential treatment programs, adolescent,
14, 237, 238, 257-258, 259. See also specific residential treatment programs;
Therapeutic communities
Resiliency, community-focused model for
strengthening, 34-35, 37
Resiliency factors against adolescent problem behavior, 24, 25-27, 33-36, 37
  attachment to conventional individuals,
    33, 34
  cognitive focus, 26, 33
  community infrastructure, 34
  empathy, 33
  family factors, 33, 34
  health-positive cognition and behavior, 33
  identifiable, 26
  individual factors, 33
  internal locus of control, 33
  personal competence skills, 33
  positive family interaction/quality of
    social ties, 34
  promotion of, 24
  psychosocial factors, 34-35

security of attachment in infancy, 34
social orientation, 33
treatment implications, 27
See also Substance abuse, mediating factors in adolescent
Resiliency focus, mitigating risk through, 25-27
Resistance, client, 222, 223, 288
managing, 283-284
overtly aggressive, 283
passive-oppositional, 283
Responsibility skills training, 282
Restorative justice, 36, 37
Rethinking report, 210
Reward Cascade, 90, 91, 103
drugs and dopamine site of action, 94
Risk:
definition, 25
mitigating through resiliency focus, 25-27
multiple exposures to, 25
Risk and drug involvement, gender comparisons across, 145, 147-150
Risk and resiliency during adolescence, 10, 11, 21
as interactive, 35
as operationally independent, 35
as opposite ends of continuum, 35
offset of, 25-27
on a continuum, 35-36
types, 36
Risk Calibration Measure (RCM), 197
Risk factors for adolescent substance abuse/delinquency, 23, 24, 37
behavioral problems, 28
biological, 27-28
child abuse/corporal punishment, 29-30
cognitive deficits, 28
community, 26
degree of parental supervision, 29
demographic, 26
depression, 28
ethnicity/race/culture, 31
family, 29-30
gang membership, 31
head trauma, 28
health behavior, 28-29
individual, 26, 27-29
insecure attachment in infancy, 29
low personal confidence skill, 28
maternal age at birth, 29
neighborhood, 31
parental/family characteristics, 29
peer associations/teen culture, 30
psychological, 28-29
psychosocial, 26, 30-31
school difficulties, 30
self-concept, 28
sensation-seeking, 27-28, 71
social orientation, 28
socioeconomic disadvantage, 30-31
sub-risk factors, 31
trauma/abuse/domestic violence experiences, 29
See also Adolescent problem behavior, risk factors for development of; Substance abuse, causes of adolescent; Risk factors for adolescent substance abuse/delinquency, models for understanding
Risk factors for adolescent substance abuse/delinquency, models for understanding, 31-33
alternative sequences, 31
co-occurring relationships, 31
equifinality, 31
multifinality, 33

reciprocal risk factors, 31
Risk-resiliency assessment, 13, 27
Risk-taking, 8, 27-28
Risky cognitions, 305
while driving under the influence, 74, 239-240, 244
Ritalin, 62, 63, 66, 68, 79, 83
Ritualism, 171
Rogers, Carl, 219, 275
Role-playing, 14, 206, 207, 299, 301, 317
problem-solving, 250, 258
Rules, 212, 225-226, 303
Rule violation effect, 229, 231-232, 307
Runaways, 29, 145, 162, 314
self-medication by, 146, 162
Running away, 29, 45, 115, 134, 145, 152, 162
Rutgers Alcohol Problem Index (RAPI), 192

S

Safety and trust, establishing treatment atmosphere of, 299, 316
Schema-focused therapy, 211
Schemas, 211
for cognitive-behavioral learning and change, 227-229, 234
Schizophrenia, adolescent:
psychotherapeutic medication for, 55
School shootings, 138, 141. *See also* Columbine High School shootings
Screening, 15
preliminary, 13
See also specific types of assessment; Assessment of juvenile offenders
Screening and Assessing Adolescents for Substance Use Disorders, 284
Screening and Assessment of Alcohol and Other Drug-Abusing Adolescents, 284
Screening for Pregnancy-Risk Drinking, 196, 197
Search Institute, 34, 37
Seattle Social Development Project (SSDP), 120-121, 132
Selective serotonin reuptake inhibitors (SSRIs), 90, 91
Self-assessment, 209
Self-attribution, 232
Self-change studies, 205
Self-concept, 28
juvenile delinquency and, 28, 122-123, 134
violent behavior and, 240
Self-defeating thought patterns, 28, 311
Self-destructive behaviors:
internalizing disorders and, 41
self-hatred, 41
self-mutilation, 41, 42
tattooing, 41
See also Eating disorders; Suicide, adolescent
Self-disclosure, 210
as treatment barrier, 277
PDS-C counselor, 275, 277
Self-efficacy, 14, 208, 224, 229, 231, 307, 311, 316
alcohol use patterns and, 213
definition, 213
during action stage of change, 213
in substance abuse/juvenile justice treatment, 213
Self-identity, adolescent quest for, 12
Self-image, enhanced:
in delinquents, 28
Self-inoculation training, 212

Self-instructional training, 206, 207, 212
Self-management methods, 206
Self-management skills, 83, 301
Self-monitoring, 208
anxiety management through, 205
Self-naming, adolescent, 168
Self-Portrait, 15, 281, 282, 299, 308
Self-reinforcement, 207, 208
Self-reinforcing feedback, 207
Self-report data, 177, 178, 179, 180, 186, 187, 190, 199, 282
as valid estimate of "true condition," 181, 199
interview (narrative), 179
psychometric test data, 179
See also Psychometric assessment instruments, guidelines for using
Self-talk, 208, 212, 226. *See also* Countering; Positive thoughts, planting; Shifting the view; Thought, exaggerating the; Thought stopping
Sensation-seeking, 8, 26-27, 171
driving while intoxicated and, 73, 74
Sensation Seeking Scale (SSS), 74
Separation anxiety, PTSD and, 51
Services Research Outcome Study (SROS), 237
Sex offenders, juvenile, 12, 153-154, 163
characteristics, 153
desistance from reoffending, 154
recidivism, 153-154
Sexual activity/promiscuity, delinquency/substance abuse and, 28
Sexual assault, childhood, 12, 152-154
adolescent sex offenders, 153
conspiracy of silence, 152
juvenile perpetrators of, 153
prevalence, 152-153
sex offense and recidivism, 153-154
status offenses and, 145
Sexual harassment, 152, 163
Shifting the view, 212, 300, 309
Simple Screening Inventory (SSI), 192
Skinner, B. F., 205
Small groups, 301
Smokeless tobacco, adolescent use of prevalence, 62
Social anxiety disorder, adolescent:
psychotherapeutic medication for, 54
Social control theory, 8, 124, 125, 141, 310
drug-crime connection and, 77
Social learning theory, 46, 56, 118, 119, 124-125, 141, 208, 213, 263
drug-crime connection and, 77, 83
Social Response Questionnaire (SRQ), 195, 291, 295, 329, 340-341
Intake Testing, 292
scoring guide and scale interpretation, 329, 342
Social responsibility, 300
Social role definition, adolescent quest for, 12
Social skills building, 210
Social skills training, 13, 206, 207, 212-213, 215, 226, 228, 300, 308
specific focus, 227
Social ties, strong and healthy:
importance of to adolescents, 34
Socioeconomic standing, 167
Solomon, T. J., 79
Spaeth, E., 106
Stages of Change and Readiness Treatment Eagerness Scale (SOCRATES), 195
Stages of change model, 5, 14, 222, 296, 308

action stage, 222, 280, 282, 283
contemplative, 280, 281
determination/preparation stage, 222, 280, 282
differentiation, 280, 285
facilitating individuals and treatment group through, 222, 280-283
integration, 280, 282, 285
maintenance stage, 222, 280, 283
precontemplation stage, 222, 280, 281
relapse stage, 222, 280
undifferentiated/global response, 280, 285
See also Challenge to change (PSD-C Phase I); Commitment to change (PSD-C Phase II); Ownership of change (Phase PSD-C III)
Stage Theory, drug-crime connection and, 77, 83
Status offenses, 115
definition, 29
girls and, 12, 145-146, 162
truancy, 29, 41, 115, 134, 145, 162
See also Runaways; Running away
Steroids, anabolic, 67
prevalence of adolescent use, 62
Strain theory, Merton's, 123-124, 125, 141, 169
innovation stage, 169, 170, 171
rebellion stage, 169, 171
retreatism stage, 169
ritualism stage, 169
Strategies for Self-Improvement and Change (SSC), 3
poor treatment outcomes for adolescents, 4
Strength-based perspective, 307
for understanding adolescent problem behavior, 5, 7-8, 11, 12, 21
to juvenile justice and treatment approaches, 36-37
See also Motivational interviewing; Restorative justice
Stress, managing, 227
Stress inoculation training, 206
Stuffing, 41. *See also* Over-controlled syndrome
Subculture of violence, 36, 119, 141
Substance abuse, adolescent, 41
drinking prevalence, 61
PTSD and, 51
recent trends, 61
scope, 61
See also specific drugs; Drugs, commonly abused; Substance abuse, causes of adolescent; Substance disorders, adolescent
Substance abuse, causes of adolescent:
age of first use, 69
conduct problems, 69
deviant peer affiliation, 71, 83
early AOD experimentation, 69
external locus of control, 70, 71
family, 69, 83
gang participation, 69
lack of health skills, 71, 83
lack of sense of purpose, 71
low self-esteen, 70
parenting style, 69
perceived life chances, 71, 83
perceived neighborhood risk, 69
personal competence, 69
positive alcohol expectancies, 69, 70, 83
psychosocial causal factors, 69
social influence, 69, 83
timing, 69
traumatic childhood experiences, 71, 83

See also Risk factors for adolescent substance abuse/delinquency
Substance abuse, criminal conduct and adolescent, 77-80
deviant peer attitudes, 77
role modeling, 77
See also Multiple pathway theory; Problem behavior theory; Social learning theory; Stage theory, drug-crime connection and
Substance abuse, mediating factors in adolescent:
assertiveness, 70, 83
family influences, 70-71
high self-esteem, 70, 83
Life Skills Training (LST), 70, 83
internal locus of control, 70, 83
self-management skills, 83
shifts in alcohol expectancies, 70
social competence, 69-70, 83
See also Resiliency factors against adolescent problem behavior
Substance abuse and juvenile justice treatment, self-efficacy in, 213
Substance Abuse Subtle Screening Inventory (SASSI), 192
Substance disorders, adolescent, 41, 56
legal substances abuse, 41
prescription drug abuse, 41
street drug abuse, 41
See also specific drugs; Substance abuse, adolescent
Substance Use Survey (SUS), 185, 192, 195, 290, 291, 292, 329, 330-333
scoring guide, 329, 334
Suicide, adolescent, 41, 42
corporal punishment and, 30
serotonin and, 45
Superpredator, 116
Systematic sensitization, 205

T

Tarasoff versus Regents of the University of California, 286
Teen-Addiction Severity Index (T-ASI), 194
Teen pregnancy:
African Americans, 151
female juvenile offending and, 150-151
Hispanic Americans, 151
Native Americans, 151
school failure and, 151
vulnerability factors, 151
Teen Substance Abuse Treatment Program (TSAT), 263-264
assessment tools, 264
components, 263
drug use testing, 264
evaluation, 264
goals, 263
in-home program, 263-264
multifamily group, 264
outcome studies, 263
primary referral source, 263
teen group, 264
Tennessee Self-concept Scale, 122
violent delinquency and high scores on, 28
Therapeutic alliance, 223, 234, 241, 244, 278-279, 283
key characteristics/elements, 278-279
Therapeutic alliance building, 210, 222-224
enhancing interest in change, 224
expanding knowledge base, 224
See also Motivational enhancement

Therapeutic communities, 14, 257-258, 259
family systems theory and, 257
first, 257
"house rules," 257-258
outcome study, 258
social learning model, 257
specific issues dealt with, 257
versus Alcoholics Anonymous, 257
Therapeutic confrontation, 223
Therapeutic feedback, 223
Therapeutic independence, enhancing client, 210-211
Therapeutic stance, 223
Thinking distortions, 311
Thinking errors, 311
identifying/changing, 209
See also specific types of thinking errors
Thinking for a Change (T4C), 14, 263, 269
Thinking report, 210, 306
Thought, exaggerating, 212
Thought arming, 300
positive, 309
Thought habits, 210, 211, 226
changing, 225
identifying, 224
See also Automatic thoughts
Thought replacement, 226
Thoughts/emotions/behaviors:
learning to control, 37
reciprocal interaction of, 210, 226, 243, 307
Thought stopping, 207, 212, 226, 300, 309, 311
Thrill and Adventure Seeking—Disinhibition and Boredom Susceptibility subscales, 74
Thrill seekers, 171. *See also* Type T personality
Thrill seeking, 27
Throw aways, 29, 145, 162, 307, 314
Time skew, 51
Tobacco, 108-110, 111
adolescent use, 12, 37
as gateway drug, 61, 83
deaths related to, 108, 111
effects on brain, 108-109
medical costs, 108
summary of effects, 109-110
See also Cigarette smoking; Nicotine; Smokeless tobacco, adolescent use of
Tolerance, teaching:
resources, 173
Tranquilizers, 147
adolescent use of, 61
prevalence, 62
Trauma History Questionnaire, 198
Trauma Symptom Checklist, 198
Treatment curriculum, PSD-C, 15
Treatment efficacy:
with juvenile justice clients, 237-238
Treatment Episode Data Set, 237
Treatment of adolescents with criminal and substance abuse problems, 14, 187
evidence for cognitive-behavioral approach to, 238-241, 244
family approaches, 252-257
individual approaches, 249-252
residential treatment, 257-258
See also specific treatments and types of therapy; Treatment of adolescents with criminal and substance abuse problems, core strategies in
Treatment of adolescents with criminal and substance abuse problems, core strategies

in:
cognitive-behavioral model for change, 224-225, 249
cognitive restructuring, 226-229
developing moral/community responsibility through CBT, 232-234
facilitating cyclic process of growth/change, 220-222
facilitating through stages of change, 222
motivational enhancement/building treatment alliance, 222-224
multidimensional screening/assessment, 220
relapse and recidivism prevention, 229-230
Treatment Outcome Prospective Study (TOPS), 237
Treatment programs, exemplary adolescent substance abuse, 14, 263-270
formats, 13
See also specific treatment programs; Adolescent Treatment Model (ATM)
Treatment Response Questionnaire (TRQ), 194, 195, 291, 295
Trigger thoughts, 307
True condition" self-report and client's, 179-181
12-step models, 69, 279. *See also* Alcoholics Anonymous
Type T personality, 171

U

U.S. Department of Justice, 159, 161
Unconventionality, adolescent problem behavior and, 8, 77
spiraling of consequences, 8
within individual at-risk youth, 8
See also Drunk driving; Risk-taking; Sensation-seeking; Social control theory
Under-controlled syndrome, 41
Uniform Crime Reports, 133-134

V

Valium, 62, 63, 83
Value confusion, 172
Values, 225, 310
Vanderbilt Study, 214
Vicodin, 65, 103, 110
Victims of crime, juvenile, 134-135
African Americans, 134
assault and, 134-135
female, 147
gang violence and, 134
Latino Americans, 134
murder and, 135
young children, 147, 163
Violence, adolescent:
as defensive posture, 28, 125
developmental perspective on, 12
gaining respect and , 239, 244, 311
learned behavior and, 169
personal responsibility for, 139, 141
social responsibility for, 139
See also specific types of violent crime; Homicide, juvenile; Juvenile violence; Juvenile violence, trends in
Violent trauma in childhood, female delinquents and, 154-157, 163
behavioral consequences, 156, 163
delinquent activity, 156, 163
depression, 156, 163
early pregnancy, 156, 163
eating disorders, 156, 163
emotional abuse, 154, 155, 163
from juvenile to adult offending, 157

gang participation, 156, 163
multidrug use, 156, 163
neglect, 155, 156
poverty, 163
promiscuity, 156, 163
psychological consequences, 156
physical abuse, 154, 155
risk taking, 156, 163
school failure, 156-157, 163
sexual abuse, 154, 155, 163
substance abuse, 156
suicidal ideation, 156, 163
suicide attempts, 156, 163
thrown away, 155-156
Visual schemas, 13

W

Watson, J., 205
Wernicke-Korsakoff Syndrome, 95
White House Office on National Drug Control Policy, 61
Wilson, Bill, 223
Worth Street Clinic (New York), 237

X

Xanax, 62, 63, 83

Y

Youth Level of Service/Case Management Inventory (YLS/CMI), 194, 197

Z

Zero-tolerance approach, 230, 232

APPENDIX A

Referral Evaluation Summary (RES)

Intake Personal Data Form

Consent for Release of Confidential Information

Client Rights Statement

Consent for Program Involvement

Health Insurance Portability and Accountability Act (HIPAA)

Parent Consent Form

Full Disclosure Statement Sample

Notice of Federal Requirements Regarding Confidentiality

REFERRAL EVALUATION SUMMARY (RES)

REFERRAL SOURCE

Name of Individual Referring Client_____ Phone_____

Date_____ Agency Name and Address_____

CLIENT DATA

Name of Client_____ Address_____

Apartment No._____ City_____. State_____ Zip_____ Phone_____

DOB_____ Age_____ Gender: [ ] Male   [ ] Female

Ethnic Group: [ ]African American [ ] Anglo-White American [ ] Asian American

      [ ] Hispanic-American   [ ] Native American

Currently Employed: [ ] No [ ] Yes   In School: [ ] No [ ] Yes

Legal Guardian _____   [ ] Mother [ ] Father [ ] Other_____

RATING OF CLIENT PROBLEMS

Referring individual is asked to rate the client on the degree of severity in each of the following areas:

	None	Slight	Moderate	Severe	Very Severe
1. Family disruption and problems	1	2	3	4	5
2. Mental health and emotional problems	1	2	3	4	5
3. School adjustment problems	1	2	3	4	5
4. Employment and/or job problems	1	2	3	4	5
5. Deviant or antisocial problems	1	2	3	4	5
6. Involvement in criminal behavior	1	2	3	4	5
7. Physical health and medical problems	1	2	3	4	5
8. Involvement with negative peers	1	2	3	4	5
9. Involvement in alcohol use	1	2	3	4	5
10. Life disruption due to alcohol use	1	2	3	4	5
11. Involvement in other drugs	1	2	3	4	5
12. Life disruption due to other drugs	1	2	3	4	5

TO BE COMPLETED BY PSD-C PROGRAM STAFF

PSD-C Staff Handling Referral_____ Intake appointment date_____

Disposition: [ ] No Show   [ ] Intake Deferred   [ ] Referred _____

[ ] Client/family refused admission   [ ] Admission to PSD-C completed

NOTICE OF FEDERAL REQUIREMENTS REGARDING
CONFIDENTIALITY OF ALCOHOL AND DRUG ABUSE PATIENT RECORDS

The confidentiality of alcohol and drug abuse patient records maintained by this program is protected by Federal Law and Regulations. Generally, the program may not say to a person outside the program that a client attends the program, or disclose any information identifying a client as an alcohol or drug abuser unless:

1)   The client consents in writing;

2)   The disclosure is allowed by a court order or;

3)   The disclosure is made to medical personnel in a medical emergency or to qualified personnel for research, audit or program evaluation.

Violation of the federal law and regulations by a program is a crime. Suspected violations may be reported to appropriate authorities in accordance with federal regulations.
Federal law and regulations do not protect any information about a crime committed by a client either at the program or against any person who works for the program or about any threat to commit such a crime.

Federal laws and regulations do not protect any information about suspected child abuse or neglect from being reported under State law to appropriate State or local authorities (See 42 U.S.C. 290dd-3 and 42 U.S.C 290ee-3 for Federal laws and 42 CFR Part 2 for Federal regulations).

Client Name_____

Client Address_____

Client Signature_____ Date_____

Witness Signature_____ Date_____

FULL DISCLOSURE STATEMENT SAMPLE

John Smith, M.A.
Certified Addictions Counselor III
Probation Officer

Mr. Smith is a probation worker with the 10th District Court, State of Texas. He has a Bachelor's Degree in Criminal Justice from the University of Maine and a Master's Degree in Counseling from Northern Colorado University. He has worked as a juvenile probation worker for 20 years and has done special work with juvenile justice clients in the area of alcohol and other drug addictions for the past five years. Although he works full time as a probation worker, he also does special drug and alcohol groups for a juvenile Day Reporting service which services juvenile justice clients who are on parole and probation.

Mr. Smith takes a client centered and cognitive behavioral orientation in counseling. He sees alcoholism and drug addiction as having many causes, including social, psychological and physical. He also feels that the social and biological genetics are important factors in the development of a substance abuse problem.

Mr. Smith has also had special training in the areas of stress management, relaxation therapy, working with depression, the counseling of juvenile offenders with substance abuse problems and cognitive behavioral approaches to working with the substance abusing youth offender. He also has specialized training and experience in working with adult criminal justice clients.

He is a member of the association of Substance Abuse Counselors of Texas and of the American Corrections Association.

PARENT CONSENT FORM

Your minor child has been selected to take part in the Pathways to Self-Discovery and Change: PSD-C, a program that helps youth prevent involvement in alcohol or other drug use and delinquent behavior or criminal conduct.

Your signature below gives the following agency permission to provide PSD-C to your child:

AGENCY

Agency _____

Agency Address _____

Agency Phone _____

MINOR

Name of Minor _____

Address_____

Signature of Minor_____

Date Signed _____

PARENT

Name of Parent_____

Address_____

Signature of Parent_____

Date Signed _____

This permission expires when minor child completes the PSD-C program.

HEALTH INSURANCE PORTABILITY AND ACCOUNTABILITY ACT (HIPAA)

On April 14, 2003, a regulation went into effect requiring all health care providers who do business with insurance carriers or transmit health information in electronic form to adhere to the Health Insurance Portability and Accountability Act (HIPAA) rules and regulations. The applicable rule for this agency is the Privacy Rule which describes how psychological and personal information about you may be used.

Under HIPAA, only the minimal necessary information is to be disclosed when individually identifiable health information is disclosed for purposes such as:

- pre-certification or pre-authorization for treatment;
- completion of insurance claim forms and follow-up as necessary;
- referrals to other professions or programs;
- filing workers' compensation or disability claims, etc.

Release of the above or other client information requires written consent and/or authorization on the part of the client, depending on the type of information to be transmitted. Exceptions include situations of:

- child abuse, neglect and endangerment;
- domestic violence and abuse;
- severe mental incapacitation, imminent threat to health or safety of self;
- imminent threat to the safety of others;
- serious injury or illness;
- or as legally or judicially required.

This agency's policy is to discuss with you any pending disclosure in advance, if at all possible, so that we both may determine what will be in your best overall interest.

At this time in Colorado, psychotherapy notes are privileged possession of the originator of the notes. However, clients and others may gain access to the less privileged general client record including such things as intake forms, billing information, appointment cards, type and frequency of treatment, diagnosis and summaries of mental status and psychometric examination data. However, this information can be released only upon your written consent. If you think your privacy has been violated you may discuss this with your therapist at any time and submit a written letter of complaint to be placed in your general therapy record. You may also call the HIPAA Compliance Office in your local area. Every effort will be made to address your issues and concerns to maintain privacy.

The HIPAA regulation is a 1500 page document. If you are interested in a more complete understanding, the publication is accessible at www.hhs.gov/ocr/hipaa.

Available to you in this agency is a summary of the most important information from the website of the American Psychiatric Association pertaining to HIPAA. Your signature below verifies that you have read and received a copy of this Notice of Privacy Rights. Thank you for your cooperation.

Client Signature_____

Date_____

Provider Signature_____

Date_____

CONSENT FOR PROGRAM INVOLVEMENT

I agree to take part in the Pathways to Self-Discovery and Change (PSD-C), which has been fully described to me. I understand that this program is between nine months and one year in length, but that I will be reviewed for continued participation in the program after completing Phase I or after two months of taking part in the program.

You also need to know that service programs such as the one you are enrolling in are not exact sciences, and that not everyone is helped by these programs. Yet, we do know that such programs, which are set up for helping people with substance abuse problems and problems with criminal conduct, have a greater chance of being successful when the client is willing to fully take part in the program.

I have been fully informed about my right to confidentiality and the exceptions to that right. I have also been informed of the ground rules and guidelines of this program and I have gone over these with my provider. My signature below is my seal for consent to be part of this program.

Agency
Name_____

Client Signature _____

Date_____

Provider Signature _____

Date _____

CLIENT RIGHTS STATEMENT

As a client in the Pathways for Self-Discovery and Change (PSD-C), you have certain rights.

First, you need to know that a qualified provider may consult with other experts on treatment issues. You are encouraged to discuss your progress in this program at any time with your provider. Unless you are a court ordered client in this program, you may end treatment at any time.

You are entitled to receive information about the methods and approaches of the program you are enrolling in. You will be an active participant in the development of your treatment service plan. You may also seek consultation from another expert regarding the appropriateness of this program for you.

You need to know that the information you give us during your treatment is legally confidential except as required by law. This confidentiality is regulated by state law, and for individuals in substance abuse programs, also by Federal law. Information about your treatment and your case can only be release upon your written request. It may be that you have been ordered to attend this program or that attendance is part of the conditions of your status in the criminal justice system (e.g., a condition of probation, parole or community corrections placement). If this is the case, and if there is a condition that a progress report must be sent to your criminal justice supervisor (e.g., probation worker), then you still must sign a written consent for such information to be released. Your provider will provide a consent form for you.

There are also exceptions to the law of confidentiality. These exceptions are as follows: if there is a "threat of harm to self or others," the person is of imminent danger to self or others, there is a suspicion of child abuse or if an individual is considered to be gravely mentally disabled. In these cases, a provider, by professional ethics and State Statutes, is obligated to protect the individual or others. In any situation where child abuse is suspected by a provider or other profession person, that suspicion must be reported to the Department of Social Services in the county where the abuse is suspected.

You need to know that sexual contact between a client and provider is not a part of any recognized therapy or rehabilitation and is never seen as acceptable under any circumstance or condition. Sexual intimacy between client and provider is illegal and should be reported to the appropriate grievance or professional licensing authority.

I have been informed of my provider's professional credentials, training and experience. I have also read the above information and understand my rights as a client.

_____   _____
Client Signature   Date

_____   _____
Provider Signature   Date

CONSENT FOR RELEASE OF CONFIDENTIAL INFORMATION

I,_____ hereby consent to communication between
　　　　　Name of Client

_____and
　　　　　Agency providing Pathways for Self-Discovery and Change - PSD-C

_____
　　　　　Court, probation, parole, and/or other agency

the following information:

_____

_____

The purpose of and need for the disclosure is to inform the above named
agency(ies) of my attendance and progress in the program. The extent of
information to be disclosed is information about my assessment, attendance at
sessions, my cooperation with the program, prognosis and other information as
follows:

_____

_____

_____

I understand that this consent will remain in effect and cannot be revoked by
me until:

_____　　　There has been a formal and effective termination or revocation of
　　　　　　　my release from confinement, probation, or parole, or other
　　　　　　　proceedings under which I was referred
　　　　　　　into the program, or

_____Consent can be revoked and/or expires on the following
　　　　　date:_____

I also understand that any disclosure made is bound by Part 2 of Title 42 of
the Code of Federal Regulations governing confidentiality of alcohol and drug
abuse records and that recipients of this information may redisclose it only in
connection with their official duties. I also release the agency disclosing
this information from any and all liability with respect to the release of this
information. My signature below provides the authority to release such
information.

Name of Client_____

Address of Client_____

Client Signature_____ Date_____

Witness Signature_____ Date_____

INTAKE PERSONAL DATA FORM

Name_____ Date_____ I.D._____

Address_____

City_____ State_____ Zip_____ Phone_____

Legal Guardian _____ [ ] Mother [ ] Father [ ] Other_____

Address of Legal Guardian_____

City_____ State_____ Zip _____ Phone: Home_____ Work_____

DOB_____ Age_____ Gender: [ ] Male [ ] Female

Ethnic Group:[ ]African American [ ] Anglo-White American [ ] Asian-American
             [ ] Hispanic-American [ ] Native American

School grade completed_____ Currently in School: [ ] No [ ] Yes

School and School Address_____

Referral Source_____ Referral Staff_____

Total Family Income_____ Source of Income and Percent:

   [ ] Father %_____ [ ] Mother %_____ [ ] Grandparents %_____

   [ ] AFDC %_____ [ ] Other _____ %_____

Birth Parents: [ ] Living together [ ] Separated [ ] Divorced
               [ ] Never married

General health [ ] Good [ ] Fair [ ] Poor Explain_____

Medical Problems [ ] No [ ] Yes Explain_____

Allergies [ ] No [ ] Yes Explain_____

Currently on Medications [ ] No [ ] Yes Explain_____

Medical Doctor_____ Phone_____ Date last saw doctor_____

RATING OF CLIENT PROBLEMS

PSD-C Admission Staff is asked to rate client on following areas:

	None	Slight	Moderate	Severe	Very Severe
1. Family disruption and problems	1	2	3	4	5
2. Mental health and emotional problems	1	2	3	4	5
3. School adjustment problems	1	2	3	4	5
4. Employment and/or job problems	1	2	3	4	5
5. Deviant or antisocial problems	1	2	3	4	5
6. Involvement in criminal behavior	1	2	3	4	5
7. Physical health and medical problems	1	2	3	4	5
8. Involvement with negative peers	1	2	3	4	5
9. Involvement in alcohol use	1	2	3	4	5
10. Life disruption due to alcohol use	1	2	3	4	5
11. Involvement in other drugs	1	2	3	4	5
12. Life disruption due to other drugs	1	2	3	4	5

APPENDIX B

Substance Use Survey (SUS)

Scoring Guide for SUS

Adolescent Self-Assessment Questionnaire (ASAQ)

Scoring Guide for ASAQ

Social Response Questionnaire (SRQ)

Scoring Guide and Scale Interpretation for SRQ

SUBSTANCE USE SURVEY (SUS)

Kenneth W. Wanberg
Author

DESCRIPTIVE INFORMATION		
NAME:	DATE:	PROGRAM:
AGE:	GENDER: [ ] Male [ ] Female	YEARS OF SCHOOLING COMPLETED:
ETHNICITY: [ ] Anglo/White [ ] Black [ ] Hispanic [ ] Native American [ ] Other		

INFORMATION AND INSTRUCTIONS ON THE USE OF THIS SURVEY

This booklet contains questions about how you see yourself. Some questions have to do with your feelings and emotions and others have to do with the use of alcohol and drugs. The information you provide will be treated as strictly confidential and will only be used by your counselors. Be as honest as you can. This will help those who are working with you to understand your concerns and questions about yourself and about your use of alcohol and other drugs. For each question in this survey, circle the letter under the answer that best fits you. **NOW YOU MAY TURN THE PAGE AND BEGIN TO ANSWER THE QUESTIONS.**

SUMMARY OF SUBSTANCE USE SURVEY (FOR STAFF USE ONLY)

1. Degree of involvement in the use of alcohol and other drugs?

Minimal   Low   Moderate   High
  0   1   2   3   4   5   6   7   8   9

2. Degree of disruption of life functioning due to the use of alcohol or other drugs?

Minimal   Low   Moderate   High
  0   1   2   3   4   5   6   7   8   9

3. Degree of mental health problems?

Minimal   Low   Moderate   High
  0   1   2   3   4   5   6   7   8   9

4. Degree of motivation for counseling or other help?

Minimal   Low   Moderate   High
  0   1   2   3   4   5   6   7   8   9

5. Level of recommended drug/alcohol services?

[ ] Prevention
[ ] Intervention
[ ] Treatment

6. Referral Source:

[ ] Juvenile Justice
[ ] School
[ ] Social Services
[ ] Medical Doctor
[ ] Parent
[ ] Mental Health Center
[ ] Therapist or Counselor
[ ] Self
[ ] School Counselor
[ ] Other: _____

7. Method of administering SUS IA

[ ] Self-administered
[ ] Face-to-face Interview
[ ] Group
[ ] Computer

8. Summary: UA PRI DRUG

ALC   ____ ____
THC   ____ ____
CC   ____ ____
AMP   ____ ____
OTHER ____ ____

9. Client I. D. Number

_____

SUS Profile Summary IA

SCALE NAME	RAW SCORE	Low			Low-medium		High-medium			High		NUMBER IN NORM SAMPLE*
		1	2	3	4	5	6	7	8	9	10	
1. INVOLVEMENT		0 1 2	3 4	5	6	7	8	9 10	11	12 13 14	15 18 50	1,334
2. DISRUPTION		0	1	2	3 4	5 6	7 8	9 10 11	12 14 16	17 20 24	25 31 77	1,334
3. MOOD ADJUST		0	1 2	3	4	5	6	7	8 9 10	11 13 28		1,334
4. DEFENSIVE		0 1 2	3	4	5	6	7	8	9	10	11 12 15	1,138
5. MOTIVATE		0 2 4 5	6 7 8	9 10	11	12	13	14	15	16 17	18	1,090
6. OADS		0 5 6 8	9 10 11	12 13 14	15 16 17	18 19 20	21 22 23	24 26 28	29 32 34	35 40 47	48 131	1,334
7. SUSR		0 1 2 5	6 7	8	9	10	11	12	13	14 15	16 17 18	1,334

DECILE RANK

1   10   20   30   40   50   60   70   80   90   99
PERCENTILE   Juvenile Justice

F-1299

382

For each of the following types of substances or drugs, including beer, wine and hard liquor, circle the letter under the answer that best fits you as to your lifetime use. If you did use the substance, write down how old you were when you first used it. *Then, on the right column of the page, for each substance, for the last SIX months you have been in the community, circle an "a" if you never had a chance to use the drug, circle a "b" if you had a chance to use it and did not, circle a "c" if you used the drug one to ten times, circle a "d" if you used it from 11 to 25 times, circle an "e" if you used it 26 to 50 times and circle a "f" if you used it more than 50 times in the past SIX months.*

Number of Times Used in Your Lifetime

Name of Drug	Never had chance to use	Had a chance but did not use	Used 1-10 times	Used 11-25 times	Used 26-50 times	Used more than 50 times	Age first used	Number of times used in last SIX months
1. Beer, malt liquor	a	b	c	d	e	f	____	a b c d e f
2. Wine, (wine coolers, maddog, Tbird, Boones)	a	b	c	d	e	f	____	a b c d e f
3. Hard liquor (gin, rum, whiskey, vodka, tequila)	a	b	c	d	e	f	____	a b c d e f
4. Marijuana (pot, weed, joint, hash, THC, fry)	a	b	c	d	e	f	____	a b c d e f
5. Cocaine (coke, crack, rock, primos, soda)	a	b	c	d	e	f	____	a b c d e f
6. Amphetamines (crank, ice, uppers, speed, crystal, bennies, white crosses, diet pills, ecstasy)	a	b	c	d	e	f	____	a b c d e f
7. Acid (LSD)	a	b	c	d	e	f	____	a b c d e f
8. Mushrooms (shrooms)	a	b	c	d	e	f	____	a b c d e f
9. PCP (angel dust)	a	b	c	d	e	f	____	a b c d e f
10. Huffed or sniffed glue	a	b	c	d	e	f	____	a b c d e f
11. Huffed gasoline	a	b	c	d	e	f	____	a b c d e f
12. Huffed paint	a	b	c	d	e	f	____	a b c d e f
13. Huffed white out/markers	a	b	c	d	e	f	____	a b c d e f
14. Sniffed rush (poppers, amyl nitrate)	a	b	c	d	e	f	____	a b c d e f
15. Heroin (horse, junk, smack, chiva, speedball)	a	b	c	d	e	f	____	a b c d e f
16. Opium	a	b	c	d	e	f	____	a b c d e f
17. Pain killers (morphine, Percodan, Vicodin)	a	b	c	d	e	f	____	a b c d e f
18. Barbiturates/sedatives (reds, blues, yellows, quaaludes, Dalmane, seconal, sleeping pills)	a	b	c	d	e	f	____	a b c d e f
19. Tranquilizers (valium, Librium, Atavan, Serax, Miltown, meprobamates, Equanil, "Ropes")	a	b	c	d	e	f	____	a b c d e f

☐

	Never had a chance to use	Had a chance but did not use	Number of cigarettes a day				Age that you first smoked
			1-5 a day	6-10 a day	11-20 a day	More than 21 a day	
20. Cigarettes/tobacco (blunt, swishers, phillies)	a	b	c	d	e	f	____

383

As a result of using or coming off of any of the above drugs (including alcohol), how often have any of the following happened to you in your lifetime? Circle the letter under the answer that best fits you. Then, in the column on the right side of the page, indicate how many times each of the following have happened to you in the past SIX months. Circle an "a" if it did not happened to you in the past SIX months, circle a "b" if it happened to you 1-3 times, circle a "c" if it happened to you 4-6 times, circle a "d" if it happened to you 7-10 times and circle an "e" if it happened to you more than 10 times in the past SIX months.

Things that have happened to you because of using alcohol or other drugs:	Total Number of Times in Lifetime					Number of times in the past six months
	Never	1 - 3 times	4 - 6 times	7 - 10 times	More than 10 times	
21. Had a blackout (forgot what you did but were still awake)?	a	b	c	d	e	a b c d e
22. Passed out (became unconscious)?	a	b	c	d	e	a b c d e
23. Tried to take your life?	a	b	c	d	e	a b c d e
24. Become physically violent?	a	b	c	d	e	a b c d e
25. Become sick to your stomach?	a	b	c	d	e	a b c d e
26. Had physical shakes or tremors?	a	b	c	d	e	a b c d e
27. Unable to go to school or work?	a	b	c	d	e	a b c d e
28. Broke the law or committed a crime?	a	b	c	d	e	a b c d e
29. Caused problems with your family?	a	b	c	d	e	a b c d e
30. Lost interest in things?	a	b	c	d	e	a b c d e
31. Stole goods or money in order to buy drugs or alcohol?	a	b	c	d	e	a b c d e
32. Felt guilty and felt bad?	a	b	c	d	e	a b c d e
33. Became very upset and emotional?	a	b	c	d	e	a b c d e
34. Saw or heard things not there?	a	b	c	d	e	a b c d e
35. Had a fast or rapid heart beat?	a	b	c	d	e	a b c d e
36. Became very nervous and tense?	a	b	c	d	e	a b c d e
37. Felt sad and cried?	a	b	c	d	e	a b c d e
38. Felt feverish, hot or sweaty?	a	b	c	d	e	a b c d e
39. Did not eat or sleep?	a	b	c	d	e	a b c d e
40. Felt tired and weak?	a	b	c	d	e	a b c d e
41. Felt rejected by friends?	a	b	c	d	e	a b c d e

2

384

For each of the following questions, please circle the letter under the answer for each question which best fits you.

	No	Sometimes	Usually	All the time
42. Have felt nervous or tense (uptight)?	a	b	c	d
43. Have felt down or depressed?	a	b	c	d
44. Have worried a lot about things?	a	b	c	d
45. Have felt upset?	a	b	c	d
46. Have gotten angry and lost my temper?	a	b	c	d
47. Haven't gotten along with people?	a	b	c	d
48. Have felt mixed up or confused?	a	b	c	d
49. Have seen or heard things not there when not on drugs?	a	b	c	d

	No	Once	Twice	More than two times
50. Have you had thoughts about not wanting to live (committing suicide)?	a	b	c	d
51. Have you tried to take your life?	a	b	c	d
52. Have you had help for emotional or mental health problems?	a	b	c	d
53. Have you had help for drug or alcohol problems?	a	b	c	d
54. Have you injected drugs (used a needle to take drugs)?	a	b	c	d

	No	A few times	A lot of times	All the time
55. Have you ever been part of a gang or involved in gang activities?	a	b	c	d
56. Have you ever been involved in selling or dealing drugs?	a	b	c	d

	No never	One or two times	Quite a few times	Many times
57. Have you gotten angry with someone?	a	b	c	d
58. Have you ever been unhappy?	a	b	c	d
59. Have you broken the law?	a	b	c	d
60. Have you ever cried or felt sad?	a	b	c	d
61. Have you ever told a lie or not told the truth?	a	b	c	d

	For sure no	Maybe no	Maybe yes	For sure yes
62. Do you **want** to stop using alcohol; or do you **want** to continue not using alcohol?	a	b	c	d
63. Do you **want** to stop using other drugs; or **want** to continue not using other drugs?	a	b	c	d
64. Do you **plan** to stop using alcohol; or **plan** to continue not using other drugs?	a	b	c	d
65. Do you **plan** to stop using other drugs; or **plan** to continue not using other drugs?	a	b	c	d
66. Do you need help with an alcohol problem or other drug use problem?	a	b	c	d
67. Would you be willing to go to a program where people get help for alcohol or other drug use problems?	a	b	c	d

END OF SURVEY. THANK YOU.

3   4   5   385

SCORING GUIDE FOR THE SUBSTANCE USE SURVEY (SUS)

INVOLVEMENT: Measures degree of involvement in different drugs.

> Scoring weights: a=0; b=0; c=1; d=2; e=3; f=4.
> Score items 1 through 19 and enter total score in box 1 and on profile.

DISRUPTION: Measures extent of disruptive symptoms resulting from alcohol or other drug (AOD) use.

> Scoring weights: a=0; b=1; c=2; d=3; e=4.
> Score items 21 through 41 and enter total score in box 2 and on profile.

MOOD ADJUSTMENT: Measures mood disruption, e.g., anxiety, depression, anger.

> Scoring weights: a=0; b=1; c=2; d=3.
> Score items 42 through 51 and enter total score in box 3 and on profile.

DEFENSIVE SCALE: Measures extent to which client defends against admitting to undesirable and negative psychosocial emotions or behavior - higher the score, the higher the defensiveness. Scores in the 9th or 10th decile range indicates high defensiveness and results might be in question.

> Scoring weights (NOTE: REVERSE SCORING): a=3, b=2, c=1, d=0.
> Score items 57 through 61 and enter total score in box 4 and on profile.

MOTIVATE SCALE: Measures plan and desire to not use alcohol and other drugs, a perceived need for help and willingness to seek help. Scores in the first and second decile range may indicate low motivation to change and seek help for AOD use problems.

> Scoring weights: a=0, b=1, c=2, d=3.
> Score items 62 through 67 and enter total score in box 5 and on profile.

OVERALL ADOLESCENT DISRUPTION SCALE - OADS

> Derive score by summing across INVOLVEMENT, DISRUPTION AND MOOD ADJUSTMENTS scales.

SUBSTANCE USE SURVEY RATING - SUSR

> The raw score on this scale is derived from summing across items 1 and 2 under the SUMMARY OF SUBSTANCE USE SURVEY part one, page one. Maximum score on this scale is 18. This is a rater scale. Put sum of these two rater items on profile.

SINGLE ITEM ANALYSIS

> Peruse all items in the SUS as to the significance of individual responses for each client.

> Attend to the more severe symptoms which measure DISRUPTION. Also, attend specifically to items 23, 24, 50, 51 and 54.

> Attend to the age of first use for drug items 1 through 20, and recency of use and symptoms of use as measured by the "Past Six Months" columns for both specific drugs (items 1 through 20) and AOD use symptoms (items 21-41).

NORMATIVE SAMPLE: Based on 1,334 juvenile offenders on probation status in the juvenile justice system.

ADOLESCENT SELF ASSESSMENT QUESTIONNAIRE - ASAQ

Kenneth W. Wanberg
Harvey B. Milkman
Authors

DESCRIPTIVE INFORMATION
(To be completed by test taker)

NAME_____DATE OF BIRTH_____TODAY'S DATE_____

DATE _____ AGE_____ GENDER: [ ] Male [ ] Female YEARS OF SCHOOLING _____

ETHNICITY: [ ] Anglo [ ] Black [ ] Hispanic [ ] Native American [ ] Other

PREVIOUS ALCOHOL OR OTHER DRUG SERVICES:

Outpatient: [ ] None   Inpatient: [ ] None
            [ ] 1-2 times   [ ] 1-2 times
            [ ] 3-5 times   [ ] 3-5 times
            [ ] more than 6 times   [ ] more than 6 times

INFORMATION AND INSTRUCTIONS ON THE USE OF THIS QUESTIONNAIRE

This booklet has some questions about how you see and think about yourself at this time. The answers you give will be treated as confidential according to the laws of the State of Colorado. Your answers will help us in working with you. Be as honest as you can. This will help those working with you around your concerns and questions about yourself and your current situation. Choose the answers that best fit you and then mark your answers with a check mark. **NOW YOU MAY TURN THE PAGE AND BEGIN TO ANSWER THE QUESTIONS.**

TO BE COMPLETED BY STAFF		
AGENCY NAME	TEST ADMINISTRATOR	CLIENT I.D. NUMBER

CURRENT SETTING (Check only one)

[ ] Inpatient treatment - private
[ ] Inpatient treatment - public
[ ] Intensive outpatient
[ ] Traditional outpatient
[ ] Juvenile corrections
[ ] Criminal justice/corrections

STATUS (Check all that apply)

[ ] Voluntary self referred admission
[ ] Voluntary agency/professional referred
[ ] Voluntary other referred
[ ] Probation
[ ] Commitment
[ ] Other court

ASAQ Profile Summary

SCALE NAME	RAW SCORE	Low 1	2	3	Low-medium 4	5	High-medium 6	7	8	High 9	10	NUMBER IN NORM SAMPLE*
1.CONTEMPLATE		0 4 6 10¦11	12	13	13	14	15	16	17		18	788
2.PSYCHSOCIAL		0	1	2 3¦4	5	6 ¦7	8¦ 9	¦10 11 12¦13	14 16¦17	18 24		798
3.COMMUNITY		0 1 2 ¦3 4	5	¦6 7	8	¦9 10¦ 11		12	¦13 14 15¦16	17 18		798
4.COLLATERAL		0 1 3 5¦ 6 7¦8 9	10	11	12	13	14	1 15	16			760
5.HELPACKNOW		0 2 5 7¦8 10 12¦13 14 15¦16 17 18¦ 19 20	21 22 23 24¦ 25 26¦ 27 28¦29 30 33									750
6.CHANGED		0 1¦2 3 ¦4 5 6¦ 7 8¦ 9	10	¦11	12	13	14				791
A.READINESS		0 1 6 9¦10 12 14¦15 16 18¦19 20 21¦22 23 24¦ 25 26 ¦27 28 29¦30 31	¦32 33 34¦35 38 44									774
B.ACTION		3 8 9 12¦13 14 15¦16 17 18¦ 19 20 ¦21 22¦ 23 ¦ 24 25¦ 26 ¦ 27 28¦ 29										774

DECILE RANK

1   10   20   30   40   50   60   70   80   90   99
PERCENTILE   Juvenile Offenders

Version 0304

1. Have you been giving some thought about making some changes in your life?

    ___a. No, not really.
    ___b. Yes, I have thought a little about making some changes.
    ___c. Yes, I have thought a lot about making some changes.
    ___d. Yes, making some changes in my life has been on my mind every day.

2. Do you feel that you need to make some changes in your life at this time?

    ___a. No, not at all.
    ___b. Yes, maybe a few changes, but I'm not sure what.
    ___c. Yes, there are few changes that I know I need to make.
    ___d. Yes, there are many changes that I need to make.

3. Do you want to stop using or continue to not use alcohol?

    ___a. No, not at all.
    ___b. Maybe I do.
    ___c. Yes, I want to stop using alcohol.

4. Do you plan to stop using or continue to not use alcohol?

    ___a. No, not at all.
    ___b. Maybe I do.
    ___c. Yes, I do intend to stop using alcohol.

5. Do you want to stop using or not use drugs other than alcohol?

    ___a. No, not at all.
    ___b. Maybe I do.
    ___c. Yes, I want to stop using drugs other than alcohol.

6. Do you plan to stop using or not use drugs other than alcohol?

    ___a. No, not at all.
    ___b. Maybe I do.
    ___c. Yes, I do intend to stop using drugs other than alcohol.

7. What would you say as to your hope of making changes in your life?

    ___a. I don't really have to make any changes.
    ___b. I have little hope I can make changes in my life.
    ___c. I have some hope I can make some changes.
    ___d. I have a lot of hope I can make some changes.
    ___e. I am very hopeful I can make changes.   1 [ ]

Now, do you feel you need to change anything in any of the following areas:

	No changes necessary	Maybe a few changes	Quite a few changes	I need to make many changes
8. Alcohol or other drug use	___a	___b	___c	___d
9. Emotional health	___a	___b	___c	___d
10. School problems	___a	___b	___c	___d
11. Job or employment problems	___a	___b	___c	___d
12. Problems with the law	___a	___b	___c	___d
13. Family problems	___a	___b	___c	___d
14. Problems with friends	___a	___b	___c	___d
15. Getting along with people	___a	___b	___c	___d

2 [ ]

Now, do you feel you need help in any of these areas below:

	I do not need any help	I need a little help	I need quite a bit of help	I need all the help I can get
16. Alcohol or other drug use	___a	___b	___c	___d
17. Emotional health	___a	___b	___c	___d
18. School problems	___a	___b	___c	___d
19. Job or employment problems	___a	___b	___c	___d
20. Problems with the law	___a	___b	___c	___d
21. Family problems	___a	___b	___c	___d
22. Problems with friends	___a	___b	___c	___d
23. Getting along with people	___a	___b	___c	___d 3 ☐

Do any of the following persons think that you need to make changes in your life?

	No	Yes, somewhat	Yes, for sure
24. Mother or mother figure	___a.	___b.	___c.
25. Father or father figure	___a.	___b.	___c.
26. Brother or sister	___a.	___b.	___c.
27. Other relative	___a.	___b.	___c.
28. Friends	___a.	___b.	___c.
29. School counselor or teacher	___a.	___b.	___c.
30. Counselor or therapist	___a.	___b.	___c.
31. Probation officer, parole office or client manager	___a.	___b.	___c. 4 ☐

32. Do you think you need help with an alcohol problem at this time?

___a. No, not at all.
___b. Maybe not, but I would like to check to see if I do have a problem.
___c. Maybe I need some help.
___d. Yes, I feel I need help.

33. Do you think you need help with problems having to do with the use
of drugs other than alcohol?

___a. No, not at all.
___b. Maybe not, but I would like to check to see if I do have a problem.
___c. Maybe I need some help.
___d. Yes, I feel I need help.

34. Would it be hard for you to stop using or to not use alcohol?

___a. No, I can stop using or not use alcohol at any time.
___b. Yes, it would be kind of hard.
___c. Yes, it would be very hard to give up using alcohol.

35. Would it be hard for you to give up using or not use drugs other than alcohol?

___a. No, I can stop using or not use other drugs at any time.
___b. Yes, it would be kind of hard.
___c. Yes, it would be very hard to give up using drugs other than alcohol.

36. Would you be willing to come to a program where people get help for problems having to do with the use of alcohol and other drugs?
    ___a. No, not at all.
    ___b. Yes, maybe I would.
    ___c. Yes, most likely.
    ___d. Yes, for sure.

37. How many times a week would you be willing to come to such a program?
    ___a. I am not willing to come at all.
    ___b. Probably once a week for an hour or two.
    ___c. Two or three times a week for an hour or two.
    ___d. Every day for an hour or two.

38. How important would it be to you to make changes in your life around the use of alcohol or other drugs?
    ___a. Not important at all.
    ___b. Somewhat important.
    ___c. Very important.
    ___d. Probably the most important thing in my life right now.

Do any of the following persons think that you need help with alcohol or other drug use problems?

	No	Yes, somewhat	Yes, for sure
39. Mother or mother figure	___a.	___b.	___c.
40. Father or father figure	___a.	___b.	___c.
41. School counselor or teacher	___a.	___b.	___c.
42. Counselor or therapist	___a.	___b.	___c.
43. Probation officer, parole office or client manager	___a.	___b.	___c.

5 ☐

44. In the past six months, have you taken action to change your life?
    ___a. No, not really.
    ___b. I have done a few things to make some changes.
    ___c. I have done a lot of things to make changes.
    ___d. I have been doing some things every day to make changes.

45. In the past six months, have you taken action to make changes in your use of alcohol or other drugs?
    ___a. No, not really.
    ___b. I have done a few things to make some changes.
    ___c. I have done a lot of things to make changes.
    ___d. I have been doing some things every day to make changes.

46. In the past six months, have you made changes in the amount or number of times you have used alcohol?
    ___a. No, I haven't made any changes.
    ___b. I have cut down on the amount or number of times I drank alcohol.
    ___c. I have stopped drinking alcohol for a few days.
    ___d. I have stopped drinking alcohol for up to a week.
    ___e. I have stopped drinking or have not used alcohol for up to a month or more.

47. In the past six months, have you made changes in the amount or number of times you have used drugs other than alcohol?
    ___a. No, I haven't made any changes.
    ___b. Yes, I have cut down on the amount or number of times I use drugs.
    ___c. Yes, I have stopped using drugs for a few days.
    ___d. Yes, I have stopped using drugs for up to a week.
    ___e. I have stopped using or have not used drugs up to a month or more.

6 ☐

48. Would you like to talk with a counselor at this time about your use of alcohol or other drugs?
    ___a. No.   ___b. Yes, I think so.   ___c. Yes, for sure.

A ☐

B ☐

THANK YOU FOR COMPLETING THIS QUESTIONNAIRE

SCORING GUIDE FOR ADOLESCENT SELF-ASSESSMENT QUESTIONNAIRE - ASAQ
SCORING PROCEDURE FOR SCALES:

1. CONTEMPLATE: Contemplating and planning change.

   Items 1 through 7 (put score in box 1)
   (a=0, b=1, c=2, d=3, e=4).

2. PSYCHSOCIAL: Change needed in Emotional and Relationship Areas.

   Items 9, 13, 14, 15, 17, 21, 22, 23 (put score in box 2)
   (a=0, b=1, c=2, d=3).

3. COMMUNITY: Change in community and social role adjustment.

   Items 10, 11, 12, 18, 19, 20 (put score in box 3)
   (a=0, b=1, c=2, d=3).

4. COLLATERAL: Client sees others as seeing him/her as needing to change.

   Items 24 through 31 (put score in box 4)
   (a=0, b=1, c=2).

5. HELP ACKNOWLEDGE: Acknowledges need for AOD help and treatment.

   Items 16, 32 through 43 (put score in box 5)
   (a=0, b=1, c=2, d=3).

6. CHANGED: Reports having taken action in making changes.

   Items 44 through 47 (put score in box 6)
   (a=0, b=1, c=2, d=3, e=4).

A. READINESS: Broad scale measuring readiness for needing help and change.

   Items 8, 9, 13, 16, 17, 21, 32 through 39, 41 and 42 (score in box A) (a=0, b=1, c=2, d=3).

B. ACTION: Broad scale measuring a commitment to and taking action to change.

   Items 1, 3 through 7, 44 through 47 (put score in box B)
   (a=0, b=1, c=2, d=3, e=4).

PUT RAW SCORES IN RAW SCORE BOX ON PROFILE AND PLOT PROFILE.
V0304

SOCIAL RESPONSE QUESTIONNAIRE - SRQ

Kenneth W. Wanberg
Author

The statements in this questionnaire address how you see yourself in relationship to other people. There are no right or wrong answers. Each person will have different responses to each of the statements. Respond to each statement as to how you honestly see yourself. Please give an answer to all statements by circling the letter under the response of your choice. Choose only one response for each statement. This questionnaire is to help you in your program of self-improvement and change. Be as honest as you can in answering the questions. The outcome is for your benefit only. Please fill in the personal information first.

NAME:		
DATE:	AGE:	GENDER: [ ] M [ ] F
ETHNIC GROUP CHECK ALL THAT APPLY: [ ] African American [ ] Anglo American [ ] Hispanic American [ ] Native American [ ] Asian American		
CIRCLE NUMBER YEARS EDUCATION COMPLETED: 6 7 8 9 10 11 12 13 14		

Now, please answer each of the following questions by circling the letter under the answer that best fits you. Thank You.

	Almost never	Yes sometimes	Yes often	Almost always
1. I take care of the things that I own or that belong to me.	a	b	c	d
2. I am a responsible person.	a	b	c	d
3. I feel in control of what I do.	a	b	c	d
4. Other people seek me out for advice or help.	a	b	c	d
5. I am (or would be) careful when I drive a car.	a	b	c	d
6. I am a good citizen.	a	b	c	d
7. I am a member of or attend clubs or groups in the community such as Girls Scouts, Boys Scouts, YMCA, YWCA, school clubs, sports clubs or church groups.	a	b	c	d
8. I try to be successful in my school work and school activities.	a	b	c	d
9. Other people see me as a person who is responsible.	a	b	c	d
10. I am honest with other people.	a	b	c	d
11. I am a person who is worthy of trust.	a	b	c	d
12. I like being part of a team.	a	b	c	d
13. I have someone that I look up to who is a good citizen.	a	b	c	d

A [ ]

Go to next page (or back side)

14. I try to work out conflict with others in a peaceful way.

	Almost never	Yes sometimes	Yes often	Almost always
14. I try to work out conflict with others in a peaceful way.	a	b	c	d
15. I try to understand the other person's point of view.	a	b	c	d
16. I see myself as someone who helps other people.	a	b	c	d
17. I try to listen to what the other person has to say.	a	b	c	d
18. I do not touch the property or things of another person without their permission.	a	b	c	d
19. I am comfortable with people of different cultures or races.	a	b	c	d
20. I try to make sure that my words or actions do not hurt other people.	a	b	c	d
21. I throw trash on the streets or out of cars, such as soda pop cans, paper, etc.	a	b	c	d

	Strongly Disagree	Disagree somewhat	Agree somewhat	Strongly Agree
22. We should all try to help each other.	a	b	c	d
23. No one has the right to touch or take other people's things.	a	b	c	d
24. There is usually no reason for people to get into physical fights.	a	b	c	d
25. If people helped each other, we would have fewer social problems.	a	b	c	d
26. It is best to just let people alone rather than help them.	a	b	c	d
27. Sometimes it is just necessary to fight.	a	b	c	d
28. Most people don't deserve to be helped.	a	b	c	d

	Not really	Somewhat honest	Very honest	Completely honest
29. Have you been honest in answering the above questions.	a	b	c	d

B [ ]   G [ ]

SRQ PROFILE

SCALE NAME	RAW SCORE	Low 1	2	3	Low-medium 4	5	6	High-medium 7	8	High 9	10	NUMBER IN NORM SAMPLE*
A. RESPONSIBLE	5	10 16¦17 18	¦19 20	¦21 22	¦ 23 24	¦ 25	¦ 26 27	¦ 28 29	¦30 31 32¦33 35 39			351
B. POS. REGARD	0	15 17¦18 20 21¦22 23 24¦ 25	26¦ 27 28	¦29 30	¦31 32	¦ 33 34	¦35 36 37¦38 40 44			347
G. GEN PROSOCIAL	0	35 37¦38 40 41¦42 44 45¦46 49 50¦51 52 53¦54 55 56¦57 58 59¦60 62 64¦65 66 68¦69 70 82									345

DECILE RANK

1   10   20   30   40   50   60   70   80   90   99
PERCENTILE   * Male Juvenile Justice

SRQ PROFILE

SCALE NAME	RAW SCORE	Low 1	2	3	Low-medium 4	5	6	High-medium 7	8	High 9	10	NUMBER IN NORM SAMPLE*
A. RESPONSIBLE	5	10 16¦17 18	¦19 20	¦21 22	¦ 23 24	¦ 25	¦ 26 27	¦ 28 29	¦30 31 32¦33 35 39			351
B. POS. REGARD	0	15 17¦18 20 21¦22 23 24¦ 25	26¦ 27 28	¦29 30	¦31 32	¦ 33 34	¦35 36 37¦38 40 44			347
G. GEN PROSOCIAL	0	35 37¦38 40 41¦42 44 45¦46 49 50¦51 52 53¦54 55 56¦57 58 59¦60 62 64¦65 66 68¦69 70 82									345

DECILE RANK

1   10   20   30   40   50   60   70   80   90   99
PERCENTILE   * Male Juvenile Justice

SOCIAL RESPONSE QUESTIONNAIRE PROFILE AND SCORING PROCEDURES
AND DESCRIPTION OF SCALES

The Social Response Questionnaire (SRQ) is a 29 item self-report questionnaire that provides a measure of two specific dimensions and one broad measure of prosociality. Scale A, RESPONSIBLE, provides a measure of responsibility towards self and towards others. Persons with high scores on this scale essentially see themselves as having self-control, of being responsible towards self and others, as being honest and trustworthy and who see themselves as being a good and responsible citizen.

Scale B, POSITIVE REGARD, provides a self-report measure of being respectful and helpful toward others and towards the community. The value of helpfulness is a strong component of this scale. As well, there is a negotiatory dimension to this scale whereby the person who scores high, values resolving conflicts in a peaceful manner and in such a manner that the rights and opinion of others are respected.

Scale G, General Prosociality, combines both dimensions A and B into a broad measure of prosocial attitudes and behavior. Persons who score high on this scale will value having a positive regard for others and a general attitude of being a responsible person towards others and the community.

Table 1 below provides a description of the three SRQ scales and the scoring procedures for these scales. Scale G essentially is a sum of the scores for Scales A and B. Table 2 provides the means, standard deviations and internal consistency reliabilities for a group of male juvenile offenders and a group of female juvenile offenders. The two groups do not statistically differ across the three scales. The profile on the second page of the SRQ is for a group of male juvenile offenders. Two profiles are given: one for for plotting pre-treatment testing; one for plotting post-treatment testing.

Description of SRQ Scales and Scoring Procedures

SCALE NAME	DESCRIPTION OF SCALES	QUESTIONS	SCORING
RESPONSIBLE	This scale measures two dimensions of responsibility: to self and towards others and the community. More specifically, it measures the perception of self as: being responsible, honest, worthy of trust; taking care of personal belongings; as having self-controlled; and as being sought out by others for advice. It also measures the perception of self as: being a good citizen; as liking to be part of a team; being careful (or would be careful) in driving a motor vehiicle; as being a member of a community group that relates in a positive way to the community; making an effort to be successful in school; looking up to another person who is a good citizen.	1 through 13	a=0 b=1 c=2 d=3
POSITIVE REGARD AND HELPFUL	This scale measures a self-perception of having positive regard and a helpful and respective attitude towards others. More specifically, the person who scores high on this scale has the self-perception of being helpful towards others, of resolving conflicts peacefully, of making an effort to understand the other person's point of view, of trying not to hurt others, of respecting the property of others, not littering in the community, of having a helpful orientation towards others and the community and seeking peaceful solutions to problems.	14 through 20 22 through 25	a=0 b=1 c=2 d=3
		19, 26 through 28	a=3 b=2 c=1 d=0
GENERAL PROSOCIAL	General prosocial involvement with others: Provides a general measure of prosocial attitudes and actions, combining a perception of self as being a responsible person towards self and others and as having positive regard and respect towards others. Persons with a high score on this scale would also see themselves as being responsible, respectful and helpful and who take a negotiatory and cooperative attitude towards others. Such persons also report being involved in positive activities in school and the community and who looks for a peaceful solutions in conflicts and who values rights of others.	1 through 20, 22 through 25	a=0 b=1 c=2 d=3
		21, 26 through 28	a=3,b=2 c=1,d=0

Table 2: Mean, Standard Deviation (SD), Internal Consistency Reliabilities (ICR) or Male and Female Juvenile Offenders

SRQ SCALE DESCRIPTION	MALE JUVENILE OFFENDER			FEMALE JUVENILE OFFENDER		
	Mean	SD	ICR	Mean	SD	ICR
A. RESPONSIBLE TOWARD SELF AND OTHERS	24.85	6.02	.79	25.75	6.61	.83
B. POSITIVE REGARD AND RESPECT	28.44	7.49	.84	29.54	7.55	.84
G. GENERAL PROSOCIALITY	53.34	12.00	.88	55.37	12.82	.89